Is There An Elephant In <u>Your</u> Church?

Or . . . The <u>Whole</u> Gospel Of Grace

Which Christ Jesus Revealed To Paul?

Leonard John Ransil

Is There An Elephant In <u>Your</u> Church? . . .

Or . . . The <u>Whole</u> Gospel Of Grace Which Christ Jesus Revealed To Paul?

Fourth Edition

The use of scripture passages and translations is explained in Appendix # 12. I enclose my own commentary of these passages within parentheses and use italics and underlining throughout the book for emphasis.

I dedicate this book to
anyone around the world
who wants to be set free from the elephant of condemnation
or who wants to jump off the treadmill of religious duty.
How?
By being set free from the Law of sin and death,
just like Paul declared in Romans, Chapter Eight.
How?
By experiencing the *higher Law of the Spirit of Life*
in the arms of our loving Father-God,
who sent Jesus to:
1) pay for and *remove* all of mankind's sin debt and
2) reconcile mankind to God, *from God's viewpoint*, and
3) offer us salvation through rebirth and
4) offer us His abundant Life through
His *whole* gospel of grace of the New Covenant,
the **finished work** of His **divine exchange**,
which He revealed primarily to Paul
who declared this reality in *2 Corinthians 5:17-21*

Leonard John Ransil
A brief bio on page 432

CONTENTS

PART THREE

A List of Charts and Diagrams by Chapters and Page Numbers

33 GRACE-BASED SONGS

FOREWARD

by Mark R. Cermak

Ever since I was a small child and as long as I can remember, I have always had lots of questions about God, the bible and church. I had questions about almost everything that was taught in church and Sunday school. "How can God have no beginning or ending?" "How can God be three persons in one?" "Is hell a real place?" "Since no one is perfect and everyone sins, is everyone going to hell?" "Why is the bible so hard to understand?" "How can a person live inside the belly of a whale?" "How did Noah get all those animals in one boat?" These and countless other questions I raised as a young child to my parents. Overwhelmed and unable to give me sufficient answers, and wanting to help satisfy my desire for the truth, my parents decided to invite the pastor of our church to dinner so that I could ask him these many questions. To my disappointment, this pastor was also overwhelmed with my curiosity. His response to me was that I was taking all of this stuff too literally and that I should appreciate it all as good stories for the lessons that are taught in them.

Perhaps you can imagine the disappointment I felt that night as I climbed into bed. Here I was, a small child being raised in a family that required that we go to church, attend Sunday school and receive the sacraments. In trying to learn the meaning and purpose of all these things, I had questions…questions that needed answers for me to consciously know that I was ready to receive any of the upcoming sacraments for which our Sunday school class was preparing us. This meant something to me because I thought it was *supposed* to mean something to me, and I was taking it seriously. I wanted…needed to understand. But in my search for understanding all I was told was that I was taking it all too literally. My parents could not provide answers, nor could the pastor of my church. I fell asleep that night deciding that none of it was worth the effort. Why search for God or study the bible or pursue the sacraments of the church if it was all just meant as some story to help us learn lessons for life? Even as a young boy, this didn't sit right with me. I wanted something *real*. I decided that night to put away my questions and stop pursuing answers to these many questions about God, the bible and the church.

It wasn't until I was in my early twenties that I began to once again pursue answers to my many questions. I was visiting my brother and his wife for a month in North Carolina. When my brother picked me up at the airport and we got in his car, the first thing I noticed was Christian music playing from his tape deck. This came as a surprise to me because I did not know my brother to be at all spiritual or religious. I don't ever remember him attending church or talking about God.

When we got to my brother's house the first thing I noticed as I was greeted by his wife was a bible on the counter in the kitchen. I was now beginning to think that there was something different about my brother and his wife. There was something definitely different from the way I remembered them. They didn't seem like the same two people that took me to parties with them growing up. I couldn't place it, but something was very different about them. What was it?

Later that first week with them, we looked in the newspaper to find something fun to do over the weekend. We saw that there was a stage play of "Jesus Christ Superstar" and decided to go. I can't remember much about the play, except for the effect that it had on me. All of a sudden, all of my childhood questions that I put on the shelf years ago came flooding back to my mind. When we got in the car I had a sense that I had come to the place where I was finally going to get the answers I had so strongly sought as a child. I began asking my brother and his wife these questions on the ride back to their house, confident that they would provide me with answers to my questions.

My brother and his wife did not have answers that night, but told me that perhaps if I joined them for church the next morning it would clear a lot of things up for me. I went to bed that night filled with anticipation and excitement.

The next morning we went to church. Before the service even began, as people were still filing in to be seated and the choir was singing, I sat there in my seat. Suddenly, out of nowhere and without any prompting on anyone's part, I began to weep uncontrollably. With my head down, eyes closed, hands gripping the seat and weeping, my brother sitting beside me saw me and put his hand on my lap. When he did that, it felt like the hand of God comforting me. In the depths of my being, as clear as day, I heard a voice saying, "It's alright. It's okay. You belong to Me now. You're Mine!"

I don't remember anything else about the church service that day. Not the songs that were sung or the sermon that was given. All I remember was how exhausted I was when I got in the car after the service…and how refreshed and clean and new I felt from head to toe! My brother and his wife knew what I was going through and asked me what I thought. I remember telling them emphatically, "I'll tell you what I think. I think I need to get me a bible!"

After a change of clothes, later that day we headed to the local mall and I bought myself a bible as well as a couple of contemporary Christian music tapes. And by the time I returned home from my visit with my brother, I had read the entire New Testament. I was coming home a changed person; a new man. I was born again!

I can remember those early days of my brand new relationship with God with such wonder. Everything seemed so promising, so full of hope. The grass was greener, the sky bluer. Everything came into focus with such clarity. I was full of life! When I read the bible, it was as if the pages opened up to me in 3D. They were alive and meaningful…and personal, as if the words on those pages were written to me and for me. It was amazing!

But over the next twenty five years something changed. What started out as a beautiful relationship with God slowly became a tedious religious duty. Gone was the wonder and the joy of enjoying a relationship with God. Something had crept in and stole the life that came with being His child. Reading the bible was no longer an eye opening experience that brought encouragement but now something that I did out of a sense of obligation and to hopefully gain a closer relationship with God. There was a sense of guilt about it all.

What happened? How did something so real and so right…something that I had sought after my whole life and finally found, something that brought such life and love and peace and joy and meaning to me become such a chore? What caused me to lose the wonder of being a child of God?

A few short years ago I met up with a friend that I hadn't seen in a long time. That friend is Lenny, the author of this book. At one of our first meetings after a long time of not seeing each other, Lenny recommended a book to me. The book was "Destined to Reign" by Joseph Prince, someone I had never heard of before. I can honestly tell you that reading that book was much like the experience I had at that church in North Carolina while visiting my brother and his wife many years ago! My eyes opened to all of the religious weight that had burdened me through the years and the negative effect that it had on my relationship with God. Joseph Prince helped me to understand my relationship with God in a way that I had never heard before, and it was all there right in the bible. I now understand the grace of God and why it is called amazing! It most certainly is!

Lenny and I have been meeting ever since. In that time he has shared with and taught me so many of the wonderful truths that you will read about in this book. It has been an honor to help him in the process of writing it. And I am very confident that his laboring over these issues will be beneficial to everyone truly seeking answers. We will all be better for it.

Lenny has taught me so much about the grace of God, His true nature, the **finished work** of Jesus, the **divine exchange**, our new nature and what all of that means to you and me as His children. (See Endnote #1.) Today I enjoy a loving and vital relationship with God, and in no small way I have Lenny to thank for it. He has blessed me with the best of all possible gifts. This is what you have to look forward to as you read this book.

As a young boy I had many questions and couldn't find answers to them for years to come. Today, I have still more questions and certainly not all of the answers. But I'm happy to tell you that many things have been made known to me that I did not know before by reading this book. The result has been a huge difference in my life, an intimate and personal relationship with God the likes of which I could not ever have imagined. This book has been a tremendous blessing to me, and I know it will be for you too.

Today I enjoy the abundant life that so many Christians talk about but so few understand, because so many wrongly believe that the abundant life is something for which to strive for, not realizing that it's something they already have.

Speaking of questions, here are a couple for you: what is the good news, and what makes it good news? I believe you'll have a much better answer to those questions after reading this book.

PREFACE

MY PERSONAL TESTIMONY: AN ESCAPE FROM BONDAGE UNDER LAW TO FREEDOM IN CHRIST JESUS.

This book, in a way, is the story of my progressive journey from hard-core legalism into radical grace, the testimony of a well-meaning person steeped in Law-mindedness who didn't know it. In 1991, the Lord began the painful but liberating process of taking off the wrappings of law-based living - not unlike Lazarus coming out of his tomb. It began with an unexpected shock! After 16 years of teaching and being principal of a Christian school, which had the specific sub-title of "A Family Formation Center," my family – my wonderful wife and four children - told me collectively that I was a lousy father.

Previously, I was basically ignorant of the Bible before I was born again and Baptized in the Holy Spirit in 1972. So, I relied on books like Larry Christenson's *The Christian Family* and ministries like "Focus on the Family" for insight on how to train my own children, the school students and also what to teach their parents how to "train up" their children "biblically." The emphasis on the external "how-to's, rather than on our new, true identity in Jesus, kept me focused on my seemingly "good" performance. But, my family's assessment, precipitated over a relatively minor family issue, was a major earthquake to me which shattered the performance-based identity on which I was standing. It presented me with a choice: reject their collective word to me (and possibly reject God's deeper reality) or view it as an attack of the devil to derail me from my God-given call. Was this God talking or rebellion afloat?

Given my life-long formation under law-based thinking, I was programmed to conclude the latter. What I was doing seemed right in my own eyes – otherwise I would not have been doing it. I was diligently applying "biblical principles" as I understood them. But …was there actually a better way to carry out what I believed God had called me to do? Or should I quit teaching His children and go back to building houses? Thanks to the lavish grace of God, I paused to ask the Holy Spirit to show me the truth - at any cost – rather than rush to a decision based on anger and pain. He led me to His still waters.

One of the most important songs that the Lord had inspired me to put to paper came in 1989, two years <u>before</u> this "crisis of call and identity." It simply invited the Holy Spirit to:

Bathe my mind with Your Truth.
Fill my temple with the incense of praise.
Cause my life to glorify Jesus.
Spirit, teach me Your ways.

This song-prayer had just welled up from my spirit almost effortlessly one day – like a butterfly out of a cocoon - and I sang and prayed it often, as well as praying "Spirit of Truth, prevail." In hindsight, I can now "see" that the Lord was busy answering those prayers, which He had originated within me. It also helped that the school motto - which I sensed He had inspired me to choose years before - was always before my eyes:

Trust in the Lord with all of your heart and lean not on your own understanding. Acknowledge Him in all your ways and He will direct your Pathways (Proverbs 3:5-6).

The Escape into Freedom

While still in mental suspension over this shock and waiting for an answer, I awoke one morning and noticed a particular book stand out on the shelf across the room. It was Dr. Neil Anderson's best seller, *Victory Over Darkness*. Little did I know then what a revolutionary renewal of my mind his writings would start to generate within me. He was the first author I had ever read who took "positional truth" seriously - a topic that most theologians ignore and most others consider to be interesting but not really relevant for our daily lives. But, as I see it now, this truth is the centerpiece of Jesus' grace-based gospel. It is His revelation to Paul of every believer's new, **unseen** identity, caused by rebirth as God's child, and the miraculous placement *into* Christ Jesus Himself, done by grace through faith alone. Jesus accomplished this miracle for us on Calvary and the details are eloquently revealed in what Paul called "my gospel" but which was really Jesus' divine revelation given specifically to Paul.

God used *Victory Over Darkness*, reinforced by the teaching of a newly arrived pastor at Grace Fellowship Church in Erie, PA., to begin to renew my mind in two foundational areas:

1) God's true nature and

2) my new nature and identity as His reborn son of God, now resurrected, alive and ascended with and **in Christ Jesus.**

This new revelation gave me the courage to allow the Holy Spirit to begin "pulling down the mental strongholds" of an identity which was wrongly based on performing "the works of the Law" in order to gain and maintain God's acceptance and approval – an impossible task – instead of by grace alone, through faith alone, in Him alone.

As the fog started to lift, I began to see that my basic human needs for security, acceptance and significance were already supplied 2000 years ago by Jesus' **finished work**, which had already radically (and unknowingly) regenerated me on the inside the moment I was reborn. I was blinded by the veil of the Law to the truth of His lavish grace and love for me – even though I had personally experienced it years before when I was first saved. To say the least, this was a radical paradigm shift which set me on a new course that has, thankfully, become the framework of a totally new kind of walk **in Christ Jesus** – receiving and experiencing His lavish love and grace through His gift of faith.

Father-God always enjoys it when we ask Him to fill in this framework of His "divine puzzle" with more and more pieces of His revelation so that we, His beloved children, can see His Big Picture the way He does. By having our mind renewed to His ways by the Holy Spirit of Truth living in and through us, God manifests the fruit of His abundant life that Jesus specifically promised – effortlessly. I know, that sounds preposterous but think about it. Does the branch of a grape vine strain to bear fruit? Neither need we! I began to tangibly experience the revelation that God's fruit-producing is the Holy Spirit's work through me, not my work for God. So, I've learned to rely more and more on Him to live through me by confidently resting in what Jesus did for us 2000 years ago, just as He learned to rest in His Father's will and supply– apart from the works of the Law. His focus was on His Father and the higher law of faith, love and liberty – the law of the Spirit of life. Jesus came to set us free from the demands of the Mosaic Law, which is good but which is not meant for us. Why? Because it arouses sin, condemns and causes death, just like it did for the Israelites for 1500 years. Part of this book is devoted to documenting that alarming fact - which many, even today, would call heresy.

The experience of fruit bearing started to happen more consistently for me when I began listening to Andrew Wommack and especially to Joseph Prince over the last seven years. Their understanding of the actual purpose of the Law is drastically different from what I was taught and formed in for the first five decades of my life. And, absorbing the revelation of what Christ Jesus has already accomplished for all unbelievers and believers for all time – Jesus' **finished work** of the Cross – has further deepened my understanding, appreciation, love and worship of such a magnanimous God. Now I *know* by revelation that He is devoted to the welfare of all mankind because He *is* Love. Believing and receiving Him by faith is the only requirement to being joined to God Himself – and all that that means. Discovering the treasures of the **New Covenant** that are already mine by being "one with Christ Jesus," fuels my appreciation and love for Him increasingly – effortlessly.

It has been this awakening over the last twenty years, out from under the shadows of the Law, into the radiant light of Father-God's lavish grace-based gospel, which compelled me to ask Him for the answers to these two questions in the spring of 2010:

1) "How did legalism get started in the church and

2) how and why has Jesus' **whole gospel of radical grace** been ignored and even maligned for 2000 years by well-meaning people like me?"

The answers will shock you – like they shocked me. But also, they will free you the way I am being progressively set free by renewing my mind through consciously abiding in Him and in the truth of His wonderful **finished work** - the **divine exchange**.

So, believer, let's discover together:

1) some of the many blessings and privileges of Jesus' **whole gospel of total grace**

2) how and why this **whole gospel** continues to be suppressed by an "elephant in the Church" - hiding in plain sight,

3) how the elephant came to be there to begin with and, most importantly

4) what to do about this "good thing in the wrong place" – possibly even in your church!

Be prepared to change your perception of God and of yourself through the revelation knowledge of the Holy Spirit. Knowing His truth about Him and about your new self **in Him** is guaranteed to set you mentally free, progressively, according to Romans 12:2.

God's abundant Grace and Peace to you and yours!

Leonard John Ransil

July 22, 2016

INTRODUCTION

Despite an apparent cover-up, there has been a doctrinal war – a schism – in the church from its very early days. This inconvenient truth has been glossed over and virtually ignored by most theologians for almost 2000 years. A few Christian historians have documented the symptoms but only a few have pin-pointed the source of the deadly disease of this doctrinal division.

Much later, Martin Luther's *original* aim in bringing false doctrine and practice to light in his Ninety-five Theses was *not* to fracture the established church but to present evidence of some doctrinal discrepancies. However, the church's stern refusal to admit and correct these seemingly minor doctrinal issues eventually revealed an existing fault line in the accepted orthodoxy itself. He had been steeped in a works-centered, religious mind–set (not unlike Saint Paul's Jewish past). Thankfully, the pain and despair of trying to become holy through law-keeping brought Luther to the end of himself and to his well-intentioned efforts at self-righteousness. He looked for a way out of his misery. How did such a drastic turn-around from law to grace happen?

As the story goes, both his confessor and his abbot advised him to teach the Bible at a local university. He plunged himself into a study of the book of Romans that, over time, helped him to come to rely on much of what Jesus' **finished work** had already done for him. He discovered that salvation and righteousness were gifts of grace from God, received by faith alone – apart from any of his efforts to earn or maintain them.

Unfortunately, the Jewish Christians in the infant church in Jerusalem did not fully grasp this reality because it was so drastically different from what they had been formed in as Jews. Circumcision and obedience to the Law were absolutely necessary to be acceptable to God under that Mosaic Covenant. I will document the details of how and why the fault line between a focus on law-keeping versus on Jesus and His **whole gospel of grace** came about and split the early church. The *intent* in showing this is the same as Luther's: <u>to expose root differences between the truth of Jesus' gospel to Paul from the **elephant of mixture**</u> that still prevails in most seminaries and churches today. Why? So that we, His church, can live in the unity of the Spirit and the bond of peace and love, already a spiritual reality **in Christ Jesus** because of His **divine exchange** with believers. <u>Our efforts to accomplish what He has already done will forever be futile and fruitless.</u> Depending on our works instead of on His performance prevents us from entering into the "rest" He invites each of us to enjoy, **in Him**.

Government agents determine counterfeit currency by first thoroughly studying the genuine. Jesus revealed to Paul the full details of His genuine **grace–based gospel** in 42 AD, which Paul later called "my gospel." (It was very different in tone and purpose from the four gospels that were written down many years later.) After that monumental event, Paul regarded the works-based system he had formerly been steeped in as "rubbish" by comparison with being immersed in the exalted Christ Jesus and enjoying the many benefits of the **finished work** of His **divine exchange**.

Actually, what you have in your hands is really three books in one. Each of the three main parts contain many important puzzle pieces which fit together progressively to unveil the whole picture of how good Father-God really is. So, we will first focus on the genuine **gospel of grace** that Jesus revealed to Paul - which Luther partially recovered for anyone in his day hungry for the truth of God's good news for mankind. Then we will explore and explain the roots and consequences of a disastrous schism in the <u>infant</u> church, caused by Judaizers <u>mixing two opposing covenants</u> (the heresy of Galatianism). How? By the connecting the dots - the clues given in the Bible and actual historical accounts - that reveal exactly when, where, why and how this disastrous division happened and how it still plagues and divides believers today. Finally, we will explore how to recognize and resist this "**the elephant in the church**" by learning how to enjoy the same realities that Jesus and Paul walked in which were minimized by this early heresy and schism. Only a few besides Paul have noticed its dangers and have been persecuted like Paul was when they dared to confront this entrenched beast.

This is Big Picture thinking, which sees the end from the beginning of God's original intent for mankind. Whether people are aware of this fact or not, each persons' own spiritual journey starts with the Fall of Adam and continues with how God reveals Himself through interactive covenants with various humans over 6000 years. It culminates with the **New Covenant** that God made with Jesus as mankind's new Representative who revealed directly to Paul how we are involved in His-story today. It has never been about what man could do for God. Rather it has always been about God revealing His <u>true nature</u> of sacrificial love through what only He was completely willing and uniquely able to do for mankind through Jesus, our last Adam.

It is the good news of our wonderful Father-God's lavish grace and mercy, motivated by agape love, that has overcome for believers the obstacles of the world, the flesh and the devil through Jesus' **finished work**. Now, all those who receive His offer of salvation by faith are joined into Himself in a forever family. We will begin this journey by first highlighting much of what Jesus has already accomplished for us in the **finished work** of His cross - the **divine exchange** - received by grace through faith in Him. It is not just Good News. It is the Best News possible!

PART ONE

CHAPTER ONE

THE GLORY OF THE WHOLE GOSPEL, UNVEILED ONLY TO PAUL BY CHRIST JESUS

QUESTION #1: Where in the Bible are we told:

1) Be it known unto you, therefore men and brethren, that through this man (Jesus) is preached to you the forgiveness of sins. And by Him, all that believe are justified from all things, from which you could not be justified by the Law of Moses.

2) I do not frustrate the grace of God: for if righteousness comes by (obedience to) the law, then Christ died for nothing.

3) I have been nailed to the cross with Christ and I live, yet not I, but Christ lives in me, and the life which I now live in my body, I live by faith in the Son of God, the (One) loving me and giving Himself over on my behalf.

4) But God, being rich in mercy, for His great love wherewith He loved us, even when we were dead through our trespasses, made us alive together with Christ - by grace you are saved - and raised us together with Him, and seated us together in Christ Jesus in the heavenlies.

5) There is therefore now no condemnation for those who are in Christ Jesus.

6) And so, from now on we know no one according to the flesh. And though we have known Christ according to the flesh, yet now we know Him in this way no longer. So if anyone is in Christ, he is a new creation; the old things passed away. Behold, all things have become new. Now all these new things are from God, having reconciled us to Himself through Christ who has given us the ministry of reconciliation. For God was in Christ, reconciling the whole world to Himself, not reckoning their sins against them. And He has placed in us the word of reconciliation. Therefore, we are ambassadors for Christ, so that God is beseeching you through us. We beg you on Christ's behalf: be reconciled to God. For God made Him who did not know sin to become sin on our behalf, so that we might become the righteousness of God in Him.

7) For though our tribulation is brief and light at the present time, it accomplishes in us the weight of a sublime, eternal glory, beyond measure. And we are meditating, not on the things that are seen, but on the things that are unseen. For the things that are seen are temporal, whereas, the things that are not seen are eternal. (See the references where these passages are found at the end of this chapter.)

QUESTION #2: What is a very important common denominator of all these scriptures? None of them are quotes from the Old Testament or any of the four gospels. To be sure, "All scripture is

23

inspired by God and profitable for teaching, reproof, correction and for instruction about righteousness so that the man of God may be complete, equipped for every good work" (2 Timothy 3:16). However, not every Bible promise or blessing or curse applies to everyone all the time.

Starting from Genesis 1:1, the Bible progressively unveils more and more about God's true nature of love in action, the devil's evil nature and destructive activity, Adam's original innocent nature, the consequences of Adam's fall for all of mankind, and God's astounding reversal of those consequences by what His Beloved Son, Jesus Christ, did for mankind on Calvary – His **finished work**. It is important to have an overview of God's Holy Word but it is also very important to understand that not all parts of the Bible apply equally to everyone automatically.

A primary example of this truth is that God gave the Mosaic Covenant *only* to the Israelites with all of its specific terms of blessings and curses which they experienced *based on their behavior*. Jesus came later and fulfilled its terms perfectly and then God replaced it with a drastically new and permanent covenant of grace that He made with Jesus, the last Adam, for *all mankind*, not just for the Jews. Jesus accomplished this and far more for us, based solely on His perfect, substitutionary sacrifice on Calvary, *not based on our behavior*. I have personally been reborn of God by His grace through faith in Jesus and, thereby, I received a very different set of covenant terms than the Israelites had, based solely on belief in Jesus' **finished work**. The covenant through Moses could not offer rebirth to anyone - let alone eternal salvation to everyone!

The seven scriptures above are exclusively from the **New Covenant** which Jesus died in our place to make possible. There are many more critical distinctions between these two opposing covenants. We will explore and emphasize these differences throughout this book and show why the all too common practice of *mixing* them is divisive, defeating and heretical, according to Jesus' revelation to Paul. This heresy is known officially as Galatianism but I will refer to it as **"the elephant in the church."** Why? Because very few realize how deadly and yet pervasive it is in so many of today's seminaries and churches and books. And even fewer people choose to confront it, as Paul was compelled to do. It is deadly because "it is no gospel at all," according to Jesus' revelation to Paul in Galatians 1:7. In Chapters Three to Five, we will investigate how this **elephant of mixture** entered the Christian church and, in later chapters, how to replace it with Jesus' **whole gospel of grace** that He revealed directly to Paul.

What Is The Whole Gospel of Jesus Christ?
When Jesus ascended into heaven, His followers believed that He would return fairly soon (see 1 Thessalonians 4:15-18). But after three decades had passed, the Holy Spirit inspired a few of His followers to start writing down many of the important teachings and events of Jesus' earthly life before all of the first-hand witnesses were martyred. Most bible scholars believe that Mark was the first to author what we now call *The Gospel According To Mark*, written in about 61 AD. (Appendix # 1 shows a chart listing the dates of when the New Testament books were written, according to the consensus of a large group of noted scholars.)

But there is one crucial fact that is rarely made clear. Paul was already teaching and writing down what he called "my gospel" years before Mark penned his book. Paul claimed in his letter written to the Galatians that <u>he received this gospel by direct revelation from Christ Jesus Himself</u> (Galatians 1:11-12). He is testifying that he did not receive it from his former Rabbi, Gamaliel, or any of the apostles in Jerusalem. Moreover, he adamantly insisted in Galatians 1:6-7 that any other gospel that differed from what Jesus had revealed to him was, in fact, *no gospel at all*. (Was Paul saying that the four gospels were no gospel at all? We will unravel this fascinating conundrum in Chapters Eleven and Twelve.)

He also called this unique revelation such things as:
"the gospel of Christ" in Romans 1:16,
"the word of Christ" in Romans 10:17 and Colossians 3:16,
"the word of God *in its fullness*" in Colossians 1:25,
"the Lords' *own word*" in 1 Thessalonians 4:15,
"the word of life" in Philippians 2:16 and 2 Timothy 2:15, and
"the glorious gospel of the blessed God which was committed to my (Paul's) trust" in
1 Timothy 1:11.

Peter himself endorsed Paul's writings as part of the scriptures, even though he acknowledged that "his letters contain some things that are hard to understand...." (2 Peter 3:16b). Well, of course they were hard to understand because Jesus revealed how believers can now participate with Him in the life of His **unseen** Kingdom while still on earth (see 2 Corinthians 4:18). It takes the Holy Spirit to overcome the limitations of the human mind to understand this new reality **in Christ**. In fact, Paul called it "walking according to the Holy Spirit." This is so different from living day-to-day by merely our <u>natural sight</u> that it requires being reborn into a whole new kingdom and outlook and ability, supplied by the Holy Spirit through His gift of grace through faith in Jesus' **finished work**. We will explore what Jesus revealed to Paul about this new way of living in Chapter Nineteen. It is the way Jesus lived on earth and He invites all believers to walk by faith in Father-God just as He did.

Apparently, Paul received this unique revelation (which was different from his earlier conversion near Damascus) in about 42 AD (which was about 9 years after Pentecost - depending on what year Jesus died). How do we know this? When he recounts this new, miraculous experience in 2 Corinthians 12:1-6, he states that this happened "fourteen years ago" and most scholars are in agreement that he wrote this book in about 56 AD (56 AD – 14 = 42 AD). (See Endnote **#2** for verification.) It was also about this time, in 42 AD, that Barnabas recruited Paul to leave Tarsus and settle in Antioch. This gave Paul the chance to begin teaching this new revelation, "the word of God in its fullness," to willing Gentiles. It was decidedly different in some important ways, and much "fuller," than what he had taught after he was reborn on the Damascus road, and what the other apostles <u>continued</u> to teach in Jerusalem for decades. We'll present these differences in much more detail in Chapters Seven to Ten.

Paul's Gospel From Jesus
It is also very important to understand that Paul began teaching these amazing, "inexpressible things," which he had heard directly from Christ Jesus, while in the third heaven, about nineteen years before Mark wrote his gospel (61 AD – 42 AD = 19 years). Furthermore, so astounding were the results of his explosive ministry in Antioch, that he, Barnabas and Titus went to Jerusalem in about 50 AD (to what we now call the First Council of Jerusalem) "... in

response to a revelation and set before them (the believers in Jerusalem) the gospel that I preach among the Gentiles (non-Jews)," according to Galatians 2:2. The council, which endorsed Paul's gospel from Jesus, occurred about 11 years before Mark wrote his book (61 AD - 50 AD = 11 years).

The book of Acts, written by Luke even later - in about 67 AD - was a fairly detailed overview of the **post-cross**, early life and teaching of the infant church – including some important parts of the emerging gospel message which I will summarize in Chapter Six. However, as we will see by comparing Paul's revelation from Jesus with the book of Acts written by Luke, Paul's gospel was a much larger and purer panorama of the **whole gospel of grace** than what was known and being preached in the Jerusalem church. One glaring proof of this basic difference is that the Jerusalem church required Gentiles to be circumcised "law-keepers" first, *before* they could become Christians. In Acts 15:5 it states unequivocally: "The Gentiles must be circumcised and required to obey the Law of Moses." And the inconvenient truth is this: that *requirement* continued in the Jerusalem church up until 135 AD. It officially ended *only* because the Romans banned the practice of circumcision there in 132 AD which sparked a three-year-long Jewish rebellion. Consequently, after crushing the revolt, the Romans drove out all the Jews (including Jewish Christians) living in Jerusalem and then destroyed, rebuilt and renamed the city. (See Endnote #3 for more details.)

However, at the council in 50 AD, Peter, James and John recognized and agreed that God entrusted Paul with the task to preach to the Gentiles the same gospel which Jesus revealed directly to him. Consequently, "… not even Titus, who was with me (Paul) was compelled to be circumcised, even though he was a Greek (not Jewish)" (Galatians 2:3). I will revisit this major doctrinal discrepancy in Chapter Five to reveal in detail just how entrenched the whole church in Jerusalem was in mixing the Mosaic law covenant with the **New Covenant** of grace. We will see here exactly when, where, why and how the **elephant of mixture** – the heresy of Galatianism – began in the early church.

A Fundamental Change

Paul's **whole gospel of grace** from Jesus was a fundamental departure from what was the norm in the Jerusalem church. (See Endnote #4 for documentation.) In practice, Jesus revealed to Paul that no part of the Law that the Jews labored under was to be transferred to Gentile believers. (Peter agreed! see Acts 15:6-11.) In addition, it was in Antioch that believers in Jesus were first called "Christians" while the believers in Jerusalem still thought of themselves just as members of a sect of Judaism – one of many Jewish sects in the city. (See Endnote #5 for more information.) The term "Judeo-Christian" reflects that early misconception. These and other major differences between the Law-based practices of the Jerusalem church and Jesus' **whole gospel of grace** revealed to Paul, have caused enormously tragic consequences in the body of Christ for 2000 years. This fault-line is commonly well understood and documented in books about early church history. However, this early schism has been generally ignored, covered over or even denied in denominational circles and theology books for 2000 years. Tragically, this has served to perpetuate rather than eliminate the heresy of Galatianism for 2000 years. Again, I will detail some of those negative consequences in Chapters Seven and Nine.

Paul did not just preach and teach this new revelation to the Gentiles. Fortunately for us, he also wrote down what Jesus personally revealed to him in many letters that comprise about one-half of the books in the New Testament but only about 25% of the New Testament's total text. Again, his earliest letter that has survived was written in about 51 AD, at least ten years before Mark wrote the first "gospel" book. In fact, scholars generally agree that Paul wrote nine of his letters before Mark wrote the shortest version of what are now officially called "the four gospels."

Are you beginning to see the makings of another serious fault-line in the early church? For 2000 years, the church has focused primarily on "the four gospels" that mainly describe Jesus' earthly life and mission while He lived under the Mosaic Covenant of Law as stated in Galatians 4:4. Fortunately, Jesus fulfilled all the demands of the Law perfectly for our sake and then all the ordinances of the Law were nailed to His cross, according to Ephesians 2:15 and Colossians 2:14. (See Endnote #6 for more documentation.) Thus, He brought an end to the Mosaic Covenant - given only to the Israelites - in order to usher in a monumentally better covenant by His blood for *all* believers, according to Hebrews 7:12 and 22. "Christ is the end of the Law so that there may be righteousness for *everyone* who believes," Paul declares in Romans 10:4. Again, God's absolutely free gift of salvation is totally based on faith in Jesus' performance, not on our efforts – or else it would not be a *free* gift and, therefore, no gospel at all.

However, Jesus revealed to Paul that there is still a "proper use" for the Mosaic Law for Jewish unbelievers, which he stated in 1 Timothy 1:8-11:

> But we know that the law is good, if a man uses it properly; knowing this, that the law is not made for a righteous (reborn) man, but for the lawless and disobedient, for the ungodly and for sinners, for unholy and profane, for murderers of fathers and murderers of mothers, for manslayers, for whoremongers, for them that defile themselves with mankind, for kidnappers, for liars, for perjured persons, and if there be any other thing that is contrary to sound doctrine, according to the glorious gospel of the blessed God, which was committed to my trust.

Notice again Paul's emphasis to his disciple, Timothy, that God entrusted the "sound doctrine *according to* the glorious gospel of the blessed God" to him. It might seem that Paul is contradicting himself in this passage when he states that the law is meant for the lawless and disobedient, and for the ungodly and sinners - in effect all **in Adam** people - when the Mosaic Law was given only to the Jews. (See Endnote #7 for more details.) He clears that up in Romans 1:32, by referencing the existence of "God's righteous decree" of a general knowledge of right and wrong, that mankind is responsible to live by on earth for the sake of civil order and relative peace.

This could be called the "principle of law" that existed long before Moses. Its origin likely comes from the "tree of knowledge of good and evil" itself which Adam ate from in the Garden (or the Noahide laws which we will discuss later). The Mosaic Covenant of Law, however, was much more specific in its demands and in God's responses to good and evil behavior. However, man's attempt to obey either a general law code or the Mosaic Law code *cannot* effect or affect mankind's eternal salvation. Why? Because it is by grace through faith in Christ Jesus' **finished**

work, not by doing the works of any law code, that unbelievers become saved (see Ephesians 2:8-9). Later, we will explore the purpose and proper use of "the law" for unbelievers, according to Jesus' revelation to Paul, in Chapter Eight. We will also contrast that "law system" with the (higher) law of the Spirit of life that Jesus revealed to Paul in Romans 8:1-2.

Father-God's Focus

Unfortunately, the church has typically focused on law-keeping and/or on Jesus' **pre-cross** earthly life and mission to the Jews instead of on the brand new terms and astounding blessings of the inclusive **New Covenant**. It is called "new" because it is a covenant of "righteousness apart from the Law," which God offers to all of mankind through Christ Jesus, as stated unequivocally in Romans 3:21-22. Yet, the Holy Spirit made it abundantly clear to Paul that God's heart and focus will forever be on the revelation and celebration of His Son Jesus and what the **unseen reality** of His **finished work** has provided for anyone believing **in Him**.

Father-God sent Jesus to make possible His *ultimate intention*, which was to have an eternal family, through the miracle of a second *spiritual* birth, received by His grace through childlike faith in Jesus' **finished work** on Calvary. It was Jesus' assignment to model and establish, through His life and His substitutionary sacrifice for mankind, the accessibility of God's **grace-gospel** offered to mankind. Jesus' assignment to Paul was to believe, receive and explain the **unseen reality** of the grace-based **New Covenant** in words that Gentiles could grasp by faith. Paul puts it this way in Ephesians 3:8-11:

> Although I am the least of all the saints, I have been given God's grace to preach among the Gentiles the unsearchable riches of Christ, and to make clear to everyone the revelation of this mystery which was eternally hidden in God who created all things, so that the manifold wisdom of God may become well-known to the principalities and powers in the heavens, through the Church - the manifold wisdom of God according to His timeless purpose, which *He has accomplished* **in Christ Jesus** our Lord.

Focusing mainly on the four gospels - *instead* of on our exalted Savior and Lord and the **unseen reality** of what He did for us - is like sleeping through the culminating act of a three act play. You miss the revelation of:

1) the fullness of who God really is,

2) understanding what He did for mankind in His **finished work** through Jesus and

3) what His gift of regeneration causes believers to *be, in* and *through* Jesus' **divine exchange** - and

4) all of what that implies for us *from God's viewpoint*.

Or, even more dramatically, emphasizing the four gospels above our **New Covenant realities** now available to us **in Christ,** is analogous to being preoccupied throughout one's whole married life with nostalgically recounting the happy years of dating and preparing for and celebrating the wedding - forever focusing on the memories of the big day by watching recorded replays. As entertaining or pleasant as those memories might be, it would be far more practical and profitable to enjoy the day to day benefits of being united with a loving spouse by experiencing the new life-style, privileges and interaction that your new marriage covenant makes legally possible. Again, Paul described the believer's new, *relational* life **in Christ** as "walking according to the Spirit" (not according to the law) in Romans 8:5-9 which we will explore thoroughly in Chapter Nineteen.

The four gospels provide an indispensable service of revealing who Father-God *really* is through how Jesus lived His life according to the Spirit while on earth. Why? Because "His Son (Jesus) is the reflection of God's glory and the exact likeness of God's being," as explained in Hebrews 1:3. The four gospels also show us who we humans are in our fallen and spiritually bankrupt condition **in Adam** - which Jesus came to reverse. While Jesus did tell Nicodemus that he had to be born again to be saved, none of the four gospels give the process because their focus is on the **pre-cross** life of Jesus. They do not unveil, describe and facilitate the mystery of rebirth into God's glorious, **unseen reality** and the implications of Jesus' **divine exchange** that is now available to anyone who trusts in His offer of salvation. Why? 1) because Calvary had not happened yet and 2) because *only* Paul was personally given a ring-side seat to the full and pure revelation of Jesus' **finished work,** which he labored tirelessly to impart to anyone who would listen. He did this despite constant opposition from the Judaizers - Jewish believers who insisted on mixing the two opposing covenants of law and grace. We will reveal their identity as major players on why the **elephant of mixture** is still in most Christian churches even today.

All Things New In Christ Jesus
Engrossed in the old days and old ways of an obsolete covenant and traditions, given only to the Jews, can't produce the good fruit of the Spirit that the new marriage covenant with Jesus Himself is intended to produce through us. Jesus made all believers "one with Him" (as He prayed in John 17:20-23) by fulfilling and replacing the Mosaic Covenant with the dramatically different terms of His New Covenant He that made with God for us. As He revealed to Paul in 2 Corinthians 5:17, His **finished work** has caused "...old things to pass away. Behold! All things have become new" for believers **in Him**. Those "new things" are the inheritance that Jesus already purchased for us. But we will not fully benefit from those "new things" that are already ours **in Christ** if we continue to focus on "the old things" of an obsolete covenant (that was never given to Gentiles) or mentally mix them with the **New Covenant** - personally and/or corporately.

What are these "new things" and how do the terms of these two major covenants differ? The seven scriptures quoted at the beginning of this chapter provide snapshots of just how radical Jesus' **New Covenant** really is. In the **big picture**, the four gospels announce and describe that His Kingdom is *going to come* and He demonstrates Father-God's heart and care for a fallen race. In Jesus' **grace-based gospel** to Paul, He reveals that His Kingdom – in the Person of the Holy Spirit – *comes down and dwells inside anyone* who becomes a reborn child of God so that they too can do the works Father-God did through Jesus – and even greater ones! Paul describes this in Romans, Chapter Eight as walking according to the Spirit instead of the flesh - which we will explore in Chapter Nineteen.

But that is just the beginning. Jesus also revealed to Paul that His **finished work** on Calvary has caused each believer to be **in Christ Jesus** Himself. Since Jesus is now seated in heavenly places next to our new Father, that means that every believer is also seated next to Father-God as well as being "one in spirit" with Him – even though he/she is still physically living on earth (see 1 Corinthians 6:17 and 19-20 and Ephesians 2:6). How much more "new" can you get than that?

Have you, believer, taken seriously Christ Jesus' Word that tells you that you are *now* seated with Him in heavenly places? This revelation was alluded to in John's gospel but clearly stated as an accomplished reality for **New Covenant** believers in Ephesians 2:6. That means that all of mankind's efforts to somehow, some day, arrive in heaven is actually the reborn believer's starting point *now,* spiritually speaking. But few Christians understand and benefit from that **unseen reality** and its implications while living on earth. Some theologians do acknowledge it as some vague concept they label "positional truth" but discount its relevance for daily living. In Chapters Sixteen and Seventeen, we will explore how consciously abiding in that glorious dimension of Jesus' **whole gospel** of salvation is now part of the new life He offers to all believers.

The following chart is included here (and later more fully explained in Chapter Sixteen) to provide a tangible representation of the **unseen reality** of the two opposing **unseen Kingdoms** with the natural, **seen realm** in the middle. God's **unseen, heavenly realm** is described above Line A. Satan's **unseen, despotic realm** is represented below Line B. **#8**

GOD'S HEAVENLY, ETERNALLY PERFECT, **UNSEEN REALM**

The "Now" Realm of God, where Christ Jesus is seated next to Father-God
with all reborn saints who are **in Christ Jesus**, enjoying the view (Ephesians 2:6),
along with myriads of ministering angels.

LINE A _

GOD'S CREATED **SEEN REALM -**
the natural Universe
God created time, space and matter in perfect order and harmony.
But Adam's Fall and the Flood caused great disorder, disharmony, disease, lack and need. Jesus laid aside His deity and took on flesh and lived here as a Man among us, to reverse the curse and provide His abundant life to us through His **finished work**.

LINE B _

The **UNSEEN** Kingdom of Darkness, originally created for the fallen angels.

Bondage, hatred, envy, deception, murder, accusation, stealing and rebellion
reign down here and seek to influence the world system and man's flesh.

1A The Three Realm Chart

Jesus' Finished Work

"Why did He do all this for us believers", you ask? It was out of His totally unselfish love for mankind, according to John 3:16-17. God has positioned us **in Him** (above Line A) and is living in us so that we can then choose to allow Him to live through us in the **seen realm.** He united us to Himself as His Body in order for us to flourish, bloom and bear the God-kind-of-fruit consistent with His Life that is lived and enjoyed in heaven – His zoë life! In other words, Jesus' **finished work** has made us *one*, united with Christ Jesus in God the Father through Jesus' **divine exchange** with us. Why? So that we can enjoy Him and share the glory of His **unseen reality** (that we are now a part of) with others in the natural, **seen realm,** here on earth! The Kingdom has come on earth in the Person of the Holy Spirit now residing in all reborn believers - even if they don't know it. Someday, the glory of God's Kingdom and reign will be *fully* manifested on a new earth after Christ Jesus returns in victory. But why wait around until then when you can enjoy His victory personally by letting the Holy Spirit live through you like Jesus did?

By becoming increasingly conscious of the person of Jesus and His **finished work**, we can then effectively be Him to others by depending on the Holy Spirit to live His "overcoming life" through us, as us. In Jesus' words, we are His branches that Father-God, the Vinedresser, grafted onto Jesus when, by faith, we were crucified, then died, buried, arose and ascended **in** and **with Christ** as new creations in our **unseen,** inner man. This is the miracle of His **divine exchange!** As we learn to hear and yield to the Holy Spirit living inside of us, He causes God's divine life - the vine's life-giving "sap" - to produce His fruit through our **seen** outer man. I call this the **butterfly life** throughout this book. And, starting in Chapter Sixteen, we will explore and explain more of why and how the experience of this God-kind-of-life is to be the *norm* for believers. It is the natural result of being a partaker of His divine nature (see 2 Peter 1:4). This is simply learning to live from the **unseen realm** above Line A.

This is how Jesus manifested the divine life of His Father to others. He was constantly tuned into His **unseen** heavenly Father and operated in the **unseen** ability of the Holy Spirit – *not* in His own human ability - as He revealed in John 8:26-29. He demonstrated His Father's nature of unconditional love, thereby confronting the popular stereotype of God being a "condemning Judge." He lavished grace, mercy and forgiveness on all receptive seekers, which was a foretaste of His **unseen** Kingdom, soon to come *into* believers in the Person of the Holy Spirit, **post-cross.** He is the same Lover who wants to live through us today to attract others to Jesus, not to ourselves. In John's gospel in particular, Jesus continuously contrasts the **unseen realm** He came from with the natural, **seen realm** in which His followers were confined. That all changed when He ascended into heaven. He sends back the Holy Spirit to live and reign within all reborn saints of God, who are also **in Him** *now,* according to Romans 5:17 and seated in heavenly places, according to Ephesians 2:6!

The question you might want to ask yourself as you go through this book is: "Am I reigning with Jesus in this life or am I laboring under the **elephant of mixture** – knowingly or unknowingly?" You will be able to better understand and definitively answer that question by the end of this book. Again, Chapter Sixteen will elaborate more on the implications of The Three Realm Chart.

Why Settle For Less Than What Jesus Paid For?

Tragically many, if not most members of the Body of Christ today, are still ignorant of Jesus' **whole gospel** of total forgiveness and lavish grace. Consequently, they have wrong beliefs about God and about themselves and about others because of a confused muddle of law and grace. They desperately need to know that God:

1) is no longer counting men's sins against them, and

2) has reconciled the world to Himself **from His point of view** because of how God regards Jesus' **finished work** on Calvary - as clearly revealed in 2 Corinthians 5:19, Colossians 2:13 and 1 John 2:2.

The doctrine of God's **total forgiveness** of all sin of all mankind for all time is such a central truth of the **New Covenant** revelation, that Chapters Thirteen to Fifteen are devoted to documenting this foundational reality accomplished by Christ Jesus' **finished work** on Calvary. This startling revelation is the extreme opposite of the terms and conditions of the performance-based, Mosaic Law Covenant. It means that, **post-cross,** a person's sins, per se, do not send him to hell because the essence of true Christianity is not about rule keeping or rule breaking like it was with the Israelite's Law Covenant. Rather, it is about accepting or rejecting a personal relationship with God Himself, now made available to all by Jesus' **finished work** for mankind 2000 years ago. But that does *not* mean that everyone is automatically going to heaven. Why? It is because personal salvation involves more than 1) Jesus' paying for, and thus removing the punishment of mankind's evil behavior and 2) Jesus absorbing God's just wrath for mankind's sins and 3) God's unilateral offer of reconciliation to mankind - from His viewpoint. Thankfully, these three things that Jesus accomplished, as mankind's second Adam sent by God, justly reversed the effects of what Adam did.

So, What Is My Part?

So again, Jesus accomplished the forgiveness of all sin for mankind, including you and me. How and when? By His sacrificial substitution for us at Calvary which paid for all my past, present and future sins - from God's viewpoint. Thereby, Jesus payment removed the negative consequences of my rebellious, evil behavior between God and me. But clearing away the rubble of a burned down house is not the same thing as replacing it with a new building. So, secondly, Jesus emphatically told Nicodemus in John 3:3-8 that no one can see or enter God's kingdom unless he is born a second time by water and the Spirit. And Jesus perfect sacrifice also made that possible for mankind to receive by faith, **post-cross**.

Rebirth speaks of being *personally* regenerated – a spiritually re-begun new creation being – this time by God, not by natural parents. Jesus makes spiritual rebirth possible for us by grace when we simply believe and accept His offer of a **divine exchange** with Him that He accomplished at Calvary 2000 years ago. My rebirth **in** and **through Christ Jesus'** death and resurrection in 1972 removed my **in Adam** sin nature and automatically established an intimate relationship with Father-God in the **unseen realm** of the spirit – one with Abba-Father as His own child. This **New Covenant** option is *offered* to everyone by grace through faith in what Jesus did for mankind as God's appointed Savior. In the **big picture**, Jesus' gift of forgiveness to all mankind is the necessary pre-requisite for Father-God's gifts of justification, acceptance, approval and security which are part of every believer's inheritance when <u>reborn</u> **in** and **through Christ Jesus.**

If God's forgiveness was not total and eternal, a believer could not walk in the assurance of permanent justification - right-standing with God - that Jesus won for all believers on the basis of faith alone, in Jesus alone. By contrast, anyone not reborn of God by His grace through faith, remains incompatible with the perfection and glory of God's nature and with heaven itself. So, thanks to Jesus, the choice is yours where you will spend eternity. As someone once said: "God cast His vote for you, the devil cast his vote against you – so now you have the deciding vote." Jesus' sacrifice restored that gift of "choice" to mankind. (See Endnote **#9** for more information on God's gift of free will to mankind.)

Personally Bonding With God
So then, on a personal level:

> … to all who received Him (Jesus), who believe in His name, He gave to them the power to become God's own children - children not born of natural blood, nor of the will of the flesh, nor of the will of man, but reborn of God (John 1:12-13).

Being born of Father-God automatically makes each of His children righteous, which is a guarantee of permanent right-standing with Him, *regardless of one's behavior* (see 2 Corinthians 5:21). That is true because **New Covenant** salvation is a free *gift* based on faith in Jesus' performance, not on one's good or bad behavior. It was not your behavior that got you saved or it would not be a free gift. So how can your behavior lose a gift? Your salvation is based only on believing and receiving what Jesus did for you, not on what you do or don't do for Him. Of course, the more you know Him, the more you will love Him and delight to walk in His wonderful plan and purpose for your life in the **seen realm**.

That is the pure, unmixed gospel of **total grace** that Jesus revealed to Paul. Law-minded Judaizers, who mixed law with grace, accused Paul of giving people a license to sin. That lie is trumpeted today by many well-meaning but deceived Galatianists in seminaries and pulpits. However, any gospel that adds man's efforts to gain or maintain <u>Jesus' free gift of full salvation</u> is *no gospel at all*. It could not be otherwise because rebirth makes the **new creation** saint spiritually united with Jesus Himself, which was the very prayer He prayed to our Father as His last "will and testament," just before He went to His death. Jesus prayed

> … that they all may be one, as you, Father, are in Me, and as I am in You, that they also may be one in Us so that the world may believe that You have sent Me (John 17:21).

Jesus' radical, **grace-based gospel** is the foundation that qualifies us to receive, by grace through faith, all the other benefits of Jesus' **finished work**, described more fully in the next chapter. I know all this is "strong meat meant for the mature" (see Hebrews 5:14) and may be a huge stretch for you, just like it was for me a while back. So let me help you "taste and see the goodness of the Lord" as we feast on His gospel truth, bite by bite, through the rest of this book.

The answers to the questions at the top of this chapter:
1) Acts 13:38-39

2) Galatians 2:21
3) Galatians 2:20
4) Ephesians 2:4-6
5) Romans 8:1
6) 2 Corinthians 5:16-21 (Chapter Sixteen will explain this wonderful passage.)
7) 2 Corinthians 4:17-18 (Paul's focus here is central to understanding the whole gospel.)

All of these scriptures were based on the revelation knowledge which Jesus gave only to Paul - a claim he made in Galatians 1:11-12, which this book will carefully document. Appendix # 12 explains the source of the translation of these and all other Bible verses used in this book.

NOTE: As an added benefit, I have included words to some of my original songs that help to reinforce many of the key points found in this book. You can find more information about these songs on my web site, www.totaltruth.org. Here are the first two:

BORN AGAIN, I've been born again.
Baptized in Jesus, I am justified in Him.
Resurrected, ascended to the heavenlies
Where I live to give all glory to Your name.

I was lost, cut off from life and mercy,
Dead to God and under Satan's slavery.
But You bought my freedom
With Your righteous blood, sweet Lamb.
Thank You Father for a privileged destiny.

Now in You, I am a new creation.
Dead to self, a living sacrifice of praise.
Holy Spirit, sanctify my outer man by grace
As I live in You through faith all of my days.
© Copyright 1993 by Leonard J. Ransil

IN YOU I LIVE AND MOVE AND HAVE MY BEING
If not for You, I would be lost and dead.
You found me, Lord, and gave me grace to choose You.
Engulfing me, You gave me life instead.

Bought by Your Blood, I'm one with You forever.
I am Your branch that draws Life from my Vine.
Just as You are, so now am I in this world.
All that I am is Yours and You are mine.

In You I live and move and have my being
Made righteous by Your perfect sacrifice.
As God's own Lamb, becoming sin to save me,
Your Holy Blood became my ransom price. © Copyright 2009 by Leonard J. Ransil

CHAPTER TWO

MORE BENEFITS OF CHRIST JESUS' NEW COVENANT OF TOTAL GRACE

Jesus' Whole Gospel Revealed To Paul

For whatever reason, Jesus revealed the full benefits of His New Covenant of lavish grace only to Paul. Understandably, he became like a pit bull, guarding His Master's treasure from anyone mixing it with law. It is the treasure in a field that Jesus spoke about in Matthew 13:44 which is worth selling everything else to obtain. That treasure and reward *is* actually Jesus Himself, revealed in His **finished work.** Father-God sent Jesus to mankind as His gift of salvation and Jesus sent the Holy Spirit to not only lead and guide us into all truth but to also teach us to understand all the things already freely given to us by God through what Jesus fully accomplished on Calvary (see 1 Corinthians 2:12). The following passage demonstrates just how passionate Paul was about the **whole gospel of radical grace** that the exalted Christ Jesus unveiled to him.

I marvel that you have been so quickly turned away from him (me, Paul) - who called you into the grace of Christ - and over to another gospel, except, there is *not* another. There are some persons (Judaizers from the church in Jerusalem) who disturbed you and who want to pervert the gospel of Christ. But if anyone, even we ourselves or an angel from heaven (not just from hell) were to preach to you a gospel other than the one that we have preached to you, let him be anathema (accursed or excommunicated in the Greek). Just as we have said before and now I say again: 'If anyone has preached a gospel to you, other than that which you have received, let him be anathema.'

For am I now trusting men, or God? Or, am I seeking to please men (the Judaizers)? If I still were pleasing men (such as the pillars in the Jerusalem church), then I would not be a servant of Christ. For I would have you understand, brothers, that the gospel which has been preached by me is not according to man. I did not receive it from any man (including Peter, James or John), nor was I taught it. I received it by revelation from Jesus Christ (Galatians 1:6-8 and 11-12).

He (God) has made us (Paul) ministers of a new covenant – not of the letter (the Mosaic Covenant) but of the Spirit because the letter (of the law) kills, but the Spirit (of God) gives life (2 Corinthians 3:4-6).

Why was Paul seemingly so "unchristian" by saying "let him be accursed" to anyone who perverts the gospel by mixing the two covenants? Because he knew, by revelation from Jesus, that all humans start off "spiritually dead to God" by being "**in Adam.**" The only remedy for spiritually dead humans is rebirth into the divine life that God gives through water and the Holy Spirit - by grace through faith in Jesus' **finished work.** By contrast, law acts like a mirror that can only *show* you an ugly pimple on your face. It gives no power or ability to fix it. God gave the law to the Israelites to point out mankind's spiritually dead *nature* **in Adam** – demonstrated by their less than perfect obedience. Again, law can only point out our sinfulness but it can't provide a remedy. It can only condemn the sinner to death because it points out his sins - and the wages of sin is death. Therefore, mixing Moses' law covenant that ministers death (and was given to reveal mankind's <u>sin nature</u> **in Adam)** with a covenant that "gives divine life," has a deadening effect. The combination nullifies both covenants and puts believers who still try to live *according* to the law (instead of according to the Spirit of life) back under the law's effect on one's own mind – condemnation. It is not God who is condemning him but his conscience, still bound to law. This deadly mixture is the answer to the "how" of the following questions.

The Veil Of Mixture

How is it possible, after almost 2000 years, so very few in the Body of Christ are fully experiencing the many wonders of the gospel of Jesus' abundant life of faith, love and liberty **in Him**? How could we, the church, make such an obvious blunder of ignoring or minimizing the glorious, present-time benefits of the **whole gospel** of the **unseen realm** for so long? How is it that believers, who are reborn of God Himself, continue to ignore the miraculous inner change - God living inside of them - and continue to regard themselves and each other as "sinners" instead of "saints of God" who sin less and less? How is it that we, who are "one with Christ Jesus in God," can still think of ourselves as "alone" or "worthless" or "failures" instead of greatly blessed, highly favored and deeply loved by the King of kings to whom we are betrothed? Why is it that we are so fixated on the **seen realm** where law reigns, when Jesus instructed us, through Paul, in Colossians 3:1-3 that:

> If, then, you were raised with Christ (reborn), set your heart on things above, where Christ is seated at the right hand of God. Set your mind on the **unseen** things above, not on things on earth, for you died and your life is hidden now with Christ in God.

Jesus (and eventually Paul) walked this way in accordance with the Holy Spirit's life bubbling in Him. Paul called it "… the law of the Spirit of life that set us free from the Mosaic law of sin and death" *and* from condemnation, according to Romans 8:1-2. Why is living this **butterfly life of grace** not commonly understood, taught and lived today? I have touched on some of the reasons already. I will document the most shocking one in the next chapter. But first, let's pause to greatly enlarge the list of the seven **New Covenant** scriptures that were presented at the very beginning of Chapter One. These amazing truths describe many more of the "new things" that already are true of every reborn saint simply because he or she is **in Christ Jesus**.

A NOTE to unbelievers: God is not angry at you. These "new things" are also offered to every **in Adam** sinner - anyone not yet reborn through Christ Jesus' **finished work**. There are only two Kingdoms, God's and Satan's. Which one do *you* want to be in forever? The latter is the *default setting* for all of mankind still **in Adam**. Thanks to Jesus **finished work**, you don't have to *remain* there. God wants *you* to be a part of His family forever. We will continue to unfold God's way to receive His free gift of everlasting salvation as we go on (or you can go to Romans 10:9-13 now to find out how). <u>Why remain a spiritual caterpillar, struggling to survive on the ground and destined for hell? You, too, can become one of God's own children - a re-created **butterfly**, enjoying the freedom of His heavenlies!</u> (The benefits of these amazing things - and far more - will become much clearer to you as you progress through this book).

Father-God's Amazing Grace Gospel

All of the following amazing scriptural truths are now *legally* true for every believer's reborn, **unseen**, "inner-being" that has been made alive **in Christ Jesus** (see Ephesians 3:16). They describe aspects of Jesus' **divine exchange** that He accomplished on Calvary for *all* believers. However, they probably don't yet describe your unsanctified body and soul - your outer-man. That mental renewal comes over time as you meditate on scriptures like those listed below. They will *greatly* help to transform your thinking to agree with how God sees you, thanks to Jesus' **finished work** on Calvary. Allow the Holy Spirit to teach and sanctify your natural mind through meditating on who you now are **in Christ**, according to these **New Covenant** truths. These scriptures declare the **Good News** that Jesus came to offer all mankind!

BE ADVISED!! The following scriptures are the meat of the Word of Christ for those who are mature **in Christ,** not for the infants who want to drink only the milk of the Word – as important as that is initially when first reborn.

> For every one that still drinks the milk (the basic rudiments of the utterances of God referenced in verse 12) is not skilled in the word of righteousness, for he is an infant. But solid food is for those who are mature, having exercised their judgment, through habit, to discern both good and evil. Therefore, having left the discourse of the beginning of Christ (His life on earth), let us move on to maturity ... (Hebrews 5:13-14 and 6:1).

This passage was written expressly to the Hebrews who were trained by the Law to think that their righteousness was based on how well they kept the Law. Consequently, "none were righteous, not even one" because no one but Jesus could keep it perfectly. The writer wants to wake up these Hebrews to realize that New Covenant righteousness is based *only* on trusting in Jesus' performance through which believers are *made* righteous as a gift, through rebirth **into Him**. Gifts cannot be earned but can be rejected. I encourage you to believe and to receive the following scriptures as gifts of God, already freely given to you, thanks to Jesus' **finished work** of His **divine exchange** with you as a believer. Feeding on the solid food of New Covenant truths like these will enable you to grow mentally strong in the Lord, in the strength of His might, by seeing yourself the way He sees you – righteous, accepted and approved **in Christ.**

> God delivered me out of the power of Darkness and translated me into the kingdom of His beloved Son (Jesus) in whom I have redemption, the forgiveness of all my (past, present and future) sins (Colossians 1:13-14, 2:13 and Hebrews 10:17-18).

> It was Father-God's pleasure to choose to adopt me as His child (Ephesians 1:5).

> He chose me **in Christ** before the foundation of the world to be holy and blameless before Him in love (Ephesians 1:4, Hebrews 10:14 and 17).

> By grace through faith **in Christ,** I have been crucified with Christ, and it is no longer I who live but Christ who lives in me. The life I am now living is His life (Ephesians 2:8-9 and Galatians 2:20).

I have been spiritually circumcised (my old, unregenerate nature **in Adam** has been permanently removed) (Colossians 2:11).

I died with Christ and, therefore, I died to the power of my old, sin-nature's rule on my life (Romans 6:1-6 and Colossians 3:3).

I have been justified (completely forgiven and made righteous **in Christ**) (Romans 5:1).

I have been reconciled to God (2 Corinthians 5:18).

I have been buried, raised and made alive **with Christ** (Colossians 2:12-13 and Ephesians 2:5)

I have been raised up **with Christ** (Colossians 3:1)

I have been put **into Christ Jesus** by Father-God's own doing (1 Corinthians 1:30).

Since I have died, I no longer live for myself, but for Christ (2 Corinthians 5:14-15)

Consequently, I am born of God (2 Corinthians 5:18).

Since I have been bought with a price I am not my own. I now belong to God. My body is now a temple of the Holy Spirit who lives within me (1 Corinthians 6:19-20).

I have been redeemed and (totally) forgiven of all my sins (Colossians 1:14 and 2:13-14).

I have been made the righteousness of God Himself **in Christ** (2 Corinthians 5:21).

I have been redeemed from the curse of the law (Galatians 3:13).

I am free forever from condemnation (from God) (Romans 8:1).

My life is now hidden with Christ in God. Christ is now my life (Colossians 3:3).

Because I am sanctified and am one with the sanctifier (Christ Jesus), He is not ashamed to call me brother (Hebrews 2:11).

I have been made complete (perfect) **in Christ** (Colossians 2:10 and Hebrews 10:14).

And God raised us up **with Christ** and seated us with Him in the heavenly realms **in Christ Jesus** (Ephesians 2:6).

I have been saved and called (set apart), according to God's doing (2 Timothy 1:9 and Titus 3:5).

I am now a recipient of His lavish grace (Ephesians 1:8).

I have been blessed with every spiritual blessing (Ephesians 1:3).

I have been given a Spirit of power, love, and self-control (discipline, sound mind) (2 Timothy 1:7).

I have been given the mind of Christ (1 Corinthians 2:16).

I have been given exceedingly great and precious promises by God by which I am a partaker of God's divine nature (2 Peter 1:4).

I have been established, anointed, and sealed by God to Christ and have been given the Holy Spirit as a pledge (a deposit/down payment) guaranteeing my inheritance to come (2 Corinthians 1:21).

I have been firmly rooted **in Christ** and am now being built up **in Him** (Colossians 2:7).

Christ Himself is in me (and I am i**n Christ**) (Colossians 1:27).

I have direct access to God through the Spirit (Ephesians 2:18).

I have a right to come boldly before the throne of God to find mercy and grace in time of need (Hebrews 4:16).

I may approach God with boldness, freedom, and confidence (Ephesians 3:12).

In Christ, I am above every name that is named (Ephesians 1:21).

How Does God See You?

Consistent with all the blessings listed above, Father-God sees me and all believers the same way He sees Jesus. Why? Because we are **in Christ**. Again, Father-God's lavish love and grace toward mankind provided Jesus and everything that His **finished work** accomplished through His **divine exchange** with me. You can make these revelations personal by praying: "Father-God, Your holy word says that I am:

Redeemed and totally forgiven of <u>all</u> my sins (forever) (Colossians 2:13 and 1 John 2:2).

Justified – in right-standing with You (Romans 5:1).

Your precious child (John 1:12; Ephesians 1:5).

Christ's friend (John 15:15).

United with You as one spirit (1 Corinthians 6:17).

A saint (set apart for God) (Ephesians 1:1).

A personal witness of Christ (Acts 1:8).

Salt and light of the earth (Matthew 5:13-14).

A member of the Body of Christ (1 Corinthians 12:27).

Free forever from condemnation (Romans 8:1-2).

A citizen of Heaven and, therefore, significant (Philippians 3:20).

Free from any charge against me (Romans 8:31-34).

A minister of reconciliation on Your behalf (2 Corinthians 5:17-21).

Seated with Christ in the heavenly realms (Ephesians 2:6).

Your beloved child who cannot be separated *from* Your love (Romans 8:39).

Established, anointed and sealed by You Yourself (2 Corinthians 1:21-22).

One for whom all things work together for good (Romans 8:28).

Chosen and appointed to bear good fruit (John 15:16).

Always qualified to approach You with freedom and confidence (Ephesians 3:12).

Able to do all things (that You lead me to do) through Christ who strengthens me (Philippians 4:13).

A branch of the true vine, a channel of Your life (John 15:1-5).

Your own temple (1 Corinthians 3:16).

Complete (perfect) **in Christ** (Colossians 2:10; Hebrews 10:14).

Hidden with Christ in God (Colossians 3:3).

Your co-worker (1 Corinthians 3:9; 2 Corinthians 6:1).

Your regenerated handiwork (Ephesians 2:10).

All because You ransomed me for the price of Jesus' blood (1 Corinthians 6:19-20).

CONCLUSION: Now, I belong to You, Lord (no longer to the devil). That is fantastic News.

It's All About Receiving All That God Has Already Done For You

Again, if you are a reborn, **new creation** saint, all of the above scriptures are true of you because you are **in Christ Jesus** – regardless of how you think or "feel" about them. This reality has nothing to do with your behavior and everything to do with being **in Christ** *by faith*. Otherwise, your salvation would be based on your performance, not on Christ's **finished work** on Calvary's cross. God's *gift* of salvation is received by grace through faith *alone*, as implied in Ephesians 2:8-9 and stated here in Romans 1:17:

> For in the gospel of Christ the gift of right-standing with God is revealed, from faith to faith, just as it was written: 'For the just (righteous) one lives by faith.'

And, did you notice this fact while praying those truths about you? Virtually none of those new things were true for anyone mentioned in the four gospels before Jesus died - including Jesus' closest disciples, Peter, James and John. Even Jesus Himself could not get Nicodemus "saved" when he came to Jesus in the middle of the night. He could just tell him what was necessary for him to "see and enter the Kingdom" – to be reborn of God – which could only happen **post-cross**, when Jesus mediated the **New Covenant** with God. That distinction clearly demonstrates how enormously different was the focus and scope of the four gospels as compared with Jesus' **whole gospel of grace**, directly revealed to Paul in about 42 AD. Of course, this does not in any way diminish the crucial role of the inspired four gospels which will be presented in Chapter Eleven.

QUESTION: Is the gospel that is revealed in the scriptures above proclaimed, taught and lived out in your church? If so, thank your pastor vociferously. If not, you may be asking, "Why not?" In all likelihood, it is probably not your pastor's fault. After all, one can't give away what he doesn't have or can't teach what he has not been taught – for whatever reason. Let's tackle the most shocking reason for this oversight in the next chapter – **the elephant of mixture** – which still goes unrecognized in much of Christendom today.

NOTE: You don't have to memorize all the blessings Jesus won for us to benefit from them. But the more conscious you are of these tangible expressions of God's love for you, the more natural it becomes to love and personally relate to Him. The following song-poem keeps me mindful of what He has done for me and keeps me in a constant receiving mode – just as Jesus enjoyed with His Father while on earth.

I RECEIVE BY FAITH ALL THE BENEFITS
Of Your Covenant today.
Now I'm under Grace, instead of Law,
To hear You and obey.

    You are my Way to Father-God
    I rest in what You've done.
    You nailed the Law onto cross,   Colossians 2:14; Ephesians 2:15
    Now Satan's on the run.   Colossians 2:15

I receive, by faith, all the benefits
Of Your Righteousness for me.
By Your Blood I'm cleansed of all my sin,   Colossians 2:13
Forgiven totally. Hebrews 13:12

    You are my Life that trumps all death,
    My Peace and Victory.
    The weight of condemnation's gone,   Romans 8:1
    Your Blood has purchased me.   Colossians 1:14

I receive, by faith, all the benefits
Of Your **finished work** today
Help me trust in You and think Your thoughts
In all I do and say.

    You are the Truth against each lie
    That battles for my mind.
    I search Your living word each day
    Receiving what is mine.   Ephesians 1:13-14

You are more than what I need each day
To live victoriously.   2 Corinthians 2:14, 1 Corinthians 15:57
Dear Jesus, as I think on You
It's amazing Grace I see.
And Your might yet Your mercy
And Your endless love for me
And Your truth that sets me free
And Your life abundantly
For You're my hope and my victory
Yes, it's amazing Grace I see!
A Sermon Song © Copyright 2009 by Leonard J. Ransil

CHAPTER THREE

THE ELEPHANT HAS A NAME

Connecting the Dots – In Christ

In the first two chapters, I presented a panorama of the amazing **gospel of radical grace** which Jesus fully revealed to Paul. Unfortunately, this gospel is not usually the primary focus today. While the reasons are many, there is a root cause, an **elephant in the church,** that few dare to face head on. See Endnote #**10.** And, since it has been protected and even fed for 2000 years, the elephant has become a cancerous carcass in the confines of the church.

Its presence greatly hinders the life-giving effects of Jesus' **whole gospel of grace**, which Paul's congregations were routinely taught, experienced and enjoyed by faith in Jesus' **finished work**. The name of this imposing elephant is the heresy of "Galatianism" - the mixture of two irreconcilable covenants - that Paul unceremoniously exposed in his letter to the Galatians. However, even after almost 2000 years, this heresy is still stifling, if not crushing, the **butterfly life** of Jesus' **whole gospel of grace** in congregations worldwide because it "seems right" to our natural way of thinking. Why? Because our ordinary thoughts are naturally geared to focus on the **seen realm** around us.

That fact is what makes the Mosaic Covenant of Law so attractive to Gentiles, even though we were never given that Law Covenant by God. It presents a tangible and seemingly doable standard to follow in order to be "good." And therein lies the trap that lures us into walking according to the flesh by focusing on the Law instead of walking according to the **unseen,** higher law of the Spirit of life, which Jesus revealed to Paul, according to Romans 8:2. These two "laws" are diametrically opposed. This is a prime example of the truth that God's ways and thoughts are far higher than our ways and thoughts, as He revealed in Isaiah 55:8-9. Father-God sent Jesus to make it possible for fallen humans to live on earth according to His **unseen** ways of the Spirit by being reborn of God - by grace through faith in Him. Rebirth automatically puts the believer in permanent right-standing with Father-God - His free gift of justification to each beloved child.

This book delves into the reason why Jesus' offer to His church to live in His abundant life on earth as He did, has **not** become the norm for the whole church over these 2000 years. The short answer is that from the very beginning of the church, most believers did not distinguish between daily life lived under the demands of the Law vs. life lived in the Holy Spirit by God's grace through faith – from first to last. By not understanding God's higher thoughts and ways of the **unseen realm** of the Spirit that Jesus revealed to Paul, the church has mostly lived in division and in defeat under Law-based thinking. Father-God would rather have His children live in unity of the Spirit and in victory in the **seen realm**, just as Jesus did. It is the difference between walking by natural sight under Law or by learning to walk according to the higher law of faith, love and liberty in the Spirit which is explained on page 54 and in Endnote # 13.

The aim of this book is *not* to further split an already fractured church but, rather, to:

1) expose a major underlying reason why such division still commonly exists today - the **elephant of Galatianism** - which routinely stomps on **the butterfly** of **grace-based** living,

2) show when and how this division began, and

3) prove that the **whole grace gospel**, that Jesus revealed to Paul and which "made all things new," is God's solution to overcome the double-mindedness of this mixture that underlies the division and animosity between denominations and among their members <u>and even inside the minds of Christians themselves</u>. It inhibits the *manifestation* of "the unity of the Spirit and the bond of peace," made possible by Jesus, according to Ephesians 4:3.

When And How Did This Division Begin?

So where did this monstrosity of mixture come from and when and how did it contaminate the doctrine of the early church? It is not hard to figure out – once you connect the right dots. Not surprisingly, the **elephant of Galatianism** walked right in with the birth of the church at Pentecost. How? Well, ignorant of its implications, virtually everyone in the early Jerusalem church - including the leaders, James, Peter and John - continued to follow the norms of the Mosaic Law that did not specifically contradict what they remembered and interpreted from Jesus' teaching while He was on earth - both **pre-cross** and **post-cross**.

And why shouldn't they do this? After all, Jesus came and lived as a Jew and complied with the practices of the Law that He lived under (unless they violated His Father's higher law of love). He had told His disciples specifically that "I was sent only to the lost sheep of the house of Israel" and that He came "to fulfill the Law and the Prophets, not to abolish them," according to Matthew 15:24 and 5:17 respectively. It is only natural that His followers would also stay on that same tried and true course as did all other law-honoring Jews. It was what God had given directly to Moses! Jesus *seemed* to emphasize the importance of the Law again when He told them "to observe all things whatsoever I commanded you" - just before He ascended into heaven (see Matthew 28:19-20).

And, when He told them to "make disciples of all nations," they naturally assumed He wanted them to circumcise the "inferior" Gentiles first before baptizing them with water as members of their new, true blue, Jewish sect. On top of all that, the Holy Spirit was *seemingly* confirming what they believed, practiced and taught with miraculous signs and wonders. They busily studied the Old Testament prophecies about what the coming Messiah would do and undergo which confirmed that Jesus was indeed the promised One sent by God. These Jewish believers were eagerly spreading the new message that Jesus was the Messiah. Law-minded Pharisees like Nicodemus and even Saul, their former persecutor, were added to the flock. How could there be anything wrong with any of these things?

Paul's Personal Paradigm Shift

Things were so amazing that, in fact, the very existence of the **elephant of mixture** in the Jerusalem church – the mixture of law with grace – was not made abundantly clear until the revelation Jesus gave to Paul during his miraculous visit to the third heaven in about 42 AD.

Jesus personally gave this plumb line - the **whole gospel of grace** - to a man willing to replace tradition with revealed *truth* and religion with a *personal relationship with God.* No doubt it took Paul some time to begin to digest such a monumental reversal of all that he had believed in, worked for, held dear and defended as an avowed Jewish Pharisee. But as this glorious revelation from Jesus progressively renewed his own mind, he could then confidently and definitively declare in Philippians 3:7-9:

> But what things were gain to me, these I have counted as loss because of Christ. Yes, indeed, and I count all things to be loss, because of the excellency of <u>knowing</u> Christ Jesus my Lord, for whom I have suffered the loss of all things and regard them as garbage, that I may gain Christ and be found **in Him**, not having my own righteousness by (trying to keep) the law, but by that which is <u>through the faith of Christ</u>—God's gift of righteousness, that comes from faith (**in Him**).

So, what exactly did he count as "loss" and even as "garbage?" Obviously, it was anything he was taught, believed in and did previously as a Jew and a learned Pharisee which contradicted what Jesus revealed to him in 42 AD and beyond. In this very passionate passage, Paul demonstrated true, **New Covenant** repentance – a mental make-over - by replacing the unacceptable mixture of law and grace he had been trusting in (and therefore teaching) with the purity of Jesus' **whole gospel of grace.** Undoubtedly, Paul's "mind renewal" was not a quick and easy process for one so steeped in law-based believing and living. He had to first replace the **elephant of mixture** in his own believing and thinking if he was going to be an effective ambassador of the **whole gospel** for his new King. And to be sure, that mental transformation was both deepened and tested for the rest of his life, starting with the still law-minded Jerusalem church and even down to his closest friend, Barnabas.

Paul made it clear to the whole world that he had won the mental battle against the strongholds of law-mindedness when he wrote: "The law is not of faith" (Galatians 3:12) in about 51 AD. For him, and for us too, that must be the line drawn in the sand. Otherwise, putting your faith in law-keeping in order to become or remain in right relationship with God, will undermine your trusting faith **in Christ Jesus** <u>alone</u>. And what He accomplished on Calvary will be of no benefit to you. In fact, focusing on law-keeping will be a detriment.

> Christ has become of no effect to you who are trying to be justified by keeping the law; you have fallen away from grace (Galatians 5:4).

That, my friend, is a serious statement. (Law-minded people typically think that you fall away from grace by sinning.)

The Mental War Between The Elephant And The Butterfly
In effect, Jesus Himself launched this "doctrinal war" when He personally revealed His **whole gospel of grace**, based totally on God's grace through faith, to a warrior like Paul. In simple terms, it is a war between walking by natural sight vs. walking in the Spirit by faith in the **unseen realm** of God's Kingdom realities. The terms of the Mosaic Law Covenant bring rewards or punishments on each person based on his or her performance. If one "keeps the Law <u>perfectly</u>," he is blessed; if one "breaks any part of the Law," he is cursed - according to the stark

terms of Deuteronomy 28:1-69. The focus on the Law is completely about one's behavior in the **seen realm.** Righteousness by the Law can only be achieved by keeping the whole Law *perfectly* for one's entire lifetime. Of course, this is an impossibility for anyone still **in Adam.** (Only Jesus lived His life without sin because He was not **in Adam** but "of God.") In short, under this works-based covenant system, righteousness was reduced to a verb - "earning right-standing with God by perfect behavior." Jesus raised the bar of difficulty in the four gospels when He included the requirement of perfect thinking, not just perfect doing. Again, only He could - and did - fulfill the requirements of the Law perfectly.

In direct contrast, God's **covenant of grace** that He offered to Abram was based on his faith in a God of the **unseen realm** who promised to give him land in the **seen realm** - the "promised land." In addition, He promised that Abram would become "the father of many nations," even though neither of these promises seemed possible in the **seen realm.** Even the very covenant that God offered to Abram was cut between God the Father and a pre-incarnate manifestation of Jesus Christ, the Light of the world, while Abram was in a trance. Everything was *done for him.* The *only* thing he had to "do" was to *believe* whatever God said was *true* in order to receive all that God promised him. His own moral behavior, *good or bad,* did not qualify or disqualify him from receiving God's blessings. Why? Because he was offered a grace-based covenant with righteousness given as a *free gift.* He just had to believe that 1) what God promised to him was true, just because *God* promised it and 2) that God could and would somehow do what He promised. Everything was based on faith in God's nature and performance, not on Abram's. That's pure grace.

Again, under this *grace-based* covenant, God freely gave Abram the *gift* of righteousness and even a new name, "Abraham" (father of many nations) because he believed that God would do what He said He would do in the **seen realm** - despite his current, childless circumstances. Consequently, God unilaterally fulfilled His covenant promises of a gift of *land* and a *son* and Abraham did nothing except *believe* and *receive.* (When he trusted in his own performance with Hagar, he got into trouble – but not with God.) That is how God operates in a grace-based covenant. Everything that is needed or "required" is supplied as a free gift.

So, whose nature and "perfect doing" do you want to depend on - yours or God's? That same choice is constantly ours today. "Faith is the substance of things hoped for, a certainty of the reality of <u>unseen</u> things" (Hebrews 11:1). The actual translation for the word "hope" in Greek is "a confident expectation of good." So we believers can be confident that all of God's promises to us about the **unseen realm** will certainly be manifested by <u>agreeing with what He says is true</u> because of who He is. His gift of faith disposes us to *agree with Him* in spite of our **seen-based** perceptions or experience when they are contrary to His direction through the Holy Spirit. But if your beliefs about Him are different than who He really is, your hopes are not based on reality. How can you receive from someone who loves you if you don't believe that they do?

Everyone Walks By Faith
Secularists would have you *think* that they walk by fact and that Christians walk by superstition or a fantasy which they equate with "faith." (They reason this way because they *believe* that only the **seen realm** exists.) But actually, *everyone* walks by faith in something or someone. The real question is "What or who is the object of *your* set of assumptions?" Said

46

another way, "In what or who do you put your trust for your well-being?" Secularists put faith *in their assumption* that their five senses perceive all of reality accurately. The Bible says otherwise by revealing the God of the **Unseen Realm**. Both views rely on some belief system.

Matthew 14:22-33 describes what happened to Peter as Jesus followed His **unseen** Father's instructions on a very eventful day. He told the disciples to board a boat and go to the other side of the lake while He went off to fellowship alone with His Father. The disciples were far from shore when a heavy wind stirred up the waves. Suddenly, Jesus came toward them, miraculously walking on the water. Peter's eyes of faith were opened by seeing Jesus do what was impossible in the **seen realm**. Peter's desire to be near Jesus drove him to request what was also impossible for him to do on his own in the **natural realm**.

Jesus knew Peter's heart and honored his request to come to Him on the water. But Peter had to first discount his normal experience that water couldn't hold him up and choose to get out of the boat by faith in Jesus' word. Peter did what was impossible in the **seen realm** because He trusted and focused on the object of his faith - Jesus - and in His invitation to "come." He could risk leaving the security of the boat because he knew from previous, personal experiences that Jesus loved him. The gift of faith to walk on the water came to Peter by him hearing and obeying the word from God that Jesus spoke to him. God's power from the **unseen realm** trumped the limitations of the **natural realm**.

So, Peter did the impossible thing that Jesus was already doing in obedience to His heavenly Father. Peter walked on wavy water. Things were fine until he took his eyes off of Jesus, the initial object of his faith, and focused on the wind and waves - his **seen** circumstances - instead. The wind and waves competed with Jesus' word for his attention. He gave in, began to sink and cried out for help - and Jesus mercifully saved him. What had happened? Peter had changed his focus from the **unseen reality** of the word of God (coming through Jesus into the **seen realm)** that temporarily had become more "real" to him. He only momentarily experienced the truth of the revelation that right *believing* and trusting in God's **unseen source** of Reality produces the fruit of right living.

So, the outcome of one's faith depends on how valid and trustworthy the "object" of that faith actually is. The **unseen reality** of God and His Kingdom is much more real than what we see down here. Jesus, the Man, stayed mentally focused on the **unseen realm** of the Spirit and He invites all believers to do the same. Only God is fully trustworthy and therefore worthy of our complete trust and focus. But wrong beliefs about who He really is can undermine our level of trust and receptivity to Him and Chapter Twenty-one will expand on who Father-God really is. The song poems on page 80 and 345 help me to stay focused on God as my ultimate reality.

Mankind's Core Problem

Although the Israelites were included under Abraham's grace-based covenant, they brashly accepted the offer of a vastly inferior law-based covenant instead - even *before* God revealed its terms Apparently they pridefully thought they were up to any challenge. (Would you sign a binding contract on a new house or car before knowing the terms? Not if you're smart.) On the other hand, why did a good God do such a seemingly "unfair thing" by offering to them a binding covenant that He knew ahead of time they could not possibly keep? Well, what might seem to be unfair and even "ungodly" to a **seen-focused**, law-minded person, was actually an act of mercy for the entire human race. God used that fifteen hundred year long "holy experiment" with the unholy Israelites to unequivocally reveal a <u>core reality</u> about mankind. God regards all unsaved humans as "**in Adam** sinners." Why? It is _not because of our wrong behavior_ which is just a symptom of the real problem. Rather, it is because all humans are born of the corrupted, unfixable seed of Adam's fallen nature. Paul succinctly explained this vital revelation from Jesus when he wrote in Romans 5:19.

> For as by one man's (Adam's) disobedience, many were made sinners, so by the obedience of One (Christ Jesus) shall many be made righteous.

If you want to be truly "fixed" forever, it is essential to first understand what mankind's root problem really is, according to God. To repeat: it <u>is not our behavior that makes us sinners, according to God</u>. No, it is _only_ because we are Adam's descendants i.e. **in Adam**. How can you fix that? _You_ can't - but Jesus can. If you want a _new_ nature and a new history and a glorious, eternal future, you _must_ be reborn of God by faith in Jesus' **finished work** of salvation. There is absolutely no other way people can be made "fit" for heaven. Only children born of Father-God can enjoy the gift of heaven, as plainly stated by Jesus in John 3:3-8.

Only God Has The Answer

Again, the Bible presents a clear revelation of mankind's core problem as well as God's only answer to man's unfixable nature: receive a totally new, regenerated nature through the **finished work** of Jesus Christ through – you guessed it – His grace by _faith alone_. In fact, all of God's **post-cross** gifts of forgiveness and righteousness and holiness are ours **in Christ** – but only by God's grace through faith, not by our imperfect efforts. The same goes for all His other blessings and privileges which He forecast in the Old Testament and then through Jesus in the four gospels. They rest on the same grace-based faith in the God of the **New Covenant** that Abraham's covenant with God did. The difference is that we have a far better covenant than even Abraham's. The benefits of this glorious **New Covenant** more fully reveal the true heart of our loving and gracious Father-God who gave His best gift to us - Jesus. We will explore the important differences between five main biblical covenants in great detail in Chapter Eighteen.

Man's Nature Is Revealed, Not God's

However, the unintended and unfortunate result of the Mosaic Law "experiment" is that people often erroneously conclude that it reveals God's nature rather than seeing God's true purpose for it. And, again, what is His true purpose for the Law? He gave it to _reveal man's unfixable **in Adam** nature and our need for Him to supply a new one._ God was loving and gracious enough to reveal man's true condition and send Jesus as the only solution. _It is Jesus, not the Mosaic Law, which reveals God's true nature._ Much confusion and distortion about who God really is and who we really are comes from Galatianism – mixing the conditions and terms of two conflicting covenants, which God _never_ intended to be mixed. Chapter Nine will explain all of this in more detail.

The natural mind of man is dominated by the **seen realm** and easily influenced by the lies of the devil and the flesh. Unless we see the **big picture** with God's eyes by faith, we will inevitably underestimate the desperateness of our **unseen**, fallen condition as a race and God's

48

unfathomable solution in the **finished work** of Christ. Believers who mix law with Jesus' grace-based Covenant are mentally putting themselves back under the law of sin and death, back under its curses, and are alienated from Christ, according to Galatians 5:3-4. It causes self-consciousness and sin-centeredness rather than Jesus-consciousness and God-centeredness. It clouds one's vision of how good God really is and often brings increasing degrees of depression and defeat rather than the experience of His overcoming victory, which Jesus revealed to Paul. True freedom from this bondage comes by hearing Jesus' **whole gospel of grace** and receiving His promise of an abundant life here on earth by grace through faith alone. It is all part of the benefits of the **unseen reality** found **in Christ** which Father-God has already freely given to all His reborn children to enjoy Him and to impact the **seen realm** as His ambassadors.

Speaking From Experience

Do you see now how imperative it is to confront this entrenched **elephant of mixture** which clouds, if not blocks, the light of Jesus' **gospel of total grace** – individually and corporately? I can personally attest to the fact that the ongoing mental battle to replace this mixture of law with the pure **grace gospel** over the past 20 some years has not been easy. But it has been greatly rewarding. The wrong concept of God which I was stuck in and, therefore, mirrored to my young family, was the "holy God of law and justice." In turn, I related to them from a corresponding "judgment mentality," shaped primarily by my religious upbringing and education that tragically mixed law with grace for the first 29 years of my life.

Unfortunately, even being saved and baptized in the Holy Spirit when I was 29 did not instantly delete or overhaul my law-centered thinking. But the groundwork was laid because I did receive a new heart and a new spirit through rebirth by grace through faith and a fuller gospel than I knew previously (see Ezekiel 36:26). I also *experienced* a new, deep hunger for God's Word and a bubbling-over of joyful thanksgiving and worship. (Ironically, it was the very thing I had resisted and had criticized those "crazy charismatics" for, during the previous four years.) I was on cloud nine for many months.

But, regrettably, no one taught me how to "divide the word rightly" according to the various covenants (explained in Chapter Eighteen) to help discern and resist any mixture of law with grace. So I continued to walk according to the holy Law that arouses sin and is the ministry of death (which will be discussed in detail in Chapter Nine) instead of walking according to the higher *law of the Holy Spirit of life in Christ Jesus*, as stated in Romans 8:2. Consequently, as I focused on the do's and don'ts of the law, especially from the Mosaic Covenant, I became even *more* committed to law-mindedness than before.

I viewed the whole Bible as a law book, confirmed by Joshua 1:8. So I was engrossed in searching for and listing all the laws in both Testaments that I *thought* I had to keep in order to "stay on the good side of a holy, law-minded God." This error only served to reinforce my negative, sub-conscious misconceptions about Him. So, I doubled my efforts on improving *my* fallible performance to please Him. The veil of the Law kept me focused on *my* performance for Jesus rather than on Jesus' performance *for me*. It kept me from discovering and learning to fully depend on and benefit from the **finished work** of Jesus' **divine exchange,** already accomplished *for* me some 2000 years ago. Instead of learning to trust and rest in His *gifts* of righteousness, acceptance and approval, I was laboring to stay in right standing with God by my own efforts. I was working to merit a gift which was already mine, as part of my rebirth **in Christ Jesus,** my Savior. It is the classic definition of well-intentioned "self-righteousness."

His Light Brings Sight

As I have already briefly shared in the *Introduction* of this book, the Lord began renewing my mind in earnest with the truth of who He *really* is and who I now am **in Christ Jesus** in 1991. Dr Robert Cornwall gave a series of talks at my church home, *Grace Fellowship International*. He made this key statement that triggered a search and subsequent revolution in my life as a reborn Christian: *"Your relationship with God is only as good as your concept of God."* Up until that point I had never systematically sorted through my assumptions – core beliefs – about who God *really* is. I had just assumed for almost 50 years that the input from my parents, siblings, teachers, and clergy - gleaned through discussions, sermons, the Bible and other books and my life experiences - was accurate and adequate. But was it? And did it really matter?

After the service was over, my doubts motivated me to ask Dr. Cornwall "How can I be sure that my concept of God is accurate?" He directed me to search out and meditate on the various names through which God reveals who He is in the Bible. That study led to a richer understanding, appreciation and reception of what He did for me as my Savior, Redeemer, Justifier, Good Shepherd, Sanctifier, Healer, etc., etc.. Then, a short while after I began my search, my wife Elaine and I were having an emotionally-charged discussion with my youngest daughter about her desire to switch to a different high school. Before long, things exploded when my oldest daughter, acting as her advocate, told me that I was a lousy father – and my wife and our other three children did *not* disagree.

I felt devastated – totally undone. It was not because of my oldest, strong-willed daughter's accusation because we had had more than a few disagreements about how to "run things" over the years and she was now living in her own apartment on the third floor. No, it was because the other four family members were siding with her too. Now that would have made sense to me if I had been an absentee father or a drunkard or a criminal. But I had purposely chosen a career as a Montessori teacher to keep me continuously involved with my family. I was the morally sound, Christian school principal of "Word of God Academy & Family Formation Center." I played by and enforced the rules and gave monthly talks to the school parents on how to "train up a child" as part of the vision and mission of the school. And here I was, being told by my whole family that I was basically a failure at the very thing I focused on – being a good Christian family man.

Parenting By The Book Of Law

In hind-sight, I now know I was internally conflicted. At school, we operated like a family of mutually supportive learners and I enjoyed the ebb and flow of relationships with the teachers, parents and students. But at home, I was much more about laws and regulations than love and relationship. I believed the Christian books that I read on parenting my children that said or implied that it was *my* responsibility to "get them to heaven." I approached it with a Mosaic Law mind-set: blessings were based on good behavior and discipline for bad behavior - like it was for the Israelites. I was relating to them and treating them like I *thought* God was relating to me and treating me.

I gave approval and affection based on their performance rather than on who they were **in Christ** which I was ignorant of at the time. I thought that we were all "sinners saved by grace" – barely. I had high standards of behavior for myself as part of my identity and expected the same from them. Who could argue with the seemingly positive results? From the outside, it looked to some like a model family, like the one in Sound of Music - before Maria came. But the letter of the law kills. Only the Holy Spirit - who is love - gives true life. In short, my identity was based on the externals of my position and performance as a teacher and a school principal, which I took pride in having and doing well at. The school climate was like a family and I received mostly positive feedback from school parents, colleagues and students who knew me up close and personal in the family-like setting.

But my own family disagreed that I was a good father and that left me stunned. I was in the dark about God's parenting process because of my law-minded bondage. Why should I try to fix what I didn't think was broken? Little did I realize then that the Holy Spirit was answering the song prayer He had inspired me to compose two years earlier which had become a favorite: *Bathe My Mind With Your Truth*. Only by the grace of God was I able to pray something like: "Lord I don't think their opinion of me is true but if it is, show me the truth." The Holy Spirit inspires prayers like that so we are softened to do things His way by letting Him live through us to bear His fruit.

A New Beginning

Not too long after that painful blowup, I awoke one morning and a particular book on our bedroom bookshelf captured my attention. The title, *Victory Over Darkness* by Dr. Neal Anderson, offered a ray of hope to my discouraged soul. God used that book and other ones later to biblically document and explain my new identity **in Christ** because of Jesus' **divine exchange**. No wonder I felt battered and shattered. I had built my identity on the shifting sands of my upright behavior and reputation, on my talents and teaching career and on people's affirmation rather than on Jesus, the only solid Rock. The more I studied and shared my discoveries with others about who we believers are **in Christ**, the more I *experienced* God's love, peace, assurance and rest which had been available all along. The warmth of His light and love was gradually melting away my law-based, self-righteousness and self-sufficiency, replacing it with a trusting reliance on Father-God's love and supply **in Christ Jesus**. It is all a part of the abundant life of freedom **in Him** that He came to give us as we learn to trust in Him for everything.

My quest for His truth about who He is and who I am **in Him** turned into a daily, ten-year-long Bible study of the terms and benefits of the **New Covenant.** The Holy Spirit incorporated over 500 key scriptures to progressively renew my mind. They solidified my understanding of who God *really is* and the roles, so to speak, of each of the three divine Persons. (I will share more about Father-God's true nature in the last chapter.) They also grounded me in the revelation of my new identity **in Christ**. I collected and scrubbed my mind with those 500 blended verses over those ten years. The revelation knowledge from those verses greatly helped supplant my stinkin' thinkin' with the truth of the Word of Christ. **#11** Since 2005, I have also greatly benefitted from more in-depth, grace-based teaching from fellow saints like Andrew Wommack and Joseph Prince and many others, recommended in Appendix #5.

After reading and assimilating a few books that used scriptures to explain my true identity **in Christ Jesus**, I saw the need to invite my pastor over to my house on Thanksgiving Day to be there as I vocalized that dawning change of mind (repentance) to my family and ask for their forgiveness for my legalistic ways. Of course, that did not erase the past hurts, but it did begin a new, more positive chapter in our family relationships. The Holy Spirit delights in "leading us into all truth" – from conflicting beliefs squashed together under the foot of the **elephant of mixture** into Jesus' **whole gospel of grace**. Jesus sent the Holy Spirit *into* us believers to progressively unveil Himself and what He did for us in order for us to come to *know* and love Him personally. This is greatly helped by understanding more and more of the implications of Jesus' **divine exchange** with us as part of His **finished work** of the cross, accomplished on our behalf. This revelation empowers us to live by grace through faith like Jesus and Paul did, depending on and abiding consciously in Father-God as our faithful and loving Provider and Justifier. We will explore all this - and much more - in later chapters.

True Sanctification Of The Soul

Now I know that all real, deep-down *lasting* change of mind – true repentance – is effortless but not necessarily easy. It happens through inviting the Holy Spirit, our Teacher, Sanctifier, Comforter and Friend to lead and guide us into all truth by revealing Jesus who is the truth. But "letting go and letting God" deal with an addiction or a wrong mind-set or a false self-image or a bad habit or a lie we have held dear for years, is often very threatening and even painful to do. Why? Because the older we are *before* being reborn, the more our outer man tends to justify and defend its acquired beliefs and habits, especially when they touch on our self-perception – our identity. (Actually, we are blind to the *true truth about anything and everything* until we come to see it from God's perspective).

But God won't force His truth and life upon us. Again, Jesus sends the Holy Spirit into all believers to reveal His truth that brings about lasting transformation on every level of our being as we invite and allow Him to have His way. He is about the sanctification process of the outer man – the earthen vessel – to progressively conform it to our inner, perfect man, now *one* with Christ and, therefore, holy and righteous. True sanctification - the process of learning to see and think like God does - results from His work in us, not from *our* efforts to fix ourselves or other people. We just have to choose to let Him have His way, in and through us. If that was not possible to do, this book would never have been written.

Let Go And Let God

Resting in that **New Covenant** revelation makes sanctification not only possible but now, even relatively enjoyable. Why? Because it is not the new, regenerated and sanctified *you* (your inner man **in Christ**) which needs reprogrammed but merely your *warped thinking and believing* going on in your natural mind which is left over from the former, **in Adam** sinner-self, now crucified and gone. You no longer have to live under the burden of trying to be your own *point of reference* or savior or justifier or defender. Jesus, the Tree of Life, came to give you His abundant life by re-creating you as His **new creation saint** through the **divine exchange** of rebirth. What believer wouldn't want be set free from the mental junk-yard of left-over bad habits and distorted mind-sets, addictions and false beliefs of his former self? How does this happen? By progressively *replacing* it all with the wealth of refreshing truth and life that are now ours **in Christ Jesus** through His divine exchange with us.

It is like opening the windows for some fresh air and getting a spring cleaning of your mind after a long winter so that you can begin to enjoy God and His countless blessings. And now that you have seen the two opposing options of law versus grace, why would you want to remain under the bondage of law-based thinking when you can live in the freedom of the **butterfly life**? And guess what. God sent His Holy Spirit into you to personally unpack for you Jesus' **whole gospel** so that you can enjoy the surpassing riches of His grace and kindness toward you because you are now alive **in Christ Jesus** if you are born again (see Ephesians 2:4-7).

It is the gracious, ongoing work of the Sanctifier, living inside of my new inner man, that reminds and convinces me of my permanent right-standing with God, thanks to Jesus' **divine exchange.** He uses both my good and negative thoughts and people and circumstances to show me Father-God's love and care - and where I am not yet fully free *mentally*. That is a very different reality and experience from being thrashed and demoralized by being mentally under the judgment of an unbending law that brings guilt and condemnation. It is the goodness of God who reveals His truth that changes our wrong mental assumptions as we yield to the ways of the Holy Spirit. Bathing our mind with His living truth of the **unseen realities,** which are now ours **in Christ Jesus**, causes right believing. Over time, this new freedom by faith in Christ Jesus' **finished work,** produces the Holy Spirit's fruit of love for God and others - right living. And even our perception of our "enemies" changes when we see them through God's eyes. Chapters One and Two offer a gold mine of His mind-renewing truth to mentally bathe in, to help you discover *how God sees you*. True Christianity is not about what *you* do for God (which is religion) but about what Jesus has already done for you - from God's perspective.

The Law As A Principle

So far in this chapter, we have been focusing mainly on the differences of two opposing covenants. They both use the word "law" but in a fundamentally different sense. God gave the Mosaic Law only to the Jews and its benefits and punishments depended on *their* performance. In contrast, God's **New Covenant** of grace and truth that came through Jesus depends on faith in *His* perfect performance, done on our behalf. We can accept His **finished work** as totally adequate to provide the blessings which *He deserves and has earned for us*. Unlike the Mosaic Law, it comes without any punishments to believers since He bore them all for *all* mankind on Calvary (see 2 Corinthians 5:18-19 and 1 John 2:2). The **New Covenant** is an expression of "the law of God's love" - "the law of the Spirit of Life" - lived by faith **in Jesus**. In summary, the Law covenant was based on *a Jew's faith in his imperfect doing.* Thankfully, the **New Covenant** is based on exercising *God's gift of faith in Jesus' perfect doing.*

Again, as mentioned in Chapter One, we can broaden the application of the Law covenant, given only to the Jews, into what author Bob George calls "the law principle" which he defines as:

> The law as a principle can be <u>any system of works</u> (God given or man–made) by which a person attempts to earn or maintain right-standing with God. #**12**

This is also a good definition for "religion" as opposed to Jesus' **gospel of total grace.** That is why true Christianity is not a "religion," or "law-system," but a personal, love-based relationship with our living God, received by His gift of grace through faith alone.

God's Higher Law That Trumps The Law Principle

But this mental conversion - from living religiously under law to living by faith **in Christ Jesus** - does *not* mean a return to "lawlessness" or license, as naysayers teach and many believers fear. Usually, believers fear this because they wrongly *assume* that the only alternative to law-keeping is lawlessness. That is a clever lie of the devil. They will remain under the devil's deception *until* their mind is renewed by seeing a third alternative - **the higher law** of the **butterfly life.** This is God's kind of life that flows from enjoying three *gifts* given through the Holy Spirit. These can't be earned, just received. (If they had to be earned, they would no longer be gifts.) They include God's gift of:

1) *Faith* – the ability to see and believe Jesus' **whole gospel of grace – the finished work** of His **divine exchange** that He revealed exclusively to Paul, which reveals the **unseen realm** of the Spirit. It is the plumb line and lens that helps us to understand the rest of the Bible from God's original intention. (More on that later.)

2) *Love* of God for you and me that motivated Father-God to send Jesus to reverse the effects of Adam's fall and fulfill His plan to have an eternal family through believing and receiving Jesus and His **finished work** of the **New Covenant** that He made with Father-God on our behalf. The Holy Spirit *is* God's Love, shed abroad into our new heart. We now can love Father-God because He first loved us. God's kind of love is the basis of the relationship among the Trinity and we are included and welcomed into that eternal family relationship as God's beloved children through rebirth. We are now one spirit with Father-God, according to Jesus' revelation to Paul in 1 Corinthians 6:17.

3) *Liberty* in Christ in the **unseen realm** because Christ has freed us from Adam's sin-nature so that we may enjoy the benefits of freedom from Satan's kingdom and from our futile efforts to earn heaven. Therefore, be established in this freedom, and don't become slaves again to the law principle.

> I, Paul, can guarantee that if you allow yourselves to be circumcised (submit to the demands of law), Christ will be of no benefit to you (Galatians 5:2).

My friend, that is another very serious statement. See page 206 and Endnote #**13** to discover where this "higher law" is found in the **New Covenant**.

The Butterfly Life From Jesus

To add substance to what may seem like a nice but irrelevant theory, let's return to the caterpillar/butterfly analogy introduced in Chapter One. One main difference between the two is that a caterpillar is forced to live *under the law* of gravity by its very nature. However, the butterfly operates by a *higher law* that allows it to fly. The caterpillar is limited to slow progress and subject to being easy prey for birds or stepped on by *elephants*. However, the butterfly can choose to either stay on the ground and be under the "gravity of circumstances" or to soar above the circumstances, which the caterpillar must endure. Butterflies have even been known to be carried great distances by the wind, just as we can be carried (mentally) by the **unseen** wind - the Holy Spirit living in us. It depends on who and what you choose to focus on. There are more details on this helpful comparison given in Chapter Nineteen.

This choice is just one of many new options for believers because we are now **new creations in Christ**. Paul used the phrase **"in Christ"** or **"in Him"** over seventy-times for a reason: it reveals the <u>foundational change</u> that Jesus accomplished at Calvary for all **in Adam** sinners who, by faith in Jesus' **divine exchange**, are crucified with Him, die, are buried then raised and ascended **with** and **in Him** – and He *in them*. That is Jesus' **whole gospel of lavish grace** in a nutshell (see Romans 6:1-11). The former **in Adam** caterpillar is regenerated by faith in Jesus – recreated as a brand new spiritual being **in Christ**. Now God regards this believer as a saint – a "holy one" – set apart into Christ Jesus by believing and receiving Jesus' **finished work**. (See Endnote #**14** for Bob George's comments on this metaphor.)

"How is this miracle legally possible?" you ask. Jesus revealed to Paul that He had fulfilled the requirements of the Law for righteousness' sake by His perfect behavior. Then Jesus "became a caterpillar," so-to-speak, by <u>becoming sin who knew no sin</u>, was crucified then died (see 2 Corinthians 5:21). Then He arose from the dead and ascended into heaven. So now, any unrighteous, **in Adam** caterpillar can be regenerated (recreated) by God into a righteous **butterfly** by faith **in Christ Jesus,** who is now his Savior, Lord and Victory. Paul pleads with the believers in Corinth - who were *previously* unfixable, **in Adam caterpillars** by nature - to awaken by faith to the *unseen reality* that they are *now* regenerated **butterflies, in Christ**. Consequently, by degrees they were able to reject their old caterpillar *lifestyle* and choose to live according to the **new creation life,** in and through the Holy Spirit living inside of them. It is the same divine life that flowed through Jesus when He lived and loved and ministered as a man here on earth, **pre-cross**. He walked by faith in what His Father told Him, loved others through the power of the Holy Spirit in Him and lived in the **butterfly life** and liberty of sonship.

Our New Option, Thanks to Jesus' Cross
Now, hopefully, you can see more clearly that the **elephant of mixture** of law with grace has influenced (if not dominated) the church from the very beginning. However, the Holy Spirit resides in every true believer to progressively live His **butterfly life** of faith, love and liberty by allowing Him to have His way in and through them. Ask Him to open up and renew your mind with Jesus' **gospel of lavish grace** which reveals our **unseen** *oneness* with Jesus and with Father-God. He will reveal to you what it means to mentally abide **in Christ Jesus** and draw on His **finished work** and, thereby, be Jesus-conscious rather than law-minded. (There is much more about how to understand and enjoy Jesus' abundant life in Chapters Sixteen to Twenty.)

In the next chapter, I will share another metaphor about three dogs to further illustrate this new reality of our life **in Christ** in the **unseen realm.** This is in direct contrast to being bound under the **elephant of Galatianism**, which can only arouse sin, bring defeat and cause death – according to Romans 7:5 and 2 Corinthians 3:7. (This bondage will be explained in much more detail in Chapter Nine.) Living the **butterfly life** is now your God-given choice as a believer **in Christ Jesus**.

The following song-poem makes a simple but profound distinction between law and grace – and what true righteousness really is, a free gift from our loving Father-God.

RIGHTEOUSNESS IN MOSES DAY

Meant keeping every law,	Romans 2:25; James 2:10
It's something only Jesus Christ can do.	Hebrews 4:15
The Law was given, not to keep,	
But prove man's sinful state,	Romans 7:7-8
So exchange it for His grace and be made new	Corinthians 5:17-21

So Righteousness, through Jesus Christ,
Is not about the Law,   Romans 3:21 & 5:5 & 9
But it's a gift that only He can give.   Romans 1:17,
It comes by faith in what He's done,
Not what you do for Him,   Romans 3:21-25a & 4:6-8
So, accept His saving grace so you can live.   Ephesians 2:8-9; Romans 10:9-13

A Sermon Song © Copyright 2009 by Leonard J. Ransil

CHAPTER FOUR

THE LAW OF THE SPIRIT OF LIFE

The last chapter addressed the difference between the defeated life of a caterpillar **in Adam** and the risen life of a **new creation butterfly**, now alive **in Christ**. Jesus revealed this fundamental difference in natures through Paul in Romans 8:1-6:

> Therefore, there is now no condemnation for those **in Christ Jesus** for the (higher) law of the Spirit of the life **in Christ Jesus** set me free from the law of sin and of death; for what the (Mosaic) Law was not able to do, because it was weak due to the flesh, God sent His own Son in the likeness of sinful flesh, and for sin, condemned sin in the flesh, that the righteousness of the law may be fulfilled in us, who do not walk according to the flesh, but according to the Spirit. For those who walk according to the flesh, focus on the things of the flesh (the **seen realm).** But those who walk according to the Spirit, focus on the things of the Spirit; for the mind of the flesh is death, and the mind of the Spirit is life and peace.

The "law of the Spirit of life" is God's **unseen, higher law** of faith, love and liberty (explained in Chapter Three and Endnote # 13) that the **new creation** butterfly can now operate in by focusing on the **unseen realities in Christ**, as Paul explained in Colossians 3:1-3. But, again, that new option is a *choice*, not an automatic result of being reborn. A butterfly can still choose to walk around under the "gravity of circumstances" (the flesh) with all the caterpillars. How? By holding on to wrong beliefs and habits and the limitations of the **seen** world which is unstable, unpredictable and is passing away, as Paul reminds us in 2 Corinthians 4:17-18. Or, the butterfly can choose to focus on the **unseen realm,** revealed by the Spirit of truth to renew his mind, in keeping with Romans 12:2 and Colossians 3:1-3.

An Analogy - The Three Big Options

My personal experience with dogs tells me that they do not all respond to people the same way. Some are mean or aggressive, some are fearful, others are friendly and loyal, etc.. One day, while I was bathing my mind with the above scripture from Romans, the outline of the following chart came to me, using my experience with dogs as an analogy. Hopefully, it will give you some additional insight into the abstractions of the above scriptural concepts. Taken as a whole, the verses above indicate that we humans who are still living on earth fall into one of three categories, spiritually speaking, described in the following chart (**4A**) as three different types of dogs, each with different characteristics.

Saint – carnal mind, lives under Law (Rm. 7:1), "dead works"	Mature Saint – lives under Grace, higher Law - a new heart	Sinner – unregenerated, slave to sin and death - condemned
Law & sin-conscious, legalistic - therefore, under condemnation **(city dog)**	God-conscious, resting in "law" of Spirit of Life - zoe Rm. 8:2 **(country dog)**	Self - centered, under license - "I can do anything I want." **(wild dog)**
walking by sensate faith, seeks approval and affirmation	walking in Spirit by biblical faith of exchanged life	walking in the flesh, selfish, "It's all about me."
fearful, needs external restraint, confessing sins to God	reconciled, fully forgiven, freedom in Christ	lawless, seeks freedom from restraint
prey to self-condemnation, judgmental, condemning others	"No condemnation in Christ," evaluates, speaks truth in love	makes own rules, whims condemns, slanders others
striving for acceptance and peace with God	accepted in the Beloved thanks to Jesus' divine exchange	self-sufficient, defiant, gangs
insecure, defensive, competitive	helpful and supportive	cold, unscrupulous
dependent on self-effort, others	dead to old self, alive to God	independent, arrogant
fearful of God/future negative)	"fear of God" (love based)	fearless, daredevil
lacks assurance of salvation	inner "witness" of assurance by the Spirit – one with Abba-Father	boastful, cocky
bound by past - looks back	consciously present to God in the "now," relational	get all the gusto now
regretful, anxious of the future	calm, patient	callous
scrupulous conscience, guilt and shame ridden	clear conscience, trusting in Jesus' finished work	seared conscience
feelings of inadequacy	adequate in Christ, "I can do..."	proud
Defensive	fruit of the Spirit - Love, joy …	Aggressive
combative, blaming	meek, rest in God	violent, destructive
self-conscious, insecure	secure and confident in Christ	confident in self, boastful
soulish, focused on the "seen"	walks according to the Spirit	soul/body led
focused on obeying the law	focused on Jesus and His life in the Spirit	focused on self, pleasure, rebellion
bound by fear, jealousy etc.	free to love - "Perfect love..."	hateful, revengeful
perfectionistic, joyless	conscientious, responsible	indifferent, careless
whines/complains/grumbles	content in Christ, a winner whose "boast" is Christ Jesus	boasts about his exploits
negative apprehension of God	at peace with God, my Father	hostile to God
battles with unforgiveness of self and others	mind renewed by the Truth, forgives from the heart	hard heart, refuses to admit to being or doing wrong

4A   The Three Dog Chart

Explaining The Three Columns

1) The **wild dog** in the right column represents a person still **in Adam** because he is spiritually unplugged from God and, therefore, is under the authority of darkness because there are only two kingdoms and all humans start off in this condition;

2) The **city dog** in the left column represents a reborn saint **in Christ** who depends on obedience to the principle of law to restrain his flesh and, thereby, hopefully earn and/or maintain right-standing with a God of justice who, he wrongly thinks, *punishes* his children when they sin and

3) The **country dog** in the middle column represents a <u>mature</u>, reborn saint **in Christ** whose mind is increasingly renewed with the **whole gospel of lavish grace** and he is *depending* on his loving Master's acceptance, approval and complete love and care for him. He loyally and gratefully responds to His Master's generosity by bearing the fruit of a Holy Spirit-led life. He understands that right-standing is God's free <u>gift</u> that can't be deserved or earned because it is the result of being **in Christ** by grace through faith alone.

The right column shows the **wild dog's** list of representative behaviors and mind-sets that characterize those who are "lawless" or ungodly because they are still **in Adam.** This sweeping category would include *anyone who is not yet reborn of God,* i.e. not **in Christ.** Therefore, it includes even very moral people who are righteous in their own eyes, based on their performance compared to others. If they do more good than bad - according to their own moral parameters - they think or hope that God will give them a pass into heaven. The Pharisees focused on the "do's and "don'ts" of religion, rather than enjoying a living relationship that Jesus came to offer to them. Consequently, they counted themselves more obedient morally than anyone mingling with sinners like Jesus did. Personally, that is the point where I started from years ago, being a "good little boy" growing up, and that is probably the hardest mind-set for God to convert – relatively speaking. God calls all of one's own self-effort to be good or holy as "filthy rags" (see Isaiah 64:6). Someone once put it succinctly: "God does not appreciate what He does not initiate." It is a polar opposite of the *free gift of His perfect righteousness*, given automatically to all who are reborn of God by grace through faith.

The left column describes the confined **city dog**, a reborn, **new creation** saint **in Christ** whose carnal (natural) mind has yet to be *renewed* by progressively washing it with the fullness of Jesus' **unseen gospel of grace**. The mixture of law and grace causes this saint to experience continuous doubts and fears because his law-mindedness is necessarily focused on himself and his own sin and its corresponding *feelings* of anxiety, guilt, shame and even self-condemnation. <u>Unfortunately, the majority of Christians still live in this self-inflicted jail.</u> It is similar to a dog corralled inside a house or a city back-yard, not free to roam and explore the hills like the country dog is free to do - if he chooses. This poisonous mixture is not consistent with the purity of the true, **grace-based gospel** of Jesus' **finished work.** All this will become clear in Chapters Eight and Nine, which present the Law's true purpose and its harsh realities. If just one saint reading this book comes to see his or her bondage to the Law the same way God does and then allows the Holy Spirit to set him or her *mentally* free by becoming Jesus-focused, heaven will rejoice.

The middle column describes **the country dog.** He represents the reborn, **new creation** saint **in Christ.** Why? Because the country dog is free to roam the hills if he wants to but he would rather stay near his master, following him around and ready to go hunting or herding etc.. He waits on and serves his master out of devotion and loyalty, not duty. Likewise, this reborn believer has a new heart for His new Lord who has now become his point of reference – *his reason for existing.* He delights in progressively renewing his mind with **new creation realities** of the **whole unseen gospel** of freedom and radical grace as Jesus intended. He is increasingly pre-occupied with God's purposes, not his own agenda and motives. By degrees, he is experiencing the transformation in the outer man that Paul urged in Romans 12:2 and in Titus 2:11 and 14 respectively when he wrote:

> And be not conformed to this world system, but be transformed by the renewing of
> your mind, that you may demonstrate what is the good and fully agreeable and
> perfect will of God.

> For the saving grace of God (Jesus) has appeared to all men … He gave Himself for
> our sake, so that He might redeem us from all iniquity, and might cleanse for Himself a
> special people, zealous for doing good.

This is nothing short of the believer seeing and relating to God as He *really* is and learning to see himself as God sees him - according to Jesus' **unseen, finished work** of grace. Jesus sends the Holy Spirit into all believers to progressively sanctify our outer man by renewing each one's mind with the truth of Jesus' **grace-based gospel.** This is the reality in which Paul and some of the Ephesians and Colossians increasingly lived. It is the *rest* found only **in Christ** which Paul was encouraging the Corinthians to yield to by faith. Their resistance stemmed from ignorance and/or unbelief in Jesus' **grace-based gospel** – which paralleled the unbelief of the Israelites described in Hebrews 4:6-11. Like the Israelites, the Corinthians were fixated on the **seen realm** which was preventing them from seeing the abundant life of the **unseen realm** Paul told them about in 2 Corinthians 4:16b and 18:

> … but if indeed our outer man is decaying, the inner man is being refreshed day by day…we
> do not look at the things which are **seen**, but at the things which are **unseen**: for the things
> which are **seen** are not lasting; but the things which are **unseen** are everlasting.

Paul's distinction between the outer and inner man, which corresponds to the **seen** and **unseen realm,** is a major revelation from Jesus to Paul that is so crucial to understanding the essence of the entire **finished work** of Jesus' **grace gospel** - which the church has largely ignored. Why? Because it makes no sense to man's carnal (natural) mind. Yet it made perfect sense to Paul once he "saw" the **unseen realm** first hand in 42 AD. He "saw" that he, himself, was a **new creation spirit-being** and *one with Christ Jesus.* He also "saw" that this was true of all other reborn saints - whether they were alive or dead physically in their outer man. (Chapters Sixteen to Nineteen will explore this vital area in much more detail.) Paul became focused on Jesus and His ways, as his *new point of reference*, rather than the ways of Law-keeping that he had been formed in and depended on as a Jewish Pharisee.

Put another way, we **reborn butterflies** can now choose to remain "grounded like caterpillars," conformed to the pattern of this **seen** world - which is necessarily law-based. Or we can become mentally conformed to the living reality of the **unseen realm** where we are seated **in Christ** right now in our inner man, according to Jesus' revelation to Paul in Ephesians 2:6. You will experience defeat or victory *in your walk on earth* as a Christian, depending on which realm you focus on primarily. Working to get God's forgiveness or to earn or maintain His acceptance and approval or to merit His blessings - or the *big one*, "trying to get to heaven" – reveals a law-based mindset that is characteristic of virtually all religions. Trying to attain what you already have as a reborn saint prevents you from enjoying the full benefits of the **New Covenant.**

Relationship, Not Religion

Thankfully, Jesus offered us relationship with God Himself instead of just another religion. He already provides all of the above benefits, "apart from us doing *any* works of the Law," as clearly stated in Romans 3:21. Your behavior does not change God's desire to bless and prosper you with His abundant life **in Christ**. But your behavior might prevent you from receiving His gifts because you are focusing on yourself and your imperfect efforts to "get" rather than focusing on Him and receiving and resting in His **finished work**, which is already yours **in Him**.

In the everyday **seen realm**, people work to merit, earn or deserve ribbons, paychecks and rewards. In the **unseen** Kingdom of our good Father, He freely gives us His treasure and rewards in the person of Jesus. Through Him alone, all blessings were offered to mankind 2000 years ago in His **finished work** of the Cross, accomplished *before* He sat down next to His Father. The only way to benefit from all He has *done* is to discover what He offers in the terms of His **New Covenant** and *believe and receive* it all as yours. Just like Joshua, who took the second generation of Israelites into the Promised Land, Jesus has taken you, believer, up into heavenly places **in Him**. We will explore all this and more starting in Chapter Sixteen. To help lubricate the process, check out the words to one of the inspired Sermon Songs from the Lord, found at the end of this chapter entitled *Oh, The Gospel Of Lord Jesus.*

As the above *Three Dog Chart* pointed out, law-minded believers are automatically focusing on the **seen realm** and always falling short of perfection in their behavior, no matter how hard they try to "be good." They or others around them think that they must depend on the fences and limits of moral standards to keep them "safe." They have yet to learn to trust in the Holy Spirit living within them, sent by Jesus to be their Teacher and Guide and Sanctifier. It does not take the power of the Holy Spirit to "know the law." The world is now full of competing religions that are based on laws and requirements. But many believers are still tricked into believing that the Holy Spirit was sent "to help them keep the Law" and to convict them of sin when they don't keep it. (We will address this misconception in Chapter Fourteen and Appendix 4.) This faulty thinking is the result of seeking religion's "do's and don'ts" rather than walking in an on-going fellowship and communication with God like the country dog does with his master. This wrong belief stems from the **elephant of mixture** which prevents living the **butterfly life** of total dependence on God's guidance by grace through faith in the Holy Spirit.

Living under law of sin and death, instead of by the law of the Spirit of life (according to Romans 8:2), is a primary reason why the rotting carcass of the **elephant of mixture** has dominated the mind of the mainstream church. This trust in the law and, therefore, mistrust in a

Spirit-led life, has prevented the church, in general, from being renewed with "the mind of Christ." Again, this is the advantage of learning to "see" God's **big picture** of what Jesus has already accomplished through His **finished work** of the cross for each believer. As Hebrews 11:1 plainly says: "Faith is the substance of things hoped for and the certainty of things **not seen**." The "things" talked about in this verse are the **unseen** *"new things"* that God sees that *He has already done* for us. But our natural senses and carnal mind cannot see them (unless the *"things"* are manifested physically, as when the angel Gabriel appeared to Mary, for example). That is why true Christianity is a walk of faith, not about law-keeping. Galatians confirms that repeatedly.

Seeing Oneself As God Does

Therefore, God supplies the sight of faith as His free gift which, when used, enables the believer to see himself from God's perspective - as a **new creation butterfly** (rather than as the caterpillar he used to be). He sees himself as now reborn of God by being crucified, risen and ascended with Christ Jesus. By first agreeing with God's view of Himself, the believer "reckons" (counts as true) the **unseen** transaction that has radically changed God's view of every believer because they are now **in Christ**, as revealed in Romans 6:11. Again, we will explore the true role of the Holy Spirit in this regard in the life of a reborn, **new creation** saint, in context, in Chapter Nineteen.

The Seen vs. the Unseen

Obviously, Paul's visit to heaven in 42 AD radically changed his perspective on everything! Paul was all too familiar with his old life under the **seen realm** of the Law – which, he discovered, actually was given to arouse sin and cause death (see Chapter Nine). What was totally new to him was the **unseen**, risen Christ Jesus appearing to him on the road to Damascus and then, some years later, in about 42 AD, showing him the **unseen realities** of eternal redemption. He off-handedly described this event by saying: "whether it was in the body or out of the body, I do not know – God knows" (2 Corinthians 12:2b). Jesus had singled him out to bestow on him His "… grace and apostleship to call all people from among the Gentiles to the obedience of faith" (Romans 1:5).

Law vs. Faith

Notice that Paul did not say "obedience to the Law," which he had previously focused on completely and had labored under as a Pharisee all of his life. Instead, he wrote about "the obedience of faith" which pertains to Paul putting his focus on the person of Jesus and His **finished work** of His **divine exchange** with us, accomplished by *Jesus'* obedient faith to His Father, dwelling in the **unseen realm.** In other words, Paul puts his faith in Jesus' obedient faith that saved and positioned Paul **in Christ**. Later on in the same chapter, he states:

> For I am not ashamed of the Gospel of Christ (the one Jesus personally revealed to him): for it is the power of God unto salvation to everyone who believes - to the Jew first, and also to the Greek. <u>For therein is revealed a righteousness of God from faith to faith as it is written: 'But the righteous (all those reborn) shall live by faith'</u> (Romans 1:16-17).

And what is the object of that faith? It is Jesus and His **divine exchange** with each believer, not faith in keeping the law. Why? Because "The Law is not of faith" (Galatians 3:12), and, shockingly, "Whatever is not of faith is sin!" (Romans 14:23), and finally: "If you walk by the Spirit you are not under Law" (Galatians 5:18). If you make the law the object of your faith, it is obviously not focused on Jesus' performance but on faith in your performance to keep it.

Paul made no reference here to his own law-keeping. Instead, he simply stated that he had believed and received the **whole gospel of grace** that Jesus had given him. He described it as the power of God Himself which makes salvation possible. Again, God freely grants right standing (justification/righteousness/relationship) with Himself to anyone who asks for it by faith, *apart from the works of the law.* It is a free gift that can't be worked for or earned or merited or maintained by us because then justification would no longer be a free gift of His love to us. It is clear, too, that Paul realized by revelation that <u>a believer cannot walk by the Spirit and by the works of the law at the same time.</u> That is true because man's works and God's grace are based on opposing covenants. (However, it is also true that when a believer walks according to the "law of the Spirit of life," he will not be "lawless" or immoral any more than Jesus was. But the good result stems from faith in Jesus and His **finished work** not from one's own efforts to be "moral" – big difference. More about this distinction in Chapter Twenty-One.)

Abraham Walked By Faith Not By Law
Again, this was the same walk of faith "process" that Paul later noted in Romans 4:3: "Abraham believed God, and it was reckoned (by God) to him as righteousness." Abraham lived over 400 years before the Law was given to Moses. Therefore, God's gift to Abraham of right-standing as "his friend" was based *only* on believing God's promise, not on obeying any behavioral standard, per se. In fact, Abraham's life was nowhere near morally perfect. Just ask his wife, Sarah, whom he turned over to two different kings to save his own neck. Also, he produced Ishmael by his own initiative, rather than waiting for God's. But, notice – God did not condemn him *because* he was under a grace-based covenant!

The heresy of Galatianism rejects the reality of God's radical grace by insisting that human effort *must* be involved somehow, someway to achieve or maintain righteousness. However, it is actually right believing and resting in Jesus' **finished work** that produces the *fruit* of right living. *Right doing does not produce right believing* and that is why behavior modification is a band-aid, not a permanent cure. All true and lasting change is initiated from inside out by the Holy Spirit, now living inside each believer. He inspires and empowers the believer to rely on the merits of Jesus' performance rather than depend on his own efforts to live right morally by depending on some code or standard that supposedly earns or "keeps" salvation.

So what about Philippians 2:12, where Paul told this church to "Work out your salvation in fear and trembling?" That sounds like anything but "effortless and joyful." This verse is often cited by law-centered preachers to "prove" that one's good works are necessary for salvation. But verse 13 completes the revelation from Jesus by saying: "for it is God *who works in you* both to will and to work for the sake of His good pleasure." In other words, because you know He loves you and has already completely forgiven and saved you through rebirth, you can now learn to trust Him to produce through you the fruit of right believing. So, as you yield to the Holy Spirit, He produces through you, as you, the works that God inspires and initiates according to His wonderful purposes for you and for others around you. That is how Jesus <u>learned</u> to respond to Father-God as He grew in wisdom and strength while on earth.

The Philippians were already grounded in their belief of the true gospel, which includes salvation as part of Jesus' **finished work** (Philippians 1:1). Abraham's experience reveals that one can't work to achieve right-standing or salvation because both are gifts from God, as reaffirmed by Ephesians 2:8-9. So now, every Christian is free to choose to walk according to the Holy Spirit by faith (rather than according to the flesh) and, thereby, bear the fruit of the Spirit, as explained in Romans 5:5-9. Respecting and valuing this underserved gift of salvation is meant to prompt a grateful response of love and joy as part of the fruit of the Holy Spirit. All this is a natural, cooperative outworking, on a personal basis, between every believer and the Holy Spirit. Psalm 2:11 puts it this way: "Serve the Lord with *reverence and trembling with joy*." This response of trusting faith (not fear) is all the more true and appropriate for us who are now alive **in Christ Jesus** under the **New Covenant** of God's totally lavish grace.

Facts vs. the Truth

Abraham simply responded to an undeserved, grace-based offer that God made to him by counting it to be true in the **unseen realm** of God's reality, even though he did not yet see the promise manifested in the **seen realm**. It was a *relationship*-based trust in the Word of one Person to another person. God, who *is* Truth and who cannot lie, said it was true. Abram's *experience* in the **seen realm** insisted it was not a fact. But Abram chose to believe the truth rather than the facts. God changed his name to "Abraham" as a sign of a new level of relationship with Him as a friend. "Seeing" with God's gift of faith enables one to do that. He lets us see into His "now" reality that is in timeless eternity. This process is a radical departure from the way we are conditioned to operate in the **seen realm**, by focusing on tangible laws and seeable facts.

Paul learned to live "by faith in the **unseen**" after receiving the **whole gospel of grace** from Jesus. Then later, he counseled the Colossians to operate this same way when he wrote:

Because you were raised together with Christ (born again), seek the things that are above, where Christ is seated at the right hand of God. Set your mind on the things that are above (the **unseen realm**), not on the things that are on the earth (the **seen realm**), for you died (with Jesus on His Cross), and your life is now hidden with Christ in God (Colossians 3:1-3).

Obviously, Paul underwent a radical change of mind – which, again, is the true definition of **New Covenant** repentance - because of his radical experiences with Jesus, first near Damascus and later in 42 AD (and probably others besides). Consequently, he was anointed to relay Jesus' **radical grace-based gospel** to us.

Chasing After What Is Already Ours

Tragically, the church as a whole has been struggling for some 2000 years to achieve what we already have **in Christ,** thanks to our Savior's **finished work** of His **divine exchange**. We can't achieve or earn the benefits of God's **unseen reality** by our efforts. They are just believed and received by Abraham's kind of trusting faith. Abraham did *not* have the same works-based mind-set that the Israelites labored under nor did he labor under the **elephant of mixture** that still beleaguers much of the church today.

The people of Israel tried to gain God's righteousness by obeying Moses' teachings, but they did not reach their goal. Why? Because they relied on their own efforts and strength rather than freely receiving God's righteousness by faith as Abraham had done (see Romans 9:31-32). That same erroneous mind-set continues to this day. I walked in it as a born again Christian for twenty years before beginning to see the disconnect. But giving up the law as a demanding "tutor," and maturing into the liberty that Father-God intends for all of His children, is worth the seeming risk of "letting go and trusting God." In fact, it is far riskier to stay under the seeming safety-net of the law, as Chapter Nine will prove. But it requires trusting Jesus' **unseen, whole gospel** over one's **seen realm** experience of works-based religion. The more you agree with what God says about Himself and about who you already are in His sight, the more maturely and freely you will operate in the **seen realm**.

The effort to learn the "3R's" in school can pay great dividends in the **seen realm**. But in the **unseen realm**, Jesus' **finished work** of His **divine exchange** supplies to all believers the following "18R's" by grace through faith **in Him**:

Repentance - agreeing with God' view of things, by faith,
Reconciliation to God
Remission of *all* past, present and future sins,
Ransomed and Rescued from the Dominion of Darkness,
Regeneration and Redemption,
Resurrection of my new spirit-self **in Christ Jesus**,
Righteousness of God **in Christ**,
Revelation of the **unseen realities in Christ Jesus**,
Renewal of the mind progressively,
Rest in Christ's accomplishments,
Riches of His lavish grace,
Reigning in life through Christ Jesus,
Ruling over Powers and Principalities **in Christ Jesus**,
Resurrection of the body after physical death,
Jesus as our Reward, all at His expense as our holy, victorious Representative!

Because Galatianism is still so rampant in the body today (even in many of the books "explaining the grace of God"), we are wasting time and needless effort by *trying to achieve what Jesus has already provided.* By continuing to teach and defend the mixture of two opposing covenants, pastors keep believers from "seeing" and "entering fully" into the benefits of the **grace-based gospel** of Jesus' Kingdom. The Mosaic Law was never given to Gentiles and is now obsolete for Jews, according to Hebrews 8:13. So why focus on what God has replaced with His **New Covenant** inaugurated on Calvary.

In the next chapter, let's see just how entrenched Galatianism was in the infant Jerusalem church (a shocking fact we touched on briefly in Chapter One) by visiting the events surrounding Peter's experience with Cornelius. It will help you begin to understand this great, historical cover-up, which has enabled the **elephant of mixture** to stay entrenched in the church for 2000 years. Consequently, this heresy has caused centuries of needless confusion, infighting, immaturity, striving, scandal and defeat. This is no small matter.

OH! THE GOSPEL FROM LORD JESUS,

Which He revealed to Paul,	Gal. 1:12, 2 Cor. 12:5
Gives the revelation of His Cross, with benefits for all.	Rom. 6:6-11, Eph. 2:16
The unseen realm that He revealed is outside Time and Space.	2 Cor. 4:18, Heb. 11:1
The privileges He won for all, are mine, through faith, by grace.	2 Cor. 5:19, Eph. 2:8-9

Yes, the Gospel from Lord Jesus, in which I now abide,	John 15:4
Is the Finished Work of Jesus who healed me when He died.	John 19:30, 1 Peter 2:24
All benefits and blessings are now mine through what He did.	Eph. 1:14
I speak them into this seen realm from unseen Truth that's hid.	Col. 3:1-3, Rom. 10:8-10

One in spirit, with my Father, because of Jesus' Blood.	1 Cor. 6:17
His grace, through faith, has justified and cleansed me like a flood.	Eph. 2:8-9, Titus 3:5
The moment I was Born Again His Life poured into me,	John 3:3
And, since I have the Holy Spirit living within me,	1 Cor. 3:16
I share His Fruit of peace and love and joy with you for free.	Gal. 5:22

Yes, the Gospel from Lord Jesus that paid for **all** my sin!	Col. 2:13; Eph. 1:7 &
Is the Great Exchange with Jesus through whom I've entered in,	2 Cor. 5:19
Into the courts of Heaven where, **in Christ**, I now abide,	Eph. 2:6
Day in day out, forever, next to my Father's side.	Heb 10:12

In the Finished Work of Jesus, there is nothing left undone.	Eph. 1:3, Heb. 4:3a
He defeated Satan's plan for me, in Him my battle's won.	Col. 1:13
I live His victory every day by speaking what is true,	Phil. 4:8
Replacing thoughts of doubt and fear – in Him, all things are New.	2 Cor. 5:16-17

One in spirit with my Father because of Jesus' Blood.	1 Cor. 6:17
His grace, through faith, has justified and cleansed me like a flood.	Eph. 2:8-9, Titus 3:5
The moment I was Born Again His Life poured into me,	John 3:3
And, since I have the Holy Spirit living within me,	1 Cor. 3:16
I share His Fruit of peace and love and joy with you for free.	Gal. 5:22

Yes, the Gospel from Lord Jesus, that gives me peace of mind,	Phil. 4:7
Is the Great Exchange with Jesus, where only I can find,	Phil 3:8b-9
A future and a hope each day when troubles come my way,	Phil. 4:6, Eph. 1:18,
I set my mind on Jesus Christ, who prompts me as I pray,	Col. 3:1-3, Heb. 3:1
Relying on His Finished work to live above the fray!	Heb. 4:9-11

Sermon Song © Copyright 2012 by Leonard J. Ransil

CHAPTER FIVE

THE ELEPHANT IN JERUSALEM

Adding A New Patch On An Old Wineskin

As already explained in Chapter Three, after Jesus ascended into heaven, His followers assumed that Judaism would continue to be the basic belief system in the early church, with an overlay of the teachings of the risen Christ Jesus, God's anointed Rabbi and Messiah. Virtually everyone in the early Jerusalem church - including the leaders, James, Peter and John – thought of themselves as members of one of many Jewish sects. (See Endnote **#15** for more documentation.) Therefore, they continued to follow the norms of the Mosaic Law that did not specifically contradict what they remembered from Jesus' **pre-cross** and **post-cross** teaching. For example, they still went to the temple to pray but they no longer sacrificed animals for their sins since they knew that Jesus had paid their sin debt on Calvary. In hindsight, we can see some hints from Jesus in the four gospels, which were written 30-60 years after Pentecost, that some **post-cross** things would be different than in the **pre-cross** days. But naturally, there would be no need to replace the entire Mosaic Law system – or so they thought.

The amazing *new things* that happened during and after Pentecost, such as fearless preaching, speaking in tongues, miraculous healings etc., were all happening in the context of their Jewish beliefs and expectations - just as miracles had occurred when Jesus lived among them. But that all began to change for Peter personally when God supernaturally connected him with Cornelius, a Gentile centurion in the Italian regiment, as described in the book of Acts, Chapter Ten. Though Jesus had ministered healings to at least two non-Jews before His death, this episode had more far-reaching implications for any Jewish believer who had the eyes of faith and really wanted to accept more of God's **unseen reality**. As always, the lens we look through determines how we interpret what we see.

Peter's Paradigm Shift

It is quite clear that God wanted to save Cornelius, though a Gentile, because He sent an angel to tell him to send for Peter. Meanwhile, God gave Peter a vision of a group of "unclean" animals being lowered from heaven. A voice told him to get up and kill and eat. But it was absolutely against the Mosaic Law to do what the voice told him to do. So, according to Acts 10:14, he replied, "Certainly not, sir! I have never eaten anything profane or unclean." Now, what does that tell you? It shows undeniably that Peter and the early church were still locked into many of the same standards they practiced as Jews before the Law was nailed to Jesus' cross (see Colossians 2:14). This crucial truth will be thoroughly documented in Chapter Ten.

However, the voice didn't applaud Peter's reply but it rebuked him: "What God has made clean, you are not to call profane." (This echoes God's original declaration at creation when He called everything "good.") And, even though God repeated the same scenario twice more, Peter was still in doubt about the meaning of this vision until the Holy Spirit told him to travel with three Gentile men, sent by Cornelius to find him. Now Peter had a choice. If he still insisted on being faithful to the Law rather than to listening to a living word from God Himself, he would have disobeyed God. Obviously, his roots in Jewish law-mindedness were being challenged.

Fortunately, by grace through faith, he passed the test. He decided to yield to God instead of depend on the Law. He invited the three Gentiles into his house as guests. (Wow! Wait until James and the Jerusalem church hears about that.) The next day, they travelled together to Cornelius' house (another no-no) and Peter said to him: "You know that it is unlawful for any Jewish man to associate with or visit a Gentile, but God showed me that I should not call any person profane or unclean" (Acts 10:28). (The Jews regarded Gentiles as "pigs.")

What a shock to Peter's system - pun intended. What does that tell you? It reveals that Peter still thought of himself as a Jew and, therefore, superior to Gentiles. He did not yet understand that he was now dead to his old self **in Adam** through rebirth and was now a **new creation** saint, seated in heavenly places **in Christ**. Why not? Because this episode took place in about 40 AD, some two years before Jesus revealed His **whole gospel of grace** to Paul. Remember that, before this revelation came, even Paul was a Judaizer, by thinking, teaching and doing many of the same things *according to the Law!* Their *assumption* was that until a Gentile was circumcised and was keeping the Law, he was profane, unclean and, therefore, unworthy to become a Christian. In effect, they pridefully believed that their heritage qualified them to receive God's many blessings. But in God's reality, it was only God's grace that enabled them to seem spiritually "closer to God" then the Gentiles were. The **big picture** truth was that they were *all* **in Adam** before Pentecost. The Mosaic Law, which they prided themselves in, could not get them saved.

God Welcomes Gentiles

But God's biggest surprise was yet to come. After finding out what God had told Cornelius, Peter declared in Acts 10:34-35: "In truth, I see that God is not partial to individuals. Instead, in every nation, God accepts anyone who fears Him, and acts uprightly." That insight is a great improvement over how Peter (and the Jews in general) viewed "Gentile sinners" - right up until he saw the vision the day before. However, his statement reveals the unfortunate mixture of covenants - Galatianism - that still prevailed in his mind. Like the rest of the Jerusalem church, Peter still believed that God accepts or rejects people on the basis of their performance or status. That implies, conversely, that "God would never accept anyone who does not fear him or does not act uprightly." That flies in the face of God's merciful prophecy through Joel 2:32a which clearly says:

And it shall come to pass, that *whosoever shall call on the name of the Lord shall be delivered* (saved)...

There is no requirement to "act uprightly" before you can be saved. Ironically, even Peter himself had publically quoted that same verse on Pentecost morning, according to Acts 3:21 (and Jesus later underscored it through Paul in Romans 10:13). Peter's wrong assumption just proves again that strongholds against the knowledge of God's merciful ways and who He really is – a gracious, gift-giving Father – die hard.

Peter's entrenched law-based mindset thought that God only hears and helps those who behave well, a carry-over from the Law Covenant of works. If that were true, no one would ever be heard or be saved because: "...all have sinned and fall short of the glory of God" (Romans 3:23). Because God is perfect, the only way He can justly declare fallen human beings acceptable enough to be one with Him - which is His ultimate goal - is for them to be perfect *by nature*. Absolutely no descendent of Adam can ever meet that required standard on his own. Jesus met that standard because He was not born **of Adam** but of God and He earned justification by His perfect performance as a human being, the **last Adam.**

Jesus now gives His righteousness as a free gift to anyone who is reborn of God and thereby receives a **new nature** by faith in what Jesus accomplished some 2000 years ago. Receiving this gift has nothing to do with one's behavior – good or bad - but everything to do with one's right believing in Jesus' **divine exchange** as one's Savior. I know that sounds like heresy to some because the **elephant of mixture** has so dominated even most theological "experts" for 2000 years.

But just think about it. Did Jesus promise paradise to the thief next to Him on Calvary based on his "upright behavior" or because of his request, made in faith in the midst of dire circumstances? Jesus certainly did not *look* like a savior, yet he called upon Jesus and was promised heaven. Now, *that* is Good News! (And notice, he did *not* have to confess all his sins first. Much more on that later.) Some may malign God's **radical grace gospel** as "easy-believeism" or "greasy grace" or "hyper-grace." But remember: it was the works-based mind-set of the Pharisees that thought God sets up obstacles to earn blessings while Jesus talked of "child-like faith." What really counts is how God views individuals personally, for only He knows each person's heart and intent. One author wisely calls the practice of adding conditions or demands to the **New Covenant** as "front-loading or back-loading" Jesus' **gospel of grace**. #16 That is exactly what was going on in the Jerusalem church and continues in most churches today.

Mixture Pollutes Purity

Mixing a performance-based message of man's imperfect law-keeping with the pure gospel of Jesus' perfect performance, necessarily nullifies both for individuals who do that. God cares about us so much that He made it possible for us to benefit fully from what Jesus has accomplished. So, He mercifully revealed to us, through Paul, how really abhorrent is this heresy, now called Galatianism. It is a perversion of the true gospel and comes with serious consequences, according to Galatians 1:8-9. Only the **whole gospel** of God's **radical grace** reveals the extent of Father-God's love and care for us. He unselfishly exchanged His precious Son's life for our sin debt and, through rebirth, exchanged His righteous nature for our unrighteous nature, from Adam. Now we, who are reborn through Jesus' **finished work,** are forever united with Father-God Himself. That was His original intent, even before creation.

Only the terms of the **New Covenant,** made in Jesus' blood, makes salvation possible to mankind. That is why the Mosaic Covenant, with its performance-based terms *had* to be replaced if mankind was to have any hope of salvation. God's reality is this: all **in Adam** humans are already condemned (see John 3:17-18). Those who foolishly put their faith in the self-effort of law-keeping of any kind to gain salvation - instead of in Jesus' **divine exchange** - remain condemned. That is why the Mosaic Law covenant was replaced for anyone now **in Christ** with a grace-based covenant at Calvary - after Jesus fulfilled it during His lifetime. However, the "principle of law" remains in force for all *unbelievers*. The Holy Spirit uses it to convict them of their evil behavior (which stems from their condemned sin-nature, **in Adam**) so that they (hopefully) cry out to Jesus to believe and receive His free gift of eternal life – salvation.

Again, to be abundantly clear, Peter's declaration above springs from the law-based message of the Mosaic Covenant. It is an accurate report of his inaccurate interpretation of why God saved Cornelius and his whole household. His perspective at that time was *not* the pure **gospel of radical grace** from Jesus Christ, revealed directly to Paul about 2 years later. On the contrary, while God loves all people everywhere, He can accept into a perfect heaven (and into His perfect Self) only those made perfect – justified, made righteous – by receiving the benefit of Jesus' performance on the cross, by faith. It is not one's obedience or disobedience to any standard that qualifies one to receive the offer of salvation. On the contrary, it is being in union with Perfection Himself by a rebirth through faith that makes a former, **in Adam** "sinner" instantly become "perfect in God's sight" and, therefore, compatible with Him and heaven too. Jesus' revelation, given exclusively to Paul in about 42 AD, makes this **unseen, in Christ reality** abundantly clear:

> But now, apart from (man's efforts to obey) the Law, a righteousness of God has been revealed, being witnessed by the law and the prophets, even the righteousness of God through faith in Jesus Christ, given to all them that believe. For there is no distinction (between Jews and Gentiles), for all have sinned and fall short of the glory of God. Being justified (made righteous) freely by his grace through the redemption that is **in Christ Jesus,** whom God set forth as a propitiation (the perfect remitting sacrifice for all sin), through faith in His blood, to manifest His righteousness (to us and through us) (Romans 3:21-25).

However, this monumental revelation was not understood and fully embraced at this point in time, even though Cornelius' conversion experience revealed Father-God's true heart and intentions.

Some Key Basics of the Gospel in Action

But in this miraculous episode, Peter did realize and experience again three important basics of the **whole gospel** of Jesus.

First, that God anointed Jesus with the Holy Spirit and power, which enabled Jesus to do mighty miracles such as "healing all those under the power of the devil" (see Acts 10:38). Of course, this "baptism of the Holy Spirit" was also what many of the believers had already experienced in Jerusalem, starting at Pentecost, according to Acts 2:4. The leaders knew it was very different from the "baptism with water for forgiveness of sins," which both John the Baptist and the disciples had administered to people, **pre-cross**. That is why Hebrews 6:2 talks about "baptisms" - plural.

Second, Peter testified that God raised Jesus from the dead. This is a key element for **in Adam** sinners to believe in order to be saved, according to Jesus' gospel, as noted in Romans 10:9-10.

Third, "… that everyone who believes in Him (Jesus) will receive forgiveness of sins through His name" (verse 43). Boom! When Peter declared that essential doctrine – that Jesus accomplished the total forgiveness of all of mankind's sins - all heaven broke loose.

While Peter was still speaking these things, the Holy Spirit fell upon all who were listening to the word. And the circumcised believers, who had come with Peter, were astonished because the gift of the Holy Spirit was also poured out on the Gentiles because they heard them <u>speak with tongues and magnify God</u>. Then Peter said 'can any man withhold water baptism on these which have received the Holy Ghost just like we have'? So Peter ordered that they should be baptized (with water) in the name of Jesus Christ. Then they asked Peter to stay with them for several days (Acts 10:45-48).

So, the take away is that Cornelius did *not* have to be circumcised first or say the "sinner's prayer" to be saved. Nor did God require him to be baptized with water <u>in order to be baptized with the Holy Spirit.</u> And notice also that this major blessing and empowerment of the Holy Spirit Himself was not limited to the supposedly "good-behaving" Cornelius but He was poured out on his entire family. Imagine – a whole family, young and old – saved, just by hearing and believing a few of the many key elements of Jesus' **whole gospel of grace**.

Totally Forgiven And Reconciled

"But," you say, "Peter did not say that Jesus accomplished the **total** forgiveness of all of mankind's sins." No, he did not spell it out then because the full benefit of the **whole gospel** was not yet revealed. But the Holy Spirit knew it and Jesus later revealed that benefit to Paul, which he recorded years later in Colossians 2:13 and which is also found as a key benefit of the **New Covenant** in 2 Corinthians 5:19, Hebrews 10:12 and 17-18 and in 1 John 2:2. By standing in as mankind's <u>last Adam</u> (1 Corinthians 15:45), Jesus' perfect, **finished work** was so powerful and complete in God's eyes that He forgave and removed the barrier of all sin caused by the <u>first Adam</u>. So now, all mankind is forgiven and reconciled to God - <u>from God's **post-cross** viewpoint</u>, as 2 Corinthians 5:19a triumphantly declares:

> God was reconciling the world to Himself through Jesus Christ, not counting men's sins against them ….

That astounding revelation, packed into just one verse and supported by others, has changed the course of human history. But, of course, even though all of mankind's sins are forgiven, each person must personally accept God's free offer of reconciliation <u>in order to be *reconciled* to God</u>, passionately expressed by Paul in verse 20b:

> We beseech you on behalf of Christ: <u>be reconciled to God</u>.

Jesus' **finished work** <u>restored</u> the *gift of choice* to all sinners to <u>be reconciled to God</u> when, *left to ourselves **in Adam***, there was no salvation possible for mankind. How painful it must be for the Trinity to watch people reject Father-God's free ticket to heaven that was bought at an infinitely high price – the life-blood of His beloved Son. God rejected Jesus on Calvary because He <u>became</u> our sin and was punished and crucified on our behalf so that we could be totally forgiven, reconciled and accepted and become His beloved children. Yet many needy, helpless sinners still foolishly say "no" to His free offer and reject His open arms. And because He is a God of love (not a dictator) He does not *force* anyone to choose to reconcile themselves to Him and be blessed in heaven eternally. God respects each person's <u>free will</u> to choose Him OR to remain alienated towards Him and to reject all His free gifts. Fortunately, Cornelius was not so foolish but responded to God's grace to seek first His Kingdom and His gift of righteousness **in Christ**, and receive all else besides, which is the essence of Jesus' **grace-based gospel**, revealed to Paul.

Undoubtedly, the experience of seeing an uncircumcised Gentile being baptized in the Holy Spirit astounded Peter and his Jewish companions. It exploded their paradigm of God's intent for mankind. To Peter's great credit, he realized it was God's lavish grace and truth in action. He went with the flow and, <u>at the risk of rejection by those back at home</u>, he remained with Cornelius for a few days. Possibly he shared his memories of Jesus' life and death and what he knew of the gospel at that point in time. Happily, there is no mention that Peter required circumcision for these reborn Gentiles. But how did all this go over with those heavily entrenched Jewish believers back in Jerusalem who did not fraternize with any uncircumcised "unclean and profane" Gentiles? (Even circumcised Gentiles were suspect, as we shall discover shortly.)

Decision Time!

Needless to say, this episode presented a major challenge to the infant church in Jerusalem which was still practicing some of the major aspects of the Law system. We can see their <u>negative</u> reaction to the **whole grace gospel** collectively on two specific occasions. **First**, when Peter returned home, he discovered that the news traveled faster than he did - and no one, <u>including the leadership</u>, was happy about his pro-Gentile behavior. And **second**, when Paul came to Jerusalem for the first church council about ten years later, Peter reminded everyone about this monumental event that he had had with God and Cornelius. His testimony helped verify that Paul's **whole gospel** was, indeed, from Jesus. We will look at this second key event in 50 AD in great detail in Chapter Seven. For now, let's look closely at the reaction of the Jerusalem church to the first event with Cornelius. Here is what Peter returned home to find, according to Acts 11:1-4:

> The apostles and the believers throughout Judea heard that people, who were not Jewish, had accepted God's word. However, when Peter went back to Jerusalem, the believers who insisted on circumcision (which included James) began to argue with him. They said, 'You went to visit men who were uncircumcised, and you even ate with them.' Then Peter began to explain to them, point by point, what had happened.

Care is taken in this passage not to reveal the names of the Judaizers (those who insisted on circumcision to be saved) as they were later called. But it is clear that, since Peter himself never had visited or eaten with unconverted Gentiles before meeting with Cornelius, no one else there, <u>including the other leaders</u>, would have ever done that either. After all, the Law was clear: a Gentile must be circumcised to be "acceptable." Again, what does this tell you? If these Judaizers were bold enough to publically accuse Peter of acting contrary to the Law, it proves again that they still regarded obedience to some aspects of the Law as essential to their walk with God. In other words, they still believed they had to <u>add their efforts</u> to Jesus' **finished work** to become or remain acceptable to God. Faith alone in Jesus' performance, by calling on His name to be saved, was not enough in their eyes that were still darkened somewhat by the veil of the Law. The **elephant of mixture** actually hides the fullness of God's grace and truth.

And further, for even a few of them to dare to accuse a man who had been part of Jesus' inner circle and who Jesus had called "rock," would suggest not only the seriousness of the accusation (in their eyes) but certainly that the other two leaders mentioned, James and John, were at least sympathetic to the accusation. Otherwise, they would not have tolerated this attack on their fellow leader. In fact, it would never have been an issue to begin with if they had understood God's true heart towards all mankind - even if it meant that no law-entrenched Pharisee ever joined them. But the plot thickens. There were two men named James among the twelve disciples. But, according to historical accounts, this particular James (the Lord's half-brother) had *not* followed Jesus as a disciple, **pre-cross**. Yet, now he, not Peter, was leading the Jerusalem church. Worse yet, he apparently remained an avowed Nazarite, committed to practicing Judaism until he was martyred in about 62 AD. (Below, we investigate more details about the life of this "James the Just," some of which are also given in Endnote #**17** and in Appendix # 10, because he is such a key figure in why Galatianism is still so entrenched today.)

A Pivotal Confrontation

Regrettably, this ugly confrontation in Jerusalem put Peter in a decidedly defensive position. Clearly, Peter was on trial before the *whole* Jerusalem church. Truth be told, this was the *beginning* of the titanic split in the early church over mixing the law with the **gospel of grace,** which still rages today. It was a preview of what Paul would have to face when he came to Jerusalem in about 50 AD to defend the **whole gospel** of Jesus Christ. Again, we will investigate that decisive event in Chapter Seven.

But remarkably, by God's grace, Peter was not intimidated, even by the leadership. He stood his ground by testifying to what God said and did that had produced such literally miraculous results. He added a brief comment to tie the event in with a promise from Jesus Himself. If nothing else, it helped to remind them that he wasn't just the water boy around there. Given what was at stake, it is very instructive to recount what Peter said to his accusers about what happened to Cornelius:

> When I began to speak, the Holy Spirit came to these people. This was the same thing that happened to us in the beginning (on Pentecost, about 6 years before). I remembered that the Lord had said, 'John baptized with water, but you will be baptized by the Holy Spirit.' When they (Cornelius and his household) believed, God gave them the same gift that He gave us when we believed in the Lord Jesus Christ. So, who was I to interfere with God?' When the others heard this, they had no further objections. They praised God by saying 'Then God has also led people who are not Jewish to turn to Him so that they can change the way they think (repent) and act and have eternal life (Acts 11:15-18).

"So, who was I to interfere with God?" Great defense, Peter! If they want to blame someone for rattling their cage - the law-based covenant from Moses - then blame God. The next verse is very telling. "When the others heard this, they had no further objections." Who were "the others"? Obviously, it was everybody Peter was testifying to, including the leadership. To repeat, they were all "Judaizers" at this point in time and understandably so. *But*, here was a God-given opportunity to renew their mind – "to change their thinking" - over to God's paradigm regarding their view and treatment of *all* Gentiles. Then, by extension, they also had a wake-up call to at least begin to question the bondage of their entrenched, law-based thinking and lifestyle.

Ironically, while they applauded the fact that Cornelius "changed the way he thought," they, themselves, did *not* fully "change the way they thought" about uncircumcised Gentiles. Peter's dramatic experience, which God personally orchestrated step by step, could and should have been enough to drop-kick the **elephant of Galatianism** out of the church then and there.

But unfortunately, James, not Peter, had the last word. Josephus records that Jesus' half-brother James was known as "James the Just" in Jerusalem because of his noteworthy faithfulness to the Law. Tradition has it that James was also known as "old camel knees" because of the calluses on his knees from praying daily in the temple. Again, he had never travelled with Jesus, **pre-cross**, but chose, instead, to remain loyal to the Jewish establishment – and, reportedly, a Nazarite to boot. He only warmed up to his rabble-rousing half-brother when Jesus appeared to him on the day of His glorious resurrection. But law-based thinking, traditions, habits and strongholds die hard unless we allow the Holy Spirit to help us walk by faith in Christ Jesus' **whole gospel** rather than by carnal sight. That is one key reason why Jesus sent the Holy Spirit to live inside of us as our Teacher and Counselor - to personally reveal Jesus' **finished work** to us in order to renew our minds to think God's thoughts.

Though Jesus had told His disciples to go out and "make disciples of all nations," James and many others chose to stay close to the temple to adhere to the traditions passed on from Moses. This was in spite of Moses' exhortation, given prophetically in Deuteronomy 18:15, 18 and 19 that Peter paraphrased in Acts 3:22-23:

> For Moses said: 'The Lord your God will raise up for you a prophet (Jesus) like me from among your own people; you must listen to everything He tells you. Anyone who does not listen to Him will be completely cut off from among His people.'

Apparently, they felt it was their duty to guard the bulk of the Mosaic Law Covenant, mixed with the gospel (as they understood it at that point in time) and defend it against challenges even from God Himself. To repeat: God expressly did *not* require Cornelius or any in his household to be circumcised before rebirth. Nonetheless, their traditions trumped God's intervention, shown by insisting that Gentiles still be circumcised before rebirth into God's family. Again, that stubborn stance, enforced by James, would lead to a later, more crucial confrontation over the opposing covenants - this time with Paul, as we will explore in detail in Chapter Seven.

The "Bare Bones Gospel"

As implied above, the infant church was operating from what could respectfully be called a **"bare bones gospel."** It was powerful enough for them to receive God, Himself, inside of them and for them to be **"in Christ."** However, there is no evidence in Acts that they understood those astounding **New Covenant realities** or many of the other major ramifications of Jesus' **divine exchange** that Paul later revealed in his letters. So the next chapter presents an outline of the essentials of the **"bare bones gospel"** being preached by the infant church in Jerusalem in order to see and understand how it differs with Jesus' **whole gospel of grace,** which we began presenting back in Chapters One and Two. We will consult Luke's account in the Book of Acts to make this important comparison between the two revelations.

The following song-poem reinforces the above message by contrasting Law vs grace and gives scriptural references for your convenience - to aid in your study of His living word.

THE ACCUSER OF THE BRETHERN

THE ACCUSER OF THE BRETHERN	Rev. 12:10
Not the God of love and grace,	1 Jn. 4:8; 2 Cor. 9:8; Eph. 1:7
Will whisper tempting thoughts to Saints with glee.	Matt. 4:1; 1 Thes. 3:5
He lies and steals by telling them to focus on the Law	Jn. 8:44; 1 Pet. 5:8; Gal.2:16; Col. 2:14-15; Rm.7:8-11,
Instead of on the One who set them free.	Gal. 5:1
The Ten Commandments aren't the key that causes victory	2 Cor. 3:3 & 9
So they were nailed to Jesus' Cross of shame.	Col.2:14-15
But Satan uses them to kill God's life of peace and joy	1 Pet. 5:8
Through groundless condemnation, guilt and blame.	Rm. 8:1; Jn. 3:18; Jn. 5:24
For the Law was only meant to show the depth of mankind's sin, -	
The rebel nature Adam passed on down,	Rm. 5:16-17, 19
To bring us to the revelation of our need for Christ	Gal.3:24; Rm. 3:9; Rm. 7:7
Who offers us His Kingdom and a crown.	Matt. 6:33; 2Ti. 4:8; 1 Pet.5:4
In Christ there is no condemnation - Jesus bore ALL sin	Rm. 8:1; Col. 2:13; Jn. 5:24
And *all* of Father's wrath at Calvary.	Rm. 5:9
Receive by faith His Kingdom and His Robe of Righteousness,	Matt. 6:33; Rm. 1:17
A Gift, through Christ, that grants true liberty.	Rm. 5:17; Gal. 5:1
Accept Him by receiving all He's done in the **unseen**	Jn. 19:30; 2 Cor. 4:18
And letting Him live through you here on earth.	Gal. 2:20
It's only possible by being one with Jesus Christ	Jn. 17:20-23
By grace, through faith, which starts with your new birth.	Eph. 2:8-9; Jn. 3:6; 1 Pet. 1:3
Then look to Jesus, not to Law, who saves and heals and keeps,	Rom. 7:6; Col. 3:1-4;
And trust in Him for all He came to give.	Jn. 10:10; Eph. 1:3-4; 13-14; Gal. 3:14
Receive His love and mercy and forgiveness of *all* sins,	Heb. 4:16; Eph. 2:4; Col.2:13
For, only by His Spirit can you live.	Rom. 8:2-5
And thank Him for re-making you a New Creation Saint	1 Cor. 5:17
An Heir with Jesus Christ, God's first-born Son,	Rom. 8:17; Gal. 4:7; Heb. 1:6
So you can live His victory, above all circumstance!	1 Cor. 15:57; Eph. 2:6
The war with Law and Satan Jesus won!	Gal. 2:19; Rm. 7:6; Col. 2:15
I glorify You, Father, Thank You Jesus Christ, my King.	1 Ti. 1:17
Sweet Holy Spirit, Counselor and Friend,	Jn. 14:16 & 15:26; Rm. 8:16
Please live your Life within me, overflowing with your love,	Gal. 2:20; Rom. 5:5 & 8:2,11
Through faith in Christ, where freedom never ends.	Rm. 1:17, Gal. 5:1

A Sermon Song © Copyright 2009 by Leonard J. Ransil

CHAPTER SIX

THE "BARE BONES GOSPEL" IN ACTS

The Various Titles of the Bare Bones Gospel

What many regard today as "the gospel message" was described by various titles in the book of Acts. These varied identifiers gives us a clue as to the expanding nature of the original understanding of the "good news" message over time. Even the very progression of what it was called is instructive.

In Acts 8:12, it was called the good news of the Kingdom;
in Acts 8:25, the gospel;
in Acts 18:26, the message of salvation;
in Acts 16:32, the Word of the Lord;
in Acts 20:24, the gospel of grace;
in Acts 20:27, the whole will of God;
and in Acts 20:32, the Word of grace.

Comparing Two Covenants

It is worth noting that what started in the list above with an emphasis on an impersonal "Kingdom" message in Acts 8:12, ended with the more personal notion of a gift of grace or favor. This is reminiscent of John's statement in John 1:17: "For the Law came through Moses; grace and truth came through Jesus Christ." Kingdom preaching tends to emphasize laws and rules and steps that must be learned and obeyed to attain or maintain the King's acceptance and blessings. In Matthew's **pre-cross** account, the word "kingdom" was used fifty-four times, emphasizing a *place*, rather than a *person*.

By contrast, grace-preaching tends to emphasize believing and accepting Father-God's loving invitation to an intimate relationship with Him - based on believing what Jesus has already done for all of mankind. In John's more relational account of Jesus' life on earth, the word "kingdom" was used only four times and he used the word "love" much more often than Matthew. Yet, both books reflect the law covenant of that period which *required* "dead people" – unplugged from God because they were **in Adam** – to love Him and each other. Conversely, under the **New Covenant** of grace from Jesus, God sends His love, the Holy Spirit, into a believer's *new* heart to empower the believer to now freely love God - and all others, like God does - because he or she is His child **in Christ**. Big difference.

Simply put the Law *demands*; grace *supplies.* They oppose each other. "The Law is not of faith" but, rather, requires man's own puny efforts to meet the impossible demands of sinless perfection. But, mercifully, "Christ redeemed us (the Jews) from the curse of the Law...." (see Galatians 3:12 and 13). So, God's grace is His *undeserved enablement* through Jesus, who has already met every demand perfectly for every believer and who meets every need with His abundant blessings, which already legally belong to the believer, simply *because* he is **in Christ**. But if you are as law-minded as I used to be, all this might sound too simple and too good to be true because you, too, are used to hearing and believing the poison of mixture. But I lovingly suggest that you do as I did when exploring this subject: depend on the Holy Spirit of truth to unfold Jesus' **whole gospel of radical grace** as you continue through this book.

The Law's True Purpose – After Adam

It is essential to remember that the demands of the Mosaic Law were given by God to reveal man's true nature, *not* God's nature! (This will be fully documented in Chapter Eight.) That is still the purpose of the Law now, a revelation that shocks most believers today like it no doubt shocked Paul at first. So he later explained this to Timothy:

> But we know that the law is good, if one makes use of it properly. Knowing this, that the law was not set in place for the righteous (saved), but for the unrighteous and the lawless, for the impious and sinners, for the wicked and the defiled (1 Timothy 1:8-9).

Again, God gave the Law to the unrighteous, **in Adam** Israelites to reveal the *hidden cause* of their rebellion which was and is mankind's fallen nature **in Adam**. When this biblical revelation is not understood, it is easy to be tricked into Galatianism and harbor distorted views of who God really is. Again, our gracious Father-God did *not* give the Mosaic Covenant to reveal His nature but to reveal our fallen nature **in Adam** that must be regenerated – replaced – for us to be compatible with God. This demand-based covenant lasted for about 1500 years and ended at Calvary when Jesus fulfilled its every demand and then the Law was abolished and nailed to the cross, according to Ephesians 2:15 and Colossians 2:14. (This crucial truth will be thoroughly documented in Chapter Ten.) This 1500 year period covers about 82% of the actual text of the Bible, from Exodus 19 to John 20. In contrast, Jesus' **grace-based gospel** given to Paul is the pinnacle of the Bible yet covers only about 8% of its pages – a 10 to 1 ratio. No wonder mixing the two Covenants is still so prevalent in Christendom. The ugly **elephant of Galatianism** carries far more weight today than the delicate **butterfly life** of pure grace.

The Lure of the Law

But besides the ten to one ratio difference in the amount of Bible text and the early stronghold of Galatianism in the early Jerusalem church, there is another more subtle reason why the **elephant** is still so prominent in contemporary Christian circles. It comes down to what one is *seeking.* Man's unaided mind cannot perceive the things of the **unseen realm** because it depends on the five senses for input. However, the **unseen realm** of God's Kingdom is, by definition, invisible to the senses and therefore impossible to understand or control with the natural mind and is, therefore, dependant on God's revelation. "The wind blows wherever it wills… so it is with everyone born of the spirit" (John 3:8). The notion of "trusting God" who is **unseen,** frustrates the unsaved, **in Adam** rebel – *the wild dog* - who is bent on "doing his own thing." Why? Because he is still **in Adam**. But even a law-focused believer – *the city dog* – finds it hard to learn to trust and depend on the lead of the Holy Spirit as a way of living day to day. Why? Because, according to 1 Corinthians 2:14,

> "… a natural man does not receive the things of the Spirit of God for they are foolishness to him and he is not able to understand them for they are discerned spiritually" (not discerned by the physical senses.)

The believer must be willing to learn to switch from depending solely on his **seen-based** senses in order to <u>learn</u> how to flow in the higher law of the Spirit of life if he is to *experience* Jesus' life and wisdom day to day like Jesus and Paul walked in.

Given mankind's unsaved condition before Calvary, it is a remarkable work of God's grace that Abram yielded to an **unseen** promise from an **unseen** God. That is why he is regarded as the Father of our faith. The Kingdom of God can only be "seen and entered into" by faith in God's declaration that both He and His Kingdom really do exist and that He is a rewarder of those who earnestly *seek <u>Him</u>* (see Hebrews 11:6). The sense of the Greek word for "seek" there is "to hunger for" and "to worship" as opposed to just "searching for" as in "hide and seek." It implies the diligence that explorers Lewis and Clark exhibited in their determination to find and map the source of the Missouri river, no matter what it took to do it. Once you get the revelation that God is your only source of true love and life (which Adam rejected), your hunger for Him will increase as you get to know Him personally. Then worship becomes a natural response. As He increases in your sight, everything in the **seen realm** will take its proper, secondary place and you will experience Him as your true source for everything that is good. Your focus will increasingly switch from <u>magnifying temporary externals to magnifying the eternal</u>, **<u>unseen reality</u>** – the Trinity that you, believer, are now one with, **in Christ Jesus**. Amen.

In direct contrast, every moral system of do's and don'ts focuses on the **seen realm** which the mind of man can readily grasp and operate in naturally - seemingly independent of God. It suits man's inherent, self-sufficient disposition (the flesh) that resulted from Adam's rejection of God's offer of permanent union with Jesus (the Tree of Life). God's life can only be received by faith through being reborn of God. I say "seemingly independent" because, in actuality, it is an illusion to think that humans or devils can exist independently of God because He mercifully sustains all things – even rebels and devils - by the word of His power, according to Hebrews 1:3. The **unseen reality** is that the continued existence of all beings are dependent on Him sustaining all things, as stated in Colossians 1:17, whether they choose to acknowledge it or not.

The reason many people - unbelievers and sometimes even believers - do not accept the full reality of the **grace gospel** of the **unseen Kingdom** is because they depend on only what they "see" and experience in the **seen realm** as the most important (if not the total) reality. I operated with this mind-set for half of my Christian life. I was focused on law-keeping until the light of His truth started to break through. While the **seen realm** is certainly important, in the **big picture** <u>it is less significant than the **unseen realm**</u> because the **seen** came from the **unseen realm** by the spoken word of God at creation. At some future point, God is going to replace this decaying **seen realm** with a <u>new earth,</u> as emphatically stated in Revelation 21:1. This revelation dawned on me one day as I meditated on this pivotal verse that Paul declared to the very carnal **(seen-minded)** believers in Corinth:

> For this reason, we do not faint. But though our outer man (soul and body) are decaying, our inner (spirit) man is renewed day to day. For the lightness of our day to day troubles work out for us a weight of a sublime, eternal glory, beyond measure. <u>And we do not focus on the things that are **seen**, but on the things that are **unseen**. For the things that are **seen** are not lasting, whereas the things that are **not seen** are eternal</u> (2 Corinthians 4:16-18). (Paul repeats this revelation in Colossians 3:1-3.)

The scripture-based lyrics of the following song-poem, poetically capture the interplay between faith and the **unseen realm** - and more:

THE UNSEEN REALM is much more real than what I see down here
For what is **seen** is passing away   2 Corinthians 4:18
True faith is the assurance that what we're hoping for   Hebrews 11:1
Will fully come to pass that glorious day   2 Peter 3:10

By grace, I fix my eyes on You so I can see what's real   Hebrews 3:1; Col. 2:17
By walking in the Spirit as You did   2 Cor. 5:7; Galatians 5:25
You rested in our Father's care, providing for each day   Hebrews 4:1-3a
By seeing what to carnal man was hid   1 Cor. 2:14; Romans 8:6-7

The gift of faith you bless me with is consciousness of You   Hebrews 11:1
And thinking on the things You're thinking of   Colossians 3:1-3
My eyes are fixed by focusing on who You really are,   Luke 11:34; Col. 3:1-2, &
                                                                        Heb. 3:1-2

Your goodness and Your faithfulness and love   Rom. 15:14, 1 Cor. 10:13, &
                                                                        1 Jn. 4:8

I'm resting in the fact that You're my Bridegroom, coming soon,
To whisk me to the marriage feast above   Revelation 19:7
I'm overwhelmed with thankfulness for all You've done for me,   Colossians 2:7
Your blood poured out in sacrificial love   John 19:34
A Sermon Song   Copyright 2009 by Leonard Ransil

(The song *True Liberty* in Chapter Eighteen that also gives insight into this **unseen reality**.)

Jesus' Gift Of Righteousness

I know, from doing this myself, that law-minded Christians operate - to varying degrees – under the limitations of depending on their natural mind to figure out what the Bible says. They typically focus on the Law that instructs what believers should "*do*" - rather than focusing on what Jesus has already "*done*" for us – by His perfect, **finished work**. They diligently do so in a never-ending effort to "please God" by trying to obey all of His "laws" in order to stay "right" with God. Like the unbelieving Israelites, carnal Christians, living *the city dog* life described in Chapter Four, put their trust in "keeping the **seen-based** laws" – which appeals to man's natural mind – according to the "standards" of their upbringing or a particular denomination etc..

The Pharisees did the same thing because they did not have the Holy Spirit within them to reveal the whole truth contained in the Old Testament about the coming Messiah. He was standing in front of them but they could not see Him. Depending on the mind of man (yours or another's) instead of on the mind of Christ, which reveals the **unseen realities** by God's gift of faith, is actually walking according to the flesh instead of living dependently on the Holy Spirit's revelation knowledge of what Jesus did for us. This common error comes from mixing opposing covenants. Under the Mosaic Covenant, an Israelite's righteousness (right standing) depended on his obedience to the Law. In the **New Covenant**, our righteousness depends on faith in Jesus' obedience to God. The former is based on man's efforts to live "righteously." The latter is based on believing and receiving the *gift* of righteousness that Jesus won for all believers. This blessing results in a life of rest and peace **in Christ Jesus' finished work** of His **divine exchange**.

This is the life **in Christ** that *country dog* believers have learned to trust and rely on as God's gift from Jesus through His **finished work.** Because of His **divine exchange** with these reborn saints, they know that He has *already* supplied His righteousness to them and has *already* met their needs in His **unseen** Kingdom. His provision is then manifested into the **seen realm,** as a life-style, by an on-going, *trusting, dependent* faith in Jesus' **finished work.** (As one of my friends likes to remind himself: "Lord, if You don't, I can't.") They value a dependent relationship with Father-God over religion. Admittedly, the Mosaic Covenant pattern (of relying on one's obedience to the external Law to earn God's blessings) sounds more logical, straightforward and "practical" than Abraham's pattern of believing Someone about something that cannot be **seen.** But God's "foolishness" is far wiser than man's supposed wisdom. The seeming "failure" of the cross is God's best example of that truth. Through rebirth, God "crossed out" the old, **in Adam** nature and supplied a new, **in Christ** nature – your new spirit-self. We will explore this wonderful reality – God's alternative to living according to the flesh - in Chapters Sixteen and Seventeen.

Wrong Believing

All this confusion, caused by the **elephant of mixture,** is usually based on the misconception that God is a law-focused Judge (as reflected in the terms of a law-based covenant that covers about 82% of the Bible) and that He uses laws to "control mankind" and that He still punishes mankind for disobedience (sin) – even under the **New Covenant.** This law-based concept of God's nature actually defines the essence of the heresy of Judaism and Galatianism that Jesus inspired Paul to totally reject in the book of Galatians. It is the same stronghold that caused the Jerusalem church to reject Paul's message of **total grace** because it 1) conflicted with their long-held tradition and doctrine of "law-based, self-righteousness" and 2) it makes no sense to the natural mind of man. However, His Kingdom and gift of righteousness can only be received by a child-like, dependent faith in Jesus and on what He has already done for mankind.

Paul made all this quite clear when he stated in Galatians 2:21:

> I do not set aside the grace of God (like others did), for if righteousness could be gained through the Mosaic Law then Christ died for nothing.

In principle, it is the same sin of unbelief that kept a whole generation of Israelites from enjoying God's Promised Land – and that promise was about something very tangible. Mentally, they magnified the giants, who they could *see,* to be bigger and more powerful than God whom they could *not see.* Then, they compared themselves to the bigger giants and lost courage and strength. In contrast, David walked by faith in his **unseen** God and so he compared little Goliath to his Big God. That choice of what to *seek* and to *magnify* is still the **main** issue in our lives today. The **unseen** Kingdom, which all reborn saints now belong to, operates by faith, love and liberty and might seem to be even more of a challenge for us than the Promised Land was for the Israelites because it is totally intangible.

But that is why Jesus sent the Holy Spirit into believers. He provides the inspiration and power to <u>magnify Jesus</u>, the Author and Finisher of our faith instead of magnifying the passing troubles of the **seen realm**. So, although the Mosaic Covenant fills so much of the Bible, it is certainly *not God's focus now* - and neither should it be ours as **New Covenant** believers. The whole purpose of the Bible was to woo mankind into a personal, living relationship with an **unseen** God, based on His interactive love through the Spirit, rather than on our imperfect obedience to the dead letter of the Law (which, remember, was only given to the Jews). Why continue to mix the two opposing covenants when we have been supplied with a new set of wonderful terms of an everlasting covenant, kept for us by Jesus?

Seeing the Unseen

But "seeing God's **unseen** Kingdom by faith" necessarily requires the revelation of the Holy Spirit to understand what only God Himself could supply to a race of rebels – His underserved favor in the Person of our Savior, Jesus the Christ. His **gospel of grace,** unveiled to Paul, is beyond natural sight by its very nature because it describes what Jesus did for us *spiritually* in the **unseen realm**. To repeat, by comparison with the concrete terms of the Mosaic covenant that covers 82% of the Bible, Jesus' **whole gospel of grace** revealed to Paul, presented in only 8% of the Bible, can seem far less significant and even illusory.

But, on the contrary, Jesus patiently informed Nicodemus in John 3:3 that he could not "see" or "enter" the Kingdom of God *unless* he became born a second time – this time by God's doing, not by his natural parents. However, since it was still the **pre-cross** period, being "born of God" was not yet possible. But, through His perfect sacrifice on Calvary, Jesus' **divine exchange** made it possible for unbelievers to *immediately be one with Him and to join Him in heaven* through rebirth - <u>by faith</u> (see Ephesians 2:6). But no one knew about that preposterous truth until 42 AD. Instead, all they had to go on was an effective, though greatly limited version of Jesus' **whole gospel of grace**. Now, let's go to the book of Acts to see what this limited **"bare bones gospel"** of the infant church looks like.

The Bare Bones Gospel in the Book of Acts

The closest thing to a summary of the essential points of the **"bare bones gospel"** preached in Acts is given in the context of a testimony to the chief priest and the Sadducees - the "supreme court" of Jerusalem - by Peter and the other apostles. They had been imprisoned for witnessing about Jesus but were miraculously freed by an angel the night before they gave this courageous testimony. The main points are underlined below.

Peter and the other apostles answered: 'We must obey God rather than people. You murdered Jesus by hanging Him on a cross. <u>But the God of our ancestors brought Him (Jesus) back to life.</u> God used His power to give Jesus the highest position as <u>leader and savior</u>. He did this <u>to lead the people of Israel to Him, to change the way they think and act</u>, and <u>to forgive their sins.</u> We are witnesses to these things, and so is <u>the Holy Spirit, whom God has given to those who obey Him</u>' (Acts 5:29-32).

Gathering the essential points of the then known gospel in Peter's summary, we see:

1) We must obey God rather than people (when they are contradicting God's word to us).

2) God raised Jesus from the dead (also see Acts 2:24 and 32).

3) Jesus is in the highest position as a leader and a savior.

4) He was sent to bring Israel back to God and to change the way the Jews think (**New Covenant** repentance) and, therefore, act.

5) He forgave Israel's sins (see point #4 below under "Additional Elements").

6) He gives the Holy Spirit to those who obey Him (see clarification in point #5 below).

Repentance Is Re-Defined Under The New Covenant

Point # 4 and # 5 signals a wonderfully new definition of the word "repentance" because of Jesus' **finished work** on Calvary. Because Jesus' perfect sacrifice fully paid the cost of all mankind's sin forever (see 2 Corinthians 5:19 and 1 John 2:2), the **New Covenant** changes the meaning and the process of repentance. The now obsolete Mosaic Law pattern required continuous repentance and sacrifices for sins, necessitated by law-breaking. But since Jesus has paid for all sin, **New Covenant** repentance has been re-defined by using the Greek word *metanoya*. This means a continuous renewing of the natural mind with the new **unseen realities** of what Jesus has *done* in order to enable believers to think like God thinks. Big difference! The former focuses on sin and self, the latter on Jesus and His finished work done for us. Jesus sent the Holy Spirit to teach and guide believers into a revelation of all His truth, which is primarily revealed in His **whole gospel of grace.** However, the Jews were trained to obey the Pharisees who were experts in the Law. So Peter is challenging that "requirement" by saying "We must obey God rather than man." That was certainly a change in thinking – repentance!

Notice also in point #5 that Peter's mind-set was still that Jesus came to save only the Jews. He probably deduced that from what Jesus said before He died, according to Matthew 15:24. "… I was sent only to the lost sheep of Israel." That is probably another reason why the Jerusalem church thought of itself only as a new Jewish "sect" - of about twenty-four at that time. (See Endnote #**18** for documentation on this key fact.) Again, they insisted that the Gentiles become circumcised before being saved. Even Paul reflected a hint of this cultural bias when he said to Peter: "We who are Jews by birth and not 'Gentile sinners' …" (see Galatians 2:15).

Again, God's ultimate intention was to offer salvation to *all* mankind through the Savior of the world, strictly on the basis of His grace through faith rather than by the "works of the Law." But this truth was not crystal clear to anyone before Jesus revealed this revelation directly to Paul on his "visit" to heaven in about 42 AD. Of course, there are many prophecies to that effect in the Old Testament but the early Jewish believers were still sorting through all of that. The four gospels contain some passages clearly based on the Mosaic Law such as "If your eye causes you to sin, puck it out" – ouch! But other passages describe what the coming kingdom will be like in the **post-cross** era of grace. This **pre-cross** mixture of messages is to be expected since Jesus was purposely born under the Law and was still fulfilling it (and then some) by obeying His Father's word to Him. But again, this mix of messages, given in the accounts of this **pre-cross** period, is *not* the purely Good News of **New Covenant** of grace given to believers who are now **in Christ**.

Additional Elements of the Bare-Bones Gospel

While the six points above are certainly key basics to the **bare-bones gospel** message, other important points are found throughout the book of Acts. I will include the references to these points to demonstrate the *progressive* nature of the apostles' understanding of this **good news** over time. (It is important to understand that new revelation of what Jesus accomplished came even after the negotiations regarding Gentile believers at the Jerusalem Council, which happened in about 50 AD and which we will be carefully examine in the next chapter.)

1) Jesus promised to give them power through what John the Baptist had called being "baptized with the Holy Spirit and fire." Jesus Himself, had received that same enabling power of the Holy Spirit in the same way when He started His ministry (see Matthew 3:11, Acts 1:8, 2:4, 10:45-48 and John 1:32-34). Unfortunately, not everyone made this "equipping" by the Spirit an essential part of the new, **post-cross** message. Jesus needed this baptism (immersion) in the Holy Spirit to <u>operate</u> with God's enabling power as a perfect man (not as God) in His earthly ministry. Therefore, how much more do we saints who still sometimes sin need this equipping? (See Endnote #**19** for more key insights.) Here is an example of what Peter and John did to rectify this oversight:

> **2)** Now when the apostles, who were at Jerusalem, heard that Samaria had received the Word of God, they sent Peter and John to them, who, when they came down, prayed for them, that they might receive the Holy Spirit: (For as yet He had not fallen on any of them: they had only been baptized (with water) in the name of the Lord Jesus.) Then laid they their hands on them, and they received the Holy Spirit (Acts 8:14-17)

And here is what Paul personally did about that same oversight in Ephesus - after his revelation from Jesus in 42 AD:

> Paul traveled through the interior provinces to get to the city of Ephesus. He met some disciples in Ephesus and asked them, "Did you receive the Holy Spirit when you <u>became believers</u>?" They answered him, "No, we've never even heard of the Holy Spirit." Paul asked them, "What kind of baptism did you have?" They answered, "John's baptism." Paul said, "John's baptism was a baptism of repentance (for forgiveness of sins under the obsolete Law covenant.) John told people to believe in Jesus, who was coming later." <u>After they heard this, they were baptized (with water) in the name of the Lord Jesus. When Paul placed his hands on them, the Holy Spirit came to them, and they began to talk in other languages and to speak what God had revealed</u> (Acts 19:1-6).

I believe it is fair to say that Jesus emphasized to Paul just how important 1) being baptized in the Spirit by the laying on of hands and 2) operating in His gifts (including tongues) are for each believer. At Paul's conversion, Ananias laid hands on him to receive sight and the Holy Spirit and *then* he baptized him with water. And, after all, if Jesus, the perfect man, depended on the Holy Spirit for His empowerment and to hear and do His Father's will, how much more is that true for anyone else, as Paul alluded to in Romans 8:2 and taught on in 1 Corinthians 12? This **unseen reality**, available to all believers, is yet another casualty from the **elephant** stomping around in the church. Our flesh prefers walking by the natural sight of the **seen realm** to "walking in the Spirit by the gift of faith" – by the "the substance (or evidence) of things **unseen**," as Hebrews 11:1 describes. (Chapter Nineteen will explore this walk much more.)

3) "All who call on the name of the Lord shall be saved" (Acts 2:20). Again, by quoting this prophecy from Joel 2:32, Peter is declaring that the time of the Messiah had come and it is not hard to be saved, because God is eager to offer this gift of grace through dependent faith, not by the self-effort of law-keeping. Paul repeats this basic doctrine in Romans 10:13. Law-minded evangelists tend to focus on "sin" and to add more steps to the salvation process than Jesus revealed to Paul because they don't start with a revelation of Jesus' **finished work**.

4) "God made Jesus (the Man) both Christ and Lord" (Acts 2:36). Therefore, He should be our primary focus *now*, not the **pre-cross** Jesus. Again, we must go to the **whole gospel** that Jesus gave to Paul to see this key revelation. Jesus says through Paul in 2 Corinthians 5:16:

> So from now on, we don't think of anyone from a human (carnal, natural) point of view. If we used to think of Christ from a human point of view, <u>we don't anymore.</u>

This is perfectly consistent with the revelation that Jesus' death and resurrection caused "all things to be made new" from God's point of view. Jesus is now the new High Priest of a new order, spoken of in Hebrews 8:1 and 9:10 respectively. In a similar vein, 2 Corinthians 5:17-18 states: "Therefore if any man is **in Christ**, he is a **new creature**: old things are passed away; behold <u>all things have become new</u>. And all (these) things are of God ...." To repeat, all this points to the **unseen realm** of **New Covenant** realities, **post cross**, *not* to the now obsolete Mosaic Law that was based on the **seen realm** and was incorporated into the four gospel books so they naturally contain various scriptures about law and some about grace. This is because Jesus spoke of the Law to the law-minded but gave grace and mercy to those seeking Him and His help. <u>This can cause confusion to those who depend on the four gospels to help them live day to day.</u> The Law parts will give you do's and don'ts but no help to obey them. Again, we will examine this dilemma in great detail, starting in Chapter Twelve.

Our Superior Post-Cross Benefits

The disciples who had walked with Jesus before His death were, no doubt, esteemed among the members of the new, Jewish-Christian "sect." (This phenomenon happens today as people who know celebrities can become "mini-celebrities" in their own little circle, just by association.) But we were not created to be our own *point of reference* instead of God. To think this way is not only a prideful, "anti-Christ" mind-set but also an "anti-self" position in the **big picture**. How so? Well, Satan successfully tempted Adam and Eve to become seemingly independent of God – to become their own gods - because Satan knew from his own personal experience that rebellion would destroy their "right" relationship with God. But ironically, by sending Jesus to rescue us from Satan's kingdom by crucifying our old, **in Adam self** (by identification with Jesus' death by faith), our loving Father-God spiritually freed us from bondage to our old self by regenerating us, through Jesus.

So now, every believer can be progressively freed *mentally* from a focus on oneself by becoming increasingly focused on Jesus and His proven love for us. This is the way of His unselfish love - agape! The trap of "self-worth-by-association" still exists among believers today.

85

How? By envying the people who actually saw and walked with the **pre-cross** Jesus. Why is that a trap? Because they fail to see how much better off all **post-cross** believers are *now* because of Jesus' victory over 1) man's sin nature, 2) sin patterns and addictions etc and 3) spiritual death. He won all this and more for everyone who believes. So, believer, let the Holy Spirit teach you His way to "enter into the rest" of Jesus' **divine exchange** – by bathing your mind in the **whole gospel** of the exalted Christ Jesus. You are important and valued and favored by God because you are in union with Jesus, not because of your status or station in this life, all of which is superficial and fleeting.

5) "Repent and be (water) baptized … for the forgiveness of your sins" (Acts 2:38a). Jesus, the Lamb of God, was sent to *take away the sins of the whole world,* according to the prophet, John the Baptist (see John 1:29). It is obvious that they understood this to mean "all of mankind's sins – past, present and future." Why? Because the perfect Lamb, who had God's authority to forgive sins on a case by case basis, **pre-cross**, was now the perfect and only Substitute needed forever. He replaced the temporary provision of animal sacrifices, slain and burnt as daily offerings in the Temple for (some) sins. Since God had mercifully accepted animal sacrifice as *atonement* (sin covering) for a full year of Israel's past sins, all the more so did God's perfect Son's selfless sacrifice of His holy blood fully satisfy God's just wrath and punishment for all sin, forever.

That revelation is a foundational part of Jesus' **whole gospel** of His undeserved mercy, grace and favor. Also, Jesus' perfect sacrifice, which He did once and for all, *must* be enough to forgive and remove all punishment for all future sins because this Lamb, sent from God, would never again be sacrificed. Otherwise, no sins committed after Calvary would be forgiven and our justification would be impossible. His **finished work** does not have to be repeated. This aspect of Jesus' **finished work** is confirmed in 2 Corinthians 5:19 and 1 John 2:2 but not fully accepted and taught in many if not most churches today. This ignorance of what Jesus accomplished for mankind keeps believers focused on the **elephant of mixture** and, therefore, on their sins and their faulty performance, rather than on Jesus. Chapter Nine will present just how deadly law-mindedness really is.

The revelation of total forgiveness of all sins was a bombshell for Jews who depended on temple sacrifices to cover (not remove) sins. This truth, which Jesus revealed definitively to Paul, is just as radical a doctrine for most Christians to grasp today. To repeat: from God's viewpoint, all the past, present and future sins of *everyone* - believers and unbelievers - were *totally* forgiven because of Jesus' **finished work**, accomplished for everyone almost 2000 years ago - even before they were born. (We will explore the scriptural proof and the ramifications of this glorious provision of Jesus' grace covenant in Chapters Thirteen to Fifteen.) But even though an **in Adam** sinner's sins are totally forgiven, he *must* choose to be reconciled to God by being born again by God in order to be qualified for and accepted into a perfect heaven.

6) Then you will receive the Holy Spirit as a gift. This promise belongs to you and to your children and to everyone who is far away. It belongs to everyone who worships the Lord our God (Acts 2:38b-39).

This scripture from Acts, Chapter 2 is significantly different from what Peter said later (chronologically), listed in point #5 above ("to those who obey Him"), because a gift does not require "obedience" (on our part), but rather faith in *Jesus'* obedience that provided His **divine exchange** with believers. This is yet another indication of "performance-based thinking," mixed with grace, which so commonly occurs due to mixing the two opposing covenants - the **elephant of Galatianism** - preached in the early Jerusalem church and, sadly, also in most churches today.

Points From Paul In Acts - According To Luke
The remaining points of the **bare bones gospel** revealed in Acts are attributed to <u>Paul</u>.

7) "Jesus is the Son of God" (see Acts 9:20). Therefore, the covenant that Jesus inaugurated in His blood on behalf of the whole world was far more important and permanent than the temporary one that God gave to Moses for the Israelites.

8) Be it known unto you therefore, men and brethren that through this man is preached unto you the forgiveness of sins. And, by him (Jesus), all that believe are <u>justified from all things, from which you could not be justified by the Law of Moses</u> (Acts 13:38-39).

Paul gave this declaration in Pisidian Antioch on his first missionary journey in about 47 AD. This is another major departure from the mindset in the Jerusalem church that believed Jesus just built on top of the foundation of the law system. Paul was saying that Jesus, the perfect sacrificial Lamb, was superior in every way to all the sacrifices, offered in the Mosaic Law combined, for those who receive – by faith alone - what Jesus did. This is a sweeping statement that opens the door into the understanding that, from God's perspective, "all things have been made new," which we will explore starting in Chapter Sixteen. Jesus' sacrifice accomplished the forgiveness of all mankind's sins - and reconciliation from God's viewpoint - so that God can offer justification (righteousness) to all who believe and receive this astounding, totally free offer.

Paul also discoursed later on the topic of "righteousness" to Governor Felix but Luke did not include what Paul said about it (see Acts 24:25). It is tragic that Jesus' **whole gospel of grace** did not take root in the Jerusalem church because the church could have walked in and maintained far greater victory in the **seen realm** and avoided an ongoing disharmony with Paul. And even more importantly, the unity of the Spirit and the bond of peace that comes from faith, love and liberty would have prevented the split between Jews and Gentiles, precipitated by James and supported by the other local Judaizers at the council in 50 AD. (We will document all this in Chapter Seven.)

An Awakening To Jesus' Whole Gospel Of Grace
The above comment about James is based on a long-term assessment of the early church. It is true that, for a short while after Pentecost occurred: "… with great power, the apostles gave witness of the resurrection of the Lord Jesus and great grace was upon them all" (Acts 4:33). There were signs and wonders of various kinds that attracted the attention of many people. However, as we now know, while our Lord's resurrection was *the* central validation of His **whole gospel**, there were many benefits for believers that were yet unknown, even to the apostles early on. Being open to all that Jesus revealed to Paul in 42 AD, by being filled and

illuminated by the overflowing life and love of the Holy Spirit, enables us, even today, to do the same "greater works than Jesus" that the apostles did at first (see John 14:12). But after Paul's time until now, these manifestations have been rarely expected and experienced by believers because the **elephant of mixture** has been allowed to overshadow the glory of the **butterfly life** over the last 2000 years. The manifestation of the gifts of the Holy Spirit have only been given lip-service for most of church history. They have not been the normal experience of most believers because they entail looking beyond the **seen realm** of law-keeping by living the **butterfly life** in the power of Holy Spirit.

Yet now, as believers are increasingly hearing Jesus' **grace-based gospel**, an awakening of the ages is beginning to spring forth world-wide and usher in the return of Jesus. Again, the Body of Christ is beginning to awaken to the 2000 year old **unseen Kingdom reality** that 1) we believers are *already* His spotless bride because our perfect Husband shed His perfect blood for us and, thereby, 2) He has caused us to be eternally righteous and favored in God's sight through His **divine exchange** and His oneness with us. This dawning revelation of God's radical **grace gospel** is renewing believer's minds world-wide and will speed His glorious return (see Revelation 19:7 and 21:2 and 9).

9) "Since you Jews reject it (the gospel) and consider yourselves unworthy of everlasting life, we are now going to turn to people of other nations (Gentiles)" (see Acts 13:46).

Martin Luther's famed struggles with unworthiness and condemnation as a monk are a metaphor of the Church's battle with and against the **unseen elephant of Galatianism.** This is still the central battle today in the Body of Christ. When a believer allows the lies of Galatianism to steal key elements of Jesus' **whole gospel** and, to that degree, he goes back under the law by relying on his own efforts or he still *thinks* that he is a worthless sinner, the devil will stomp on him with guilt and condemnation. But, saints of God, because of Jesus' **divine exchange**, we are not caterpillars any longer but **butterflies**, alive, risen, ascended **in Him** and, therefore, free and in love with Christ Jesus in our inner man! Bathe your mind with the revelation of Jesus' **whole grace-based gospel,** revealed only to Paul, so that you will be firmly *established in His gift of righteousness* through the truth of His **finished work.**

10) Speaking to a crowd of men in Athens about their "unknown God," Paul made this bold declaration:

> Just as some of your own poets have said: 'For in Him (God) we live, and move, and exist, for we are of His offspring.' Therefore, since we are His kind (His creations, not His children until reborn of God), we should not think that this divine being is made of gold or silver or precious stones, or the engravings of art from the imagination of man. … He has appointed a day on which He will judge the world with justice, through the man (Jesus) whom He has appointed, offering faith to all, by raising Him from the dead. (Acts 17:28-31)

This is a tantalizing verse because it can be wrongly interpreted to mean that everyone is automatically a child of God, which is a heresy that I will address in Chapter Thirteen. But Paul intriguingly alludes to a major truth of the **whole gospel** by ironically quoting a Greek poet. One of the main points of Jesus' revelations to Paul is that **in Adam** sinners are offered the choice to be reborn **in Christ** and, thereby, to become a **new creation** being and, thereby, an actual child of God. Obviously, this drastic change in identity was not wholeheartedly accepted in the Jerusalem church or they would certainly *not* have continued to cling to Judaism for their identity. This passage also points out that God raised the *man* Jesus from the dead and He would judge the world with divine justice. But fear not, saints of God. Since all believers **in Christ** are totally forgiven of all sins and forever <u>justified</u>, there is every reason to thank God for that great day yet to come. There is no condemnation for those who are **in Christ** by grace through faith. Jesus exchanged His righteous nature as a Man for your unrighteous nature **in Adam** – forever.

11) Paul was testifying "… to both Jews and to Greeks about the need for 1) a change of mind towards God (**New Covenant** repentance), and 2) faith in the Lord Jesus Christ" (see Acts 20:21). This is very close to the simplicity of the process he records in Romans 10:9-10 in order to be saved. Without spelling it out, Paul is inviting them again to change their thinking about God being primarily a Judge (as generally portrayed in 82% of the Bible under law) to His real nature - a Father of love - who sent His beloved Son to make it possible for **in Adam** sinners to become reborn saints **in Christ Jesus**. The **elephant of mixture** sways believers and unbelievers alike to have a bad opinion of God because they wrongly think that He is against them for their bad behavior. But He did not send Jesus to condemn an already condemned mankind but to save mankind from their Adamic nature, as John 3:16-19 clearly states. Why would a God of love send His Son to ransom someone He hates? Why would He forgive and reconcile *all people in the world* to Himself through Jesus if He hates all or even some of the people in the world? That is nonsense from the devil. Ask the Holy Spirit to reveal God's true heart towards you and renew your mind about Father-God's true nature. We will focus on this crucial revelation of God's goodness as a fitting and final chapter of this book.

12) "Be baptized, and have your sins washed away as you call on His name" (Acts 22:16). This is Paul's account of what Ananias told Paul the day he was saved. This is yet another confirmation that it was generally understood that all of a believer's sins – past, present and future - are totally forgiven thanks to Jesus' sacrifice. Unfortunately, not all believers rest in that assurance today because of the **elephant of mixture.** We will address that dilemma in Chapters Thirteen and Fourteen. But also note that Ananias' elementary understanding of the process of how to be saved includes being baptized with water. It was a carry-over from John the Baptist's ministry that the disciples imitated, **pre-cross.** This is not the baptism that Cornelius received first when he was saved with his whole household. Yet, it was what Peter followed up with after Cornelius' Baptism in the Holy Spirit. Neither one is "required" in the rebirth process that Jesus revealed to Paul, found in Romans 10:9-13. Water baptism does not *cause* rebirth. It is an outward sign of an inner transaction of rebirth in the **unseen realm** by grace through faith between God and the seeker. Going under water (especially by immersion) <u>symbolizes</u> the death and removal of the Adamic "old man" and then rising out of the water <u>symbolizes</u> being regenerated into a **new creation** child of God by grace through faith in Jesus as your Savior.

CONCLUSION: There is some overlap in all these points above, of course, because Acts reflects the dynamic interaction of a living God with His new children, rather than a doctrinal statement of a dry religion. My purpose in listing these various points of the **bare-bones gospel** is not to minimize its power or importance but to serve as a basis of comparison with Jesus' revelation to Paul of His **whole gospel** message presented earlier, in part, in Chapters One and Two. As should be evident to you by comparing the two messages, the infant church in Jerusalem was not operating in the fullness of Jesus' glorious revelation of His **good news** given to Paul - and unfortunately, neither is much of the Church today.

A Radical Conversion Is Available

Instead, much of the Body of Christ functions much closer to the basic list above rather than Jesus' **whole gosp**el of lavish grace, love and liberty - by faith. This debilitating condition will not change, personally or corporately, until 1) the mixture of these two incongruous covenants is seen for the double-minded Galatian heresy that it is and 2) the believer's mind is progressively transformed by the truth of the **whole gospel of radical grace** unveiled by Christ Jesus. A drastic mind renewal like Paul experienced – **New Covenant** repentance – is necessary and this is accomplished over time by the Holy Spirit of truth for all who ask Him to have His way. The conversion of my mind began in earnest when I began to pray the song He gave me: "Bathe my mind in your truth." Can you see now why any other gospel that differs from His **post-cross** revelation to Paul - including the four gospels - is not <u>purely</u> good news?

Now, before you blow a holy gasket, please carefully read Chapter Twelve where I provide many examples of what I mean by the "mix" of law-based passages with grace-based passages found throughout the four gospels. Remember, they describe the period still "under the law" so it is inevitable that some things which were said and done in that time period – even by Jesus Himself - do *not directly apply* to the **post-cross** believer. Why? Again, because we have a decidedly new and *superior* covenant of total grace - signaled by a change in the priesthood - that Jesus graciously inaugurated later in His own blood, shed on Calvary, for our sake not His!

To help you discern this mix of law-based verses from grace-based verses in the four gospels, it is first necessary to 1) complete (in the next chapter) the story mentioned earlier of Paul's appearance before the First Jerusalem Council and 2) to establish, in Part Two of this book, a clear, scriptural understanding, given to Paul by Jesus, of why God gave the Law and what He intends it to accomplish. <u>If believers use it differently than He intends, they risk falling from grace by going back under law and, consequently, they come under a curse</u>, according to Galatians 3:10. The **elephant of mixture** is a menace to the **butterfly life** - a fact that Jesus made very clear to Paul, as will be documented in Chapter Nine. As you will see in coming chapters, I am *not* antinomian – i.e. "against the Law" - even though it arouses sin and causes death, just as it is meant to do for **in Adam** sinners. But I am opposed to using it *against* believers, based on Jesus' revelation to Paul, according to 1 Timothy 1:7-9a. Moreover, I am definitely *for* the higher Law of faith, love and liberty, described in Chapter Three, because that is how God's Kingdom operates.

The following song-poem contrasts some aspects of the Law covenant with the **New Covenant** of grace.

MERCY, NOT JUSTICE

Jesus Christ did not come down to show how bad you are.
The Law of Moses does that very well.
It brings to light your "Adam self," at enmity with God,
Condemned to die and on your way to hell.

Law's justice, not mercy, has proven man is "lost"
But Jesus came to save us by bearing all the cost.

If mercy, not justice, is what you're looking for,
Jesus Christ, your Savior, has opened Heaven's door.

For Jesus came to free you from the Law of sin and death
By nailing Satan's weapon to the tree.
And being crucified to pay for all of mankind's sins,
He's offering you Life abundantly.

Through Mercy, not Justice, He made all things brand new.
The Lamb of God forgave you - which proves His love for you.

It's Mercy, not Justice that Jesus came to give
And when He lives within you, then you will also live!

For He's God's gift to anyone who sees their need for Him
A Savior sent to set all captives free.
Accept Him as your only Lord, who rose triumphantly,
Receive, by faith, His Life and Victory.

Through mercy, not justice, He gave His life for you.
His Spirit living in you will teach you what to do.

All glory and honor to Jesus Christ the King!
Ask Jesus to live in you and be your Everything!
Sermon Song © Copyright 2009 by Leonard J. Ransil

CHAPTER SEVEN

PAUL DEFENDS JESUS' WHOLE GOSPEL OF GRACE

A Brief Recap

The previous chapter presented an overview of the basic gospel message – the **bare bones gospel** - found in the book of Acts. Taken as a whole, this new *news* spawned a revolutionary excursion into dimensions of the **unseen realm** that had not been open to any of Jesus' disciples before they were reborn of God at Pentecost. They personally experienced such things as being baptized in the Holy Spirit and speaking in languages they had never studied yet were understood by Jewish pilgrims. They saw 3000 people being saved by grace through faith - like they, themselves just were – in response to a Holy Spirit-inspired sermon from Peter, a fisherman. Later on, God manifested signs and wonders in and through them like Jesus had done, **pre-cross**. All this was such a radical shift from the shock and deep despair that had overwhelmed them when Jesus was crucified and buried less than two months earlier, only to see Him risen, appear at different times, then ascend out of sight for good. Talk about a roller-coaster ride.

This new life certainly was an improvement over the many rituals and demands of the Mosaic Law that they had grown up with. A major change was the revelation that God had accepted Jesus' sacrificial death for all their past, present and future sins, which meant that they were forever forgiven because of Jesus' perfect sacrifice for their sins (see Hebrews 10:17-18). Wow! What a relief to know that they no longer had to buy sacrificial animals for their unintended sin or risk death from an intended sin or depend on a Jewish high priest's performance to remain in God's favor every year. All they had to "do" was *believe* and receive Jesus' **divine exchange** which made them righteous in God's sight forever. But, needless to say, these and other new beliefs, which differed so drastically from the constant demands of the Law, were viewed as a threat by the Jewish establishment. Additionally, the disciple's insistence that Jesus was alive, the man whom the Sanhedrin had condemned and crucified as a blasphemer, was suspect to say the least.

As an example, soon after Paul's conversion, the Jews in Damascus and then the Grecian Jews in Jerusalem tried to kill him because he was proving from scripture that Jesus was the Messiah. The believers in Jerusalem quickly shipped him back to his hometown of Tarsus so that things could return to a relatively peaceful co-existence between the Jewish establishment and the leaders of the Jerusalem church, as recorded in Acts 9:19-31. We will examine this strategy more below.

The Excitement And The Pain Of Change

There certainly were a lot of changes to get used to and there continued to be more surprises, good and bad. As already discussed in Chapter Five, the Jerusalem church was in turmoil over Peter's experience with Cornelius's unorthodox conversion in about 41 AD. Why? Because it all happened without this Gentile and his whole family first converting to Judaism and being circumcised. But even that momentous event, obviously orchestrated by God Himself, did not reverse a deep-seated prejudice against Gentiles - even among the church leadership. They gave

Peter a pass after a confrontational examination but they continued to require Gentiles to become circumcised before they could be reborn of God by faith. Apparently, in their minds, Jesus' perfect sacrifice that demonstrated God's pure mercy, grace and unconditional love for *all* mankind was just too good to be true. The veil of the Law continued to limit their understanding of just how good and inclusive God's offer of salvation really is. Some still think that way today.

Fortunately for us, about one year later, Jesus revealed many glorious dimensions of His **finished work** of redemption in the **unseen realm** to Paul, using many "unspeakable words" and "surpassing revelations" as he recorded in 2 Corinthians 12:4 and 7. Then, over about a 20+ year period, Paul unveiled the implications of these wondrous revelations that he emphatically declared to be "*the gospel of Christ,* for it is the power of God to *everyone* believing, both to the Jew first and to the Greek," as he wrote in Romans 1:16. This "new news" magnificently fleshed out the **bare-bones gospel** found in Acts. Among those revealed mysteries, which had been hidden until then, was 1) the Law was nailed to the cross and, therefore, was no longer in force for Jewish Christians (see Colossians 2:14) and 2) by replacing the law-based covenant with a grace-based covenant, God made it possible for both reborn Jews and Gentiles to enjoy equal right-standing in His sight by faith alone.

While a majority of Christians even today still think they need the **elephant of mixture** to stay on God's good side, God did not give the Mosaic Law to the Jews to get them to heaven. The reason was simple: perfection is required for relationship/union with God because He is perfect. But the Law could not provide that because the **in Adam** Jews could not keep it perfectly, even by their best efforts. And even if any could have kept it perfectly, the terms of the Mosaic Covenant did *not offer* eternal life. That was not its purpose. Furthermore, why would the Holy Spirit help a believer today, keep "operational" what was 1) only given to the Israelites, 2) nailed to the cross and 3) made obsolete, according to Hebrews 8:8 and 13? And, as we will prove below, even James, the bishop of Jerusalem, denied that he had authorized Judaizers to direct Gentiles in Antioch (not in Jerusalem) to be circumcised and to keep the Law. As someone has succintly stated, "The law condemns the best of us; grace saves the worst of us."

Again, the law only tells you what is wrong with you or wrong with what you are doing; it can't help you fix you or your behavior. For example, if a road sign posting the law says the speed limit is 35 mph and you are going 50, the sign won't apply your car's brakes for you. You have to decide what you will do. And state troopers are paid to "fine" speeding drivers, not pull them over to tell them how well they are driving. The law offers no power to obey it nor give you encouragement when you do. The Mosaic Law was based on fear of punishment, not on love for God. Why hold on to something that operates negatively and arouses sin when we can flow in the love and liberty of the Spirit by faith? (We will examine more of the Law's true purpose and scope in detail in the next chapter).

So, given the many reasons above, it is obvious why the law is not our friend even though the Jerusalem church insisted on enforcing it. We would all still be under it if Jesus had not revolutionized Paul's thinking with a mind-transforming visit to heaven in about 42 AD. Again, the dichotomy is undeniable in this statement which Paul made after his heavenly visit:

Be it known unto you therefore, men and brethren, that through this man (Jesus Christ) is preached to you the forgiveness of (all) sins and, that by him, all who *believe* are justified from all things, from which you could not be justified by the law of Moses (Acts 13:38-39).

Wow! "… by Him (Jesus), all who believe are justified from all things…" But, how can that be true? It is because Jesus' **finished work** changed "righteousness" from a *verb to a noun* - from a "*work*" under Law to God's *free gift* - received by grace alone through faith alone. That is light years apart from the impossible goal of trying to achieve and/or maintain justification – union with God – by constant trial-and-error-obedience to the law-based covenant of Moses. Then Paul backed up this bold declaration with a prophecy quoted from Habakkuk 1:5, warning them just how radical Jesus' **whole gospel** really is by saying:

You despisers! Look and wonder and be scattered! For I am working something in your days, a deed which you would not believe, even if someone were to explain it to you (Acts 13:40-41).

Again, that "something" was right-standing with God by simply believing and receiving Jesus' gift of salvation and trusting in His **finished work** rather than trusting in one's constant, failing efforts to obey the Law perfectly. This is exactly Jesus' point, definitively stated through Paul in Romans 3:21-28, written in about 56 AD:

But now, <u>apart from the law</u>, the righteousness of God, to which the Law and the prophets have testified, has been made manifest. And the justification of God, through the faith of Jesus Christ, is *in* all those and *over* all those who believe **in Him** for there is no distinction. For all have sinned and all are in need of the glory (and the perfection) of God. <u>We have been justified freely</u> by His grace through the redemption that is **in Christ Jesus**, whom God has offered as a <u>propitiation</u> (total payment for and removal of all sin), through faith in His blood, to reveal His justification for the remission (forgiveness) of the former offenses, and by the forbearance of God, to reveal His righteousness in this time, so that He, Himself, might be both "just" and *the Justifier* of anyone who has faith **in Jesus Christ**. So then, where is your self-exaltation? It is excluded. Through what Law? That of works? No, but rather through the <u>law of faith.</u> For we conclude that a man is justified (made righteous) by faith, without any works of the (Mosaic) law.

Do you see the opposing terms of the two Covenants? It all boils down to "the law of (human) works" versus the "law of faith" in God's works – Jesus and His **finished work** of justification by grace through faith. This monumental revelation can hardly be stated any more clearly and directly than that! However, the **elephant of mixture** of law with grace still permeates most of the church today, even though Luther rediscovered this core doctrine of Jesus' **whole gospel** – by "*sola fide*" – by faith alone. After receiving this revelation, he bravely fought the **elephant** keepers and protectors of his day – like Paul did in his. Scholars generally think that the above account, taken from Acts 13:38-39, occurred somewhere between 46-48 AD which is about 4 to 6 years after Jesus' revelation to Paul and about 2-4 years before the Council of Jerusalem, held in about 50 AD. Scholars argue over which came first - the council in

Jerusalem or when Paul confronted Peter in Antioch - because the accounts of the two events in Galatians and Acts differ in this key point and in many others as well, as we shall soon see.

I will assume that Paul's account is accurate chronologically because he wrote Galatians very soon after 50 AD and said specifically that he was not lying about these very important matters. On the other hand, Luke wrote his account in Acts about 17 years later and he gives the impression that the council meeting fully resolved all doctrinal disagreements between the Jerusalem church leadership and Paul. (See Endnote #**20** for more insight on James.) That is decidedly not the case, as I will soon show, which explains how the **elephant of mixture** nearly stomped Jesus' **grace gospel** out of existence in Antioch after Paul confronted Peter sometime *after* the council. But before we explore that sad episode, let's look first at the following account of the central controversy that precipitated the first council of the early church.

The First Jerusalem Council In 50 AD

Paul tells us in Galatians 2:1-2 that:

> Next, after fourteen years, I went up again to Jerusalem, taking with me Barnabas and Titus. And I went up according to a revelation, and I debated with them about the gospel that I am preaching among the nations, but privately to the ones of reputation, lest I run, or have ran, in vain.

Paul didn't choose to specifically clarify what revelation he was responding to. Some commentators speculate that it was just God's direction to go up to Jerusalem. But Luke's version states that the Antioch church commissioned Paul to go to Jerusalem to resolve the very heated doctrinal disagreement. So, I personally think the "revelation" mentioned in this verse was the **whole gospel of grace** message that Paul had received from Jesus. By this time, he had assimilated "the gospel of Christ" well enough to present it coherently to his doubting, double-minded brothers, who were still clinging to much of the Law and mixing it with grace.

As yet, those in the Jerusalem church had no clue that they were individually **"in Christ"** and were part of His Body on earth – let alone "seated in heavenly places" **in Him**. While the two camps agreed on the **bare bones gospel,** as described in the previous chapter, we also know now that they came from two opposing sets of assumptions on other non-negotiables, much like it was with Luther and the established church of his day. Again, the account of the council in Acts, written in about 67 AD by Luke (who apparently served as Paul's companion and physician at times) differs significantly in content and tone regarding the doctrinal conflict, as we shall see below.

To be sure, the bottom line issue and one main reason for this book you are reading is to prove that 1) there existed, early on, a major doctrinal war over radically opposing viewpoints of enormous importance and 2) unfortunately, this war has been mostly wall-papered over for 2000 years - at great harm to sinners and saints alike. This stinking carcass of a double-minded **elephant** has been rotting in the Christian church ever since its birth at Pentecost in about 33 AD. Fortunately for us today, Paul's love for Jesus and his passion for the truth of Jesus' **whole gospel of grace** compelled him to travel to Jerusalem to present this revelation and its corresponding fruit of the Holy Spirit in the lives of the Gentiles in the Antioch church. Those who side with the truth of Jesus' **whole gospel of grace** as Paul did, will readily see the fault-line in the following comparison of two different accounts of the same council meeting, held in about 50 AD.

Please remember that, for years, Paul had been an anti-Christ Pharisee. But even after his conversion to **the bare bones gospel**, he still mixed law and grace along with everyone else. Why? It is because there was no other alternative before Jesus' revelation of the **whole grace gospel** to him in 42 AD. Therefore, he perfectly understood where the church leaders were <u>still</u> coming from because he had walked in their shoes as a believer until his visit to heaven. Again, the church leadership in Jerusalem was, at first, understandably ignorant of the **whole gospel** truth. But sadly, they remained resistant to the treasure of Jesus' **whole gospel** which the following comparison of accounts by Luke and Paul documents.

The Controversy: Must Gentiles Be Circumcised Before Salvation?
Luke's version in Acts 15:1-5:

> And certain ones that came from Judea, were teaching the brothers, '<u>Unless you are circumcised according to the custom of Moses, you cannot be saved.</u>' Therefore, when Paul and Barnabas had a <u>fierce discussion and discord</u> with them, they decided that Paul and Barnabas, and some of the others, should go up to the apostles and priests in Jerusalem concerning this question. Therefore, being sent by the church, they traveled through Phoenicia and Samaria… . And when they had arrived in Jerusalem, they were received by the church and the apostles and the elders, reporting what great things God had done with them. But some, from the sect of the Pharisees <u>who were believers,</u> rose up saying, 'It is necessary to circumcise and instruct them to keep the Law of Moses.'

As I pointed out in an earlier chapter, Peter's experience and testimony of God sovereignly saving the Gentile, Cornelius, and his whole household, should have settled this major doctrinal issue long before, thus making this council meeting unnecessary. But the church leadership chose to regard Cornelius' God-orchestrated conversion as an exception to the "rule" - an anomaly - rather than proof that Jesus' **New Covenant** offer of grace-based salvation is for all nations. Therefore, they refused to slay the **elephant of mixture** years before now. Worse yet, they allowed the strident, law-based Pharisees who were regarded there as believers (though Paul called them "false brothers") to stir up strife and discord at the council meeting. Paul's following description of the same setting shows just how intense this battle really was. Clearly, Jesus' radical **grace gospel** was on trial, just like Peter had been years before. And, to his great credit, Peter boldly endorsed Paul's revelation and ministry from Jesus, as we shall soon see.

Paul's version of Galatians 2:2-5

> And I went up according to a revelation, and I presented to them the Gospel that I proclaim to the nations, but privately to the ones seeming (good), lest I run, or have ran, in vain. But even Titus, who was with me, was not compelled to be circumcised, even though he was a Gentile. <u>False brothers</u> were secretly sneaking in to spy on our liberty, which we have **in Christ Jesus**, so that they might reduce us to <u>slavery</u> (back under

Law). We did not yield to them in subjection, even for an hour, in order that the truth of the Gospel would continue with you (the Galatians).

Peter Defends Jesus' Gospel Given to Paul

Luke's version in Acts 15:6-11:

And the Apostles and elders came together to consider this matter. And after a great debate had taken place, Peter rose up and said to them:
"Fellow brothers, you know what happened some time ago (with Cornelius). God chose me so that people of other nations could hear the gospel and believe. And God, who knows hearts, testified to them by giving them the Holy Spirit, just as He did to us. And he made no distinction between us and them, purifying their hearts by faith. Now, therefore, why do you *test God* to impose a yoke (the Law) upon the necks of the disciples, which neither our fathers nor we have been able to bear? We believe that we are saved through the grace of the Lord Jesus Christ, the same way that he saves them (purifying their hearts by faith)."

Bravo, Peter! Obviously, he totally agreed with Paul's policy: do not impose circumcision or the Law on the Gentiles. He also recognized the central problem with the Mosaic Law and put his assessment in the form of a question that we should be asking law-minded preachers and teachers today: "… why do you tempt God to impose a yoke (the Law) upon the necks of the disciples, which neither our fathers nor we have been able to bear?" He was stating what had become obvious to him – the Law, including circumcision - was not needed to be saved and, to think so was to "test God." Peter's forceful speech was a slam-dunk for **Jesus' grace gospel** by stating that "we are saved through the grace of the Lord Jesus Christ … purifying their hearts by faith."

But James was not about to concede that there was no need for *some* kind of law or standard. (After all, how could he keep the church in line or measure people's "holiness" unless they are judged according to some code? It would put the Pharisees in the group out of business.) And, unfortunately, James had the last word that made law-keeping *seem* more bearable – but it was still the heretical mixture of law with grace. Even a *little* leaven of the Pharisees contaminates the whole loaf, as Paul pointedly stated in Galatians 5:9. Here are James' own words.

James' Edict

Luke's version in Acts 15:12-21:

Then the entire multitude was silent. And they were listening to Barnabas and Paul, describing what great signs and wonders God had wrought among the Gentiles through them.
And after they had been silent, James responded by saying: "Brothers, listen to me. Simon Peter has explained in what manner God first oversaw how to take out from the Gentiles a people (Cornelius and his household) for His name. And the words of the Prophets are in agreement with this, just as it was written: 'After these things, I will return, and I will rebuild the tabernacle of David, which has fallen down. And I will rebuild its ruins, and I will raise it up, so that the rest of men may seek the Lord, along

with all the nations over whom my name has been invoked, says the Lord, who does these things.' To the Lord, His own work has been known from eternity.

Because of this, I judge that those who were converted to God from among the Gentiles are not to be harassed but instead that we write to them, that they should keep away from:

1) things defiled by false gods,

2) from sexual sins,

3) from eating the meat of strangled animals,

4) and from eating bloody meat.

After all, Moses' words have been proclaimed to every city for generations. His teachings are read in synagogues on every Sabbath."

Notice that James' reference point was Moses, not Jesus, and that he boldly used his leadership position and reputation to unilaterally formulate what should be done and why. Because of his Jewish faith and Nazarite life-style, James was aware of the Noahide laws that pre-dated Abraham and Moses. Simply stated, Jewish tradition holds that after the Flood, God gave Noah a series of seven universal "laws" which all mankind should obey. (Some Rabbis also taught that they were then given again to the Israelites at Sinai before the actual Mosaic Law was given.) Six of the seven laws are exegetically derived from passages in Genesis, and the seventh one, which requires the establishment of courts, was added later. The Jews believed that Gentiles who faithfully kept these laws would benefit from an afterlife. So, in James' very Jewish mind, he was upholding the Torah and doing the Antioch Gentiles a favor by telling them what God (supposedly) *requires* them to do.

Of course we know now, in hindsight, that the **New Covenant** changed everything, "making all things new" in the way God views mankind, thanks to Jesus. Law-based religion is an enemy of the law of faith that Jesus revealed to Paul. So Paul naturally disregarded James' direction to the Gentiles under his care because he knew that the law of the Spirit of life had set him and all believers free from law-mindedness, which arouses sin and causes death. (We'll explore much more about this in the next chapter.) Paul later addressed the issues in this edict from a grace-based perspective in 1 Corinthians 10:23-33 and Romans 14:6, which are a great example of how to apply Jesus' **grace-based gospel**. By ignoring James' demands, Paul deftly guards each believer's freedom **in Christ** from the demands of the Law, protecting the **butterfly life** that lives by the Holy Spirit's higher law of faith, love and liberty, **in and through Christ Jesus**.

The Four Laws Sent By Letter
Luke's version in Acts 15:22-29:

Then it pleased the apostles and elders, with the whole church, to choose men from among them, and to send them to Antioch, with Paul and Barnabas. They chose Judas, (who was surnamed Barsabbas) and Silas, who were leaders men among the brothers, They sent them with the following letter written by their own hands:

99

'The apostles and elders, brothers, to those who are at Antioch and Syria and Cilicia, brothers from the Gentiles, greetings!

Since we have heard that some, going out from among us, have troubled you with words by saying "Be circumcised and keep the Law" to whom we gave no such direction, it pleased us, being assembled as one, to choose men and to send them to you, with our most beloved Barnabas and Paul, men who have handed over their lives on behalf of the name of our Lord Jesus Christ. Therefore, we have sent Judas and Silas, who themselves also will, with the spoken word, reaffirm to you the same things. For it has seemed good to the Holy Spirit and to us to impose no further burden upon you other than these necessary things. Keep away from:

1) things defiled by false gods,

2) from sexual sins,

3) from eating the meat of strangled animals,

4) and from eating bloody meat.

You will do well to keep yourselves from these things. Farewell."

Was it really the Holy Spirit that inspired this edict that contradicted, in principle, what Jesus revealed to Paul and to Peter earlier or was it just their Jewish tradition that "nullified the Word of God" (see Matthew 15:6)? Jesus came to set us free from the yoke of bondage to the law. Why would the Holy Spirit endorse something that He 1) inspired Peter to call an unneeded yoke that they could not keep and 2) inspired the writer of Hebrews to declare "obsolete" and passing away (see the details in the next chapter)? And again, amazingly enough, James seems to agree by issuing the following disclaimer:

Since we have heard that some, going out from among us, have troubled you with words by saying "Be circumcised and keep the Law" to whom we gave no such direction.

Exposing the Elephant – A Double Standard

Hopefully, the Jerusalem church leadership was not guilty of authorizing such a message to Gentiles beyond Jerusalem. But they *were* guilty of enforcing that direction in Jerusalem. And that fact is precisely where the confusion for 2000 years was solidified. There is really a double message from James going on here. So, which should the church follow? First James says in this passage that we (presumably the Jerusalem leadership) gave no command to the Gentiles in Antioch (by way of the Judaizers who came from James, according to Paul) to "Be circumcised and keep the Law." If that is an authoritative directive from the first bishop of the Jerusalem church in agreement with its leadership (especially Peter and John) to Gentiles, then why are we teaching the Ten Commandments today as a necessary part of Christianity? James specifically did not include a list of the Big Ten in his edict. And he agreed, therefore, by implication, that keeping the Mosaic Law had *nothing* to do with Christianity, per se. (Chapter Nine will examine the negative effects for Christians who foolishly put themselves under the Law.)

Yet, James flip-flopped by giving the Antioch Gentiles just a "necessary" *small yoke,* carried over from Noah. But necessary for what? The only necessary yoke is to be yoked to Jesus, not to law or tradition. Fortunately for the Gentiles under Paul, only James kept the "big yoke" of 613 laws only on himself (through his own lifestyle as a Nazarite) and on the Jerusalem church. Again, the Gentiles there were *required* to be circumcised and to obey the whole Law before they could get saved – despite how God demonstrated the opposite with Cornelius and his whole household. James continued to tie one's faith and the works of the Law together. Apparently for James, if one was *not* focusing on learning about and doing the deeds of the Law, his faith was obviously "dead" – (maybe not yet saved?) - according to James 2:26, as commonly interpreted even today.

So, for James, the measurement of a Christian's faith and righteousness *before God* was how well he kept the Law. But Jesus taught Paul that righteousness is a gift from God through faith alone **in Jesus Christ** to all who believe. Again, Jesus made it clear to Paul that righteousness from God is *apart* from law-keeping and comes through faith alone **in Christ Jesus**, according to Romans 3:21-22. Martin Luther literally staked his life on this revelation.

So, which policy do you think should have been the *norm for the whole church from day one?* Now we know the truth about all this because of what Jesus revealed specifically to Paul in 42 AD. Christianity is not to be mixed with Judaism because the **elephant of mixture** nullifies both covenants. Tragically James' teaching and example carried far more weight in the infant church than Paul's did, as can be easily deduced from Paul's letters. And this pained Paul greatly because he personally received Jesus' **revelation** on this vital doctrine that separates Christianity from all religions, including Judaism. Paul forcefully and painstakingly presented this **New Covenant reality** in his preaching, teaching and writings. And the Judaizers persecuted him relentlessly. (Some even think that they were the "thorn in his flesh" which Paul wrote about.)

What Is The Root?
Reliance on law-keeping is rooted in the human *fear* that, if there is no Law – no standard of behavior – believers will "go wild." Question: Did Abraham or Isaac or Jacob or his son Joseph "go wild" before the Law was given? Well, that depends on what standard you use, Mr. Policeman. But God was not playing "policeman" with Abraham like He did later with the Israelites. Instead, He demonstrated His true heart by giving the gift of righteousness to Abraham and to his descendants who *believed* God's promises, not who tried to for them. That is still true for us today, provided that we, too, believe and receive Jesus who *is* God's gift of righteousness to believers, given by Father's generous grace - *not* by keeping some code or standard. This is why it is absolutely vital that we know which covenant God offers to us today and how to enter into it through Jesus, not through law-keeping. This is what Jesus revealed to Paul in Romans 4:13-17

For the Promise to Abraham, and to his posterity, that he would inherit the world, was not through the law, but through the righteousness that comes by faith. For if those who are of the law (the Jews) are the heirs, then faith becomes empty and the Promise is abolished. For the law works unto wrath. And where there is no law, there is no law-breaking. Because of this, it is from faith, according to grace, that the Promise is ensured for all posterity, not only for those who are of the law (Jews), but also for those who are of the faith of Abraham, who is the father of us all, according to what has been written by God (in Genesis 17:5) 'I have appointed you the father of many nations.' Abraham believed Him who revives the dead and who calls those things that do not exist (in the **seen realm**) into existence (from the **unseen realm**).

Remember: All this happened to Abraham over 400 years before Moses and the Law came on the scene. Yet, Abraham was friends with God under that grace-based covenant. Now, because of Jesus' **finished work**, believers today are under another grace-based covenant that is far better than Abraham's and has no connection with the Israelite's covenant – especially for Gentiles who were never given that law-based covenant to begin with. (Chapter Eighteen will present all this and its central importance in great detail.) So again, for we believers today (who are under grace, *not* the Mosaic Law, thanks to Jesus), knowing and resting in God's perfect love for us casts out fear of "going wild" and replaces it with the higher law of:

1) faith in God's faithfulness and **finished work** through Jesus,

2) His love for me despite my behavior, which then motivates me to respond in love and

3) the liberty in the Holy Spirit, sent to help us to will and to do Father's good pleasure.

Believers who learn to listen to and rely on the Holy Spirit will "keep the law," even if they never heard of the Noahide laws or the Big Ten. How do I know? Well, as we just saw above, James said that Paul's Gentiles did not need to know the "big yoke" and Paul even ignored the "little yoke" James tried to foist on them.

Relying on teaching the law to reborn saints (instead of teaching the higher law of the **New Covenant** of grace and encouraging them to be baptized in the Holy Spirit like Paul did) is the coward's way out. It denies the need to trust in a relationship with the Holy Spirit and replaces it with external do's and don'ts. That is Judaism, not Christianity and bad consequences result when the two are mixed – the heresy of Galatianism.

So obviously, James and Paul were not on the same page, although this has been inexplicably believed and proclaimed by the general church for 2000 years. However, Paul knew otherwise when he commented in Galatians 2:12 that *James sent* some members "of the circumcision" who caused Peter and others to draw back from eating with the Gentiles because they were afraid of the Judaizers. Again, the timing of this episode is debated. But at least in Paul's mind, James was behind a fundamental policy disagreement on a *major* doctrinal issue which essentially split the unity of the church into two factions. The Jewish believers enforced parts of the Law in Jerusalem and even in other cities while the Gentile believers were taught the **gospel of grace** by Paul, as we shall see in more detail in the following scriptures.

Luke's version in Acts 15:30-32 and 35:

And so, having been dismissed, they went down to Antioch and, gathering the multitude together, they delivered the epistle. And when they had read it, they were gladdened by this consolation. And Judas and Silas, being also prophets themselves, consoled the

102

brothers with many words, and they were strengthened. … Paul and Barnabas stayed in Antioch preaching and teaching the gospel, the Word of the Lord, with many others.

Paul's version in Galatians 2:6-10:

> But from those (leaders) who <u>seemed</u> to be something (of what kind they were means nothing to me for God does not accept the face of a man). And those <u>seeming</u> to be something <u>added nothing to</u> what I shared. But on the contrary, they had seen that the <u>gospel *of* the uncircumcision</u> to the Gentiles was entrusted to me, just as the gospel *to* the circumcision (the Jews) was entrusted to Peter (James not mentioned). For he who was working the apostleship to the Jews in Peter, was also working in me among the Gentiles. And so, when they had acknowledged the grace that was given to me, James and Cephas and John, who <u>seemed</u> to be pillars, gave to me and to Barnabas the right hand of fellowship, agreeing that we would go to the Gentiles, while they went to the Jews, asking <u>only</u> that we should be mindful of the poor, which was the very thing that I also was eager to do.

Three comments

1) Again, Paul ignored James' edict (which was based on law, not on grace through faith) indicated by his own summary of this council. Instead of listing James' edict, he substituted a comment about helping the poor, which he had done more than once by collecting money for the church in Jerusalem. In other words, he turned the other cheek, even though he saw, first hand, that they were not faithful to Jesus' **gospel of pure grace**, a pattern which pained him greatly. Also, notice that Paul specifically mentioned Peter (but not James) as the one God was working through to reach the Jews. He knew Peter was more grace-minded because he supported Paul's defense of Jesus' **whole gospel** at the council and had refrained from suggesting any extra "burdens" be added to the **grace gospel.** Peter acknowledged publically that the Law was a *burden they could not keep.* But the flesh in us loves a good challenge to prove what we can do to "earn points." (How else do you explain "competition" since it does not exist in heaven?)

It is also clear that Paul was not all that impressed with their "seeming" status as pillars etc. After all, how can one be a true pillar of Jesus' **pure gospel of grace** when he is living under the curse of the law by his own testimony and practice? Even a baby elephant can crush a butterfly. Paul's revelation from Jesus obviously made him a resolute "hardliner" – like Jesus was with the **pre-cross** Pharisees. Having been a Pharisee, Paul now knew just how deadly was the leaven of the Pharisees – the mixture that Jesus warned his disciples about before He died. Obviously, they really didn't get it, despite James' disclaimer, so the confusion, caused by the **elephant of mixture**, continues in most churches today. Is this elephant in <u>your</u> church?

2) Apparently, they stayed faithful to this mutual agreement to split the ministry. The Jerusalem church leaders focused on the Jews, there and abroad, as their letters strongly suggest – particularly the letter by James. Understandably, it contains a "double-minded mixture" of law with grace, more than the epistles by Peter and John. Tragically, this agreement forged a *doctrinal split* in God's growing family of the redeemed <u>that set a precedent for **division** rather than for the unity of one mind and heart, desired by Father-God.</u> God's vision is for "one Body with one Head" - which is Jesus. Like any good father, God likes to see His kids get along. The unintended consequences of this doctrinal schism have been a scandal to the watching world ever since. Worse yet, the mixture of opposing covenants suppresses maturity in those saints who still wrongly believe that their performance determines their degree of righteousness and holiness. They lack the revelation that both are gifts from Jesus as part of His **divine exchange** with them as explained in 1 Corinthians 1:30 and Hebrews 5:13.

3) Of course the Gentile believers in Antioch were relieved that they would not have to be circumcised. But it was Paul who saw the **big picture** and had to take a stand to keep his flocks from being infiltrated by even the "little yoke" of the **elephant** – the mixture which was alive and well in Jerusalem. The following confrontation with Peter proves that the war was ongoing – even after the seeming "truce" at the council, implied in Luke's account. **Elephants** are hardy beasts! (Of course, this is based on the assumption that Paul's chronology of these two events was correct. But even if Luke was correct and the episode with Peter described below happened first and precipitated the first council in 50 AD, the above observations still hold true.)

Paul Stands Alone for Jesus' Gospel

So, later for whatever reason, Peter decided to visit Paul and the Antioch Church – maybe at Paul's invitation or maybe because James wanted a report of happenings there. All was fine at first because Peter was over his phobia of uncircumcised Gentile believers (thanks to his experience with Cornelius' miraculous conversion). He was enjoying their fellowship and even having meals with them. However, he was not over his phobia of James. Paul describes his second battle in the deepening doctrinal war, where he pulled no punches with Peter in defense of Jesus' **whole gospel of grace**. Paul clearly knew what was at stake and proved his willingness to defend the purity of Jesus' **whole gospel** – even against recognized church leaders who came on his turf – according to this account in Galatians 2:11-16 and 19-21:

> But when Cephas (Peter) had arrived at Antioch, I stood against him to his face, because he stood condemned. (Why?) Because, before some came from James, he ate with the Gentiles. But when they came, he drew apart and separated himself, being afraid of those who were of the circumcision group (sent by James). And the other (reborn) Jews joined him in his hypocrisy, so that even Barnabas was led by them into hypocrisy. But when I saw that they were not walking uprightly by the truth of the gospel, I said to Cephas in front of everyone: 'If you, being a Jew, are living like a non-Jew and not like the Jews, how is it that you compel the Gentiles to live like the Jews? By natural birth, we are Jews, and not Gentile sinners. And we know that man is not justified by the works of the law, but only by the faith of Jesus Christ. And so we believe in Christ Jesus in order that we may be justified by the faith of Christ and not by the works of the law. For no flesh will be justified by the works of the law'. ...

> 'For through the law, I have become dead to the law, so that I may live for God. I have been nailed to the cross with Christ. I live; yet now, it is not I, but truly Christ who lives in me. And though I live now in the flesh (physical body), I live in the faith to the Son of God, the One loving me and who delivered himself (to the cross) for me. I do not reject the grace of God. For if (a believer's) justification is gained by law-keeping, then Christ died needlessly.'

Fearless courage! Paul was the only one left standing to defend Jesus' **whole gospel**. Even Barnabas, who had befriended him in Jerusalem after his conversion and had brought him from Tarsus to Antioch and who had repeatedly heard Paul teach Jesus' own gospel, deserted him. But, by keeping his mind on things above, not on things of earth (see Colossians 3:1-3), Paul was, in principle, inspired to wield the same Sword of the Spirit that Peter had previously wielded when defending his experience with Cornelius to the Jerusalem church, by saying - "… who was I, that I could withstand God (Acts 11:17b)?" (If this episode happened before the council, maybe it woke up Peter enough to stand with Paul at the council.)

Fear Of James Instead Of God

It is abundantly obvious from this episode that James must have been an imposing figure to these reborn Jewish Christians - including even Barnabas - to exhibit such a fear of Judaizers (and also fear of James by extension, even though he had not personally come down from Jerusalem). But Paul knew that "the Law is not of faith" – or of love or of liberty. Rather, its demands arouse fear, torment and bondage and can even cause disease and death to those under it. This scenario is an early example of far too many saints today who live under the fear of a man (or a woman) using the club of Law to control them in order to maintain his own traditions and build his own kingdom. If, in fact, James operated like that in the early church – as this scenario would suggest - it can certainly happen in churches today where leaders depend on imposing laws and requirements on their flocks - possibly with the best intentions, like I did with my family - out of ignorance of Jesus' **whole gospel** of faith, love and liberty.

Unfortunately, law-minded Christian leaders and parents who exalt the Law, often end up misusing their authority. They cause the sheep to rely on them and their instructions and rules instead of teaching them to rely on the administration of the **finished work** of Jesus by the Holy Spirit living in them, which gives all believers an equal standing of righteousness and blessing before God. Paul knew from his own experience that "the letter kills but the Spirit gives life." And, correspondingly "it was for freedom that Christ has set us free, so stand firm and do not submit again to the yoke (law) of slavery" - as he declared in 2 Corinthians 3:6 and Galatians 5:1 respectively. The book of Galatians is Paul's eloquent diatribe against the **elephant of mixture** that continuously threatened to stomp out Jesus' **grace-based gospel**, which Paul was painstakingly sowing and defending throughout his later life. Unfortunately, that same **elephant of mixture**, preserved and promoted by law-minded believers like I was, has limited, if not smothered, the **butterfly life** of lavish grace in many if not most quarters of the institutional church throughout the centuries.

Thankfully, Paul did not let his astonishment and distresses over what happened in Galatia demolish his confidence **in Christ**. Some might think his words to Peter, as rendered in the Amplified Bible, might be overstated or even untrue: "But when Cephas came to Antioch, I protested and opposed him to his face for he was blamable and stood condemned" (Galatians 2:11). After all, did not Jesus tell Paul in Romans 8:1 "therefore there is now no condemnation for those **in Christ Jesus**? For the (higher) law of the Spirit of life has set you free from the (Mosaic) law of sin and death." How could Paul seemingly contradict himself by telling Peter that "he stood condemned"?

It is because Paul was operating from the **big picture** of Jesus' **grace gospel**. By siding with Law in this way, Peter had "fallen from grace" and, thereby, subjected himself mentally to "the law of sin and death" which reigns in the **seen realm**. By withdrawing from the truth of what God had miraculously shown Peter regarding the Gentiles (which was a major paradigm switch for him), his unbelief made him again subject to the constraints and curses of the Law that he reverted back to out of fear of man. This is a constant choice for all of God's redeemed – to walk by the **unseen** Spirit under grace or walk by natural sight under aspects of the Law and/or man's tradition, which greatly appeals to our self-sufficient flesh.

Again, this did not mean that Peter was "condemned to hell" but condemned - by his own unbelief - to the consequences in the **seen realm** of going back under the curses of law-based religion. The devil is quick to use the negatives that the law causes against believers who submit to law-keeping to try to please God. They, in some way or other, attempt to gain or maintain God's acceptance, approval and/or right-standing. This futile effort is the self-righteousness of "dead works" which even believers (including Peter, James and John) can be tricked into pursuing. How? By not understanding and relying on Jesus' **finished work** of **total grace**, by which He freely supplies God's gifts of righteousness and holiness by faith alone. The former is "religion," the latter is the essence of Christianity – which is being *one* **with Christ in God** and trusting in His doing (*not* in one's own behavior) for right-standing with God. Paul was the first to be shown this glorious light of the **whole gospel** but he certainly did not keep it hidden under a basket. He preserved it for anyone willing to die *mentally* to the counterfeit of mixture like Paul had done and embrace the **total truth** of Jesus' pure **gospel of lavish grace**.

No account is given of Peter's immediate reaction to Paul's rebuke but, no doubt, he now more clearly understood Jesus' differentiation between law and grace revealed to Paul. This dove-tailed, of course, with his experience with Cornelius. Ultimately, he endorsed Paul's writings by calling them "scriptures" in 2 Peter 3:16. But, at this point in time, he and the "men sent from James" now knew for sure that what Paul was preaching and doing in Antioch was still *unacceptable* in the Jerusalem church under James. How tragic! Paul had to draw a line in the sand to preserve the wonderful fruit that the Holy Spirit produced among the *uncircumcised* Gentiles under Paul's ministry.

The Motive Behind Compromise - Peace At Any Cost

Paul wrote many more cautions to the Galatians – and to us – about the dangers of mixing the two opposing covenants. He even ventured to guess the motive behind why those in the Jerusalem church chose to keep, feed and even promote this **elephant of mixture** to Jews in the Diaspora. It shows that even a good thing – the Law - can be the enemy of the best. By holding on to what Jesus had replaced with His **whole gospel of total grace**, they caused enormous grief, not only to themselves, but also to Paul virtually everywhere he traveled. He put it this way:

> These people (Judaizers sent by James) who want to make a big deal out of a physical thing (circumcision) are trying to force you to be circumcised. Their only aim is to avoid persecution because of the cross of Christ. It's clear that not even those who had themselves circumcised did this to follow Jewish laws. Yet, they want you to be circumcised so that they can brag about what was done to your body. But it's unthinkable that I could ever brag about anything except the cross of our Lord Jesus Christ. By his

cross, my relationship to the world and its relationship to me have been crucified (Galatians 6:12-14).

This is Paul's no nonsense assessment of the motives of James and his followers in contrast to what now compelled him – especially since 42 AD. He states that they have rejected Jesus' **whole gospel of grace** (which he had clearly presented to them at the first council) to save their neck from persecution and to brag about how many Gentiles they circumcised. Paul sensed that they greatly feared happening to them what had happened to John the Baptist, Jesus, James the less and Stephen. Recall that Stephen was stoned for declaring that Jesus was the Messiah while Saul (now Paul) witnessed and applauded his execution, just before Saul's conversion. And, even worse in their eyes, was what happened after Stephen was murdered, which Luke recounts here:

> Saul approved of putting Stephen to death. On that day widespread persecution broke out against the church in Jerusalem. Most believers, except the apostles, were scattered throughout Judea and Samaria. Devout men buried Stephen as they mourned loudly for him. Saul tried to destroy the church. He dragged men and women out of one home after another and threw them into prison. The believers who were scattered went from place to place, where they spread the word (Acts 8:1-4). (Given the timeline, this would have been the "Bare Bones Gospel.")

No doubt this terrifying experience was ever on the minds of the apostles, Peter, John and James, the leader, all of whom had stayed in Jerusalem despite Jesus' direction to "flee persecution" in Mathew 10:23 and "Go into all the world …" in Mark 16:15. James apparently was not there at that commissioning and, as a very committed Nazarite Jew, he wanted to stay near the Temple. No doubt, his choice to apparently continue living as a highly respected Nazarite, as discussed in Chapter Five, served to only reinforce his personal and pastoral insistence on defending his Jewish roots, which protected the **elephant of mixture** in the infant church by default.

In the **big picture**, it meant being sympathetic with the law-promoting Pharisees in his congregation and also with the Jewish establishment in the city. This served to help keep the peace, avoid riots and, hopefully, martyrdom. Ironically, despite all his peace-keeping efforts, James was martyred when, according to Hegesippus (and later quoted by Eusebius), James' non-Christian Pharisee friends called on him to publically denounce Jesus. Instead, he shocked them by endorsing Jesus and they killed him. (See Appendix # 10 for an historical account of James' lifestyle and death).

Paul Feared No Man

Paul himself had personally experienced this tension soon after his conversion. In his zeal for Jesus, he began stirring things up again like Stephen had done. As a result, the Jews in Damascus tried to kill him because he was in the synagogues proving from scripture that Jesus was the Messiah. The disciples there hustled him over the wall of the city in a basket and then he went boldly into the heart of the battle – Jerusalem. The disciples were afraid of him at first but Barnabas took charge and he testified to the apostles about Paul's conversion. But did Paul learn his lesson from his first brush with death in Damascus?

And he (Paul) was with them coming in and going out at Jerusalem. And he spoke boldly in the name of the Lord Jesus, and debated with the Hellenistic Jews but they tried to kill him. So when the brothers learned about this, they brought him down to Caesarea, and sent him away to Tarsus. Then the churches throughout all Judaea and Galilee and Samaria had peace, and were edified. And, walking in the exceeding fear of the Lord, and in the comfort of the Holy Ghost, their numbers multiplied (Acts 9:28-31).

In other words, when a saint was on fire with the Sword of the Lord in his mouth, the rabid anti-Jesus Jews in Jerusalem who strove to defend and protect Judaism, pushed back so hard that the remaining Jewish church members were intimidated and chose to keep a low profile. Instead of fearlessly operating like a thermostat that influences - if not controls - the climate, they settled for being a thermometer that just records the temperature, reacting instead of leading. And predictably, the earlier overflow of Jesus' abundant **butterfly life**, which was so evident at first, was gradually *suppressed* by the weight of the Law and tradition, held onto by well-meaning, peace-loving, Jewish Christian leaders who settled for accommodating the **elephant of mixture.**

Ironically, the insistence on circumcision by Jews and Jewish Christians alike disgusted the Romans rulers so much that they banned the practice in about 132 AD. This fueled a general Jewish rebellion against Rome who then destroyed Jerusalem in 135 AD. To add insult to injury, the Romans then rebuilt it into a Roman style city, which they renamed *Aelia Capitolina*. All Jews were banned from returning to the city by the penalty of death. So the church was then governed by Gentile bishops, who ended the practice of circumcision (see the text and Footnotes in Chapter Ten). But even that cataclysmic episode was not enough to slay the **elephant of mixture**. If anything, it was reproduced elsewhere when the Jewish Christians of Jerusalem were forced to relocate and took their law-minded mixture with them. It is even possible that some of them showed up wherever Paul went and opposed him.

Paul, however, repeatedly proved his tenacity to the **total truth** of Jesus' **grace-based gospel**. His intensity and willingness to die for it was likely a big reason (among others) that God specifically picked him to receive the revelation of His **whole gospel of grace** in 42 AD. Who else but Paul was willing to forsake everything he had and believed in, for the sake of knowing and loving and serving Jesus his Lord and spreading His **whole gospel**? And he never quit, in spite of the opposition constantly stirred up by Satan, the Anti-Christ, through law-centered believers and unbelievers alike. Opposition came from Peter visiting Paul in Antioch, from James and company in Jerusalem, from Barnabas, his closest friend, and from legalistic Jews wherever Paul travelled. The scenario was repeated later in history against tenacious saints like Tyndale, Hus and Luther and continues today against those who dare to confront the **elephant in the church** in all its many forms. Remember: any other gospel that contradicts the one Jesus revealed to Paul is "no gospel at all" ... his words, not mine.

So far, we have surveyed Jesus' **whole gospel of grace** in the first two chapters, investigated Acts to see the outline of the *basic gospel* early on, and noted the growing division and turmoil between the leaders of two founding churches, Jerusalem and Antioch, which has been papered over for 2000 years. That controversy centered on opposing views of the relevancy, purpose and use of the Law. So, Part Two of this book will focus on

1) what Jesus' revealed to Paul regarding the Law's **post-cross** purpose,

2) its differences with the **New Covenant** and

3) the specific dangers of mixing the Law with the **whole gospel** of Christ Jesus' **New Covenant realities.**

NOTE: The first song poem below, entitled **In Christ**, captures the essence of Jesus' **grace-based gospel** – being **in Christ Jesus.** The second one declares that Jesus is man's only Savior – so let Him be that for you in every situation.

Jesus died to sin forever
To free me from its slavery.
Death no longer masters Jesus.
What's true of Him is true for me...YES

    In Christ, I was crucified and buried.
    In Christ, I was raised and justified.
    In Christ, I ascended to the heavens.
    Through Him I am being sanctified.

The life He lives He lives to God,
Sharing it abundantly
With all who died to self by faith
And live in Him **dependently**...YES

    In Christ, I am totally forgiven!
    In Christ, all my guilt and shame are gone!
    In Christ, I am Righteous and accepted!
    It's His Finished Work I'm resting on!

Jesus died to sin forever
To free me from its slavery.
Death no longer masters Jesus.
What's true of Him is true for me...YES

    In Christ, I partake of God's own nature.
    In Christ, I'm reborn of His own seed.
    In Christ, I'm at peace with God my Father.
    In Him I have everything I need.

The life He lives He lives to God,
Sharing it abundantly
With all who died to self by faith
And live in Him **dependently**...YES

In Christ, I Have Power over Darkness
In Christ, by His Spirit not my might.
In Christ, I'm above all circumstances.
Where I go I bring God's light.

Jesus died to sin forever
To free me from its slavery.
Death no longer masters Jesus.
What's true of Him is true for me...YES

In Christ, I am sent to earth from heaven
In Christ, as a prophet, priest and king.
In Christ, I'm recruiting for my Master.
He deserves my thanks in everything.

All glory to my Father who remade me.
Worthy is the Lamb who ransomed me.
Holy is my Friend and Sanctifier.
You abound triumphantly. (3x)
© Copyright 1995 by Leonard J. Ransil

THE ONLY THING THAT REALLY WORKS
Is the **finished work** of Jesus
The only thing that really works is what He did for all.
The only thing that really works is Jesus' sacrifice
That reversed the curse that came through Adam's Fall.

Chorus
>   The curse of death from Adam's sin passed down to you and me.
>   But Jesus took our place, by grace, and bore our every blow.
>   He cancelled all of mankind's debt by dying on a Tree
>   But He won't force His love on you, so there's something you must know.

The only thing that really works is the **finished work** of Jesus.
You must believe He died for you to give you righteousness.
It's part of Jesus' **finished work** which gives you His new life
That opens up your heart towards Him to share His holiness.

The only thing that really works is the **finished work** of Jesus.
Abundant Life He came to give to all of Adam's Seed.
By grace through faith, Lord, I receive all You have done for me.
By resting in your **finished work** that meets my every need.
© Copyright 2012 by Leonard J. Ransil

PART TWO

CHAPTER EIGHT

THE PURPOSE OF THE MOSAIC LAW – IN DETAIL

Wrong Assumptions Can Lead To Heresy

First, I want to reiterate a very important distinction I made earlier regarding the span of the Mosaic Covenant. For most of my life I assumed that the period of the Mosaic Law Covenant ended with Malachi, the last book of what we call the Old Testament, and the **New Covenant** began with what we call the New Testament, beginning at Matthew 1:1. It was a shock to realize that the Mosaic Covenant overlapped into the New Testament and actually ended at the cross when the **New Covenant** was mediated in Jesus' own blood. (In simple terms, a person's will/testament is executed when he dies not when he is born.) This common but erroneous assumption that the Mosaic Law ends with Malachi causes untold confusion about Jesus' earthly ministry (described in the four gospels) which I will discuss in Chapter Eleven. Missing the implications of this subtle but crucial overlap can readily lead to mentally mixing the two covenants of law and grace – further reinforcing the heresy of Galatianism.

Fixing The Fall Of Mankind

Second, it is helpful to understand that one of Jesus' many purposes in coming to earth was to *fulfill* the Mosaic Law, given *only* to the Jews for a specific reason in the **big picture.** We learn from Jesus' revelation to Paul, later on, that Jesus could give the gift of right-standing with God to all who believe **in Him** because He, Himself, remained sinless throughout His life (until He became our sin on Calvary.) Therefore, He was legally declared righteous by Father-God because this Son of Man was the only man who kept the spirit of the Law perfectly. He could not have legally fulfilled the Law if He was not subject to its demands. Adam had caused mankind's fall because he ate of the wrong Tree - which was a type of the Law, "the knowledge of good and evil." Yes, God had declared everything He created to be "good." But this Tree was *not* good for man. If God had intended man to live under the slavery of the Tree of Law instead of in the freedom of the Tree of Life (Jesus), He would have complimented Adam for his choice.

Instead, God mercifully removed Adam and Eve from the garden, probably to prevent them from eating from the Tree of Eternal Life which might have caused them to "burst." Why? Because Jesus said in Mark 2:22 that "No one pours new wine into old wineskins. If one does, the new wine will burst the skins and both the wine and the wineskins will be ruined." Because of Adam's rebellion, he was no longer fit for eternal *life*, the Spirit of Christ, to enter him. God's only remedy is that the old, **Adamic nature** must be crucified with Christ, by faith in what Christ Jesus did for mankind, in order to be made fit for God's habitation as a **new creation in Christ** through regeneration.

By living in the higher law of faith, love and liberty in His Father, Jesus could perfectly fulfill the Law because He had not been born **in Adam** like we are, but was miraculously conceived and *born of God* by the ministry of the Holy Spirit through Mary. So again, before any human can become compatible with the perfect, higher life of heaven, "he must receive birth from (God) above," according to what Jesus revealed to Nicodemus in John 3:3.

Now, from what source was Jesus getting His words of wisdom and direction? Was it from the books of the Law, which He would have probably memorized as a Jewish boy? No, because the Law is rooted in the **seen realm** and was given to put demands on **in Adam** humans. Again, the law principle is meant for all who are still rooted to the earth - **in Adam** sinners. (Adam is the Hebrew word for "earth".) But it is *not* meant for those who are one with God **in Christ**, through rebirth, and are now seated with Him in the heavenlies. **#21.** Jesus spelled this revelation out in John 3:31-34 by saying:

> The One (Jesus, Himself) who comes from above is above all. The one who is from the earth (Adam - and all in him) belongs to the earth and speaks as one from the earth. The One who comes from heaven is above all. He testifies to what He has seen and heard (in the **unseen realm** and from His Father).... For the One whom God has sent, speaks the words of God, for God gives the Spirit without limit.

The "words of God" are not necessarily identical to "the words of the Law" in a given situation and Jesus explained that He listened to His Father's ongoing, living words when He said "The words I have spoken to you are spirit and they are life," recorded in John 6:63. Father's words of life (that come through the still, small voice of the Holy Spirit, according to 1 Kings 19:12) are in direct contrast to how He described the word of the Law to Paul in 2 Corinthians 3:6 and Galatians 3:10a respectively: "For the letter kills but the Spirit gives life!" and "All those who rely on observing the Law are under a curse ...."

Jesus came to reverse the effects of the curse of law-minded thinking and living. This is still a death-dealing alternative to God-focused living. Jesus trusted in and followed His Father's words of life, rather than depending on following the dictates of the Law or even His own, unilateral thinking. He reiterates His source of inspiration and power for daily living in John 7:16 and 8:28b-29 by revealing His secret:

> My teaching is not my own. It comes from Him who sent me. ...

> ... I do nothing on my own but speak just what the Father has taught me. The One who has sent me is with me. He has not left me alone for I always do what pleases Him.

So it is obvious that He was not operating as God, per se, but as a man, *constantly* focused on His Father's living and active word to Him from the **unseen realm.** Even at the temple courts in Jerusalem, when He was only twelve years old, "everyone who heard Him was amazed at His understanding and His answers" according to Luke 2:47.

Now, through His **finished work**, Jesus has made it possible for **in Adam** humans to be born of God too – by faith in Him, *not* by faith in one's attempt to keep the Law perfectly. Jesus was fulfilling (or completing) the requirements of the Law during the thirty-three year period of His life. That period ended when He willingly died on a dead tree, fashioned and erected by fallen, law-minded humans. This tree, soaked in His holy, royal blood, was the instrument on which He:

1) "became our sin" and paid our sin debt in full

2) absorbed God's just wrath and all the curses of the Law against mankind and

3) freely offered us His new, abundant life – the eternal life of God.

<u>The Son of God became the Son of Man so that the sons of man can now become the sons of God</u> – apart from law-keeping - because He kept it perfectly for us. Jesus' righteous, earthly record is now every reborn believer's own record - from God's viewpoint - because of being in union (identified) with **Him** and now alive **in Him**. That is fantastic news! And, in turn He says to us: "My sheep (all those **in Christ**) hear My voice. I know them and they follow Me" (John 10:27). Notice that the Pharisees knew the Mosaic Law backwards and forwards but did not hear Jesus' voice as His sheep do. They mistakenly viewed Him as a law-breaker rather than One who kept the <u>spirit</u> of the law perfectly *by walking according to the Holy Spirit.* This is the law of faith, love and liberty in His Father and which replaced the Mosaic Law system given only to the Israelites.

Our Loving And All-Wise God

So, one could say that Jesus' earthly life was a crucial time of transition that ended the 1500 year period of the Mosaic Law Covenant which the Israelites had foolishly agreed to keep, even though God knew they could not do so. "Well then," you might ask, "wasn't God being cruel for giving them something they couldn't do then punishing them for not doing it?" Predictably, you are thinking like a human, not like our all-wise Father-God. He always works from the **big picture** of what is best in the long run, both for mankind in general and for individuals in particular, as they yield to Him in faith. He who *is* Love, does all this within the context of us humans constantly exercising <u>His gift of a free will</u>, which He gave to mankind as a part of being originally made in His image and likeness (see Genesis 1:26). (Also see Endnote #**22** for more insight into God's gift of free will.) (Of course, the possibility exists that, from God's viewpoint, Adam lost that original perfect image and likeness at the Fall. Genesis 5:3 specifically says that Seth was in the image and likeness of Adam and we now know that the **in Adam** nature is our core problem as humans. Is this why Jesus told the Pharisees that the devil was their father?) At any rate, now, being reborn of God (not just born of Adam) is a pre-requisite for eternal oneness with God and being welcomed into a perfect heaven by being **in Christ**.

God's Big Picture Ways, Not Our Selfish Ways

So, what might seem cruel to us, from our limited vision of self-interest, was actually very merciful to the human race in general and even to the Israelites specifically – given their "Egyptian" heart still **in Adam.** They deserved death rather than deliverance - as does the whole human race. But that has never been God's will for mankind. Death is part of the devil's plan in his efforts to steal, kill and destroy the human race. The following is a very brief overview of how God chose to patiently work with man's fallen nature to eventually offer a permanent reconciliation to a race of **in Adam** rebels.

After Adam's fall, God was able to launch the process of reconciliation with rebellious mankind in earnest when Abraham believed and accepted His promise to make him the father of many nations (see Genesis 17:4). Abraham's grandson, Jacob, fathered twelve sons, all of whom survived a severe famine through God's merciful intervention. God turned the eleven sons' intrigue and treachery against their own brother, Joseph, to work for the good of the whole family. Pharaoh permitted them to settle in a prime part of Egypt, called Goshen, and they became known as the "Israelite Nation" because God changed Jacob's name to "Israel." However, over their 400+ year stay, they were enslaved under increasingly tyrannical pharaohs and finally, when they cried out for deliverance, God mercifully sent Moses to set them free.

Previously, Abraham had walked with God by faith under a unilateral, grace-based covenant which provided protection, abundant provision and many blessings - in spite of Abraham's **in Adam** nature and sinful behavior. Unfortunately for his descendants, 400+ years of slavery under the cruel "gods" of Egypt apparently wiped out any memory of the goodness and mercy of Abraham's God. Eventually, in desperation, they cried out to this God who orchestrated a series of ten plagues to persuade the stubborn Pharaoh to release the Israelites from slavery through Moses' leadership. He delivered them from Pharaoh's clutches by miraculously parting the very deep Red Sea. But the Israelites reacted to this miraculous deliverance - and to God's care for them in all the challenging conditions of the desert - with complaining and unbelief rather than with gratitude and a trusting faith (like Abraham's earlier response to God had been). Nonetheless, our longsuffering God put up with their tantrums and graciously met their needs in the desert for some fifty days.

A Performance-Based Reward System
What happened next was a crucial turning point in how the Israelites would relate to God for the next 1500 years and what also often colors how people view God even today. These events are recorded in Exodus, Chapter Nineteen and Chapter 20:18-21.

In the third month of the departure of Israel from the land of Egypt, in that day, they arrived in the wilderness of Sinai. Thus, setting out from Raphidim, and going directly to the desert of Sinai, they encamped in the same place, and there Israel pitched their tents away from the region of the mountain. Then Moses ascended to God. And the Lord called to him from the mountain, and he said: "This you shall say to the house of Jacob, and announce to the sons of Israel: <u>'You have seen what I have done to the Egyptians, in the way I carried you upon the wings of eagles and how I have taken you for Myself. If, therefore, you will hear my voice, and you will keep my covenant, you will be to me a particular possession out of all people. For all the earth is mine. And you will be to me a priestly kingdom and a holy nation.'</u> These are the words that you will speak to the sons of Israel." Moses went, and calling together those greater by birth among the people, he set forth all the words which the Lord had commanded. And all the people responded together: <u>"Everything that the Lord has spoken, we shall do."</u>

And when Moses had related the words of the people to the Lord, the Lord said to him: "Soon now, I will come to you in the mist of a cloud, so that the people may hear me speaking to you, and so that they may believe you continuously." Therefore, Moses reported the words of the people to the Lord, who (then) said to him: "Go to the people, and sanctify them today, and tomorrow, and let them wash their garments. And let them be prepared on the third day. For on the third day, the Lord will descend, in the sight of all the people, over Mount Sinai. And you will establish limits for the people all around, and you will say to them: 'Take care not to ascend to the mountain, and that you do not touch its parts. All who touch the mountain, shall die.' Hands shall not touch him, but he

116

shall be crushed with stones, or he shall be pierced through with darts. Whether it be a beast or a man, he shall not live. For when the trumpet begins to sound, perhaps they might go up toward the mountain."

And Moses came down from the mountain to the people, and he sanctified them. And when they had washed their garments, he said to them, "Be prepared on the third day, and do not draw near to your wives." And now, the third day arrived and the morning dawned. And behold, thunders began to be heard, and also lightning flashed, and a very dense cloud covered the mountain, and the noise of the trumpet resounded vehemently. And the people who were in the camp were fearful. And when Moses had led them out to meet God, from the place of the camp, they stood at the base of the mountain. Then all of Mount Sinai was smoking. For the Lord had descended over it with fire, and smoke ascended from it, as from a furnace. And the entire mountain was terrible. And the sound of the trumpet gradually increased to be louder, and extended to be longer. Moses was speaking, and God was answering him. And the Lord descended over Mount Sinai, to the very top of the mountain, and he called Moses to its summit. And when he had ascended there, he said to him: "Descend, and call the people to witness, lest they might be willing to transgress the limits, so as to see the Lord, and a very great multitude of them might perish. Likewise, the priests who approach toward the Lord, let them be sanctified, lest He strike them down." And Moses said to the Lord: "The people are not able to ascend to Mount Sinai. For you testified, and you commanded, saying: 'Set limits around the mountain, and sanctify it.' And the Lord said to him, "Go, descend. And you shall ascend, and Aaron with you. But let not the priests or the people transgress the limits, nor ascend to the Lord, lest perhaps He may put them to death." And Moses descended to the people, and he explained everything to them.
Then all the people considered the voices, and the lights, and the sound of the trumpet, and the smoking mountain. And being terrified and struck with fear, they stood at a distance, saying to Moses: "Speak to us, and we will listen. Let not the Lord speak to us, lest perhaps we may die." And Moses said to the people: "Do not be afraid. For God came in order to test you, and so that the dread of Him might be with you, and you would not sin." And the people stood far away. But Moses approached toward the mist, in which was God.

In the underlined verses in the top part of this passage, God reminds what He did to the mighty Egypt that had enslaved them and also "how I (God) have taken you for Myself." So why would God choose to defend these ungrateful ragamuffins against a civilization that everyone marvels at today? Did He just want the underdog to come out on top, like many sports fans prefer to see? No. It is because of His faithfulness to the covenant that Abraham received by faith, about 430 years earlier. These ex-slaves were descendants of a man who believed God's promises when other mightier civilizations gave their allegiance to false gods. God is a covenant-making and a covenant-keeping God, as we will present in depth in Chapter Eighteen. So, God honored that earlier covenant by delivering them from the clutches of the Egyptians. So why didn't He just continue to offer these Israelites the same grace-based covenant that Abraham had enjoyed?

The likely reason is that this "stiff-necked" people obviously did not trust Him like Abraham had, otherwise they would not have whined and complained against God during the first 50 days in the desert. They chose to walk by sight rather than by faith in God's demonstration of goodness on their behalf. So, rather than abandon them or return them to Egypt as they yearned for, He offered them a Law-based covenant that <u>depended on their behavior</u> rather than on His lavish grace like He had offered to a wiser, more co-operative Abram over 400 years earlier. Here, again, are the two initial terms in nutshell:

> <u>If, therefore, you will hear my voice, and you will keep My covenant, you will be to me a particular possession out of all people. For all the earth is mine. And you will be to me a priestly kingdom and a holy nation.</u>

Who wouldn't like the wonderful promises stated there. But the key difference from the Abrahamic covenant is that they themselves had to keep the terms of the covenant to get the promised blessings. God was offering them a works-based relationship with Him rather than a grace-based relationship between Him and Jesus. Big difference. Deuteronomy, Chapter 28 lists the specific blessings that God offered to them *if* they would obey the terms of the covenant <u>perfectly</u>. But, if and when they did not keep the covenant agreement, they would be subject to an even longer list of punishments and curses. Obviously, their confidence in *their own* ability to behave perfectly blinded them. Even before they saw the specific demands of this new covenant, they boldly said: "<u>Everything that the Lord has spoken, we shall do.</u>" It would be similar to an "I dare you" challenge today that might cause a prideful person to choose a regrettably disastrous outcome.

Trusting in Their Law-keeping, Not In God

Their pride was evident in two ways: 1) they foolishly agreed to accept this law-based covenant *before* they knew the lengthy list of laws they would have to keep *perfectly* and the terrible curses if they fell short and 2) their track record over these first fifty days in the desert should have proven to them they could not do much of anything well – let alone perfectly - for any length of time. So, as I stated above, God, who knows the end from the beginning, knew that they could not keep this solemn covenant which they freely chose to accept, being confident in their own ability. "Pride goes before the fall" (Proverbs 16:18).

The rest of the underlined passages above focus on the reaction of the Israelites to God's awesome power. They saw Moses ascend by faith into the fiery display on the mountain and return unscathed. But rather than rejoice in the presence and power of the true God wanting to relate with them too, they wrongly viewed this spectacle as a <u>threat to their well-being</u>. God had delivered them from their enemy and personally cared for their needs in the desert. But their <u>wrong concept of who God really is</u> prevented them from experiencing all that God had for them. What drew Moses to God caused fear and needless alienation in them.

God Gave the Law to Reveal Man's True Nature In Adam

So, again, why didn't He stop them or, better yet, not offer this inferior covenant to them in the first place? Such a good question deserves His wise answer. First, He did that to show them (and *all* mankind) what was evident to Him since Adam's fall but what was *not* yet evident to them. It was the fundamental fact that mankind's "troubles" are, ultimately, *not* the result of "law-breaking behavior" but of a fallen **nature** – the result of being descended from and, therefore, **in Adam**, mankind's original parent. <u>Since this root cause of evil is hidden in the</u> **unseen realm** <u>of the man's spirit, (not just in the soul) it is impossible for mankind to detect it apart from God's divine revelation.</u>

Consequently, it is also impossible for mankind to fix that corrupted nature by any human effort such as "behavior modification." Therefore, God mercifully established this performance-based covenant *only with the Israelites* to unequivocally *reveal* the root cause of mankind's wrong behavior. And what is that? An evil, rebellious *nature*, caused when Adam, <u>as mankind's</u> <u>representative</u>, rejected God's truth and perfection by choosing to believe the devil's lies. The Old Testament talks much about man's evil heart. Jesus not only explained the root cause of that to Paul in 42 AD but also how His **divine exchange** provides believers with a totally new nature – a reborn spirit being, compatible with God Himself. (Chapter Sixteen presents the details of this incomparable revelation.)

Not even the apostles, who had lived and travelled with Jesus as His disciples, **pre-cross**, understood the true cause of evil human behavior and so they continued to try to keep some aspects of the Law to "stay right" with God, **post-cross**. Ironically, such law-keeping does the exact opposite, according to Jesus' **whole gospel**: "… when the commandment came, sin sprang to life and I died. I found that the very commandment that was intended to bring life actually brought death" (Romans 7:9b-10). Remember, "The Law is not of faith" (Galatians 3:12). Therefore, "anything not of faith is sin" (Romans 14:13). (See the next chapter for a more complete overview of the hazards of law-based "Jewish Christianity," the **elephant in the church**).

Secondly, God gave the Israelites a law system that they could not keep perfectly because, otherwise, they (and we) could never come to know mankind's desperate need for God's only solution for man's root problem - the coming Savior, Jesus Christ. (Jesus used the Law to reveal this to the "rich young ruler" and their conversation will be explored in Chapter Twelve.) Again, Jesus is the only one that could and did make possible the total removal of every believer's old, **in Adam** nature when it is crucified with Jesus – through identification by faith. Then he is regenerated – reborn of God – as a totally new creation **in Christ Jesus**. Astoundingly, the sinless Jesus *became* mankind's sin so that each and every unbeliever, by believing in and receiving Jesus' **divine exchange**, instantly becomes a "partaker of *His* divine nature" and then able to love God wholeheartedly from his new, **unseen** spirit-self (see 2 Corinthians 5:21 and 2 Peter 1:4).

The Divine Exchange

How awesome is that? This transformation "from being a caterpillar to becoming an all new **butterfly**" spiritually speaking, is preposterous foolishness to the natural mind of man, yet that is the essence of the **total grace gospel**. Through rebirth by faith, Jesus

> 1) gives His perfect righteous nature in exchange for the unbeliever's evil nature **in Adam** (by dying to the old, spirit- self accomplished *instantly* through rebirth),

> 2) exchanges His abundant life for the unbeliever's death on the cross by faith and

3) exchanges His earned blessings and favor with God for the unbeliever's sins, curses and rejection.

That is why it is called by its Greek superlative "euaggelion" which means "nearly too-good-to-be-true-news." We will explore the depths of this glorious revelation much more fully, starting in Chapter Sixteen.

Any "gospel" which adds *any* mixture of law-keeping with Jesus' perfect, comprehensive, **finished work** on Calvary to attain or maintain righteousness is no gospel at all. This revelation from Jesus becomes clear once you comprehend the details of our initial, **unseen** condition as **in Adam** sinners the way God does. Again, the Bible reveals that all humans are sinners because of being **in Adam**. They can become "saints who still sometimes sin" only through rebirth as a new spirit-being **in Christ Jesus**. Righteousness under the Mosaic Law Covenant required a lifelong, sinless performance. Righteousness under Jesus' **New Covenant** in His blood requires 1) His perfect performance on earth, then 2) Him giving Himself as a gift to all who believe and receive Him by faith. Mercifully, **New Covenant** righteousness is not based on a saint's fallible performance but only on accepting and being united with God's free gift of Jesus, Who then instantly *becomes* the believer's wisdom, righteousness, holiness and redemption in God's eyes, according to 1 Corinthians 1:30.

The Ultimate Goal of Jesus' Gospel – Relationship with God Himself
To put it another way, in His mercy, God sent His own Son, whose sacrifice of His perfect self on Calvary made it possible to *become* what we could never, ever accomplish by ourselves – united with a perfect God. Jesus made that request at the Last Supper when He prayed for us to His Father: "that they all may be one as you, Father, are in Me, and I in you, that they also may be one in us ..." (John 17:21). That has always been Their desire for all of mankind. Everything that Jesus said and did had that unfathomable goal in mind, agreed upon with His Father before Jesus left heaven to come here as a man. Since the Mosaic Law system could only reveal (not fix) man's perverted nature **in Adam**, the Law was nailed to the cross for believers and a completely new, grace-based covenant was given to God's reborn children, thanks to Jesus' **divine exchange** (see Colossians 2:14 and Ephesians 2:15).

In Summary
In simple terms, what is God's purpose for giving a standard that a sinner can't keep? It is to reveal man's true nature of Darkness **in Adam** in order to bring him to the end of depending on himself. And why is this necessary? So that he will come to believe and depend on Christ Jesus *alone* as God's only trustworthy provision for salvation and true life. Only then will a prideful, self-sufficient person be willing to admit his core problem and accept the only true answer for his depraved nature **in Adam** – Jesus' gift of a new, righteous nature, available only by rebirth *through* Christ Jesus, the last Adam.

And, unfortunately, sometimes things have to get pretty bad before some people get desperate enough to wake up to their intrinsic need for God. For example, when I do prison ministry locally, the women often testify that incarceration was the best thing that ever happened to them. Why? No, not because of the free room and board but because it was the only time in their lives that they 1) slowed down long enough to see the mess their bad choices had made for themselves externally and 2) to allow God to reveal how bad off spiritually they were **in Adam**. It was an important wake-up call to give up the "games" and get serious with God, their loving Creator and Savior. "He who keeps his life shall lose it; he who loses it for my (Jesus') sake and for the **whole gospel of grace** will find it," according to Mark 8:35. He alone is the Tree of Life.

"But what about good people who keep the Law," you ask? "Even Jesus said only the sick need a doctor." True, but He also clarified that when He said, "Only God is good" in Luke 18:19. By revealing this **unseen** fact of man's depravity **in Adam**, He was putting His finger on the same core problem. Because of Adam, everyone's core, which is his spirit-self, was "unplugged" from God, the only source of true "goodness" and life. Adam was still enjoying "bios" life physically but was dead to God spiritually by becoming one with Darkness. Only when we humans get plugged back into God, through rebirth, and receive His gift of righteousness, will we fulfill the purpose for which He created us originally, which is to be in joyful union with Him and His family of new creation saints, forever **in Christ Jesus.**

Only Perfect People Are Welcome In Heaven

Here is yet another way to see this very important matter. We know from the Bible that God is perfect, heaven is perfect and God even made a perfect garden for Adam and Eve to live in and be in daily fellowship with Him. That is no fairy tale. God would not kid around with such an important indicator of how really *good* He is. So, heaven is perfect yet mankind automatically became complicit with Adam's treachery when he rebelled as mankind's representative from God's viewpoint. Therefore, what must happen for any person to become compatible with perfection again so that he or she can be one with God? Now you know the answer – give up trying to earn heaven and simply receive the **finished work** of Jesus' **divine exchange** by believing He did it all for you. In Chapter Nineteen, we will explore the practicalities of this new freedom of "walking in the Spirit," just like Jesus Himself walked.

In this chapter, we examined the <u>main purpose and function</u> of the Law Covenant in God's grand scheme of His salvation process for mankind from various angles. In doing so, we can now understand what Paul meant in Romans 3:31: "Do we nullify the Law by this faith (in Jesus)? Absolutely not! Rather we uphold the Law." Jesus upheld the law by keeping the spirit of the Law perfectly for our sakes so that He could give us His "earned" righteousness as a gift. Then the Law was abolished in His flesh (for believers) when He became sin and then <u>paid for</u> and <u>removed all the sin from mankind, accoding to 2 Corinnthians 5:19</u>. Now we are to uphold the Law *only* to do what God intended it to do - to bring the Jews (and all mankind) to see their need for mankind's Savior, Christ Jesus. The law principle can do the same for unbelievers today <u>if it is used properly</u>. But it should never be used to punish, browbeat or control any believer. Why? Jesus made this clear to Paul who wrote 1 Timothy 1:8-9 to set the record straight:

> We know that the Law is good if one uses it correctly, by knowing this that the law is not meant for a righteous one (justified **in Christ**) but the law is laid down for the lawless, rebellious, ungodly and sinful ones … .

In other words, the law principle of the knowledge of good and evil and its consequences (condemnation) is for the *unrighteous* – for those still **in Adam**. Now it is time to explore, in much greater detail, why and how the Law is *hazardous* to a believer's spiritual health and maturity whenever it is mixed with Jesus' **whole gospel of grace**. Here is another song-poem that explains the differences between law and grace and what God supplies to us as believers **in Christ Jesus.** It makes a good outline for sermons and witnessing.

THE LAW IS GOOD BUT MAN IS NOT   Rom. 7:12 & 16, Mk. 10:18; &
Because of Adam's Fall,   Rom. 5:14   Rom. 3:12
His sin caused death and hopeless misery.   Rom. 6:23, Rom. 5:15, Jn. 3:18
But You sent grace and mercy in the form of Your own Son   Jn. 5:23, 1 Tim. 1:2
Restoring mankind's hope for victory.   1 Cor. 15:19, Col. 1:27

When Jesus Christ came down to earth to conquer sin and death,   Rom. 8:2, 6:18 & 22
He brought an end to Law for righteousness.   Rom. 10:4, Gal. 3:13 & 2:21
For Law arouses sin, produces wrath and causes death   Rom. 7:5 & 8, Rom. 4:15, & 6:23, &
If you rely on it for righteousness.   Gal. 2:16   2 Cor. 3:7-9

Becoming sin and dying and then rising from the grave   2 Cor. 5:21, Matt. 27:50 & 28:6
He proved that He was God who came to earth.   Jn. 8:58
The Law had done its job in showing mankind's need for Him.   Rom. 7:7, Gal. 3:24
So He nailed it to the cross and gave rebirth.   Col. 2:14, 1 Pet. 1:3

When asked by Nicodemus what He meant by a "rebirth."   Jn. 3:4
This Savior of the human race replied: Titus 3:5-7
"By water and the Holy Spirit is a man reborn."   Jn. 3:5, Titus 3:5
The only way he can be justified.   Jn.3:3, Gal. 3:24, Gal. 2:19-21, &
                                                 Rom. 4:5

So Jesus, You fulfilled the Law to be my righteousness   Matt. 3:15, 2 Cor. 5:21, Rom. 3:26
Your precious blood has paid for ALL my sin.   Eph. 1:7, Col. 2:13, Heb. 8:12
So death no longer has the sting of endless misery   1 Cor. 15:26, 54-55, Rom. 6:9, &
For now Your very Spirit lives within!   1 Cor. 3:16, 6:20   2 Tim. 1:9-10

God sent You, Holy Spirit, so that You could live through me   Acts 2:4, Jn. 6:63, Gal.3:3-5
And keep my eyes on Jesus – my new way.   Col. 3:1Rom. 7:6, 8:6
His living words renew my mind so I can think like Him.   Rom. 12:2, Eph. 5:26, Col. 3:1-3,
You help me hear what Jesus has to say.   Rom. 1:5, 10:17 and Gal. 3:25

His words of Life replace the Law that I could never keep.   Acts 13:39, Rom. 3:23, Heb 10:9
I live by faith in all that He has done.   Rom. 3:26, Heb. 8:13, Acts 13:39
Like Abraham who trusted God to give him righteousness,   Rom. 3:22, 24, 28, Jn. 3:16-18
I'm righteous in You, Father, through your Son.   2 Cor. 5:17 & 21, Gal. 3:22

I thank You for the gift of faith and love and liberty,   Rom. 3:27, Matt. 32:27-40,
The "higher Law" that Moses could not give.   Gal. 5:1-6, Rom. 8:2 & 13:8-10,
This time, You sent a Savior King to rescue me from death,   Jn. 3:16, 1 Jn. 4:14, Col. 2:12-14
Because of Him, this prodigal now lives!   Rom. 4:17, 6:13, 8:11, Jn. 10:10
Sermon Song © 2009 by Leonard J. Ransil

CHAPTER NINE

THE HARSH REALITIES OF THE LAW

"The Law was given through Moses; grace and truth came through Jesus Christ" (John 1:17).

A Recap of the Law's Purpose

Chapter Eight detailed God's revealed purpose for the Law and proved that only Jesus' **finished work**, not man's law-keeping, is God's answer for not only salvation but also for man's every need. Since that is a central premise of this book, a brief recap of God's purpose for giving the Law will set the stage to better understand why there are grave consequences when believers mix the two opposing covenants.

The God of Abraham, Isaac and Jacob gave the Mosaic Law to a specific group of people for a specific purpose for a specific period of time – to reveal their need (and therefore mankind's need) for a sinless Messiah whom He would send later. In fact, immediately after Adam's fall and throughout the Old Testament, God often indicated through His prophets that He would send a savior because He knew that Adam's treachery would cause all of His descendants to *be* sinners due to *being* **in Adam**, not because of bad behavior, as Romans 5:19a makes clear.

Unless that corrupted nature was somehow fixed or replaced, all imperfect human beings would forever remain unplugged from the intimate relationship God desires to have with all humans. But mankind could not comprehend just how deep the breach was in the **unseen realm**, let alone how to fix it. God still mercifully interacted with various people for 2500 years to prepare the way for the Savior's coming. Again, the law principle was, and still is, an important tool – properly used as God intends – to reveal to an unbeliever his true, depraved nature **in Adam**. God gave the law-based Covenant to the Israelites to prove that no amount of self-effort could qualify such fundamentally flawed humans to become compatible with Him.

The only way is to trust Him for salvation through Christ Jesus, the last Adam. God found fault with the people (because of their unfixable sin nature and consequential behavior) under the Mosaic Covenant of Law and promised that He would eventually make a **New Covenant** with radically new terms. It offers a **new nature** to **in Adam** sinners through rebirth by faith that makes them **new creation** saints, perfectly compatible with Him forever (see Jeremiah 31:31-34, Hebrews 8:8-13 and Ezekiel 36:26-27). Chapter Sixteen will explain how God does this for receptive humans.

But notice that God gave the Mosaic Law *only to the Jews*, never to the Gentiles. So how did parts of it, such as the Ten Commandments, become so central to church life today? By now, you know the answer! The **elephant of mixture - grace mixed with law** - marched into the church through the law-minded leadership in Jerusalem. They mistakenly assumed that they must obey at least some parts of it in order to remain in union with God. They failed to comprehend the obvious fact that God declared Abraham to be righteous (in good standing with

Him) just by him believing in God's promise, not by Abraham's obedience to a law system that began over 400 years later. In the **big picture**, the Mosaic Covenant was, on one hand, a *necessary step* to reveal man's true condition and need for a savior. Yet, on the other hand, it was a regression in many ways from the grace-based covenant God gave to Abraham. And, in hindsight, the Law-based covenant is most certainly vastly inferior to the new, grace-based covenant believers are meant to enjoy now – without any mixture of the two. (See Endnote #**23** for more information on why this heresy was rooted in Jerusalem.)

So why did Jesus, through Paul, make such a big deal about mixing the two covenants of law and grace? Before exploring what Jesus revealed to Paul about this very important question, let's first look at a helpful illustration.

When a person goes to get help from a doctor because of some serious physical problem, the cause may not be obvious. So the doctor orders an x-ray of the problem area to determine the root cause. While the x-ray might reveal the cause of the trouble, it cannot fix it - and no one expects it to. That is not its purpose. But this good tool can also be destructive if used wrongly. In fact, if the exposure is too long or continuously repeated, the radiation could damage healthy tissue or mask the original condition - or worse. Simply put, a good thing wrongly used can cause bad results.

A Wrong Focus Causes Wrong Results
And so it is when a believer **in Christ Jesus** continues to focus on the Law instead of on Jesus and His **unseen, finished work**, which replaced the Mosaic Law with God's higher law of faith, love and liberty as described in Chapter Three. But this vital switch in focus would have been impossible for believers to figure out if Jesus would have not revealed this **new reality** option to Paul in 42 AD. It seems so counter-intuitive because the system of laws that we have in the **seen realm** are necessary and often very helpful. They can serve to promote social order and a modicum of peace and safety in a basically chaotic and confusing world which was caused by Adam's fall. Think of a "Wild West" town before a sheriff arrives "to bring law and order."

But realize, too, that any law, by itself, cannot *cause* good effects. It is powerless to do so. To be effective, a law must be known and then obeyed by "law-abiding" citizens who, typically, are under the fear of negative consequences from the local "law-enforcement" authority." In other words, there will be *consequences* if one is "caught" breaking a particular law. (Most people only follow the laws they know will be "enforced." There are many civil laws "on the books" that most people don't even know about.) Not stopping at a red light can get you a ticket that brings some form of punishment or, worse yet, cause a minor or serious accident. The traffic light was installed to prevent crashes but it cannot do that unless it is "obeyed." Man's laws are generally made to control people's behavior through <u>fear of punishment</u> in order to achieve some desired outcome in the **seen realm** – good or bad.

But Jesus' **grace-based gospel** is not merely about the **seen realm**, which is the focus of the Mosaic Law, but primarily about the **unseen realm** of God's Kingdom that operates far differently and now includes all believers - thanks to Christ Jesus. The gospel of His **divine exchange** enables believers to enjoy the benefits of His new and abundant life on earth as long as they continue to *depend* on Jesus and His righteousness from faith to faith, as stated in Romans

124

1:17. But experiencing ongoing victory in the **seen realm** can be minimized by going back under the law by depending on one's own human resources and efforts instead of depending on Jesus' **finished work** by faith. "The righteous shall live by faith" in Jesus' works, not in theirs.

Paul – Before and After

No doubt Paul, formerly a Pharisee of Pharisees, initially *assumed* that the Mosaic Law was still fundamental to the conversion experience with Jesus that he enjoyed while near Damascus because it, too, had come from God originally. Jesus was seemingly just adding a new layer to the solid foundation of Judaism that stood for 1500 years. But his thinking radically changed in about 42 AD when Jesus exploded his assumptions. It was such a revolutionary change that Paul later wrote that "... all things are made new" (see 2 Corinthians 5:17). Jesus turned everything-right-side-up for Paul – including his new understanding about 1) what the Law could *not* do – fix one's Adamic nature - and 2) the great harm to believers who are continuously focusing on the Law (just like being exposed to x-rays) rather than focusing on Jesus. "For the letter (of the Law) kills but the (Holy) Spirit gives life" (2 Corinthians 3:6). Prayerfully invite the Holy Spirit to use the following sequence of scriptures to unveil these vital concepts that explain why the **elephant of mixture** is so dangerous. Jesus' **grace gospel** is not meant to be just information *for* your mind but cause a transformation *of* your mind to think like God thinks.

The Good Law Cannot Make A Man Good

Moses was up on the mountain with the Lord forty days and forty nights.... he wrote the terms of the covenant—the Ten Commandments—on the <u>stone </u>tablets (Exodus 34:28).

The Law is holy and the commandment is holy and righteous and good (Romans 7:12).

That old system of law etched in *stone* <u>led to death</u>, yet it began with such glory that the people of Israel could not bear to look at Moses' face. For his face shone with the glory of God, even though the brightness was already fading away (2 Corinthians 3:7).

We know that the law is spiritual; but I am unspiritual, sold as a slave to sin (nature of **Adam** before rebirth) (Romans 6:14).

For what the law was powerless to do in that it was weakened by the sinful nature **(in Adam),** God did by sending His own Son in the likeness of sinful man to be a sin offering for all sin (Romans 8:3).

… by observing the law no one will be justified (Galatians 2:16).

The former regulation (the Mosaic Covenant) <u>is set aside because it was weak and unprofitable</u> (for the Law made nothing perfect), and a better hope (the **New Covenant**) is introduced by which we draw near (have access) to God (by union with God **in Christ**) (Hebrews 7:18-19).

Referring back to the above analogy: The Law is to an unbeliever what an x-ray is to a corpse. It can reveal the *cause* of death but it can't raise the corpse to life. Nowhere in the Bible does the Law offer eternal life to the Israelites. It was all about relating to God in the **seen realm** as **in Adam** sinners, spiritually dead to God and subject to blessings and cursings based on their behavior.

God's Remedy For Spiritual Death

But now a righteousness from God, apart from law, has been made known … This righteousness from God comes through faith in Jesus Christ to all who believe (Romans 3:21-22).

For we maintain that a man is justified (made righteous - right with God) by faith apart from observing the law (Romans 3:28).

God's Purposes For The Mosaic Law

What, then, was the purpose of the law? It was added because of transgressions, which the sacrificial system temporarily covered, until the Seed (Jesus) to whom the promise referred, had come (Galatians 3:19).

If there had been a law given which could have given life (not caused death), then righteousness would have come from the Law. But the scripture locked up all things under sin's power so that the promise (the receiving of the Spirit – verse 14), by the faith of Jesus Christ, might be given to all those believing. But before faith (in Jesus Christ) came, we were kept under the Law, having been locked up from that faith about to be revealed (when Jesus came). So, the law was our trainer until Christ (came), that we might be justified by faith **(in Him).** But now that faith has come, we are no longer under a trainer (the Law) because you are all sons of God through faith **in Jesus Christ,** for as many were baptized **in Christ,** you put on Christ…. you are all one **in Christ** (Galatians 3:21-28).

Additionally, by way of an analogy, as long as an heir is a child, he is no different (in practice) than a servant. Though he is the lord of all the estate, he is under tutors and governors until the time appointed by the father. Even so, when we were children, we were in bondage under the principles of the **(seen)** world. But when the fullness of the time had come, God sent forth his Son, made of a woman, made under the law, to redeem those who were under the law (the Jews), that we (Jews) might receive the adoption of sons (through rebirth). And because you (Galatians) are now sons (too), God hath sent forth the (promised) Spirit of his Son into your hearts, crying, Abba, Father. Therefore, you are no longer a servant, but a son and if a son, then an heir of God through Christ (Galatians 4:1-7).

These last two lengthy passages from Jesus' revelation to Paul recorded in Galatians, point to a God-orchestrated transition from the covenant of the Law which was meant to function as a trainer over an immature "son," the Israelites. They were still **in Adam,** so the Law was given to prepare them for the time when Jesus inaugurated a covenant of grace, based only on faith **in Him.** Some major benefits included in the **New Covenant,** given to every new believer who is automatically justified by Jesus' blood, was to become God's son through rebirth and to receive the Holy Spirit (in place of the Law) as the believer's personal "trainer," – Teacher, Guide, Guard, Sanctifier, Comforter etc.. Jesus sent Him to do everything for the believing son that the Law could never do. Why? Because, again, the law only tells you what you do wrong but can't give you any help to do what is right or to fix yourself. It only arouses sin-consciousness and a *feeling* of condemnation in the soul. However, the Holy Spirit comes to teach you about your right-standing with God because you are a new, reborn being **in Christ** – which is the true state of your new self, *apart from your behavior*. And your behavior will reflect your godly sonship in Christ by letting Him live His life through you, as you. Chapter Nineteen will explain this **New Covenant** reality more fully.

Hagar and Sarah

And, just in case Paul's explanation was not yet clear enough, he then presented an unmistakable contrast of the two opposing covenants of law vs. grace by recounting the following story of Abraham's two wives and corresponding sons that every Jew knew by heart, retold in Galatians 4:21-31:

> Tell me, you who want to be under the law, are you not aware of what the law says? For it is written that Abraham had two sons, one by a slave woman and the other by a free woman (whose name was Sarah which means "grace" in Hebrew). His son by the slave woman was born in the ordinary way; but his son by the free woman was born as the result of a promise. These things may be taken figuratively, since the women represent two covenants. One covenant is from Mount Sinai and bears children who are to be slaves: This is Hagar. Now Hagar stands for Mount Sinai in Arabia and corresponds to the present city of Jerusalem, because she is in slavery with her children. But the Jerusalem that is above is free, and she is our mother. For it is written: 'Be glad, O barren woman, who bears no children; break forth and cry aloud, you who have no labor pains; because more are the children of the desolate woman than of her who has a husband.'
> Now you, brothers, like Isaac, are children of promise. At that time the son born in the ordinary way persecuted the son born by the power of the Spirit. It is the same now. But what does the Scripture say, brothers? 'Get rid of the slave woman (the Law) and her son, for the slave woman's son will never share in the inheritance with the free woman's son.' Therefore, brothers, we are not children of the slave woman, but of the free woman (the **New Covenant** of grace, **in Christ**).

And his next sentence in Galatians 5:1 is the climax of Paul's exhortation:

> So, stand firm in the freedom by which Christ Jesus has made us free and do not be held captive by the yoke (the Mosaic Law) of slavery.

The underlined sections reinforce the conclusion in the earlier scriptures above: There is the Jerusalem in the **seen realm** that is in slavery to the Law. But the true believer's "mother" is the new, **unseen** Jerusalem that is free of bondage to the Law and, therefore, the believer is the child of the Promise because he is "born by the power of the Spirit of God." He is often persecuted by those still under law. So, Paul is telling those still locked up under law, living in the **"seen"** Jerusalem church (literally and/or figuratively), to take seriously what Jesus has already accomplished through rebirth for us and live in the freedom of the Spirit-led life, not under a law-led life that causes death. This passage parallels Paul's painful description of a Jewish Christian struggling under law as recorded in Romans, Chapter Seven. His agony is in stark contrast to a new-found freedom **in Christ**, expressed in Romans 8:1-4:

Therefore, there is now no condemnation for those who are **in Christ Jesus**, because through Christ Jesus the (higher) law of the Spirit of life set me free from the (Mosaic) Law of sin (nature) and death. For what the Law was powerless to do in that it was weakened by the sinful nature **(in Adam)**, God did by sending His own Son in the likeness of sinful man to be a sin offering. And so he condemned sin (nature) in sinful man, in order that the righteous requirements of the law might be fully met in us (by faith in Jesus alone), who do not live according to the sinful nature (now crucified, dead and gone) but according to the Spirit.

So now that every believer's former, **in Adam**, nature is gone, God wants His children to live according to the life of the new Teacher and Sanctifier, the Holy Spirit living inside of them. But what if a believer is ignorant of the blessings of the Spirit-led life or chooses to mentally stay under the law like the Jerusalem church obviously did? Let's look at some of the likely consequences.

The Dire Consequences of Law-mindedness For A Believer
God gave the Law to the Israelites through Moses to bring to light what was hidden to man in order to make clear how desperately mankind needs a savior - as was described in Chapter Eight and above. But now, let's explore how harsh and harmful the Law is for the *believer* who focuses on the old "trainer" (performance-based law-keeping) instead of relying on the Holy Spirit for guidance and sanctification of the outer man, according to the law of faith, love and liberty in God's **unseen** Kingdom – the **butterfly life.**

According to the following scriptures, the <u>Law</u>:

1) **IS THE STRENGTH OF SIN**: The strength of sin is the Law (1 Corinthians 15:56).

2) **REVEALS SIN**: I would not have known what sin was except through the law (Romans 7:7).

3) **AROUSES SIN**: … when we were controlled by the flesh (sarx), the sinful passions aroused by the law were at work in our bodies, so that we bore fruit for death (Romans 7:5).

4) **CAUSES SIN-CONSCIOUSNESS**: …no human will be justified in God's sight by observing the law for through the law comes consciousness of sin (Romans 3:20).

5) **BRINGS GOD'S WRATH**: ... for the law brings wrath. <u>However, where there is no law, there is no transgression</u> (Romans 4:15).

6) **BRINGS DEATH:** (The Ten Commandments, which were written on stone, are) "the ministry of death" (2 Corinthians 3:7). "But sin, seizing the opportunity afforded by the commandment, produced in me every kind of covetous desire. For <u>apart from law, sin is dead.</u> Once I was alive apart from law; but when the commandment came, sin sprang to life and I died. I found that <u>the very commandment that was intended to bring life actually brought death.</u> For sin, seizing the opportunity afforded by the commandment, deceived me, and, <u>through the commandment, put me to death</u>" (Romans 7:8-11).

7) **BRINGS A CURSE**: "All who rely on observing the law are under a curse, for it is written: 'Cursed is everyone who does not continue to do (perfectly) everything written in the Book of the Law'" (Galatians 3:10).

A Summary Of The Collective Purpose Of The Law

The Law was given to arouse sin, bring guilt and to trigger condemnation for those **in Adam** in order <u>to bring them to the end of themselves</u> so that they surrender to Jesus' gift of salvation by grace through faith in the **finished work** of His **divine exchange**!

Please note: The devil also tries to get the believer to focus back on the Law, rather than on Jesus. If a believer swallows the deception, Satan can then discourage the righteous saint with unfounded *"feelings"* of guilt and separation from God by lying to his mind, which causes him to think that he is now under a curse and God's condemnation. Then he <u>thinks</u> he must do some religious works to get back into God's "good graces." That deception is Satan's main strategy against a true Christian who is, by definition, in constant <u>spiritual</u> union with Christ Jesus by faith alone, apart from his behavior. Knowing about and relying on Jesus' **divine exchange** by faith alone, equips His Saints to discern, resist and defeat the enemy's deception and attacks. Chapter Twenty will elaborate on being victorious in this area, known as spiritual warfare.

The Law Is Opposed To Faith

THE LAW IS NOT OF FAITH: "The law is not based on faith; on the contrary, 'The man who does these things (rely on the law) will live by them'" (Galatians 3:12).

The unbeliever and the carnal Christian lives by (and therefore, is under) the Law - the things he sees and does in the **seen realm** - not by faith in God's **unseen, Kingdom realities**. We described this struggle using the *Three Dog Chart* in Chapter Four. "But, without faith (in God) it is impossible to please God (let alone to be justified)" (Hebrews 11:6).

PLEASE NOTE: God supplies the gift of faith to hear of and believe in Jesus' **finished work** - His **whole gospel of grace** (which is based on how heaven operates) - to fully benefit from His New Creation realities available **in Christ** while here on earth. When a believer accepts just the **bare bones gospel** of salvation, he is immediately regenerated from being dead **in Adam** to being alive **in Christ**. This change in his nature repositions him into heavenly places – even if he does not know about this new, **unseen** reality, according to the Ephesians 2:6 revelation from Jesus.

But discovering and believing in the benefits of the **whole grace gospel** of Jesus enables the believer to progressively *experience* Jesus' abundant life and victory in the **seen realm** by receiving what Jesus Himself deserves because of the believer's new, legal position, **in Christ**. Experiencing the amazing realities of God's **unseen Kingdom** on earth the way Paul learned to walk, comes from *knowing* about and *reckoning* as <u>true for you</u> what Jesus has already legally done for you in the **divine exchange**. That is how what is *already true* for you *legally* **in Christ,** becomes *vitally* true by personal experience in the **seen** realm. Focusing on the Law instead of on Jesus, frustrates this whole grace-based process of faith in what Jesus did and puts the believer (mentally) back under the curse of the Law which is based on the believer's faulty performance.

WHATEVER IS NOT OF FAITH IS SIN "… for whatever is not of faith is sin" (Romans 14:23b).

The Bottom Line

1)The Law *cannot justify* a sinner.

2) However, it can bring *grave consequences* upon the saved saint who puts himself under the Law through accepting mixture (which will be explained more fully in the next chapter). While his eternal salvation is not at stake, his *experience* of Jesus' victory over Darkness and His offer of abundant life - received by letting the Holy Spirit live through him on earth - are minimized. Most importantly, it deprives the saint of enjoying a *vital,* ongoing, intimate relationship with the Trinity, free of all guilt and condemnation from Father-God.

So again, since God nailed the Law to the cross, according to Colossians 2:14, does the Law principle have any use today? Absolutely: it is to be used properly, as needed, in ministering to those *still in Adam* to:

1) help them realize, by grace, their true, *fallen condition* before God in the **unseen realm**,

2) help them come to recognize their desperate need for Jesus as their only hope for salvation, and then

3) receive Him by faith. This process is in cooperation with the Holy Spirit, <u>who convicts the unbeliever of his sin of unbelief</u> in Jesus, the world's only true Lord and Savior, who arose from the dead (see John 16:8-9).

Jesus Christ Is The End Of The Law For The Righteous Ones - The True Believers

However, as noted at the end of the last chapter, Paul revealed to his disciple Timothy that <u>the Law is *not* for the righteous saint **in Christ**.</u> Let's let Jesus' **whole gospel** to Paul tell the wonderful story of our freedom **in Christ**:

> But we know that the law is good, if a man uses it properly, knowing this, that the <u>Law is not made for a righteous man</u>, but for the lawless and disobedient, for the ungodly and for sinners … (1 Timothy 1:8-9).

> For Christ is the end of the law for righteousness to everyone that believes (Romans 10:4).

Christ Jesus fulfilled the just requirements of the Law and, thereby, He became "the end of the Law" for those who receive His gift of justification/righteousness through being reborn of God by faith alone.

So again, because of Jesus' perfect sacrifice, God legally "nailed the Law to the cross" for it was "weak and unprofitable" (useless) in making anyone perfect (see Colossians 2:14 and Hebrews 7:18-19). Therefore, Jesus' crucifixion accomplished the believer's crucifixion by faith and also "the crucifixion of the Law" for the believer. Consequently, where there is no Law, sin is not imputed, according to Romans 5:13. That is awesome news. How did He do all that?

> Christ redeemed us from the curse of the law by becoming a curse for us, for it is written: 'cursed is everyone who is hung on a tree.' He redeemed us in order that the blessing given to Abraham might <u>come to the Gentiles</u> through Christ Jesus, so that, by faith, we might receive the <u>promise of the Spirit</u> (Galatians 3:13).

> For He (Jesus) is our peace who has made the two (Jews and Gentiles) one, having destroyed the barrier, the dividing wall of hostility, <u>by abolishing in His flesh, the Law with its (Ten) commandments and regulations</u> (Ephesians 2:14-15).

No Contradiction, But Completion
"But wait a minute!" you might say. "Jesus Himself said in Matthew 5:17-18:"

> Do not think that I have come to abolish the Law or the Prophets. I have not come to abolish them but to fulfill them. I tell you the truth, until heaven and earth disappear, not the smallest letter, not the least stroke of the pen, will by any means disappear from the Law until <u>everything is accomplished</u>.

Yes, Jesus' **pre-cross** statement certainly does seem to contradict all these **post-cross** statements revealed to Paul as quoted above. This is precisely a case in point to show just how different the two covenants are - divided by the **finished work** of the cross. If you think in **big picture** terms as God thinks, you will see the connection. Do you see it? The key is in the last phrase: "... until everything is accomplished." Think back to Jesus' last words on the cross according to John 19:3, written down by the only disciple who was there with Mary:

> When He received the drink, Jesus said <u>'It is finished.'</u>

That is the moment when He "accomplished everything" - <u>from God's "now" viewpoint</u>, not from ours. This is the actual fulfillment of what Jesus prophesied to His hearers in John 17:4b when He said "<u>I have completed the work that You (God) gave me to accomplish (even though He had not yet died)</u>." For Jews, that marked the "end of the Law," which was nailed to the cross and signaled the inauguration of His new **grace-based** covenant, won for all mankind, Jews *and* Gentiles, by His shed blood. This is a perfect example of the supreme importance of <u>dividing the Word rightly</u> - according to what covenant a particular text belongs. A text taken out of context can con you into believing wrongly.

Law-minded people use Matthew 5:17-18 to "prove" that we are still under the Law because heaven and earth have not yet passed away. They also might cite Luke 16:17 which reads, "It is easier for heaven and earth to disappear than for the least stroke of a pen to drop out of the Law" where, unfortunately, the qualifying phrase at the end of Matthew 5:18 was omitted - "... until everything was accomplished." But notice that Luke *does* say in verse 16 that there has been a major change: "The Law and the Prophets were proclaimed until John (the Baptist). Since that time the <u>good news of the gospel of the Kingdom</u> is being preached, and everyone is crowding his way into it." But remember, this "crowding" did not actually happen until Pentecost.

131

Now, according to Jesus' own assessment of John in Luke 7:28, "... among those born of women, there has not risen anyone greater than John the Baptist." (This would include Abraham, Moses and David - and all the other luminaries of the Old Testament that the Jews lionized.) "Yet, he who is least in the Kingdom of heaven is greater than him." The reason that the "least" one is greater than even John the Baptist is because all people, including John the Baptist, were still **in Adam, pre-cross.** Therefore, they could not yet be in the Kingdom - which Jesus was just then announcing and demonstrating with signs, wonders and the forgiveness of sins individually. Then, after He fulfilled the law covenant to earn righteousness with God by living sinlessly, He gave Himself to us as a gift on Calvary. Remember: the Law was given through Moses (and could not make **in Adam** sinners righteous). However, grace and truth came to earth in the person of Jesus Christ to bring an eternal *new order* for reborn, **new creation** believers, made righteous by His blood by grace through faith in Him alone (see John 1:17 and Hebrews 9:10).

The juxtaposition of "the Law was given by Moses" vs. "grace and truth came" implies that "truth" was not on the side of law even though it was initiated by God. If the Law embodied truth as the end all and be all like the Pharisees insisted, Jesus would not have opposed them for thinking so. However, Jesus operated by *faith* in His Father's direction, lived out through the Holy Spirit's power, which demonstrated God's grace and truth and *love* that produced *freedom* for those in bondage. The law puts a person who focuses on it under the ever deepening bondage of guilt and condemnation that is meant for unbelievers, *not* for believers who are **in Christ**, according to Romans 8:1. (More detail on this topic is presented in Chapter Fourteen, page 222.)

Again, all but four chapters of the four gospels, as we traditionally call them, were under the **pre-cross** time period of the Mosaic Law – which was given *only* to the Jews - and must be understood that way or wrong conclusions can easily be made. (Many more of these differences will be presented in Chapter Twelve.) Let us rejoice that we believers are under grace and truth, *not* under Moses' Law Covenant. The following scriptures continue to document this revelation.

Released From The Mosaic Law

For if a law had been given that could impart life, then righteousness would certainly have come by the Law. But the Scripture declares that the whole world is a prisoner of sin (**in Adam**), so that what was promised, being given through faith in Jesus Christ, might be given to those who believe" (instead of by obedience to the Law) (Galatians 3:21-22).

Before this (gift of) faith came, we were held prisoners by the law, locked up until faith should be revealed. So the Law was put in charge to lead us to Christ that we might be justified by faith. Now that faith has come, we are no longer under the supervision of the law (Galatians 3:23).

Now we are to be under the supervision of the Holy Spirit if the Spirit lives in you... (Romans 8:9).

But now, by dying to what once bound us (the **in Adam** nature), we have been released from the law so that we serve in the new way of the Spirit, and not in the old way of the written code (the Law) (Romans 7:6).

For **in Jesus Christ**, neither circumcision nor uncircumcision has any value, but faith shown by works of love (Galatians 5:6).

And you, being dead in your sins and the uncircumcision of your flesh, God made you alive with Christ. He forgave us all our sins, having cancelled the written code (The Big Ten) with its regulation that was against us and stood opposed to us. He took it away, nailing it to the cross (and thereby), disarmed the principalities (who use the law as a club of condemnation)… (Colossians 2:13-14).

He (Jesus) has made us able ministers of the **New Covenant** - not of the letter (of the law) but of the Spirit. <u>For the letter kills but the Spirit gives life</u> (2 Corinthians 3:6).

…because through Christ Jesus the "law" of the Spirit of life set me free from the Mosaic Law (that causes) sin and death (Romans 8:2).

How Did All This Happen To Me?
Through the law I died to the law so that I might live for God (an **unseen** transaction) (Galatians 2:19).

I have been crucified with Christ and I no longer live, but Christ lives in me. The life I live in the body, <u>I live by faith in the Son of God</u>, who loved me and gave Himself for me. I do not set aside the grace of God, for if righteousness could be gained <u>through the law,</u> Christ died for nothing (Galatians 2:20-21).

By now it should be crystal clear that life **in Christ** - true Christianity - is not about us working to gain or maintain right-standing with God by law-keeping but about believing in and receiving His free Gift of salvation through Jesus' **finished work.** That is counter-intuitive to the world's system of "no pain, no gain." The difference is because of Adam's rebellion - which changed how things work in the **seen realm.** Before that fatal fall, Adam experienced nothing but God's free gifts of love, acceptance, provision and pleasure - abundantly - by believing, receiving and enjoying them, <u>not by striving for and earning them.</u>

This distinction brings us to one last major point before we move on. Obviously, Adam was not under the Mosaic Law - which came about 2500 years later. But, unfortunately, he put his faith in Satan's word instead of in God's loving warning about eating of the only Tree in the garden that represented *Law*. This was the introduction of the general "principle of law" that put the human race under the curse of law-mindedness, as presented in Chapter Three. God did not put it there for Adam to eat but as a test of trusting faith – because <u>knowing good and evil, per se, was not "good for him"</u>- or for us - in the **big picture.** He and Eve had to be removed from the garden for their own long-term protection - as explained in Chapter Eight. His<u>unbelief</u> led to rebellious disobedience which lost the blessings of living in a perfect world. Instead, he had to strive and toil to provide food for Eve and their family. Wrong believing and mistrusting God's direction leads to wrong living. This is the first instance of the law causing the spiritual death of a man and a woman.

The Letter Kills But The Spirit Gives Life

In other words, he fell from the lofty experience of depending on a loving God's continuously perfect supply – His divine welfare – down to slaving under the dominion of the devil, forcing him to depend on his own imperfect efforts to meet his family's needs. That is the essence of switching from a grace-based life of authority and power **in Christ** - which depends on God's love and provision - to the curse of a law-based focus on morality and independent self-effort, consumed with meeting one's needs and wants. Jesus is the only man that ever lived totally free of that bondage because He was not born **in Adam**. <u>He lived by the higher law of *faith* in His Father's *loving* care through the Holy Spirit who kept Him in the *freedom* of righteousness, peace and joy.</u> He knew that the Mosaic Law was only a shadow of the liberating **New Covenant** He was soon to mediate for us on Calvary.

Now, once again, Jesus is our Tree of Life, the central figure of our **New Covenant** of grace. But we can still spoil His offer of abundant life and blessings, here and now in the **seen realm**, by continuing to choose the **elephant of Galatianism** – instead of resting in the **finished work** of His **divine exchange** as He intends. And, as we shall continue to see in the next chapter, mixing law with grace is a costly deception that robs believers of Jesus' full victory on earth, bought for us by His perfect sacrifice.

This song-poem proclaims who to focus on and why.

JESUS CAME HERE AS A MAN to pay for mankind's sin	Jn. 1:14, Rm.11:27, 1 Jn. 3:5
And bring Man back to Father-God and guide us from within.	Eph. 2:16, Jn. 16:13
The Ten Commandments aren't to be the focus of our faith.	Rm. 7:4, Col. 3:1-4, Heb. 3:1-3
The do's and don'ts of Law arouses sin.	Rom. 3:9 & 4:15 & 7:5-7
The Law brings condemnation onto those who look to it.	2 Cor. 3:9
Relying on the Law will do you in.	Gal. 3:10, 1 Cor. 15:56,
The Law is good but causes death, exposes sin and strife.	Rm 7;12 & 14 & 9-11, 2 Cor. 3:7
In Christ is now a "higher law" - the Spirit who gives life.	Rm. 7:6 & 6:15 & 8:2 & 14 & 3:28
For Jesus kept the Law for us to be our righteousness	Rm. 10:4, Gal. 4:4-7, Heb. 4:15
And gives this gift to all who will believe.	Eph. 2:8-9, Heb. 11:7
The more you know His love for you	Jn. 3:16-17, 2 Cor. 3:16-17,
And what His cross has done,	Eph. 1:3-8 & 2:4-7
The more of who He is you will receive.	2 Cor. 3:18
So, focus on the One who gives His life abundantly	Jn. 10:10
And let him open up your eyes to see <u>reality</u>.	Col. 3:1-3, 2 Cor. 4:18
O King of Life and Mercy, I receive your Liberty.	Gal. 5:1
By faith I take You as God's gift of righteousness for free!!	2 Cor. 5:21, Rm. 5:17, 10:6, 14:17, &
A Sermon Song © Copyright 2009 by Leonard J. Ransil	1 Cor. 1:30

CHAPTER TEN

THE TURNING POINT: JESUS, THE TREE OF LIFE, SET US FREE FROM THE TREE OF LAW

The Mosaic Law vs. the Law Of Christ

Paul took great pains to distinguish between the Mosaic Law and the **"Law of Christ,"** which was an alternate phrase he used to name the <u>higher law</u> of the Spirit of life of the **unseen Kingdom**, as quoted in Galatians 6:2 and 1 Corinthians 9:21 below. This very important insight becomes clear by depending on the Bible to interpret the Bible in these few passages. We have:

1) freedom *from* the Mosaic Law (given only to the Jews), because Jesus:

    a) <u>fulfilled</u> the Law (Matthew 5:17 and Acts 3:18) and then, once fulfilled, He

    b) <u>abolished</u> it in His flesh according to Ephesians 2:15

    c) by <u>nailing it</u> to the cross, according to Colossians 2:14 and finally, in Hebrews 8:13, the Law was declared obsolete #[24] and

2) freedom *from* <u>the principle of the Tree of law</u> for both Jews and Gentiles which Jesus accomplished for all believers when they died to their old, **in Adam** self by faith at rebirth through identification with Jesus on Calvary. Paul makes much of his new-found freedom through Jesus' **grace gospel** in these words:

… Stand fast in the liberty by which Christ has made us free, and do not be entangled again with the yoke (the Law) of bondage. Behold I Paul say unto you, that if you are circumcised, Christ shall profit you nothing. For I declare again to every man that is circumcised, that he is a debtor to do the whole Law (Galatians 5:1-3).

Whosoever of you are justified by the Mosaic Law, then Christ is of no effect (no help) for you; you are <u>fallen from grace</u>. For we, through the Spirit, wait for the hope of righteousness by faith. For, **in Jesus Christ**, neither circumcision nor uncircumcision has any strength, but faith expressed by love (Galatians 5:4-6).

Bear one another's burdens, and, thereby, you will fulfill the **Law of Christ** (Galatians 6:2).

… Though I be free from all, yet I have made myself a servant to all people so that I might win more (to Jesus.) And to the Jews, I became as a Jew, that I might save the Jews. To them that are under the Law (of Moses), (I became) as under the Law, that I might save them that are under the Law; to them that are without Law (the Gentiles), (I became) as without Law - not being without the (Mosaic) Law of God, but <u>under</u> the **Law of Christ** - that I might save them that are without the Law (the Gentiles). … And this I do for the Gospel's sake, that I might partake of it with you (1 Corinthians 9:19-23).

For the sake of clarity, let's contrast the opposites described in these passages:

Under the Mosaic Law	**Under the (higher) Law of Christ-Grace**
1) entangled with a yoke of bondage	1) freedom of Christ
2) circumcision - Christ profits you nothing	2) through the Spirit …
3) a debtor to the whole Law	3) righteousness by faith
4) justified by Law – no benefits from Jesus	4) **in Christ Jesus**, sharing His life
5) fallen from grace	5) faith expressed by Love
	6) bear one another's burdens
	7) to save others for the gospel's sake
	8) a partaker (of God's best) with you.
	9) not *without* the (Mosaic) Law of God (which has its use on unbelievers)

10A   A Basic Covenant Comparison Chart

"But wait a minute. I thought the Law given through Moses was the only Law of God." Friend, it depends upon what covenant period one is living in. We already discussed the Principle of Law represented by the Law Tree in the garden and the harsh realities of the Law that came through Moses. There were various other codes associated with the Torah. It is interesting to note that the Jews have never actively sought converts to Judaism because the Torah prescribes a "righteous path" for Gentiles to follow, known as the "Seven Laws of Noah." They are a set of moral imperatives that, according to the Talmud, were given by God as a binding set of laws for the "children of Noah" – that is, all of humanity.

Maimonides, a respected 12th century Jewish scholar, explains that any human being who faithfully observes these basic moral laws earns a proper place in heaven. The four "laws" that James tried to pass on to the Antioch Gentiles at the Jerusalem council are based on this law code. Likewise, denominations today have their law formulations drawn from parts of the Bible such as the "holiness doctrine" or Canon Law. They all share one thing in common: mankind's fleshy tendency to try to earn God's approval or blessings by one's own efforts. It is the Tree of Law with new leaves.

The Benefits of Law In The Seen Realm

However, there were many advantages in the **seen realm** for the **pre-cross** Israelites living under the Law Covenant as compared with other nations at that time. As long as they obeyed the terms, they were:

1) greatly blessed, given a land flowing with milk and honey,

2) protected from their enemies and harsh climate conditions,

3) treated to a superior life-style through the dietary and hygienic laws etc.,

4) not required to sacrifice their children to false gods and, best of all,

5) blessed to have the true God of the universe manifested in their midst.

But those blessings were dependent on the level of obedience of the high priest and of the people themselves to keep the Ten Commandments and the other 600+ laws perfectly, as we noted above. Rebellion (which they were prone to because they were still **in Adam**) was often met with dire punishments, as prescribed by the specific terms of that covenant. Only God's merciful inclusion of a complex system of animal sacrifices for their continuous sinning, kept them from being justly destroyed. As it was, they suffered humiliating military defeats and sometimes even exile for rejecting God by periodically turning to idols over the course of about fifteen-hundred years.

In contrast, the grace-based covenant, which God gave to Abraham previously, was far better since God did all the work and let Abraham rest and receive His blessings by simply a trusting faith, which God credited to him as righteousness – the same as it had been with Adam before his fall. And, again, Abraham was not punished for doing wrong, even when he fathered Ishmael through Hagar and twice gave his wife, Sarah, to foreign kings to save his own neck. On the contrary, God blessed Ishmael and Abraham was given material blessings by both kings. Why? Because the terms of the covenant he was under were based on God's gifts of grace and mercy, received by faith, not on Abraham's perfect behavior.

The Wonderful Terms of the New Blood Covenant from Jesus

So Jesus' revelation to Paul is that Abraham's covenant was based on the <u>freedom</u> that only grace can give and was, therefore, far better than the <u>unbearable yoke</u> of living under the Mosaic Law - as Peter described it in Acts 15:10. Yet, far better still are the terms of the **New Covenant** which Jesus cut with God on our behalf as our perfect High Priest. This is the **Law of Christ,** according to the **grace-based gospel** of Christ, which totally replaced the covenant of the Mosaic Law - which only Jesus could and did keep on our behalf. This **New Covenant** could also be called the *Covenant of the Higher Law,* which consists of the three key elements that we listed in Chapter Three and are listed in points #1, #3 and #5 in the above comparison of the two covenants, namely freedom, faith and love.

By receiving God's gift of salvation (Jesus) through God's gift of faith, each believer now can enjoy freedom from:

1) bondage to Satan's kingdom,

2) bondage to the Mosaic Law (or from the principle of law-keeping) to remain righteous,

3) slavery to the world system that is based on selfishness,

4) the dominance of one's former sin nature **in Adam** - now crucified and gone and

5) freedom from the control of one's flesh - by choosing to walk according to the Spirit's life in us.

By contrast to the Jews bound to the Mosaic Law, believers now are automatically qualified by Jesus' **finished work** to enjoy the glorious privileges, blessings and inheritance of Jesus' abundant life, through the Holy Spirit. Here are the simple terms of the **New Covenant**, which are in stark contrast with the demanding terms of the Mosaic Covenant, now obsolete for Jewish believers:

> This is the **(New) Covenant** that I will make with the house of Israel, after those days, says the Lord. I shall put My (higher) laws into their minds, and I will write them upon their hearts, and I will be God to them, and they shall be My people. No longer shall a man teach his neighbor or his brother, saying, 'Know the Lord,' because they shall all know Me, from the least to the greatest, <u>because I will be merciful to their unrighteousness, and their sins and their lawless deeds I will remember no more.</u> By saying 'new,' He has made the first (Moses' Covenant) old and <u>obsolete</u> and what is old will soon disappear (Hebrews 8:10-13).

Spelled out, point by point, we see God's marvelous promises to all **New Covenant** believers:

1) "I will put My laws (Christ's higher law of faith, love and liberty) into their mind and write them upon their hearts." This reference to "My laws" can't mean the Big Ten because verse thirteen says the Mosaic Law is now "obsolete." Why would God write something on our heart that is obsolete and was nailed to the Cross (because it arouses sin and causes death)? Paul also speaks of the law of righteousness by faith in Romans 9:30-31 which ties in nicely with "the law of Christ."

2) "I will be God to them" (an Abba-Father of love and mercy, protection and supply).

3) "They shall be My people." (Now, believers are no longer in spiritual union with the devil by being **in Adam** but one with Father-God, as verified in 1 Corinthians 6:17)

4) "They shall all know Me, from the least one to the greatest one of them" (a personal, intimate, Spirit to spirit oneness with the Trinity through rebirth by faith).

5) "I will be merciful to their unrighteousness, and their sins and their lawless behavior I will remember no more." (The permanent forgiveness of all sins for all time, through Jesus' blood, belongs to every believer by being **in Christ**, who *is* our righteousness. This truth is verified in 2 Corinthians 5:19 & 21 and 1 John 2:2)

6) *Therefore:* "… by saying 'new,' He (God) has made the first (covenant of Law) old and obsolete and what is old, will soon disappear."

NOTE: this last line in this prophecy became literally true for Jewish believers in 70 AD when the Jerusalem temple was destroyed by the Romans. Consequently, no more animal sacrifices could be offered for sins. The offering of animals, which was an essential feature of the Mosaic Law for forgiveness of sins, was *replaced forever* with a totally new, grace-based covenant by the blood of the perfect Lamb, Christ Jesus. Glory!

Hallelujah! Gone is the heavy, unbearable yoke - the demands of the Mosaic Law, including the Ten Commandments, on Jewish believers – and the curse of the Tree of Law on all believers. We are now free to focus on Jesus, who met every demand perfectly for all believers and gave us the merit of His obedient life and His righteousness as a free, underserved *gift*. We are now free to gratefully receive and enjoy all the benefits that He has won for all believers. But sadly, many if not most believers have been trained - indoctrinated - to focus on the **elephant of mixture** instead of living the **butterfly life in Christ.** They *mentally* cling to the conflicting terms of these *two diametrically opposed covenants* – just like the infant Jerusalem church did. (See Endnote #**25** for more important information on covenants.) To paraphrase Paul's expression again: this mixture is *no gospel at all*. "I, Paul, say unto you, that if you are circumcised, Christ shall profit you nothing," stated emphatically in Galatians 5:1-3. (His words, not mine.)

A Detailed Comparison Of The Two Opposing Covenants

The next chart (**10B**) greatly expands the basic covenant chart (**10A**) into a much bigger panoramic comparison between the Mosaic Law Covenant of works and Jesus' **New Covenant** of grace in order to thoroughly document just how superior the new one is over the old, obsolete one and also to prove how illogical and frustrating it is to try to mentally live under the foot of the **elephant** that squishes these two opposing covenants together. Seeing them side by side will demonstrate that combining them together actually nullifies both and confuses us about the true nature of God and what true Christianity is founded on – Christ Jesus' **finished work**. You will find much more about this in Chapter Eighteen.

Mosaic Covenant 2 Cor. 3:14	New Covenant 2 Cor. 3:6
Came by Moses John 1:17	Came by Christ Heb. 8:6, 9:15
Fulfilled by Christ Mat. 5:17-18	Now in force Heb. 8:6, 10:9
Ended by Christ Rom. 10:4	Established by Christ Heb. 8:6, 10:9
Abolished at the Cross 2 Cor. 3:13	Continues gloriously 2 Cor. 3:11
Law of sin Rom. 7:5-6	Law of righteousness Rom. 9:30-31
Law of the flesh Rom. 7:5-6	Law of the Spirit Rom. 8:2
Not of faith Gal. 3:2	Law of faith Rom. 3:27
A shadow Col. 2:14-17	The reality Heb. 10:1-18, Col. 2:14
Cannot justify Gal. 2:16	Fully justifies Acts 13:38-39
Law of works Rom. 3:27	Law of grace and faith John 1:17
Brings wrath Rom. 4:15	Saves from wrath Rom. 5:9
Leaves imperfect Heb. 7:19	Makes perfect Heb. 7:19
Powerless to save Heb. 9:9, 10:4	Saves to uttermost Heb. 7:25
Brings a curse Gal. 3:10	Redeems from the curse Gal. 3:13
Exposes sin Gal 3:19	Removes all sin Rom. 4:1-8
God Remembers sins Heb. 10:3	God Forgets sins Heb. 8:12, 10:17
Yearly atonement covers sin Heb. 10:3	Eternal atonement Heb. 10:14
No salvation Heb. 10:2-4	Eternal salvation Heb. 5:9, 10:10
Perfected nothing Heb. 7:19	Perfects believers Heb. 7:19, 10:14
No mercy Heb. 10:28	Complete mercy Heb. 8:12
Entangles Gal. 5:1	Makes free John 8:32, 36
Earthly tabernacle Heb. 9:2	Heavenly tabernacle Heb. 8:2
Imperfect mediator Gal. 3:19	Sinless mediator 1 Tim. 2:5
No inheritance Rom. 4:13	Eternal inheritance Heb. 9:15
Instituted upon animal blood Heb. 9:16-22	Instituted upon blood of Christ Mat. 26-28
Cannot give life Gal. 3:21	Gives abundant life John 6:63-68
Ministration of condemnation 2 Cor. 3:9	Ministration of righteousness 2 Cor. 3:9
Non-redeeming Heb. 10:4	Redeems Gal. 3:13, Heb. 9:12-15
Non-pleasing Ps. 40:6	Pleasing to God Heb. 10:5-18
Ministry of death 2 Cor. 3:7	Reconciliation ministry of life 2 Cor. 5:18
Circumcision Ex. 12:48	No circumcision Rom. 4:9-12

10B An Expanded Comparison Chart of Two Covenants

As already discussed, the Law is of the **seen realm** and so, to the degree that a believer is focused on the Law, to that same degree he is necessarily focused on himself and his sins (and/or probably on other people's sins) instead of on our **unseen** Savior, Christ Jesus, our covenant keeper and justifier. Again, Paul described this as "falling from grace by going back under law" to try to stay right with God. To depend on law-keeping is to *deny* the revelation that believing and receiving the gospel of **Jesus' finished work** is all that is needed to become and remain in right-standing with God. Again, Jesus denounced this common, works-based heresy when He stated through Paul: "The Law is *not* of faith" (Galatians 3:12). "Anything not of faith is sin" (Romans 14:13).

The key to get out and stay out of this double-minded quagmire is to "rightly discern and divide the word of truth:"

1) according to which of the two covenants – Moses' Law Covenant or Jesus' grace-based covenant - were in force at the time of any New Testament passage in question and

2) by determining if the New Testament author was still believing in and, therefore, possibly including elements of the mixture that was erroneously believed and accepted by the Jerusalem church.

(Another way to ask question #2 would be: Does this New Testament passage contradict what Jesus revealed directly to Paul and is, therefore, not the gospel?) If this two-fold test is not consistently applied, falling prey to the **elephant of mixture** is likely, if not inevitable. How else could this destructive heresy have been tolerated, and even pampered in Christendom for some 2000 years?

A Doctrinal Conundrum

The logical, doctrinal question to point #2 would be: "Does that mean that some of these Bible books are not the inspired and inerrant Word of God?" That is an extremely important question and requires a wise, full-orbed answer from a **big picture** perspective.

First of all, as Galatians makes abundantly clear, out of all the authors in the New Testament, Paul is the only author that insists that "his gospel" came directly and only from Jesus and, therefore by implication, was the only whole gospel by which all other New Testament writings must be judged for **New Covenant** saints. Secondly, Peter agreed at the Jerusalem Council in about 50 AD that God gave Paul this gospel and Peter singled out Paul's writings as being "scripture" when he wrote in 2 Peter 3:15-17:

> Bear in mind that our Lord's patience means salvation, just as our dear brother Paul also wrote to you with the wisdom that God gave him. He writes the same way in all his letters, speaking in them of these matters. His letters contain some things that are hard to understand, which ignorant and unstable people distort, as they do the other Scriptures, to their own destruction. Therefore, dear friends, since you already know this, be on your guard so that you may not be carried away by the error of lawless men and fall from your secure position.

Peter admits that Jesus revealed to Paul "some things that are hard to understand." That is because those were the **unseen things** about the **unseen Kingdom** that those steeped in the Law had trouble accepting. Remember, even Paul's superior knowledge of the Law did not equip him to see these **unseen realities** before Jesus revealed them to him in 42 AD. Peter also acknowledged that there were "ignorant and unstable people" distorting Jesus' gospel given to Paul which would bring them to destruction. This may be the reason Peter eventually left Jerusalem and joined Paul in Rome. Peter was willing to be shown the truth of the **whole gospel of grace** but others were not. Otherwise, the Jerusalem church, led by James, would have *immediately* stopped requiring Gentiles in Jerusalem to be circumcised after the council in 50 AD. But, again, the practice continued in the Jerusalem church for another 85 years – until the city was destroyed over that very issue, as we will review in greater detail shortly.

Finally, Peter warned against the possibility of being "carried away by the error of lawless men." This is an ironic statement in three ways. First, it implicitly refuted the objection of some Jews who reasoned that Paul was lawless "because he preached against the Law." As Peter began to understand the "hard things" that Jesus had revealed to Paul, he realized that Jesus' **New Covenant** replaced the Law in favor of the higher law of the Spirit of life, as Paul stated in Romans 8:1-2. Secondly, it was ironic because the leaders in Jerusalem were actually causing the reborn saints in Jerusalem to <u>fall from grace</u> by holding on to much of the obsolete Law. It is an historical fact that the Jewish bishops of Jerusalem were known as the "bishops of the circumcision." (See Endnote **#26** for the names of these early bishops etc.) Thirdly, the practice of circumcision infuriated the hated Romans who, ironically, finally banned the practice which then triggered a Jewish revolt in 133-135 AD.

The Romans retaliated by attacking Jerusalem and banished <u>all Jews</u> from the city under penalty of death if they returned. Unfortunately, the Jewish believers took their mixture with them to other lands. But this officially ended circumcision in Jerusalem and the church continued under Gentile bishops - since Christianity itself was not banned. The Gentile bishops were probably glad to comply with the Roman ban on circumcision for obvious reasons. The Romans then rebuilt the city into a Roman outpost and renamed it Aelia Capitolina. To add insult to injury, they erected temples to their gods in God's holy city.

However, thanks to Paul's insistent stand against the **elephant of mixture**, Jesus' **whole gospel of grace** survived the doctrinal war, though it has never really flourished as God intends. Elephants are hardier than butterflies. Paul was so adamant about what Jesus revealed to him that he told the Galatians that even if an angel from heaven or he himself ever deviated from Jesus' gospel, they were to discount that as heresy – and, therefore, no gospel at all.

Now, as I will prove in Chapter Twelve, the four gospels about Jesus' life, necessarily and understandably include many references to the two opposing covenants. Why? Because it was a time of *transition* of removing the old wineskin and bringing in the new wineskin. So, among the many "new things" in the coming **New Covenant,** reborn saints would become temples of the Holy Spirit living within them, without them bursting apart.

Mixture Explained

"So, because the four gospels have a 'mixture' of references to both covenants, does that mean they are not inspired and are not inerrant?" <u>No, not at all</u>, because they are written records that describe some of the many wonderful events the writers personally witnessed or heard about and remembered and then recorded them, some 30 to 60 years *after* Jesus arose. Many inaccurate statements by people were accurately stated such as "Jesus has a demon" or "He is a blasphemer." The same could be said for other books of the Bible that recorded the events of the Old Testament. They are not "the gospel" that Jesus revealed to Paul, per se, for the majority of them were written during the heyday of the Law - and "the Law is not of faith." But that does not make them less inspired or in error. They were written about different time periods of salvation history for different purposes under many different covenants by many different people who saw things from their unique perspective and insight as God gave revelation progressively for 6000 years. Believers have the Holy Spirit in them who teaches and reveals God's purposes.

Ultimately, all the books in the Bible point to Jesus in various types and shadows but they are also different in many ways from Jesus' culminating revelation to Paul of the **whole gospel of grace**. (Appendix 7 provides a link to a web page that describes how Jesus can be seen in every book of the Bible.) The confusion of mixture comes when believers replace Jesus' **grace-based gospel** revealed to Paul with the four gospels as though these **pre-cross** accounts of Jesus' life on earth are the core and essence of **New Covenant** Christianity. Remember, the **New Covenant** was inaugurated on Calvary - not when Jesus was born.

Since Jesus gave the **whole gospel** revelation only to Paul, and since it was not fully embraced by the Jerusalem church leadership, it stands to reason that there could also be some "mixture" in books written by those leaders of the Jerusalem church – especially since they were writing primarily to the Jews, as agreed upon at the Jerusalem council. They could only write consistently with what they believed and taught progressively at any given time since they were not writing prophecy, per se, but letters to fellow Jewish believers. But remember, by rejecting the full benefit of Jesus' revelation to Paul, these Jewish Christians of that early period still clung to the *heretical requirement* of circumcision, for both Jews and Gentiles, before they could be saved. Also, they chose to still live under some of the other demands of the obsolete Law. As we have already proven in previous chapters, the Law was <u>radically different</u> from the grace-based **New Covenant** that Jesus revealed to Paul.

That fact alone should be reason enough to routinely discern whether any given passage in letters written by the other apostles might contain "mixture" of one degree or another. If they do, it is an accurate snapshot of what they believed at that time, therefore, what they were teaching and writing about. We must keep in mind that Paul insisted that anything that opposed what Jesus revealed to him was not the true gospel. Since what he shared at the Jerusalem council was not fully embraced by James, in particular, <u>we must be alert to any discrepancies that are likely to be found in the letters sent out to Jewish believers during that early time period</u>, while they were still debating over and sorting out the **whole gospel** of Jesus. (That is why we need the Holy Spirit to <u>guide us into all truth as He reveals it</u>.)

In fact, Paul wrote his letter to the Galatians as a warning to them (and to us) to be on alert for mixture from the Judaizers because the deception was affecting his own sheep in Galatia.

Even Peter and Barnabas were guilty of yielding to the influence of mixture embedded in the Jerusalem church under James. Herded together, the "sacred cows" of works-based thinking, which were unwittingly carried over from Judaism, constitute the heresy of Galatianism. It is hard to shake off 1500 years of teaching and tradition that you were formed in from infancy and which is the lifestyle of relatives and friends living around you. None of Jesus' own family or even His disciples began to understand what He was really about until He ascended. And even then, most clung to their old ways. Maybe that is one extra reason why Jesus told his disciples to go into other parts of the world in order to make disciples in all nations. But besides Paul, how many of them and other missionaries since them <u>have taken Jesus' **whole gospel of grace** to the world</u>?

So again, it is important to remember that the other apostles typically taught the **bare bones gospel** rather than the **whole, infallible gospel** according to the glorious revelation from Jesus to Paul that was not known by any man until about 42 AD. In fact, the Holy Spirit is still *progressively* unveiling some of the magnificent depths and riches of Jesus' wondrous **New Covenant** gospel today. He wants to renew our minds to what <u>has been there all along</u> – Jesus' **whole gospel** of His **divine exchange** - but which we have overlooked or not believed or even rejected because we have been embracing the **elephant of mixture** instead of living His **butterfly life of grace** by faith in Him.

This book was written to equip the saints with a clear understanding of Jesus' own **grace-based gospel**, revealed directly to Paul, which is <u>absolutely and *only* what is necessary to be accepted and made righteous forever by God through rebirth</u>. It springs from my own search to seek and find and focus on the **unseen realities** of Jesus' **New Covenant**. This search has continued for more than twenty years of daily repentance - the renewal of my own mind with the **Word of Christ** - to mentally escape from the yoke of bondage from the mixture of law with grace. Walking in the freedom that Jesus purchased for believers requires that we discern a mix of references to opposing covenants - even if it is presented in some New Testament passages, especially (and understandably) in the four gospels. Again, Jesus' **whole gospel** to Paul is to be <u>the plumb line to discern all the other Bible books</u> – not to mention what is being taught today.

However, I do not condemn theologians and pastors and teachers who still believe and teach the web of mixture like I believed in and taught for much of my life - and still can fall prey to occasionally. It is to be expected, given how pervasive this heresy has been for 2000 years and how entrenched it is today. Furthermore, civil societies must have some rules and regulations to maintain peace and order in the **seen realm**. Anarchy and chaos are marks of the devil, not of God. But, in regards to Jesus' gospel of the **unseen realm**, my hope is to alert anyone who has unknowingly esteemed mixture above Jesus' revelation to Paul, that it is the "wood, hay and stubble" that Paul warned against in 1 Corinthians 3:12. It keeps you under a curse which Paul specifically warned against in Galatians 1:8 and <u>repeated</u> in verse 9. It also makes the many benefits of Jesus' **whole gospel** of little or no effect for you while on earth. Why? Because the knowledge of His **unseen Kingdom realities** must be personally reckoned as true and combined with His gift of faith in order to receive to the fullest what Jesus has already done so that we can walk in daily victory in this **seen realm.**

The Leaven Of Mixture

For example, how can you benefit from the revealed truth of God's unconditional love, acceptance and approval of you (because you are truly His reborn child) yet sin-conscious (instead of Jesus-conscious) because you are still Law-conscious? That mental stronghold makes you prone to believe that your acceptability to God is based on your behavior, not on Jesus' **finished work**. And how can you rest in His gift of eternal justification and union with Father-God (see 1 Corinthians 6:17) if you still believe that you must regularly confess your sins to get back in fellowship with God who forgave all your sin even before you were born or saved, according to 2 Corinthians 5:19 and 1 John 2:2? Ignorance or unbelief in Jesus' **finished work** will leave you <u>searching and asking for things that Jesus already gave you as a gift</u>.

And, regrettably, much of the church has been brain-washed to think that the "sinner's prayer" must include a confession of sins to be valid. If so, Paul misquoted Jesus when he wrote Romans 10:9-13 because it includes the confession that Jesus is Lord but *nothing* about confessing one's sins. In fact, you won't find Paul focusing on sin-confession in *any* of his letters because it requires taking your focus off of Jesus and putting it back on your performance – law-keeping. On the contrary, he encourages every believer, in Colossians 3:1-3, to set his mind on the **unseen realities** above, not on himself and his sin. Do you see again how the law/grace mixture gums up the works and causes defeat by diverting your attention from Jesus' **divine exchange** with you, back to law-keeping and self-analysis which actually arouses sin and causes condemnation and even death? How can that be good news?

In Chapter Twelve, we will apply the two point "test," which I presented above, in order to understand, in context, that what Jesus said in the four **pre-cross** gospels sometimes *contradicts* the terms of the **New Covenant** that we examined above. Again, contradictions are to be expected because the *terms of the two opposing covenants* were so drastically different. But first, the next chapter will highlight the many wonderful benefits of the four gospels. They reveal God's loving nature through His merciful redemption plan for mankind. Jesus accomplished all that by His earthly life, ministry, death and glorious victory over sin and death, hell and the grave – all orchestrated for our benefit.

The following song-poem explains what happens at rebirth and how to enjoy it **in Christ Jesus**. The scriptures are there to prove I am not making this wonderful stuff up. It is all great news.

I WAS CRUCIFIED AND BURIED THEN AROSE WITH YOU, Rom. 6:3-4, Col. 2:12, Col. 3:1
Dead to sin, alive to God through You.   Rom. 6:6-7, Col. 3:3,
Reborn by your grace – <u>G</u>od's <u>R</u>ighteousness <u>A</u>t <u>C</u>hrist's <u>E</u>xpense, 1 Pet. 1:23, 1 Jn. 5:18, 2 Cor, 5:18-21
A child of God, now free to worship You.   Jn. 1:12, 1 Jn. 3:1-2, Rom. 8:14-15, &
                                                  Gal.3:26

Thank you Jesus, my Redeemer,   Gal. 3:13, Eph. 1:7, Col.1:14
By your blood You paid for all my sin.   Col. 2:13, 1 Jn. 2:2
One in spirit with my Father,   1 Cor. 6:17, 2 Cor. 5:18, Heb. 2:11
And your Holy Spirit lives within.   1Cor. 3:16, 2 Cor. 1:22, 1 Tim. 1:17

Now triumphant, You are seated next to Father-God,   Eph. 1:20, Heb. 1:3 & 8:1 & 10:12
And, by grace, I'm seated there in You.   Eph. 2:6, Col. 2:12, Col. 3:1, Phil. 3:20
No longer of this world, I'm here to walk by faith in You   1 Pet. 2:11, 2 Cor. 5:7
And let You reign in me to share good news.   Rom. 5:17, Col. 1:12, Heb. 13:16, &

Matt. 28:19

Thank you Jesus, my Salvation 2 Tim. 2:10, Titus 2:11
Condemnation's gone, I'm under grace. Rom. 6:13
Free to love You and to serve You, Gal. 5:1, 2 Cor. 5:14-15
As a holy saint before Your face. Eph. 1:4, 4:24, Heb. 3:1, Eph. 1:1

I am resting in Your **finished work** that's mine through You, Heb. 4:11
Abiding in the life we share above. Jn. 15:4, Eph. 2:6
Your righteousness and peace, enjoying what is good and true, Rm. 14:17, Jn. 10:10, 2 Cor. 5:21, &
Your faithfulness and everlasting love. 1 Cor. 1:9, 1 Jn. 4:8   Phil 4:8

Thank you Jesus, King and Bridegroom, 2 Thes. 3:3
Coming back to catch me up with You. Jn. 3:29
Holy Spirit, my Sanctifier, 1 Thes. 4:16-17, 1 Cor. 15:5
Do within me what You need to do. 1 Pet. 1:2, 2 Thes. 2:13
Sermon Song © Copyright 2009 by Leonard J. Ransil

CHAPTER ELEVEN

THE MAIN PURPOSE AND BENEFITS OF THE FOUR GOSPELS

The Life of Jesus According to Mark, Matthew, Luke and John

Correctly understanding which covenant Jesus lived under in His earthly life has major implications when considering the context, the value and the purpose of the four gospels. Of the eighty-eight chapters of the combined four gospels, only four chapters focus on Jesus' crucifixion, resurrection and beyond – the **New Covenant** era. He did not just coincidentally live during what turned out to be a crucial thirty-three year transition period. Rather, He came down to die in order to *cause* the transition that brought an end to the Mosaic Law Covenant so that He could inaugurate on Calvary the "all things new" covenant of radical grace through His shed blood.

Now, while we thankfully do *not* have the demanding terms of the law covenant that He lived under, there are, of course, still some great benefits that can be gained from reading the four gospels that describe Jesus' life and ministry in the **seen realm**. Note: I say this in spite of Paul's caution in 2 Corinthians 5:16, as mentioned in the last chapter: "to no longer regard Christ from a worldly (natural) viewpoint." I believe that Paul wrote that warning because when a sinner **in Adam** is reborn of God through faith in Jesus' substitutionary sacrifice, he receives a new, re-generated (re-begun) nature and position **in Christ** in the **unseen realm** that no human had ever enjoyed before Calvary. Paul was concerned that believers would yearn to return to that **pre-cross** period again - an impossibility - rather than understand, benefit from and enjoy *all* that Jesus *has done* for believers by His **finished work, post-cross.**

Jesus indicated the coming change in covenants when He said in Matthew 11:11:

> I tell you the truth: among those born of women, there has not risen anyone greater than John the Baptist; yet whoever is least in the kingdom of heaven is greater than him.

Wow! What a game-changing statement. Even the least one that will be in His coming Kingdom - **post-cross** - is better than the greatest human that ever lived **pre-cross** (except for Jesus Himself). That, of course, included even His closest disciples who would eventually become His reborn apostles at Pentecost. Unfortunately, they remained ignorant of the *fullness* of that glorious, **post-cross,** inner transformation until Jesus revealed it to Paul in 42 AD. Consequently, Paul, the former "persecutor of Jesus" (see Acts 9:5) did not live in or yearn for or hold on to the past (like some of the other apostles did) but counted it as rubbish in comparison to knowing and flowing with the Spirit of Christ Jesus who now lived inside of him.

In some ways, it was probably easier for Paul to make a clean break with his past than for those who had walked and talked with Jesus and were probably revered for that experience. The Holy Spirit inspired four men to write separate accounts of Jesus' life, death, resurrection and ascension for our instruction and edification. *But*, we should **not conclude** that Jesus' use of and fulfillment of the law while He lived on earth proves that we should mix law with grace now.

Why? Because Jesus strongly warned against that deception through Paul in Galatians. We will also see Jesus' strong rebukes about that in John's gospel below.

Our Loving Abba-Father

Perhaps the greatest overall benefit of the four gospels is that they provide a tangible picture of Father-God's true nature of love and mercy. As we shall prove below, Jesus lived His life in direct connection and obedience to His Father-God and, consequently, mirrored God's heart for a fallen, hurting mankind, still lost **in Adam**. He called them "sheep without a shepherd." Worse yet, because they were **in Adam**, they were sheep under the spiritual dominion of the devil - the wolf who is an enemy of the good Shepherd, Jesus Christ. As I stated earlier - and this cannot be said too often - the Mosaic Covenant of law was given to reveal man's true nature, not God's! The sometimes terrifying images of God's just actions, (under the demanding terms of the law covenant), all too often leave a residue of false impressions about our loving Father-God when the Word is not divided correctly - according to what *covenant terms* were in force at that time. This revelation is too important to miss so let's briefly review again how it plays out in the Bible.

For example, God offered a free, grace-based covenant to Abram which he received by faith apart from any works. God counted his response as righteousness – right-standing with God – given as a free gift (see Genesis 15:6). (See Endnote #**27** for more important insights on this key revelation.) Even though Abraham later lied to King Abimelech about his wife in order to save his own neck, God did not condemn him or take back the gift of right standing for his "sin" but actually defended him before the king (who did no intentional wrong). He not only got Sarah back but was enriched by the very king who he had deceived. He even prayed for Abimelech who was healed. That is a vivid example of how a grace-based covenant operates. Since it is God's free gift, it can only be received and sustained by faith in God, not by faith in one's efforts (see Genesis 12:14-20 and 20:2-18).

The terms of the Mosaic Covenant were based on the exact opposite dynamic. Righteousness was not a free gift but a reward earned by good behavior and lost by bad behavior until the sin of the individual – or the nation - was acknowledged and forgiven through the sacrifice of substitutionary animals. Under this law-entrenched covenant, the wages of sin was death, which God mercifully allowed to be paid by the shedding of the life blood of an animal - except for serious, intentional actions such as killing someone. In that case, "an eye for an eye or a tooth for a tooth" was required. Punishment of some form had to follow sin *because* the terms of that covenant required it. If God ignored the terms, He would be breaking the covenant and He would be unjust. The sacrificial system was a way to provide a modicum of grace so that God's desire to manifest His holy presence in the midst of sinful people could be justly accomplished. But, as we saw before, God did not offer this covenant to be mean and punitive but to demonstrate the depravity of mankind's **in Adam** nature – and, therefore, man's need for a personal savior.

Again, under the terms of our grace-based **New Covenant**, which God made with Christ Jesus for anyone who believes it and receives it, all of God's wrath and just punishment for sin has been received and paid for in the body of Christ Jesus, the perfect Lamb. In fact, He paid all the wages of all sin for all mankind for all time on Calvary. His righteousness in God, which He earned through perfect obedience while on earth, also belongs to every believer because he is **in**

148

Christ, the last Adam. The terms of this **New Covenant** (as we saw in Chapter Ten) even state that, because of Jesus' **finished work**, God no longer remembers "their sins and lawless acts," according to Hebrews 10:17. That, my friend, is total grace from a loving Father-God.

Clearly, God's two **grace-based covenants** that were cut with 1) a prefigurement of Jesus on Abraham's behalf and 2) the man Jesus on our behalf, are poles apart from the law-based covenant with Moses and the Israelites. *Ignoring that key insight can easily result in warped concepts about God that mirror the devil's lies about God in Eden.* (The differences between the last two covenants are extreme enough that some heretics in the past concluded that there must be two distinct Gods – the cruel God of the Old Testament as opposed to Jesus, the loving God of the New Testament.) Again, any mixture of the terms of two opposing covenants is not the true**, grace-based gospel** of Christ Jesus. We will do a detailed comparison of the five major covenants in Chapter Eighteen to make clear how God chooses to interact with mankind.

Emmanuel – God With Us

For much of my life, I labored under conflicting concepts of God due to a confusion about the covenants etc. Then I realized that the best evidence of God's true nature is revealed by looking at the personality and life of Jesus who "… is the reflection of God's glory and the exact likeness of God's being …." (Hebrews 1:3a), and who is "… the image of the invisible God," (Colossians 1:15). Of course, this description refers to Jesus' loving nature and servant-heart, not necessarily to His physical appearance, per se. Jesus Himself underscored this union with God when Philip asked Him to show them His Father:

> … I have been with all of you for a long time. Don't you know Me yet, Philip? Anyone who has seen Me has seen the Father. So how can you say, 'Show us the Father?' Don't you believe that <u>I am in the Father and the Father is in Me? What I'm telling you doesn't come from Me. The Father, who lives in Me, does what He wants</u>. Believe Me when I say that I am in the Father and that the Father is in Me (John 14:9-11).

Again, it is all about believing in God's **unseen Kingdom realities,** which He graciously reveals to those who seek Him, rather than about relying on our limited perception of the **seen realm.** But Philip was not yet reborn of God, therefore his concept of God was formed primarily by the demands of Mosaic Law which today comprises over 90% of the Protestant version of the Old Testament. While we now know from Jesus' gospel why the Law Covenant was given, they lacked that **big picture** revelation. So, overall, God's displays of wrath and His just punishment of the Israelites - based on their vacillating levels of obedience to the law - was the exact opposite of how Jesus related to them. From that perspective, their unbelief in Jesus, who was equating Himself with God, is certainly understandable. The point is, even though Jesus lived with them in the **seen realm**, God's gift of faith was still necessary for them to regard Him - while in human form as a man - as God's Son, manifested in the **seen realm**.

Walking By Faith

The same is true for everybody, from Adam to the last baby yet to be born. All must walk by faith in God's **unseen** truth of His Word, instead of relying on **seen** "facts," in order to see, enter and enjoy God's **unseen Kingdom** by faith. Even Jesus, as a man, walked this earth depending on the voice of His good, loving Father – a walk of trusting-faith right through His horrible death, believing that His Father would raise Him back to life. And God's goodness and faithfulness prevailed over Satan's attempt to eradicate, by crucifixion, mankind's only means of salvation from eternal condemnation and punishment, when God raised Jesus out of the grave. And it is this monumental miracle of salvation, which is offered to all mankind, that the four gospels testify about and document - for all of mankind's instruction and benefit. That alone should erase all doubts about Father-God's goodness and love for mankind in general and for believers personally.

Taken as a whole, the four gospels weave a tapestry of "when, where, why and how" Jesus accomplished the greatest feat of human history – though He looked like a colossal failure on Good Friday. Even His resurrection did not fully explain *everything* that He had accomplished by these dramatic events. And the disciples were again disappointed when Jesus ascended into heaven - once again shattering their expectations of His earthly triumph over Rome etc. However, the light of truth began to dawn on them, starting at Pentecost. They, too, were baptized in the Holy Spirit like Jesus had been and experienced signs and wonders.

But until Jesus' revelation to Paul in about 42 AD, much of what Jesus had actually accomplished at Calvary remained hidden to them. It was beyond comprehension that His humiliating death had actually reconciled <u>all</u> of mankind to the holy and just God of the Israelites - from His viewpoint. The God that gave the Law to Moses, with its harsh realities, was the same loving and merciful Abba-Father who sent Jesus to fulfill and replace it with a new and living way to Himself - Christ Jesus - despite the excruciating pain and cost to both of them. But given the abominable mess Adam got us into, it was God's divine way to justly ransom and redeem a family that He desires to be with Him forever.

Jesus' Victory Is Our Victory
The four gospels also demonstrate God's almighty power over His enemies, the fallen angels, who conspired to destroy God's plan for mankind, only to have the tables turned on them at Calvary. Satan tried to destroy Jesus' mission earlier killing infants in Bethelem and by tempting Him in the desert, only to be thwarted by this perfect Man's faith in His Father, though weakened by hunger. He passed the test that the first Adam had failed so He proved to be our true Champion. He also delegated His **pre-cross**, God-given authority and power over demons and diseases to His **in Adam** disciples. Then He sent them out to preach about the coming **unseen Kingdom** of God and to heal the sick to back up their statements (see Luke 9:1-2).

Jesus, Friend Of Sinners
Also, the four gospels show unequivocally that Father-God truly loves **in Adam** sinners or else He would not have sent His best gift to earth to take our place and punishment. Jesus demonstrated this even before He reconciled mankind (from God's point of view) at Calvary. Everyone was automatically an **in Adam** sinner by nature when He lived among them. Nonetheless, He befriended them, healed many, forgave their sins on a case by case basis, shared His Father's wisdom with them, fed them and even ate with them. He saw and met their spiritual and physical needs despite the rigid culture of the Law Covenant. He confined His ministry primarily to the Jews rather than going on extensive missionary journeys to the Gentiles – which He told His followers to do later, according to Matthew 28:19.

150

The Basic Conflict of Opposing Covenants Is Demonstrated

But we also see Jesus' pointed rebuke to those who insisted on staying law-minded rather than grace and truth–minded. They viewed the system that Moses handed down to them as superior to anything or anyone else – including the One standing in front of them. Consequently, holding on to and trusting in a **seen realm** system of rules, prevented them from seeing the Messiah by using God's gift of faith.

Law-dependent living always seems more reasonable, reliable, practical, predictable, stable and controllable than the give-and-take dynamics of relationship – especially with an **unseen** God. And here was a man claiming to be the Son of God yet breaking their cherished Sabbath rules and challenging their entrenched traditions which the Pharisees routinely used to put themselves into a comfortable position of power and prestige. The law was there to show them their rotten nature. But they used it to cover it over with a veneer of self-righteous actions that appeared to be "holy." Jesus' public rebukes were the first tangible indication from God that this "system," by which they were trying to gain and maintain right-standing with God by their own doing, would become obsolete for Jewish believers – after He fulfilled it.

Jesus gave many parables of how the coming **unseen** Kingdom would operate – which was very different from their way of thinking. What Jesus could see and hear and draw from through the Holy Spirit remained hidden to them, all because they could not "see" or "enter" without being reborn of God. So Jesus' parables stirred a spectrum of responses, depending on what pre-conceived agendas and mind-sets they each had. Even the disciples, who were closest to Jesus, expected Him to establish an earthly kingdom and make them overseers. Consequently, they were thoroughly disillusioned at His death. Their faith was **seen-focused**, looking for what He would do to improve their status in the **seen realm**. The four gospels tell it like it was for Jesus to live among fallen humans and put up with their selfishness in all forms, yet love them anyhow. Jesus is the gracious heart of Father-God on parade.

Much has been written to explain the unique purpose and style that each author of the four gospels had in presenting Jesus' life. Together, they provide rich insight into God's **big picture** of why He sent His only Son to earth, so there is no need to examine those different slants in detail here. Suffice it to say that the three gospel books of Matthew, Mark and Luke are called "synoptic" gospels because they are similar in many respects and, taken together, offer a fuller picture of the day to day life and ministry of Jesus while on earth than if looked at individually. Yet each has a different emphasis and degree of detail. Many scholars agree that Matthew emphasizes the Kingdom; Mark presents Jesus in a servant role; Luke in a fellowship role. For our purposes, we will take note in the next chapter of examples of the intertwined passages of law and grace found in these synoptic gospels.

From An Unseen Source

However, the gospel of John is substantially different from the other three books because John offers a more intimate and penetrating presentation of Jesus in His **unseen** relationship with Father-God and the impact of the Holy Spirit living in Him while on earth. This **unseen** dimension of relationship is what Jesus came to make available to all believers, **post-cross.** John also portrays Jesus as much more bold in stating and proving His divine linkage and authority than do the authors of the synoptic gospels. John's unique slant deserves special attention here because, in his book, Jesus' words unveil more of the workings of His Father's **unseen realm** rather than focusing on law-keeping in the **seen realm** like the Pharisees were pre-occupied with.

Instead of starting with Jesus' genealogy or His birth or the birth of His cousin, John the Baptist, John first presents some **unseen** dimensions of Jesus as the Word of God, creator of all and the life of God, coming as a man to give eternal life and light to a race of rebels who are dead to God and lost in Darkness. This was not about what man could do for God (try to obey the law) but what God would do for any person who would just believe and receive what God offered through Jesus – including becoming a child of almighty God Himself. And before the end of Chapter One, John reveals Jesus as the "Lamb of God who takes away (not just covers) the sin of the whole world," the Messiah, the Son of God and the King of Israel who is baptized with the Holy Spirit. (See Endnote **#28** for an important clarification.) The dramatic explosion of all this revelation of Jesus' unique identity, sets the stage for presenting a wealth of the marvelous words and works of the world's Savior who was a willing representative and faithful *expression* of His loving Father while He lived among us on earth.

John continues to enlarge this theme of Jesus' intimate connection to His **unseen** Father-God throughout the book by recounting Jesus' own words about Himself, such as:

John 3:31: The One (Jesus, speaking about Himself) Who comes from above is above all. The one who is from the earth belongs to the earth and speaks as one from the earth. The One who comes from heaven is above all.

John 8:42: I came from God and now am here. I have not come on my own but He sent me.

John 5:39: By myself I do nothing. I judge only as I hear and My judgment is just, for I seek not to please Myself but Him Who sent Me.

John 5:19: I tell you the truth, the Son can do nothing by Himself; He can only do what He sees His Father doing because, whatever the Father does, the Son also does.

John 10:37-38: If I do not do the works of my Father, do not believe in Me. But if I do them, even if you are not willing to believe in Me, believe the works, so that you may know and believe that the Father is in Me, and I am in the Father.

John 6:38: For I have come from heaven not to do My will but to do the will of Him who sent me.

John 7:16: My teaching is not My own. It comes from the One Who sent Me.

John 8:23: You are from below; I am from above. You are of this world; I am not of this (**seen**) world.

John 10:30: I and the Father are one.

John 8:47: He who belongs to God hears what God says.

John 6:46: No one has seen the Father except the One (Jesus) who is from God. Only He has seen the Father.

John 3:12: I have spoken to you of earthly things and you do not believe Me; how, then, will you believe if I speak of heavenly (**unseen**) things.

John 8:55: Though you do not know Him (God), I know Him. … I do know Him and I keep His word.

John 18:36: My Kingdom is not of this world. If it were, My servants would fight to prevent My arrest by the Jews. But My Kingdom is from another place.

John 3:13: No one has ever gone into heaven except the One Who came from heaven – the Son of Man.

John 14:3: I am going there to prepare a place for you (His believers). I will come back and take you with Me so that you may also be where I am. (Note: This promise was fulfilled spiritually in Ephesians 2:16.)

While these and other passages reveal Jesus' oneness with Father-God, a few also point out that mankind is not of the same sphere that Jesus came from and that is precisely why we all need a savior. We were created to live in that **unseen**, heavenly sphere and be compatible with God but Adam's fall disconnected mankind from God spiritually - as explained previously. So John unveils God's solution and the means to that solution: it is to offer the same oneness with God that Jesus enjoys and that He prayed for so that all who believe <u>in Him</u> can share His life, as stated in John 17:21. The means is by sheer grace through faith in Jesus' **finished work** at the cross (not obedience to the law) which is freely given to humans through the miracle of rebirth that Jesus described to Nicodemus in John 3:3-6:

In reply (to Nicodemus) Jesus declared, 'I tell you the truth, no one can see the (**unseen**) Kingdom of God unless he is born again.' 'How can a man be born when he is old?' Nicodemus asked. 'Surely he cannot enter a second time into his mother's womb to be born!' Jesus answered, 'I tell you the truth, no one can enter the (**unseen**) Kingdom of God unless he is born of water and the Spirit. Flesh (of natural human beings) gives birth to flesh, but the (**unseen**) Spirit gives birth to (regenerates a dead-to-God) spirit.

Of the four books, John's gospel is the clearest **pre-cross** forerunner of the true **gospel of grace** that Jesus would later reveal to Paul in its fullness to share with the other believers in Jerusalem – including John. For example, being "born again" to see and enter an **unseen Kingdom** was certainly a revolutionary concept for the Jews to swallow. They were still **in Adam** and they focused on Moses' performance-based law system as a sure means to righteousness. Consequently, they were unable to personally experience the **unseen realm** - apprehended by faith - that Jesus lived from and which even Abraham had enjoyed to a limited degree.

If anyone there had been attuned to the drastic difference between the two opposing covenant "systems," they could have sensed the transition from the Mosaic Covenant to the **New Covenant**, signaled by the many comments of Jesus that John reports in his book. The way Jesus freely related to His Father was the new and living way of a grace-based relationship between God and reborn saints which was soon to replace the way of the law that causes death. As Paul put it succinctly in Romans 8:2 "… the (higher) law of the Spirit of life set me free from the (Mosaic) law of sin and death."

The Law Is Not Of Faith – The New Covenant Is

The Holy Spirit, testifying through John, wastes no time in implying a dichotomy between Moses' covenant of law and the coming covenant of grace that Jesus embodied when John wrote in John 1:17: "For the law was given through Moses; grace and truth came through Jesus Christ." This is a monumental declaration that defines the battle lines between the rigidity of the law-minded Jews versus the relational-based flow of our grace-minded Savior who would soon usher in a new, eternal, blood-covenant that manifests the truth of who God really is. The Pharisees argued that the true way was Moses. But Jesus presented Himself as the only true way to God, His Father, by saying:

> … I am the way, the truth and the life. No one comes to the Father except through Me (John 14:6).

> If you hold to My teaching (not to the law) … you will know the truth (which they thought they already knew) and the truth will set you free (from the curse of the law) (John 8:31b-32).

> But when He, the Spirit of truth, comes, He will guide you into all truth (John 16:13).

> (Father) Sanctify them (the disciples) by the truth; Your word is truth (John 17:17).

All this implies that the law was not identical to the total truth - which Jesus represented and presented - which He would later send the Holy Spirit to teach them, **post-cross.** It is He, the Spirit of truth, who sanctifies while the law only condemns. It is He who sets free through the truth of Jesus' **finished work,** while the law is powerless to help and actually arouses sin and causes death, as already explained in Chapter Nine.

John also records Jesus' on-going verbal battle with the Jewish leaders who were bent on defending Moses and the law system that he had mediated between God and the Israelites 1500 years before. This was a fitting juxtaposition because Jesus was sent by God to be the new mediator between God and all humankind. This was another reason why the law had to be removed because it was a barrier, a "dividing wall of hostility," between the Jews and Gentiles, according to Ephesians 2:14. The hostility, in part at least, came from the prideful superiority the Jews felt over the Gentiles who did not have the benefit of any covenant with God. (Of course, it was an unfounded pride because the Jews did not keep the law covenant – let alone originate it.) Over time, the exchanges between Jesus and the Jewish leaders became increasingly heated each time they accused Him of breaking the law or having a demon. Finally, when Jesus claimed to be one with God (though He operated here as a man), their anger boiled over. Blinded by the law, their response was *death* – "crucify Him" – not *life*. The following is a flow of verses that describes their progressive hostility.

> The Jews persecuted Jesus because He was doing these things (healing people) on the Sabbath (John 5:36).

> Some of the Pharisees said, 'This man is not from God, for he does not keep the Sabbath.' But others asked, 'How can a sinner do such miraculous signs?' So they were divided (John 9:16).

> (Jesus said) 'Has not Moses given you the law? Yet not one of you (Jews) keeps the law. Why are you trying to kill me (break the law by killing an innocent man)?' 'You are demon-possessed,' the crowd answered. 'Who is trying to kill you?' Jesus said to them, 'I did one miracle, and you are all astonished. Yet, because Moses gave you circumcision … you circumcise a child on the Sabbath. Now if a child can be circumcised on the Sabbath so that the Law of Moses may not be broken, why are you angry with me for healing the whole man on the Sabbath? Stop judging <u>by mere appearances</u> (by the law, based on the **seen realm**), and make a right judgment (according to God's perspective) (John 7:19-24).

Jesus got His direction from Father-God, not from the law, so the "right judgment" He referred to was acting according to the higher law of faith, love and liberty - not according to the Mosaic Law, per se.

Moses Versus Jesus
The Pharisees declared in John 9:28: "We are disciples of Moses."

> (Jesus said) 'You diligently study the (Old Testament) Scriptures because you think that by them you possess eternal life. These are the Scriptures that <u>testify about Me</u>, yet you refuse to come to Me to have life (even though they had the Law)… but I know you. I know that <u>you do not have the love of God in your hearts</u>. I have come in My Father's name, and you do not accept Me … But do not think I will accuse you before the Father. Your accuser is Moses, <u>on whom your hopes are set</u> (not on God, whom they do not know). If you believed Moses, you would believe Me, <u>for he wrote about Me</u>. But since you do not believe what he wrote, how are you going to believe what I say?' (John 5:39-47)

What a shocking, public indictment against the law-minded Jews who were harassing Him. Actually, Jesus did them a great service by pointing out that what they were depending on (diligently studying Moses' law-based covenant) for receiving eternal life was futile. It did not produce a love for God in their hearts. And, ironically, the one that they were depending on, Moses, would actually be their accuser because they missed the focal point and purpose of what he wrote about – to reveal Jesus as Messiah who would come to provide eternal life. So, their wrong believing produced wrong living, even though they were sure it was "right living" as moral law-keepers.

Christianity is *not* about focusing on "right morals" per se. It is about a right relationship with God, offered with His unearned gift of righteousness. Whenever Jesus is received and depended on, "right morals" come as a by-product - the fruit of a Spirit-led life in Christ Jesus. Put simply, God's grace-based covenant is about His performance (never the believer's) in which the believer puts his confidence. Again, if he puts confidence in his own behavior – good or bad – he is under the curse of Galatianism – the **elephant of mixture**.

In your own Law it is written that the testimony of two men is valid (John 8:17).

Notice, Jesus said "In your own law" not "in my Father's law." He distances Himself from the law because He knows that after He fulfills it, it *should* no longer be the focus of attention for any **New Covenant** Jewish believers. Instead, He, the glorified Lamb of God, along with all that He has accomplished for mankind, will rightly be the center of attention for all eternity. But, instead of making Jesus their new focus, the Jews cited Abraham and even God as their Father, trying to justify themselves by their heritage. Of course, Jesus knew they really needed Him, because He is the only way to God - not Moses or Abraham. But Jesus shocks them with His revelation of who their father really is – because they are still **in Adam** – even though they "know the law." But He knew from His Father's revelation "what was in a man" - the fallen, **in Adam**, nature (see John 2:25). So, John writes:

> To the Jews who had believed Him, Jesus said, 'If you hold to My teaching, you are really My disciples. Then you will know the truth (as opposed to the Law which they already knew), and the truth will set you free (by being reborn **in Christ**).' They answered him, 'We are Abraham's descendants and have never been slaves of anyone. How can you say that we shall be set free?' (Remember: They did not know they were **in Adam** and, therefore, under the dominion of **unseen** Darkness.) Jesus replied, 'I tell you the truth, everyone who sins (**pre-cross**)is a slave to sin. Now a slave has no permanent place in the family, but a son belongs to it forever. So if the Son (Jesus, referring to Himself) sets you free, you will be free indeed.'

> 'I know you are Abraham's descendants... (But) If you (really) were Abraham's children,' said Jesus, 'then you would do the things Abraham did. As it is, you are determined to kill Me, a Man Who has told you the truth that I heard from God. Abraham did not do such things. You are doing the things your own father does.' 'We are not illegitimate children,' they protested. 'The only Father we have is God himself.' Jesus said to them, 'If God were your Father, you would love Me, for I came from God .... You belong to your father, the devil, and you want to carry out your father's desire (to kill

Jesus). He was a murderer from the beginning, not holding to the truth, for there is no truth in him. ... He who *belongs* to God hears what God says (rather than being focused on the law). The reason you do not hear is that <u>you do not belong to God</u> (through rebirth) (John 8:31-37, 40-42, 44 and 47).

The difference is unmistakable. Only when one "belongs to God" can he then love God. Until one belongs to God by rebirth, he belongs to the devil, no matter what his earthly heritage is. Why? Because there are only two Kingdoms in the **unseen realm** and, as Jesus told Nicodemus earlier: "You *must* be born of the Spirit (not just physically) to see and enter My Kingdom" (a capsule summary of John 3:3-8). Of course, they could not "belong to God" yet because they were all still **in Adam** in this **pre-cross** scenario. But the implication is that if they later became "born of God," **post-cross**, it would be His voice that they were to listen for and obey by the Spirit rather than focus on the limited and limiting law. Why? "For the letter (of the law) kills but the Spirit gives life" (2 Corinthians 3:6). (This distinction harkens back to Adam's choice between eating from the Law Tree vs. the Tree of Life – Jesus.) The heated exchange continued:

> (Jesus said) 'I tell you the truth, if anyone keeps My word, he will never see death.' ... At this the Jews exclaimed, 'Now we know that You are demon-possessed! Abraham died and so did the prophets, yet You say that if anyone keeps your word (not the Law, per se), he will never taste death. Are you greater than our father Abraham? He died, and so did the prophets. Who do you think You are' (John 8:51-53)?

We now know that by saying "My word" Jesus did not mean the Law for He often "broke their perception of the Law" which scandalized and alienated those who chose to honor the law above Jesus. This phrase also demonstrates that "keeping His word" was not the same thing as "keeping the Law" because the latter has no guarantee that a law-keeper "will never see death." On the contrary, the law causes death because no one (but Jesus) can keep it perfectly, which is required for works-based righteousness. In effect, Jesus jerked away the rug of the law they were standing on and then stunned them again with verse 58: "I tell you the truth, before Abraham was born, I Am." That was just too much. They trusted and believed what their five senses told them instead of listening to and heeding His revelation regarding His **unseen** origins. Therefore, they rejected Him who *is* eternal life. Knowledge of the law is no substitute for knowing Him, just as Paul had discovered at his own conversion. In fact, their dependency on the law blinded them from knowing Jesus accurately, as this passage reveals:

> 'Has any of the rulers or of the Pharisees believed in Him (Jesus)? No! But this mob - that knows nothing of the law - there is a curse on them' (John 7:48-49).

How ironic is that! According to Jesus' revelation to Paul: "All who rely on the law are under a curse, for it is written 'cursed is everyone who does not do everything written in the book of the law'" (Galatians 3:10). If they had been honest with themselves, they would have realized that the law automatically puts them under a curse, according to its terms because they could not - and therefore did not - keep it perfectly. That revelation could have caused them to seek the world's Savior – like the law is meant to do. Instead, it blinded them. It is only those who repented – changed their mind regarding Jesus' identity and focused on Him instead of the Law - who actually received His reward. But the confrontation got even uglier:

He who hates Me hates My Father as well. If I had not done among them what no one else did, they would not be guilty of sin. But now they have seen these miracles, and yet they have hated both Me and My Father. But this is to fulfill what is written *in their law*: 'They hated me without reason" (John 15:23-25).

As soon as the chief priests and their officials saw Him (Jesus), they shouted, 'Crucify! Crucify!' But Pilate answered, 'You take Him and crucify Him. As for me, I find no basis for a charge against Him." The Jews insisted, "We have a law (given only to the Jews), and according to that law He must die, because He claimed to be the Son of God (John 19:6-7).

So why are "Gentile" believers *today* typically under so much law if it was not given to them originally but only to the Jews? Again, it is because the **elephant** was first unknowingly accepted, then promoted and defended by the Jewish Christians in Jerusalem as documented in the Book of Acts. Then, when Jesus revealed His **whole gospel of grace** to Paul in 42 AD, it was not fully embraced by the leaders of the Jerusalem church – just like Jesus' **pre-cross** word to the Pharisees was not believed in and received.

The Alternative to Law - Hearing His Voice

And so it still is today, unfortunately, because long held traditions of men are often valued more than Jesus' **whole gospel of grace**. I was steeped in these traditions for over half of my life and learned the hard way that: "the law kills but the Spirit gives life," according to 2 Corinthians 3:6.

(Jesus said) 'I am the good shepherd; I know My sheep and My sheep know Me - just as the Father knows Me and I know the Father - and I lay down My life for the sheep. I have other sheep (non-Jews) that are not of this sheep pen. I must bring them also. They too will listen to My voice (not the Law, for only the Jews were given the Law), and there shall be one flock and one Shepherd' (John 10:14-16).

Again, I suggest that you do what I do – to invite the Holy Spirit of truth to continually *renew your mind* by triumphing over and replacing any remnant of the dangerous **elephant of mixture** with Jesus' pure **gospel of radical grace**. The song-poems found at the end of many chapters of this book have greatly helped me do just that - so I included them in this book for your benefit.

The Obedience Of Faith vs. Obedience To Law

Another significant difference in John's gospel from the synoptic gospels is the Holy Spirit's emphasis on faith in the **unseen** promises of Jesus about the coming **New Covenant**. This is obvious by just comparing the number of times the following words are attributed to which writers as listed in the *NIV Strongest Concordance*. John uses faith-based words about the **unseen realm** almost 1/3 more times than the other 3 writers combined. Here is the breakdown:

UNSEEN Focus in John's gospel		UNSEEN Focus in other 3 gospels	
"BELIEVE" in John's Gospel	55	in the other three combined	31
"BELIEVES" in John's Gospel	13	in the other three combined	3
"BELIEVED" in John's Gospel	19	in the other three combined	2
"FAITH" in John's Gospel	7	in the other three combined	33
Totals: in John's Gospel	94	in the other three combined	69
Number of chapters in John's	21	in the other three combined	68
Average per chapter in John's	4.5	in the other three combined	1

11 A A Comparison of The Four Gospels

So, John's gospel highlights the dynamic of *believing in the **unseen realm*** over four times more <u>per chapter</u> than the other three gospels combined. In the book of Romans, the word "faith" is listed 40 times. It is not that Jesus did not talk about the **unseen Kingdom** in the other three gospels but He did so <u>descriptively</u>, using parables to 1) describe what it is like and 2) declare that it was *going to come*. But John's emphasis was on what is necessary to *enter* and then to *participate* in that **unseen Kingdom** - faith. We enter by *rebirth* through faith, as Jesus told Nicodemus. We *participate* by being made one with Jesus, which He prayed for just before He died: "Father, make them who believe in Me, one **in Me** as I am one in You" (John 17:21). When you are **in Christ,** the King of kings, you are in God's Kingdom 24/7/365 and the Kingdom is also in you because a king's kingdom is wherever the king lives.

God's emphasis on simply *believing* and *receiving* - a living faith - is what all of God's grace-based covenants are founded on and by which Abraham was made righteous. Again, in contrast, the Mosaic Covenant is not based on faith in God's performance but on one's own performance for righteousness and that is why it had to be replaced to make way for another, far better covenant. The **New Covenant** is a gift offered to anyone who chooses to believe in Jesus' perfect, substitutionary performance, done *for* them. This faith-emphasis is the key to entering into and living by the <u>higher law of the Spirit of Life</u> through <u>faith</u> that operates by <u>love</u> and lived in <u>liberty</u> – apart from one's own lifeless works.

It is for freedom that Christ set us free…. The only thing that counts is faith, expressing itself through love…. So, I say, live *by the Spirit* (not by the Law) and you will not gratify the desires of the flesh (Galatians 5:1a, 6b and 16).

Man's self-sufficient flesh likes to glory in its own accomplishment, independent of God, and fights to hold on to the supposed need for the law. But the Lord does not participate in glorifying one's flesh, which wars against the spirit of a believer. Only Jesus' **gospel of lavish**

grace through faith, enables believers to manifest God's glorious nine fruits of the Spirit - which reveal and glorify God. Chapter Nineteen presents more on this very important topic.

James On The Fringe

Jesus' half-brother, James, did not travel with Jesus during His public ministry so he did not personally witness Jesus' verbal battles with the Pharisees. Again, according to historical accounts, James was apparently committed to a Nazarite spirituality and life-style that focused on keeping the law even more strictly than the Pharisees. He spent much time in the Temple and so did not witness these exchanges that clearly point out Jesus' opposing view with the Jews over the purpose of the law and its dangers for those who rely on it for righteousness. But James probably heard about these skirmishes from his Pharisee friends.

As was clear from his words and actions later on, James remained sympathetic to the Pharisees' biased pre-disposition towards the law and enforced some of it in the Jerusalem church when he became its leader. Regrettably, apparently John did not speak up and stand with Peter and Paul at the Council to resist James' insistence on giving the little yoke of "four token laws" to the Gentiles under Paul. Therefore, it is likely that John, himself, had not yet fully understood the implications of Jesus' battle with the law-minded Jews, **pre-cross**. But he did so later when he wrote what we now call "John's gospel" in about 87 AD.. It all became much clearer to him as he received what Paul and/or the Holy Spirit taught him over time about the necessity of rebirth etc..

The Birth Of The Elephant

Unfortunately, James obviously did not recognize who Jesus really was, **pre-cross** (unlike John the Baptist) and so he was not discipled by Jesus. Because he was a Nazarite from birth, the Pharisees endorsed James as an especially "holy" man and called him "James the Just." Under the Mosaic Covenant, such a title meant basically that he kept the law better than anyone else so he was regarded as more "righteous" by his behavior (not by receiving the gift of righteousness from God like Abraham had enjoyed.) Ironically, what they failed to understand was that, **pre-cross**, James was still an **in Adam** sinner and his half-brother, Jesus, was actually the only righteous One in God's eyes because He came directly from God and was "one" with His Father. Again, the second most important human, **pre-cross**, according to Jesus, was not Abraham or Moses or David or James or even Mary but John the Baptist, according to Luke 7:28.

This is what happens still today when people focus on the **seen** "worth" of others, based on their appearance or status or talents or potential or performance rather than as God sees them in the **unseen**. It is not complicated. If you are **in Adam**, you are an unrighteous sinner condemned to hell because your spiritual parent is Adam, according to Romans 5:19. If you are **in Christ**, you are a righteous saint because your spiritual Parent is now Father-God Himself. The allusions to this **unseen reality** in John's gospel only become clear and relevant to us when we see them spelled out in Jesus' **whole gospel of grace** to Paul.

James' devotion to the Law blinded him to who Jesus really was **(pre-cross),** the exact representation of God come in the flesh. This kept him from hearing God's word through Jesus about the coming, **unseen Kingdom**. Consequently, his ignorance of Jesus' exchanges with the Law-keepers (and James' life-long sympathy with their pro-law bias) led him to perpetuate a

160

dependence on the law system among the Jewish Christians, **post-cross**. John's gospel, written years after James' death, shows that adherence to the law *blinds* one to the truth of the living word heard through the Spirit who gives life (while depending on the letter of the law brings death).

The next chapter will provide many examples of where Jesus used the law correctly as a *mirror* to show law-minded people their self-righteousness. Why? To motivate them to give up that mind-set (repent) and rely on Him for His *gift* of true life and righteousness instead. However, in many other instances, He showed grace and mercy to people who looked to Him (instead of to the law) for help in many forms. So the **pre-cross** texts of the four gospels document a mixture of instances of Jesus using law with some (like the rich young ruler in Luke 18:18-23) while showing grace to others (like the boy with an evil spirit in Luke 9:38-43).

Transitioning To The New Covenant
This mixture characterized the transition period, **pre-cross**, when Jesus was fulfilling the law perfectly by walking according to the Spirit within Him. He did this by consistently operating in the <u>higher law of faith in Father-God, and in His love and liberty</u>, *as His Father directed* – according to each individual's request or need. Again, "The Law came through Moses but grace and truth came <u>through</u> Jesus Christ" (John 1:7). Jesus *gave the law* to those who wanted a religious set of rules to obey to "become holy" by their own efforts. Again, He held it up like a mirror to show them that they could not perfect themselves. (The Sermon on the Mount is a case in point. He raised the bar much higher than the rigid demands of the Mosaic Law by saying a person sins by *thinking* wrongly, not just *doing* wrong like the Law indicated.) However, Jesus *gave grace* to those who were desperate for God's help and looked to Jesus for deliverance and healing, instead of depending on their flesh for self-righteous law-keeping.

Could it be that those who make the Law their standard of the truth, are, thereby, not actually glorifying Jesus who is the Truth? If the Ten Commandments are a part of the Universal Moral Law that people must depend on for becoming or staying righteous, why did God call these same Commandments, which can only condemn mankind, the "ministry of death" and nail them to the cross? Can you be righteous without focusing on the Law? Why did God tell Adam not to eat of the Tree of the Knowledge of Good and Evil (if it was the way to eternal life)? (If you want to see my answers go to endnote #**29**.)

The next chapter will consider how to avoid a potential pitfall of *misinterpreting* the four gospels as a seeming endorsement of the **elephant of mixture.**

This song-poem helps me keep in mind what Jesus did to give me a new identity **in Jesus,** and expresses my gratefulness for His love and mercy towards me.

161

I BELONG TO YOU, JESUS
Purchased by Your death on a tree.
I belong to You, Jesus,
Loving me so patiently.

    Crucified my rebel heart
     With all its brokenness and shame,
    But raised me up, alive in You
    To glorify Your mighty name.

Jesus, Servant King, come to set all captives free.
Jesus, Lamb of God, thank You Lord for including me.

I'm complete in You, Jesus,
You're my joy, my righteousness.
I'm at peace in You, Jesus,
Trusting in Your faithfulness.

    Melted by Your love for me,
    I yield to all You say and do.
    Pour through me Your loving-kindness
    As I live for only You.

Jesus, King of Kings, come to set all captives free.
Jesus, Saving God, thank You Lord for choosing,
Thank You Lord for saving,
Thank You Lord for including me.
© Copyright 2003 by Leonard J. Ransil

Chapter Twelve

Potential Pitfalls In The Four Gospels

Discerning The Four Gospels

The previous chapter highlighted some of the many benefits of the four gospels. However, it is hazardous for Christians to focus on the four gospels as though they comprise Jesus' definitive statement on the <u>essence</u> of Christianity. Why? Because the commands and demands of Moses' Law-based system are intertwined with some terms and parables Jesus used to describe the new, grace-based covenant that He would inaugurate later at Calvary. This patchwork of two opposing covenants combined within the same books can be confusing and misleading to the undiscerning believer. Why? Because he might conclude that he, too, is under the law like Jesus and His disciples were at that time period and, therefore, he should do *all* that Jesus commanded *them* to do. But that is not true for a believer today because he is under the **New Covenant** of grace, not law. The performance-based law-covenant was given *exclusively* to the Israelites through Moses. God never formally offered that covenant to any Gentile nation, according to Ephesians 2:11-13.

> ... be mindful that, in times past, you were Gentiles (non-Jews) according to the flesh, and that you were called uncircumcised by those who are called "the circumcised group" in the flesh (Jews), which was performed by man, and that you were, in that time **(pre-cross)**, without Christ, being foreign to the way of life of Israel, being foreigners to the (Jewish) covenant, having no hope of the promise (given to Abraham), and were without God in this world. But now, in Christ Jesus, you, who were in times past far away, have been brought near (to God) by the blood of Christ. (See Endnote **#30** for more about Gentiles in Jerusalem.)

And, as you now know, the Mosaic Covenant was nailed to Jesus' cross - according to Jesus' revelation to Paul in 42 AD - and was replaced with a totally new, grace-based covenant, ratified by His perfect blood and available to both Jews and Gentiles. So, again, if the Law was abolished after Jesus fulfilled it at Calvary and if it was never given to any Gentiles by God, why do most Christian leaders today insist on feeding the **elephant of mixture** to reborn believers by teaching the Ten Commandments? One big reason - that no doubt influenced the Jerusalem church to teach them - is because Jesus used them on some **in Adam** people in the four gospels.

However, He used them *only* for their intended purpose during His earthly life, **pre-cross**, when the Mosaic Law was still in force for the Jews. So, the assumption has been made for some 2000 years that <u>whatever things Jesus taught regarding the Law, **pre-cross,** all Christians are still obligated to focus on today</u>. But, again, what was God's intended purpose for the Law? Most Christians today would say something like "They are God's standard to keep in order to please Him by helping me live a holier life." If you have read Chapter Eight, you now know that is not God's true purpose for the Mosaic Law Covenant. The Law's purpose was to reveal mankind's nature **in Adam** and demonstrate that no one can earn God's blessings or heaven by his or her performance because no one can ever meet God's standard - perfection. <u>God's salvation and righteousness are gifts to be received not rewards to be achieved.</u> When Jesus referred to the Law, He used it to bring those Jews, who were depending on their efforts at Law-keeping to be righteous, to see their need for Him as the only way to be put in permanent right-standing with God.

Unfortunately, most Christians today are not taught to discern the four gospels through the lens of their new position as reborn, righteous saints **in Christ,** under a totally **New Covenant.** They still just accept all of Jesus' words printed "in red" as commands written to them, as though they are **in Adam** Jews. To make matters worse, many are under pastors who use the "whip of the law," like Calvin taught, to keep them "in line." (See Appendix #3 about the shocking mixture of law for believers in John Calvin's writings.) They are trusting in the law to do what it *can't* do instead of trusting the Holy Spirit to do what He was *sent* by Jesus to do through us, as us. That mind-set of law-based righteousness is what grieves the Holy Spirit. That is not Jesus' true **gospel of lavish grace.** It comes from man's soulish reasoning and traditions and mental strongholds carried over from a focus on fleshy law-keeping. This monster is the **elephant of mixture** that even Paul had believed in and taught until he learned the truth about Galatianism directly from Jesus in about 42 AD.

God's View, Post Cross

Again, God's view of His beloved children **in Christ** is that they are greater than was any Old Testament person born of woman - **pre-cross.** These are Jesus' own words in Luke 7:28 that described reborn saints in the **New Covenant**:

For I (Jesus) say to you: among those born of women, no one is greater than the prophet John the Baptist. But he who is least in the kingdom of God (born again) is greater than he is.

This clearly shows Jesus' view of how superior would be the results of the coming, grace-based **New Covenant** over the Mosaic Covenant which He was in the process of fulfilling and replacing. Without this enlightened view of Jesus' **finished work** from God's perspective, believers can easily be misled when they do not divide the word rightly according to Jesus' **divine exchange** with them. His cross made all **unseen** things *new* for believers so not *all* of Jesus' words in the four gospels apply directly to believers today. I will prove that revelation below. Believing that *all* of Jesus' words in the four gospels do apply to every believer, is one of the main reasons the **elephant of mixture** has so dominated the mind of the church for some 2000 years.

This legacy of error and confusion can *only* be corrected today by esteeming Jesus' **whole gospel** given to Paul above all the other books of the Bible and using it as God's plumb line to properly interpret all its other books. Why? Because it is Jesus' own description and commentary on the culminating Third Act of the Bible, His redemption of mankind. It is the most important event in mankind's existence, but Jesus' revelation to Paul still continues to have a lesser spotlight than the stories in the Old Testament or the words of Jesus in the four gospels for most Christians today. Yes, all the **pre-cross** books are the inspired word of God. They give hints about the coming Messiah. They also indicate that something of great consequence was about to unfold. Nonetheless, the four gospels, when compared to Jesus' **whole gospel** given to Paul, are but *shadows* of the **unseen,** eternal reality found only in the **finished work** of Christ Jesus' **divine exchange.** Again, this is why Paul exhorted the church, saying:

164

So from now on we regard no one from a worldly (natural, carnal, **seen level**) point of view. Though we once regarded Christ in this way, we do so no longer (2 Corinthians 5:16)

That perspective needs to be our *starting point* as **New Covenant** Christians.

The First Church Schism Was Caused By A Mixture Of Law With Grace

The **elephant of mixture** will only be exposed and overcome by the sword of the Holy Spirit which is Jesus' **gospel of radical grace** that includes the revelation of the Holy Spirit residing in every believer. Had the **whole gospel of radical grace** been understood, received, honored and applied by all of the leadership at the Jerusalem council in 50 AD, the **elephant of mixture** would not have gained a permanent foothold that caused a tragic schism in the infant church which has undermined "the unity of the Spirit in the bond of peace" for some 2000 years. Jesus gave Paul the revelation of what He *had accomplished* on Calvary which had united Jews and Gentiles into one, unified Body in the **unseen realm in Christ**. Ephesians 2:14-19 describes what Jesus' **finished work** accomplished in the **unseen realm** from God's view point. He desires that unity **in Christ** to be manifested in the **seen realm** as His life in and through His Holy Spirit. However the mixture of opposing covenants by law-minded church leaders has greatly hindered that expression of His will in the **seen realm** for 2000 years. Again, this is what Jesus did from God's viewpoint:

> For He (Jesus) is our peace. He made the two (Jews and Gentiles) into one by abolishing the law of commandments and requirements in His flesh, thereby dissolving the wall of separation that caused hostility (between Jews and Gentiles) so that He might create, in Himself one new man (the church) out of these two, making peace and (then) reconciling both (Jews and Gentiles) to God, in one body, through the cross, slaying this hostility in Himself (by becoming sin). When He first came (on earth), He preached peace to you (Gentiles) who were far away, and peace to those (the Jews) who were near. For by Him (Jesus), we both have access, in the one Spirit, to the Father. Now, therefore, you are no longer strangers and by-standers. Instead, you are citizens among the saints in the household of God (Ephesians 2:14-19).

What Did Men Do With God's Vision For Unity?

Again, Jesus came to abolish in Himself the **pre-cross** split between the world's only two people groups, Jews and Gentiles (as viewed by God). He accomplished that task by "abolishing the Law of commandments and requirements" on Calvary in the **unseen realm** for all true believers because they are made one **in Christ** through rebirth by the "unity of the Spirit." Undoubtedly, this "unity of the Spirit" that Jesus died to provide would be manifest here in the **seen realm** more consistently if all believers understood and lived in the ramifications of Jesus' **divine exchange** that makes all believers one **in Christ** automatically – from God's perspective.

But tragically, the infant Jerusalem church led by James, maintained the split in the **seen realm** by 1) mixing the obsolete covenant of works (that they had lived under with Jesus, **pre-cross**) with the **New Covenant** of pure grace by requiring circumcision for even Gentiles before salvation and by 2) dividing up the work of the ministry by the same two people-groups as before - rather than by geography etc. Thereby, James frustrated the grace of God in this regard by continuing the "split" between Jews and Gentiles in the **seen realm**. How? He assigned Paul to go to the Gentiles and he, Peter and John would minister to the Jews. So, what God had joined together **in Christ**, man tragically put asunder on earth. That first "church split," engineered by James and practiced by the Jerusalem church until 135 AD, set an example and precedent for a *spirit of division* ever since, over big issues like "What is the true gospel?" or "How are we justified in God's sight?" and over small ones like music styles or the color of a new carpet in a church.

The **elephant of mixture** of opposing covenants was innocently welcomed into the infant Jerusalem church through ignorance at first. Regrettably, it was not recognized as the heretical monster that it is and, therefore, was not fully eradicated at the Jerusalem Council - despite Peter's testimony about Cornelius' conversion and Paul's presentation of Jesus' **whole gospel of radical grace**. James was not content to yield to God's wisdom coming through these two hand-picked leaders. Instead, he had to add the leaven of the "knowledge of good and evil"- four of the seven laws of Noah that he believed all humans must be under. Galatianism has increasingly dominated much of Catholic and mainline Protestant doctrine and practice. (One of the ways this plays out is that some denominations see the Bible as one, whole covenant that automatically and equally applies to all believers.) And, again, another contributing factor is the *assumption* that the **pre-cross** "red-letter" words of Jesus must be held in higher esteem than His direct revelation of the **New Covenant** of His **whole gospel of grace** to Paul, **post-cross**.

Wrong Focus Leads To Wrong Beliefs

So, we will now explore why the church's tendency to focus *primarily* on the **pre-cross** part of the Bible is flawed and naturally leads to many wrong conclusions. The same confusion would happen if one would emphasize the first two acts of a play over the third and final act. Or, worse yet, discount act three as irrelevant or too complicated or not acceptable in one's denomination or too "abstract." Now, typically, the first two acts of effective dramas provide necessary factual background and a growing tension that sets the stage for the third, culminating act – in this case, Jesus' **gospel of grace**. In God's salvation story, the Second Act focuses on Moses' Law Covenant, which ends at Calvary. It reveals the need for a Hero to save mankind from 1) a slave master (the devil), 2) a corrupt nature (by being **in Adam**) and 3) the consequences of imperfect behavior (sinning). However, just pointing out the problems that exist in a dysfunctional situation does not resolve it. In this case, Act Two only lays bare the colossal mess that Adam got us into. But it is the Third Act - our **New Covenant** deliverance and blessing **in Christ Jesus** – that reveals the heroics of our Champion, who vastly outshines the negatives that the devil and Adam instigated.

Admittedly, Jesus' revelation to Paul might, *at first glance*, seem too mysterious or impractical to solve mankind's three great dilemmas listed above, or even to overcome our struggles in daily life. But that is a common lie from Satan, the Word Thief. He knows it spells his undoing when believers hear, believe in and receive **Jesus' whole gospel**. Jesus sent the Holy Spirit specifically to help believers understand the secrets and gifts of the **unseen Kingdom** that Jesus described to Paul and which he then revealed in Act Three, the **New Covenant** – the **Word of Christ**. Believers are now citizens *spiritually* of God's **unseen Kingdom**, not of this **seen** world which is only temporary, as Paul explained in this key passage:

166

… We do not look at the things which are seen but the things which are not seen. For the things which are seen are temporal but the things which are not seen are eternal (2 Corinthians 4:18).

In principle, this is a parallel verse to 2 Corinthians 5:16 quoted above. This revelation is a thematic *fulcrum* in Jesus' **grace gospel** and represents a sea change in focus. Some parts of the four gospels are focused on how to please God and live on earth as His people by obeying some set of commandments and traditions. But other times, Jesus changed the *focus* from Moses' Law system for Jews to exhorting His hearers to

First of all, seek God's (**unseen**) Kingdom and His righteousness and all else will be provided for you (Matthew 6:33).

You probably have sung this verse many times like I have. But have you contemplated its true meaning? What does it mean to seek something that is not tangible and to seek His "righteousness" that can't be achieved by our "doing" because it is *His* righteousness, not ours, which this verse tells us to seek. (This is an obvious contrast to the Mosaic Law which was all about "being righteous by good behavior.") Elsewhere, Paul tells the Colossians to "Set your minds on things above, not on things of this earth." Both Jesus and Paul stress the importance of focusing on God's gifts of His Kingdom and His righteousness, received by faith through rebirth, rather than by self-focus.

We believers are then to be ambassadors of God and of His **unseen Kingdom,** now that He resides in us (just like the Holy Spirit did in Jesus), starting at our rebirth. Again, the <u>end</u> of the four gospels marks the *transition point* in the Bible from a law-based covenant of "never finished works" (Act Two) to a grace-based covenant of rest in Jesus' **finished work** (Act Three). Consequently, there are verses and parables throughout the four gospels that either 1) focus on law or 2) describe the coming Kingdom and its grace-based covenant (which was yet to be cut between God and Jesus on Calvary), <u>according to who Jesus was speaking *about* or speaking *to* during that time period of about three years.</u>

Correctly Dividing God's Holy Word

Discerning these differences in the four gospels might sound too cumbersome or technical to the casual reader. But it is a helpful and necessary process to insure a correct, grace-based interpretation that enables right believing which, then, produces the fruit of right living. Myles Coverdale offered this wise advice to believers to properly exegete scripture:

It shall greatly help ye to understand the Scriptures if thou mark not only what is spoken or written, but of whom and to whom, with what words, at what time, where, to what intent, with what circumstances, considering what goeth before and what followeth after. #**31**

So the following parables from the four gospels are examples of law–based thinking, presented here to sharpen your discernment of how to rightly divide the Word by

1) paying attention to conflicting sets of terms of the two opposing covenants – law vs. grace - and by

167

2) using scripture to interpret scripture and by

3) rejecting the temptation to personally adopt or hold on to any law-based thinking that occurs inevitably in the four gospels.

Ask and trust the Holy Spirit to teach you, knowing that He would not have you believing and living under the yoke of a works-based covenant that you, as a Gentile, were *never given* and which is now obsolete for all Jews, **post-cross**. (Appendix #2 offers an example of the radical differences in the two covenants and their implications for believers in the context of the *Our Father* prayer.)

A Worthless Servant Or A Friend

Our first example of law-centered thinking in the four gospels highlights a central truth of the Bible which reveals that man's true nature and identity is as a sinner because of being **in Adam**. Jesus taught the following parable, found in Luke 17:7-10, from God's **pre-cross** perspective of fallen mankind.

But which of you, having a servant plowing or feeding cattle, would say to him, as he was returning from the field, 'Come in immediately; sit down to eat?' Instead, would you not say to him: 'Prepare my dinner then get ready and serve me, while I eat and drink; and after I am done, you shall eat and drink?' Would he be grateful to that servant for doing what he commanded him to do? Of course not. So too, when you have done all these things that I told you, you should say: 'We are worthless servants. We have just done our duty.'

Similarly, in Luke 11:13 Jesus said to those listening to Him, including the disciples: "If you, then, being evil, know how to give good gifts to your children ..." Jesus minced no words. He labeled the disciples - and mankind in general – as "useless, unworthy, worthless, unprofitable" (legitimate translations of the same Greek word) and "evil." Since these are the specific words of Jesus (written in red), they have been branded on the minds of true believers for almost 2000 years as part of the **pre-cross** "gospel according to Luke." Why would Jesus say what seems so contradictory to His normally kind and gracious manner to the sinners He encountered day to day? It is because He was being *honest about the spiritual condition of all mankind* since all were still **in Adam**. In fact, those harsh words were actually better than what His audience really deserved, since they were rebels by nature and at enmity with God. But let's see if that harsh assessment is echoed in John's gospel or, most especially, in Jesus' gospel revealed directly to Paul.

I will no longer call you servants, for the servant does not know what his Lord is doing. But I have called you friends, because everything whatsoever that I have heard from my Father, I have made known to you. You have not chosen me, but I have chosen you. And I have appointed you, so that you may go forth and bear fruit, and so that your fruit may last. Then, whatever you have asked of the Father in my name, He shall give to you. This I command you: that you love one another (John 15:15-17).

168

At this point, Jesus was talking to His disciples who were still **in Adam**. The difference is that He was *speaking prophetically,* in anticipation of what His perfect sacrifice would do for them <u>when they became reborn of God</u>. He knew they could not obey the command to love God or each other with God's kind of unselfish, agape love, **pre-cross**. They proved that by their disloyal behavior right up to His crucifixion on Calvary. However, this kind of unselfish love for God and for others would begin to be *possible* when they became new creations **in Christ** by rebirth and, thereby, received the Holy Spirit, who is God's love personified. John explains this in his **post-cross** letter, in 1 John 4:9-16:

> The love of God was made apparent to us in this way: He sent His one and only Son into the world that we might live through Him. In this is love: not that we loved God, but that He loved us first and sent His Son as a propitiation for our sins. Dear friends, since God loved us that much, we also ought to love one another. No one has ever seen God; but if we love one another, God lives in us and His love is perfected in us. We know that we abide **in Him**, and He in us, because He has given us His Spirit. And we have seen and testify that the Father has sent His Son to be the Savior of the world. <u>Whoever confesses that Jesus is the Son of God</u>, God lives in him and he in God (by rebirth). And so we know and rely on the love God has for us. God is love. Whoever abides in love, abides in God, and God in him.

By now, that revelation should sound familiar to you as the fulfillment of Jesus' prayer in John 17:21 which is the *key* to understanding Father-God's will and redemption plan for all mankind. Whoever "confesses that Jesus is the Son of God, God abides in him and he in God." (Notice, it is not about "confessing sins.") Therefore, he is no longer a "servant" or just a "friend," like Abraham had been, but now he is a *justified son* of God – a member of God's own family along with Christ Jesus, our Savior and elder Brother. This is made clear in the prophetic, **pre-cross** statement of John 1:12:

> … to all who received Him, to those believing in His name, He gave the privilege (right, freedom) to become children of God - not of natural descent, nor the will of the flesh nor the will of man, <u>but born of God.</u>

Remember, none of this was possible or fathomable, **pre-cross**. And by being God's adopted child, these are manifold benefits for every believer's life on earth and for his or her future after physical death, a few of which are explained next:

> In this way, God's love is perfected among us so that we will have confidence (not fear of punishment) on the day of judgment, because, <u>as He is so also are we in this world</u> (because we are one with Jesus). There is no fear found in love. Instead (God's) perfect love (for us) casts out fear, because fear has to do with punishment (which Jesus absorbed in our place). Whoever fears is not perfected in (the revelation of God's) love. Therefore, let us love God, because God loved us first (1 John 4:17-19).

And Jesus even demonstrated His love for His "useless, unworthy servants" personally by washing their feet – a servant's job - before they were reborn. He even washed Peter's (who later denied, with cursing, that He ever knew Him) and Judas' (who betrayed Him then hung himself), knowing what they were about to do (see John 13:1-38).

Wow! Thanks to Jesus' **finished work**, believers are not "evil" or "unworthy" or "useless" or just a servant, dutifully plodding along and subject to the just punishment by an angry ruler (as some regard God). Believers need not fear judgment because God loved and forgave the whole world full of sinners before anyone was **reborn in Christ,** according to 1 John 2:2 and 2 Corinthians 5:19. Believers are now enabled and free to love God, others and oneself because of what His perfect love for us accomplished on our behalf. And it is on the basis of God's love, demonstrated in Jesus' **divine exchange** with us (see 2 Corinthians 5:21), that all the blessings Jesus revealed to Paul are ours **in Christ Jesus** - many of which were already presented in Chapter Two. Jesus pours it on with His **New Covenant** words through Paul in Romans 5:17:

> For though, by the sin of the one man (Adam), death reigned through that one man, yet so much more will those who receive both God's abundant provision of grace and of the gift of righteousness reign in life through that one man, Jesus Christ.

Wow, again! Through rebirth, a formerly "unworthy, evil servant" receives God's gift of righteousness to reign in life **in and through Christ Jesus** – here and now. That, my friend, is His amazing **grace gospel!** That is why He told us to seek first His **unseen Kingdom** and accept His gift of righteousness through rebirth which makes us joint heirs with Christ Jesus. This, in turn, *entitles* us to all the benefits of His infinite inheritance, here and beyond, because we are one with Him. What is true for Jesus, our elder Brother, is now true for us *because* we are **in Him.** This is His amazing **grace-based gospel!**

But you will **not** learn all of this truth (and so much more) by just focusing on the four gospels – even on John's gospel. That is why Jesus revealed His **whole gospel of grace** to Paul in 42 AD who, then, passed it on to all who would listen to him. Without that magnificent revelation, you might spend your entire Christian life believing the lie that you are just an unworthy sinner/servant, just barely saved by grace. But the truly good news, believer, is that you are a **new creation** child of God and a joint-heir of heaven, living **in the victorious Christ Jesus -** and He, the Spirit of Christ, is living in you as His temple!

And there is more. "Blessed are they who are invited to the wedding feast of the Lamb" (Revelation 19:9a). The formerly "unworthy servants," now reborn of God, will be collectively the Bride of Christ and enjoy a glorious, eternal wedding feast with Christ Jesus, our triumphant Groom. For believers, living consciously by faith in God's **unseen**, **big picture** panorama, "This is the worst it gets." That is why, like Paul, you can "rejoice in the Lord always" because you are secure **in Christ**, regardless of your present circumstances in the **seen realm**.

The New Covenant Terms Are The Key To The Total Truth
Do you see now how important it is to clearly understand the terms and consequent privileges of our **New Covenant** with God which were somewhat forecast in John's gospel but not yet operational? Accurately distinguishing the two opposing covenants will keep you from being confused and defeated by mixing the **New Covenant realities in Christ** with the terms of the abolished Law Covenant that was never intended for Gentiles. Renewing your mind with Jesus' **whole gospel of grace** will progressively set you free from wrong believing in your outer self as you are already free in your inner man **in Christ!** Just always remember that none of God's infinite blessings come by your own doing but they are all free and unmerited gifts of

God's abundant grace, given to anyone who believes and receives God's offer. An ever-deepening revelation of what Father-God did for us - through Jesus' **finished work** of His **divine exchange** - will automatically inspire gratitude and worship out of an ever deepening love for our wonderful Father-God.

And since we are now His sons (instead of being evil, unworthy servants), our love for such a gracious Father-God impels us to serve Him wholeheartedly. How? By doing the works He has specifically called each of us to do in spreading the **whole gospel** of Christ Jesus (see Ephesians 2:10). There is a huge difference between being a worthless servant toiling dutifully under law, as described in Luke's gospel, versus being a beloved son with a new a spirit and new servant-like heart, responding out of love for our Savior and Lord and our new Father by the enablement of the Holy Spirit. Right believing produces the fruit of right living, rather than futile, fleshy, dead, self-initiated works, done to try to earn heaven or maintain God's approval.

But, again, many believers remain law-minded and duty bound because they believe that everything Jesus said in all four gospels automatically applies to them "because Jesus said it – and it is even written in red!" A believer's wrong beliefs about God, or about himself, inevitably comes from a failure to divide the **pre-cross**, law-based covenant period from the **post-cross**, grace-based covenant which all believers are now *legally* under **in Christ**. But having legal rights to something does not automatically mean that one benefits from them. Being given a graduation gift of a new car by your rich father and officially owning it when registered with the state, is *not* the same thing as getting into it and actually driving and enjoying it.

The Giver Is The Gift

But when it comes to receiving God's **unseen gifts**, there is altogether another level of intimacy and enjoyment involved. That is because, in His Kingdom, the Giver is also the gift and that drastically changes the dynamics from what we experience in the **seen realm**. Down here, your natural father is not the same as the new car. While the car was a result of the relationship and the generosity of your father, he is not the car. You can enjoy him without the car in view and can enjoy the car without him being near.

However, in God's **unseen** Kingdom, the "gifts" are expressions of the person of God as Father, Savior, Sanctifier, Counselor – and on and on. To experience a spiritual gift from God is to experience God Himself as part of the **"in Christ"** relationship which the **New Covenant** is built on and pre-supposes. Jesus does not just give me His "wisdom." Rather, He *is* my wisdom, according to 1 Corinthians 1:30, which is now mine to draw on consciously because of our intimately connected relationship. I may refuse to rely on Him as my wisdom in a particular situation but He is constantly available because He offered Himself to me (and to all mankind) 2000 years ago and is always available to all who open themselves up to trust in and depend on Him to any degree. After all, He is my life, whether I see Him that way or not.

From His perspective in the **unseen reality**, His **divine exchange** with me took all my bad and gave me all His good. But *experiencing* His gifts over time in the **seen realm** comes by entrusting myself to Him in rebirth and beyond. How? By believing He loves me personally and is my good and faithful Father-God, a rewarder of those who *seek* ("hunger for and worship" in the Greek) Him diligently – intentionally, consistently – as an ever-present, ever-loving

171

companion. But that surrender of yourself to Him is either hindered or facilitated by your concept of just who God really is.

How Accurate Is Your Concept of God?

In your mind, is God a law-giver and judge, who makes constant demands on His "unworthy subjects," who must then try to measure up and "be holy" in order to be blessed – as the Mosaic Covenant required of the Israelites? Or is He a merciful Father who loves all of mankind enough to 1) sacrifice His only beloved Son to propitiate (forgive and remove) all the sins of us evil, **in Adam**, unworthy, rebellious slaves of the devil then to 2) offer rebirth to anyone believing and receiving Jesus as Savior?

The **elephant** of law-mindedness gravitates inevitably toward the former concept of God; the **butterfly life** of grace-consciousness revels in the latter. Your concept of God and what He has done for you through Jesus is <u>crucial</u> to how much you are willing and able to receive from an infinite supply of Himself and all that implies. Your receptivity is proportional to how loving and, therefore, trust-worthy you believe (deep down) He really is. The more you renew your mind with the total truth of the **whole gospel of grace**, the more you will be able to experience and rest in *all* the gifts that He has already supplied to *you* in His **divine exchange** – the giving of Himself as the great Giver. It is your choice, believer and unbeliever, how much of Him you will receive experientially in the **seen realm**. Chapters Eighteen to Twenty-One will explore all this in much more detail.

Jesus Raises The Bar Of The Law

Let's examine another example of a focus on law that often occurs in the four gospels. Compare what we read above about the **post-cross** assurance of our Father's unconditional love for us (and the fact that Jesus has been punished for all our sin) with the following **pre-cross** passage from Matthew 5:27-30:

> You have heard that it was said, 'You shall not commit adultery.' But I say to you that anyone who looks at a woman lustfully has already committed adultery with her in his heart. If your right eye causes you to sin, pluck it out and throw it away. It is better for you to lose one member of your body than for your whole body to be thrown into hell. And if your right hand causes you to sin, cut it off and throw it away. It is better for you to lose one part of your body than for your whole body to go into hell.

Whoa. Since this quote pertains to the **pre-cross** period of the Mosaic Law, we should expect to find an endorsement of the Ten Commandments. But Jesus' words go far beyond the big Ten by saying that even just entertaining lustful *thoughts* is adultery. And, of course, if you break just one law, you break the whole law – according to the terms of that covenant. And what is Jesus saying that the Jewish sinner should do to uphold the requirements of the law? The unthinkable act of gouging out one's eye and throwing it away. Why? <u>So that what is left of you does not end up in hell.</u> That is a brutal but accurate picture of the law – a stern, unbending standard which demands perfection in everything *because* perfection is the required standard for acceptance into heaven!

So how many believers that you know have obeyed Jesus' command by gouging out an eye (or their brain) after using it to sin? And if they lusted again, gouged out the other one? Or cut off their right hand when they stole something – anything? That is really the full force of the law. When I ask law-minded believers if they obey that standard perfectly, they side-step the issue by saying that Jesus did not really mean that. A common response is: "It is just a figure of speech." If so, where do you draw the line? How low do you pull down the pristine requirement of perfection to accommodate your own, doable standard? That is exactly what the Pharisees tried to do and Jesus called them on it - repeatedly.

Spiritual Quicksand

Do you see the quick-sand that law-based requirements inevitably put you in – especially when we are talking about "perfection?" But one of the reasons law-thinking is so popular in Christian circles, even today, is that it gives an illusion of being independently in charge of yourself (and of others, if that happens to be your motive) instead of being totally dependent on God's grace-based covenant - Jesus' **divine exchange**. The flesh is famous for trying to meet our needs independently of Jesus Christ. Believers who are insecure because of their faulty concepts of God and/or of themselves, look for the security blankets of power and control over people through laws (such as "standards of excellence" as they are often called), or a "holiness doctrine" or dress codes or worship music played perfectly or proper food, manners and hygiene etc., etc., etc. – enforced on self or others to "please God." Does that nonsense sound like Jesus or the Pharisees?

These requirements are used as "standards" that other believers have to meet to be "acceptable" and therefore accepted. (I pity the flock under a perfectionistic pastor.) This thinking displays man's conditional love, controlling others by enforcing man-made rules and regulations. Or, worse yet, some disobediently resuscitate God's law code (even though it was made obsolete for Jewish believers) in order to make sure that believers are morally pleasing to God. It is all about a head full of law rather than a new heart full of love. Ironically, this lie is what displeases God the most for it puts the curse of "living under law" back on the believer's, shoulders, the very thing that Jesus explained through Paul in Galatians 3:10:

> All who rely on observing the law, are under a curse, for it is written: 'Cursed is
> everyone who does not continue to do everything written in the Book of the Law.'

Some of the symptoms and earmarks of "living under law" were given in "the dog chart" in Chapter Four. The left column is a snapshot of what law always produces, which is a focus on self and the outer, **seen realm.** This trap is a substitute of what really matters to God – living by grace through faith in the higher law of the Spirit of life, out of a conscious oneness with Him **in Christ Jesus**. But because of almost 2000 years of rarely challenged mixture, many church leaders assume that their job is to make and enforce laws over their congregations to cause or to force compliance – renamed "holiness." They are in the "sin-management business" – their own and their flock's.

But not only is it *not* how God operates, but controlling and manipulating other people's will is actually a form of witchcraft. Our free will is a precious gift from God which He respects and honors. It is a key element of His image in us as humans, which makes true, reciprocal love towards Him possible – once we become reborn, **new creations**. And, of course, rebirth itself is a person's choice, despite the doctrine of predestination that some denominations erroneously teach. In Chapter Eighteen, we will explore God's alternative to law-based relationships (with Him and others).

God Is Love

God is no respecter (prejudiced pre-selector) of persons because agape love is inclusive, not exclusive, kind and not self-seeking. Would He be "just" if He played favorites? Yes, Jesus did say "You have not chosen Me but I have chosen you" (John 15:16). But since we know from 1 Timothy 2:4 that it is God's will that "all men be saved and come to the knowledge of the truth (Jesus)," it is clear that He wants all people to be in love with His Son and be with Him in heaven. So, if that is God's desire, will all mankind end up in heaven - as Universalists believe and teach?

Well, I will answer that question with a question. Does Jesus' desire to have us as His bride override our choice in the matter? In a truly Christian wedding, both parties must freely choose to give themselves to the other person by saying "I do." God intends marriage to be a covenant of *mutual* surrender to each other. (Again, the vital importance of understanding God's view and purpose for covenants will be presented in Chapter Eighteen). We know now that Jesus wants to be "one" with you and me. Therefore, He provided that *option* at Calvary by paying mankind's sin debt and reconciling mankind to Father-God, according to 2 Corinthians 5:18-19. But verse 20 puts the ball back in our court. We must *choose* to be reconciled to God. And how is that accomplished? By each **in Adam** sinner making a choice to accept God's offer of rebirth by God's grace through faith in Jesus who revealed to Paul that:

He who unites himself with the Lord is one spirit with Him (1 Corinthians 6:17).

Why would He create you in His image, which includes having a free will, only to violate it by *forcing* you into (or preventing you from) making a marriage covenant with Jesus? Jesus proved beyond any possible doubt that He loves you. Now you are free by His love-based sacrifice on Calvary to give yourself to Him in return. So now, you can either:

1) stay locked up **in Adam** as a "wild dog" (described in the right-hand column of the chart in Chapter Four) or

2) saved but still be held captive (mentally) by law, like a "city dog" (in the left-hand column) or

3) live a Jesus-centered life as a "country dog," experiencing and resting in the favor of God's love and acceptance.

Jesus came to set us free from whatever bondages hold us – big or small. It is for freedom that Christ Jesus came to offer the benefits of the **butterfly life in Him,** lived according to His higher law of the Spirit of life. Again, much more about that **New Covenant reality** will be explored in Chapter Eighteen.

Our Freedom Is In Christ Jesus

Controllers in church circles, who use law through force of personality or will etc. (as I did with my children in the early part of my Christian life), usually do so because of ignorance of:

1) who God really is,

2) how much He loves them,

3) what Jesus has accomplished through rebirth for all believers, and

4) how God regards His precious children – the same way as He regards Jesus!

A rigid, domineering mind-set can be passed down by training and modeling through generations - and even through nationalities. Again, this all too common problem often results from viewing the fifteen hundred year period of the Mosaic Law as a portrayal of God's *character* – seemingly a harsh judge, sometimes punishing disproportionately to the "crime." Then the image is carried over into today, **post-cross**, by saying "God is the same yesterday, today and forever." This warped assessment denies the truth that God is always motivated by other-centered, sacrificial, relational, *agape love*, regardless of how it looks on the surface to self-centered, **in Adam** humans who are against God by nature. Don't let the world's system or your self-centered flesh or your experience under an unloving parent or the devil's lies about God, or any other distortion, define who God really is for you.

Believing that God's response to that sad period of **pre-cross,** Jewish history reveals His character or defines Him, is like deciding that a parent's effort at disciplining a blatantly rebellious teenager defines the parent's character. It ignores all the parent's sacrifice and (hopefully) loving care given freely for years and the pain a child's rebellion causes both siblings and mature parents. The prodigal son did not repent (change his twisted perception of his father) until he became desperate enough to appreciate how <u>gracious</u> his dad really was. God gave the law to graciously reveal mankind's desperate, **in Adam** condition under Satan's enslavement. Why? To wake us up to the truth of our need for Jesus' salvation. It is not "the law" but <u>Father-God's proven love and grace to mankind that defines Him because He *is* Love</u>. Amen.

God Is Never The Problem

Our good God did not cause humans to be rebellious and obnoxious - Adam did. And that occurred only after God gave him a perfect world to live in and the choice to personally relate to God daily. He gave only one command – and the freedom to violate it – showing that God is not a law-imposing tyrant as some mistakenly believe but a <u>freedom-giving, risk-taking lover</u>. He desires to bless all who will yield to His wonderful plan for them by providing an eternity of perfect relationships and infinite blessings because His new family is one with Him. <u>That is the true image of our Father-God</u>. We will see much more evidence of who He really is in Chapter Twenty-one.

Unfortunately many, if not most, Christians unconsciously labor under a negative view of God. Why? Because of the terms of the Law Covenant which required God's "just" response to the Israelite's stubbornness and idolatry. Their escapades fill over 82% of the Protestant Bible.

"Sinners in the hands of an angry God" sums up their warped perspective of who He is. Fortunately for us, Jesus *exchanged* what we deserved (God's angry judgment and wrath) with what Jesus deserves (Father-God's loving-kindness), in spite of our Adamic nature and rebellious behavior.

We now know that the Law Covenant was a temporary phase (Act Two) of the whole salvation drama. Here is what God knew would happen:

The Law was added so that sin might abound (the law arouses sin) but where sin abounded, grace abounded much more (Romans 5:20).

Notice that sin increased (and began to be imputed) when the Law was given to the Israelites. They received just punishment from God while it was in force. But again, grace and truth came in the Person of Jesus to replace the sin-arousing Law with the **New Covenant** of Love, not with increased punishment. God replaced the Law with His higher law that supplies faith in God's love for us which brings liberty through relying on Jesus' perfect performance for our justification.

Notice that increased sin was *not* met with ever increasing "justice" to suppress sin but ultimately with super-abounding grace – Jesus – who took all the just consequences of all sin and gave us total forgiveness and the free offer of oneness with God Himself. God *does* justice but He *is* love who shows mercy. Believers no longer have to fear His *justice* but can bask in the unconditional love of our wonderful Father. Why? Because the gift of "justification" and "righteousness" are the same word in Greek. Now *you*, believer, are a righteous-one (or just-one) of God *because* you are **in Christ** who is our righteousness, according to 1 Corinthians 1:30. Don't doubt that Good News! Believe and receive it as being as true for you as it is for Jesus.

No negative concept of God needs to dominate a believer's mind any longer if he "divides the word rightly." Let the truth of who God really is demolish any lies and mental strongholds that oppose the accurate knowledge of God's loving nature. How? By focusing on Jesus and His **divine exchange**, all of which is a gift from Father-God, offered to all humankind. There is now no need to pluck out your eye or cut off your hand because all sin of all mankind was forgiven (and no longer remembered by God) at Calvary, according to 2 Corinthians 5:19 and Hebrews 8:12 and 10:17. Therefore, now anyone can freely choose to be reconciled to God through rebirth and bask in the *experience* of Father-God's love as His beloved child by faith in Jesus and in His **finished work.** Again, we will more fully answer this all important biblical question "Who is God According to the Bible?" in our final chapter.

But Jesus Gave The Law To The Rich Young Ruler

"But wait a minute," you might be saying, "Jesus told the rich young ruler to keep the Law and we must do what Jesus commands." Well, let's look at that **pre-cross** passage to see *why* he gave him the law because it reveals, once more, God's true purpose for the Law. All three synoptic gospels contain the account (with some slight variation, which is not unusual). But we will look at Mark 10:17-27 because it was apparently the earliest written account and arguably the most personal of the three.

As Jesus started to leave, a man ran up to him and fell on his knees before him. 'Good teacher,' he asked, 'What must I do to secure eternal life?' 'Why do you call me good?' Jesus answered. 'No one is good except God alone. You know the commandments: Do not murder, do not commit adultery, do not steal, do not give false testimony, do not steal, honor your father and mother.' 'Teacher,' he declared, 'all these I have observed from my youth.' Jesus looked at him and loved him.

'One thing you lack,' he said. 'Go, sell whatever you have and give to the poor, and you will have treasure in heaven. Then come, follow me.' At this the man became sad. He went away grieved, because he had great wealth. Jesus looked around and said to his disciples, 'It is difficult for the rich to enter the kingdom of God! The disciples were wondering at his words. But Jesus said again, 'Children, how hard it is to enter the kingdom of God! It is easier for a camel to go through the eye of a needle than for a rich man to enter the kingdom of God.' The disciples were even more amazed, and said to each other, 'Who then can be saved?' Jesus looked at them and said, 'With man this is impossible, but with God, all things are possible.'

There is so much in this poignant passage to indicate it is in the **pre-cross** period of Jesus' ministry. For starters, Jesus focused on the man's greeting before addressing his question by asking a rhetorical question: "Why do you call me good? No one is good except One - God." We already read where Jesus called His hearers "evil" and even "children of the devil" so this "bad news," (describing man's fallen nature) was a consistent part of His overall message, **pre-cross**. But it caused shock, if not resentment, among the Jews because it contradicted the popular notion that at least some of their ancestors were "great men of God" (i.e. "just") and therefore "good" in God's eyes. How could they be "God's own people" and not be "good"? And this man, down on his knees, certainly thought that he was "good" because (he said) he kept all the commands (that Jesus mentioned) ever since his boyhood.

He was obviously well trained in the Jew's "performance-based" covenant, indicated by how he phrased his question: "What must *I do* to inherit eternal life?" (The correct question under the **New Covenant** would be: "What must I believe to receive eternal life?") Since he asked a law-based question (rather than faith-based), Jesus gave him a law-based answer. (His answer would be far more understandable than the one Jesus gave to Nicodemus – "be born again.") But first, "Jesus looked at him (through eyes of grace) and loved him." He did not chide or condemn him for his reliance on the Law because that was the expected norm under Moses' Covenant and it was still in force for the Jews.

Yet, Jesus did not leave him ignorant - or mistaken - either. He used the Law on this **in Adam** sinner lovingly, to give him a second chance to realize and admit his need for a Savior, rather than to continue to rely on his flesh to accomplish the "dead works" of law-keeping to try to earn eternal life. Jesus pushed him beyond his limit by raising the difficulty level, (though not to the standard of perfection which is required in order to "earn heaven by works") by suggesting that he sell all he owned, give (at least some) to the poor … and follow Him. That way, Jesus would be his <u>only</u> focus, his security, his provider, his reward - his God. He was offering him a "faith-walk" experience into the inner circle with Himself and His disciples in exchange for what he was *depending on* – his wealth, status and reputation. <u>His *real* problem regarding wealth was</u>

not that he *had* wealth but that his wealth had *him*. Jesus was offering him freedom from the false security of his wealth in the **seen realm** by putting his focus and dependence on Jesus, our only true treasure and reward.

In this exchange with the rich young ruler, Jesus used the Law as God intends to:

1) bring him to the end of his self-sufficiency,

2) show him his true condition and

3) see if he was really serious.

Again, Jesus used the demands of the law as a *mirror* so the man could see his true condition **in Adam**. Jesus' challenge revealed that, deep down, this man selfishly coveted things more than God and the wisdom of how to "get to heaven." He turned away sad. He was offered an eternal relationship with Jesus Himself and clung to his "stuff" instead. Hopefully he had a change of mind (repented) later – before it was too late.

Is Money Evil?

So then Jesus used the situation to say that it is (or at least can be) hard for a rich man to enter His Kingdom. (In fact, it is impossible for anybody while **in Adam**.) They were amazed at this revelation which shows that they were not paying attention to His dire assessment of mankind's fallen condition – whether rich or poor materially. They were conditioned by the terms of the Law to think that if you are rich, (like David had been) it was because God was blessing your good behavior, and, by extension, an indication that He would allow you into His Kingdom when you died. Conversely, bad behavior brought on God's punishment which did not bode well for your future. Jesus exploded their assumptions by saying that even the rich can have trouble entering heaven. (As always, He was operating from God's view of their **in Adam** condition.)

Now, thoroughly confused, they asked: "Who then can be saved?" Their question provided a teachable moment so Jesus gave them the bottom line: "With man it is impossible (to be saved), but not with God because with God, all things are possible" (Mark 10:23-27). His comment was designed to bring the disciples to the end of themselves, too, by changing their wrong beliefs (repenting) in order for them to think the way God thinks. Again, it is not just *hard* but impossible for any human, "rich or poor, good or bad, smart or dumb" to save himself with wealth or works or anything else of his own doing. That contradicted everything they believed in as Jews under their performance-based Judaism. Paul elaborated on this revelation when he stated: "I do not set aside the grace of God, for if righteousness could be gained by keeping the law (self-effort), then Christ died for nothing" (Galatians 2:21). "The law is not based on faith" (Galatians 3:12). "Anything that does not come from faith is sin" (Romans 14:23). Those revelations ought to end all discussions about holding on to any part of the **elephant of mixture.** But long-held strongholds resist the truth of the **whole grace-based gospel**, so Jesus sent the Holy Spirit to renew our mind with Father-God's perspective. So, ask and allow Him to "bathe your mind with His truth."

God Is Good, Not Stingy

When I heard Mark 10:17-27 read in church many years ago, my law-mindedness concluded that Jesus favored poor people over rich people. That idea was reinforced by a few church sermons I heard on the book of James which implied that the poorer one is, the holier he is - and that the rich were automatically evil. I did not know enough of the Bible to realize that God made people like Abraham and David and Solomon and even the Israelite slaves (coming out of Egypt) very materially rich. My ignorance of the truth caused me to think wrongly about rich people (defined in my mind as anyone richer than my family's middle class status) when I was young. I even made vocational choices based on that perspective. It was all part of the "lowly caterpillar syndrome" that is wrongly sold as "humility." That false concept still plagues those routinely opposed to any notion of "prosperity." Yet, if you ask them, they will probably tell you that they want their children and grandchildren to be healthy and prosperous - rather than sick and poor.

The Apostle John had the same loving attitude towards his friend Gaius in 3 John 2 when he wrote: "Beloved, I hope you are doing well (prospering) in all things and are in good health just as your soul prospers." Does God want less for His children than loving parents want for their children and that John wanted for his friend? If God was a stingy withholder and a nasty Judge, as many people wrongly think, would He have risked giving Adam dominion over His perfect earth? Or would He have handed over His beloved Son to a bunch of murderous, **in Adam** rebels and offer them heaven to boot?

After I repented – changed my mind to agree with God about His true character - it became very clear to me that Father-God likes to bless His children abundantly because He is a loving Giver at heart. And the more we are convinced of His outrageous goodness and lavish grace, the more we are properly disposed to receive all that He has already given to us, **in and through Christ Jesus' finished work**. Then, like Abraham, we can freely bless others as we are blessed. If poverty is so wonderful, why are there campaigns to "eradicate poverty?" In actuality, poverty is part of the bondage of the Adamic curse that Jesus broke when He submitted to being crucified on a tree, revealed in Galatians 3:13.

The problem comes when a believer *focuses selfishly* on health and/or wealth in the **seen realm** rather than focusing on the **unseen** Provider of divine health and wealth and all His other blessings as part of Jesus' inheritance given to believers. Ultimately, Father-God is the only focus worth having because He is the only source of all good things. Again, Jesus made this very clear when He said: "Seek first the Kingdom of God and His righteousness and all else will be given to you" (Matthew 6:33). If you are reborn of God, you are already in God's **unseen Kingdom** and are automatically righteous in His sight. Therefore, you are a legal beneficiary of Jesus' **finished work** and the challenge now is learning how to rest in what He *has done* and let the Holy Spirit live this new life **of Christ** through you. How? By walking according to the Holy Spirit's wisdom and ability rather than depending on your fleshy, self-centered perspective. God invites us to enter into His rest by letting Him become *our point of reference and supplier*. We will explore that mental switch-over later, in Chapters Sixteen to Nineteen.

Obviously, the rich young ruler was attached to having and getting wealth and Jesus was just mercifully pointing that out. Jesus wanted the rich young man to get free of what he was clinging to deep down – temporary "stuff" rather than God. He was his own point of reference and, unfortunately, he decided to keep it that way. He valued the **seen** creation above his **unseen** Creator because he did not know Father-God's lavish love for him and that He wanted to provide for him like He did for Jesus and His followers. Tragic!

Must Believers Faithfully Obey All Of The Commandments In The Four Gospels?

One specific **pre-cross** passage that stresses law-keeping is only found in Matthew's gospel, in what is known as "The Great Commission." It records Christ Jesus' last words (according to Matthew), immediately before His Ascension into Heaven and reads as follows:

Now the eleven disciples went to Galilee, to the mountain where Jesus had told them to go. And seeing Him, they worshiped Him; but certain ones doubted. Then Jesus came to them and said, 'All authority in heaven and on earth has been given to me. Therefore go forth and disciple all nations, baptizing them in the name of the Father and of the Son and of the Holy Spirit, teaching them to obey all I have commanded you. And behold, I am with you always, even to the consummation of the age' (Matthew 28:16-20).

One can only guess why the same commissioning "orders" were not thought significant enough to be included in all four gospels and in Acts, where the event was also described. And curiously, this event, described in Mark 16:9-20, is *not* found in "the most reliable early manuscripts and other ancient witnesses" according an NIV footnote for that passage. And, even more curious, Mark's account about Christ Jesus' ascension made no mention of "teaching commandments," even though there are many other phrases similar to Matthew's account. Likewise, neither the gospel of Luke nor the book of Acts makes any mention of "teaching commandments" in their respective account of Jesus' ascension. And the gospel of John makes no mention of the event at all. It is also very curious that, according to Matthew, some of the eleven "doubted" even though they worshipped Him.

More puzzling still is why Matthew makes no mention of Jesus' very important directive to wait in Jerusalem for what turned out to be the birth of the church – Pentecost – which Luke included both in his gospel and in Acts. So, bottom line, Matthew added the "teaching commandments" phrase to Mark's account but neither one included the direction to wait in Jerusalem (although Mark's account mentions that converts "will speak in new tongues" – which were given at Pentecost.) Also, "obey all that I have commanded you" would include gouging out one's eye etc. when it causes a believer to sin or requiring a rich person sell all he owns. That is *not* good news but clearly one of Jesus' many commands for law-keepers to add to the list.

Why the differences? One explanation is that Matthew's theme was "the coming Kingdom" and how can you have a kingdom without commandments? Given his tax-collector training and law-based Jewish mind-set, this is what he would be listening for and remembering from Jesus – or adding, as the case may be. But we now can contrast this law-centered account with the **big picture** presented above in Chapter Nine about:

1) the Mosaic Law's "harsh realities" and

2) that it was intended only for Jewish unbelievers, *not* Jewish believers or Gentiles and

3) why God abolished the Law for Jewish believers which had been a barrier between Jews and Gentiles and

4) just how magnificent is God's replacement – Jesus' **New Covenant** of lavish grace.

Yet Matthew's account is another instance where just one verse in just one of the four gospels is often used to stomp on or compromise the **butterfly-life** of Jesus' **grace gospel**. It requires a working knowledge and revelation of Jesus' **finished work** to discern what parts of the **pre-cross** four gospels are life-giving to the New Covenant believer and what parts are not. I strongly suggest that when feasting on the meat of God's word, be sure to avoid swallowing the bones of the law which will give you more than just indigestion. The Law ministers death and condemnation to the believer according to Jesus' revelation to Paul, as recorded in 2 Corinthians 3:7-9.

Ironically, eating actual elephant meat today is now illegal in most, if not all, parts of the world. But spiritually, the **elephant of mixture** is a steady diet for most believers. They focus on the dead letter of the law that kills, according to 2 Corinthians 3:6. Hopefully, dear saint, you will benefit from the testimony of my deliverance from the bondage of mixture into the freedom of Father-God's lavish **grace gospel**. How? By renewing your mind as needed on the pure meat of Jesus' **whole gospel of grace**, which is totally good news. Christ Jesus sent His Holy Spirit of truth within you to lead you into all truth. So invite Him to have His way in you and through you.

The Parable of the Pharisee and the Tax Collector
To some who were relying on themselves as being righteous and who looked down on everybody else, Jesus told this parable: 'Two men went up to the temple to pray, one a Pharisee and the other a tax collector. The Pharisee stood up and prayed to himself: 'God, I thank you that I am not like other men - robbers, evildoers, adulterers - or even like this tax collector. I fast twice a week and give a tenth of all I get.' But the tax collector stood at a distance. He would not even look up to heaven, but beat his breast and said, 'God, have mercy on me, a sinner.' I tell you that this man, rather than the other, went home justified before God. For everyone who exalts himself will be humbled, and he who humbles himself will be exalted' (Luke 18:9-14).

Based solely on this parable, one could understandably deduce that, to be continually righteous, – in right-standing with God – one must agree with God that he is a wretched sinner and must, therefore, continually ask for mercy. If he ever thinks otherwise, he is no longer acceptable to God because, according to this parable, given by Jesus **pre-cross**, there are only two self-concepts possible. And what Christian wants to disagree with Jesus? Thus, most Christians typically believe and say today, 2000 years later: "I am a sinner saved by grace." They reinforce the conclusion by misusing Paul's caution: "… Do not think of yourself more highly than you ought," found in Romans 12:3. Bottom line: this is (supposedly) the only truly accurate and "humble" thing to confess over oneself. If a reborn believer would think and say otherwise, he would automatically be classified as a proud Pharisee, since Jesus gave only two possibilities in this parable. And as everybody knows: "God opposes the proud but gives grace to the humble. Therefore, humble yourself under the mighty hand of God …" (1 Peter 5:5).

The common conclusion from all of this "biblical thinking" is that the believer is still a wretched caterpillar - unworthy, broken and desperate to get a crumb from a mighty God. Why? Because he is (supposedly) still a rotten sinner in the hands of an angry God. He is "double-minded, unstable in all his ways so he can't receive anything from the Lord" – as James would say in James 1:7-8. This description, and even worse, was preached by Jonathan Edwards (which is thought by some, even today, to be the greatest sermon ever given in America. After all, it was credited for starting the first Great Awakening in America.) Believer, is any part of this **pre-cross** assessment still your belief and confession, deep down? If so, that is *not* good news. You are agreeing with the Accuser of the brethren, not with God.

So Who Are You, Really?

Again, *some* of that would be true of you *if* you are still **in Adam** instead of reborn of God (All of God's just *anger* against mankind was poured out on the body of Jesus at Calvary.) It is an accurate and fitting description of your former "state of being" before the holy God of the universe. It was quite appropriate for Jesus to say that about everyone He connected with *before* he died. "There is none righteous, no not even one," "for all have sinned and fallen short of the glory of God" (Romans 3:10 and 23). The verdict for everyone **in Adam** is that they are condemned to hell forever. That is the desperate state that the whole human race begins in, thanks to being **in Adam.** Now that is *really* bad news.

Two Kinds Of Righteousness

So, in fact, that was the **unseen**, spiritual condition of *both* of these men in the parable. The only important difference was that the Pharisee was oblivious to this fact because he trusted in his law-keeping and so believed himself to be righteous. His self-righteousness masked his actual state of unrighteousness in God's eyes. However, the tax collector had the grace and courage to acknowledge the truth of his desperate condition - to the degree that he understood it. Therefore, the honest tax collector's "righteousness" was not the same as New Covenant righteousness, - based solely on Jesus' **finished work** - which had not yet happened. Rather, he implicitly agreed with God's assessment (repentance) that he needed a savior because he admitted that he could not meet the requirement of performance-based righteousness which demands perfect law-keeping under that covenant. By grace, he realized that his only real hope was in receiving mercy and forgiveness as underserved gifts from God.

The Pharisee's brand of *behavior-based* righteousness is also reflected in many of the proverbs in the Bible. For example, some people are labeled as "just" while others are called "wicked." (See Endnote **#32** for more on Abraham's kind of righteousness.) The assessment was based on their external behavior, not on their **in Adam** nature. Therefore, in God's **big picture**, both men were still **in Adam sinners** because the **seen-based**, law covenant could not fix any man's **unseen** nature problem. So people just evaluated other people based on their words and deeds, period. (That was also James' primary focus in his life as a Nazarite, in his ministry, and in his book - and why he was called "James the Just.")

However, Jesus astounded the Jews because He could see people's true heart/spirit condition - sinners still **in Adam**, spiritually dead to God, as implied in John 2:25. But fortunately for us all, He did not come to enforce the law but to fulfill it and replace it with the **New Covenant.** Instead of condemnation, He came with grace and truth in order to finally set sinners free by rebirth, as John 3:17-18 happily reveals. And remember, it was the Pharisees, not the "sinners," who angered Jesus. Why? Because they were only focused on obedience to the **seen** law for performance-based righteousness. They missed "seeing" the righteous One who came from the **unseen Kingdom** to fulfill and replace what they erroneously <u>depended</u> on for their own "righteousness" – the Mosaic Law – which, again, is the strength of sin and results in death.

But the true gospel explains that Jesus was sent by Father-God to offer to everyone the opportunity to "be saved" from certain damnation – caused by being spiritually united with Adam who is mankind's original "Federal Head" by default. Jesus came, not to condemn the world – because everyone was already condemned **in Adam** – but to remove all the effects of what the first Adam caused by his rebellion (see John 3:17-18). Jesus came as the suffering Servant to forgive and to absorb all of humankind's sin, and God's just wrath and punishment for *all* sins, in His human body by actually becoming sin. In doing so, Jesus, the last Adam, restored the ability for people to personally choose or reject Him - Tree of Life – a privilege that was lost to mankind by Adam when he rebelled as mankind's legal Representative before God.

Consequently, from God's divine viewpoint, Jesus' **finished work** removed the "negatives" against all mankind and only a person's *refusal* to personally believe and accept God's offer of rebirth will keep him or her **in Adam** and, therefore, condemned to hell because of *unbelief.* But Jesus accomplished far more than just remove the "negatives" and restore individual choice. When a sinner chooses to be reborn by grace through faith, his or her former, **in Adam** nature, which defines every human as a sinner from God's viewpoint, becomes a "partaker of divine nature," according to 1 Peter 4:13 It is a **divinely orchestrated exchange,** described in 1 Peter 1:23: "For you have been born again, not of perishable seed but of imperishable seed, through the living and enduring Word of God (Jesus, Himself)." How? Again, because Jesus *became* the sin of all mankind as God's replacement for Adam. Jesus is man's new Federal Head and Savior. This **divine exchange** enables believers to enjoy Jesus' righteous standing before God by being united to Him. When He arose, all believers arose with Him by faith in what He did. Simple. Profound. Awesome. (Chapter Twenty-One provides more details of this astounding transaction that made our redemption possible.)

Eternal Life, Eternal Righteousness

So, under the new and everlasting covenant, all believers are permanently righteous just by accepting and relying on Jesus' performance, not on theirs. Now God regards them as saints, alive to Him - not as sinners still dead to God. Therefore, it is no longer truthful or "humble" for any believer to deny God's re-creative handiwork by still calling himself "a sinner, saved by grace." One cannot be **in Adam** and **in Christ** simultaneously because true Christianity is all about fundamentally *being* a **new creation** (having a regenerated, re-begun nature) *not* about behavior. Thinking and saying otherwise dishonors the enormous sacrifice Jesus paid for your redemption and right-standing with Father-God. Put simply, **New Covenant** righteousness is about right *being* not about right *doing*. However, right believing will eventually produce the fruit of right living the more a believer becomes *mentally* established in God's revelation and implications of Jesus' **divine exchange**.

So why do believers still believe and even profess being a sinner? It is because of wrong beliefs and traditions that fail to divide the word rightly by distinguishing between the two opposing covenants. Again, this can happen easily by reading the four gospels without discernment. What is true for **in Adam** sinners is no longer true for **in Christ** saints because of Jesus' **finished work**. His **pre-cross** parable of the publican and Pharisee *did not include this third option because it was not yet a post-cross, New Covenant reality.*

Now, thanks to Jesus, reborn-of-God-humans are instantly transformed from a caterpillar nature, as a sinner **in Adam**, to a **butterfly nature** as a "perfect saint"- in one's inner spirit-man - by being made one with Jesus in His crucifixion, death, resurrection, and ascension into heaven. Calvary "made all things new" spiritually for all believers. But this **unseen reality** of being **one with Christ** can only be "seen" by *using* the eyes of biblical faith which God gives to believers as standard equipment. Only Jesus' gospel to Paul provides the complete revelation of who every believer actually *is* **in Him.** (Jesus' revelation to Paul about every believer's new spirit-man **in Christ** is explained in Chapter Sixteen. Ignorance or denial of this core reality is one of the root causes of mixture, doubt and unbelief in the church today.)

So what *was* true for you when **in Adam** is no longer true for you if you are **in Christ**. Jesus' **finished work** added a new possibility - a third category besides "Pharisee" or "Publican" - in the **post-cross, New Covenant.** To continue to say that "I am a sinner, saved by grace" after being reborn of God, is to be mentally "squashed" under the lies of the **elephant** of Galatianism. Again, this is the mixture of the **pre-cross,** Mosaic covenant of works with the astonishing effects of Jesus' cross, according to His **whole gospel**. What was true, **pre-cross,** for all mankind is no longer true for the redeemed, **post-cross** believer. The confusion stems from not discerning the major difference between one's "sin nature **in Adam**" with one's "perfect, **new nature in Christ**" - the last Adam, according to Hebrew 10:14. Jesus could hardly make the distinction any more clear when He revealed this through Paul in 2 Corinthians 5:14 and 16-17:

> For Christ's love compels us, because we are convinced that one died for all, and therefore all died. ... So from now on we regard no one from a worldly (natural, carnal, **seen level**) point of view. Though we once regarded Christ in this way, we do so no longer. Therefore, if anyone is **in Christ**, he is a new creation; the old has gone, the new has come!

To Repeat The Wonderful Good News

Jesus is revealing to us what happened in the **unseen realm** on Calvary. Again, He was commissioned by God to be the *new representative of the whole human race* – replacing the first Adam. Therefore, when He died*, all died (spiritually) with Him* to the **in Adam** nature (just like we all had died spiritually to God when Adam fell) - as a legal reality, from God's viewpoint. However, it must be received individually, by faith, in order to become a vital, personal reality through rebirth. For all who believe, the old, **in Adam** nature (the old man, one's former spirit-self that was one with Darkness) was crucified with Christ then *died* just as He died and was *buried* just as He was buried. It was so depraved and corrupt that it could not be "fixed" but had to be eliminated. Then, when Jesus arose, you, believer, were regenerated - re-begun - as a **new creation** spirit-being, perfect and one with Christ Jesus in your new, inner man. Again, for a believer to regard himself otherwise – as still an **in Adam** sinner – is to deny that such an **unseen**, fundamental transaction took place because of Jesus' perfect **divine exchange** with him. Jesus left nothing undone in order to make you, believer, one with Father-God which was His stated prayer and goal in 1 Corinthians 6:17 and John 17:21.

Could it be stated any clearer than that? From God's viewpoint - who always sees things correctly - the believer is fundamentally different from when he was **in Adam**, even though there may be no immediate, visible changes on the outside. If that was not true, no believer could be united with **Christ**. For a believer to look at himself from a worldly perspective is to make the mistake of using his sensate sight to define himself and other people, when God's definition of him and others is the only true perspective. Again, that is why Paul no longer regarded others from the perspective of the **seen** flesh, (including Jesus in His **pre-cross** humanity, as he states in 2 Corinthians 5:16 cited above.) It is simply a matter of being humble enough to agree with what God sees and says is true – even *if* it does not seem true to you at first. And when you ask Him to show you what is true, He will bath and renew your mind to begin to see the **unseen realities** of His Kingdom as He does. "Holy Spirit, bathe my mind with your truth." That is how the content of this book came to be written.

Insisting on regarding oneself from a carnal viewpoint is to reject God's assessment (which is based on the **unseen reality**) in favor of temporary facts in the **seen realm**. The latter is based solely on the believer's self-centered focus on his unsanctified outer man and his behavior. That is also what the Book of James focuses on primarily. It is precisely this mental stronghold of *focusing on one's seen self and on one's behavior* (based on following people's laws rather than depending your relationship with Father-God) that defines "dead works" biblically. This focus corresponds to the "weak and poor principles of this world's system," which ultimately came from the carnal knowledge of the "Tree of Good and Evil" in the Garden. This "law sandwich" is still being peddled by the devil today, which Jesus condemned through Paul in Galatians 4:4-9 as follows:

But when the time had fully come, God sent his Son, born of a woman, born under law, to redeem those under law (the Jews), that we (Jews and Gentiles) might receive the full rights of sons. Because you are sons, God sent the Spirit of His Son into our hearts, the Spirit who calls out, "Abba, Father." So you (Gentile Galatians) are no longer a slave, but a son; and since you are a son, God has made you also an heir. Formerly, when you did not know God, you were slaves to those who are not gods by nature. But now that you know God - or rather are known by God - how is it that you are turning back to those weak and poor principles (of the Law)? Do you wish to be enslaved by them all over again?

Receiving God's gift of eternal redemption through Jesus' monumental accomplishment causes each believer to be a cherished son and an heir of God because he is one spirit with Him, **in Christ Jesus**, according to 1 Corinthians 6:17. We are to get our sense of worth and direction from the Holy Spirit, as God's children, rather than depending on the rules and regulations and vain philosophies of unbelievers.

If a believer continues to confess that he is a "sinner" because he still behaves imperfectly, he will continue to carry out that self-perception into action - sinning - even though God no longer defines him that way. He is, in effect, agreeing with the devil's condemning mantra that goes something like this:

You are still an unworthy caterpillar because your behavior disqualifies you from really being a son of God. Nothing you can do really pleases God because He demands perfect obedience and holiness. You may as well quit trying, curl up and die.

Do you see the lie? The devil wants you to keep thinking that your right-standing and acceptance with God is still based on your day-to-day rule-keeping rather than on Jesus' perfect life and sacrifice which is now the basis of God's gift of righteousness to you – regardless of your outward behavior. God's free gift is based solely on your *belief* that God accepts Jesus' perfect doing (not your imperfect doing) as your basis for eternal redemption, a righteous relationship, and an eternal inheritance **in Christ**. When you accept that **divine exchange** by faith, you are, thereby, "born of God" which qualifies you for *all* that Jesus accomplished for you by identification with Him. Again, your new identity has nothing to do with your behavior and everything to do with believing and receiving what Jesus did for you 2000 years ago - including making you a holy (set-apart) saint, a child of Father-God and joint-heir **in Him**.

Freedom Comes From Believing God's Truth About You

The believer's fundamental nature change can only be understood by the supernatural sight of faith in Jesus' **whole gospel** that reveals the **unseen realm** to any believer who accepts what Jesus showed Paul as real and relevant. The four gospels do not reveal the actual terms of the **New Covenant** but just give hints of what the coming **unseen Kingdom (post-cross)** would be like. But this "preview" is also mixed with the curses and consequences of living under the law system which was inadequate for justification because it depended on a sinner's failed efforts and performance. That is why God found fault with the Mosaic Covenant and why Jesus would soon replace it with a **New Covenant** for believers as part of His **finished work** on the cross.

The difference between an **in Adam** sinner and a saint **in Christ** is that the sinner cannot do anything but sin because of his **in Adam** nature. A saint, however, no longer *has* to sin because of his **new creation** nature - though he still might because of his soulish, stinkin' thinkin' and the self-sufficiency of the flesh. As a saint renews his mind with the **whole gospel of grace** to understand, by revelation knowledge, who he now is **in Christ**, he will be far more likely to use the overcoming power of the Holy Spirit to walk free of habits and patterns and mind-sets that plagued him as a sinner **in Adam**. Since he is no longer a caterpillar, he can choose to soar like a **butterfly** in the wind of the Spirit-led life – just like Jesus learned to do.

Bondage-Breaking Truth

Even in the midst of sinning, the Holy Spirit will remind you that "you are the righteousness of God in Christ Jesus." As you yield to this revelation and speak it out by faith, you will increasingly experience the freeing power of this word of truth to release you from a sin habit or addiction etc. The living and active word of truth about who you now are – a saint **in Christ** even while you sin – will remind you of how *God* sees you and will give you an upward call to live out of your new, perfect spirit-self that is united to the Lord. This is the reality that Paul constantly reminded the Corinthians about to help them overcome various sin patterns from their old lifestyle. As you become established in this revelation of being united with Jesus and, therefore, righteous in Him, your mind will be progressively freed from the grip of law and sin-consciousness and guilt and condemnation. Why? Because your natural mind can't focus on two things at the same time. The revelation that you are "dead to sin (the Adamic nature) and alive to

God" will become experiential in your outer man. Sinning will progressively lose its dominion over your soul and body as you learn to walk according to the Holy Spirit. The more you focus on Jesus and focus on the truths of the **unseen reality**, which you are now a part of according to God, the less attractive will be the mud puddles of the world, the flesh and the devil. As the song says: "And the things of earth will grow strangely dim in the light of His glory and grace." We are now privileged to be participants in His glory and grace and ambassadors of His message of lavish grace.

Seeing yourself as God's precious child, provides the affirmation so sorely needed to live consistently in the **seen realm** according to who you now actually are in the **unseen realm**, thanks to being **in Christ Jesus**. Because He is your righteousness, you *are* now the righteousness of God **in Christ**, according to 2 Corinthians 5:21. It is not merely "imputed to your account (separate from you, as some teach). Rather, Jesus' righteousness is imparted to you because you are *one* with Him who has become your righteousness. Over time, believing God's **unseen** truth and affirmation about you will trump the **seen** facts and transform your behavior from inside out! That is a work of the Spirit of truth, sent to reveal and convince you of the truth of who you now are **in Christ**.

As you meditate on this revelation, you will progressively experience the sanctifying process of your soul and body as God's own ambassador and temple. This process is **New Covenant** repentance – the renewing of your mind to agree with what God says about you by faith, not by your sight. The more you agree with God, you will increasingly understand what Jesus has personally already accomplished for you. This continuous increase of right believing will produce the Holy Spirit's fruit of right living – an outer demonstration of your new, righteous, spirit-being self, alive and in union with Christ Jesus. This glorious reality, unveiled by Jesus to Paul, will be explained in greater detail in Chapter Sixteen.

Can The Grace Gospel Be Twisted?

Is it possible for believers to be deceived to think that Paul is actually reinforcing the law for believers? Such an interpretation is possible if you let the **elephant** of law-mindedness walk around in your head. That is exactly what I did for much of my life. One example was my faulty understanding of a scripture where Paul instructed Timothy, one of his dearest disciples, to: "Study to show thyself approved unto God, a workman unashamed, rightly dividing the word of truth" (2 Timothy 2:15). Of course, Paul was referring to the **grace gospel** that he received directly from Jesus, which he called "the law of Christ" in Galatians 6:2 and the "gospel of Christ" in Romans 1:16. (We know that he was not referring to any of the four gospels because they were not written yet.) Again, one's interpretation of what Paul was writing to Timothy will necessarily depend on which set of "lenses" (which mindset) a believer is looking through: the law's dark-tinted glasses *or* the crystal clear, grace-based glasses of Jesus' **whole gospel**.

Given my law-centered, religious upbringing, I naturally saw everything through my dark "law glasses." Therefore, I interpreted the above scripture to mean that it is necessary for me to study the Bible daily to get and maintain God's *acceptance* and *approval* and *righteousness*. I wrongly thought that it was just one of the many *demands* that God expected me to live under and consistently fulfill as a workman ("toiler" in the Greek) so that He would not become ashamed of me. If I didn't read and study the Bible regularly - daily in fact - God would not be pleased with me. But, as long as I was diligent in this and in all the other (supposed) duties of a Christian, I believed that I did not have to fear that God would be ashamed of me! Instead, God would *reward my efforts* with His many blessings as a sign of His approval. I just had to make sure that I "divided the word correctly" by finding out what other demands (laws) in the Old and New Testament I must do to please God even more. I even made lists of "commands" found in Paul's writings. Sound familiar?

My Fears Relieved

But when I put on Jesus' grace-based glasses, the ones Jesus put on Paul, Eureka! I "saw" that Paul was actually urging Timothy to study "my gospel" (2 Timothy 2:8), the "gospel of Christ" (Philippians 1:27). It is Jesus' **whole gospel of lavish grace** that Paul had taught Timothy and had even written down – *to unveil the benefits* of Jesus' **finished work.** Since Timothy was a reborn saint, he was already totally accepted and approved – justified and righteous – *apart* from his behavior, because he was now *one* with Christ Jesus, just as Paul stated so clearly in Romans 3:21-22. Father-God saw him the same way as He regarded Jesus, since he was now **in Him** and, therefore, He was already pleased with him because he was also "one spirit with the Father." And, best of all, what was true for Timothy, **in Christ**, was also now true for *me* too! Wow!

Therefore, since I was now under God's abundant, grace-based **New Covenant**, just like Paul and Timothy, I would never, ever have to be under the law of sin and death again. A growing revelation of Jesus' higher Law of faith, love and liberty gradually freed my mind from law-centeredness. By reading grace-based books listed in Appendix 5, I gradually realized that I did not have to be mentally bound to the law that

1) was impossible for me to keep,

2) arouses sin,

3) is the strength of sin,

4) causes death and

5) brings on guilt and shame – all of which we covered in Chapter Nine.

Rather, by feeding on (not toiling for) the benefits of Jesus' glorious revelation of **Jesus' whole gospel of grace**, I, too, could forever rest from my own efforts to gain or maintain right-standing with God. Instead, since rebirth made me the righteousness of God **in Christ** - as His *gift* to me - I could live by faith in His love for me and in His freedom from my former self, purchased for me by Jesus' **finished work** which has replaced the burden of law-keeping. Glory!

Furthermore, because the law is not for the righteous (1 Timothy 1:9), there was, from now on, *no* condemnation from God because

1) Jesus forgave all of my sin for all time and

2) the law was nailed to the cross (Colossians 2:14 and Ephesians 2:15) and

3) no sin is imputed to me by God when there is no performance-based law (see Romans 4:15).

I was now permanently positioned **in Christ Jesus** (Romans 8:1 and Ephesians 2:6). Paul also exhorted Timothy (and me) to guard Jesus' gospel with the help of the Holy Spirit inside of him:

> With faith and love for Christ Jesus, consider what you heard me say to be the pattern of accurate teachings (Jesus' gospel). With the help of the Holy Spirit who lives in us, guard the Good News that has been entrusted to you (2 Timothy 1:13-14).

Guard it from what or whom? In context, protect it from the lies of the world system, his own flesh, the devil and the Judaizers, led by James, who were still circumcising Gentiles in the Jerusalem church (and, by extension, those pushing a law-focus today). The battle still rages today wherever Jesus' **whole gospel**, given to Paul, is mixed with the terms of the Law Covenant which do *not* apply to **new creation** believers.

Again, this travesty also happens when people mistakenly assume that *all* of Jesus' statements in the **pre-cross** four gospels are to be automatically followed today, even though He was primarily speaking to **in Adam** Jews who were still under the law. Many more examples of **pre-cross** realities found in the Old Testament and in the four gospels that were updated at Calvary for believers **in Christ** are in the left-hand column of the following chart (**12A**). The radical changes, caused by Jesus' **divine exchange**, are in the right-hand column. Allow the Holy Spirit to renew your mind by slowly reading each line – out loud is even better – and let faith and gratitude rise up in your new heart, believer, by hearing His life-giving truth. We will explore more facets of His truth in later chapters.

PRE-CROSS life of JESUS under Law		POST-CROSS JESUS' Gospel to Paul
Old Things In ADAM		**"All Things New" In CHRIST**
Main focus is Jesus' SEEN life on earth		Main focus is UNSEEN Realm's benefits
Jesus prayed for our oneness with Him	F	He achieved it - Jn. 17:21 - for believers
Recorded the events of Calvary		Jesus revealed what He accomplished
He was crucified, buried, raised		The same for believers in Him - by faith
Satan had legal dominion over the earth	R	Jesus defeated Satan, restored Dominion.
Satan lies about God's nature and motives		Knowing Jesus, sets believers free
All Under Slavery	E	**All Things New In Christ**
Satan steals, kills and destroys		**In Christ**, Satan is under believer's feet
In Adam, mankind condemned to Hell	E	**In Christ,** believers seated in heavenlies
Mankind in Darkness at birth		Reborn saints walk in the Light - Jesus
All are Sinners and unrighteous by nature		Made righteous **in Christ** by faith in Him
Jews under the Mosaic Law	D	Believers under New Covenant of Grace
Jews under Law's heavy yoke, Acts 8:10		"My yoke is easy" – the law of the Spirit
God seen as distant Law enforcer - Judge		God is Abba-Father, revealed in Jesus
The Law demands but cannot help		The Mosaic Law was nailed to the Cross
Constant efforts to earn God's acceptance	O	Believers are accepted in the Beloved
The Gentiles were "lawless"		Higher law is Faith, Love and Liberty
Mixture of Law and Grace		Pure Grace – Jesus' Revelation 2 Cor. 12
Stuck here on earth, destined for Hell	M	Seated **in Christ** in the heavenlies Eph. 2:6
Under circumstances - **in Adam**		Above circumstances - **in Christ**
None born again – all **in Adam**		Rebirth offered at Pentecost – **in Christ**
Self and sin-centered		Unselfish and God-conscious **in Christ**
The wages of sin is death	IN	Sinless Jesus became and removed our sin
Jesus forgave sins to individuals		Jesus' death paid for all sin of all mankind
Constant confession of sins		God no longer remembers our sins
Reconciliation based on daily sacrifices		I am reconciled to God by Jesus' Blood
Under the curses of Dt. 28	C	Jesus' Cross removed all curses in Dt. 28
Righteousness won by perfect behavior		Righteousness is a gift from Jesus
Perfection is required but impossible		His perfection is supplied to all saints
All blessings were based on one's efforts	H	All blessing based on Jesus' performance
The Holy Spirit came on some		The Holy Spirit inside every true believer
Mysteries of the Kingdom kept hidden		Kingdom mysteries revealed to the saints
Jesus foretold coming of the Kingdom		His Kingdom is Him - inside each saint
The Law says "You must do."	R	Jesus declared "It is Finished." Done!
The Law says "You have to …"		Now, saints "get to …"
The Law demands & requires perfection		Jesus supplies righteousness & perfection
Kingdom closed to even Jesus' disciples	I	Rebirth enables believer to see and enter
Blind to the **Unseen Realm**		The **Unseen** revealed by eyes of faith
Disciples' good works were "dead works"		Greater works than Jesus' now possible
Disciples merely followed Christ	S	Believer is now **in Christ** and He is in him
Salvation was not yet possible		Jesus opened the veil to heaven
Sinners are incompatible with God		Believers one in spirit with Father-God
All sinner's efforts just "dead works"	T	The Spirit of Life produces His fruit in us

12A Pre-Cross – Post-Cross Chart –Freedom In Christ

How refreshing it is, believer, to bathe your mind in Jesus' **divine exchange**. It is proof positive of His steadfast love for you and me, as our elder Brother, our suffering Savior, our servant-King and our Lord. There is nothing you can say or do to merit such sacrificial gifts of love, acceptance, approval, righteousness and significance from the God of the universe. It is all a free, underserved gift. And, because it is impossible to be justified (made righteous) by one's good works, a true believer can't become condemned by God (i.e. "unjustified") by doing bad works. Why? Because, in the **New Covenant**, righteousness is *a gift from God, received by grace through faith in His **finished work*** of salvation. If justification was still "works-based" (like it was under the Mosaic Law), it would not depend on God's free, unmerited gift of salvation through Jesus' **finished work**. Instead, it would be earned or lost based on one's daily performance. Condemnation is the result of still being **in Adam** and rejecting His **finished work** by the sin of unbelief.

So, believer, which gospel are you <u>believing in and depending on</u> – Jesus' good news of the pure **grace gospel** revealed to Paul or the combination of law-based passages and graced-based revelations found side by side in the four gospels?

Is There An Elephant In Your Head?

If you are a reborn Christian who still believes that you are a "sinner saved by grace," then please *repent* (change your thinking) by agreeing with God about the new, righteous you, **in Christ**, in whom all things are new, *spiritually*. Yes, that includes *you*, believer. It would be impossible to be **in Christ** and *not* be righteous and perfect because Light and Darkness do not mix. As it says definitively in 1 John 1:5: "God is light and in Him there is no Darkness" - none. You would be "contaminating" Christ Jesus, the holy One of God, if you were anything less than perfect in your inner man, as stated clearly in Hebrews 10:14 and received by faith.

Believe Jesus' **whole grace-based gospel** revealed to Paul about who you now are **in Christ**, which was described in detail in Chapter Two, so that you can see the way God now regards you, thanks to Jesus' **finished work** on Calvary. Chapter Fifteen will examine this truth in greater detail but before going there, a thorough scriptural exploration of God's gift of total forgiveness of *all your past, present and future sins* is presented in the next two chapters to help you renew your mind, as needed, about this core reality. That will then pave the way to fully embrace the revelation of your true identity **in Christ**, presented more completely in Chapter Sixteen. The best is yet to come!

Jesus made it possible for fallen humans to abide **in Him** automatically through rebirth. It takes no effort because you are now <u>placed</u> **in Him**. But that is not the same as being mentally conscious of that **unseen reality** and resting in it. The following two song-poems go together scripturally and musically. The first is Jesus' invitation to <u>consciously</u> live **in Him**. The second asks Him to teach us believers how to "enter that rest" **in Him** *mentally* – and come to rely in all that He has done for us.

ABIDE IN ME, and I will abide in you (2X)
A branch cannot bear any fruit of itself.
It must remain on the tree.
Neither can you bear any fruit of yourself.
You must remain in Me.
© Copyright 1994 by Leonard J. Ransil

TEACH ME HOW TO REST in You, O Lord,
Gladly yielding to Your sovereignty.
Teach me how to rest in You, O Lord,
Trusting in Your love for me.

I was nothing without You,
I was doomed to failure and shame,
But in You I can do all Your love calls me to
For the sake or Your glorious name.
© Copyright 1991 by Leonard J. Ransil

CHAPTER THIRTEEN

A THEOLOGY OF GOD'S TOTAL FORGIVENESS IN THE NEW COVENANT

The overwhelming evidence in Jesus' **grace gospel** is that God has forgiven all mankind of all sin for all time because of Jesus' **finished work**, according to 2 Corinthians 5:18-19 and 1 John 2:2. Why, then, are so many Christians confused and even in doubt about this magnanimous gift? The primary reason is named in the title of this book. The **elephant** of Galatianism, which is the heretical mixture of two opposing covenants, is still being paraded around in many, if not in most, churches today. It became entrenched because the early church was not in full agreement of what comprises Jesus' **whole gospel of grace**. Most early believers did not fully understand, value and accept what Paul taught and wrote about, as described in Chapter Ten. Kingdom realities can only be seen, entered into, appreciated and progressively received by God-given faith.

But not every Christian is aware of or eager for experiencing all that the **New Covenant** supplies. For example, it is shocking that, after almost 2000 years, the baptism of the Holy Spirit and the gifts of the Spirit (which are part of the **bare bones gospel** experienced at Pentecost by those in the Jerusalem church) are not welcomed and enjoyed by all Christians. Likewise, God's **total forgiveness** of mankind's past, present and future sins, based on Jesus' perfect, substitutionary sacrifice, is not believed by every Christian or often shared with unbelievers. It all comes from *unbelief* – the failure to agree with what Jesus revealed to Paul.

Two Contemporary Heresies

Before presenting a scriptural case to support this foundational doctrine of **total forgiveness** of mankind, some clarification is in order so that there is no misunderstanding. God has totally forgiven all sin and reconciled the world to Himself (from His viewpoint) because of Jesus' perfect sacrifice. But this does not mean everybody is now automatically going to heaven – by default. If an **in Adam** sinner is to benefit from God's amazing gifts of His grace, he must believe and receive the Giver of these gifts, his Savior and Lord of all, Christ Jesus. Otherwise, by default, he who is justly condemned already by still being **in Adam** will suffer eternal consequences in hell. It is not God's will that anyone should perish. Jesus came to offer salvation to everyone. But each person must choose to accept God's free offer to be united with Jesus in spirit and in truth because heaven is based on entering into an eternal relationship with God and His family. In order to qualify for heaven, Jesus emphatically stated that every human must be born of God, not just of man, according to John 3:3.

Two popular heresies contradict this truth and, therefore, attack the true gospel of Jesus Christ. The first is the lie that "All humans are automatically children of God and, therefore, part of His family." This notion became ingrained through popular songs like *He's Got The Whole World In His Hands* and the line "little ones to Him belong" in *Jesus Loves Me This I Know*. (As a worship leader for 40+ years, I have become increasingly careful to compose and to choose songs that declare the truth of Jesus' gospel to Paul.) The implication in the lyrics is that we are automatically all brothers and sisters by reason of natural birth and, thereby, belong to God who is everybody's father. This is a false premise that denies the truth in Genesis that God created Adam and Eve as part of His creation, not as part of an eternal spiritual family. There was no human family *fathered* by God before Jesus came to make that possible through rebirth, **post-cross**. Genesis makes it clear that all mankind is part of God's *created* human race – and there is only *one* natural race, with Adam as our original "human father." His rebellion caused the whole race to be under the power of Darkness until we each, individually, are reborn and transferred into the **unseen Kingdom** of God's beloved Son, *only* by grace through faith in Jesus' **finished work, according to** Colossians 1:13. John 1:12-13 is the clearest **New Covenant** statement of the only way to become God's child and, thereby, part of God's family:

> Yet to as many as received Him (Jesus), to those who believed in His name, He gave authority (the right) to <u>become</u> children of God, who were born not of (human) blood, nor of the will of flesh nor the will of man, but <u>born of God</u>.

In effect, God established a new blood-line and a new spiritual race when Jesus became the first of many brothers at His resurrection. On the cross, Jesus, the sinless man who knew no sin, became sin and received God's full wrath and full punishment for *all* of mankind's sin and received the consequent wages of sin, which is death, as our perfect Substitute, according to 2 Corinthians 5:17-21.

Then He was raised from the dead, no longer as the sin-filled Son of Man but as the justified Son of God in the human form of the exalted and last Adam. He willingly includes all who receive regeneration by faith in His redemption process – His **finished work**. He is the only human being able to fully qualify all **in Adam** human beings for sonship in God. How? First, by fulfilling the law perfectly (which we could not do) with His life, lived on our behalf and secondly, by satisfying the sin-debt for all mankind and then, thirdly, freely giving a new nature to those who believe and receive what He accomplished on their behalf. He, Himself, *is* eternal, abundant life – the Tree of Life. Bottom line: You can only become a child of God by being born of God through Jesus, His Son, by grace through faith.

This explains why the second popular heresy, called Universalism, is also not true. Universalism is the belief that all mankind is automatically saved because of what Jesus did for the whole world. However, no **in Adam** sinner is qualified to be compatible with God's perfection unless he/she personally accepts Jesus as God's only Savior for mankind and is, thereby, reborn of God. Jesus came in the flesh 2000 years ago to offer everyone His gift of rebirth to become God's adopted child, made possible by Jesus' **finished work**. Son-ship with God was never automatic or universal, even with Adam. Union with Jesus would have been his if he had chosen to eat the fruit of the Tree of Life – Jesus. Likewise today, only Jesus is the way to God and heaven, received by choosing to accept Him as your life-giving Savior and Justifier, by grace through faith.

The Reality Of Total Forgiveness In Christ Jesus
We will explore the process and outcomes of God's amazing miracle of rebirth in Chapters Sixteen to Eighteen. But for now it is important to understand that, from God's viewpoint, this new unity with Jesus through regeneration enables God to <u>legally regard all believers as He regards Jesus Himself</u>. What Jesus deserves, believers can now also enjoy just by being **in**

Christ – received by a trusting faith, not by self-effort. If the believer's reborn spirit-self was not automatically perfect, no oneness or intimate fellowship with God would be possible (see Colossians 2:10 and Hebrews 10:14). **Total forgiveness** of *all* sin was a necessary pre-condition to accomplish Father-God's ultimate goal for us - of being one spirit with Him forever (see 1 Corinthians 6:17). This miracle happens immediately upon rebirth, *not* "someday in the sweet by and by" as many people have been erroneously told through sermons, books and songs. (See Endnote #**33** for more clarification on this vital topic.) Likewise, God's eternal life is not merited by living a "good life" and then given at death as a reward. Rather, it is God's gift of Himself to a spiritually dead, **in Adam** sinner upon rebirth. Remember, the Giver is the Gift.

More amazing still, God forgave *all* of mankind's sin according to His perfect knowledge of mankind's total sin debt, not according to our limited awareness of our own sin debt. That is a huge difference. Due to our corrupt thinking, we are often not aware of our personal sins of omission and might even try to justify (excuse) a sin we are aware of. If God exacted justice on us for our total sin debt that He fully knows about (instead of heaping it all onto Jesus who became our sin and fully paid it off), no one could endure it. And, even if He did offer to accept a payment from us for our individual sin debt, what payment do we have to offer because we are bankrupt without Him? Fortunately for us, He desires to have a family of redeemed saints living with Him, instead of a mob of condemned slaves who are forced to pay for their own sin-debt in hell, eternally. The choice is now ours, thanks to Jesus.

There is yet another key reality that hinges on properly understanding this major doctrine of **total forgiveness** which is central to victorious, Kingdom living. Jesus reveals it through Paul in Colossians 3:13 and Ephesians 4:32 respectively:

> … bearing with one another and forgiving one another, if there is any complaint against anyone, even as, indeed, the Lord forgave you … and be kind and tenderhearted, having forgiven each other, even as also God, **in Christ,** forgave you.

Our concept of how God perceives and treats us generally dictates how we see and treat others. If we falsely believe that God forgives us for each sin only when we confess it and then ask for His forgiveness, then we are likely to hold on to unforgiveness of others until they ask for forgiveness – if then. To be sure, there are a few New Testament scriptures from Matthew, Peter and John that would *seem* to suggest (as many believers still think) that we must constantly seek God's forgiveness or that it is conditional. So I will address those verses in the next chapter. But we will first focus on what Jesus revealed to Paul as the authoritative word about this essential doctrine.

A Scriptural Case For The Gospel of Total Forgiveness

Now, working backwards from the reality of a believer's unity with God by being **in Christ**, it is obvious that any **post-cross, New Covenant** scripture that does not seem to conform to Jesus' **whole gospel of grace,** revealed only to Paul, must be re-interpreted, using Jesus' *whole gospel* as the only true plumb line. And what does Jesus' **post-cross** revelation to Paul say about **total forgiveness**? The following scriptures supply the definitive answer.

Paul's only recorded <u>sermon</u> that explains the core message of Jesus' gospel is found in a lengthy passage in Acts 13:14-52, given in Pisidian Antioch (not to be confused with his home base of Antioch) a few years before the doctrinal struggle that happened at the Jerusalem Council in 50 AD. First, he gives a brief overview of selected events and notable people in Hebrew history. Then he briefly describes Jesus' death and resurrection as that which fulfilled key Old Testament prophecies. Then he boldly addresses a central concern of his Jewish and Gentile audience by declaring in verses 38-39:

> Therefore, my (Jewish) brothers, I want you to know that, through this One (Jesus), the forgiveness of sins is proclaimed to you. Through Him, everyone who believes is justified (acquitted, innocent, free, and righteous) from everything you could not be justified from by the Law of Moses.

To especially the Jews, this was a radical bombshell, a total replacement of all that they had been taught to depend on in order to become and stay justified before God. They understood that Paul's "good news" presented a major doctrinal shift from relying on the Law of Moses to believing in a Man who Paul implies is superior to Moses and has fulfilled the Messianic prophecies. But he did not stop there. He warned them not to reject this free offer of justification, received by faith apart from observing the law, by citing a fitting Old Testament verse from Habakkuk 1:5:

> Take care that what the prophets have said does not happen to you: Gaze among the nations, and see. Admire, and be astounded. For a work has been done in your days, which no one will believe when it is told (Acts 15:40-41).

This was a defining moment for them. Either they stay with Moses' performance-based system or now rely on Jesus' **grace-based gospel** for justification. They realized there was no middle ground – no mixing of the two. Either trust the ongoing sacrificial system based on their constant efforts to obtain forgiveness/justification *or* accept this preposterous offer that another Man did it all for them already. All they had to "do" was be willing to believe and receive His gift. Predictably, some followed Paul and Barnabas out and received even more truth from Paul. The others waited until the next Sabbath to hear more. But when the whole city turned out to hear Paul, the leaders became jealous and publically contradicted him. So, once again, Paul minced no words:

> …We had to speak the word of God to you (the Jews) first. Since you reject it and do not consider yourselves worthy of eternal life, we now turn to the Gentile nations for this is what the Lord has commanded us: 'I have made you (Paul) a light for the Gentile nations that you may bring salvation to the ends of the earth' (Acts 13:46b-47).

No doubt this and many other confrontations with the Jews, wherever Paul went, galvanized his resolve to preach the **whole gospel** of God's grace and freedom that Jesus had revealed to him, even if it meant confronting Peter or James later on. He personally met and knew Jesus in whom he now firmly believed. Fortunately, some courageous Jews and many Gentiles in various cities did receive the gifts of **total forgiveness** and righteousness through faith in Jesus. The following **fourteen scriptures** (noted as "**points**" and which span the next seven pages) are taken primarily from Paul's letters of encouragement and instruction to those early believers. They confirm and amplify the grace-filled message of Jesus' **whole gospel**.

Point 1) Ephesians 1:7-8 … in whom (Jesus) we have redemption through His blood, the forgiveness of sins, according to the riches of His grace which He lavished on us in all wisdom and prudence.

Point 2) Colossians 1:13-14 … For He (God) has rescued us from the dominion of Darkness and transferred us into the Kingdom of His beloved Son (Jesus) in whom we have redemption, the forgiveness of sins.

Jesus paid for the redemptive ransom, which bought us from slavery under Satan (and dealt with the sin nature **in Adam)** by the cost of His own divine blood so that God could legally place all who believe and receive His accomplishment into His Kingdom. The transaction had to include the forgiveness of *all* sins so that no sin will ever contaminate Him or His perfect Kingdom.

Point 3) Colossians 2:13-15… And you, being dead in your sins and in the uncircumcision of your sinful nature, He (our Father-God) made you alive together with Him (Jesus), <u>having forgiven you *all trespasses*, blotting out the handwriting of ordinances</u> (the Mosaic Law) <u>that was against us, and was contrary to us, and took it</u> (the Law) <u>out of the way, having nailed it to His cross;</u> thus having stripped the **(unseen)** rulers and authorities (from using the law against us), He displayed them in public, triumphing over them in it.

It is absolutely crucial to understand that the handwritten ordinances refer to the Ten Commandments, which were the only part of the Law hand-written on stone tablets. Jesus called these "the ministry of condemnation" and "the ministry of death" because they are "the ministry that condemns men" (see 2 Corinthians 3:7-9). Since Jesus came to "set the captives free," He would naturally want to remove anything and everything that causes bondage, condemnation and death to believers. That is why the Law in general - and the Big Ten specifically - was nailed to the cross and replaced by the higher law of faith, love and liberty **in Christ**.

This same truth is repeated in Ephesians 2:14-18 where Jesus reveals how He made possible the fulfillment of the prayer for God's spiritual union with both Jewish and Gentile believers who were divided by the Law Covenant. The short answer is that He abolished it as described here:

For He Himself (Jesus) is our peace, who has made the two (Jews and Gentiles) one and has destroyed the barrier, the dividing wall of hostility, <u>by abolishing, in His flesh, the Law with its Commandments and regulations.</u> His purpose was to create in Himself one new man out of the two, thus making peace, and in this one body to reconcile both of them to God through the cross, by which he put to death their hostility. He came and preached peace to you who were far away (the Gentiles) and peace to those who were near (the Jews). For, through Him, we both have access to the Father by one Spirit.

Now again, you may be still wondering how this can be true when Jesus Himself said in Matthew 5:17-20 that He did not come to abolish the Law but to fulfill it. I already touched on this passage in Chapter Nine under the section "No Contradiction But Completion on page 131."

But, I will more fully unravel this seeming contradiction between the two passages regarding the Law in the next chapter on page 222 that deals with that topic specifically.

> **Point 4)** 1 Peter 3:18… For Christ died for sins, once for all, the righteous (Jesus) for the unrighteous (mankind) to bring us to God, being put to death in the body but made alive in the spirit.

Peter understood that Jesus died to pay for all the sins of the unrighteous - all mankind for all time - because he knew that the wages of sin is death. Since Jesus only died once, <u>He must have paid for all sins at that time</u>, or else all those born after Calvary could never be made righteous – unless He came back to die again. No more animal sacrifices are needed because the perfect Lamb of God is now our righteousness - thanks to His **divine exchange** with all who believe **in Him** as their Savior.

> **Point 5)** Romans 8:1-4… There is therefore now no condemnation for those who are in Christ Jesus for the (higher) law of the Spirit of life in Christ Jesus has made me free from the (Mosaic) law of sin and death. For what the law was powerless to do, in that it was weakened by the flesh, God sent His own Son in the likeness of sinful flesh, and, concerning sin, condemned sin in the flesh (His own body at Calvary) so that the righteous demand of the law might be fulfilled in us (who also died and arose with Christ Jesus, by faith), who are not walking according to the flesh, but according to the Spirit.

Jesus did what the Law cannot do – save **in Adam** sinners. The "righteous demands of the Law" are fulfilled in those who walk by the spirit-man **in Christ**, not by the natural (outer) man, trying to do the impossible – keep the (obsolete) law perfectly.

> **Point 6)** 2 Corinthians 5:17-18 … Therefore if any man is **in Christ**, he is a **new creature**. Old things have passed away. Behold, all **(unseen)** things have become new. And all things are of God, who has reconciled us to Himself by Jesus Christ, and has given to us the ministry of reconciliation. For God was **in Christ**, reconciling the world to Himself, not imputing their trespasses unto them and has committed to us the word of reconciliation.

A Shocking Revelation

This scripture is an astounding statement that includes God's gift of reconciliation toward the *whole world* (from His standpoint) and that He is no longer imputing sins – absolutely none – to mankind, because Christ Jesus paid the just debt for all sin in full. In other words, all people are fully acquitted because of the value that God places on His Son's blood which has totally paid mankind's sin debt as the last Adam. If this was not so, the phrases "and all things are of God, who has reconciled us to himself by Jesus Christ," and "for God was in Christ reconciling the world to Himself" would be null and void the moment after Jesus' substitutionary death when people continued to sin. God's grace-based gift of reconciliation would be meaningless if "future" sin debt still counts against mankind.

The lie that an **in Adam** sinner is forgiven *only* of his past sins upon rebirth, contradicts one of God's most important revelations of Jesus' **whole gospel of grace**: *all of mankind's sin has* *been totally forgiven and "remembered no more"* by God. Why? Because of Jesus' **finished work**. That is certainly one of the most radical, revolutionary terms of the **New Covenant**: "… for I will forgive their wickedness and I will remember their sins no more," as unequivocally stated - not once but twice - in Hebrews 8:12 and 10:17. The "will" word quoted here is part of a **pre-cross** prophecy in Jeremiah 31:31-34 which promised the benefits of Jesus' redemptive sacrifice and **finished work** – which now belongs to each believer **in Christ**.

These terms are now a **post-cross** reality for mankind as a part of the necessary condition to be legally reconciled to God Himself, even as God was in harmony with Adam before he rebelled. Jesus legally paid for and removed the offense of mankind's personal "sin barrier" that we are all guilty of due to our own behavior. What remains for an unbeliever to *personally* benefit from this fulfilled prophecy is to "be crucified with Christ," through rebirth by faith alone, which replaces his **in Adam** nature with a regenerated, **new nature in Christ.**

That is why Paul did *not* include "confessing one's sins" as a necessary part of Jesus' "salvation formula" (so to speak) in Romans 10:9-13. What he stressed was a "confession" or proclamation of one's *heart-based* belief in the Lordship and resurrection of Jesus Christ. Jesus' glorious victory over "the law of sin (nature) and death" is declared and celebrated in all of Paul's writings – not just over people's soulish sins and mistakes which might continue until they die. This **New Covenant** revelation is one more proof (and an indictment) against the law-focused, sin-conscious mindset of mixture that has diseased the Church for two millennia. The **elephant of mixture** is so ponderous and intimidating – like James was in Jerusalem – that the **butterfly life of grace** has rarely escaped the cocoon before it gets stepped on. No wonder Luther called the book of James "the book of straw" – maybe because it rhymes with law. (Just kidding – he wrote in German.)

All this is so contradictory to Judaism, which is based on one's "obedience to the law" as the day to day <u>determiner</u> of one's connection with God. Therefore, it is no wonder that the church in Jerusalem hung on to their roots in Moses rather than "risk God's wrath" – as the **elephant of mixture** inclined them to believe and expect. The irony is that their continued inclusion of the Law for maintaining reconciliation and righteousness (which are **post-cross** gifts that cannot be earned) progressively minimized (if not prevented) a vibrant, victorious, faith-based experience with God as time went on. James operated as a self-appointed watchdog, on the look-out for sinning (law-breaking) rather than appreciating the liberty that faith and love **in Christ** produces through the "law of the Spirit of life."

Predictably, the Book of James focuses on law-keeping, (rather than on grace-based living) because he believed it, lived it and, therefore, wrote about it to the Jews who were still practicing the law zealously. In a nutshell, James still held on to the "knowledge of good and evil" rather than only to the "Tree of Life" – Jesus' **whole gospel**. But since law is far easier for the carnal mind to understand than Jesus' revelations, most Christians are attracted to that book like I was rather than to "Paul's gospel" from Jesus. If you use James' book as your primary lens to interpret Jesus' gospel, you will be feeding the **elephant of mixture,** which undermines true Christianity. I share more about that in Appendix #10.

The Carnal Mind's Main Objection To Radical Grace

What then? Shall we sin because we are not under law but under grace? By no means (Romans 6:15). Shall we go on sinning that grace may increase? By no means! We died to sin (the **in Adam** nature). How can we live in it any longer?" (Romans 6:1-2)

Because Paul was trained to be law-minded from his youth, he could anticipate the objections from the Jewish Christians who still viewed parts of Moses' Law Covenant and circumcision as indispensible for righteousness. He probably wrestled with the above questions himself while processing the revelation from Jesus in 42 AD. In typical fashion, he answers these logical objections with God's **big picture** perspective presented in Romans, Chapter Six. This chapter explains the **unseen** "mechanics" (so to speak) of Jesus' gospel and sets the stage to say in Chapter Seven what the Law does and does not do, and then, in Chapter Eight, what His **finished work** has fully accomplished for each believer in the **unseen realm**. No one who focuses on the Law will be able to properly "see" or appreciate Romans, Chapter Eight because it requires God-kind-of-faith. And, remember, the "law is not of faith." That was the essence of the stumbling block for the Jerusalem Church and is still true today for believers conditioned by the **elephant of mixture**.

Paul explains to the Gentile Romans that

> … though you used to be slaves to sin (the **in Adam** nature) you wholeheartedly obeyed the form of teaching to which you were entrusted (Jesus' **whole gospel** taught only by Paul). You have been set free from sin (the **in Adam** nature) and have become slaves to righteousness (as part of being one with Christ) (Romans 6:17-18).

Paul did not commend them for "obedience to the Law" because he did not give them the Law. Instead, he taught them Jesus' **whole gospel** that can only be comprehended by faith. So he commended them for their "obedience that comes from faith" which Paul specifically cited in Romans 1:6.

And what were the specifics of this new "form of teaching?" Paul outlined them in Romans 6:2-11 where he briefly explains the "mechanics" of what happens at rebirth. First, the old self is crucified with Christ to get rid of the Adamic sin nature and, second, this transformation from a caterpillar to a butterfly, enables the reborn saint to live **with** and **in Christ**. Therefore, Jesus (who became sin) and the believer both died to the sin nature once and for all. Now, the believer is free to live unto God as a **new creation**. This transaction is done in the **unseen** and can only be **"seen"** by faith so Paul makes a pivotal statement in Romans 6:10-11:

> The death He (Jesus) died, He died to sin (the **in Adam** nature) once for all (mankind); but the life He lives, He lives to God. In the same way, count yourselves dead to sin (the **in Adam** nature) but alive to God **in Christ Jesus** (as a **new creation**).

True Life and Freedom In The Spirit

In other words, every believer is to regard what happened to Jesus on Calvary as now also true for himself, through being identified with Jesus, by faith. Reckoning this reality as now true for you, believer, empowers you to live accordingly, out of the **new creation** spirit-being that

200

you now <u>are</u> **in and through Christ Jesus**. You are now risen and ascended on high with Him, according to Ephesians 2:6. Over time, as you renew your mind with that **New Covenant** reality **in Christ**, right believing of who you *now* are **in Christ** will produce right living through you, according to the law of the Spirit of life. Why? Because you will progressively yield yourself to the Holy Spirit to live and speak through you, as you, manifesting the fruits and gifts of the Spirit of Christ, who came to live in you and who wants to reign in and through you.

This revolutionary way to believe and live is the out-working of the radical **gospel of grace** – the very way Jesus walked on this earth, **pre-cross**. He was not rooted in the **seen realm** - like all **in Adam** people necessarily are (and carnal Christians function from) - but rooted in His Father and in His **unseen Kingdom**. He lived by faith, love and liberty in His Father, not by "following the law." That is why He seemingly "disobeyed" the law. For example, He touched a leper and healed people on the Sabbath and forgave the adulterous lady when the Law required stoning her. All these actions were "against the Law." Nevertheless, Jesus listened to His Father's voice and He adhered to the higher law – His Father's heart of love for all mankind - which actually *more* than fulfilled the negative "demands" of Moses' Law. By doing what His Father told Him, Jesus kept the spirit of the higher law that gives life rather than the letter of the law that brings death.

Why Does God Hate Sin?

"So are you saying that God no longer hates sin and it does not matter if a believer sins?" No, on the contrary. **First,** God still hates the fact that not all have *personally* benefitted from what His Son did for them and, therefore, many are still **in Adam** because of ignorance or unbelief. That is the root cause that makes mankind subject to sinning. **Second,** God hates sinning because it still can cause negative consequences – including physical death - in the **seen realm**, even for believers and it can scandalize unbelievers.

Third, God also hates sinning because it can open the door to the devil into the lives of even His saved children when they choose some form of bondage such as fear or some addiction etc. like Adam did. Do you think God enjoyed removing Adam and Eve from the perfect Garden spot of the world that He specifically created for them? But Adam's fall did not surprise Him or "offend" Him. Instead, God directed His just anger at the Seducer and cursed the ground, not Adam, per se. Adam put himself under the curse of the law Tree by choice, despite God warning beforehand. Mercifully, God quickly promised to provide a Deliverer who would, in the fullness of <u>His time</u>, overcome the devil's rule over mankind and God prophesied the Deceiver's eventual demise.

Fourth, God still hates sinning far more than how loving fathers hate to see the bad consequences which come from their children's poor choices or from some disease they catch because it undermines their well-being. Our unselfish Father-God is not pre-occupied with Himself or His glory – like humans tend to be. How do we know? If He was self-centered, He would not have gone to the enormous trouble and heart-ache to create humans who could choose to be insulting and rebellious towards Him. He is as other-centered as Jesus described to Paul in 1 Corinthians 13:4-8b which reveals that love is not self-seeking and does not keep a record of wrongs, among many other wonderful things. The fallen mind and flesh of man excels at impugning and blaming our blameless God. But, after rebirth, a believer has the grace to see and experience the truth of how loving, trustworthy and faithful Father-God really is. Again, we will explore more revelation about Him in Chapter Twenty-one.

Unfortunately, a common notion among law-minded Christians is that God hates sin because He is personally offended by it and punishes all who commit sin – even believers (see Appendix # 11 for an example of this wrong idea). This mental stronghold is a direct carry-over from the **elephant of mixture** of two mutually exclusive covenants, as if Calvary made no fundamental difference. As you can tell, I never tire of pointing out this glorious, **New Covenant** reality.

This common misconception denies three key aspects of Jesus' **finished work** for mankind, stated in 2 Corinthians 5:18-21and 1 John 2:2, which echo the terms of the **New Covenant** described in Hebrews, Chapters 8 and 10 as follows. God was:

A) "reconciling (the population of) the whole world to Himself **in Christ**," and

B) "not charging their trespasses to them (mankind)."

C) "not remembering (mindful of) their sins anymore." (Under the Law covenant He remembered their sins to the third and fourth generation.)

Both were accomplished by a one-time, unilateral sacrifice of Jesus' own blood to cause this amazing two-fold benefit - from God's point of view in the **unseen realm**. Why would God be offended by sins and punish people for them today since He is fully satisfied with what Jesus accomplished on Calvary and, consequently, is NOT charging **any** sins against us. Furthermore, why would God be personally "offended" by what He is no longer mindful of? This rotten carcass of confusing mixture which is still festering in people's minds, is a mockery of the redemptive blood of God's precious Son.

D) the only thing standing in the way of salvation for *any* person is to "be reconciled to God" by believing and receiving what He offers as a free gift – Himself.

Tragically, living under the deception of Galatianism effectively nullifies the radically new terms of Jesus' **grace gospel** for individuals – the *free* offer of justification and oneness with Him without any required works on our part.

The benefits of Jesus' **whole gospel** is not dependent on one's performance (as it was under Moses' Law Covenant) but on believing and receiving the results of Jesus' performance and **miraculous exchange** offered on Calvary. As mankind's new representative sent by God, He became our sin and received all the just wrath and punishment that mankind deserved. That merciful transaction on Calvary made "all things new" for mankind from God's point of view.

Father-God could justly and legally do that because Jesus was the last Adam whom He sent to be our new, *redemptive* representative to God - just as the first Adam was mankind's first representative and legally caused mankind's fall from grace. When anyone believes and receives Jesus (and, therefore receives the benefits of His **finished work),** he or she is reborn of God and automatically receives and becomes "the righteousness of God **in Christ**," as 2 Corinthians 5:21

declares. So, again, what is true for Jesus is true for him or her too. That, my Christian friend, is the most glorious gift possible because He qualifies you for heaven as a joint-heir, by grace through faith alone!

So, there has been a glorious yet **unseen** sea-change of covenants, from God's viewpoint. But this monumental event is compromised, if not negated, by carnal, law-based thinking that wrongly defines and, thereby, dishonors the true nature of God and of Jesus' **finished work.** How? By mixing the two opposing covenants. Why? Because doing so nullifies the intended effects of both covenants for the misguided believer. This is the **elephant of mixture** that Paul sought to slay in his letter to the Galatians. But it was kept alive and fed to the Jerusalem Church by James and the other "Hebrew bishops" who oversaw that flock until their demise in 135 AD. Some scholars believe that Paul was so out-numbered after he corrected Peter at Antioch (when even Barnabas sided with the Judaizers sent by James) that he soon left there to spread Jesus' **whole gospel** elsewhere and wrote Galatians as a rebuttal to the Judaizers in Jerusalem.

Righteousness Apart From Works
Point 7) Romans 4:6-8 ... Even as David also pronounced blessing upon the man to whom God reckoned righteousness apart from works, saying, 'Blessed are they whose iniquities are forgiven, and whose sins are covered. Blessed is the man to whom the Lord will in no way charge (reckon) sin.'

This amazing statement was made by a man still formally "under the Law Covenant" but who had apparently experienced, by grace through faith, a direct, relational connection to God on the basis of "reckoned righteousness." Apparently, David reckoned/believed and received as true, the gift of righteousness from God just like Abraham had done. So, though he was not yet **in Christ** per se, he foreshadows the glorious **New Covenant's** provision of **total forgiveness** of all sin. Remember: in the **big picture** of the **unseen** *"now"* realm of God, Jesus was slain "from the founding of the world" to make possible this gift that Abraham and David received by faith, **pre-cross** (see Revelations 13:8).

Point 8) Romans 5:18-19 ... Therefore, as by the offence of one man (Adam) judgment came upon all men to condemnation, even so, by the righteousness of one man (Jesus), the free gift came upon all men unto justification of life. For as by one man's disobedience the many were made sinners (**in Adam**, by nature), so by the obedience of one shall the many be made righteous (**in Christ**, by belief in His perfect sacrifice).

Point 9) Hebrews 7:27 ... (Jesus) did not need to daily ... offer up sacrifices, first for His own sins, and then for the people's: for this He did once, when He offered up Himself, ... Hebrews 9:28a ... So Christ was offered once to bear the sins of many ... Hebrews 10:12 ... But this man (Jesus), after He had offered one sacrifice (Himself) for (all) sins forever, sat down on the right hand of God; ... Hebrews 1:3b ...when He had, by Himself purged (all) our sins, He sat down on the right hand of the Majesty on high; ...

These verses tell us plainly why Jesus Christ was offered on Calvary – "to bear the sins of many" – and He only had to do it *one* time – "one sacrifice for sins forever." Then, by sitting down in heaven in a position of "rest," He indicated that He had completed what He was sent to do – "purge our sins by Himself." With His last breath on the cross, He had declared "It is finished," again reinforcing the truth that nothing more had to be done (such as dying at the end of the world to forgive all the sins committed after Calvary). Since all sins of all believers living today were in "future time," when Jesus paid that massive debt for *all* of mankind's sins, all of our future sins have already been paid for and forgotten as noted in "C" above. God does not waste time looking at my sins but He regards me as He does His precious Son – righteous.

> **Point 10)** Hebrews 2:17 … Wherefore it behooved Him (Jesus) in all things to be made like His brethren, that He might become a merciful and faithful high priest in things pertaining to God, to make propitiation (payment for or "forgiveness" of a debt) for the sins of the people.

God justly received and was satisfied with Jesus' substitutionary death as more than adequate payment for the sin-debt of the whole human race owed to God, which then made it possible for individuals to be regenerated, redeemed, justified, and adopted into God's family by faith in Jesus and His **finished work**.

> **Point 11)** Hebrews 8:11-12 …for all shall know Me, from the least to the greatest. For I will be merciful to their unrighteousness and their sins and their iniquities will I remember no more … Heb 10:17-18 … And their sins and iniquities will I remember no way by no means (a double negative in Greek). Now, where remission of these is, there is no more offering for sin (necessary).

> **Point 12)** 1 John 2:2 … And He (Jesus) is the propitiation (He appeased the offended one who is now favorable toward the offender) for our sins and not for ours only, but also for the sins of the whole world … 1 John 2:2… I write unto you, little children, because your sins are forgiven you for His name's sake … 1 John 4:10 …God … sent His Son as an atoning (satisfying) sacrifice for our sin debt.

> **Point 13)** Revelations 1:6 Unto Him (Jesus) that loved us, and washed us from our sins in His own blood and hath made us kings and priests unto God, His Father. To Him be glory and dominion forever and ever.

> **Point 14)** Acts 26:15-18… And I (Paul, at his conversion) said, 'Who are you, Lord?' And he said, 'I am Jesus whom you are persecuting. But rise, and stand upon your feet: for I have appeared to you for this purpose, to make you a minister … to open their (the Gentile's) eyes, … that they may receive forgiveness of sins, and an inheritance among them which are sanctified by faith into me.'

From Paul's initial, **post-cross** encounter with Jesus, he knew he was commissioned to tell the Gentiles the benefits of Jesus' **finished work**, including the forgiveness of *all* sins. The Gentiles in Paul's congregations (unlike in Jerusalem) did not labor under the burden of the Mosaic Law (unless infiltrated by Jewish Christians from Jerusalem like happened in Galatia). Therefore, they could immediately walk in the undeserved benefits of the **New Covenant** without needing to unlearn the **seen**-centered, Mosaic Law system of self-righteousness by works. Upon rebirth **into Christ**, they were automatically justified – were made righteous **in**

Christ - which qualified them to receive all of God's blessings as His **new creations**. They did not have the handicap of the Law system to hamper their **experience** and maturity. May God raise up a world-full of pastors and teachers who faithfully live in and declare Jesus' **whole gospel of grace** to usher in His triumphant return.

The Lamb Is The Focus

Before dealing with the New Testament scriptures listed in the next chapter that *seem* to contradict the doctrine of God's "**total forgiveness** of all sins," it is instructive to first review an example of the process (and typology) of how an individual, under the Mosaic Law, was forgiven of his "unintentional sins" (committed accidentally or in ignorance of the Law) - found in Leviticus 4:32-35.

> If he (who sins unintentionally) brings a lamb as his sin offering, he is to bring a female without defect. He is to lay his hand on its head and slaughter it for a sin offering at the place where the burnt offering is slaughtered. Then the priest shall take some of the blood of the sin offering with his finger and put it on the horns of the altar of burnt offering and pour out the rest of the blood at the base of the altar. He shall remove all the fat, just as the fat is removed from the lamb of the fellowship offering, and the priest shall burn it on the altar on top of the offerings made to the Lord by fire. In this way the priest will make atonement for him for the sin he has committed, and he will be forgiven.

The sinner who sinned unintentionally (for example, causing an accidental injury or who discovered, after the fact, that he had unknowingly broken a commandment) was to bring an unblemished (perfect) female lamb to a priest who thoroughly inspected the animal (not the sinner) to be sure it was perfect. The focus was on the qualifications of the lamb, not on the sinner, who was obviously not "perfect" i.e. not righteous. When the sinner laid his hand on the righteous lamb's head, there was an **unseen exchange** between the two, from God's viewpoint. The sinner's unrighteous sin was imputed to the lamb and the lamb's **spotlessness** was imputed to the sinner, who then went away forgiven and (temporarily) justified before God – until the next "unintentional" sin. The priest oversaw the process to make sure all of the Law's requirements were fulfilled. The burden for discovering the unintended sin and buying the perfect lamb and initiating the process was totally upon the sinner.

Now, the above case was for "unintentional sin." But how was it for a defiant rebel in the camp? Well, it was far worse for such a person, according to Numbers 15:30-31:

> But anyone who sins defiantly, whether native-born or alien, blasphemes the Lord, and that person must be cut off from his people. Because he has despised the Lord's word and broken his commands, that person must surely be cut off but his guilt remains on him.

In this case, the defiant sinner (one who intentionally broke a law) was excommunicated from God's only covenant people - made an outcast with no hope for forgiveness. In some cases, such as doing work on the Sabbath, death by stoning was the punishment, according to Numbers 15:32-38. Now, before you say "I'd never be that dumb," remember that the punishment under the Mosaic Law system was based on one's behavior, not on his **in Adam** condition. You now know that such an evaluation, when based only to one's behavior, was superficial. (However, if

God was punishing them only on the basis of mankind's position **in Adam**, they (and we) would all be justly under condemnation and legally subject to death.) And that is how it was with the **in Adam** Israelites, living under the outer trappings of the Law Covenant which offered a temporary covering, *not a removal*, of their sins. It is only by the grace and mercy of God, even under those seemingly "harsh" (but just) conditions, that any of them, including Joshua and Caleb, were spared. (See Endnote #**34** about God's provision for grace in the Cities of Refuge.)

All Things New

But now, **post-cross**, every believer and unbeliever is forgiven of all sins – unintentional and intentional - according to God's complete and accurate knowledge of all of mankind's sins - not just according to each person's own accounting or memory. The perfect Lamb's perfect sacrifice perfectly forgave all mankind's sin and qualifies every one believing in His substitutionary work on Calvary for rebirth. He is justified as part of the terms of Jesus' **New Covenant** of lavish grace. Also, Christ Jesus was simultaneously God's appointed High Priest who fulfilled all the Law's requirements for His own **pre-cross** life and death *and* for every believer's **post-cross** new, abundant, God-Life **in Him**.

Now, given how mercifully superior are the **New Covenant** terms for believers today, solely thanks to Jesus' **finished work**, why would anyone want to risk mixing these grace-based terms with those of the Mosaic Law? As Paul remarked in Galatians 3:1 "O foolish Galatians! Who has bewitched you?" Now you know the answer to that question: the Judaizers from Jerusalem sent by James. Such is the blindness that law-based obedience promotes and which regrettably still grips much of the Body of Christ today. This heretical preoccupation with law robs the believer of operating in the higher law of the "obedience *of* Christ" which produces:

1*) faith* - to see, understand, receive and enjoy the stupendous benefits of Jesus' **finished work** as part of the believer's legal inheritance **in Christ**;

2) *love* - to grasp the extent of Father-God's love, proven by sending Jesus who left nothing undone for us - and to respond to Him and to others out of His love, shed abroad in our new heart in the Person of the Holy Spirit, the way Jesus lived on earth;

3) *liberty* - to enjoy an unencumbered response to let the Spirit of Christ live through us as His grateful worshippers - and as His ministers of reconciliation - to a forgiven yet condemned world of unbelievers (those still **in Adam**). These three laws of the Spirit of life are summed up in Galatians 5:1-6. (See Endnote #13 that gives more details about these three aspects of the higher law of the Spirit of life).

Freedom Is Now Possible For All Mankind

Taken as a whole, all the above scriptures verify one of the basic doctrines of Jesus' **grace gospel**. It is, namely, that God, through Jesus, has reconciled the world to Himself because of Jesus' perfect sacrifice which totally satisfied God's just wrath and totally paid for the just punishment due for all the sins of all mankind for all time. Why such **total forgiveness**? So that individuals can now freely choose to be reborn of God and personally receive all the glorious benefits of Jesus' **finished work.** They include Father-God's fantastic gifts like justification and the habitation of the Holy Spirit and freedom forever from all guilt and condemnation by being **in Christ Jesus**.

Again, simply put, Jesus, our elder Brother, <u>exchanged all His good for all our bad</u>. What a wonderful Savior! However, there are a few scriptures that *seem* to contradict this key doctrine of **total forgiveness** of all sin and, consequently, cast doubt and even fear that this amazing, almost "too-good-to-be-true-gospel," might not really be true. Therefore, we will present those scriptures and:

1) apply the principle of "dividing the Word rightly" according to what covenant they were written under and

2) keep in mind the fact that not all New Testament writers fully understood and embraced the **whole gospel** that Jesus revealed to Paul in 42 AD.

Therefore, we will use Jesus' **whole gospel of grace,** revealed to Paul, as the only sure plumb line to discern the truth from the possible mixture of messages in other New Testament books that we already discovered is the case in the four gospels, as demonstrated in Chapter Twelve.

This song-poem is a capsule of Jesus' **finished work** and a thankful response to Him.

AMAZING GRACE, <u>G</u>OD'S <u>R</u>IGHTEOUSNESS
<u>A</u>t <u>C</u>hrist's <u>E</u>xpense for me.
You paid the ransom I could not
To buy my Liberty.

You bore God's wrath and every curse
While dying on a Tree.
With You, I died and rose again,
Brand new, alive and free.

My outer man has yet to know
Full freedom from all sin.
Yet You forgave me totally
And now reside within.

There's nothing I can say or do
To earn your lavish grace.
Instead, I trust your finished work
That nothing can erase.

I thank you, Lord, for all You have done
Far more than my eyes can see.
By faith in You I now receive
Your life abundantly. A Sermon Song © Copyright 2009 by Leonard J. Ransil

CHAPTER FOURTEEN

SCRIPTURES WHICH SEEM TO CONTRADICT TOTAL FORGIVENESS

A Brief Review

One of the major points of this book is that only Paul was given the full revelation of Jesus' **whole gospel** by the risen Christ Jesus Himself in about 42 AD. A second central point is the historical fact that the Jerusalem church was under the control of a succession of fifteen Hebrew bishops – starting with James – until 135 AD. (See Endnote # 27.) All of them required that Gentiles first be circumcised before they could be saved. They also taught both the Jews and Gentiles to observe the Ten Commandments and some other aspects of the law <u>in order to remain in right-standing with God</u>. Regrettably, this **elephant of mixture** of the two covenants, now known as the heresy of Galatianism, still afflicts the majority of church members today.

One of the main reasons that mixture is still tolerated, and even promoted, in the general church is the refusal by some to realize the superiority of Jesus' **whole gospel** of the **New Covenant**, directly revealed to Paul, over all other parts of the Bible. When this fact is ignored, it is then virtually impossible to "rightly divide the word of truth." Jesus' revelations to Paul of what He accomplished on Calvary and beyond for believers, should trump any conflicting differences between previous covenants and their corresponding terms.

The differences are relatively minor among all the major grace-based covenants recorded in the Bible. The only major covenant that has an opposing set of terms is of course, the Mosaic Law Covenant because being in right standing with God is based on man's efforts, not on God's unmerited grace. Thankfully, it is not for believers today. Why? Because it was never given to the Gentiles by God and it is now obsolete for Jewish believers, according to Hebrews 8:13 and 1 Timothy 1:9. As already proven, it was based on the Israelite's faith in their own ability to keep the law perfectly (as the terms required) rather than on God's ability and faithfulness to fulfill what He generously promised according to the terms of the various grace-based covenants. This basic difference makes the Law Covenant diametrically opposed to Jesus' **New Covenant** and, therefore, they should not be mixed together. In fact, while the law is good and eternal, Jesus reveals this truth through Paul in Romans 7:4:

> And so, my (reborn) brothers, you also have become dead to the law through (identification at Calvary with) the body of Christ (by faith) so that you might belong to another, to Him (Jesus) who was raised from the dead in order that <u>we might bear fruit to God</u>.

The Dead Reborn

Again, Paul was not addressing Gentiles in this passage but those "who know the Law" – the Jews. They regarded themselves as "married" to the Law which is why they were so reluctant to give it up. Without disparaging the Law or the first relationship, Jesus revealed to Paul that Jews could become "married" to Jesus without committing "spiritual adultery" when, by faith, they agree to die to the Law with Jesus on Calvary and be raised with Him in newness of life in the Holy Spirit because of the **divine exchange** of natures.

The fruit Paul is pointing to is described in Galatians 5:22-23 as the fruit of the Holy Spirit "against which there is no law." Why? Because it is produced by the Holy Spirit through the believer's new spirit-self **in Christ**, *not* through obedience to the law, which can only produce "dead works," as revealed in Hebrews 6:1. We are to repent – have a change of mind – from "dead works" by no longer living under the law mentally but by living under grace through faith in "the law of the Spirit of life," now that we have "died to the law of sin and death" and are alive **in Christ** (see Romans 8:2). And don't fall for the lie that the Holy Spirit wants you to focus on the Law so He can help you keep it. Again, why would He, the Spirit of Truth, want you to focus on something that was not given to the Gentiles and was declared "obsolete" for reborn Jews in Hebrews 8:13? Remember: "The strength of sin is the Law" (1 Corinthians 15:56). "The law was added so that sin might increase" (Romans 5:50). We are now married to Jesus! So focus on your loving husband, not on a harsh, unbending standard that no one can perfectly keep. Jesus sent the Holy Spirit to *convince* us of our righteousness **in Christ** - apart from law-keeping - because it is His gift to us by being united with Him who now *is* our righteousness.

What believer in their renewed mind would want to knowingly live under the demands of the law, which arouses sin and causes death, when Jesus has freed us to live in the higher law of the Spirit of life? The main reason believers do not experience this freedom is because of the blindness and confusion caused by the **elephant** of Galatianism that mentally stifles, if not crushes, the **butterfly life in Christ Jesus**. The devil uses this obsolete system to blind believers from seeing the truth of what Jesus has accomplished. The main purpose of this book is to help renew every believer's mind to Jesus' **whole gospel** of **radical grace** like the Holy Spirit is doing for me as I learn to live in the higher law of Christ, summarized by Paul in Galatians 5:1-6.

Given this review, it will be obvious to you how to rightly interpret the majority of the following scriptures that seem to contradict the **gospel of grace**, revealed in the wonderful terms of the **New Covenant** found in Hebrews 8:8-13, as outlined in Chapter Thirteen. First, I will present three scriptures from the **pre-cross** period of the four gospels that deal with the need for "confessing" and/or the forgiveness of sins. (Wherever the same event occurs in more than one of the four gospels, only one occurrence will be discussed.) Then I will discuss at length 1 John 1:7-10 written in the **post-cross** period.

Pre-Cross Examples Of The Forgiveness Of Sin

1) Luke 3:3... "He (John the Baptist) went into all the countryside around the Jordan preaching a baptism of repentance for the forgiveness of sins." What an astonishing statement! This was a major departure from the dictates of the Law for how sins were to be treated during the previous fifteen hundred years, as was briefly described in Chapter Thirteen. For many sins, death was the automatic punishment with no negotiation possible. The only hope was to escape to a city of refuge. For unintended sins, some kind of sacrifice was routinely required. Now, here comes a wild-looking man named John ("grace" in Greek) merely water-baptizing people to facilitate forgiveness of sins. For those who had eyes to see, this was a signal that a totally *new order* was about to replace the sacred tradition and practices of the Mosaic Covenant of Law.

210

This relatively short transition period of about three years, which foreshadowed the coming **New Covenant**, saw an explosion of changes to the status quo, triggered by John and fulfilled by Jesus.

The Jews were proud of their law covenant with God, viewing themselves as superior to all other nations, including the hated Romans. They were blind to the fact that the Law kept them in bondage because it actually aroused sin and caused death because they were **in Adam** sinners. It was powerless to make them holy but they thought that their sincere attempts to keep it were the reason for their assumed righteousness and holiness.

Again, they missed the fact that God had declared Abraham "righteous" 430 years before the Law had been given *and* the fact that he had lied twice about his wife, Sarah, *and* gave her over to two different kings to save his own neck. Yet, with all his "sin," there is no record of him "confessing his sins" to regain righteousness before God. Why? Because right-standing with God was His gift received by faith – not something Abraham "worked" to earn or keep. Jesus explained through Paul that, "Where there is no law, sin is not imputed because there is no transgression" (Romans 4:15b). The **post-cross, New Covenant** would again be based on God's *offer* of pure grace but this time to **all mankind** (not just to Abraham and his natural seed). But, for that to happen, "all things had to be made new" on Calvary.

John baptized with water for the forgiveness of sins and Jesus' disciples administered that as well, according to John 4:1. But John exclaimed that when the Messiah came, He (Jesus) would "baptize with the Holy Spirit and fire." Soon after, Jesus was the first human to receive that monumental blessing – the indwelling of the Holy Spirit - because He was without sin. Only when **in Adam** humans are reborn **in Christ** are they then made a holy vessel, a new wineskin, and, therefore, able to have the Holy Spirit immediately come to dwell within their new spirit-self. If law, sin and the "confession of sin" would have remained the focus in the **New Covenant** (instead of confessing the lordship of Jesus over the law of sin and death) then believers could not be worthy temples or "containers" of the Holy Spirit. No Darkness can be mixed with Him, who lives within every believer's regenerated, perfect spirit.

More Examples
2) John 1:29... "The next day John (the Baptist) saw Jesus coming toward him and said: 'Look, the Lamb of God who <u>takes</u> away the sin of the world'". Forgiveness, in this **pre-cross** scripture, is presented as an on-going process, so it seems to contradict the truth that Jesus sacrifice *has* forgiven all sins of the whole world, including those not yet committed. But that is what one *should* expect as a commentary on what Jesus actually did **pre-cross**. He forgave sins on a <u>case by case</u> basis to enable healing, etc. But God's ultimate plan through Jesus' sacrifice was to forever remove the sin barrier between God and mankind so that even *all* those who would never see Jesus physically after His ascension would still enjoy God's forgiveness of all sins. But, remember, His **finished work** that accomplished mankind's total forgiveness did not happen until Calvary. So this verse is consistent with the **pre-cross** transition period while Jesus ministered on earth.

3) Matt 6:15... "But if you do not forgive men their trespasses, neither will your Father forgive your trespasses." Again, this **pre-cross** statement of Jesus is perfectly consistent with being under a performance-based covenant of works – the Mosaic Law - which was soon to pass away for Jews. Forgiveness under these terms is directly tied to how well you forgive others – tit for tat. This verse is a follow up to what we now traditionally call "the Lord's Prayer." This title has caused it to be enshrined as a focus of attention, even though it is based on a covenant system that is now obsolete for Jews. However, on the plus side of this progressive revelation, Jesus' words represented a major challenge to the law system because it added the dimension of horizontal forgiveness *between people* that was not a specific part of the Law Covenant. It actually made receiving forgiveness harder because it added another condition, *internal* to the person.

Before Jesus introduced this temporary stipulation for forgiveness (which no longer included animal sacrifices for his disciples), the sole emphasis under the Law was whether one's *actions* broke the law and what process was necessary to be forgiven – if possible – including restitution to another person. But nowhere in the Law Covenant was vertical forgiveness by God tied to horizontal, interpersonal forgiveness with others. In effect, Jesus temporarily added another layer to the burden of "works" while, at the same time, He signaled another positive change coming in the **New Covenant**. Later, through Paul, Jesus specifically instructs us in Colossians 3:13 "To forgive as God forgave you," which He did for *all* people living **post cross,** even before they were born, according to 2 Corinthians 5:18-19 and 1 John 2:2. Have you ever heard that good news taught in YOUR church?

That obviously refers to His **New Covenant** through which He made "all things new." He forgave us 2000 years ago when He, as the perfect Lamb, was sacrificed for all sins (see Hebrews 9:26b and 10:12). Thankfully, His **total forgiveness** of all of mankind's sins, provided on Calvary, no longer requires that we first forgive others before we can be forgiven. That, again, would be a return to a mixture of the two covenants because a believer's forgiveness would still depend *conditionally* on his own efforts. God's total forgiveness would no longer be a free gift but depend on something we must earn by our "works." Most of the prayer in Matthew, chapter six has already been fulfilled in Jesus' prayer to Father-God, found in John 17:21, and cited earlier. So why would we be asking for things we already have **in Christ**? (Much more insight about the "Our Father" prayer is in Appendix # 2.)

Post-Cross Confession of Sins To God
1 John 1:7-10 But if we walk in the light, just as he is also in the light, we have fellowship with one another, and the blood of Jesus Christ, His Son, cleanses us from all sin. If we claim that we have no sin, we deceive ourselves, and the truth is not in us. If we confess our sins, He is faithful and just to forgive us our sins, and to cleanse us from all unrighteousness. If we claim that we have not sinned, then we make him a liar, and his word is not in us.

Many, if not most, preachers and teachers in most Christian denominations today teach that this passage is written by John to born-again believers as a *necessary* condition for staying in right relationship and/or in fellowship with God. (Some people combine those two concepts, some do not.) This common interpretation of verse nine states that 1) God's forgiveness of one's sins and 2) His cleansing from all unrighteousness are directly dependent upon whether or not the believer first confesses specific sins not yet confessed. The implication and logical corollary (that is generally taught) is that God will not forgive a believer's sin unless and until he confesses each one specifically and asks Him for forgiveness – hopefully, on a daily basis so the sins don't "accumulate" which could result in "backsliding" or a "hardened heart." This process is what is generally understood as "biblical repentance" in most Christian circles today, especially among Catholics. Popular teachers like John F. MacArthur also teach similar ideas, as discussed in Appendix # 11.

So, to restate again what is often <u>understood</u> by this passage: in order to stay right with God, one must confess to God every sin he commits, on an ongoing basis, for the rest of his Christian life. Why this requirement? Because, according to one <u>common interpretation</u>, every time a believer sins (especially "intentionally," as the Law distinguished), he loses fellowship with God (if not his "righteousness" too) and must "repent of his sins" to get back into fellowship with God – or more drastic still, be "born again, again."

It is obvious that such believing is based on a **focus on the law** because sin *presupposes* that there is a law that has been broken. (All this *stems* from Adam eating of a right/wrong Tree – pun intended.) But here is the catch. The only valid reason a "law enforcement officer" can give you a ticket for speeding is that there exists a law against going over a specified speed limit. If there is no law against "speeding" on that particular road, then obviously there can be no violation/transgression for traveling at any speed on that road. *You can't break a non-existent law. i.e. "sin."* Jesus clarified this truth through Paul in Romans 4:15b "And where there is no law, there is no transgression" and in Romans 5:13b "But sin is not taken into account when there is no law (which brings punishment from God)." Believers are now under the higher Law of faith, love and liberty of the **New Covenant**, in which all deserved wrath, punishment and condemnation from God (not from man) for sin has been <u>fully satisfied and paid for</u> by Jesus, and <u>fully forgiven and forgotten by God</u>, according to Hebrews 8:12 and 10:17-18.

But Paul also warns that a law-focus causes a believer many problems (as explained in detail in Chapter Nine) such as in Galatians 3:20: "No one will be declared righteous in His (God's) sight by observing the law; rather, <u>through the law we become conscious of sin</u>." If by wrong believing, regarding the true purpose of the law, a *believer* focuses on the law that cannot save him, he obviously is not focusing on the One who *has* saved him. Saved him from what? From condemnation from God, regardless of his behavior, because he is **in Christ Jesus,** *not* under law, from God's viewpoint. If a believer goes back under law *mentally,* he falls from grace but not "out of Christ." His conscience might condemn him for his foolishness but God does not.

Unwittingly, by focusing on the law (and therefore on his sins) rather than on Jesus, he is inviting guilt, condemnation and, possibly, even a spiral into depression like Martin Luther battled against for years under the weight of sin-consciousness caused by a law-focus. That is the trap Paul warned the Galatians about. They were bewitched by the Judaizers. Therefore, since the law can't make a believer righteous but can only remind him that his behavior is not perfect, it was nailed to the cross. So, believer, set your mind on Jesus and on what He has done for you, not on the obsolete <u>law principle</u> that you died to when you became married to Christ when reborn. Tragically, one single verse - 1 John 1:9 - has been used to negate the **fourteen scriptures** cited in the previous chapter that document God's gift of total forgiveness to the whole world through Jesus, the last Adam.

God removed the law for Jewish believers so that they can see and appreciate who they *now* are **in Christ Jesus**. His righteous performance on earth, offered to both Jews and Gentiles, becomes theirs by identification with Jesus by faith. His flawless track record, accomplished while He lived on earth, is now every believer's track record before God by the same legal transfer that happened when Jesus became our unrighteous "sin-package" in *exchange* for His righteous life and total forgiveness. Admittedly, it is an infinitely "unfair" **divine exchange.** But such is <u>the unending expanse of Father-God's other-centered, sacrificial love and lavish grace for us helpless humans</u>. It is this profound revelation that Paul prayed would be imparted to the Ephesians (and to us) that is found in Chapter 3:14-19:

> By reason of this grace, I kneel before the Father of our Lord Jesus Christ, from whom His whole family - in heaven and on earth - is named that, according to the wealth of His glory by His power, He may strengthen you with His might in the <u>inner man</u> through His Spirit so that Christ may live in your hearts through faith, having been rooted in and founded on love, so may you be able to comprehend, with all the saints, what is the width and length and height and depth of the love of Christ, and even be able to know that which surpasses all knowledge, so that you may be filled with all the fullness of God.

This passage strains to convey Father-God's immeasurable love that He offers to every believer. And He wishes that every believer would receive His fullness, by faith, so that God Himself becomes experiential to him. It will take eternity to fully understand and appreciate the value of His unconditional love, manifested in and by Jesus, Who won for all believers Daddy God's unconditional, eternal acceptance. This is a gift to every believer, regardless of his behavior, because <u>it was not his behavior that won his acceptance to begin with</u>. It is only by God's gift of grace through faith.

And it was strictly by God's grace through faith that Mary chose to receive and nurture Jesus Christ within her womb (not within her spirit yet) as a baby for nine months. He returned in an infinitely more important and powerful way within her <u>new spirit</u> and in all those present at Pentecost. However, neither did she nor did anyone else understand <u>His entrance into them and their entrance into Him</u> until the exalted Christ Jesus revealed that mystery to Paul in about 42 AD. Believers are not just re-created "image-bearers" but also God-carriers and *one* with Him forever. These **new creation** realities which begin at rebirth, instantly change sinners into saints - caterpillars into **butterflies** - by an unfathomable spiritual metamorphosis, given to affect the outer man as well, over time. Again, how can believers who begin to grasp this revelation continue to regard themselves as sinners when God regards them as perfect in His spotless Son, according to Hebrews 10:14?

Grace Upon Grace

Your new spirit-self **in Christ** is righteous in God's eyes, not because of your present outward behavior, but because of Jesus' behavior almost 2000 years ago and the **divine exchange** that you agreed to by faith by being reborn into Him. His **finished work** alone has fully qualified you for heaven where you now reside and reign **in Him**, according to Ephesians 2:6. Of course, God desires you to live according to the <u>new you</u> who lives **in Christ** so that you can benefit from <u>all</u> He has done for you and also to avoid giving place to the devil who is still out to steal, kill and destroy the gift of Jesus' abundant life here on earth. But you are no longer in league with this deceiver or under his dominion. You now have Jesus' revealed truth, authority and power to resist his lies and enforce Jesus' victory over him and his minions. So don't be seduced again by his lies into wrong believing. We will explain this area of spiritual warfare more fully in Chapter Twenty.

So again, mentally going back under a focus on the law through wrong believing (instead of staying under grace), necessarily causes a believer to be law/sin/self-conscious instead of Jesus conscious. Focusing on rules and codes and laws does not fix the sin problem but only arouses more sinning which reveals that there *is* a problem and results in *feeling* guilty, condemned and estranged from God. It also indicates that the believer is focused on himself and on his imperfect behavior. God's grace-based solution for every true believer for the "sin and self problem" is to be continuously conscious of Jesus and **His finished work.** Why? Because He has accomplished the total forgiveness of all sins already and has given every believer God's "righteousness, peace and joy in the Holy Spirit – the Kingdom of God," as defined in Romans 14:17.

This assurance by <u>faith</u> empowers the believer to bask in God's <u>love</u> and walk in the <u>liberty</u> of a cleansed conscience, now free from useless rituals that law-consciousness requires (confession of sins to God etc.) which are "dead works," left over from a system that had no power to fix the "sin and self problem." Again, if attempted obedience to the law system (and introspection) can make a believer righteous, perfect and holy, then Christ Jesus' sacrificial death was meaningless. Jesus' revelation through Paul put it this way in Galatians 2:21:

> Do not set aside the grace of God (by going back under the law) for if righteousness could be gained through the law, Christ died for nothing.

First John, Chapter One Explained

So, does 1 John 1:9, cited before, contradict Paul's gospel that he received directly from Christ Jesus? In the **first place**, chapter one of 1 John was *not* written to Christian believers but to, as yet, unconverted Jewish Gnostics who erroneously believed <u>that they were sinless.</u> That is the reason John stated twice within three verses: "If we say that we have no sin ...." No orthodox Jew or reborn Christian would entertain such nonsense because the doctrine of sin is a foundational part of both belief systems. If there was such a thing as "having no sin," there would be no need for Moses' sacrificial system in Judaism or our Savior's sacrificial death on Calvary. It is denying the central truth of Adam's fall in the Garden. However, the lie that "there is no such thing as sin" was a foundational doctrine of a popular heresy of that time - Gnosticism - that John was publically combating when he wrote this letter to the Diaspora Jews in about 85-90 AD. Appendix #4 gives a detailed explanation of this heresy.

Secondly, if you notice, John did not open this letter with the customary greeting to a particular person or group as he did in his two other short letters and which was generally customary. Rather, the first chapter is his testimony that he had known Jesus Christ personally, followed by a proclamation that, unless you realize by grace (through the conviction of the Holy Spirit who might use the Law) a need for a savior due to your **in Adam** "sin condition," you, obviously, won't ask to be saved by Jesus and, therefore, can't be in a spiritually-based fellowship with true believers. In contrast to his opening chapter, he specifically addresses the remaining chapters to "my dear children." This implies that you can't be one of John's spiritual children under God the Father unless you are saved by grace through faith first.

Thirdly, if the ongoing confession of sins to God, as discussed in 1 John 1:9, was supposed to be a *central doctrine* for Christians to "stay right" with God – as the Catholic church made it become – then how did the early church survive spiritually from Pentecost (about 33 AD) to when John wrote his letter (about 90 AD)? If God's gift of justification/ righteousness (both come from the same Greek word) and also fellowship with God depends on a believer's constant efforts to "confess his sins" (instead of confessing Jesus) to keep close "sin accounts" with God, then the gift of justification is no longer a gift by grace through faith but a "work of the law," based conditionally on one's diligent efforts.

Fourthly, if a believer's ongoing confession of his sins was a requirement of Jesus' **New Covenant**, then Jesus either forgot to tell Paul (or Paul ignored His directive) because nowhere in Paul's writings is the confession of sins even mentioned, let alone "required." In other words, Paul would have done a great disservice to the church by not including such an important "doctrine" in every one of his letters. In fact, as noted previously and worth emphasizing again, Paul did not even include a requirement to "confess one's sins" in order to be saved, according to Romans 10:9-13. Why? Because Jesus revealed to Paul just how totally forgiven and reconciled mankind is from God's viewpoint – thanks to Jesus' **finished work** (again, see 1 John 2:2 below and 2 Corinthians 5:18-19).

Fifthly, John knew from his days before Jesus came that if a Jew who sinned took a perfect lamb to a priest, and the proper process and **exchange** was made, the sin was no longer on the sinner but transferred to the lamb. The sinner did not have to "confess his sins" to God in the process. The sin was covered in God's eyes because of the **exchange** of his sin for the lamb's spotlessness (perfection) – from God's viewpoint. And John also knew that Jesus was Father's *only* Lamb who perfectly and completely paid the price for and forgave and removed all of mankind's sins on Calvary. In fact, John was there to witness, first-hand, what it cost Jesus to provide mankind the freedom from our sin debt. Consistent with this revelation of mankind's forgiveness, John writes the following verses below (and already quoted in Chapter Thirteen) from 1 John. Please note that these quotes are from the very same letter that needlessly causes so much guilt and condemnation for many, if not most Christians. Why? Because they *misunderstand* John's intent for its first chapter. So, to set the record straight again, this is what Jesus, the Lamb, accomplished for mankind in God's eyes, according 1 John:

> 1 John 2:2 … And He (Jesus) is the propitiation (payment and removal of punishment) for our sins and not for ours only, but also for the sins of the whole world…

> 1 John 2:12… I write unto you, little children, because your sins are forgiven you for His name's sake …

> 1 John 4:10 …God … sent His Son as an atoning sacrifice for our sin debt.

Clearly, John knew that confession of sins was not needed for any true believer because, on Calvary, Jesus paid the sin debt for the population of whole world, *not* just for believers. Jesus revealed this doctrinal reality to Paul in 2 Corinthians 5:18-19, over 30 years before John wrote this letter. Either Jesus' perfect sacrifice as mankind's last Adam paid the sin total debt of all people for all time - or for no one at all. Why? Because it is the only sacrifice for mankind's sin that He will ever make.

Note: The fact that most of the world's population do not even know they have an **in Adam** sin-nature *and* had a sin debt to the God of the Bible, let alone that Jesus has already paid for all sins, stands as an indictment of the ignorance of the church of what Jesus has already mercifully accomplished for mankind. That ignorance, in turn, has prevented believers from spreading the **whole gospel of grace** to the world because they don't know it themselves! So, most people in the world still believe that "the gods" are angry at them and must be appeased.

The fourteen scriptures already quoted in Chapter Thirteen document God's merciful gift of total forgiveness for everyone through Jesus' **finished work**. What remains for each person is to personally choose to be reconciled to God by rebirth, as Paul pleaded for in 2 Corinthians 5:20b. Jesus came to save a condemned world **in Adam.** He is the only ticket to heaven because of who He is and what He did for mankind. Any other gospel is no gospel at all.

Lastly, the Jerusalem leaders in 50 AD agreed that they would proselytize the Jews and that Paul and Barnabas should proselytize the non-Jews. Presumably, they honored this gentleman's agreement when they wrote their various books/letters, now contained in the New Testament. Consequently, it is just being consistent to realize that Paul's writings were written primarily to Gentile believers and that James, Peter and John's letters were aimed at the Diaspora (Jews scattered abroad) and included some of the "mixture" of both covenants (law and grace) common in the Jerusalem church as indicated by the insistence on circumcision for even Gentiles.

They regarded themselves as just another "Jewish sect," not members of a distinct and revolutionary new belief system that Paul preached and lived. #**35** So, it follows that the radical, **grace-based gospel** of Christ Jesus was not *fully and purely* presented and explained in their letters – written to Jewish believers and unbelievers alike. This fact is vital to keep in mind to avoid reaching wrong conclusions about what is the true doctrine of radical grace for **New Covenant** believers that Jesus revealed to Paul in about 42 AD. This is why Luther regarded James' letter as a "book of straw." It did not center on Jesus and *His* **finished work** but focused on the Jewish believer's behavior - which keeps one centered on self and sin. (For a more detailed explanation of 1 John 1:9, see APPENDIX #4.)

So, like Paul, I never tire of meditating on and teaching and singing about the fantastic news that Jesus Christ "became sin who knew no sin" and, thereby, absorbed in His person all the punishment and wrath of God, justly due to all mankind for all sin for all time. From God's standpoint, all of mankind was totally forgiven and reconciled to God when Jesus declared "it is finished." All one needs to do now is believe and receive rebirth and the fullness of Jesus' **finished work** "by grace through faith" (see 2 Corinthians 5:19, Ephesians 2:8-9, Titus 3:5 and Colossians 3:1). That is how wonderfully *good* Jesus' **whole gospel of grace** really is.

The Ministry Of The Holy Spirit

The following passage has been interpreted by many to define the role of the Holy Spirit as a type of "policeman" whose job is to be on the lookout for sin and convict *anyone,* on the spot, who commits a sin. But let's read it objectively, looking through the lens of Jesus' **whole gospel of grace** to rightly divide this important passage.

> 5) John 16:5a and 7-11... Now I am going to Him (Father-God) who sent Me (Jesus) ... But be assured that it is for your benefit that I am leaving you. For, unless I go away, the Counselor cannot come to you. But when I go, I will send Him to you. And when He (the Holy Spirit) comes, He will convict the world concerning sin (nature), and concerning righteousness, and concerning judgment: concerning sin (nature), because they (the world) do not believe in Me (Jesus); concerning righteousness, because I am going to my Father, and you (the disciples) will see me no more; concerning judgment, because the prince of this world is judged.

When we realign the text to allow the two disjointed sections to flow together point by point, it becomes clear that John is addressing three different audiences. It reads:

"And when He (the Holy Spirit) is come:

1) He will convict the (**in Adam** people of the) world concerning sin, because they (the world's people) do not believe in Me (Jesus);

2) and concerning righteousness because I am going to my Father, and you (the disciples) will see me no more (Jesus leaves them so that He can send back the Holy Spirit on Pentecost when those disciples will be made righteous by rebirth.)

3) and concerning judgment because the prince of this world (Satan) is judged." (Satan was judged and defeated by Jesus' victory at Calvary, as predicted by God's declaration in Genesis.)

Scholars generally believe that John's gospel was written in about 85-95 AD, over fifty years after Pentecost (see Appendix # 1). As discussed in Chapter Thirteen, it focused primarily on the words, miracles and the identity of the **pre-cross** Jesus, yet included descriptions and inferences of the **unseen Kingdom** (which was yet to come) more than the other three gospels. Here, in the **first** of three scenarios which John presents, the Holy Spirit's true purpose for the Law is demonstrated: *convicting the **in Adam** sinners of the world of the sin of underlief in Jesus so that they will then (hopefully) see their need to believe and receive Him as their Savior.*

NOTE: The word "convict" typically has a negative connotation, associated with "judgment and punishment for wrong doing." Convicts are in prisons. But the Greek word can also mean "convince" someone of something – good or bad. That translation could also be used in point one above "to convince the people of the world that they are lost sinners without Jesus". The negative sounding word "convict" is used by most translators in the first point because it is consistent with the mood of doom that hangs over the unsaved who are condemned **in Adam**. It drives home the idea that the unbeliever is "in the wrong" and if there is no change of mind about Jesus (repentance), he will end up in the wrong place - hell. The law principle is still in force for "lawbreakers" – those who are still **in Adam** sinners by nature - to "wake them up" to their desperate need for the Savior's redemption.

The Ultimate Consequences Of Unbelief

Even though God provided total forgiveness of all of humankind's sin on Calvary, God cannot ignore one's *unbelief* (rejection) toward Jesus because He is mankind's only ticket to heaven which is all about relationship with God Himself. God's gift of free will, given to each human being, allows individuals to accept or reject God's gracious offer – which is to become one with Him through rebirth by faith. Again, God honors each person's free will to reject God's gift of a Savior and His **finished work** and, thereby, remain eternally apart from Him by remaining **in Adam** and under Satan's control. <u>Remember</u>: There are only two kingdoms and everyone begins in the Kingdom of Darkness as **in Adam** sinners.

Now it is true that 1 Timothy 2:3-4 assures us that "It is His (God's) will that all men be saved and come to the knowledge of the truth." However, the Bible also reveals that many refuse the invitation (for example, see Matthew 22:2-14). Forcibly dragging rebellious sinners (who are at enmity with God by nature) into heaven against their will would not make for a heavenly experience for God or anyone else there. And, it follows, that heaven would no longer be "perfect." In His Sovereignty, God chose to grant to angels and to mankind the gift of free choice and He has patiently endured the painful cost of this gift – man's option to personally reject His perfect will. Such is God's great risk – rejection by those He created and loves – even after He spent the price of His beloved Son's redemptive blood. He went to this extreme so that He could have an eternal, love-relationship with free-willed, yet bankrupt humans who accept His gracious invitation to be reborn of God, Himself.

The Assurance Of The Holy Spirit

In the **second point** of the passage, Jesus addresses disciples who will not see Him on earth after His ascension because He is going to the Father who sent Him, according to verse 5. However, <u>He assures them that the Holy Spirit will come to them to reveal and *convince* them, as new believers, of their righteousness **in Christ** once they are reborn</u>. Jesus is going to the Father so that He can send the Holy Spirit back to teach and guide them into the benefits of Jesus' **divine exchange** of the **New Covenant** with God. Jesus wants His disciples to let the Holy Spirit convince (reveal and teach) them about the benefits of His gift of justification (or righteousness) that He will give them at Pentecost as part of their rebirth **in Christ** - received by faith alone. This is different from the purpose of point one which was ultimately to <u>convince unbelievers</u> that they need to believe in Jesus so that they, too, can be justified **in Him**.

Unfortunately, this wonderful passage has been twisted by law-minded people to say that "Jesus sends the Holy Spirit to convict believers of their sin so that they can confess their sin and get back into fellowship with God." Then they might use a **pre-cross** passage such as Nathan coming to David to "convict him" of his sin with Bathsheba as a type of the Holy Spirit's work. <u>But Jesus' cross has changed everything</u>. "God was **in Christ** reconciling the world to Himself, not imputing their trespasses to them" (see 2 Corinthians 5:19). Why? Because God is Love:

> For God so loved (the people in) the world that He gave His only Begotten Son (Jesus) that <u>whosoever believes **in Him**</u> will not perish but have everlasting life. For God did not

send His Son into the world to condemn (the people in) the world but so that (the people in) the world might be saved through Him (John 3:16-17).

How? By believing and receiving His gift of righteousness through rebirth - through His **finished work** of redemption, offered to all.

Satan Will Finally Be Judged

In the **third point**, Jesus discloses that Satan is the prince of this world (because he deceived Adam into giving to him the dominion over the earth that God had delegated to Adam). For his treachery, Satan will finally be thrown into the lake of fire, created and reserved for him and his followers. Hell was not established for man but for Satan and the one third of God's angels that he fooled into rebelling against God. However, Adam's allegiance to Satan required that all who remain **in Adam** (because of unbelief in Jesus) must go to where Satan goes, since that is the only alternative to God's Kingdom. You would be wise to make sure that is *not* your destination. Be reconciled to God once and for all!

So, summarizing John 16:5a and 7-11, God sends the Holy Spirit to:

1) convict the **world's population** of sin through the law principle in order to reveal man's need for a savior – even as He used the Law Covenant to prove that to the Israelites – so that "everyone who calls upon the name of the Lord shall be saved" (Romans 10:13), and to

2) convince **believers** of their permanent, righteous standing (not condemned) before God because of their faith in Jesus' **finished work** of His **divine exchange**. This assurance of being Father-God's sons and heirs is the work of the Holy Spirit whom Jesus sends into each believer to renew his or her unsanctified mind, revealed in Romans 8:15b-16 as follows:

> For the (Holy) Spirit himself renders testimony to our spirit that we are the sons of God. So if we are sons, then we are also heirs, certainly heirs of God, but also co-heirs with Christ … and to

3) assure the Church that **the devil** and all his fallen angels (but not true believers) will suffer God's judgment and eternal punishment for all their rebellion against God and all the evil they have done against mankind.

Did Jesus Abolish The Law?

Now, you may be wondering how can it be true that the Holy Spirit 1) does not convict the believer of breaking the law (sinning) and that 2) Jesus has replaced the Mosaic Law itself (for Jewish believers) with "the law of the Spirit of Life" when Jesus Himself said in Matthew 5:17-20:

> Do not think that I have come to abolish the Law or the Prophets. I have not come to abolish them but to fulfill them. I tell you the truth, <u>until heaven and earth pass away</u>, not the smallest letter, not the least stroke of a pen, will by any means disappear from the Law <u>until everything is accomplished</u>. *Anyone* (who is under the 613 Jewish laws) breaks <u>one</u> of the least of these commandments and teaches others to do the same will be called

least in the kingdom of heaven. But, whoever practices and teaches these commands, will be called great in the kingdom of heaven. For I tell you that <u>unless your righteousness surpasses that of the Pharisees and the teachers of the law</u> (which is based on their imperfect performance), you will certainly not enter the kingdom of heaven.

Well, you already know the reason why both statements are true, now that you understand the **pre-cross/post-cross** division of the two opposing covenants. Jesus came to first fulfill all the righteous requirements of the good, Mosaic Law - which no one else could keep perfectly. He accomplished this feat by living a sinless life on earth so that He could legally maintain His right standing with God as a perfect Man *and* as the perfect, sacrificial Lamb, who Father-God sent as our *substitute* in order to accomplish our redemption. (If He would have sinned when He was tempted, we would have lost all hope for salvation because only He, as a perfect sacrificial Lamb, could totally pay for mankind's sin-debt for all time.)

Once He fulfilled the Law with His perfect obedience to God – including even death on a cross – *the law principle <u>had</u> to be "abolished" for believers* (not for unbelievers) so that Satan could no longer use it to falsely accuse and condemn believers. How? By tempting them to take their eyes off of Jesus and focus, instead, on law-keeping. Again, that is the very reason that Paul warned the reborn Galatians that if they continued to focus on, come under and, thereby, mix the law with the perfect **New Covenant**, they would *fall from grace* and experience accusation and condemnation from the devil (but not from God) and nullify both covenants for themselves.

Paul knew that this gospel of grace was the *opposite* of the religion of Judaism that he was formed in as a Jew. Joshua 1:8 instructs the Jews to "meditate on the Law, day and night." The purpose of that instruction was supposedly to keep the Jews from sinning. But Jesus showed Paul that the Law is actually <u>the strength of sin</u> because it is a perfect standard that no one but Jesus can keep perfectly. Failure to keep any part of the law breaks the whole Law. That leads to guilt and condemnation for anyone under the Law.

For there to be "no condemnation **in Christ**," according to Romans 8:1, God replaced the Mosaic Law as a means of righteousness for Jews (and He never gave it to Gentiles.) Jesus spoke the words in the passage above in the **pre-cross** period. The law was still in force for those He was speaking to - the Jews of His day. But it is not to be our focus as believers who are free from the Law of sin and death, **post-cross.** This is very good news because Jesus tells us through Romans 4:15b that "… where there is no law, there is no transgression."

Again, why would the Holy Spirit convict believers of sin when they are not under a performance-based law system but **in Christ** and all of mankind's sin already forgiven and forgotten? It is *not* the Holy Spirit but the law-minded clergy who *think* in and who teach the **elephant of mixture**. In so doing, *they* (not the Holy Spirit) keep believers both self and sin-conscious and, thus, they cause condemnation in the Body of Christ. It is they who are helping the devil to do his dirty work of "accusing the brethren day and night." Law mindedness leads either to defeat and depression or to self-righteousness because it takes the believer's focus from Jesus and puts the focus on himself (or on others) and on the quality of his own (or other's) performance. It is all based on the **seen realm** rather on God's **unseen** Kingdom realities.

Also, notice that the <u>worst case scenario</u> for *"anyone who breaks one of the least of these commandments* and teaches others to do the same, (they) will be called least in the Kingdom of heaven"* (not sent to hell). Obviously, grace-based teachers are not teaching lawlessness when they are preaching Jesus and His **finished work** of grace and the <u>law</u> of the Spirit of life. But legalists often accuse them of that because they are not pushing the obsolete Mosaic law on believers. They assume that if you don't teach believers the law, they will <u>go wild and become</u> "<u>lawless</u>." *But legalists are walking in fear, not in grace.* The truth is that when believers have a revelation of God's love for them, it casts out the spirit of fear and bondage to law and enables them to walk in harmony with God like Jesus lived. It is the <u>goodness</u> of God, not the law of God, which leads people to a lasting change of mind (true repentance) about who God really is and what He did through Christ Jesus. The letter of the law kills but Jesus' **whole gospel** revealed to the saints by the Holy Spirit gives life and bolsters our <u>faith</u> with His truth that sets believers <u>free</u> to <u>love</u> the Trinity.

He said "<u>anyone</u>" in Matthew 5:19 quoted above (which includes unbelievers) because Jesus paid the price for all sin at Calvary, even for **in Adam** sinners. So their sinning is now *not an issue* from God's point of view. <u>It is their **in Adam** nature and their *unbelief* in Jesus'</u> salvation that keeps them from being saved, <u>not their sinning, per se.</u> *However*, if they become born again by repenting (changing their mind) from unbelief to belief in Jesus (see Romans 10:9-13), their sinning ways, (if continued) would result in them being "least" in the Kingdom, yet saved from the devil's kingdom forever. On that basis, the "good thief," who Jesus promised to take with Him to paradise after they both died, would be one of the "least," (probably meant in terms of "rewards"). Why? Because he bore no good fruit of the Holy Spirit while being **in Adam** all of his life - until he professed belief in Jesus.

All Things New

"But wait a minute. Heaven and earth have not yet disappeared. I am living on the earth right now so the law principle has not passed away." (This is a follow up to this conundrum addressed in Chapter Nine.) Well, that is true for those still **in Adam** but not for those **in Christ**. Why? Because unbelievers are still under the law principle but believers are now under grace through Jesus' **finished work**. What seems to be correct from our limited point of view is sometimes not true from God's viewpoint. He alone sees the fullness of the **unseen realm** where everything is "now" for Him and He knows just how monumental Jesus' **finished work** truly is <u>in His sight.</u> When Jesus said on Calvary *"It is finished,"* that obviously meant a lot more to God than to our carnal minds, which are limited to the **seen realm.** Again, Jesus revealed to Paul in 2 Corinthians 5:17-18 that:

If anyone is in Christ he is a new creation; the old things have passed away. Behold, <u>all things have become new</u> and all are from God....

So, could that be what He meant by saying "till all things are accomplished" in Matthew 5:18? Jesus is now seated at God's right hand, indicating that He *has finished* all that we needed Him to do. And we also know from Jesus' revelation to Paul that the law has now *"passed away" for believers* (not for unbelieving Jews) because "the law was nailed to the cross" and "He (Jesus) is the *end* of the Mosaic Law" which was weak and inadequate to bring people to perfection. And we know that both Peter and James told Paul in 50 AD that Gentiles were not to be given the Law of Moses.

In God's view, the **New Covenant** began a *new era or age* - the age of God's abundant grace toward mankind because of what Jesus did as the last Adam. This revelation is also indicated in Hebrews 9:10b which says that the Law was in effect "…until the time of setting things right has been imposed." (The NIV translation says: "… until the time of the new order.") God has set things right through Jesus in the **unseen realm**. From God's viewpoint, there is a new race of redeemed humans in heaven and on earth right now. We are His sons and daughters, no longer of the Adamic race.

That revolutionary change has not yet effected the physical globe of dirt that we stand on. But it certainly has changed the **in Adam** "dirt" that we were united with. But don't expect to see the fullness of all this with your natural eyes until Jesus returns. Why? Because only those who believe and receive Jesus through rebirth are saved by grace through faith into the new race and the eternal rewards of the new age which began at Pentecost. Only through Jesus do we receive the gift of His righteousness by being *one* with Him. That gift cannot be earned by keeping any law principle. (And, as you now know, *having* those gifts of the Holy Spirit is not the same thing as *manifesting* them by letting Him live His life through you, which is the focus of Chapter Eighteen.)

However, the law principle still has the same useful purpose that it had in Jesus' day – to reveal an unbeliever's **in Adam** nature and motivate him to look to Jesus as the promised Savior. But once an **in Adam** sinner has changed his thinking from unbelief to belief in Jesus – and, thereby, is reborn by God's grace through His gift of faith – *he no longer needs the law*. In fact, it's death dealing properties as the "ministry of death" etc., as already explained in Chapter Nine, will have negative consequences meant *only* for unsaved sinners - to bring them to the end of themselves. Since the believer has already died to his old, **in Adam** self, as Jesus explains through Paul in Romans, Chapter 6, he need only to reckon it as true for him by believing that it *is* true because Jesus revealed what He has accomplished. It is a necessary part of *experiencing* the transformational, **divine exchange** that already occurred in the **unseen realm** upon rebirth.

The law did its job to bring you, believer, to Christ Jesus, but you are now dead to the law principle from Adam (by being crucified with Christ through rebirth by faith) and married to Jesus, as revealed in Romans, Chapter 7. Now, you are a **new creation saint in Christ Jesus** that will never again be under God's condemnation because you belong to Christ Jesus – as agreed to by believing and receiving Him as your own Savior and Lord. Father-God sees you and treats you as united with Christ Jesus forever. Ask the Holy Spirit to help you see yourself as God does. Chapters Two and Sixteen to Twenty will help you in the process of renewing your mind to agree with God on who you now are **in Christ Jesus.**

Satan's Club Removed From Believers

From another angle, Colossians 2:15 is a revelation of the inner drama between the two **unseen** Kingdoms – Light and Darkness. It describes Jesus' victory over the powers of Darkness, doing what conquerors do to the vanquished: first, disarm them so that they can do no more harm, and then parade them before the celebrating citizens - in this case, the heavenly angels (and possibly those with Abraham who were waiting for Jesus to rescue them). But notice what weapon was removed from Satan, the accuser of reborn believers. Jesus stripped away the Law from Satan then it was nailed to the cross. And where there is no law, sin (and its resulting condemnation) is no longer imputed.

However, the Accuser, (the devil) continues to tempt believers with the law so that they take their eyes off of Jesus. The strategy worked with Adam in the perfect garden so why not continue to use it against believers in this imperfect world? A believer can then become mentally subject again to Satan's schemes and condemnation through ignorance of the **whole gospel**, even as the Jerusalem church did. Paul was furious with the Galatians who were apparently succumbing to the same temptation – even though the Law was never given to them as Gentiles. The **elephant of mixture** is still alive to bewitch unaware believers who are not established in the truth of our loving Father-God's total forgiveness, acceptance and approval of them because of Jesus' **finished work**.

Which gospel are you believing – Jesus' good news revealed to Paul or the bad news of the law that is interspersed with Good News in the four gospels? If you have been a victim you can now be a victor!

Be Finally Persuaded

Hopefully the truth of all the scriptures listed in these last two chapters has forever convinced you of the **New Covenant** reality that God has totally forgiven the sins of the whole world, thanks to Jesus' perfect sacrifice for mankind. Let them bathe your mind in this vital reality so that you become *established* in the freedom of the **grace gospel** for yourself, personally. Renewing your mind with this revelation that you are totally forgiven – vertically from God's viewpoint – is absolutely essential to enjoy the reality that "Therefore, there is now no condemnation for those **in Christ Jesus**," as emphatically stated by Paul in Romans 8:1. (This revelation will empower you into the freedom of forgiving others just as God has completely forgiven you. More on this in the next chapter.)

But many law-minded teachers, preachers and authors will argue to the contrary because they parrot what they have been told all their lives. And that is precisely how the **elephant of mixture** has prevailed for almost 2000 years over the "law of the Spirit of life" - **the butterfly life** – that Jesus revealed to Paul, described in Romans Chapter 8. That is because law-minded believers are afraid of being set free "from the law of sin and death" because they wrongly believe that moral laws are necessary guard rails so that believers won't go off the straight and narrow. They would rather trust in their efforts to keep the law (even though they admit, as Calvin did, that it is not possible to do so perfectly) than to *trust in being sealed in and kept by the Holy Spirit*. We will examine the fallacy behind those guard rails in Chapter Nineteen.

Now it is time to contrast that wonderful truth of the total forgiveness of all of our sins with the need to give and receive forgiveness for sins on the horizontal level – person to person, when appropriate. But as difficult as forgiving others may seem at times, it is far easier for a believer to flow in the river of forgiveness towards others when he is *fully convinced* of God's total forgiveness of all sin for him and, consequently is righteous **in Christ Jesus**. Reveling in God's **total forgiveness** of all your sin – past, present and future - will supply you with the grace to freely give and receive forgiveness horizontally with all others – even as Jesus has forgiven them already. So now let's turn our attention to the importance of <u>horizontal forgiveness</u> for spiritual health for one and all – as the following song celebrates and which is the topic of the next chapter.

This song-poem is a prayer, asking the Holy Spirit to have His way in various ways.

LORD HELP ME LIVE as one fully forgiven
And rest in joy because my debts You've paid.
Reborn through You, God's wrath no longer
Safe in Your arms, now I am not afraid.
Your grace abounds, so I forgive all others.
I thank You for Your freeing love each day.

You loved me when I was a helpless sinner.
You died for me so I could live in You.
Your perfect love casts out all fear and hatred.
Help all who know You see things as You do.
We're one with You, partakers of Your Nature,
So live through us and help us rest in You.

Spirit of God, You now abide within me.
Renew my mind in places not yet free.
Bring forth Your fruit that gives my Father pleasure,
Sharing Your Truth that sets all captives free.
Covenant Bread, I eat and share with others
So You can feed this hurting world through me.
© Copyright by Leonard Ransil 2007
(This can be sung to Finlandia)

CHAPTER FIFTEEN

OUR NEED FOR
HORIZONTAL FORGIVENESS OF SIN

Vertical vs. Horizontal Forgiveness

So far, this book has focused primarily on revealing who God really is as demonstrated in the Person and **finished work** of Jesus and His Spirit living in us, as presented in Jesus' **whole gospel** to Paul. Secondarily, we have also traced where that pure, **whole gospel** was compromised historically by the mixture of law with grace. In presenting all this, we focused on the revelation of the *vertical relationship* with Father-God that Jesus made available to mankind through His **whole gospel of grace**. The basic premise is that right believing in Jesus' **whole gospel**, lived out through the Holy Spirit's **unseen** "law of the Spirit of life," will increasingly manifest the fruit of right living in the horizontal **seen realm** of the believer's outer man.

As we saw in the last two chapters on **total forgiveness**, a key part of right believing is that "God was **in Christ**, reconciling the world to Himself, not charging their trespasses to them..." as Paul declares in 2 Corinthians 5:19. All that remains is for each individual to choose to personally accept God's offer of salvation, by grace through faith in Jesus, to have His reconciliation become mutual. This can be greatly hindered by wrong concepts of who God really is, which can come from hearing sermons and songs and reading books that mix the opposing covenants – producing Galatianism. By contrast, believers can be very effective ambassadors of God's gift of total forgiveness and reconciliation when they are steeped in Jesus' **whole gospel** of His **radical grace**.

Distinguishing between Vertical And Horizontal Forgiveness

Now it is time to shift the focus of *vertical* forgiveness and reconciliation, accomplished by God through Jesus, to the *horizontal* plane of forgiveness of sins between people. It is seemingly a very different topic – except for one knotty fact. Jesus tied the two together in the "Our Father" prayer, **pre-cross**, explained in Matthew 6:12-15. This passage *seems* to negate all the scriptural evidence for total, unilateral forgiveness and reconciliation from God towards mankind at Calvary, which we covered in the last two chapters.

But to come to such a conclusion is to miss the extremely important fact *of when it was said and to whom.* Context is the key to proper interpretation. As noted, this passage is from a **pre-cross** period when Jesus and the Israelites were living under the Law. All that changed with the coming of the **New Covenant**. Tragically, the church has been clinging to the "Our Father" passage as though it was addressed to *believers*, not to the **in Adam** disciples, **pre-cross**. Thankfully, that is *not* true, as I explain in detail in Appendix # 2. Our forgiveness from God *totally* depends on what Jesus *has done* for mankind, not on how well we forgive others. (That is not to say that horizontal forgiveness is not important – as we will soon see.) This is just one more example where making the four gospels one's focus for right believing and living, is to risk mixing the terms of two opposing covenants – Galatianism – thereby missing the benefits of Jesus' **finished work.**

However there is another passage that *is* **post-cross** and has been interpreted by the Catholic church in such a way as to seem to negate God's **total forgiveness** of mankind's sins *vertically* and affect people's forgiveness of sins *horizontally* as well. Consistent with the thesis of this book, any **post-cross** verse that seems to contradict Jesus' direct revelation to Paul in 42 AD, requires proper discernment, especially when it *seemingly* contradicts all the overwhelming scriptural evidence for **total forgiveness** from God presented in the last two chapters. So, let's have a look.

> **1)** John 20:21-23… Then said Jesus to them again, 'Peace be to you! As my Father has sent me, so I send you.' And when he had said this, He breathed on them, and said to them: 'Receive the Holy Spirit: <u>whosoever sins you forgive, they are forgiven them; and whosoever sins you retain, they are retained.</u>'

Again, this scripture is a **post-cross** statement by Jesus, given to His disciples before His ascension, but not to Paul. On the face of it, it *seems* completely inconsistent with Jesus' revelation to Paul about **total forgiveness** of all mankind's sins at Calvary that the fourteen scriptures listed in Chapter Thirteen present and confirm. Moreover, historically, this single scripture has been used by the Roman Catholic Church to, in effect, negate all those fourteen scriptures from Jesus' **whole gospel of grace.** Taken collectively, they unequivocally guarantee that all the sins of all mankind were paid for and fully forgiven at Calvary, 2000 years ago, as part of His **finished work,** as stated in 2 Corinthians 5:18-19. Even in 1 John 2:2 (written by the same author of the scripture quoted above), John says that Jesus is the payment "for the sins of the whole world."

Nonetheless, the Roman Catholic Church interprets this single scripture to mean that a bishop or priest is delegated by God to decide (in administering their required sacrament of Penance) whether or not to absolve a person from the sins that he or she confessed to him. This policy is specifically stated in # 1441 in the *Catechism of the Catholic Church*, endorsed by the pope in 1992. So, according to this doctrine, it is the role of duly ordained clergy to first hear the confession of a person's sins and then to either grant or retain God's forgiveness – known as "absolution." They see themselves as necessary mediators between God and man – as was true in Judaism but which Jesus replaced when He became God's eternal High Priest. Now, we dealt with the notion of "confessing sins to God" in # 4 of the previous chapter by proving that such a "requirement" is not found anywhere in Jesus' **whole gospel of grace** revealed to Paul, **post-cross**.

So, how can we maintain the integrity of this verse with the other fourteen scriptures? We can do what lawyers do – make a key distinction between seemingly opposite positions. We can do what the Roman Catholic Church has not done - distinguish between *vertical* forgiveness from God to all mankind, which Jesus provided 2000 years ago, vs. *horizontal* forgiveness between people that is an ongoing process. Unfortunately, some have mixed the two together by not dividing the word of God according to the terms of each respective covenant. (Chapter Eighteen explains those differences in detail.)

Now, understanding this distinction, what does God say about horizontal forgiveness between His children? Well, we have His very clear word through Paul: "And be kind to each other, tenderhearted, having forgiven one another *just as God*, for Christ's sake, *has forgiven you*," according to Ephesians 4:32. Now this will cause confusion if you still wrongly think that you are not forgiven by God until you ask forgiveness for each and every sin and, therefore, don't have to forgive people until they ask. And more confusion will come if you think it is okay to retain forgiveness rather than freely give it – even *ahead of time* (as an attitude of your new heart) as Jesus did for us 2000 years ago.

As you can now understand, <u>the way of the Holy Spirit</u> is for us to be "… kind to each other, tenderhearted, having forgiven one another just as God, for Christ's sake, <u>has forgiven you</u>." Exercising that choice is the way of the higher law of <u>faith</u> in His power to do that out of <u>love</u>, the way that Father-God and Jesus love you, and, thereby, experience the <u>liberty</u> from anger, bitterness, rage etc. against others. (In contrast, the Mosaic Law required an eye for an eye and a tooth for a tooth – how nice!)

The Role Of The Priest In The Mosaic Covenant Gives Insight For Today

The role of a Levite priest as a mediator in the Mosaic Covenant - that required animal sacrifices to forgive unintended sins - was certainly necessary. But, again, even there, <u>the priest did not judge whether the sinner was forgiven</u> but only whether his *sacrifice* was perfect - without blemish. If the sinner went through the proper ritual with the priest, he was forgiven, regardless of what the priest thought of him. The basis for forgiveness under this *inferior* covenant was not about the priest inspecting the sinner but only about inspecting the lamb to be sure it was spotless.

So the question becomes: did Jesus our perfect High Priest, by this single passage found in John 20:21-23, put the determination of the efficacy of His perfect blood-sacrifice, shed for the sins of the whole world, back into the hands of intermediary, fallible humans to decide, on a case by case basis, if God has forgiven a believer's individual sins or not? Roman Catholics, of course, say "yes" to defend the Sacrament of Penance (or Reconciliation, as it is sometimes called). Obviously, this doctrine denies the doctrine of **total forgiveness** for the whole world (let alone for God's own children) which Jesus personally revealed to both Paul and John, as presented and proven in previous chapters.

Now, we believers are assured in Hebrews 10:8-18 that:

1) all the continuous sacrifices under the Law Covenant, which could never take away sins, "have been set aside" (verse 9) and that

2) by the will of God, believers "… have been *made holy* through the sacrifice of the body of Jesus Christ *once, for all*" (verse 10) and that

3) "… when this priest (Jesus) had offered, for all time, one sacrifice for sins, He sat down at the right hand of the Father."

He sat down because He, as the perfect Man, High Priest and Sacrifice, fully and finally paid for the *forgiveness and removal* of all of mankind's sin that was a major barrier between man

229

and God. Bottom Line: Righteousness is a <u>gift</u> from God, received by grace through faith, not *earned* or *maintained* by confessing one's sins to God or to anyone else.

4) "... God was in Christ, *reconciling the whole world to Himself, not imputing their trespasses to them,* and He gave us the ministry of reconciliation" (see 2 Corinthians 5:19). Astoundingly, for 2000 years, the church in general has been ignoring/denying much of Jesus' **finished work** by saying that God is still imputing sins to mankind - the exact *opposite* of Jesus' direct revelation to Paul. The **elephant of mixture** has all but eclipsed the light of many key truths of the **whole gospel** of Christ Jesus. No wonder many believers are still under so much fear, anger, guilt, shame, bitterness and condemnation – and often pass it on to others, or quit going to church. This condemnation is not coming from Abba-Father. Because of wrong believing, the Accuser of the brethren has had a field day, causing and using all this confusion for 2000 years.

What Did Jesus Mean?
So, considering the overwhelming evidence supporting God's **total forgiveness** of all sin for all time for all mankind, I <u>suggest to you in my paraphrase</u> that Jesus was telling His listeners in John 20:21-23, **post-cross**, that, *in effect:*

> *Before* I died, I told you that you are forgiven *according to how you forgive others* (see the "Our Father" in Matthew 6:9-15 and explained in Appendix # 2). But now, because of what I did for you on Calvary, you are now totally forgiven of all your sins *forever* and are reconciled to My Father. Also, you now have the gift of peace with Me and My Father, from Our perspective. Choosing to refuse to extend the gracious gift of forgiveness to others who have offended you will <u>not</u> affect Our relationship and forgiveness toward you. You are unconditionally forgiven, even if your forgiveness towards others is still conditional. You are no longer under My former word to you, **pre-cross**, because I have made <u>all things new from My Father's point of view!</u>

So, I believe that, Jesus' **finished work** eliminated the negative stipulation that based God's forgiveness of the disciples sins on how well they forgave others sins, *horizontally.* (Remember: this stipulation was not even on the radar in the Mosaic Covenant nor was it ever given to us Gentiles.) So now, **post-cross**, John 20:21-23 is an update from Jesus' earlier requirement of conditional forgiveness given to the disciples (in the "Our Father" prayer) to a *choice* to forgive or retain offenses done against oneself. Again, we believers are not under the demand of *conditional* forgiveness or any other condemnation for the unloving behavior of not forgiving others like God forgave us through Jesus' sacrifice, on Calvary. The revelation of such mercy and love from God actually freed many of the early saints to forgive their persecutors – even while they were being tortured and killed.

Believing in and receiving His perfect love, **total forgiveness**, acceptance and approval casts out all *fear* of punishment, which brings torment, stated in 1 John 4:18. Knowing and believing this revelation from Jesus will set you increasingly free to love and forgive others, just like Jesus did in the liberty of the Holy Spirit's power while on earth. By believing rightly about God's gift of **total forgiveness**, you will much more readily and freely forgive others *horizontally* <u>out of gratitude for how God now views and treats you – as His forgiven child.</u>

Correspondingly, when believers question or doubt God's forgiveness for their sins and are not secure in His unconditional acceptance and approval (based on Jesus' **finished work,** not on their efforts) they are likely to treat others the same way – if not worse.

So, to repeat, Jesus is both our High Priest and our perfect Lamb, who did over and above all that was necessary to gain every believer's permanent justification (acquittal) of all past, present and future sins, according to Hebrews 10:12. Therefore, there is no longer any sacrifice or "confession of sins to God" necessary for believers to stay in right relationship with God. Jesus' work on our behalf is finished! So, again, since this single, **post-cross** scripture – John 20:21-23 - must not refer to our *vertical* relationship with God regarding the "sin issue," what then does it mean? Well, the only other area that forgiveness of sins that is in question is *between people* who have the free choice to withhold or grant forgiveness to others when offended.

Therefore, on a person to person basis, John 20:21-23 can be best understood to mean that, on the *horizontal* level, we each have the <u>choice</u> to give or retain forgiveness toward the sins of other people. It is a matter of one's free will. Again, now that believers have received the presence and power and love of the Holy Spirit within them, they can now choose to "<u>forgive as the Lord has forgiven you</u>" – <u>even ahead of time like Jesus did for us on Calvary</u> - by refusing to take offence over the words and actions of others. This is the same freedom of the **butterfly life** that Jesus walked in and it now belongs to all those **in Christ**. In this fallen world, <u>offences are inevitable</u>.
The question is, will you *react* in the flesh or *respond* through the Holy Spirit as Jesus did?

The devil wants you to hold on to unforgiveness because it opens the door to bitterness and depression by focusing on another's sin and your personal "hurt" instead of on Jesus. Whether one focuses on his own sin or on the sins of others - instead of on Jesus - it is still being law and carnally minded (fleshy) rather than being led by the higher law of faith, love and liberty in the Spirit, by abiding consciously **in Christ**. In other words, the believer is letting his outer, soulish self dominate his true, inner, spirit-self **in Christ** by walking according to his flesh. (I'll present much more on this differentiation in Chapter Sixteen.)

Another Burden Lifted

Additionally, the **post-cross** revelation of **total forgiveness** also removed the trepidation that the disciples probably had over the **pre-cross** parable of the unforgiving servant found in Matthew 18:21-35. It was sparked by Peter's question: "Lord, how many times shall I forgive my brother when he sins against me - up to seven times?" That probably seemed like a mountain for Peter but Jesus amazingly upped the ante to seventy times seven. Then He launched into a **pre-cross** parable which featured an unmerciful, unforgiving, servant who threw his debtors into prison for just a fraction of his humongous debt which his king had mercifully just cancelled. The **pre-cross** consequence of his sin of unforgiveness was frightening. His king became justly angry and "delivered him to the torturers until he should pay all that was owed." That was a hopeless impossibility because the only one who could bail him out was the same <u>king</u> who gave the sentence.

Again, the king's reaction was consistent with the law-based covenant of works: you get back what you dish out. If you bless, you get blessed; if you curse you get cursed. There was as yet no righteous High Priest, no perfect Substitute, and no elder Brother to remove the sin-debt and give him freedom from his old in Adam self and the demands of the inflexible Law. That was the Law-based covenant terms that they were steeped in and defended all their lives. It was focused on justice - not on God's love and grace like Abraham had experienced – in order to reveal man's true self-centered, loveless nature, **in Adam**.

Pentecost brought their rebirth that *legally* released them from the bondage of the Law to the freedom of the **New Covenant in Christ Jesus**. But the fullness of the gospel was not revealed until 42 AD and it was *experientially* theirs only in proportion to how much they individually and/or corporately exchanged law for grace by faith in Jesus' **finished work**. Paul's plea to the Galatians was not to cling to any part of the law (like the Jerusalem church was doing) but reject the law system as a means or guide to try to become or to stay righteous. He wanted them to keep Jesus (not the law) on their radar screen instead. This same choice is continually ours today. That same mental metamorphosis – the change over from having one's mind-cluttered and confused by the **elephant of mixture** to the freedom of the **butterfly life -** is no small thing! One main purpose of this book is to help you to progressively renew your mind to be in sync with Jesus' glorious **gospel of radical grace**.

More On Horizontal Forgiveness

2) James 5:15-16… And the prayer of faith shall save the sick, and the Lord shall raise him up; and if he has committed sins, they *shall* be forgiven him. Confess your faults one to another, and pray one for another, that you may be healed. The effectual fervent prayer of a righteous man avails much.

Considering all that has been documented so far about James' insistence on mixing the two opposing covenants of law and grace, it is obvious why he is still talking about getting one's sins forgiven by God in the future tense by writing "… they (his sins) *shall be* forgiven him." He is writing to Jews who "know the Law," to use Paul's telling phrase in Romans 7:1. However, he is not presenting Jesus' **whole gospel of grace** (which replaced the law for Jewish believers) but encourages his Jewish readers to still focus on much of it. How can you tell? A focus on "sins" presupposes a focus on the Law. Again, James does not mirror Paul's full revelation of **Jesus' finished work** which reveals what Jesus has already *done* for all mankind – believers and unbelievers - so that they can reckon it as true and receive it all by faith. Instead, James is consistent with his commitment to law-mindedness as a Nazarite by focusing primarily on what works one must *do* to receive from God and stay in right-relationship with Him.

No Strings Gospel

Notice that even in Jesus' **pre-cross** ministry, when appropriate, He first forgave people's sins before He healed them. They never had to "confess their faults" to Jesus first to be healed but they just *looked* to Him who then did all that was necessary. And that was during the period of the inferior Law Covenant, **pre-cross**. How much more does His lavish grace abound to anyone who earnestly believes and receives what Jesus offers in His **New Covenant**, won for us by His precious blood. To avoid being deceived by mixture, be sure to "divide the word rightly" by reading James and all the other New Testament books through the lens of Jesus' **whole gospel of unmerited grace,** revealed only to Paul. Don't settle for less than the fullest revelation as you interpret scripture with scripture.

Person To Person Forgiveness of Sins

Now, regarding *horizontal* forgiveness between humans, James instructs his Jewish readers to "confess your faults one to another, and pray one for another, that you may be healed." It is, of course, important to seek forgiveness when one has offended another human being for the sake of restoring a healthy relationship of trust, if possible. But did even the lack of *horizontal* forgiveness among the Jews who Jesus healed keep them from being healed first? It is typical of our unrenewed mind, steeped in law rather than grace, to assume all vertical and horizontal hindrances must be removed <u>before</u> we can receive any good thing from God. We can easily forget that while we were yet sinners - **in Adam** enemies of God - Jesus died for us anyhow and, thereby, forgave all our sins and reconciled us to God - from His divine viewpoint. How much more does His grace abound toward all who are now **in Christ Jesus** (see Romans 5:6-11).

Apparently, James knew relatively little of this wonderful **gospel of God's lavish grace** – or chose not to fully embrace by faith what he was told by Paul. Now, one could surmise that James wrote his book in the late 40s AD and therefore did not have the benefit of Jesus' revelation of the whole gospel given to Paul. However, we know that James did hear it explained by Paul, at least somewhat, at the Jerusalem Council in 50 AD. So then, how can we explain James' insistence on holding on to circumcision – even for Gentiles – after the Council where James publically agreed not to give the Law to Antioch Gentiles? This would seem to be a case of "double-mindedness," which, James says, "causes a man to be unstable in all his ways and not able to receive anything from the Lord." <u>Walking according to the Law is certainly not walking by faith</u> **in Christ Jesus,** as Paul made clear. James' decision to enforce circumcision of Gentiles in Jerusalem continued to be enforced for about eighty-five more years. Clearly, the **elephant** was walking around in James' mind <u>or he would not have said one thing to Paul at the council and done the opposite thing in Jerusalem.</u> Who do you think tolerated, if not welcomed, the unrepentant Judaizers who were zealous for the Law into the church? It certainly was not Paul.

Why have we papered over that historical fact that helped justify the mixture of Galatianism for 2000 years? <u>Blaming a "minor disturbance" on a few unhappy Judaizers in the Jerusalem church (instead of on law-minded leadership) and claiming it was all resolved in 50 AD is not the truth.</u> There is a major skeleton in the closet of our early beginnings as a church and it is about time that we honestly admit it. Only by knowing and facing the truth squarely, and openly acknowledging this gross cover-up (exposed by Paul's account in Galatians), can the church in general hope to *exorcise* the elephant and come into the full freedom of Jesus' **whole gospel,** received and championed by Paul.

Grace Abounds

After Paul had time to process the amazing **grace gospel** from Jesus, he did not condemn saints or sinners for their behavior but reminded the saints that they were the righteous ones **in Christ,** called and equipped to bear the fruit of the Holy Spirit, rather than fulfill the lusts of the flesh. He knew by revelation that, thanks to Jesus, "there is now no condemnation for those **in Christ Jesus**" (see Romans 8:1) so he ministered life, not death, to them accordingly. He knew from his personal encounters with Jesus how to deal with terrible sinners, like he was when he condoned Stephen's murder and hunted down other Christians. He contrasted God's character, revealed through Jesus, with the law-minded Jews that he had once emulated when he wrote in Romans 2:3-4:

But, O man, when you (Jews) judge those who do such things (sin) as *you yourself also do,* do you think that you will escape the judgment of God? Or do you despise the riches of His goodness, patience and forbearance (love and grace)? Do you not know that the kindness of God leads you to repentance (a change of mind)?

He knew that you catch more flies with honey than with vinegar. Law-mindedness breeds a judgmental mentality that alienates rather than draws. Yes, there were many instances in the 1500 period of the Mosaic Law that God was angry with the Israelites for their sins of rebellion and disobedience. But that was then **(pre-cross)** and this is now **(post-cross),** which makes all the difference. Remember: all believers (and the whole world) are now *not* under the judgment and wrath of God for their sins, thanks to Jesus' **finished work**. However, a believer's law-based, judgmental attitude and harsh words of condemnation can further alienate believers and sinners who already wrongly think that He is angry at them. Thanks to Jesus, sinners are *not* in the hands of an angry God like the Israelites were. Those who model and teach that heresy (that I used to think was the truth) are doing the Accuser's work for him. He is out to steal, kill and destroy the message of the **whole gospel of God's lavish grace** offered to all mankind.

The answer, believer, is to allow the Holy Spirit to express His love and compassion through you to others – even to law-hardened unbelievers like Paul himself had been. He learned from Jesus that "…where sin abounds, grace abounds far more" (Romans 5:20b). That revelation is the natural fruit of bathing your mind in Father-God's love for you personally, proven by what Jesus has already accomplished for *you.*

Paul modeled a grace-based approach when a particularly perverted instance of sexual immorality came to light, described in 1 Corinthians 5:1-5. Under the Law, this man would have to be stoned to death to "rid the camp of him." It is a "circle the wagons to avoid the wrath of God" mind-set. However, Paul initially directed the leaders there to gather together in the name of our Lord Jesus and, with the power of the Lord present, "hand this man over to Satan for the destruction of the flesh (not for the destruction of the man himself) so that his spirit may be saved in the day of the Lord Jesus." Then, in a second letter to them, Paul wasted no time to direct them to "forgive and comfort him so that he will not be overwhelmed by excessive sorrow. I urge you, therefore, to reaffirm your love for him" (see 2 Corinthians 2:7-8). We don't know the specifics of what happened between the man and the Holy Spirit before Paul sent the second letter. But the outcome was far more grace-based and encouraging for *all* the saints there than if the man had died on the spot like happened with Ananias and Sapphira. Paul mirrored God's heart to restore fallen mankind, not condemn them.

The forgiveness and comfort that Paul advised was "horizontal" for the hurt and bad example that man's behavior caused to both individuals and to the community as a whole. But notice that he did *not* command the man to "confess his sins to God" to be forgiven and reconciled back to God Why? Because Paul knew that God had already forgiven and reconciled that man (and the whole world) to Himself. Paul was relying on the goodness of God, shown by the community, to lead this saint **in Christ** to repentance – a change of mind as to who he was **in Christ**.

It was the same loving-kindness and identification that brought me to repentance out of the occult and after years of law-based parenting with my children. Again, God is about restoration, not condemnation, as clearly stated in Romans 8:1: "Therefore, there is now no condemnation for those who are **in Christ Jesus**." And all who are still **in Adam** are, consequently, already condemned because of what *Adam* did in the Garden - not because of what God did there. God offers the gift of faith and righteousness to all so that no one has to remain condemned **in Adam**. John 3:16-18 spells this out clearly.

> For God so loved the (people in the) world that He gave His only-begotten Son, so that all who believe in Him may not perish, but may have eternal life. For God did not send His Son into the world, in order to condemn the world, but in order that the world may be saved through Him. Whoever believes in Him is not condemned. But whoever does not believe <u>is already condemned</u>, because he does not believe in the name of the only-begotten Son of God.

Even as Jesus showed compassion for the woman caught in adultery, **pre-cross**, Paul was motivated by God's love for the good of each individual, the love and acceptance we all long for that is typically missing among legalistic saints – <u>especially for saints caught in a serious sin</u>. Jesus, through the Holy Spirit's ministry, seeks to restore, not reject, the offender, no matter the sin. "While we were yet sinners (lost **in Adam**), Christ died for us." Paul was engulfed in the love and vision that Jesus has for all people in all conditions – the **whole gospel of lavish grace**.

However, the other apostles were not as consistently grace-based as Paul was. Consequently, their beliefs, words and actions, which were accurately recorded in the Bible, sometimes brought condemnation instead of horizontal forgiveness – just like wrong beliefs can cause in the Body of Christ today. The **elephant** keeps stomping on the **butterfly life** of grace. We will continue this investigation of Galatianism's negative impact on horizontal forgiveness by exploring two accounts in Acts to get some insight about Peter's limited understanding of Jesus' **whole gospel of lavish grace** before the council in 50 AD.

Peter's Limited Understanding Of The Whole Gospel

On the whole, Peter understood much more of Jesus' **whole gospel** than James did because he personally witnessed the salvation of the uncircumcised Gentile Cornelius – and his whole household - just after Peter spoke these words, recorded in Acts 10:43:

> All the prophets testify about Him (Jesus) that everyone who believes in Him receives forgiveness of sins through His Name.

He was astonished that these heathens received the baptism of the Holy Spirit and spoke in tongues without "confessing their sins" or being circumcised or even being baptized with water. That was not supposed to happen according to his limited revelation of the gospel. So, given Peter's first-hand experience, what did he believe about the "forgiveness of sins," **post-cross**? Did he grasp the fact that God forgave the sins of the whole world because of Jesus' sacrifice?

Well, we know that despite his experience with Cornelius, Peter was still strongly influenced by the mixture of covenants due to:

1) having walked with Jesus for three years while living under the Mosaic Covenant and not having the same, full revelation that Jesus gave to Paul of the revolutionary change in the **unseen realm** that Calvary caused and

2) his continued association with the Jerusalem church and apparent endorsement of circumcising Gentiles before salvation, insisted on by James and

3) that he "went to the temple at the time of prayer" (Acts 3:1) and

4) Paul's rebuke when he drew back from eating with the Gentiles in fear of the Judaizers sent by James, as recorded in Galatians 2:12.

As we saw previously, the definition of "repentance" for a law-based person is based on "the confession and/or contrition of sins" rather than the **New Covenant** concept of simply "a change of mind." It is apparent that Peter still labored under this confusion on the topic of God's forgiveness of the sins of the whole world on more than one occasion. Again, all this is understandable because Jesus' revelation to Paul occurred in 42 AD and the following two episodes happened even before Paul was converted and also before Peter's experience with Cornelius' glorious conversion.

Unfortunately, these following accounts in Acts have also served to reinforce the **elephant of mixture** for many believers because they occurred **post-cross** and through the ministry of Peter, who is traditionally regarded as a "pillar" of the early church. Therefore, it is necessary to interpret these events in light of Jesus' **whole gospel** revealed to Paul. Why? So that Peter's mixed view, which undermines God's **New Covenant** of mercy, is no longer absorbed and practiced unwittingly.

> **3)** But a certain man named Ananias, with his wife Sapphira, sold a field, and he was deceitful about the price of the field, with his wife's consent. And bringing only part of it, he placed it at the feet of the Apostles. But Peter said: 'Ananias, why has Satan tempted your heart, so that you would lie to the Holy Spirit and be deceitful about the price of the land? Did it not belong to you while you retained it? And having sold it, was it not in your power? Why have you set this thing in your heart? You have not lied to men, but to God!' Then Ananias, upon hearing these words, fell down and expired. And a great fear overwhelmed all who heard of it. And the young men came up and removed him and carrying him out, they buried him. Then, about three hours later, his wife entered, not knowing what had happened. And Peter said to her, 'Tell me, woman, if you sold the field for this amount?' And she said, 'Yes, for that amount.' And Peter said to her: 'Why have you agreed together to test the Spirit of the Lord? Behold, the feet of those who have buried your husband are at the door, and they shall carry you out!' Immediately, she fell down before his feet and expired. Then the young men entered and found her dead. And they carried her out and buried her next to her husband. And exceeding fear came over the entire Church and over all who heard these things (Acts 5:1-11).

Now that we have seen just how good and gracious God really is, as displayed in the person of Jesus, the last verse should tip you off to the fact that this was not a "grace-filled" episode for this couple or the church. Was what this couple did worse than what Peter had done when he cursed and then swore three different times that he did not know Jesus just before He was crucified? Is lying to God about money worse than denying and rejecting the God-Man and friend who came to save him? These questions are not asked to make light of their sin but to make much of Jesus' **finished work**. But law-mindedness is quick to judge and condemn even the best of us when grace is there to save and restore the worst of us.

If Peter had been fully grace-minded - like Jesus was toward him - Peter would have known that "... where sin abounds, grace super-abounds" because he certainly experienced it continually for three and one half years, **pre-cross** (see Romans 5:20). What caused Peter to frame this as a "test" and a "lie" against God and the Holy Spirit, rather than just a lie to Peter, himself? Apparently, the revelation that God *had already* forgiven their sins through Jesus' sacrifice for this couple was <u>nowhere</u> on Peter's radar. His accusatory (and likely angry) tone would be enough to give anyone a heart attack, especially coming from Jesus' right-hand man.

Additionally, we know from Jesus' revelation to Paul, found in 2 Timothy 1:7, that Father-God has not given us a spirit of fear but of love, power and a sound mind (or self-control.) Some might argue that the Greek word for "fear" or "terror" in Acts 5:1-11, can and should be translated "awe" or "reverence." But the choice of words in a translation is usually governed by the translators pre-disposition and assumptions of their concept of God. Judge for yourself whether your loving, Father-God wants you to be terrified of Him while seated next to Him **in Christ** or at peace with Him as your Abba-Father. Do you see how He really has made all things totally opposite from the Judaizers point of view!

Condemnation Is Not From God

As we know from many other previous instances, Peter was quick to jump to conclusions and speak without thinking. We also know that "life and death are in the power of the tongue." Was it God who caused this couple's death over a sin already forgiven by the shed-blood of Jesus at Calvary or was it from the *condemnation* in Peter's pronouncement (after he received a word of knowledge of this man's sin) that struck "exceeding fear" (as the Greek indicates) in both the couple and all of the church? Again, the gifts of the Holy Spirit revealed in the **post-cross New Covenant** are given for edification, not to cause terror or bring condemnation, fear and *death* to believers. Again:

> For we have not been given a spirit of (negative) fear of God but of love (for God), power and a sound mind (2 Timothy 1:7).

This event is reminiscent of the **pre-cross** time when James and John wanted to call down fire from heaven, like Elijah had done, to destroy some Samaritans who did not welcome Jesus. But Jesus rebuked them for their harshness – even though they were still under the Mosaic Law (see Luke 9-54-55). Again, "For God did not send His Son to condemn (the people in) the world but to save (the people in) the world through Him" (John 3:17). The mixture of the opposing covenants apparently still played havoc with the minds of the apostles, just like it does in the church today. Here is yet another example of that of what that elephant looks like in Peter's life before 50 AD.

4) Acts 8:13 and 18-23... Then Simon (the sorcerer) himself <u>believed</u> also. And when he was baptized, he continued with Philip and beheld with wonder the miracles and signs which were done. And when Simon saw that, through the laying on of the apostles' hands the Holy Ghost was given, he offered them money. Saying, 'Give me this power also, that on whomsoever I lay hands, he may receive the Holy Ghost.' But Peter said unto him, 'May your money perish with thee, because you thought that you could purchase the gift of God with money. You have no part in this ministry because your heart is not right in the sight of God. Repent therefore from your wickedness, and ask God if, <u>perhaps</u> the thoughts of your <u>heart may be forgiven</u>. For I perceive that you are in the gall of bitterness, and a bundle of unrighteousness.'

Now, according to the account, Simon was saved and, therefore, a righteous, precious saint, though obviously still ignorant in the ways of God's **unseen Kingdom**. He needed to be discipled, not condemned. He had previously been active in the devil's kingdom as a popular sorcerer with a great following. So, when he saw what seemed like even better "magical powers" than his, he did what was normal to his unrenewed mind – try to buy the "secret power." He did not discern that this **unseen** power which God gives freely to set captives free is diametrically opposed to the devil's counterfeits. (Remember, Pharoah was fooled too until Moses' snake ate all the magicians' snakes) The devil can lure and ensnare anyone ignorant of the differences in the two opposing, **unseen Kingdoms** and then make his victims pay in more ways than one.

Mercy Triumphed Over Justice

Something similar happened to my wife and me when we were told how wonderful Edgar Cayce was because he read through the Bible every year and his weird messages, given during trances, often healed people when obeyed them. We *reasoned* that he was *doing* "good things," therefore, he must be "good." After all, doesn't the Bible say that "By their fruits you will know them?" Thankfully, the Holy Spirit did not condemn us for our ignorance. Instead, He sent a woman to our door who had been in our Cayce study group but had just got saved and she related her experience which helped us see our error. Then later, shortly after I was saved, we believed that my wife was hearing messages from my deceased mother through a "prophetic gift" when it was actually a demonic spirit speaking through her. Later we received wise counsel (about Satan's schemes) rather than condemnation and renewed our minds (repented) with the truth. Fortunately, I was not told I was "wicked and obviously not saved" or that I was "a bundle of unrighteousness" or that "I had to be born again, again" etc. So I can sympathize with Simon's ignorance of the truth as a new believer. Jesus came to give us God's mercy and revelation, not condemnation and punishment.

But Peter's response to Simon had the familiar ring of judgment that comes from being *mentally* "under law instead of grace" and not seeing people the way God sees them, **post-cross**. He was quick to condemn because that was the doctrine he was steeped in from birth – just like Paul had been. While Peter did not order Simon to be stoned as the Law dictated, neither did he operate out of the **whole gospel revelation of grace** that Paul was given sometime after this episode. Consequently, Peter was obviously not yet aware that Simon was "the righteousness of God **in Christ**," or of his new position **in Christ**. Rather, he saw Simon "according to the flesh" which Jesus later cautioned us about through Paul in 2 Corinthians 5:16a with these words: "So now, know no one after the flesh (by natural sight)..." Had Peter looked at Simon the way Jesus looked with love at Peter after his betrayal (even though Peter was still **in Adam**), Peter would have reminded Simon of Father-God's mercy, love and acceptance towards him, thanks to Jesus' **finished work** of His **divine exchange**. That assurance would have encouraged him to learn to depend on and allow the Holy Spirit, already inside of him, to live through him and do greater works than Jesus did.

That grace-based revelation would likely have helped bring this seeking saint to a mental make-over about God and about himself. Unfortunately for Simon, Peter could not give what he did not yet fully understand at that point – Jesus' **whole gospel of grace**. But mercifully, he later saw God's unmixed grace in action through Cornelius' conversion, and later still, in Paul's sharing at the council and then later in Paul's writings, which, again, Peter declared to be part of the scriptures. He, too, would eventually discover that "… it is the kindness of God that leads to repentance" for everyone, not just him, and that the "substance" that truly matters is found **in Christ**, not in the shadows of the Law (see Romans 2:4b and Colossians 2:17b).

"But wasn't Paul harsh with Peter at Antioch when he called him a hypocrite in public?" Yes, just like Jesus was harsh with Peter when he tried to talk Jesus out of following God's plan for Him. So Jesus said to him (and to the devil) "Get behind me, Satan!" as reported in Matthew 16:23. But, in neither case, was Peter condemned to hell or did he die on the spot. And it is important to note that in both cases, Peter was using his carnal thinking (or worse) to deter *others* from hearing and following God. That is a different matter than having a personal, hidden sin and, therefore, might need to be addressed publically. Also, these two episodes did not result in an "exceeding fear" of God, which often causes mental estrangement or alienation from God or within the church. People may "turn to God" or change their behavior after a "fire and brimstone" diatribe. But how will that experience shape their view and relationship with God, long-term? Will it foster intimacy or distance? And, what concept of God will they pass on to others? Will it be a law and judgment-based terror of God, like many people now have, or be a grace and love-based freedom **in Christ?**

Discerning The Word Of God

5) This same confusing **elephant of mixture** that depends on one's *sight* and *self-effort (flesh)* under law (rather than depending on Jesus' **finished work** under grace) also carries over into other areas besides horizontal forgiveness. It can also be seen in a *translation* of 2 Peter 1:5-9 where the choice of words and mistaken context in this translation exhorts Christians:

> … to make every effort to add to your faith goodness; and to goodness, knowledge; and to knowledge, self-control; and to self-control, perseverance; and to perseverance, godliness; and to godliness, brotherly kindness; and to brotherly kindness, love. For if you possess these things in increasing measure, they will keep you from being ineffective and unproductive in your knowledge of our Lord Jesus Christ. But if anyone does not have these things, he is nearsighted and blind, and has forgotten that he has been cleansed from his past sins.

However, the following translation is much more consistent with the Greek text and its context (that actually starts in verse 2). It provides a much more grace-based rendering of recognizing and relying on Jesus' **finished work**. It begins with verse 3 and ends with verse 10:

Grace and peace be multiplied to you by a full knowledge of God and of our Savior, Jesus Christ. And through this full knowledge of Him, His divine power has given to us all things of life and godliness, having called us through (His) glory and virtue, by which means He has given to us very great and most precious promises, so that by these things you may become sharers in the Divine nature, fleeing from the corruption of lust (craving of the flesh) in the world (system). In addition to all this, (He) having brought in all eagerness to supply to your faith, virtue and to virtue, knowledge and to knowledge, self-control and to self-control patience and to patience, godliness and to godliness, brotherly love and to brotherly love with agape love – God's love - (all supplied by the Holy Spirit as He lives His life through us, as us.) For these things, <u>already being in and abounding in you</u> (because you are **in Christ** and He in you), will keep you from idleness and unfruitfulness in the full knowledge of our Lord Jesus Christ. But he, in whom these things are not present (mentally), is blind and groping, being forgetful of his purification of (all) his sins in times past (at Calvary.) Because of this, brothers, be all the more diligent, to make sure of your calling and election, because, by (mentally) abiding in these things, you will not ever fall.

The first translation is consistent with the law-based thinking of Peter's Jewish audience who are accustomed to trying to produce works acceptable to God. It has him admonishing the Jews to "…<u>make every effort</u> to add goodness to your faith etc…" However, the emphasis in the second translation is on what God **has done,** starting in verse 3, and, therefore is already ours, **in Christ.** It is important to come into the full knowledge of all that we have **in Him** so we do not remain blind and shortsighted of His **finished work** and fail by focusing back on the Law to try to "collect these things" by our efforts. Remember, the gifts are the same as the Giver. If we have Him then we have them. But we may not be using our eyes of faith to see as God sees and respond accordingly as He leads. More about that in Chapter Nineteen.

Compare both translations with Jesus' revelation to Paul in Romans 15:14 which states: "I am convinced, my brothers that you are full of goodness, complete in knowledge and competent to instruct one another." (Remember, few if any Gentiles were schooled in the Old Testament) Why the difference in perspectives? Because, **pre-cross**, each person was deemed to be just or "good" by the evidence of his good works. That was Paul and Peter's roots as Jews but both had a better grasp of the **finished work** of Jesus than James did, demonstrated by what he held on to. The second translation is much more in line with the **whole gospel** from Jesus. The overall sense is that these gifts and blessings listed in the passage by Peter are already *in* you (just as the life of the vine is in a branch) rather than things that you have to strive to get by your efforts.

Again, the second translation reinforces Jesus' revelation to Paul that God, <u>the Holy Spirit, was *in* each believer to produce His fruit</u> – not just "with him" or "on him." The latter was the case in the Old Testament and was the way the Holy Spirit manifested Himself at Pentecost when He appeared above them. (The confirmation that the Holy Spirit <u>lived in them</u> happened when they "spoke in tongues." But there is no written evidence that they actually *grasped* the significance of that miraculous, **New Covenant** reality until Jesus' revelation to Paul in 42 AD.)

Furthermore, the first translation reads as though Peter is giving a list of "things" that can (or must) be added to one's faith - as though they can be owned by a person and must be accumulated in a certain sequence like charms on a bracelet. Jesus' revelation was that they are

New Covenant gifts and fruits that are produced by the life of the Holy Spirit living in and through a believer who is focused on Jesus and His **whole gospel**, not on his own "efforts for God." This is one more example of how "all things have been made new" spiritually in the **unseen Kingdom** that we now are a part of as believers - because of the Jesus' **divine exchange** with us.

The subtle differences in these translations betray how deep seated and wide-spread is the influence of law-mindedness - even in the minds of translators in their choice of particular words and phrases. (That is why I chose not to stick to any one particular translation in writing this book. Popular author N. T. Wright uses quotes from his own translation, as noted in Appendix # 12). There is no substitute for knowing the genuine **grace-based gospel** revealed to Paul and using that as a plumb line to discern the translations of the New Testament books. When a text implies that the believer must earn or strive for any Kingdom benefit and blessing by his own effort – even though it was already paid for and given in Jesus' **divine exchange** - you will know that it is not Jesus' **gospel of grace**. Likewise, there is no substitute for relying on the Holy Spirit to "lead and guide you into all truth" to help you discern the genuine **butterfly life in Christ Jesus** from the **elephant of mixture.** Be open to receive the Holy Spirit's revelation knowledge of God and then let Him live His life through you, just as Jesus did.

6) Later on, in the same passage above, the first translation reads:

> But if anyone does not have these things, he is nearsighted and blind and has forgotten that he has been cleansed from his past sins (2 Peter 1:9).

This popular way of translating this passage has led many believers to think that only a believer's past sins (before he was saved) are forgiven at rebirth, implying that on-going confession and forgiveness of current and future sins are still required, a notion contrary to the full revelation of Jesus' **finished work**. It is possible (though unlikely) that Peter might have believed that wrong notion when he wrote this passage. But it is far more likely that he knew that Jesus' single, perfect sacrifice <u>paid for all future sins</u> when he came to write down this passage, <u>years after his experiences noted above</u>, and that it has been wrongly translated from the Greek. A much better rendering, given in this second translation, reads:

> For he who does not <u>have</u> these things <u>within</u> is blind – being shortsighted –and is forgetful of his purification of his sins in times past (on Calvary).

This translation is based on the actual Greek text. This wording changes the emphasis from only "one's past sins" being forgiven to the revelation that Jesus has forgiven all his sins (and the sins of all mankind) in times past – meaning at the cross in about 33 AD. The latter translation is far more consistent with Jesus' **finished work** of the **New Covenant** terms found in 2 Corinthians 5:19, 1 John 2:2, Hebrews 8:12 and repeated in 10:17. Either way, Jesus' direct revelation to Paul should be <u>the plumb line</u> by which the entire Bible is interpreted. Why? In order to <u>accurately understand God's true heart and His full redemption plan in all its particulars and fulfillment</u> as explained in the "Third Act" of the Bible. The first two acts do **not** give the "full knowledge of God" as Peter writes about above. (The next chapter elaborates on this analogy of the Bible as being a dramatic three act "play."

In Summary

The last three chapters focused on the *extremely* important topics of

1) God's **total forgiveness** of all of mankind's sins at Calvary and

2) the enablement of the Holy Spirit to gracefully walk in horizontal forgiveness between people by knowing total forgiveness of all sins from God.

We have quoted a total of twenty-three scriptures to confirm the truth of these wonderful, **New Covenant** benefits - when properly discerned by "rightly dividing the Word," according to their respective covenant contexts. If the **elephant of mixture** is still walking around in your mind like he did in mine for almost fifty years, I suggest you do what I have been doing for the last twenty plus years: scrub your mind with these three chapters, asking the Holy Spirit to bathe your mind with His total truth, the **grace gospel** of Christ Jesus. Again, it is the doorway into seeing the splendor of the **unseen Kingdom** of God that Paul exhorted the struggling Corinthians to focus on when he wrote in 2 Corinthians 4:18:

So we fix our eyes, not on what is **seen** but what is **unseen**. For what is **seen** is temporary but what is **unseen** is eternal.

That is the **unseen Kingdom** which all believers now belong to, whether they mentally comprehend that or not. Paul is actually pointing to the **New Covenant** realities that can only be seen by God's gift of faith - the ability to see the way God sees. Jesus directly revealed to Paul that, in the **unseen** realm, His **finished work** has made *"all things new" spiritually speaking.*

The final chapters of this book will help to "fix your eyes" even more on Jesus and some of those *new things* that He disclosed to the saints through Paul. We listed many of them in the first two chapters but did not elaborate on them. By doing so in the next chapters, your eyes of faith will get increasingly "fixed" – pun intended. Get ready, believer, for the ride of your new life!

And here is the first installment to set the stage – a poetic picture of how much Father-God loves you, forever proven by what He accomplished for *you* through Jesus on the altar of Calvary and beyond.

YOUR LOVE FOR ME IS HIGHER than the heights of any sky,
It's deeper than the depths of any sea.
Your love for me is bigger than the total universe
You proved it when You shed your blood for me.

O Precious Lamb You paid the price to reconcile the world,
A Savior sent by Father-God above.
For only You could do what was needed to be done,
To bring me to His outstretched arms of love.

There's nothing that I did or was that earned Your selfless Love,
A rebel only int'rested in me.
But when I died and rose with You, a new creation saint,
You came to love through me, abundantly.

2000 years ago You paid for all my sin and shame,
Forgiving everything I'll ever do.
It's not cheap grace but lavish love that paid my monstrous debt,
So in thanks to You, I forgive all others too.

Your love for me was costlier than all the gold on earth
And brighter than the diamonds in the sky.
Your love for me is surer than all of human love.
I'm one with You, the apple of Your eye.
Sermon song © Copyright 2010 by Leonard Ransil

PART THREE

CHAPTER SIXTEEN

ALL THINGS ARE NEW, SO WHICH YOU ARE YOU?

A Three Act Play – The Big Picture

As you know by now, a key contention of this book is that Jesus' **whole gospel** of the **unseen realm,** unveiled only to Paul, is the constitutional core of all major **New Covenant** Christian doctrine, by which all the other books of the Bible should be interpreted. As we saw earlier, the Bible can be viewed as a three act play to help grasp the relative importance and meanings of the various covenants and events described in the Bible. The first two acts of any good play set the stage for the climax - the resolution of a conflict or a mystery - and reveal who did what, when, why and how. And so it is with the Bible. The third act, which centers around Calvary and beyond, reveals the true cause and nature of the conflict between God and mankind that began in Act One in the Garden. Then it unfolds God's merciful resolution to the conflict which, in turn, demonstrates His wisdom, power, goodness, holiness and loving nature that is meant to benefit all mankind.

It is the most important drama ever conceived because it is about every human's past, present and eternal future in relation to God, to self, to other people and to Satan. By default, every human necessarily participates in this drama whether they know about it or not. Do you think that, in a drama of this magnitude and seriousness, our loving Creator of both the stage and us humans wants us to know that, *unless something radically changes*, we are all doomed to endless torment **in Adam** instead of enjoying God's abundant life and love forever? Of course He does! The Bible's worthy purpose is to unveil God's true nature and mankind's true purpose, through the Greatest Story ever conceived and revealed progressively in the Bible. It is God's **big picture** in a book. And Jesus sent the Holy Spirit into His reborn saints to transform our minds to see and think more and more like God does.

Act One includes Genesis 1:1 to Exodus 19, an overview of creation, the fall of man, the world-wide flood, God's grace-based covenant with Abraham, the events that led Abraham's decedents into slavery in Egypt and, finally, their miraculous deliverance from Pharaoh by God's grace. This period was about 2500 years long and is recorded in only about 6% of the Protestant Bible's total text of 66 books. Genesis 2:7 reveals that:

> The Lord God formed man from the clay of the earth, and he breathed into his face the breath of life, and man became a living soul.

Note that Adam was created from the earth, not "born of God" and, therefore, he was not God's child. He interacted with God before and after his fall but he was not "one" with God as a "partaker of His divine nature" and so he did not enjoy the same relationship with God as regenerated saints do today. This vital relationship probably would have happened if he had chosen to eat of the Tree of Life – Jesus. Instead, he chose to eat of the Tree of Law and became spiritually separated from God, as previously discussed.

Act Two begins at Exodus, Chapter 19, where the Israelites accepted the Law Covenant given to Moses (which supplanted the grace covenant they were under through Abraham, described in Act One). It includes the four gospels and ends at Calvary when Jesus fulfilled the Law of Moses by identifying with our Adamic sin nature and when the Law was nailed to His cross with believers. His words "It is finished" signaled the end of the *old order* and looked toward the beginning of the **New Covenant** era. Again, this period was about 1500 years long and covers about 82% of the Protestant Bible.

Act Three begins with Jesus' triumphant resurrection from the dead and the start of the **New Covenant** in His own blood. Again, the exalted Christ Jesus made this **New Covenant** with Father-God on our behalf as mankind's new Representative, the last Adam. His sacrifice for mankind paved the way for humans to be "born of God" for the first time in history and enjoy spiritual intimacy with God that Adam missed by eating from the Tree of Law. This culminating Act Three also includes the miracle of Pentecost which was the birth of the **New Covenant** church and describes the *new order* where "all things are made new" for all those **in Christ**, according to Hebrews 9:10 and 2 Corinthians 5:16-17 respectively.

Jesus said much about the coming **unseen Kingdom** in the four gospels at the end of Act Two. His words were fulfilled when He, the triumphant King of all Kings, sent the Holy Spirit to establish His Kingdom *inside* each believer. He is sent by Jesus to teach and guide and guard and sanctify and express Himself through the believer's "outer man" as we choose to yield to Him. His coming into humans was obviously a "brand new thing" that makes everything new spiritually, in a personal way, for every **new creation** saint **in Christ.** God now resides *inside* each believer, which makes *intimacy* with God possible as an experiential reality for believers! This Third Act includes the eventual return of our triumphant Christ Jesus back to earth again in the future to establish His Kingdom on a new earth. The Old Testament, and the four gospels in Act Two, speak of what is to come in veiled ways that remain veiled to all those still **in Adam** and to believers who stay focused on the Law. In Act Three, Jesus revealed the mysteries of His Kingdom primarily to Paul. They are described in detail as a *present-time reality* in his **post-cross** books that comprise about 12% of the New Testament. Paul's books (even if we include Hebrews) comprise only about 7% of the total Bible. But, taken together, they are the *primary* books that present Jesus' **whole gospel of grace**.

Spreading the Whole Gospel

It is imperative in these last days that the Body of Christ focus on Jesus' **whole gospel** to best understand and communicate to a world of spiritually dead people what Jesus *has already done* for them as mankind's new Representative, and what God *wants to do in them*, by faith **in Christ Jesus**. Why? So that they can become part of God's family and the new order – His **unseen Kingdom** - *forever* (see John 1:12 and Hebrews 9:12).

Tragically, for two thousand years, the Christian church as a whole, has focused much more on Act One and Two, the tangible part of the Bible (with a great emphasis on "keeping the law") and far less on the **unseen realm** revealed by Jesus to Paul which all true believers are automatically a part of, **in Christ.** Believers generally have been taught to think that the new order does not begin *for them* until they die and go to heaven - or when Jesus returns physically to establish His Kingdom on earth. But is that God's view? Absolutely not. How do we know?

Because our triumphant Lord and elder Brother, Christ Jesus, has **finished His work** - which still includes helping unbelievers to be reconciled to God by rebirth and by putting believers **into Himself.** So now, all believers are **in Him** and, therefore, <u>seated</u> next to Father-God, Who is now also our Abba-Father.

Reign Now Or Only Later?

So, salvation is not a matter of "waiting around to die to go to heaven." Rather, it is about Jesus, our spiritual Head, reigning on earth through us, His risen body of believers, who have already ascended **with and in Him**, by faith, according to Ephesians 2:6. This is the fullness of His revelation to Paul that explains how His **unseen Kingdom**, which is inside every believer, has now "come to earth" so that our King can reign through us, His body, even before He returns physically. As He revealed through Paul in Romans 5:17b

> … how much more will those, who receive God's abundant provision of grace and the gift of righteousness, reign in life through the one Man, Jesus Christ.

How do we reign in this life? By believing and receiving:

1) the Holy Spirit's revelation of "God's abundant provision of His **New Covenant** of grace," which becomes legally ours by rebirth, and

2) His "gift of righteousness" that qualifies us to operate in His empowerment.

Jesus' New Order

Through His death, resurrection and ascension, Jesus overcame:

1) the world system, based on selfishness,

2) the devil, who infected Adam with his prideful nature, and

3) Adam's sin nature on Calvary by becoming sin, dying and then rising Justified for us!

Through rebirth, Jesus has included all believers into His victory, making us overcomers because we have "come over **into Him**" who is now our victory. God's true life is found only **in Christ Jesus**, who *is* the Tree of Life, and in the ability of the Holy Spirit living through us, as us. He works effortlessly from inside out to produce His fruit of unselfish love. He is the Vine and we are His branches, re-created to bear the fruit that He produces through us as we intentionally yield to Him. Of course, all this is not automatic. We believers now have the choice to walk according to the self-sufficiency and lusts of our **flesh** in the outer man or walk according to the life and leading of the Holy Spirit, <u>resident in our inner man</u> as described in Chapter Nineteen, based on Romans, Chapter Eight. (There was no such choice while being **in Adam**, before rebirth.)

His new life of faith, love and liberty lived in and through us, as us, is meant to be a vivid testimony and proof to **in Adam** sinners that there is another Adam, the last Adam, Who is alive and well. God sent Him to save the world, not to condemn the people of the world, like the devil does through his lies and accusations. Instead we are God's ambassadors and ministers, sent to announce *to* the whole world that Jesus purchased the monumental gift of forgiveness and reconciliation *of* the *whole world* to God Himself (from God's viewpoint). All that remains is for sinners to choose to be reconciled to God. If all this wonderful news *still* sounds too good to be true, let's see again what Jesus revealed to Paul in 2 Corinthians 5:17-21, a pivotal scripture describing aspects of His **divine exchange:**

> So if anyone is a new creature **in Christ** (through rebirth), what is old (the **in Adam** nature) has passed away (crucified and buried – gone). Behold, all things have been made new spiritually. All is from God, having reconciled us to Himself (from His viewpoint) through Jesus Christ, and having given us the ministry of reconciliation (to tell the world of this amazing change) that God was **in Christ,** (at Calvary) reconciling the world to Himself, not charging them with their sins. And He has placed the Word of reconciliation in us. Therefore, we are ambassadors for Christ, so that God is exhorting you through us. So, we beseech you on behalf of Christ: Be reconciled to God.

And what is the just basis of this astounding, unilateral transaction of total forgiveness and reconciliation from God's viewpoint? Verse 21 unveils this exhilarating revelation:

> For God made Him who did not know sin to *be*come sin for us, so that we might *become* the righteousness of God **in Him**.

God's message of forgiveness and reconciliation is best understood by others when we are a living demonstration of His love that made Jesus' **whole grace gospel** available to all mankind. As we yield to the Holy Spirit living through us, His love is the power that attracts sinners to God's goodness and truth and can lead people to **post-cross** repentance - a changed mind - towards who God really is. They will come to understand that He wants to set all captives free from all bondages. The freedom and power to love others as God does, comes from knowing God's lavish love for you, believer, and for all unbelievers too. It is not about my puny might or power but by the glorious might and power and love of the Holy Spirit, who I am now one with, expressing Himself through me as I yield to Him.

But, again, this is not proof that all of mankind automatically goes to heaven because of God's lavish generosity, as Universalism insists. If that were true, there would be no need to commission believers to exhort sinners to "be reconciled to God." And this exhortation would also be unnecessary if God operated in *absolute* sovereignty (defined as negating His gift of free will and choice to mankind by orchestrating every last detail of our day-to-day lives by absolute, *sovereign* predestination.) No, neither of those extremes represent Jesus' gospel to Paul. Instead, we who have heard, believed and received this fantastic news of forgiveness and reconciliation of the whole world, are instructed to declare and demonstrate Father-God's magnanimous love and forgiveness to **in Adam** sinners because of Jesus' **finished work.** Why? To inspire them to taste and see how good Father-God really is, which will lead those who truly *hear and believe* Jesus' **grace-based gospel** to say "yes" to God's invitation to heaven through rebirth. But how can they hear the truth of Jesus' **grace-based gospel** if it is mixed with error that causes fear and doubt about God's nature of sacrificial love? In Adam sinners are not in the hands of an angry God, thanks to Jesus perfect sacrifice.

But maybe this perspective of being totally forgiven, reconciled and now able to consciously *abide in* a victorious God is as new to you as it was to me twenty plus years ago. As I already described in Chapter Three, my law-entrenched catholic training at home, in church and at school majored more on rules than on relationship – especially when it came to God. I had a mental mixture of a God who looked down from above with a measure of "divine providence," watching out for me with His guardian angels and Saint Christopher etc. But on the other hand, He would send me to hell if I did not go to Sunday Mass for no "valid" reason – unless and until I would go to confession on Saturday afternoon to get forgiven. I liked singing at daily mass "to get close to where God was and to please Him." But the senior priest was none too friendly and was a stern administrator of the parish. My general experience was that everyone around me accepted and approved of me because of my family status, appearance and performance. Sound familiar? It is the "system of the world," not at all how God's Kingdom actually operates.

Transformation By Revelation – Not Just Information
Part of my ongoing journey of mentally replacing my law-centeredness with grace-mindedness included personalizing and putting music to Paul's inspired prayers for his churches (and for us) to receive the same benefits as they did from Jesus' **whole gospel of grace**. Music greatly helps me to remember and share the revelation of key scripture verses as I make music in my heart to the Lord and as a local worship leader. Below is one of those song-prayers that regularly enable me to receive fresh revelation of different aspects of Jesus' **whole gospel** which progressively renews my mind to think God's thoughts after Him:

FATHER OF GLORY, please give me Your Spirit
Of wisdom and knowledge so that I can know You well.

Please let the eyes of my heart become enlightened
So that I can come to know the great hope of Your call.

And all the riches of Your inheritance
And the greatness of Your power in me who believes.

This is the power that raised Christ from the dead
And enables Him to reign with You forever. Amen.

Glory and honor and wisdom and knowledge
And power and riches are Yours forevermore.

Alleluia - alleluia - alleluia - alleluia
From Ephesians 1:17-20 © Copyright 1987 by Leonard Ransil

Like Paul prayed for his flock, I regularly ask the Holy Spirit to reveal to me what Jesus has already accomplished for me – His invitation to know and experience the riches and power of His resurrected life that is the key to victory in the **seen realm**, regardless of the facts. You see, in God's realm of the **unseen**, His truth always trumps any facts that are opposed to His **total truth**. All believers are automatically one with God, **in Christ**, and, therefore are qualified and equipped by the Holy Spirit living in them to reign over the temptations of the world's system, the flesh and the devil (the *facts* of the **seen realm)**, just as Jesus did while physically on earth. He lived that way, not by the dictates of the Mosaic Law or by His human soul power, but by dependent faith in His Father's direction through the Holy Spirit, living and loving through Him, to tangibly personify and demonstrate who His Father really is. Again, heaven found expression through the man Jesus and revealed how *good* Father-God really is. Now, as His reborn children, we have the privilege and power to also be an expression of God's love and goodness to others here on earth

Seeing The Way God Sees

To avoid detours and traps common to carnal man, Jesus revealed to Paul that we should no longer focus on the **seen,** earthen-vessel aspect of ourselves or that of other people, *including the pre-cross Jesus* (see 1 Corinthians 5:16 below). Instead, focus on the exalted Christ Jesus in the **unseen realm,** above Line A (in the chart in Chapter One and repeated below) by God's gift of faith – the way God sees. This is nothing short of a "mental makeover" by seeking to increasingly see the reality of the **unseen realm** – the way God views unbelievers and believers – according to the Holy Spirit's wisdom, not according to the flesh. He has been waiting patiently for His Bride to learn to walk by faith (instead of relying on one's natural sight) which unveils the hidden reality of what Father-God sent Jesus to accomplish nearly 2000 years ago by His **divine exchange** with us.

> So, from now on, regard no one according to the flesh (**seen** perspective). Even if you have known Christ after the flesh (His **pre-cross** life on earth), we no longer regard Him that way. … For God made Him (Jesus) who did not know sin to become sin for us, so that we might become the righteousness of God **in Christ** (2 Corinthians 5:16 and 21).

Why would Paul make such a drastic statement? Is it just because he didn't spend three years with Jesus like the other apostles did and wanted to minimize their celebrity appeal? Of course not. That would be the very same focus on the self-centered flesh that he warned against. He was not preoccupied with his own reputation or status or circumstances but with *Jesus* and the **whole gospel of grace** that Jesus revealed to him. Again, he was making the point that Jesus, operating as a man on earth and who people knew before Calvary, is not the same man after Calvary. Why? Because Jesus, the perfect man, **became sin,** identifying Himself (becoming one) with our Adamic nature. Why? He did that to erase our ancestral, spiritual link to the fallen Adam, by which mankind is regarded as "sinners" by God, according to Romans 5:19.

> For, just as through the disobedience of one man (Adam), many were established as sinners, so also through the obedience of one Man (Jesus), many shall be established as justified (righteous).

This means that, through Jesus' obedience to God's plan for Him as our new and perfect Representative and Lamb, *He exchanged His righteous nature on Calvary with mankind's corrupted, in Adam nature* – i.e. the **divine exchange**. Then Jesus, who "became our sin," was then sacrificed on the altar as the unrighteous Lamb, onto whom all mankind's sins had been placed. This miraculous, once-and-for-all-time event happened at the very same time the Passover Lamb was being sacrificed in the Temple at Jerusalem. The parallel to the sacrifice of the innocent lamb by the priest for one year of Israel's sin under the Law was meant to be an unmistakable confirmation that His sacrifice took away *all* sins of the *whole world*. Jesus'

finished work put an end to condemnation for all of our individual "sinning." God regarded Jesus' sacrifice of Himself as a <u>sufficient payment for the sins of the whole world, legally reconciling mankind to Himself from His viewpoint.</u>

As has been stated repeatedly, the only barrier left for each person to receive salvation is to <u>choose to be reconciled to God</u>. How? Through the *free gift* of rebirth by grace through faith in Jesus' **finished work**, according to Romans 10:9-13. Jesus' **finished work** cannot be added to by our efforts or it would not be a free gift of His grace. <u>Simply believe that what Jesus did for you is now true for you and receive His life and His free, **New Covenant** benefits.</u> Jesus' victory began a <u>new race</u> of totally re-generated, spirit-beings which are all His reborn saints and who are automatically "the righteousness of God **in Christ**." Paul put it this way:

> Therefore, since you have risen together with Christ, seek (hunger for, worship) the things that are above, where Christ (and you, believer) is seated at the right hand of God. Set your mind on (focus on, meditate on) the things that are above, not on the things that are upon the earth. For you have died and so your life <u>has been hidden with Christ in God</u>. When Christ, your (Tree of) life, appears, then you also will appear with Him in glory (Colossians 3:1-3).

Why is walking by God's kind of sight so important? Because, again, from God's viewpoint, *all* eternally important things originate from the **unseen realm** – above Line A (see below) - <u>and all things (in the Holy Spirit) have been made new</u> for the reborn believer. Paul reinforces this reality in 2 Corinthians 4:18 that is quoted often in this book. Once you grasp the revelation of what has happened to you through Jesus' **divine exchange,** you will understand that living out of your new, **unseen self** (like Jesus lived out of His uncorrupted, **unseen** human spirit on earth, **pre-cross**) is now the "natural" thing for you to do too. Why? Because you are now a **new creation** saint, seated in the **unseen** heavenlies **in Him**. What is true for Him as God's perfect Man is now true for you too. Wow! Have you ever heard about that **New Covenant** reality in your church?

Seeing The Unseen

The following chart (**16A**) (already presented in Chapter One) will help to put some substance to your faith by helping you concretely visualize the two **unseen kingdoms** that the Bible reveals. The lines are there to distinguish the three realms but actually the two spiritual kingdoms coexist in the **seen** universe, between the Lines A and B. **#36**

GOD'S HEAVENLY, ETERNALLY PERFECT,
UNSEEN REALM

The "Now" Realm of God, where Christ Jesus is seated next to Father-God
with all reborn saints who are **in Christ Jesus**, enjoying the view (Ephesians 2:6),
along with myriads of ministering angels.

LINE A _

GOD'S CREATED SEEN REALM -
the natural Universe

God created time, space and matter in perfect order and harmony.
But Adam's Fall and the Flood caused great disorder, disharmony, disease, lack and need.
Jesus laid aside His deity and took on flesh and lived here as a Man among us, to reverse the
curse and provide His abundant life to us through His **finished work**.

LINE B _

The UNSEEN Kingdom of Darkness,
originally created for the fallen angels.

Bondage, hatred, envy, deception, murder, accusation, stealing and rebellion
reign down here and seek to influence the world system and man's flesh.

16A The Three Realm Chart

.

Since this new view applies to seeing Christ Jesus differently *because* He is now risen, ascended and exalted, it certainly must also apply to everyone **in Christ**. "As He is, so are we in this world" (1 John 4:17b). This revelation is the truth that is meant to reshape our perspective about *everything*. This is an example of what it means to walk by biblical faith, not by natural sight. Without this kind of spiritual sight, we can't fully benefit from all that Jesus has done for our outer man while we live on earth. That is why He gives you the gift of faith for free so you can come to "see" the truth of how free you are **in Christ Jesus,** according to Jesus' **whole gospel**. So again, ask the Holy Spirit to bathe your mind in His truth so you can fully benefit from all that Father-God has provided in Jesus' **finished work** through His **divine exchange** with *you*. Fortunately, your mind doesn't have to know about every detail of every blessing first before you can receive from God. The Giver is the gift and you are united with the Giver. So you can start agreeing with God by praying the song-poem *I Receive By Faith All The Benefits*, found at the end of Chapter Two.

Renewing Our Mind To See God's Amazing Love, Goodness and Grace

The unique premise of true Christianity is that Father-God *is* love and that He wants a big family. So He wants to include all willing human beings into an eternal, harmonious relationship with Him as His beloved children and, consequently, be partakers of the divine nature of the Trinity and in fellowship together. As 1 John 4:13-17 declares:

> In this way, we know that we abide **in Him**, and He in us because He has given to us from His Spirit. And we have seen, and we testify, that the Father has sent His Son to be the Savior of the world. Whoever has confessed that Jesus is the Son of God, God abides in him, and he in God. And we have known and believed the love that God has for us. <u>God is love</u>. And he who abides in love, abides in God, and God in him. By this, love has been perfected with us so that we may have confidence on the day of judgment. <u>For as He is, so also are we in this world.</u>

This has been Father-God's <u>ultimate intention</u> before He created the universe. His desire to have an eternal family and His plan to bring it about might seem to have been forever ruined by Adam's disastrous choice to eat of the Tree of Law instead of the Tree of Life. But Father-God sent Jesus at the right time to eliminate every hindrance so that all humans can now freely choose to believe and receive the privilege of a personal, eternal, love-based relationship with the only true God.

A Radical Change Of Mind

How different Jesus' **grace gospel** is from the all too common view that every believer is still "a wretch, a caterpillar, a poor sinner, hoping to somehow make it to heaven." Why hasn't this monumental reality of Jesus' **whole gospel of total grace** blanketed the whole world by now? The simple answer (one main premise of this book) is that the **elephant of mixture** has consistently eclipsed the **butterfly life** of radical grace *which is Jesus' true and only gospel of salvation*. The persecution and rejection of the purity of Jesus' **grace-based gospel** has been relentless, starting with the Jerusalem church against Paul, two-thousand years ago. It was the beginning of "denominationalism." It is the war between "sense-based faith," which is focused on the **seen realm**, versus "God-based faith," which sees and operates from the **unseen Kingdom** in His resurrection power, living in each believer in the person of the Holy Spirit. But each believer must choose to willingly yield to and depend on His ministry, God's resurrection life living in and through him, to enjoy the fruit He desires to produce to "bring heaven to earth." This is what it means to "rest" in Jesus' **finished work** rather than depend on one's efforts to live the Christian life.

Another way to describe it is that most believers still allow their sense-based soul and the self-sufficiency of the flesh to *dominate their **new creation** spirit self, which is the true core of every saint in Christ*. Why? It is because the church has consistently rejected the true, tri-part identity of the reborn, **new creation** saint that Jesus revealed to Paul. Whenever the unsanctified, **seen-focused** mind of one's soul is allowed to dominate the fully sanctified and perfect re-created spirit of a believer, "dead works" of the flesh will follow - even the doctrines of demons – instead of the fruit of the Spirit. It is primarily out of ignorance of the **whole gospel** that "My people perish for lack of knowledge" (Hosea 4:6).

That truth can be updated to: "My saints (those **in Christ**) suffer and are defeated in the **seen realm** for lack of My revelation of what the **finished work** of My Son Jesus' cross, death, resurrection and ascension has caused them to **be** in *My* sight. They keep viewing everything from their limited sensate/natural experience - instead of from My viewpoint. I regard each one as I regard My Son Jesus because they are **in Him**" If you think that this statement is not God's perspective then ask the Holy Spirit to reveal to you what the above prayer song from Ephesians 1:17-20 really means as well as Paul's prayer in Ephesians 3:16-19. Then let Him have His way.

Sensate Knowledge Versus Revelation Knowledge

Said yet another way on the corporate level, Acts One and Two have dominated the consciousness of the Church because sensate knowledge – the traditions and biases of various denominations that make the **gospel of grace** of little or no effect - abounds in the Body of Christ in various ways and degrees. How do I know? I grew up in that mixture, was steeped in it – like a teabag in lukewarm water – and only could begin to break out of the mold when I experienced a drastic, internal overhaul by rebirth and being baptized in the Holy Spirit in the spring of 1972. But I soon went back under law, thinking I was "following Jesus" by focusing on the four gospels and being guided by other people who focused on "trying not to sin" and "trying to be moral" and "trying to manage sin" by focusing on law-keeping. That focus took my eyes off of Jesus, the Tree of Life, and put them back on myself, even though I was no longer **in Adam**.

I did not advocate sinning then and do not advocate it now. But I now know that such a pre-occupation with "the sin issue" (instead of on Jesus' redemption victory) keeps the focus on one's self and one's faulty performance rather than on Jesus and His perfect performance that He lived on our behalf. But freedom comes by discovering that His **finished work** has *fully* dealt with "the sin issue" to God's complete satisfaction. When did the breakthrough into Jesus' **whole gospel of grace** finally happen for me? When I began to pray and sing and meditate on what Paul prayed for the Ephesians and, thereby, began to discover:

1) who God really is,

2) who I *now* am **in Christ** and

3) the crucial importance of understanding and *resting/abiding* in my position **in Christ** *consciously.* When people ask me how I am doing, I say things like. "I am flourishing" or "I am triumphant – and my outer man is doing well too." I regularly remind myself *Whose* I am and where I am – seated in heavenly places, enjoying the view. That's how the "things of earth" take their proper place in the Big Picture.

Why did Jesus provide His power and authority and blessings to us, His saints, if we are to just sit around, waiting for Him to return? Why do believers still complain and confess defeat and lack and ignorance and failure and brokenness and sickness and fear when Jesus has *legally* paid for His Body to be freed from all that bondage and more? Did He fail in His mission to "set the captives free" and give His "abundant life," even though He said "It is finished?" Or are we missing a lot of His salvation benefits that He *has* already won for us **in Him**?

Freedom From A Slave Mentality Of Works

God sent a reluctant Moses back to the most powerful kingdom of his day to free the descendants of Abraham, trapped by destitute conditions and a slave mentality. By the blood of lambs, spread on their doorposts as a sign of faith, God preserved from death the first born sons of all those who believed and acted on His word of warning. And He freed them from Pharaoh's enslavement. They walked out of Egypt <u>healthy and rich</u> on the dry sea-bed of a 500 foot deep land-bridge in the Red Sea and benefitted from God's care for 50 days under a grace-based covenant – all the way up to Mt. Sinai when they enslaved themselves to the Law Covenant. Likewise, God sent Jesus to set all captives free from the devil and all bondage and walk in freedom - just like Jesus, the last Adam, walked free here on earth by depending on His Father. This is only possible under the grace-based **New Covenant** in which God supplies everything that is needed for life and godliness, according to 2 Peter 1:3. And it becomes our experience only as we learn to trust Him and be receivers of Jesus' **finished work**, walking according to the Spirit of grace, the **butterfly life** - not according to the **elephant of mixture**. We will focus on this reality in Chapter Nineteen.

Yes, we are to "go and make disciples (not just converts) of all nations" but what "laws" are we preaching as the *gospel* and teaching those converts to obey? Is it some behavior-based code of dos and don'ts - **the elephant of mixture** - which no one can keep perfectly and which is the ministry of death and brings defeat and condemnation on believers, according to 1 Corinthians 3:7 and 9?

OR

Is it Jesus' higher law, revealed in His **whole gospel of grace**, with signs and wonders from the **unseen realm** that the Holy Spirit wants to produce as evidence of His **unseen** Kingdom? We can't live and teach something unknown to us. If the elephant is walking around in your mind, that mixture is what you will live and preach and teach and share and live – instead of the **butterfly life** of Jesus' **whole gospel of grace**.

Tip-offs to Mixture

There is no shortage of books on the topic of grace, written by many popular authors, that I have read over the years to find freedom from the law. But there is often still mixture to some degree - tipped off, for example, by telling reborn saints that they are just "sinners saved by grace." #37 Another major tip-off is that "we humans are comprised of only a soul and a body," which rejects Jesus' revelation to Paul that is necessary to properly understand the **big picture** of the **whole grace gospel**. Again, the problem persists because the doctrine of most denominations focuses on the law-related "sin problem" and "what must *I do or not do* to avoid sinning?" - rather than on the revelation of the **finished work** of Jesus' **divine exchange** with believers. This in turn comes from focusing primarily on the four gospels or even the Mosaic Law directly – Act Two. I addressed the error of the first tip-off earlier in Chapter Twelve. Now it is time to focus on the second major tip-off <u>which is one of the biggest deceptions</u> that the Body of Christ has needlessly debated and wrestled with for two-thousand years because of sense-based thinking and traditions that are not founded on Jesus' revelation to Paul in 42 AD.

Jesus Unveils Man's True Nature

The *great mystery* of man's tri-part nature and his identity - either being **in Adam** or **in Christ** - is unveiled in Act Three of the Bible, as one might expect. As with most dramas, there are many confirming clues scattered throughout Acts One and Two. But they only make sense when the mystery is "unraveled" and revealed by the Holy Spirit in Act Three. It is all part of the "inexpressible things" that Jesus showed Paul when he saw, first-hand, that "all things have been made new" spiritually. God now lives *inside* believers. But *where* inside?

It should be no surprise to you, by now, that all things in the **unseen realm** can only be initially apprehended by the gift of Kingdom-faith, which bypasses the limits of the sensate mind. Likewise, comprehending and receiving into this **seen realm** the fullness of the **unseen** benefits of His **finished work,** hinge on accepting God's view of *you* … **in Adam** before regeneration and **in Christ** after your rebirth. Since God created your **unseen** self, it requires relying on His gift of faith - just like your salvation did – to accept what your unaided mind cannot begin to fathom, the reality of the **unseen realm**. Let's discover how God has equipped us to abide **in Him** and Him in us - in the **unseen.**

Who Is The Believer In God's Eyes?

Hopefully, you recognize the following key scriptures, first quoted in Chapter One. Please read them over again prayerfully, inviting the Holy Spirit to bathe your mind in His truth.

> I have been nailed to the cross with Christ: nevertheless I live; yet not I, but Christ lives in me. The life which I now live in the flesh (the body), <u>I live in the faith of the Son of God</u>, who loved me, and gave Himself for me (Galatians 2:20).

> And so, from now on, we know no one according to the flesh (how they appear in the natural, **seen** realm). And though we have known Christ according to the flesh, yet now we know Him in this way no longer. So if anyone is **in Christ** (by rebirth), he is a new creation; the old things passed away (the old Adam nature is gone). Behold, they have become new. Now all this is from God, having reconciled us to Himself through Christ, and who has given us the ministry of reconciliation. God was **in Christ**, reconciling the whole world to Himself, not reckoning their sins to them. And He has placed in us the word of reconciliation. Therefore, we are ambassadors for Christ, so that God is beseeching through us. We beg you (those yet not reborn of God) on Christ's behalf: be reconciled to God. For, God made Him (Jesus) who did not know sin to be sin on our behalf, so that we might become the righteousness of God in Him (through rebirth) (2 Corinthians 5:16-21).

> Therefore, there is now no condemnation for those who are **in Christ Jesus** (Romans 8:1).

> But God, being rich in mercy, for his great love wherewith He loved us, even when we were dead through our trespasses, made us alive together with Christ (by grace you have been saved), and raised us up with Him, and made us to sit with Him in the heavenly places, **in Christ Jesus** (Ephesians 2:4-6).

So far in this book, we have presented these and many other scriptures that do not make sense to your unaided, natural mind because they describe an **unseen reality** that is beyond the **seen** world and, therefore, beyond your normal human perception and experience. The scriptures above are marvelous revelations from Jesus which describe God's view of *only reborn Christians.* If you are now **in Christ**, instead of **in Adam**, you are necessarily a **new creation**, according to God. He says further that "old things (about you) have passed away." So, according to God's spiritual perspective, what are the old things about you, believer, that have "passed away" and what "all things about you have become new?" The following explanation begins at the beginning, a very good place to start.

In **Act One**, God clues us in to the fact that, during the days of creation, He said: "Let us make man in our image and likeness" (Genesis 1:26). In **Act Three**, Jesus further reveals that God is a Spirit being. "God is a Spirit and those worshipping Him must worship Him in spirit and in truth" (John 4:24). "And the Lord is the Spirit and where the Spirit of the Lord is there is freedom" (2 Corinthians 3:17). Notice that God does not describe Himself as a "soul" nor did He have a physical body until Jesus "became flesh." Therefore, man must also be a spirit being or he would not be "in God's image and likeness." Jesus confirmed this when He revealed man's true, tri-part nature in 1 Thessalonians 5:23 where Paul prays: "May your whole spirit, soul, and body be preserved blameless at the coming of our Lord Jesus Christ." He would not write down such a prayer if he was not aware of a distinction among the three parts.

Biblical Differentiation

In the Bible's original languages of Hebrew and Greek, the words ruach or neshamah (Hebrew) and pneuma (Greek) are translated as *spirit.* The words nephesh (Hebrew) and psuche (Greek) are translated as *soul.* There would not be two different words used if they had identical meanings, as the context in what Jesus showed to Paul makes crystal clear. **#38**

This tri-part revelation is confirmed again by the inspired writer of Hebrews who declares:

> The word of God is living and powerful, and sharper than any two-edged sword, piercing even to the division of soul and spirit, of joints and marrow... (Hebrews 4:12).

If man is only a body and soul, as most believers are told today, the Word would divide the soul from the soul – cutting it into two parts. However, by naming them as distinct parts the inspired writer reveals that they are *not identical.* To drive home the point, he emphasizes this difference with an analogy using the illustration of the human skeleton. From outside appearances, a bone is a bone is a bone. But when the bone is sawed in two, a distinct, totally different substance inside – in form and function - is revealed. Marrow is too soft to hold up a human body but it is vital to the creation, health and function of the bone. Likewise, if you want to be strictly literal, one's "joints," where the bones and cartilage meet, are even more different in form and function from bone marrow. In context, the proper relationship among the three distinct parts of man, from God's point of view, can be expressed this way: man is a spirit being (as God is) who has a soul and lives in a body.

As you ask the Holy Spirit of God to reveal this and other key **unseen realities** He wants to show you in Jesus' *whole* **gospel of grace**, you will be fascinated by how the **unseen** things of an

unseen Kingdom fit together like a jig-saw puzzle. Paul explained this new dimension this way in 1 Corinthians 2:6-14:

> We do speak wisdom among the mature, but not the wisdom of this age or of the rulers of this age who are coming to nothing. Instead, <u>we speak of God's secret wisdom, a wisdom that has been hidden and that God destined for our glory before time began</u>. None of the rulers of this age understood it, for if they had, they would not have crucified the Lord of glory. However, as it is written: 'No eye has seen, no ear has heard, nor entered into the mind of man what God has prepared for those who love him' - but God has revealed these **unseen realities** (of His gospel) to us by His Spirit.
>
> The Spirit searches all things, even the deep things of God. For who among men knows the thoughts of a man except <u>the man's spirit within him.</u> In the same way, no one knows the thoughts of God except the Spirit of God. We have not been given the spirit of the world but the Spirit who is from God, <u>that we may understand the things given to us freely by God.</u> This is what we speak, not in words taught to us by human (natural, **seen**) wisdom but in words taught to us by the Spirit, <u>expressing spiritual truths in spiritual words</u>. The man without the Spirit does not accept the things that come from the Spirit of God, for they are foolishness to him, and he cannot understand them, <u>because they are spiritually discerned.</u>

Believer, your "born of God, spirit-self" is now compatible with and in union with the Holy Spirit – unlike your unsanctified soul and body. Your regenerated spirit-self is the "new wineskin" into which the Holy Spirit is poured. Your unrenewed soul and body would explode like an old wineskin if the Holy Spirit was poured directly into either or both of them. Of the three parts of your soul – the mind, will and emotions – it is your natural mind that must be renewed with God's perspective in order to see the way God sees and to think His thoughts like He wants you to be able to do. Again, this process is called "**New Covenant** repentance" and is part of a believer's inheritance. The Holy Spirit wants to renew our mind with the mysteries that were kept hidden, **pre-cross,** by using the "mind of Christ" available to all believers by regularly inviting the Holy Spirit to have His sweet way!

> And who can know the things that are of a man, except the <u>spirit</u> which is within that man? So also, no one knows the things which are of God, except the Spirit of God (1 Corinthians 2:11).

We are spirit beings that are either 1) **in Adam** and, therefore, in union with the **unseen Kingdom of Darkness** because of Adam's fall or 2) **in Christ** and, therefore, also in union with Father-God and the Holy Spirit in the **unseen Kingdom of Light** by being reborn children of God by faith in Jesus. As believers, we now live in God and He lives in us. When Adam rebelled by eating of the wrong Tree, he came under the devil's dominion because his spirit-self, designed to be united with God by eating of the Tree of Life, became "dead" to the possibility of an intimate, spirit-to-Spirit union with God. However, his soul and body were still functional and could speak with God like Adam did after the fall.

But man's soul was darkened with the veil of the Law Tree and alienated from God. The only way to escape this sub-human state is to be re-born of God – to be regenerated as a new spirit-being that is automatically one with Christ in God Himself. Spiritually, this is a far better arrangement than what Adam apparently experienced, pre-Fall. Again, he was of the earth and not "one" with God the way we are, **post-cross**. Now we can feed freely from the Tree/Bread of Life - Jesus - in the spirit realm which, then, enlightens our natural mind to the realities of the **unseen realm**. Here are many more scriptures that confirm the believer's **new creation**, tri-part nature **in Christ**.

Man Is A Spirit - ruach or neshamah (Hebrew) and pneuma (Greek)

1) But it is the spirit in a man, the breath of the Almighty that gives him understanding (Job 32:8). (The context describes the "understanding" of the **unseen** ways of God that only His revelation can provide, received first by a man's spirit.) A Ransom (Jesus) will save him and restore his righteousness by grace, not by his works (Job 33:24-26).

2) For I am full of words and the spirit within me compels me (Job 32:18).

3) The spirit of man is the lamp of the Lord (Proverbs 20:27).

4) I will give you a new heart and put a new spirit in you (Ezekiel 36:26a).

5) That which is born of the flesh (the body) is flesh; that which is born of the Spirit is spirit (John 3:6).

6) The spirit is willing but the flesh is weak (Matthew 26:41).

7) Jesus perceiving in His spirit … (Mark 2:8) (A word of knowledge from God.)

8) He (Jesus) sighed deeply in His spirit (Mark 8:12).

9) Mary said: "My soul magnifies the Lord and my spirit rejoices in God my Savior" (Luke 1:47). (See Martin Luther's commentary on this below).

10) Jesus said: "Father, into your hands I commend My spirit" (Luke 23:46).

11) He (Jesus) was deeply moved in spirit (John 11:33).

12) Stephen prayed: "Lord Jesus, receive my spirit" (Acts 7:59).

13) Being fervent in spirit (Acts 18:25).

14) Whom I (Paul) serve in my spirit (Romans 1:9).

15) But if Christ is in you, your body is dead because of sin, yet your spirit is alive because of righteousness (Romans 8:10).

16) The Spirit himself bears witness with our spirit (Romans 8:16).

17) What man knows the things of a man except the spirit of man which is in him (1 Corinthians 2:11).

18) For anyone who speaks in a tongue does not speak to men but to God. Indeed, no one hears (understands him); but in (his) spirit he speaks mysteries (1 Corinthians 14:2).

19) If I (Paul) pray in a tongue, my spirit prays but my mind is unfruitful (1 Corinthians 14:14). (See Endnote #**39** for what Paul had to say on this important topic.)

20) So it is written: "The first man Adam became a living being; the last Adam, a life-giving spirit" (1 Corinthians 15:45).

21) They refreshed my spirit as well as yours (1 Cor. 16:18).

22) Again, Paul prayed "I pray that out of His glorious riches He may strengthen you with power through His Spirit in your inner being (spirit) so that Christ may dwell in your hearts through faith" (Ephesians 3:16).

23) Moreover, we have all had human fathers who disciplined us and we respected them for it. How much more should we submit to the Father of our spirits and live (Hebrews 12:9).

A Puzzling Question

If I am reborn, yet still only an imperfect, unsanctified soul/body person, how is it possible that I am justified (righteous) by being spiritually united with the all holy Christ Jesus? And how can I be seated with Him in the heavenlies, next to Father-God, *right now,* as revealed by Jesus through Paul in Ephesians 2:6? Wouldn't I be contaminating both Jesus and heaven by association? My sensate experience of my <u>outer self</u> is that I do not always think God's thoughts, don't always have holy feelings and don't always make godly choices. Yet, I am assured in Hebrews 10:14 that "… by one sacrifice, He (Jesus) made <u>perfect forever</u> those who are being sanctified." I know now by faith that same truth applies to me as a believer **in Christ.** <u>But I do not experience myself being absolutely perfect</u>, even on my best days. And, of course, that is true for all believers - before we die physically. It does no good to pretend otherwise. <u>So, how can both of these opposing conditions be true of me at the same time.</u>

God's Profound Answer

Here is where Jesus' revelation of man's tri-part nature is so helpful. Both conditions can co-exist because an unbeliever becomes a believer when, by believing in Jesus, "… the Holy Spirit gives birth to his (or her) spirit" – not to his soul or body (see John 3:6). This is a transaction in the **unseen realm** that is *symbolized outwardly* by baptismal immersion where the whole person is put under water (the grave) then "arises" out of the water as a regenerated being with God-kind-of-life which is eternal. The actual **unseen** process is described in Romans Chapter 6. Again, from God's viewpoint in the **unseen**, each believer was "reborn of God" when, by God's grace through faith in **Jesus' finished work**: 1) he was supernaturally crucified with Jesus, 2) he died, 3) he was buried, then 4) he arose as a **new creation** spirit-being, and 4) he ascended into the heavenlies, with and **in Christ Jesus**.

Put simply, while still a sinner, he said "yes" to God's grace and God did the rest – just by agreeing to be identified with Jesus, mankind's only Savior and Lord. This fulfilled Jesus' prayer for him in John 17:21. <u>Since he is **in Christ**, what is true for Jesus, as Man, is now true for him.</u> Because Jesus is seated in heavenly places, so is the believer because he is **in Christ**. It is true because God's word says it is true through rebirth. God's **unseen** truth is true, <u>independent of your soul/body experience.</u>

So, don't expect this glorious transaction to make sense immediately to your sense-based mind any more than the revelation that "God made Him (Jesus) who knew no sin to *become* sin for us, so that we might become the righteousness of God **in Him**" (2 Corinthians 5:21). It is all possible because of a legal, **divine exchange** of positions and conditions on a Spirit to spirit level, not on a soul to soul level. That is why a believer is regarded by God as "perfect" even while his mind thinks bad thoughts. He functions on two levels – the **unseen** and the **seen**. It behooves every believer to now regard himself as God does – according to this direction through Paul in Romans 6:6-8 and 11:

> For we know this: that our old (spirit) self has been crucified with Him (Christ) so that the body of sin (the **in Adam** nature) could be destroyed, so that we should no longer serve sin (the old nature) because anyone who has died has been justified (acquitted) from sin (the old nature). Now if we have died with Christ, we believe that we will also live with Him. … <u>So also, count yourselves dead to sin (the old nature) but alive to God in Christ Jesus our Lord.</u>

In other words, since you, believer, are now **in Christ** instead of **in Adam**, regard yourself as an adopted son of God Himself, not as a slave of Satan like you were **in Adam**. You no longer have an Adamic sin-nature but are a partaker of God's divine nature and *one in spirit* with Father-God, according to 1 Corinthians 6:17. Therefore, allow the Holy Spirit to live through you, because you are now **in Christ**. Why? So that you can operate in the **seen realm** as Father-God's already righteous and worthy prince or princess in His **unseen Kingdom**, loving Him out of a grateful heart that delights in carrying out His wishes. *Faith that works through love brings liberty – the fruit of the higher law of faith and love in Christ.* In His awesome, **unseen Kingdom**, the **unseen** Giver is the same as the gift. Jesus is your righteousness, as well as your wisdom, and redemption and holiness, because you are now "one" with Him through the rebirth of your new spirit-self, according to 1 Corinthians 1:30. (One of my favorite privileges is to introduce Christians to themselves – according to how Father-God sees them.)

The Holy Spirit Sanctifies Our Soul

This new spiritual reality, where "all things have been made new," is obviously not pointing to your still corrupt mind that needs renewed, or to your emotions that fluctuate like the weather, or to your will that sometimes makes choices according to wrong beliefs and thoughts or to the appetites of your body which need channeled. But that disorder of the soul and body can now be addressed and progressively sanctified as you direct them from the leadership position of your new, regenerated inner man - your new spirit-self, which is one with the Holy Spirit living within the *new you*. Jesus sent Him to specifically sanctify your outer man – soul and body - to progressively reflect who you already *are* in the **unseen realm, in Christ Jesus**. It is not by <u>your effort</u> but by authorizing and yielding to the Holy Spirit to do what Jesus sent Him to accomplish as He lives *in and through* you, as you. Your role is to fix your spiritual eyes of faith on Jesus and receive all the benefits of His **finished work** by renewing your natural mind with Jesus' **whole gospel of lavish grace.** What you look at intently and magnify, you "become" - for better or worse. Paul puts it this way in 2 Corinthians 3:17-18:

> Now the Spirit is the Lord and wherever the Spirit of the Lord is (inside of you), there is liberty. Yet truly, all of us, <u>as we gaze upon the unveiled glory of the face of the Lord, are transfigured into the same image</u>, from one glory to another. And this is done by the Spirit of the Lord.

Wow! A mirror can reflect the glory of the sun only when it is pointed toward it. Likewise, beholding the Son of God and soaking in the rays of the glory of His love which shines on you continually (by including you in His **finished work**), will warm and melt your wayward soul and body so that the Potter can properly refashion your outer self for His purposes. The life of the Holy Spirit within you operates like the sap that flows from the root – Father-God – through the Vine – Jesus – through you - the branch - as a connected extension of the Vine, producing the fruit of the Holy Spirit (see John 15:4).

Jesus describes this living fruit as His love, joy, peace, patience, kindness, goodness, faithfulness, gentleness and self-control. This flow of His life is the result of being led by the Holy Spirit to seek and to focus on Jesus and the things above rather than on the **seen realm** - which can stimulate the cravings of the five senses of the soul and/or the appetites of the body. This is how to feast on the Tree of Life (rather than on the Tree of Law that shrivels the soul and diseases the body). We were never meant to live under the law which arouses sin and causes death. Rather, we are now re-created to flourish as God's **butterflies** in the glow and reality of GRACE – God's Righteousness At Christ's Expense.

My Reborn, Inner Man

What is an appropriate response for so great a salvation from our King who has now made it possible to be *one* with Him and to worship Him "in spirit and in truth?" I can personally attest to the power and delight of worshipping God in the Spirit. The first time it happened was on the night I was reborn and baptized in the Holy Spirit in Richmond Virginia, April 1972. I had resisted yielding to salvation for four years and repeatedly told my saved wife, Elaine, that God did not need or want all that emotional, jubilant, charismatic worship at the prayer meetings that she attended. I was mentally turned off by all the enthusiasm because I was used to the traditional, "reverent" choir music that I sang in church for over twenty years. Additionally, I played sax and drums in Pittsburgh night clubs etc. and crooned secular dance band tunes that were relatively calm and sedate (pre-rock & roll). Imagine my astonishment when my prayer to receive the baptism of the Holy Spirit - "Lord, I'll take anything you want to give me" – was answered with a gusher of joy and grateful praise and worship from the inside out (see John 7:38b).

I know that it was not from my mind which had no time to change opinions, but out of my newly regenerated, inner spirit-self. Instantly, God turned a soulish singer to a psalmist who now delights in worshipping Him with "... psalms, hymns and spiritual songs, singing and praising in my heart to the Lord" (Ephesians 5:19). The hundred-plus songs I have received since that time help me and fellow-worshippers to renew our minds with the knowledge of the truth of Jesus' **whole gospel** that progressively sets and keeps saints free. How? By focusing on, celebrating, and enjoying the **finished work** of Jesus' **divine exchange** which made me united with Him.

So, again, here is where it is essential to believe Jesus' full revelation to Paul, which describes man's true, tri-part nature. Accepting this revelation opens the door to understand "... the mystery kept hidden for ages and generations but now disclosed to the saints" (Ephesians 1:26). Why? So that we can fully yield to and benefit from the blessings of Jesus' **whole gospel of grace** while still on earth. Both Paul and Peter reinforce this vital truth with references to our "inner being," as follows:

> May He grant you, according to the riches of His glory, to be strengthened by the power of His Spirit in the <u>inward man</u>. (Ephesians 3:16).

> And so, I discover the law, by wanting to do good within myself, though evil lies close beside me. For I am delighted with the (higher) law of God, according to the <u>inner man</u> .... (Romans 7:21).

> For you, there should be no unnecessary adornment of the hair, or surrounded with gold, or the wearing of ornate clothing. Instead, <u>a hidden person of the heart</u>, with the incorruptibility of a quiet and a meek <u>spirit</u>, which is of great value in God's sight (1 Peter 3:3-4).

Even Peter (who is still in the habit of imposing laws and traditions) equates the inner self with one's spirit. Do you see it yet? There must be a third category, besides soul and body, for all these above scriptures to be true and relevant to us. James insisted on following the Mosaic Law - including external circumcision. In direct contrast, Jesus let Paul see past the **seen realm** and get to the heart of the matter. It is the inward reality of exchanging one's old, **in Adam** heart of stone (which is separated from God) with a new heart of flesh that is open to God by rebirth in the Spirit of Christ Jesus.

> A man is not a Jew if he is only one outwardly, nor is circumcision merely outward and physical. No, a man is a Jew if he is one inwardly; and circumcision is <u>circumcision of the heart</u>, by the Spirit, not by the written code. Such a man's praise is not from men, but from God (Romans 2:28).

This verse corresponds to the birth or regeneration of a believer's spirit-self that Jesus revealed to Nicodemus, as we explored previously. Unfortunately, the Church has debated and battled over this revelation of man's true nature for many centuries. Why? Because **seen-focused** believers, depending on the human mind to *try* to figure out **unseen** things of the Spirit realm, will naturally come to wrong conclusions. Why? Because the **unseen realm** can only be understood by God's gift of faith (spiritual sight) in what He reveals about it, not by human understanding. That is how and why Abraham was reckoned righteous before God. He believed an incomprehensible promise that was already an **unseen reality** in the mind of God who lives in the eternal "now."

Agree With God

I strongly encourage every believer to discover who God says you are, regardless of what your outer man or the devil or other people say. God paid the infinite price of His own Son to make every believer already compatible with Him in the **unseen**, spirit realm. The more that you become conscious of that revelation of God's goodness and His personal love for you, the more you will fall in love with Him and be enabled to progressively love others the way He does – without the yoke of trying to "keep the law."

You will find yourself operating effortlessly in the freedom of the higher law of faith, love and liberty – the manifestation of the life of the Holy Spirit of grace. It will not be without a battle – the battle between the real you and your soulish thinking that needs to be progressively renewed by the truth of Jesus' **whole gospel of lavish grace**. But you can rejoice because Jesus sent the Holy Spirit to lead you to victory over your sense-based thinking by revealing Jesus and His **finished work** of the **divine exchange** that He has accomplished for you! Then you will be thinking more and more like God does – using the mind of Christ that is available to all believers as part of their inheritance **in Christ Jesus.** And you will progressively *experience* peace between you and God and, therefore the peace of God, which surpasses all (natural) understanding, and helps to keep your heart and your mind on Christ Jesus who you now belong to. The more that you become aware, established and secure in that stable, **unseen reality**, the more you will experience the overflow of joy through the Holy Spirit.

So, through Paul, Jesus has revealed two fundamental mysteries of:

1) man's true make-up (a spirit-being who has a soul and lives in a body) and

2) man's identity (either **in Adam** or **in Christ**).

This truth allows all of the other **unseen** puzzle pieces of the **big picture**, called salvation history, to fit together for believers who accept those two key truths. Again, they are two of the many realities hidden in the **unseen realm** that can only be apprehended by faith in Jesus' **whole gospel of lavish grace.** But all this will not make any sense to your natural mind, at first, since spiritual realities cannot be discerned (figured out) by the human mind that is unaided by God's revelation knowledge.

It's like trying to watch TV by using a radio. The right waves are coming from the TV station but the radio is incapable of benefitting from a strong TV signal. And so it is with our outer man. Being reborn of God enables the believer to be united in spirit with the Spirit of Christ Jesus and, therefore, live on His "wave length" in order to receive *from Him* everything that we need for life and godliness, as we let Him lead and guide us. The Holy Spirit was sent to illumine the mysteries in the scriptures that were kept hidden, **pre-cross,** but which are now disclosed to the saints (Colossians 1:26). We can now yield our mind to the inspiration of the Holy Spirit's wisdom as Paul chose to do, starting at his initial conversion. He was willing to set aside his previous, ingrained beliefs and traditions <u>to embrace the new realities of the Spirit of Christ</u>. The **unseen realm** is apprehended only by God's gift of child-like faith, the way He designed His life to be received, starting with Adam. (It is tragic that most believers in the Jerusalem church were not as receptive to Jesus' **whole gospel of grace** as Paul was.)

In Summary

At this point, all of this revelation knowledge, starting from Chapter One, might be "boggling your natural mind," so here is a re-cap. The natural mind is one part of every person's soul. It depends on the body's five senses for all its input, as 1 Corinthians 2:14 clearly reveals:

> … the natural man does not receive the things that come from the Spirit of God for they are foolishness to him and <u>he is unable to know them because they are discerned spiritually</u>.

Because of Adam's fall, every human begins as an **in Adam** sinner who is dead-to-God, but who is a spirit-being by nature. When a sinner accepts God's gift of faith in Jesus, he is instantly crucified, dies and is buried and he becomes a regenerated, **new creation** spirit-being, alive **in Christ Jesus** - all by identification with Christ's **finished work** of His **divine exchange** - by God's grace through faith. There may be little or nothing that his soul or body experiences at that time, but he is now "one spirit with the Father **in Christ**," according to 1 Corinthians 6:17. He is perfect and complete and seated **in Christ** in heavenly places because of being identified with Jesus – born of God as a **new creation** spirit-being, as Paul describes in Ephesians 2:6.

The believer's outer man - his body and his soul, consisting of his mind, will and emotions - are not fully unsanctified and, therefore incapable of being "one spirit with God." Our soul-based thoughts, choices and feelings constantly fall short of perfection. Our perfect, all-Holy God cannot be united with unholy flesh - our imperfect outer man. It is not that our soul and body are "evil," per se. They are just not yet perfected and so fall short of perfection. In Romans 6:19, Paul exhorts believers to consecrate our body to righteousness.

Nonetheless, God the Father fulfilled Jesus' prayer in John 17:21 through:

1) the miracle of rebirth through identification with Jesus' **finished work** and

2) by sending the Holy Spirit into the believer's perfect spirit-being.

This is the new wine skin that Jesus said was necessary in order for a human to be filled with "new wine" – the Holy Spirit. Consequently, this living, reborn saint is no longer **in Adam**, but is now compatible and in eternal fellowship with God Himself because he is now **in Christ Jesus**. Paul expressed this big, **unseen reality** in Ephesians 2:4-10 this way:

> Yet still, God, who is rich in mercy, for the sake of His exceedingly great love with which He loved us - even when we were dead (to God) in our sins - has enlivened us (spiritually) together **in Christ**, by whose grace you have been saved. And He has raised us up together, and He has caused us to sit down together in the heavenlies, **in Christ Jesus**, so that He may display, in the ages soon to come, the abundant wealth of His

grace, by His goodness toward us **in Christ Jesus.** For by grace, you have been saved through faith. And this is not of yourselves, for it is a gift of God. And this is not of (man's) works, so that no one may boast. For we are His handiwork, re-created **in Christ Jesus** for the good works which God has prepared for us to walk in.

There is no way this could be true right now if we were just body/soul humans. This passage reveals that **in Adam** sinners are dead in transgressions and only saved due to God's grace by faith in His **grace gospel** – not by self-effort. God makes these dead-to-God sinners "alive" with Christ in their new spirit-self and raises them up, one with Christ, and He seats them with Christ Jesus in the **unseen**, heavenly realm - **in Christ**. God counts each believer as His own, re-created workmanship **in Christ Jesus.** He enables His "good works" (which He has already prepared for each believer to do) as a loving response to God for His gift of salvation, (*not* to earn or maintain it) according to Ephesians 2:10. His full salvation package is all a gift of grace, received by faith alone. Now you can see that a believer's position **in Christ**, who is seated in the heavenlies, is not just a hopeful possibility for some far off day, but is now "... the reality found **in Christ**" for all reborn believers, as stated in Colossians 2:17.

So believer, you now have a choice to either

1) ignore or

2) remain in doubt and/or unbelief about Jesus' revelation of your tri-part being, or

3) agree with God and ask Him to teach you how to operate mentally from your *position of victory*, **in Christ Jesus** in the **unseen realm,** over any "condition" or circumstance in the **seen realm,** with the wisdom, power and authority of God – just as Jesus walked on earth according to the Holy Spirit's higher law of faith, love and liberty.

And we have known and have believed the love which God has in us. God is love and the one abiding in love abides in God and God in him. By this (abiding in God), love has been perfected in us, that we have confidence in the day of judgment, that <u>as He is so are we in this world</u> (1 John 4:16-17).

Believer, you can now operate in the love of the Holy Spirit *from* a place of authority, power and victory – your heavenly position **in Christ** – enforcing, by agreement with Jesus, what He has already done to conquer the world, the flesh and the devil. Our flesh foolishly tries to gain victory through soul-based efforts. Jesus' **finished work** was *finished from His perspective* some 2000 years ago. All there is left to *do* is to yield to the life and power of the Holy Spirit living in you by welcoming this new reality as true for you. Ask Him to help you renew your mind with who God really is and with who you now are **in Christ** and let Him manifest His life through you, as you, in the **seen realm.** How? By setting your mind on things above (like Jesus constantly did) rather than on things of earth, because you have died to whom you once were and are now raised up **in Him**, according to Colossians 3:1-3.

<u>The progressive switch-over from a soul-directed life-style, lived "according to the flesh"</u> (that always falls short of God's best) <u>to "living life according to the Spirit" is, itself, to be</u>

orchestrated by the Holy Spirit. Jesus sent Him to personally lead and guide you into all His truth by renewing your mind with Jesus' **whole gospel**. So continually invite Him to have His way in and through you as Jesus did. Again, this transformation of the outer man is what Jesus described to Paul in Romans 12:2 and 5:17. Reborn saints are already fully transformed in their new spirit-self because they are united with perfection Himself and, therefore, righteous. But, reigning "in life through the one Man, Jesus Christ" is for those who "receive God's abundant provision of grace and the gift of righteousness" and then progressively *learn to walk* in that "present truth reality", just as Jesus and Paul walked in it. We explore that process in more detail in Chapter Nineteen.

The following is a song-poem that makes the point that our new spirit-self, now one with the Holy Spirit, is what God originally designed to direct our outer man (soul and body) by the mind of Christ. This is now possible because we saints have the option to intentionally benefit from the truth and wisdom of Jesus, our Tree of Life, so that we can mentally come to understand who we now are **in Him** and *consciously abide* **in Him** and His **finished work,** just as He focused on His Father while on earth. The "Word" cited in the first line speaks primarily about Jesus' **gospel of grace**, as you can tell by the **New Covenant** references.

THE BATTLE IN MY MIND IS WON by feeding on Your Word. Eph. 6:12-18 and 5:26, Rom. 12:2
It keeps me focused on the truth, replacing lies I've heard.   2 Cor. 10:3-5
I have an earthen vessel – a body with a soul,   2 Cor. 4:7, Heb.4:12, 1 Thess. 5:23
But I am one with You, Lord, a spirit You control.   1 Cor. 2:12 and 6:17, Gal. 5:18, &
   Rom. 8:6 & 14
We tell my soul what it should think, what choices it should make. Ps. 103:1, 2 Cor. 10:5, Phil. 4:8
We tell my body what to do – to live for Jesus' sake.   Rom. 6:19 and 12:1
By thinking on Your gospel, I'm thinking more like You.   1 Tim. 4:15, 1 Cor. 2:16
Through faith, I see *reality*, what always has been true.   Heb. 11:1, Col. 2:17

By learning who You really are, I'm seeing more of You,   Eph. 2:4, 1 Jn. 4:8, 1 Cor. 1:9
Appreciating what You've done and all you bring me through.   1 Pet. 2:3, 2 Cor. 9:15, Tit. 3:5
So, I thank you Lord for loving me and blessing me each day.   Rom. 15:29, Eph. 1:3
You are my peace and victory, my truth my life my way.   Phil. 4:6-7, 1 Cor. 15:57, Jn. 14:6
Sermon Song © Copyright 2009 by Leonard J. Ransil

Much of the above revelation of our tri-part nature was new to me until some twenty years ago. If it is new to you, you may be wondering why you have not heard this vital revelation presented in your church or Bible study. The reason is that there has been a long-standing debate over man's nature, both inside and outside of the church. Mankind has struggled to answer life's most important questions such as "Who am I, why am I here on earth and where am I going?" Only God knows the right answer to all of those key questions and He put the answers in the Bible so we could discover them. Unfortunately, the church has sometimes looked to secular philosophers for their opinion rather than depended on God for His wisdom and revelation. Consequently, there has been much debate in the church for almost 2000 years regarding man's nature and purpose. The next chapter presents a brief, historical overview of this doctrinal controversy and debate to help clear up any doubts or questions about this extremely important doctrine that Jesus revealed to Paul.

CHAPTER SEVENTEEN

THE DOCTRINAL WAR OVER MAN'S NATURE

By now you can possibly understand why the revelation of the tri-part **new creation** being **in Christ** has had such opposition for the last thousand years. The bi-part vs. tri-part battle rages as much as ever today. Why? Because the devil knows that when the saints of God **in Christ** embrace this revelation, the devil's use of the club of law over the church will be spiritually discerned for what it really is. The saints will start living out of their true, new spirit-self, led by the Holy Spirit who is available to all who dare to believe and receive Jesus' **whole gospel of lavish grace**.

"What battle?" you ask. "I never heard of any battle over this doctrine in my church. All I have ever heard all of my life is that I am a soul with a body." Well then, that is a good indication that the fullness of Jesus' **grace gospel** of the **unseen realm** that Paul preached is not understood and taught in your church. The **elephant of mixture** is probably alive but unrecognized in your church. Sadly, most seminaries and denominations have followed suit with the Catholic Church and dismissed the biblical tri-part reality. So let's engage in a brief history lesson to trace the debate over this vital issue, beginning with a few of the early church Fathers, as quoted from *A Dictionary of Early Christian Beliefs*. You will see from the following seven quotes, by three of these revered church Fathers, Titian, Irenaeus and Augustine, that they, indeed, believed Jesus' revelation to Paul about our tri-part nature.

The Tri-part Distinction Of Body, Soul And Spirit

1) Titian c. 160 AD, B., 2.70

May your whole spirit, soul, and body be preserved blameless at the coming of our Lord Jesus Christ (1 Thessalonians 5:23). The word of God is living and powerful, and sharper than any two-edged sword, piercing even to the division of soul and spirit (Heb 4:12). We recognize two kinds of spirits. One kind is called the soul, but the other is greater than the soul. It is an image and likeness of God. Both existed in the first men. So in one sense, those were material. But, in another sense, they were superior to matter.

2) Titian c. 160 AD, B, 2.70-71

The soul is not in itself immortal, Oh Greeks, but mortal. Yet it is possible for it not to die. To be sure, if it does not know the truth, it dies. It is dissolved with the body, but rises again at last at the end of the world with the body, receiving death by punishment in immortality. But, again, if it acquires the knowledge of God, it does not die, although for a time it is dissolved. ... The soul does not preserve the spirit, but is preserved by it. The dwelling place of the spirit is above, but the origin of the soul is from beneath.

3) Irenaeus c. 180- E/W 1.4

When the number is completed that He had predetermined in His own counsel, all those who have been enrolled for life will rise again. They will have their own bodies, their own souls, and their own spirits, in which they had pleased God.

4) Irenaeus c. 180 AD, B/W 1.532

What was his (Paul's) object in praying that these three - that is, the soul, body, and spirit – might be preserved to the coming of the Lord, unless he was aware of the reintegration and union of the three.

5) Irenaeus c. 180, B/W 1.533

To die is to lose vital power and to become thereafter breathless, inanimate, and devoid of motion. . . . But this event happens neither to the soul (for it is the breath of life) nor to the spirit, for the spirit . . cannot be decomposed, and is itself the life of those who receive it.

6) Irenaeus c. 180, B/W 1.534

The complete man is composed of flesh, soul, and spirit. One of these does indeed preserve and fashion the man - the spirit. It is united and formed to another - the flesh. Then there is that which is between these two - the soul. The soul is sometimes indeed raised up by it, when it follows the spirit. But sometimes the soul sympathizes with the flesh and falls into carnal lusts.

7) Saint Augustine b. 354 A.D., d. 430 A.D. Taken from his book: Faith and the Creed. Chapter 10 *Of the Catholic Church, the Remission of Sins, and the Resurrection of the Flesh* Section 23.

… inasmuch as there are three things of which man consists—namely, spirit, soul, and body - which again are spoken of as two, because frequently the soul is named along with the spirit; for a certain rational portion of the same, of which beasts are devoid, is called spirit: the principal part in us is the spirit; next, the life whereby we are united with the body is called the soul; finally, the body itself, as it is visible, is the last part in us. (source: http://www.newadvent.org/fathers/1304.htm)

It is obvious from these seven quotes, taken from the writings of these three highly regarded early church fathers that they were in basic agreement with Jesus' revelation to Paul on this crucial doctrine of man's tri-part nature. That is not to say that some others of their day might not have agreed with them. But Saint Augustine was held in very high esteem among later fathers of the church for his biblical scholarship and pastoral insight. Therefore, it is fair to say that there was a general consensus for the validity of this tri-part doctrine for many centuries. So what historical events caused the overthrow of this revelation to what we have today – a mostly opposite consensus?

As we know from church and European history, there were many pressing issues for the struggling church over its first eleven hundred years such as the split in vision and doctrine that became solidified at the first Church Council in 50 AD (as documented in this book), heresies to refute, political intrigue, infighting, wars, scandals, the so-called Dark Ages, and finally a major public schism that split the church itself in 1054 AD. Therefore, the tri-part doctrine went basically unquestioned until Thomas Aquinas (1225–1274) came on the scene and, in time, became more highly regarded than Augustine. (See Endnote **#40** for some disturbing information about Thomas Aquinas' writings.) About that time, too, the Greek classics were enjoying a rebirth after being all but lost during the "barbarian invasions."

Aquinas Triumphs Over Jesus' Gospel

Unfortunately, Aquinas chose to exalt the opinion of the heathen Aristotle's bi-part view of man above the revelation that Jesus gave to Paul and affirmed by St. Augustine. In turn, it stirred a debate over this key doctrine until the Roman Catholic Church Council of Vienna, which began in 1311, officially reviewed this central doctrinal issue, along with other pressing concerns of the day. An excerpt, focusing on their conclusion about man's nature, is quoted below, taken from:

Introduction and translation (from Latin) taken from Decrees of the Ecumenical Councils, ed. Norman P. Tanner

Decrees
Adhering firmly to the foundation of the catholic faith, other than which, as the Apostle testifies, no one can lay, we openly profess with holy mother church that the only begotten Son of God, subsisting eternally together with the Father in everything in which God the Father exists, assumed in time in the womb of a virgin the parts of our nature united together, from which he himself true God became true man: namely the human, **passible body** and the **intellectual or rational soul** truly of itself and essentially informing the body. And that in <u>this assumed nature</u> the Word of God willed for the salvation of all not only to be nailed to the cross and to die on it, but also, having already <u>breathed forth his spirit</u>, permitted his side to be pierced by a lance, ... But when they came to Jesus and saw that he was already dead, they did not break his legs, but one of the soldiers pierced his side with a spear, and at once there came out blood and water. He (John the Apostle) who saw it has borne witness—his testimony is true, and he knows that he tells the truth—that you also may believe.
We ... declare with the approval of the sacred council that the said apostle and evangelist, John, observed the right order of events in saying that when Christ was already dead one of the soldiers opened his side with a spear. ... In order that all may know the truth of the faith in its purity and all error may be excluded, we define that anyone who presumes henceforth to assert defend or hold stubbornly that the rational or intellectual soul is not the form of the human body of itself and essentially, is to be considered a heretic. (Bold and underlined words added for emphasis)
(source: http://www.ewtn.com/library/councils/vienne.htm#09)

Restated positively by removing the word "not," the Decree declares that "the rational or intellectual soul is the form of the human body of itself." Boiled down from all the esoteric verbiage, it is saying that the nature of man consists of only the soul and the body. This was decided <u>in spite of the admission that Jesus had breathed forth His spirit</u> at Calvary. By implication, there is no distinction between the spirit and the soul. Worse yet, anyone who says otherwise is anathema, Greek for "under a curse." It can also mean "excommunicated" – the equivalent, in their thinking, of no longer being a part of the Body of Christ and, therefore, hell-bent.

This unfortunate doctrinal conclusion of the 1311 Council, enforcing bi-part over tri-part as the definition of man's nature, is still held by the Roman Catholic Church, according to the current, official Catholic Catechism, quoted as follows:

365 The unity of soul and body is so profound that one has to consider the soul to be the "form" of the body: 234 i.e., it is because of its spiritual soul that the body made of matter becomes a living, human body; spirit and matter, in man, are not two natures united, but rather their union forms a single nature.

366 The Church teaches that every spiritual soul is created immediately by God - it is not "produced" by the parents - and also that it is immortal: it does not perish when it separates from the body at death, and it will be reunited with the body at the final Resurrection.235

367 Sometimes the soul is distinguished from the spirit: St. Paul for instance prays that God may sanctify his people "wholly", with "spirit and soul and body" kept sound and blameless at the Lord's coming.236 The Church teaches that this distinction does not introduce a duality into the soul.237 "Spirit" signifies that from creation man is ordered to a supernatural end and that his soul can gratuitously be raised beyond all it deserves to communion with God.238
(source: http://http://www.scborromeo.org/ccc/p1s2c1p6.htm)

In short, the Roman Catholic Church still insists that there is no "duality of the soul," which is their way of stating that there are **not** two distinct parts or named entities, even though the decree above states this about Jesus "… having already breathed forth His spirit." They use the words "soul" (nephesh in Hebrew, psuche in Greek) and "spirit" (ruach or neshamah in Hebrew, pneuma in Greek) interchangeably even though there are five different Hebrew and Greek words in the original languages for two distinct concepts. This is like saying that the words "joints" and "marrow" mean exactly the same thing when, of course, they don't.

Personally, I find it enormously disturbing that the Roman Catholic Church would reverse such a pivotal doctrine – which Jesus revealed to Paul, and whose writings were endorsed by Peter as "scriptures" - on the word of Thomas Aquinas. Why is this a problem? Well first, he based his conclusions on the "wisdom" of the Greek heathen, Aristotle (384-322 BC), who lived over three centuries before Jesus revealed the truth to Paul. Secondly, near the end of his life, Thomas made this astounding statement regarding the veracity of his own writings: "Such secrets have been revealed to me (during a long "ecstasy" at Mass in 1273) that all I have written now appears to be of little value." He took this event so seriously that he refused to write anymore, so he never finished his most highly regarded work, *Summa Theologica*. He died two years later at only forty-nine years of age. It is a mystery to me why *any* of his writings are so highly valued since he did not value them himself. Nonetheless, he is regarded as a Doctor of the Roman Catholic Church. Why would anyone in their right mind regard Aristotle over Augustine – let alone over Saint Paul who was speaking for Jesus. (If you have a good, Bible-based reason, please send me an e-mail, found at totaltruth.org, and I will re-evaluate my comments.) (See Endnote **#41** for more on Aquinas' life.)

Martin Luther Weighs In

Understandably, with such a heavy-handed decree and threat of excommunication over every Catholic's head (forbidding any departure from the bi-part doctrine), no one strayed from the reservation – until Martin Luther took issue with many key doctrines. In 1521 AD, while in the midst of a major push back from the Roman Catholic Church, Martin Luther penned a very important work on the *Magnificat*, Mary's agreement to become the mother of Jesus. In this lengthy work, he took great pains to describe his understanding of man's <u>tri-part nature</u>, signaled by Mary's opening line in Luke 1:47; "My soul magnifies the Lord and my spirit rejoices in God my Savior." Luther first distinguishes the <u>functions of the three parts</u> and then parallels them with the temple in Jerusalem as a metaphor. It is a lengthy quote but given the <u>extreme importance</u> of this doctrine, which is central to understanding Jesus' **whole gospel of grace**, the entire section from his book is included here as follows:

> The first part, the spirit, is the highest, deepest and noblest part of man. <u>By it he is enabled to lay hold on things incomprehensible, invisible, and eternal.</u> It is, in brief, the dwelling-place of faith and the Word of God. Of it David speaks in Psalm 51:10, "Lord, create in my inward parts a right spirit" — that is, a straight and upright faith. But of the unbelieving he says, in Psalm 78:37, "Their heart was not right with God, nor was their spirit faithful to him."

> The second part, or the soul, is this same spirit, so far as its nature is concerned, but viewed as performing a different function, namely, giving life to the body and working through the body. In the Scriptures it is frequently put for the life; for the soul may live without the body, but the body has no life apart from the soul. Even in sleep the soul lives and works without ceasing. <u>It is its nature to comprehend not incomprehensible things, but such things as the reason can know and understand (in the seen realm). Indeed, reason is the light in this dwelling, and unless the spirit, which is lighted with the brighter light of faith, controls this light of reason, it cannot but be in error.</u> For it is too feeble to deal with things divine. To these two parts of man the Scriptures ascribe many things, such as wisdom and knowledge — <u>wisdom to the spirit, knowledge to the soul</u>; likewise hatred and love, delight and horror, and the like.

> The third part is the body with its members. Its work is but to carry out and apply that which the soul knows and the spirit believes.

> Let us take an illustration of this from Holy Scripture. In the tabernacle fashioned by Moses there were three separate compartments. The first was called the holy of holies: here was God's dwelling-place, and in it there was no light. The second was called the holy place: here stood a candlestick with seven arms and seven lamps. The third was called the outer court: this lay under the open sky and in the full light of the sun. In this tabernacle we have a figure of the Christian man. <u>His spirit is the holy of holies, where God dwells in the darkness of faith, where no light is; for he believes that which he neither sees nor feels nor comprehends.</u> His soul is the holy place, with its seven lamps, that is, all manner of reason, discrimination, knowledge and understanding of <u>visible and bodily things</u>. His body is the forecourt, open to all, so that men may see his works and manner of life.

Now Paul prays to God, who is a God of peace, to sanctify us not in one part only, but wholly, through and through, so that spirit, soul, body, and all, may be holy. We might mention many reasons why he prays in this manner, but let the following suffice. When the spirit is no longer holy, then nothing else is holy. This holiness of the spirit is the scene of the sorest conflict and the source of the greatest danger. It consists in nothing else than in faith pure and simple, for the spirit has nothing to do with things comprehensible, as we have seen. But now there come false teachers and lure the spirit out of doors (from inside the Holies of Holies); one puts forth this work, another that mode of attaining to godliness. And unless the spirit is preserved and is wise, it will come forth and follow these men. It will fall upon the external works and rules, and imagine it can attain to godliness by means of them. And before we know it, faith is lost, and the spirit is dead in the sight of God.

Then commence the manifold sects and orders. This one becomes a Carthusian, that one a Franciscan; this one seeks salvation by fasting, that one by praying; one by one work, another by another. Yet these are all selfchosen (sic) works and orders, never commanded by God, but invented by men. #42

Ironically, the same fleshy divisions now exist in the Protestant world today that Luther cited in the Catholic world and increase within both groups every century. It all points back to the **elephant of mixture** – the direct result of men depending on man's unaided, sense-based mind, rooted in the **seen realm,** to understand the workings of the **unseen realm** of the Holy Spirit, which is only discernible by a believer's spirit-man with the help of the Holy Spirit by grace through faith.

I leave it to you to decide for yourself, in counsel with the Holy Spirit, which view of man's nature is heretical. But be assured that this is a pivotal doctrine for accommodating the central truth of Jesus' **grace gospel** that declares that believers are complete/perfect and totally righteous **in Christ** and seated in heavenly realms with Him upon rebirth. Likewise, the Holy Spirit of God Himself resides in each reborn believer - despite the condition of his unsanctified soul and body. The logical question that must be answered by those holding to the bi-part doctrine is: in what perfectly compatible, holy place in your imperfect body and soul is perfection Himself residing? Must not an old wine skin be recreated to accept the new wine so that the believer does not "burst" with God's very presence? What part of a believer is radically new and compatible with God Himself?

You already know my answers to those vital questions. Accordingly, we will continue to use Paul's tri-part view of man's nature as a key to unlock many of the mysteries hidden in the "new things" about believers, which Jesus revealed only to Paul, in the next chapter. And be assured, believer, that whichever doctrinal position you hold, I will not curse you as a heretic because I gladly embrace the **whole gospel** of Jesus' mercy and grace. He has already forgiven and forgotten all our sins so this does not effect your salvation, just your level of victory on earth!

This next song-poem, set to an upbeat, country western melody, covers a lot of theological territory presented in this book. (My songs come in many musical flavors.)

NOW, I'M A WINNER NOT A SINNER I'm a saint not an ain't
Thanks to Jesus who has set this captive - free.
I'm the head, not the tail,
Anchored now behind the veil
Learning how to live in Jesus' victory.

Holy Spirit, Counselor and Friend,
Keep me faithful to the very end.
Day by day, Lord, have your way in me
As You lead me to my destiny.

Well it's not just what I see that defines reality
For my human mind can't see the things above.
But Your promises are true
And, by faith, they're mine through You
Who enables me to live Your life of love.

It's by faith, Lord, in Your living Word,
And obeying what I know I've heard,
That Your promise of abundant Life
Overcomes all tragedy and strife.
© Copyright 1997 by Leonard J. Ransil

CHAPTER EIGHTEEN

A NEW COVENANT,
A NEW POSITION,
A NEW REALITY

Thinking Like God Thinks

Now, let's first focus on some of the many amazing implications that naturally flow from Jesus' revelation about man's tri-part nature, which we discussed in the previous two chapters. All this might seem like a flight of fancy if your mind has not been renewed by Jesus' revelations to Paul about the workings of the **unseen realm**. All believers **in Christ** are automatically equipped with the supernatural gift of biblical faith to accept the **whole gospel of grace**. But you can be hindered from receiving this revelation knowledge if you, believer, insist that the revelations must first make sense to your natural mind - especially when the revelation is not only about the **seen realm** but the **unseen realm** of heaven that you are now a part of, **in Christ**. Fortunately, we can ask the Holy Spirit to bathe our natural mind in His truth so that we can begin to mentally "catch up" with the **post-cross** realities found **in Christ** that are the essence of Jesus' **whole gospel of lavish grace**.

You have the mind of Christ available to you but thinking His way is possible only by using God's gift of faith. When God says that "My thoughts are not your thoughts" in Isaiah 55:8, He is speaking of an **in Adam** mind-set that functions apart from divine revelation. Now, part of the "all things new" reality of the **New Covenant** is the choice to begin to think more and more like God thinks. Wouldn't any truly wise father want his child to think like he thinks? Of course! And this is especially true with Father-God who, in fact, has already supplied us with His Wisdom in the person of His Son, who is every believer's "wisdom from God and righteousness, holiness and redemption," according to 1 Corinthians 1:30.

But like everything else in Daddy's Kingdom, legally possessing the benefits of Jesus' **finished work** and vitally enjoying them is not the same thing. Believing and receiving them, as *personally meant for you,* is the power and purpose of His gift of faith. It is the sight to see the way He sees. It may be likened to someone supplying you with a computer to access the **unseen** internet "highway" which is impossible for you to access by just using your brain power. The Holy Spirit is the teacher Jesus has given to all believers. We benefit from His ministry to us by:

1) hearing Him unveil the **whole gospel,** as revealed in the "word of Christ" given to Paul, and then

2) yielding to His guidance as we let Him live through us to enjoy the benefits of God's **unseen Kingdom**, all by a faith-based relationship with God.

God Relates To Us Through Covenants

The predominant way God chooses to relate to mankind, in general, is through covenants. There are many examples presented throughout the Bible. But before looking at two charts that present an overview of the Bible's five main covenants, it is helpful to understand how covenants operated among peoples in early times. Like contracts typically do today, covenants were "cut" to make binding agreements between two or more people or groups for mutual benefit. For example, a weaker tribe might offer to make a covenant with a stronger tribe for protection from other warring tribes in exchange for supplying food or other services etc. But a *big* difference with contracts made today is that if a person or group violated any of the terms of the covenant agreement, they paid for it with their life, signified by the mingling of their blood, flowing from a cut in each one's wrist or hand in a prescribed ritual.

In the following chart (**18A**) the left column lists the common points of many ancient covenants. The right column is a parallel list of just some of the ways Jesus' **New Covenant,** cut with Father-God for *our* benefit, corresponds to terms of a typical covenant cut between the ancients. Please take the time to observe and reflect on how each step in this ancient ritualistic process has a corresponding parallel truth in the **unseen realm** of what Jesus did for us in His **finished work.**

Nine Steps in the Old Testament Blood Covenant	Old Covenant "revealed" in the New Covenant – Jesus' divine exchange!
1 Exchange of clothes.	1 Jesus provides believers with a "robe" of righteousness, a **divine exchange** for our filthy rags of **in Adam** self-righteousness and w are also clothed **in Christ**, our holy armor.
2 Exchange of weapons.	2 The tongue – a restless evil exchanged for "the Sword of the Spirit," speaking the Word of God. Our bodies now can be "a weapon of righteousness."
3 Cut animal(s) in half and walk in a figure eight around them; walking in the blood. "May God do this to me if I violate the covenant." (While Abram slept, Jesus was the Light or firebrand). (Birds of the air came as a type of the devil to hinder the process)	3 Jesus took our just beating and scourging and God's wrath and curses and death by becoming sin Who knew no sin and exchanged all that and more for abundant, eternal Life in Him. Also, Jesus exchanged our slavery under Satan for victory and authority over Satan and his minions.
4 Cut right hands or wrists and mingled blood to become blood brothers. (A remnant is a handshake). Breaking oath meant death.	4 Jesus' hands were not just cut but nailed in our place and he bought our Justification so that He could reconcile us to God and extend His right hand of fellowship to each new member of His family. He is our Blood Brother.
5 Ashes or dirt used to make a scar – a permanent mark as a sign and reminder of the covenant in blood.	5 His nail scarred hands are a permanent part of his glorified body, an eternal reminder of His gift to us, a New and Better Covenant with better promises – eternal Life in Him. He gave us beauty for ashes and a garment of praise in exchange for a spirit of heaviness (the law principle.)
6 An exchange of names.	6 He gave us a new name written down in glory and written in the Lamb's book of life.
7 Declare assets and liabilities – and exchange them in principle "What is mine is yours & what is yours is mine." I give you myself, in effect.	7 He exchanged His righteousness for my sin nature and sin behavior; my poverty for His infinite riches; my sickness for his health; my death for His life.
8 Covenant meal – a sign of fellowship.	8 He reversed my "exclusion from the covenants" and now I enjoy the blessings of Holy Communion as a provision for the health of my outer man.
9 They plant a tree as a memorial and sprinkle blood on it.	9 Jesus bled and died on a dead tree so that I could be made alive in Him and be protected by His Blood from all evil which is the New Covenant "Pass-over"

18A Nine Steps Of Blood Covenants

Again the left column in the above chart (**18A**) is a basic model of the many covenants in the Bible which God made at various times to further His divine plan of salvation. The following two charts below (**18B** and **18C**), are an overview of the five main covenants recorded in the Bible for our instruction and benefit. A quick look at the <u>top</u> of each column reveals a glaring truth alluded to in earlier chapters: <u>*only* the Mosaic Covenant in Chart **18C** was founded on a performance-based law system</u>. Again, the Israelites' good behavior brought blessings; their bad behavior brought curses, according to the specific terms of that covenant. Worshipping false gods usually resulted in exile. The reason was simple; rejecting God's ways meant rejecting His protection from their enemies - **seen** and **unseen**. This 1500 year experiment, which takes up 90% of the Old Testament and 82% of the whole Protestant Bible, proved beyond question that man's **in Adam** nature was corrupt beyond cure. Each human must be born of God to be compatible with God, which we now know, by revelation, is what Jesus came to earth to make possible. The other four covenants are founded on God's grace-based initiative and so demonstrate just how good He really is.

Act One: The Bible's First Three Main Covenants

The first three of the Bible's five main covenants, named in the next chart (**18B**), were all in the Bible's First Act. Note that all three were covenants based *ultimately* on God's <u>grace and mercy</u>, on behalf of mankind. It includes some details about the time periods in history. There was no formal law *officially* in force, so God did not routinely impute sin and punish mankind for sinning as He did under the *very specific* terms of the Mosaic Covenant with the Israelites. Romans 1:18-24 alludes to what could be called the law principle that the world was subject to. But by comparison to the specifics of the Mosaic Law system, it was generally a period of grace - rather than of pure justice for every wrong committed. Even though mankind's gross evil with fallen angels before the world-wide Flood required judgment, God did not wipe out mankind but spared one family to continue with His long-range salvation plan. (No doubt, God's mercy frustrated Satan - named the "god of this world" because he had usurped Adam's delegated dominion over the whole earth through deception. He certainly would have preferred mankind's total destruction or consignment to hell instead of what happened at Calvary when God fulfilled His prophecy He had declared against Satan at Adam's Fall in the garden.

Note: Chart **10B** on page 140 also compared and contrasted these two covenants.

4000 BC 3000	BC 2000	BC 1500 BC
ADAM 4000-3070 BC MERCY and GRACE He ate of the "Law Tree" Causing the "Fall"	**NOAH** 2885–1935 BC MERCY and GRACE	**ABRAHAM** 2166-1991 BC MERCY and GRACE
NO LAW so <u>Sin NOT Imputed, -</u> but all were "dead" spiritually	NO LAW so <u>Sin NOT Imputed</u> **	NO LAW so <u>Sin NOT imputed</u>
Adam "ushered" from the Garden, which was God's great mercy! Romans 5:12-15: "Therefore, just as sin entered the world through one man (Adam) and death came through sin, in this way, death came to all people so all sinned. Sin was in the world before the (Mosaic) Law was given, but sin is not charged against anyone's account when there is <u>no law</u>. However, death reigned from the time of Adam to the time of Moses, even over those <u>who did not sin by breaking a command like Adam had done</u>. He is a pattern of the one to come But the gift (Salvation) is not like the trespass. For if the many died by the trespass of the one man (Adam), how much more did God's grace and the gift that came by the grace of the one man, Jesus Christ, overflow to the many!"	2235 BC **THE** **F** **L** **O** **O** **D** A "special Judgment" to save the human race from self-destruction. ** For without the law, sin was dead. Romans 7:8	Romans 4:13, 15-16. . ."For the **promise**, that he should be the heir of the world, was **not** to Abraham, or to his seed, **through the law,** <u>but through the righteousness of faith</u> … **the law works wrath: for where there is <u>no law</u> there is no transgression".** "Therefore the **promise** is of faith (not man's effort), that it might be by grace; to the end the promise might be sure to all the seed; not to that only which is of the law (Jews), but to that also which is of the faith of Abraham; who is the father of us all (Jews and Gentiles)…"

18B The First Three Main Covenants

Acts Two And Three: Moses' Law Covenant Versus The New Covenant of Grace

Moses' Law covenant, in the left column of the chart **18C**, corresponds to Act Two of the Bible. Act Three is Jesus Christ's blood covenant in the right column, cut with Father-God on our behalf. Jesus' **whole gospel**, revealed only to Paul, explains in marvelous detail just what Jesus accomplished for mankind, His **finished work** of the **divine exchange**. It is the reception by faith of this glorious, legal transaction, accomplished almost 2000 years ago, that exchanges one's rotten, **in Adam,** spiritual core for a **new creation** spiritual core through the rebirth process, forecast by Jesus to Nicodemus. Again, Jesus did all the hard work for us on Calvary and He offers all that He purchased through His perfect sacrifice to anyone who believes and receives all that He accomplished for mankind - for free. As you read through each column, notice how different these two covenants are from each other – even though both are originated by God.

1500 BC goes to	33 AD 1000 AD 2000 AD on...
MOSES 1526-1406 BC **COVENANT TERMS:** "Do good, get good, Perfection required!) "Do bad, get bad." Judgment, Wrath, Curses!	**JESUS' NEW COVENANT, made with GOD for US!** C **GOD'S LAVISH MERCY and GRACE:** R **GOD'S RIGHTEOUSNESS** O **At CHRIST'S EXPENSE.** S **CHRIST JESUS is the END of the LAW. **** S Sin is NOT Imputed
MOSAIC LAW PERFORMANCE – BASED **Sin is Imputed**	**The "HIGHER LAW" of Faith, Love, Liberty** Romans 8:1-2 replaces the MOSAIC LAW which Jesus nailed to the Cross - Colossians 2:13-15 ****
The blessings for obedience: Deut 28:1-2: "And it shall come to pass, if you shall listen diligently to the voice of the Lord your God, to observe and to do <u>all</u> of His commandments which I command you this day, that the Lord your God will set you on high above all nations of the earth. ….. And <u>all these blessings</u> shall come on thee, and overtake thee: …" **The Curses for disobedience**: Deut 28:15: … "But it shall come to pass, if you will not listen to the voice of the Lord your God and observe and do <u>all</u> of His commandments and His statutes which I command thee this day then <u>all these curses</u> shall come upon you and overtake you: …" The blood of animal sacrifices covered accidental or unintentional sins. An "eye for and eye"… for intentional sins. James 2:10 "For whoever keeps the whole (Mosaic) Law yet stumbles on just one point is guilty of breaking the whole Law.	**The Blessing of Righteousness** via faith in the Blood of Christ Jesus, our Savior and Lord! Romans 5:16-21: "The gift of God (salvation) cannot be compared with the result of Adam's sin. The judgment followed one sin and brought condemnation, but the gift followed many trespasses and brought justification. For if, by the trespass of the one man (Adam), death reigned through that one man, how much more will those who receive God's abundant provision of grace and of the gift of righteousness, reign in life through the one man, Jesus Christ!" "Consequently, just as one trespass resulted in condemnation for all people, so also one righteous act resulted in justification and life for all people. For just as through the disobedience of the one man the many were made sinners, so also through the obedience of the one man the many will be made righteous." "The law was brought in so that sinning might increase. But where sinning increased, grace increased all the more, so that, just as sin reigned in death, so also grace might reign through righteousness to bring eternal life through Jesus Christ our Lord." **** Col 2:13-15: "And you, being dead in your sins and In the uncircumcision of your flesh, He (Jesus) has made you alive together with Him, having forgiven you <u>all</u> trespasses, blotting out the handwriting of ordinances (the Law) that was against us and was contrary to us. He (Jesus) took it out of the way, nailing it to the cross thereby, having spoiled Principalities and Powers, He made a public display of triumph over them." ** Romans 10:4

18C   Last Two Main Covenants

Jesus' New Covenant, outlined in the right column, is the "all things new" grace gospel of Jesus that deserves center stage in the mind of every believer. Why? In order to begin to fathom the height, the breadth, the width, the length and the depth of Father-God's agape love for him or her (see Ephesians 3:18). Jesus specifically sent the Holy Spirit to live inside every believer to help him or her grasp the benefits and privileges of the divine exchange that is the framework of Jesus' New Covenant.

> But we have not received the spirit of this world, but the Holy Spirit who is of God, so that we may <u>understand the gifts</u> that have been given to us by God (1 Corinthians 2:12).

As we now know through revelation of the Big Picture, the Mosaic Law was given primarily to reveal mankind's core problem – the **in Adam** nature – so that man's need for a savior became evident. In the meantime, the Law actually aroused sin and caused death. Yet God wanted to be near His chosen people so He inaugurated the sacrificial system to provide a temporary covering for their sin. This provision was in effect for the Jews until Jesus' perfect, substitutional sacrifice for all of mankind at Calvary.

God ordained the following process for sin-forgiveness, to temporarily satisfy His justice at that time in history, which is just a shadow of what Jesus' cross would later accomplish for mankind permanently. The sinner demonstrated his faith in God's promise of forgiveness by complying with the process. The priest carried out the required process and the sinner got the benefit. All he had to do was supply the perfect lamb and believe it was sufficient. No "confession of sins" was required - but bringing a lamb to the priest was an admission of a sin problem. This whole process was just one of the many prescribed rituals of the Mosaic Covenant, which:

1) the <u>Israelites made with God</u> (**bilateral**),

2) was for a <u>specific time period</u> (**temporary**)

3) <u>required that certain conditions be met</u> *before* the blessing was given (**conditional**).

So, in this ritual, for example, a spotless lamb had to be supplied by the sinner. If the rules were carefully followed, the person's sin was exchanged for the lamb's spotless (righteous) condition and the person went away justified because the sin was covered by the life's blood of the sacrificed lamb.

God honored that process (which He gave only to the Israelites) <u>in anticipation</u> of what Jesus would do later as mankind's new representative *to take away all the sins of the whole world.* God could justly do this through Jesus' bloody sacrifice at Calvary, where He inaugurated a totally **New Covenant** with mankind's new representative Jesus Christ, the Lamb supplied by God. <u>The terms of this New Covenant are drastically different than the Mosaic Covenant because of</u>

<u>1) who Jesus is and</u>

<u>2) what He accomplished for mankind as God's spotless Lamb.</u>

So now, all reborn believers benefit from a radically **New Covenant,**

1) which was made between Father-God and Jesus (**unilateral**)

2) which is not temporary but permanent (**eternal**) and

3) in which He fulfilled all the conditions (**unconditional**).

Therefore, in accordance with Romans 10:9-13, there is nothing left for any unbeliever to "do" to be reborn into this **New Covenant** of Father-God's Kingdom except, by grace through faith in Jesus, to:

1) speak in agreement that Jesus is Lord of the universe – because He proved it by His resurrection, orchestrated by God His Father and

2) believe for and receive His gift of rebirth into righteousness and speak in agreement that you are now saved through rebirth and set free from your old **in Adam** nature.

Then, ask the Holy Spirit, who now lives in you, to teach you and lead you into all truth which He will by progressively renewing your mind to think and see the way God does, now that you are His child. Why? So that you can enjoy Jesus' promise of His abundant life as He defines it in both realms.

Positioned In Christ

These many gifts and privileges of redemption are the "all things new" of the **divine exchange** that has qualified us, as **new creations,** to be **in Christ Jesus** (instead of being **in Adam**). Therefore, believers are automatically positioned **in Him** in heavenly places as joint-heirs of God's Kingdom *now*. What is now true for the exalted human side of Christ Jesus, **post-cross,** is also true for all reborn saints because of Jesus' **divine exchange.** This miraculous transaction is the permanent and radical difference between being **in Adam** to being **in Christ.** (See Endnote # **43** for a summary and explanation of why this is called a radical gospel.) Jesus' accomplishment made the Mosaic Covenant of Law obsolete for the Jews because it was based squarely on their self-effort. (And, again, God never intended the Mosaic Law, including the Ten Commandments, to be given to any Gentiles. It was the Judaizers who insisted on that.)

That **elephant of mixture,** and the resulting schism in 50 AD, snuck in through the policy and practices of the infant Jerusalem church. Christ Jesus cut the **New Covenant** with God for *both* Jews and Gentiles as mankind's perfect Representative. It is based solely on Jesus' monumental effort of a sinless life that culminated at Calvary. It is fully completed and offered to anyone who simply believes and receives Jesus as Savior. Our part is to count it *done* and rest in the **unseen reality** of His **divine exchange** with us (see Romans 6:11). Before exploring some of these glorious truths of Jesus' accomplishments for us, let's do a quick review of an Old Testament story that is recorded, starting in 1 Samuel 18, to give insight into how Jesus' **New Covenant** operates for us by His gift of grace through faith, not by our effort.

David and Jonathan

Before David became king, he and King Saul's son Jonathan made a covenant, sealed in their own blood, in which David promised to never cut off kindness toward Jonathan's family. After both King Saul and Jonathan died in battle, King David remembered this covenant and, according to 2 Samuel Chapter 9, he asked if any of Jonathan's family still lived. Jonathan's only son, the crippled Mephibosheth, wrongly believed that David was against him, so he was hiding away in fear. He was found and brought before King David who blessed him with a place at David's own table. Moreover, David generously restored all the land that had belonged to his grandfather, Saul, back to Mephibosheth.

The binding terms of the blood covenant between David and Jonathan were made on Mephibosheth's behalf, even though he knew nothing about them. David honored his promise to Jonathan by seeking out his son. In doing so, Mephibosheth exchanged a life of fear, unbelief, poverty and loneliness for one of blessing, favor, riches and fellowship with the King of the land. His new *position* replaced his helpless, impoverished condition, because David remembered and honored his covenant promise to Jonathan. It had nothing to do with Mephibosheth's fruitless efforts and everything to do with David honoring a covenant of grace.

This true story of Mephibosheth parallels the city dog column in Chapter Four. Many believers today mentally labor under the law in some way and, therefore, have a distorted opinion about God as the *cause of their troubles.* An underlying fear or suspicion that God is aloof, or arbitrary or even cruel, is typically caused by living under the **elephant of mixture** in ignorance or doubt and unbelief. But, again, Paul declares in 2 Timothy 1:7 that "God has not given us a spirit of fear, but of power and of love and of a sound mind."

Why would He do that if He is not *for* you and wants you to think His thoughts about His true nature and about your new spirit-self, now positioned **in Christ Jesus?** You, believer, have a far greater <u>position</u> and package of benefits than Mephibosheth ever enjoyed. They are available to you because of the terms of the blood covenant between Father-God and your elder Brother, Christ Jesus. These blessings are part of the **unseen Kingdom reality in Christ,** *not* of this **seen** world, per se. That is why Paul exhorts you and all believers in Colossians 3:1-4 to focus on Jesus and His **unseen realm,** not on the things of earth, because of *Whose* you are now and, therefore, *who* you are and *where* you are - **in Christ Jesus.**

> If, then, you were raised with Christ (reborn of God), seek (worship, hunger for, inquire after) the things that are above, where Christ is seated at the right hand of God. Think about (interest oneself in, set your affection on, meditate on) the things that are above, not the things that are upon the earth. For you have died, and so your life has been hidden with Christ in God. When Christ, your life, appears, then you also will appear with him in glory.

This passage is, in one small way, reminiscent of Joshua 1:8 that exhorted the Jews to meditate on the Law day and night (and be careful to perfectly do *everything* written in it) in that it told the Israelites what to *focus* on. However, that covenant was never given to Gentiles and the focus is now to be decidedly different for everyone included in the **New Covenant.** The Law's focus, is (and always was) on what *one should do and not do* in the **seen realm**. the **New**

Covenant's focus for believers is all about focusing on what *Jesus has done* for us and operating from the **unseen realm** of the spirit, through the Spirit. In case you think Paul was just fantasizing or being unrealistic, he describes how he mentally handled the persecution and trials he endured in 2 Corinthians 4:17-18 as follows:

> For though our tribulation is, at the present time, brief and light, it accomplishes in us the weight of a sublime eternal glory, beyond measure. And we are contemplating, **not** the things that are **seen**, but the things that are **unseen**. For the things that are **seen** are temporary, whereas the things that are **not seen** are eternal.

Paul clearly depended on and operated from the **New Covenant** benefits of the **unseen, divine exchange** that he consistently experienced through and **in Christ**. His position **in Christ** was not just some theological pipe-dream for the sweet bye and bye. It was a *now* reality that he walked in consistently because he learned to *rest* in the **New Covenant** realities, personally revealed to Him by Jesus. For the first time in mankind's history, God had obligated Himself to a perfect Man, the last Adam, who He sent to earth in order to represent and save mankind from destruction. Jesus showed and shared His accomplishments with Paul for all to read and believe and enjoy on earth today. But it begins with focusing on and magnifying Christ Jesus, your righteousness, instead of focusing on and magnifying your circumstances in the **seen** realm.

So, like Paul, I am now a **New Covenant** receiver who is **in Christ Jesus**, my covenant maker and covenant keeper with God. Therefore, I can now experience the benefits of the same covenant rights with God that Paul walked in. Legally, what belongs to Jesus, by virtue of His Covenant with Father-God, is now also mine because I am **in Him**. It is a legally established, **unseen reality,** based on the grace-based terms of the **New Covenant**. Even though I am not perfect in my outer man, all the blessings and benefits that belong to Jesus are also legally mine *now* because I shared, *through rebirth,* in Jesus' perfect obedience of His life and death etc. via *identification,* by grace through faith. Now, I am grafted into the Vine, Jesus Himself, by His doing, not by mine. His **divine exchange** with me and you, received by faith, is that glorious, legal basis.

Vital Basis to Receive Jesus' Unseen Benefits

How are all the **New Covenant** benefits consistently received? By yielding yourself over to Jesus - just as Jesus surrendered Himself over to God as His caretaker, provider, resurrection life, His all in all etc. through the ministry and communion with the Holy Spirit. In effect, *you are mentally switching over from you being your own point of reference to "God within you" becoming your point of reference.* This is the practical process of walking in a daily, interactive relationship with Jesus and Father-God through the Holy Spirit. But before describing that walk more in Chapter Nineteen, we first need to better understand the importance of being seated with Christ in God that Jesus revealed to Paul in Ephesians. Theologians call it "positional truth" which simply means that God relocated believers from being spiritually destitute and shackled **to Adam** in Darkness to now being spiritually rich and free **in Christ** in the heavenlies, who also placed Himself inside all believers.

That "relocation" to heavenly places **in Christ** qualifies every reborn believer to be a joint-heir with Christ Jesus and, thereby, enjoy the rights and privileges of Jesus' **divine exchange.**

This is the legal basis of inheritance that is already yours by being *one* with Christ Jesus, the King of kings. As you learn to trust in and cooperate with the flow of the life of the Holy Spirit, <u>your new reference point</u>, you will experience the **unseen** benefits of Jesus' victory in the **seen realm.** He will lead and guide you into knowing Him and receiving all the truth and revelation needed to set your outer man progressively free from fleshy mind-sets, addictions, bad habits etc.. You will experience over time, that Jesus' yoke of a grace-based walk is, indeed, easy and that His burden is light. Why? Because it is living according to the higher law of the **butterfly life in Him,** rather than under the burdensome **elephant of mixture** that is still so common in Christianity today. Might there be some misunderstanding and even persecution for consciously abiding in Jesus? Possibly, but His strength is more than sufficient and His rewards are far greater.

The Divine Exchange

So, now that you just saw a few of the highlights of Jesus' **New Covenant** of grace in the charts above, it is time to present many more details of the grace-based, "all things are new" covenant of God's **unseen realities** that He intends for His children to believe and receive and walk in. The benefits in the next chart (**18D**) are all part of what Jesus called His "abundant life" that He came to freely give to anyone who would receive Him, who *is* our Tree of life. I now invite you to meditate on the following chart titled *"The Exchanged Life In Christ"* that focuses on Jesus' **divine exchange** made with each believer. It is expressed in the endearing terms of our intimate relationship with Him, orchestrated by Father-God and empowered by the Holy Spirit.

JESUS, this is what You did for me under the Mosaic Law & through Your Divine Exchange with me . . .

. . . so that I can now live in You forever under your New Covenant of lavish Grace

You loved me first, while I was a sinner — so that I can love You now as a saint in You
You came into a sin-filled world — so that I can love You now as a saint in You / **THE** / to place me in You in the Heavenlies
As Your confidence was in Your Father — so that my confidence is now in You
You rested in Father-God's care — **E** — so I can now rest in His peace and Love
You were secure in Father's love — and my security is now in You, Jesus
You focused on Your Father, not on Law — **X** — so that He can be my focus now, too
You perfectly met all the Law's demands — freeing me from the law of sin & death
You fulfilled the Mosaic Law — **C** — so it was nailed to the Cross
You obeyed the Law perfectly — to give me Your Righteousness as a gift

H

L A B O R   TO
" MY YOKE IS EASY,

A

E N T E R MY REST
MY BURDEN IS LIGHT"

You became my sin 2 Cor. 5:21 — **N** — to give me Your everlasting Righteousness
You took my place of execution — to make me alive forever in You
You were forsaken by Father-God — **G** — to make me now fully accepted in You
You were condemned to die — to free me totally from all condemnation
You were bound then scourged — **E** — to set me free from all bondage
You were scourged with whips — so that by those stripes, I have been healed
You bore a crown of thorns — **D** — to give me Your helmet of salvation
You were punished beyond recognition — to absorb and pay for all my just punishment
You were crucified in shame — to fully pay for all my guilt and shame
You were rejected by family & friends — **L** — to make me one with You and Your Body
You bore all my curses on Calvary's Tree — to provide me with every spiritual blessing
You shed Your sinless Blood for me — **I** — to make me a totally forgiven saint in You
You shed Your Blood for my protection — so I am now fully protected by Your Blood
You included me in Your death — **F** — so I am now risen and ascended in You
You became my perfect High Priest — to give me all the blessings that You deserve
You died as my elder brother — **E** — to make me a part of Father-God's family
You died as a pauper — to make me a joint-heir of heaven in You now
You finished Your work and sat down — so that I can rest in all that You did for me
You were obedient, even unto death — **IN** — to give me Your Life and full salvation
You are God's beloved Son — and now I am as loved by God as You are
You disarmed all Principalities — and triumphed over them by the Cross
You descended into Hell — **C** — to rescue me from the power of Darkness
You overcame the grave and Hell — and transferred me into Your Kingdom
You crushed the serpent's head — **H** — so Satan is now under my feet in You
You totally defeated Satan — and sent the Holy Spirit to reign in me
You conquered Death itself — **R** — so now Your Love for me casts out all fears
You were my holy Substitute — so You are now my Holiness 1 Cor. 1:30
You sent the Holy Spirit as my surety — **I** — so now I have Your assurance of full salvation
You came as God's Grace and Truth — so now You are my Way, my Truth, my Life
God is totally pleased with You — **S** — and now also with me because I am in You
Though rich, You became poor — to make me ever prosperous in You
God nailed the Mosaic Law to the Cross — **T** — and gave me a New Covenant in Your Blood
Jesus came to save you and all mankind — so believe and receive His free gift of Life

Thank-You Father-God, Jesus and Holy Spirit

18D   The Exchanged Life In Christ Chart

Seated With Christ Jesus - Location is Everything!

As a believer, when God calls you His reborn child and a "**new creation**," He means it. You are regenerated or "re-begun," not just remodeled or refitted. The old, corrupted seed, which you once were **in Adam,** is now crucified, dead, buried - *gone*. If you wonder how that could possibly be true then also ask yourself how is it that the perfect man Jesus Christ *became* sin. Then how did He, who *was* sin, arise out of the grave *sinless* and qualified to go into a sinless heaven? He did so by the same God-given transformation and resurrection power that raised the new, non-sinner you, now **in Christ Jesus**, out of the grave and into heaven as well. Jesus' **divine exchange** took your place as a sinner **in Adam** and gave you His place as a saint **in Christ Himself**. Every believer is "re-positioned" by God's resurrection power **into Christ** when reborn from above by His grace through faith alone. Jesus documented that reality, motivated by God's love for us, through Paul in Ephesians 2:4-6 which says that

> But God, being rich in mercy, because of His vast love with which He loved us, even though we were dead in our sins, made us alive with Christ. It is by His grace (through faith) that you have been saved. And God raised us up with Christ and seated us with Him in the heavenly realms **in Christ Jesus**.

Obviously, we are welcome at His heavenly table – with the wedding banquet yet to come.

Jesus' Whole Gospel

All this, my friend, is the *third* triumphant part of the **whole gospel** of Christ Jesus. It is rarely mentioned or discussed because bi-part biased believers (who only believe they are a soul in a body) have no part of their imperfect outer man to connect to this present, **unseen reality**. They know that their body is not yet in heaven, nor is their soul (natural mind, will and emotions) compatible with the perfection of heaven. So, this vital **New Covenant** reality is stashed in the theological dust-bin of "positional truth" because it makes no sense to their unrenewed mind. Yet, they dare not deny it to be true since Paul wrote it down. But, at best, they regard it as an irrelevant "anomaly" to be discovered and appreciated when believers "go to heaven at death." Again the religious mind, contaminated with the droppings of the **elephant of mixture**, misses a vital key to understanding the monumental, transformational effect that the **finished work** of Jesus instantly imparts to a newly reborn saint **in Christ**. He is already where Jesus is, seated in heavenly places, next to Father-God. A believer's starting point in heaven is what religious people hope to arrive at when they die.

Did you catch that revelation? Again, by being regenerated as a new spirit-being, which makes us united with Christ in Heaven, God has given to us, as the *starting point* of His new, abundant, heavenly life **in Christ**, what is the attempted *arrival point* for the religions of the world. Wow!

God's gift of righteousness qualifies every believer to operate *now* from His heavenly position of power and authority as an adopted child of God *over* every **unseen** principality and power of Darkness that he was *under* just nano seconds before his rebirth. It is the very same Holy Spirit power and authority that Jesus walked in on earth as Father-God's Representative. Now, everyone **in Christ Jesus** is God's ambassador of reconciliation thanks to the perfect, completed, **finished work** of Jesus' **divine exchange.** What remains for the believer is to learn how to walk according to the Spirit's leading and guidance as Jesus learned to walk.

Holy Spirit Empowered Living

So, Jesus' promise of abundant living, as He defines it, is not about your efforts here but about His Holy Spirit's performance through you - just as it was about His performance through Jesus while He reigned in life - even on the cross. We are the trophies that He won for Father-God, risen and ascended on high with Him. Now, we no longer have to work and struggle to get victory. Instead, we get to learn how to cooperate with the Holy Spirit who lives His victorious life through us to manifest His royal fruit of love, joy, peace, patience, gentleness, goodness, meekness, kindness, faithfulness and self-control. Taken together, this fruit is an expression of the nature and life of Christ Jesus in God - the abundant life of heaven - which we are now in holy union with as righteous, spirit-beings.

A Sinner No More

Again, how could you be a sinner in God's eyes and be seated next to Him in heaven? The answer is: you are no longer a sinner when you changed positions through His lavish GRACE - God's Righteousness At Christ's Expense - believed in and received by His gift of faith. Put simply, faith is the disposition to believe and receive all God wants to give you - even before there is any evidence of it manifested in the **seen realm.** The more we receive from Him the more He gives - and He delights in doing so.

Can you see now how important it is to mentally rise above the "ceiling" of the **seen realm,** like Jesus and Paul did, and revel in the victorious position of the **butterfly life in Christ Jesus,** whom you are already *in* as a new, spirit-being? Striving to get to heaven is a mirage; the reality **in Christ** is given to us to rest in and enjoy and operate from, enabling us to bring a taste of heaven (Jesus) into this **seen realm.** This truth, apprehended by faith, facilitates the reception of all the other "new things" that are part of your legal inheritance **in Christ.** He paid for them so why not benefit in every way possible so that you can manifest God's goodness and be a blessing to others who are looking in all the wrong places for treasure? Jesus is our treasure and reward, as the following song poem declares:

YOU ARE MY TREASURE AND REWARD, the keeper of my soul
I'm one in spirit with You Lord, for You have made me whole.
For, of myself, was no good thing, without You I was dead.
Now You're my life, my peace and joy, my victory instead.

I thank You for Your love for me, for Your gift of righteousness.
I'm set apart to live for You, my life and holiness
You are my purpose and reward, the why and how I live.
You are my Source of only good so I welcome all that You give.
Sermon Song © Copyright 2009 by Leonard Ransil

Sit

Watchman Nee summarized this vital revelation of our position **in Christ,** found in Ephesians 2:6, with a single word: **Sit!** Mentally sitting **in Christ,** next to Father-God, allows you to consciously abide and bask in His engulfing love that will heal any misgivings about who Father-God really is at His core. He **is** love - personal, unconditional, sacrificial, committed, totally accepting, engulfing, consuming, enjoyable and eternal! Ask the Holy Spirit to bathe your mind in Father's love and goodness that removes all mental barriers to your Abba-Father, "Daddy" God. As you ask and allow the Holy Spirit to melt away any resistance to wholly identifying with Jesus and Father-God, you will increasingly be persuaded and then come to an inner certainty, reinforced through experience, of what Paul prayed for us in Ephesians 3:14-19:

> For this reason I kneel before the Father, from whom His whole family in heaven and on earth derives its name. I pray that, out of His glorious riches, He may strengthen you with power through His Spirit in your inner being, so that Christ may dwell in your hearts through faith. And I pray that you, <u>being rooted and established in (His) love</u>, may have power, together with all the saints, to grasp how wide and long and high and deep is the love of Christ (for me), and <u>to know this love</u> that surpasses knowledge -- <u>that you may be filled to the measure of all the fullness of God</u>.

Did you catch that revelation? Paul is praying a Holy Spirit inspired prayer for you and me that we each grasp how wide and long and high and deep is the love of Christ (for you and for me), and to know this love that surpasses knowledge - *that you may be filled to the measure of all the fullness of God.* Wow! It was because of that "knowing" - through his spirit-oneness with God Himself - that Paul counted everything else he had focused on before 42 AD as rubbish, by comparison. It is beyond the mind - through one's new spirit-self **in Christ** - that the link happens by faith and can now be rested in and enjoyed, regardless of what is going on in the **seen realm** with your outer man. This may sound to some like a new form of Gnosticism that the apostle John wrote against in his letters. But heresies always contain some kernel of truth in order for them to appear true. But the genuine gospel that Jesus revealed to Paul is all about us being *of* the **unseen realm** while still being *in* this **seen realm.** It is a *"duality of positions"* (not duality of natures) that was not possible to us before Jesus' **divine exchange** with believers. It is all part of "all things are new" **in Christ.**

Living In God's Reality

The **seen realm** cannot provide true life because it is a passing reality. Whatever we choose to focus our mind on tends to shape and solidify our thinking and believing, absorbing our time and treasure – for better or worse. But only Jesus deserves to be our main focus because He is our very life, <u>our all in all</u>. Resting and abiding and basking **in Him** consciously can become a wonderful habit - and more life-giving than the preoccupations with a job or sports or food or country or even one's family etc. They are all a blessing from God but they are "externals" that can compete for our attention and allegiance to Jesus, our continuous only source of true life and refreshment. The more we see everything through God's eyes like Jesus did, the more we are able to appreciate the "externals" without the danger of them becoming idols to us. He alone is our true, eternal reality, internally and externally, and our reason for being! Only true liberty is available to all reborn saints who choose to focus their faith-eyes on Jesus. Believer, He is the author and finisher of your faith, who wants to unveil to you the *whole revelation* of what He has already done for you - His **divine exchange** (see Hebrews 12:2 and also the first song poem - below).

By meditating on all that Jesus' love for you has already accomplished by His **finished work,** you will renew your mind with God's revelation of who you now are **in Christ Jesus.** This revelation, through the Holy Spirit, will, in turn, enable you to increasingly live what many refer to as "holy living" because it puts your focus on Jesus rather than on yourself. The wellspring of *true* holiness is tapped by seeing your new spirit-self as a righteous and holy being **in Christ** who *is* your righteousness and holiness, wisdom and redemption, according to 1 Corinthians 1:30. It's not about "pursuing holiness" but about consciously abiding in Him who already *is* your holiness.

Rightly defining yourself as God sees you will renew your mind with His truth which will then empower you to live consistently out of who you already are - a **new creation** saint who is *one* with Christ Jesus and Father-God. It is impossible for *you* to live the Christian life. Only the Holy Spirit can do that through you because Jesus is the Vine and you are a branch, grafted into Him to bear *His* perfect fruit, not your imperfect works of the flesh. So, let go and let God have His wonderful way in and through you!

Reflecting Father-God's Love

Again, Jesus exchanged all His good for all your bad **in Adam** so that you can now *bear* His good fruit because you *are* good - **in Him**. He took rubbish and made a diamond so do not demean His handiwork as being anything less than wonderfully perfect and beautiful in His sight. You are now of His royal DNA, so walk in the glow of your new Father's doting care and affirmation and increasingly reflect your new, royal parentage in your outer man. Remember, by His doing, you are a partaker of God's divine nature! We will delve more into "walking according to the Spirit" in the next chapter.

Below are the words to three more song-poems that summarize some of the realities of God's **unseen Kingdom** that we just covered.

TRUE LIBERTY FROM ALL I SEE
Is the sight to see the way You see.
This gift of faith You give for free
Helps me know the truth
Of Your love for me.

For all I see and taste and feel
Are not what will stay forever real.
It's only You, my liberty,
Who is my true life, eternally.

You're my all in all, redeemer King,
You're my righteousness, so to You, Lord, I sing
A song of praise and thanksgiving
For who You are, You're my Everything.

Now all I see just fades away
When I focus on You night or day.
I set my mind on things above
Where I live in You, my unfailing love.
© Copyright 2010 by Leonard Ransil

Jesus, You became my sin, through Your death, we rose again,
GREATLY BLESSED, HIGHLY FAVORED, DEEPLY LOVED.
Father's wrath You received, by His grace, I believed,
Now I'm seated with You, high above.

So I thank You for Your love for me.
And rest in all You've Done for me
Absorbing all my punishment,
And every curse on Calvary.
It's You, Lamb of God, that I love.
By your stripes I am healed, my salvation is sealed.
GREATLY BLESSED, HIGHLY FAVORED, DEEPLY LOVED.
And my future is secure for Your promises are sure.
We are One - like an hand in a glove.

So I thank You for Your love for me
And rest in all You've done for me.
Your **finished work** has set me free,
And I am New because of You.
I worship You, Lord, with songs of love.
 © Copyright 2010 by Leonard J. Ransil

I'VE BEEN ADOPTED BY THE ONE TRUE GOD
Was picked before the world began.
I've been adopted by the One, True God,
As a part of His glorious plan.

Justified by the blood of God's Holy, Righteous Lamb.
Set apart, and glorified, I am one with the Great "I Am."

I am the Righteousness of God, **in Christ**,
A gift from God, by grace through faith.
I am the righteousness of God **in Christ**.
As He is so am I in this world

I'm alive under grace and abiding in the Vine.
By His Covenant of Blood, I am His and He is mine!

I am a new creation, priest and king,
Reborn of God by grace through faith.
I am a new creation, priest and king
Sent to speak words of Life to the dead.

So I boast in the Lord Who has made all things brand new.
If you ask Him and believe, you'll be in God's Kingdom too.

I've been adopted by the one, true God,
Was picked before the world began.
I've been adopted by the One, True God,
As a part of His glorious plan.
Sermon Song © Copyright 2009 by Leonard J. Ransil

CHAPTER NINETEEN

WALKING BY THE SPIRIT IN FAITH, LOVE AND LIBERTY

A Review Based on Romans Chapter Seven

We can tell from the context of Romans, Chapter Seven, that Paul was specifically addressing Jewish Christians "for I am speaking to people who know the law." Again, he is not speaking to Gentile believers because God never intended the Gentiles to be under the Mosaic Covenant of Law. But, tragically, Gentiles in Jerusalem were required by the early Jerusalem church to go under law by being circumcised before they could become Christians. Paul was furious about this heretical mixture. So, in Romans 7:2-4, Paul exposed this deception by using the *analogy* of a woman who was married to the law. (Jewish Christians still saw themselves bound to it, as though married.) Yet, she needed to become wedded to Christ Jesus to be saved. (The law cannot save her but can only condemn imperfect humans.) Since the holy Law can't "die" (thus allowing her to legally marry Jesus), Jesus supplied her with a death to her **in Adam** self by identification with Him on the cross by faith, apart from her performing any works required by the law.

Her old spirit-self, **in Adam,** died (by being crucified with Christ, by faith) and it was buried with Him. Her new self arose with Him and now she lives **in Christ** as a **new creation** spirit-being. So now, she is legally married to Him and is seated in the heavenlies since she is no longer who she used to be, spiritually speaking. And who is the "she" Paul is referring to? Everyone who is reborn of God by faith. That, my friend, is Jesus' **whole gospel** in a simplified nutshell which He made possible for both Jews and Gentiles by His **divine exchange**. But if all this is so wonderful, then why the turmoil and anguish of soul that Paul took pains to describe towards the end of Chapter Seven? I am glad you asked. This is the inevitable result when anyone trusts in his law-keeping to please God or to reach perfection through obedience to its impossible demands. The turmoil that Paul describes here is a graphic illustration of being stomped on by the **elephant of mixture.** God sent Jesus to perfectly fulfill that "weak and inadequate covenant" of law (see Hebrews 7:18) and offer to mankind a glorious new, everlasting covenant that <u>He keeps for us</u> as part of His **finished work** on the cross.

Position Is Everything

So, a sinner's **divine exchange** with Jesus, received by faith, changes everything for him in the **unseen realm** as a reborn believer **in Christ.** Again, his old starting point of being in Darkness and trying to get to heaven by his futile efforts is now reversed. How? Because every believer's new position, located in the **unseen** reality of being *seated* **in Christ** in heavenly places, is his *starting point.* But that is only the beginning, not the whole picture, of course. Why? Because, believer, while you *are* a reborn spirit-being **in Christ Jesus**, you still have an unsanctified soul and live in an earthly body until that dies – or Jesus returns first. In other words, you no longer belong to this world, spiritually speaking, but you still function in it. But, again, thanks to Jesus' **divine exchange**, your *starting* point as a **new creation in Christ** is religion's attempted *arrival* point - heaven. Spiritually, you now partake of His divine nature instead of the nature of your former self, which was in league with God's enemy. Once you agree with God that you are now a **new creation** spirit-being, yet still living in an imperfect body and soul on earth, you may be asking: "Okay, so how do I walk victoriously in the **seen realm**." No doubt, Paul had the same question and needed Jesus to help sort out what really happened to him when reborn. He described this holy transaction in Galatians 2:20:

> I have been nailed to the cross with Christ. I live; yet now, it is not I (my old, **in Adam** self), but truly Christ, who lives in me (in my new spirit-self, **in Christ**). And though I live now in the flesh (my physical body in the **seen realm**), I live in the faith of the Son of God, loving me and who gave Himself for me.

The way to receive the Tree of Life Himself has always been the same - *by faith*. Adam could see and experience the perfection of God all around him and he knew nothing of evil. Yet even he had to walk by faith, trusting that God's view and His *living word* was better than any contrary word – be it from Satan, Eve or his own mind coming from his natural sight. Paul reinforces the importance of walking by faith in God's viewpoint in Romans 1:17: "For in it (Jesus' Gospel) the righteousness of God is revealed from faith to faith, even as it has been written 'The righteous shall live by faith'" (from Habakkuk 2:4). The **unseen realm** can be apprehended only by a trusting faith in God's living revelations of what He has done for us.

In Chapter Eight of Romans, Paul launches into explaining some of the benefits of the **divine exchange** of natures - from formerly being **in Adam** to now being **in Christ**. God intends that the radical change in both our *new nature* and *new position* **in Christ** should impact our earthly *condition* as well. We can now live free of condemnation that was caused by being a sinner **in Adam**. As already explained in Chapter Three, we are empowered to live in the far higher **butterfly life** - the "law of the Spirit of life **in Christ Jesus**." This is His life of faith, love and liberty that He offers to live through us, as us, by depending on the Holy Spirit sent by Jesus, *not* on the law principle. It is the way of freedom that Jesus lived on earth which enabled Him to perfectly fulfill the demands of the Mosaic Law that He was born under. He did that by focusing on Father-God by faith, *not* on the law principle itself, which is not of faith. The following passage in Romans 8:1-17 is a major revelation from Jesus, giving God's alternative to living under the demands of any code or law system that always causes death. Jesus made this possible by His **divine exchange** with us.

God's Higher Law Of The Spirit In Romans, Chapter Eight

Therefore, there is now no condemnation for those who are **in Christ Jesus** for the (higher) law of the Spirit of life **in Christ Jesus** has freed me (Paul) from the (Mosaic) law of sin and death. For the law (being) powerless because it was weakened by the (selfish) flesh, God sent His own Son in the likeness of sinful flesh and because of sin, and concerning sin, condemned sin in the flesh (when Jesus became sin on the cross) so that the righteousness of the (Mosaic) law (which Jesus kept perfectly) might be fulfilled in us (who arose with Jesus from the grave - justified) who are not walking (living day to day) according to the (selfish) flesh (the sarx, not my former self), but according to the (new, regenerated) spirit (which is now in union with the Holy Spirit).

NOTE: The remainder of this passage, verses 5 to 17, is in a double column format below. Please follow the numbering system of #1 to #12 in **Chart 19A** in order to understand the **contrast** Paul makes between *living according to the flesh* (the odd numbers in the left column) versus *living according to the Spirit* (the even numbers in the right column). Appendix # 15 has more about the "sarx" ie. the flesh.

Living by the selfish flesh (sarx)	**Living by the Holy Spirit's love**
#1 For those who are in agreement with the flesh, they are mindful of (focused on) the things of the flesh (the **seen realm**).	#2 But those who are in agreement with the spirit (by the gift of faith) focus on the things of the spirit (the **unseen realm**)
#3 For the mind set on the flesh is death (because the **seen realm** is passing away).	#4 But the mind set on the spirit is (eternal, abundant) life and peace.
#5 And the (natural, unrenewed) mind of the flesh is hostile towards God for it is not subject to the (higher, **unseen**) law of God, nor can it be. So those who are in the flesh are not able to please God.	#6 But you are not in the flesh but in the spirit if, indeed, the Spirit of God lives within you (by being reborn of God).
#7 But if anyone does not have the Spirit of Christ, he does not belong to Him.	#8 But if Christ is within you (through rebirth), then the body is indeed dead to sin, but (your) spirit truly lives, because of justification (the gift of Jesus' righteousness). But if the Spirit of Him (God) who raised up Jesus from the dead lives within you, then He (God) who raised up Jesus Christ from the dead shall also enliven your mortal bodies, by means of His Holy Spirit living within you. Therefore, brothers, we are not debtors to the flesh, so as to live according to the flesh.
#9 For if you live according to the flesh, you will die.	#10 However, if you put to death the deeds of the flesh by the (power of the) Spirit, you shall live. For all those who are <u>led by the Spirit of God</u> are the sons of God
#11 And you have not received, again, a spirit of servitude in fear (under Law).	#12 but you have received the (Holy) Spirit of the adoption of sons, in whom we cry out: "Abba, Father!" For the Holy Spirit Himself renders testimony to our spirit that we are the sons of God. But if we are sons, then we are also heirs: truly heirs of God, but also joint-heirs with Christ, if we share in His sufferings (are persecuted if necessary) that we may also share in His glory (Romans 8:17).

19A Walking According To The Flesh   Or According To The Spirit

If you followed the flow of the numbers from #1-#12 in the two columns above, Paul's contrast is easy to see. We are no longer under the penalty of sin before our holy God because Jesus perfectly paid that penalty - in advance of all our sinning - in His flesh. He agreed to *become sin* and, consequently, was "justly" condemned in our place on the tree. We are now free to live by a trusting faith as God's redeemed children in the love and liberty of our faithful Father-God, just as Jesus lived on earth, doing *even greater works* than He did, in response to the ongoing guidance and protection of the Holy Spirit.

Wow! Can that really be true? What could "doing even greater works than Jesus did" possibly mean? Well, think about it. We can do the greater work of *facilitating* the rebirth of others - which Jesus could not do for Nicodemus, **pre-cross.** Why? Because He had not yet physically and spiritually accomplished the **divine exchange** in the **seen realm** on Calvary. Sure, He raised Lazarus from physical death, **pre-cross** but he later died physically again. But Jesus could not get anyone "saved" into heaven until He accomplished the crucifixion of the Adamic nature and rose from spiritual death. Now, thanks to Christ Jesus, we get to announce the really good news of total forgiveness and reconciliation from God to all mankind and to facilitate His free gift of salvation that He offers to all willing unbelievers. Again, the only "requirement" is that they personally believe and receive Jesus and what God offers through Him, according to Romans 10:9-13, in order to be "reconciled to God."

The Veil of The Law

Now, just in case you are not yet convinced that living according to the Mosaic Law prevents you from walking according to the Holy Spirit, let's read what Paul had to say to the Corinthians who were apparently confused about this issue too. Why? Possibly because the Judaizers from Jerusalem were doing in Corinth what they had done in Galatia - stirring opposition almost everywhere Paul traveled. In the context of 2 Corinthians 3:6-18, Paul said that the Law ministered death and condemnation to the Israelites, but the Holy Spirit gives to us the exact opposite – life. Jesus came to *free mankind* from death and condemnation in every form (including from the Mosaic Covenant for the Jews), and to supply mankind with a brand new, totally revamped covenant of grace. Now, starting in verse 14, Paul explains that the Law has a dulling effect on the human mind because it acts like a veil – a mental hindrance – to seeing the higher, **unseen** law of the Spirit that Jesus came to provide to those who put aside their law-mindedness and look to Him for salvation and guidance. He says it this way:

… (the Israelite's) thoughts were rendered dull, and even to this present day, the same veil remains unlifted when they read the old covenant because (only) through Christ is it taken away. To this day, in fact, whenever Moses is read, a veil lies over their hearts. But whenever a person turns to the Lord (is reborn), the veil is removed. Now the Lord is the Spirit, and where the Spirit of the Lord is, there is freedom (from depending on one's performance for righteousness). All of us, gazing with unveiled face on the glory of the Lord, are being transformed into the same image from glory to glory as from the Lord who is the Spirit (2 Corinthians 3:14-18).

But the process of liberation of the believer's mind through the sanctification of the Holy Spirit is not automatic. It can be hindered if the believer *falls from grace* by mentally going back under the ministry of death and condemnation by focusing back on the Law as a "standard" to follow. That was the cause of the mental battle Paul was describing at the end of Romans, Chapter Seven, written only to "those who know the Law" – the Jews. But that mental turmoil and anguish, caused by law-mindedness, sets the stage for the **whole gospel's** way to freedom **in Christ,** described in Romans, Chapter Eight, explained above.

Now, all of us who are alive **in Christ** are enabled, by the Holy Spirit living inside of us, to walk and live according to His peace and direction for He is in union with our new, regenerated spirit-self. Walking according to the <u>Spirit, in union with our new spirit-self,</u> overrides the dictates of our unsanctified natural mind that is not fully renewed to think like God thinks and sees. He does not force His ways on us like other influential forces like to do. Some people, our flesh, the devil, our appetites, wrong mind-sets, old habits, etc. pressure us to pursue ways that are not life-giving. Seeing the **unseen realm** with eyes of faith and pausing to ask the Spirit for His view and power, enables us to operate from the "mind of Christ" that is <u>always</u> life-giving and available to the listening saint. This is not the burdensome "have-to's" of the Law but the "get-to's" of our Friend, Guide, Teacher and Sanctifier of our soul, the Holy Spirit.

The Secret Of Victorious Living On This Earth

Jesus is our wisdom <u>who we can now choose to consciously abide in and draw from continuously.</u> *Or,* we can rely on our own limited understanding and walk according to "the flesh" (the sarx, in Greek). *The former is another way to describe walking and living according to the direction and control of the Holy Spirit.* The latter is as futile as trying to get to Hawaii on a bicycle. Why even try that when the **butterfly life,** supplied **in Christ Jesus,** empowers you to fly above the pull of circumstances and the lusts of the flesh by keeping your mind on:

1) who God really is, the One who loved you when you were still a rebellious sinner,

2) what He has done for you by giving you a new nature **in Christ**, and, therefore,

3) who you now are – God's holy of holies – your spirit-self where God Himself dwells

> For though, by the one offense (Adam's fall), death reigned through one man (Adam), yet so much more the ones <u>receiving the abundance of grace</u> and <u>the gift of righteousness</u> (justification), <u>reign in life through the one (man) Jesus Christ</u> (Romans 5:17).

So, how do we reign in this life? Again, we do so by heeding Jesus' instruction through Paul, stated in 2 Corinthians 5:16:

> And so, from now on, we know no one (including oneself) according to the flesh, though we have known Christ according to the flesh (externals), yet now we know Him in this way no longer.

This perspective comes from the gift of divine faith – the ability to see Father-God, Christ Jesus, others and ourselves *as God does,* with spiritual eyes rather than with merely carnal-based thinking. This is the essence of operating from a "transformed mind, the mind of Christ." Again, <u>right believing about who God is, what He *has done* to and for you, and who you now are **in Him**</u> will increasingly produce the Holy Spirit's fruit of right living in Him. Jesus revealed this

301

secret when He pictured Himself as a vine to which we are attached as fruit-bearing branches. We can invite the life sap of the Holy Spirit's life to flow through us to produce the overflow of good fruit, rather than "dead" efforts – the works of the flesh. This is exactly how Jesus learned to walk on earth, listening to His Father and living according to the life-giving power of the Holy Spirit operating through Him.

When He was baptized in the Holy Spirit and fire, Jesus heard His Father's voice of love and approval: "This is my beloved Son with whom I am very pleased." Father-God now speaks that same approval to all believers **in Christ Jesus,** not based on your good or bad performance but based only on your position and righteousness **in Him**. Jesus knew who His Father was and listened to His loving voice, learned what He was called to do and trusted the Holy Spirit to live Father's divine life *through* Him. Consequently, He manifested the fruit of heaven's kind of life. *We now have the same option – to progressively see and think as God does*, as we let the Holy Spirit live through us as His righteous fruit bearers and ambassadors – children of the King of kings – because of His abundance of grace.

It is another way of describing the privilege of "walking according to the Spirit" rather than by one's limited and unsanctified carnal mind, i.e. the flesh. Again, this is how Jesus learned to walk in the Spirit while on earth. He was intentionally *dependent* on His Father's provision and direction "acknowledging Father-God in all His ways" so that He could direct Jesus through the Holy Spirit living within Him. Again, Jesus was *always* Father-conscious (not Law conscious) for He did nothing unless His Father told Him (see John 5:19). Jesus did not try to do His own works to get God's approval. He was *already* righteous and approved - before He began His ministry. And so is every reborn, new creation saint (from God's view) because he is **in Christ**, who now *is* the believer's righteousness. Jesus came to do the works of His Father as a dependent ambassador of God's will and Kingdom. Similarly, we have the privilege of being God's ambassador, His "… handiwork, created in Christ Jesus for the good works which God has prepared for us, in which we should walk," according to Ephesians 2:10. It all springs from walking by grace through faith in Jesus' **whole gospel**.

The Freedom Of Focusing Only On Jesus
To the degree that a believer is still law-conscious and, therefore, self-conscious (rather than Jesus-conscious) he will be focused on how he behaves according to some "standard." This focus easily leads him to continually estimate an *imagined* fluctuating acceptance and "approval rating" by God. It is based on his performance (works) which determines his "holiness quotient" and his current level of "closeness to God." In short, this is a fleshy self-consciousness which is pre-occupied with one's doing. This is the heresy of Judaism. True Christianity focuses on Jesus and relying on His **finished work** to live a Holy Spirit-led life of grace – just as Jesus did. We are not still on earth to "live *for* God" but here for Him to live through us, as us, responding to His love by yielding to what He leads us to do. That is why Christianity is not a religion but a living relationship of love, lived by faith in the only true God who *is* our liberty.

In contrast to living mentally under law, the believer who trusts in Jesus' **divine exchange** is increasingly convinced of how good God really is. This revelation frees him to enjoy fellowship with all three persons of the Trinity in a loving relationship because he knows that what is true for Jesus is now true for him too – just because he is **in Christ**. Jesus fulfilled and removed the

302

Tree of Law so that every believer could walk by faith in the freedom of His love and intimate fellowship. Jesus revealed the alternative to law-based religion to Paul, revealed in 1 Corinthians 6:12 and 10:23:

All things are lawful for me but not all things benefit. All things are lawful for me but I will not be mastered by any. All things are lawful for me but not all things benefit. All things are lawful for me but not all things build up.

Jesus sent the Holy Spirit to live within each believer to renew our minds to what is truly beneficial according to the ways of God's love in His Kingdom, not according to the ways of the world system or our unsanctified, natural mind. True life flows from the unity and "rest" of a love-based relationship with God and with His children. In contrast, religion imposes law-based requirements and demands, which can't be kept perfectly, and so cause condemnation and the *feeling* of separation from Father-God. It comes from the treadmill of religious activity rather than in the restful relationship of the "country dog" relying on and doting on his master – who is now his point of reference.

As the gift of God's love is increasingly believed in and received, the believer is freed and empowered by the Holy Spirit to respond in love to God and to others - and "… against such things (the nine fruits of the Holy Spirit) there is no law," as Paul joyfully declared in Galatians 5:22. While the law's job was to point out sins and to condemn, God's love, grace and truth, given to others *through* us, demonstrates God's Kingdom of righteousness, peace and joy, only found **in Christ Jesus**. Magnifying Jesus, instead of human sins and foibles, keeps us in the flow of God's love for others – as opposed to being a judgmental fault-finder like the law-minded Pharisees. Paul had been a die-hard Pharisee so he knew what their focus on the law produced. Because he was reborn of God and walked by faith, according to the Holy Spirit, he provides us with some insight on what this new way of living looks like on a day to day basis, described in Philippians 4:4-8.

Rejoice **in the Lord** always. Again, I say, rejoice. Let your gentleness, (patience, moderation) be known to all men. The Lord is near (inside you). Have no anxiety about anything. Rather, in all things, by prayer and supplication with thankfulness, let your petitions be made known to God. And, thereby, shall the peace of God, which exceeds all (natural) understanding, guard your (new) hearts and minds **in Christ Jesus.** Concerning the rest, brothers, meditate (ruminate) on whatever is true, honorable, just, pure, lovely, reputable, virtuous and praiseworthy.

Paul learned to be content and rejoice in all things because he kept his mind on God's **big picture** that is beyond the limitations of the **seen realm**. He knew *Whose* he was and *who* he was and *where* he was positioned – **in Christ**. Magnifying the negatives of this world instead of Jesus, keeps one in bondage and defeat. The **butterfly life** is superior in every way. Yes, sometimes there is need to offer what some call "tough love." I had to do that as an elementary school principal. But it will only bear good fruit in the context of a loving relationship. If you have a God-given opportunity to love a person that way, trust the Holy Spirit to show you if, what, when and how to speak His truth in love like Jesus did. Jesus did not enforce the law and, so, participate in stoning the woman caught in adultery like the law-minded Pharisees were eager to do. Instead, He listened to His Father and treated her with love and respect to demonstrate Father-God's goodness, which brings about true, **New Covenant** repentance – a change of mind.

And if following the Holy Spirit's lead doesn't bring about an immediate turn-around, at least you will be giving them the aroma of God, not the flesh. You planted a seed of truth and light that He can use to woo him or her, over time, to Jesus, who is their Savior, not us. You are God's ambassador of His good news of total forgiveness reconciliation, not His policeman. If you are focused more on "upholding the law" (like I used to be) rather than the welfare of the person, you are not living by God's gift of the higher law of faith, love and liberty like Jesus consistently lived. For your welfare and those around you, I suggest that you ask the Holy Spirit to bathe your mind in His love, forgiveness and peace so that you naturally let Him have His way in and through you.

Living In God's Freedom Is A Choice

If all this seems familiar to you, it may be because I touched on some of this in Chapter Four entitled "The Law of the Spirit of Life." I contrasted the lives of two believers using the analogy of the *city dog* and the *country dog* and emphasized the importance of the renewing of one's mind by a revelation of Jesus' **divine exchange**. The chart (**4A**) on page 54 might be helpful to you (as it continually is to me) as a reminder of how fundamentally different the results of these two ways really are. They are as different as the Mosaic Covenant is from God's **New Covenant** with Jesus. The topics I covered after that chapter were designed to help you:

1) better understand the differences between the two opposing covenants of law and grace and the hazards of mixing the two and

2) realize that God has supplied a new "operational law" to believers, "… the (higher) law of the Spirit of life" that Jesus revealed to Paul, found in Romans 8:2 and in Galatians 5:1-6. It is based on an eternal love relationship with God by His grace through a trusting faith (not by one's faith in rule-keeping) which leads to liberty.

It is the **butterfly life** of Jesus' grace-based covenant. I use the metaphor of a butterfly for two important reasons. First, its four stage life-cycle includes the drastically opposite natures and positions of a crawling caterpillar and a flying butterfly. The butterfly can't skip the caterpillar stage any more than we humans can skip the **in Adam** stage. But a key difference is that, with butterflies, the metamorphosis is a process that automatically produces a butterfly according to God's design. However, with us humans, we all would have remained as **in Adam** "caterpillars" if Jesus' **finished work** on Calvary would not have restored free choice to mankind to accept or reject God's invitation of salvation. Now, we humans can choose to:

1) remain as **in Adam** caterpillars by refusing His invitation to heaven through rebirth or

2) become reborn butterflies who are positioned in heaven but who can still choose to keep crawling around in the flesh, under the law and circumstances on the earth, fatalistically, until we die physically or

3) be reborn butterflies that learn to fly – to live according to the Spirit of life which we were re-created to do and to reign victoriously from our new spirit-self's position **in Christ** by consciously receiving God's abundant grace and being established in His gift of righteousness.

These are the same three choices presented in the three dog chart, with corresponding results listed in each category. Whatever you choose to focus on - such as the world system, the flesh, the law, yourself, others, the devil etc., *or* on Jesus – will produce corresponding outcomes in the **seen realm**. Whatever you mentally magnify will become bigger and bigger to you, absorbing your energy, time and treasure. What you choose to focus on can all but blot out other interests from your mind. Even for believers, wrong believing can produce awful consequences on earth. But right believing produces the Holy Spirit's fruit of right living, here and forever.

More About Life As A Butterfly

You have probably noticed by now that this book has not focused primarily on the unbeliever as much as on the believer who is unwittingly caught in the confusion of trying to live in the quagmire of mixing the two opposing covenants – law vs grace. They are as opposite as a caterpillar is from a butterfly. This incompatibility between the two covenants is analogues to two pairs of opposing forces found in the **seen realm** - namely, gravity and drag, versus lift and thrust - which operate continuously. The law of gravity pulls the butterfly towards earth, and drag slows it down. But the combined forces of lift (which overcome gravity's pull) and thrust, (which overcomes drag) frees the butterfly to enjoy flight.

Before the Wright brothers could invent a machine that flies, they had to figure out what natural forces butterflies and birds were instinctively using that enabled them to overcome the downward pull of gravity and drag. Wind tunnel experiments etc. revealed that the right proportions of lift and thrust could do for humans sitting in machines what birds and butterflies do naturally in order to fly. So, while the Wright brothers could not bring a permanent end to the law of gravity (thankfully), they did discover the mechanics of an alternative "higher law" that enabled them to fly with the butterflies and birds – as long as they provided the required amounts of lift and thrust. However, it takes much effort and expense for humans to counteract the law of gravity because we are not anatomically equipped like butterflies and most birds are.

Similarly, it is not possible for an **in Adam** sinner, who is dead to God spiritually, to live according to God's life in the Spirit. He is still "of Darkness" rather than "of Light in the Lord," and "of earth" rather than "of heaven." But thanks to Jesus' **divine exchange**, walking according to the Spirit is now a privilege for all reborn saints. We are fully equipped to hear God's voice and enabled as **new creations** to live by the carrying power – the lift and thrust - of the Holy Spirit residing within us and wants to live through us, *as us*. This is what it means to operate by faith in what Jesus has already done for us rather than search aimlessly for true life and love and meaning in the chaos of a world system that is corrupt and passing away. While we are still operating *in* this **seen realm**, thankfully we are no longer *of* it because we are now reborn *of* God.

What Did Jesus Focus On?

When Jesus was presented with the challenge to feed thousands of people, He didn't focus on the enormous size of the crowd or the small amount of available food. If He had focused on the **seen** circumstances, He would only get a **seen-based** answer. No, He looked to His **unseen** Father and thanked Him for the provision that He knew was already supplied in the **unseen realm**. How did He know that? Because He was always abiding consciously in His Father as a lifestyle. He went where Father directed and met people's questions and needs with Father's answers and ability and supply - not with His own. Jesus relied on an **unseen** supply of "lift and thrust" from an **unseen** Kingdom that overcame the lack in the natural realm. He brought a manifestation of heaven to earth – as we are now equipped to do as justified and empowered saints **in Him**, by being an expression of His abundant life living in us which is meant to overcome the drag and gravity of circumstances. We are ambassadors of Jesus' **whole gospel** of forgiveness and reconciliation from God.

That is what living in His victorious "resurrection life" is all about. But, sadly, most believers still live like caterpillars under the "gravity" of the Law of Moses – or other self-imposed rule systems - because of ignorance or unbelief. But Jesus has provided deliverance and freedom from the yoke of law at great expense (His blood) and effort (His cross).

But the preponderance of the **elephant of mixture** has so bewitched the church in general for almost 2000 years that Jesus' offer of liberty **in Him** seems threatening or even blasphemous to law-focused people, saints included. The caterpillar-mindset keeps millions of butterfly saints crawling around on the ground, easily stepped on by the world system, the flesh and the devil himself. That is not Christianity; it is works-based religiosity. Jesus drank the cup of the cross to free all those who would believe **in Him** from the curse of a **seen-focused** life – which is no life at all. As quoted in previous chapters, the *Law is not of faith and whatever is not of faith is sin,* which results in various forms of "death" - even while living on earth. Jesus came to reverse all that by the option of abiding **in Him** consciously, which is another name for "walking in the Holy Spirit," who provides true, abundant life.

Transforming The City Dog's Mind
You can take the city dog out of the city but it requires a mind renewed by a revelation of our Savior's love and provision - fully revealed in the **finished work** of His **divine exchange** - to take the "city" of out of the dog. Only then can a believer *mentally* come to be at rest and peace in the Master's constant love and presence. It sure beats the alternative of relying on one's own imperfect efforts that the self-sufficient flesh prefers. But only believing and receiving Jesus' radical **grace gospel** can produce the inner peaceful <u>rest</u> known by the country dog. The following passage from Colossians 2:2-5 is a great summary of Jesus' **grace-based gospel** and why Paul diligently labored to spread this fantastic news wherever and whenever he could.

> May their hearts be comforted and united in love, so that they may have abundant riches of the full assurance of understanding in order that <u>they may know the mystery of God, namely, Christ,</u> in whom are hidden all the treasures of wisdom and knowledge. I tell you this so that no one may deceive you with grandiose words. For though I may be absent from you in body, <u>I am with you in spirit</u> and delight to see your order and the firmness of your faith **in Christ.**

So what is the mystery of God? It is Christ Jesus - whose Spirit is in all believers and is our only "hope of glory," as revealed in Colossians 1:27. He remains a mystery to all who refuse to believe that He *is* who He says He is and He *did* what He came to do – the **divine exchange** that we can now receive and rest in by a walk of trusting faith. Man's natural sight is in opposition to the way God sees – the sight He calls "faith" – which is the ability to see beyond the natural into the **unseen** truth of who He really is and what He has actually *done* **in and through Christ Jesus.** God *has* "made all things new" from His vantage point, according to 2 Corinthians 5:17 and He cannot lie. And, consistent with His gracious nature, He has given believers His fantastic "will and testament" – the **New Covenant gospel of radical grace** – an inheritance that legally belongs to all believers as part of Jesus' **finished work.** But only by faith, reckoning His work as true for you, can you live/abide in and benefit *practically* from it in the **seen realm** and, thereby, impact the world by manifesting His true, Kingdom life.

Manifesting Jesus

Zombies repulse people who are looking for true life. God's abundant life, which He wants to live through us as His branches, is meant to be a manifestation of Him to the world - just as Jesus displayed His Father to the world. He offers to reign through us with His pulsating life of grace, truth, love, glory, authority and power in order to reveal to doubters who He really is. Before Jesus returns to earth, the earth is to be "full of His glory" through His children exhibiting the life and fruit of His **unseen Kingdom** as a testimony to His goodness, meant to benefit all mankind. To repeat: we, who are hidden spiritually **in Christ** in God in the heavenlies, are still physically here on earth to reveal His hidden "treasures of wisdom and knowledge" of what Jesus has done for mankind. This **unseen reality** is hidden to unbelievers. So Father-God desires that all believers be fruitful branches of Jesus, our Vine, manifesting the irresistible fruit of righteousness, peace and joy of a Spirit-led life **in Him.** Then unbelievers can taste and see Jesus through us and be delivered from Darkness into God's glorious Kingdom of Light, by grace through faith **in Him.**

Abiding Consciously In Jesus

But how do you get there from where you are mentally right now? Paul had the challenge of communicating Jesus' revelation of the **unseen reality** of the gospel given to him to save spiritually dead, **in Adam** Gentiles. What did he consistently preach? Certainly not the Law but the absurdity of the cross of Calvary, which is the narrow way that leads to life – Jesus. Once reborn, Jesus' grace-based message given to Paul has the power of God to progressively renew every believer's mind with what Jesus has already done for him so that he can enjoy the full riches of complete understanding and personally know Jesus and His **whole gospel.** This is the amazing mystery that He wants disclosed to *all* the saints and to unbelievers alike.

Feeding saints the dead carcass of mixture, instead of unveiling the mystery of Jesus' **butterfly life**, lived *in, with, through, and by the Spirit of Christ Jesus,* limits (and can even prevent) the manifestation of His will and life that we, as royal ambassadors of His **unseen** Kingdom, are sent throughout the earth to declare. 2 Corinthians 3:6 reveals that "the letter (of the law) kills but the spirit gives life." The **elephant of mixture** that the Jerusalem church was promoting was actually the deception "of fine sounding arguments" that appeals to the sense-based, natural mind but causes sin and death. Paul was delighted to see that the Ephesians and Colossians (unlike the Galatians and the Corinthians) were holding firmly to Jesus' **whole gospel** and ordering their outer life accordingly, in response to God's love, not to the law. Then he continues in Colossians 2:6:

So then, just as you received Christ Jesus as Lord (by grace through faith), *continue to live in Him*, having been rooted and built up **in Him,** established in the faith (Jesus' **grace gospel**) as you were taught, and overflowing with thankfulness.

Notice the progression: to *continue* to

1) live **in Jesus** just the way you first received Him – by God's gift of faith - not by natural sight or effort, and

2) be rooted and built up **in Him** – an illustration of one firmly planted in the rich soil of His grace and truth and maturing and progressively yielding the pleasing bounty of His life-giving fruit as His beloved branch, and

3) be established in Jesus' **grace gospel** that only Paul fully taught, and

4) be overflowing with peace and thankfulness from experiencing the abundant life of an "overcoming" saint who has *come over* **into Christ** - delivered out of the pit of slavery **in Adam** and out of fear and death caused by religiosity.

With such a glorious offer of the fullness of Jesus' abundant life, why would anyone want to go back under the **elephant of mixture** that Paul describes in this revelation found in Colossians 2:8-11:

> Be careful that no one takes you captive through empty and deceptive philosophy (wrong believing), which <u>depends on</u> men's traditions and the basic elements of this (**seen**) world rather than on Christ. **In Christ** (now ascended) dwells <u>all the fullness of the Deity in bodily form, and *having been filled*, you are **in Christ**</u>, who is the head over every power and authority. **In Him** you were also circumcised, in the putting off of the sinful nature (the **in Adam** nature, nailed to the cross), not with a circumcision done by men's hands but with the circumcision done by Christ (by identifying with His crucifixion and death by faith).

Do you grasp what this actually means? "**In Christ** dwells all the fullness of the Deity in bodily form and, **having been filled,** you are **in Christ**" - and so is every reborn believer. Therefore, what is true for the ascended Man, Christ Jesus (who is also fully God) is also true for every believer (who is *not* God, per se, but a sharer in His divine nature, according to 2 Peter 1:4). How about *that* for "making all things new?" That is what it means to be a son *of* someone – an offspring and sharer of that person's nature. A dog cannot share in the nature of a man unless he becomes "of man" which is not possible. An **in Adam** man cannot share in the nature of God - unless and until he is reborn of God. That revelation is the solution to the human dilemma of eternal separation from God caused by being **one with Adam.** Only God Himself can and did eliminate the infinite chasm through Jesus' **divine exchange** with believers!

True believers are, by definition, "born of God." So why settle for less than what Jesus has purchased for you by believing in human traditions and the deceptions of religion or in the "basic elements and ideas of this world" <u>that come from man's natural mind and mere appearances.</u>

Believer, *reject the lie* that you are still a sinner by nature or that you are not totally forgiven and accepted in our beloved Redeemer, Christ Jesus. Don't let that deadly mixture of unbelief undermine your faith but "be established in the faith" of the **whole gospel of grace** that Jesus taught through Paul. Renewing your mind by thinking with the mind of Christ will revamp your belief system to line up with the truth. Knowing the truth about God and about the new you will set you free from any of the self-imposed or church-imposed constraints of the city dog. Step into the freedom of the **unseen Kingdom Life** of the country dog who delights in His loving Savior and Lord. For, through Him, God has already provided everything we need for life here and for godliness above, **in Him**.

Switching From Dogs to Goats and Sheep

In case all this sounds too theoretical, the following two contrasting illustrations of "life in the spirit" will provide additional spiritual insight. The first illustration comes from an article written in 1992 as an attempt to realistically describe the "difficulties" of walking in the spirit, based on Galatians, Chapter Five. The Catholic writer, who was baptized in the Spirit, was correct in pointing out the twin dangers of legalism and license. He defined legalism as "trying to earn God's favor by keeping the law," and license as "abusing our freedom by giving in to our selfish desires." He writes further that "legalism comes from good intentions and hidden pride. License comes from bad intentions and open pride. The flesh (as this author defines it) … is the force of gravity that tries to pull us off the high ground." (Note: He does not explain what the flesh actually is.) He illustrates the tension between the two extremes of legalism and license with the word picture of a "hogback trail" along the top of a mountain ridge, pictured below as **19B**. (Since I have never seen one up close, I am relying on the writer's description of what distinguishes it from other mountain trails.)

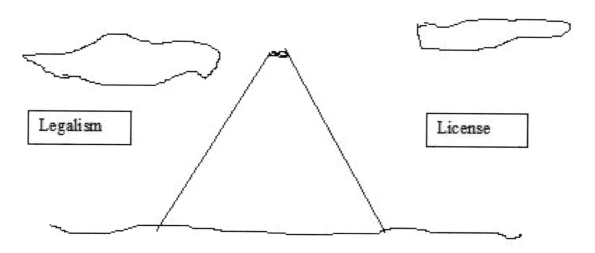

19B   A Hogback Trail – end view

Notice that the ridge of the mountain does not come to a point but has a relatively very small, flattened space all along the ridge. According to him, this trail is sometimes no wider than a foot path, making it possible to have one foot sliding down one side of the treacherous slope and the other foot down the other side. The two sides of the ridge, says the author, represent the lure of the law on one side and the lure of license on the other. He contends that the selfish flesh likes both sides but resists the "life in the Holy Spirit" represented by the narrow path. This picture, he insists, is consistent with Jesus words "… narrow is the path that leads to life" in Matthew 4:17.

While this may seem right to our natural experience and to the pitfalls that trouble an unbeliever, it is not the spiritual position of a believer from God's viewpoint. I agree that "narrow is the way" for those who Jesus was addressing - **pre-cross**. There is only one way for an unbeliever to be saved and come *into* the knowledge of the truth – Christ Jesus, through rebirth. Again, there is absolutely no other possible path to God or to heaven than by being reborn of God by grace through faith **in Christ Jesus.**

But, after rebirth takes place, is the narrow hogback trail (and its two treacherous slopes) fit for a reborn, dependent sheep or for stubborn goats? Goats naturally find it appealing to test and trust their skills to climb the slopes. God designed them that way. However, Jesus did *not* describe *humans* as skillful, independent goats but as sheep *needing a shepherd*. Why? Because He knew just how foolish, helpless and wayward we can think and behave in this fallen world because of our self-centered flesh (sarx, in Greek) and unsanctified soul – our outer man. (If a sheep gets turned over on his back, he is helpless.)

God knows how helpless and dependent we actually are in the Big Picture. But we don't always want to admit that by pridefully thinking that we are "strong in ourselves." Unfortunately, the immature, self-dependent, law-minded *believer*, the "city dog," still strong in his own soul-power, might take the challenge (like the Israelites did) of walking on the narrow trail - according to the flesh. In that case, he will have to do some slipping and sliding and tumbling until he is finally convinced that only his Good Shepherd has already provided a much better place **in Himself** – a pasture of rest and peace and protection for His sheep to feed on, pictured in diagram **19C**.

Just how much rescuing and mind-renewal an immature believer needs will depend on how much he still relies on his ignorant, stubborn, faithless and selfish flesh (mind-sets, attitudes and appetites left-over from the crucified former self) and natural thinking to lead him. That is why Jesus sent the Holy Spirit into our new, perfect, regenerated spirit – to renew our mind with His truth, the revelation of the **whole gospel of grace**. As we willingly yield and let Him renew our *minds* with His truth and to direct us, He will gladly lead and guide us into the experience of His lush green pastures of abundant life - His righteousness, peace and joy in the Holy Spirit – which our inner man already enjoys **in Christ**. The good fruit will be His unselfish love for God, for the new self and for others, the way Jesus lived on earth.

That is why Paul remarked "When I am weak then He is strong." And when are we "weak?" From God's viewpoint, *always*. He knows the strength of the opposition – the world system, the selfish flesh and the devil. Our unsanctified natural mind, no matter how intelligent or disciplined or moral it might seem be, is no match for this collective threat to the well-being of our vulnerable outer man. That is why He has already given us His righteousness, peace and joy that "passes all understanding" - the Kingdom of God - in our inner man to operate from. This benefit for the soul is found only through life **in Christ Jesus**, whose loving care protects us from the treacherous peaks of the mixture of legalism or license – even though our stinkin' thinkin' prefers them. This is the essence of the mental battle that can rage between the wisdom of the Holy Spirit who is living in our spirit-self and the mixture of truth and lies and emotions and circumstances and confusing choices that can trouble our unsanctified body and soul.

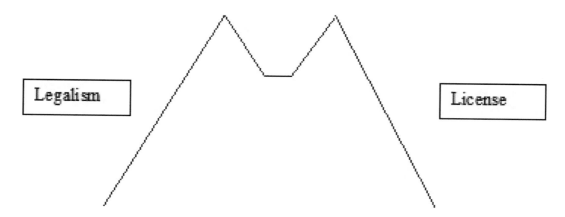

19C Our Good Shepherd's valley of rest and refreshment for His sheep, alive **in Him**

Beholding Jesus

God's **unseen Kingdom** is part of the "all things new" change in the landscape that we, as His saints, are now a part of – the landscape of the **heavenly realms** which becomes more obvious and experiential to the degree we consistently set our mind on things above like Jesus did. This option is the **unseen reality**, only found **in Christ**, since we died and are now alive **in Him**, according to Colossians 3:1-3. This is *not* the "valley of the shadow of death" because spiritual death has been defeated for those **in Christ**. (Endnote **#44** explains the difference between "sin" and "sinning" in Jesus' gospel to Paul.) This is the **unseen** valley of life, described in Psalm 23:1-2, with its overflowing streams of living water, i.e. the Holy Spirit. He is now alive *in* us, not just to sip from occasionally when we are desperate but to "swim in" (be baptized/immersed in) like Jesus was - letting Him carry you and refresh you and enliven you from inside out.

The following is an *updated* word picture, based on Psalm 1:2-3, but seen through the lens of Jesus' **grace gospel**. It reveals what the **unseen** valley's true life is like, which is now fully available to us by faith **in Christ Jesus,** our Good Shepherd:

> Blessed is anyone who delights in the (higher) law of the Lord and meditates on Jesus, (the fulfillment and replacement of the Mosaic Law for the Jews), day and night. Jesus is the tree of life, who we are now one with, which has been planted beside the running waters of the Holy Spirit, who provides His fruit in His time. Jesus' leaf will never wither and die. And in all things a believer does, in and through Jesus, he will prosper.

I know I have switched from caterpillars and butterflies to sheep, but the former is where we believers start because our natural mind is first formed in the caterpillar stage of being **in Adam** in Darkness and in the fallen world's foolish and corrupt system. But the Holy Spirit's mission is to sanctify and transform our <u>outer man</u> into a cooperative servant of our new, reborn spirit-self (who is already perfect **in Christ**, according to Hebrews 10:14). Why? So that Christ will be formed in my unsanctified outer man, which is progressively "being made holy," even as the Holy Spirit is already in union with my inner, holy and perfect spirit-self. The fleshy, goat-life of self-effort frustrates that transformation of my soul. However, the dependent life of a willing sheep focused on Jesus, the Good Shepherd (like the country dog, waiting on his master), progressively changes into the maturity of a resting, yet productive saint, bearing the Holy Spirit's fruit, by grace through faith, rather than the counter-productive works of the self-centered flesh.

Effortless Change

All real and lasting change that Jesus made possible at Calvary for all believers is effortless. Why? Because it is accomplished by the working of the Holy Spirit, living His life through a yielded vine/butterfly/sheep, rather than by the deception of the **elephant of mixture** or by the self-effort of one's self-centered flesh. (Remember: if you prefer, you can take the daily challenge of staying on top of the narrow hog trail by focusing on avoiding legalism or license to accomplish any "character change." But then *you* will have to expend your energy to constantly maintain that position – or slip down the mountain.) All the Holy Spirit needs is our ongoing agreement and permission. "Yes Lord, have your way, Holy Spirit. "Thank you Jesus." By learning to depend on and rest in the Holy Spirit's wisdom, direction and power from within (right believing), every saint can then dedicate his soul and body – God's temple – to be *instruments of his or her righteous* inner spirit-self – which is already *one* with **Christ** (see Romans 6:13). Listening to and yielding to the Holy Spirit, like Jesus did, will progressively bear the good fruit of right living. This is God's ordained way to victorious, holy living in the **seen realm** - even as your holy, spirit-self is already victorious in the **unseen realm,** seated with Christ in the heavenlies.

Right believing **in Christ Jesus** and His **whole gospel of grace** will inevitably lead to right living - the **butterfly life**. When you work, God rests; but when you rest **in Him** and in a revelation of His love and **finished work**, He is free to work in and through you, as you. Jesus accomplished all that needs to happen some 2000 years ago and our part is to believe and receive and cooperate with all that He has done. As recorded in John 4:34: "Jesus said: 'My food is that I may do the will of Him who sent me and that I may finish His work.'" He finished the work of salvation at Calvary, from God's viewpoint. Nothing that you or I *do* can improve upon His perfect work, done on our behalf. (It would be like you trying to fix the Mona Lisa painting with a hatchet.)

Learning to Rest In Jesus

At one point in Jesus' ministry, recorded in John 6:28-29, a crowd asked Him:

'… What should we do, so that we may perform the works of God?' Jesus said to them, 'This is the work of God, that you <u>believe</u> **in Him** (Jesus) whom He (God) sent.'

They were trying to figure out how to multiply food and do the other miracles that Jesus did. His answer was the same as it has always been – by believing, trusting, depending on the **unseen reality** of Father-God and His Word, Who is now alive in every reborn saint. In this particular case, they were looking *at* the man Jesus Himself. He had laid His deity aside and took on human form to make possible the greatest miracle of all - salvation for all who simply believe **in Him** as the living Word - the **gospel of grace**. Jesus the Man walked by faith in His Father through the ability of the Holy Spirit to will and to do our Father's good pleasure – from boyhood to Calvary and beyond. He invites everyone to do the same, **in and through Him.**

But **in Adam** sinners can only **enter** the covenant Father-God made with the last Adam through the gift of rebirth by faith in His **finished work.** Any other human work is as filthy rags by comparison to His qualifying work – which has always been the case. So give up your efforts to "clean yourself up" or "save yourself" or "become holy" or "come closer to God." Instead, believe Him, receive His rebirth and learn to rest in His never-ending love for you and His gifts of righteousness and holiness that are now yours and true of you *because you are reborn into union with Him by faith.* Trust in the security of His hidden "valley-life" where there is righteousness, peace and joy in the Holy Spirit. That, my friend, is the **unseen reality** of God's **eternal Kingdom**, now within you. It is the highlands for **butterflies** who abide consciously **in Christ Jesus.** What else could Paul's advice to "set your mind on things above" mean? God's Kingdom is where He is, and He is in you and you are **in Him.** That is the glorious reality of our **New Covenant** from Christ Jesus. Awesome!

The Divine Escape

Some people travel to the mountains to escape the soulish confusion of human demands and threats and anxieties and round-the-clock news etc. But peace *with* Father-God and the peace and rest that He supplies to reborn saints who learn to walk in the revelation of all that Jesus has done, provides the true refreshment that our weary, unsanctified outer man desperately needs. Worshipping all three Persons of the Trinity "in spirit and in truth" for who They are and for what They have accomplished for me helps sanctify my mind as I focus on Them – whenever and wherever I am. Singing songs, hymns and spiritual songs to Father-God about who He really is and about His **finished work,** which is now mine **in Christ Jesus,** wells up gratitude and love for God spontaneously. Nothing refreshes me more than Jesus-centered thinking and worship, inspired and enabled by the Holy Spirit. May the song poems, found in many of these chapters, bless and refresh you in this way.

Hopefully it has become clear to you by now that struggling under a mixture of law and grace prevents the sense of peace and freedom that Abba-Father wants all His children to continually enjoy **in Christ Jesus.** My prayer is that you agree with God and be done with the deception of mixture by asking the Holy Spirit to renew your mind to the **whole gospel of lavish grace** in order to set you (and the church) free in these last days. The next chapter will present Jesus revelation to Paul on how to stand against the lies of the devil and enforce Jesus' victory over Darkness with the truth of Jesus' **divine exchange.**

Here is a simple song-poem that invites the Holy Spirit to <u>have His way in you</u>. He inspires requests like this so that He can supply what is best for us day by day from the storehouse of Jesus' **finished work**. Believers already please Father-God just by being in His beloved Son. The following song refers to our walk in the outer man.

HELP ME TO PLEASE YOU
In all I think in all I do and say.
Holy Spirit have Your way.

Help me to hear You
No matter where I am, each night and day.
Holy Spirit have Your way.

Let me see as you see, help me love with Your love
You're my potter, O Lord, I'm Your clay.
Holy Spirit, my Sanctifier, Holy Spirit, have Your way.
© Copyright 2003 by Leonard J. Ransil

CHAPTER TWENTY

STAND WITH CHRIST JESUS AGAINST THE WILES OF THE DEVIL

"Jesus came that He might destroy the works of the devil" (1 John 3:8).

The true core of Christianity is all about our literal location/position spiritually – being **in Christ** and Him in us - then being renewed mentally to the **unseen reality** of our new spirit-self now seated **with Him** in heavenly places, according to Ephesians 2:6. Of course, this is all foreign to a believer's unsanctified soul that had been enslaved by the old, **Adamic nature** which has been crucified with Christ and is now gone. Why is it foreign? Because our outer man can only think and form beliefs by the perceptions of the five senses or by our imagination which is also primarily dependent upon sensate experiences. The natural mind is unable to perceive and directly connect with the **unseen realm** except by such things as 1) receiving divine revelation of truth by hearing or reading the Word of Christ or 2) when Christ Jesus physically appeared to the disciples, **post-cross**, or 3) when a spirit being – a good angel or evil demon - takes on a physical appearance or 4) by demonic activity against those under his dominion or influence.

Therefore, the natural mind of man is not reliable in comprehending and distinguishing between the hidden workings of the two, opposing, **unseen Kingdoms** - light versus dark. That is why a believer needs the Holy Spirit's discernment and power to successfully resist the devil's lies and temptations. He can masquerade as an angel of light and deceive us as easily as he did Adam if we depend on our natural thinking. As always, walking according to the Holy Spirit is only done by grace through faith, supplied as gifts, to enable us to reign in the **seen realm** as we saints already do with Him in the **unseen realm – in and through Christ Jesus**.

Enforcing Jesus' Victory

So, the only reliable way to walk victoriously on earth is through the gift of the discerning of spirits, which Jesus revealed to Paul in 1 Corinthians 12:10, and enforcing Jesus' victory over Darkness through the authority and power of the Holy Spirit who resides in each believer. The manifestations of the Holy Spirit, which Paul enumerated as "gifts," are actually a part of God's equipping of His saints so that we can bless others and reign in this **seen** life through Christ Jesus, according to Romans 5:17. And when we reign **in and through Him,** the world system, the flesh and the devil can't override our true self. We are winners, even if our outer man is martyred, like happened to overcomers like Stephen, Paul and Peter, who made God their point of reference. In other words, they put their focus on Christ Jesus and their eternal citizenship in God's **unseen Kingdom** rather than on this passing world.

Historically, the institutional church has generally preferred the **elephant of mixture** and ignored or even denounced and martyred those believing and walking according to the Holy Spirit's direction, power and gifting. Dr. Eddie Hyatt chronicles this doctrinal struggle in his inspiring book titled *2000 Years Of Charismatic Christianity*. Depending on law-keeping, instead of on the liberating work of the Holy Spirit, results in "deadness" and even depression and defeat in both personal and congregational life. Just because a church has a lot of activities to keep people busy does not mean that believers are enjoying Jesus' abundant life as He defines it.

Ignorance Is Not Bliss

Any believer who remains ignorant of God's equipment and strategy in the battle going on within his mind (as opposed to his perfect spirit-self **in Christ**), is easy prey to deception – just like Adam was. Jesus understood who was tempting Him in the desert and used the sword of the Spirit, the Word of God, to declare the truth of how things work in the **unseen realm** to thwart the devil's lies. Again, Jesus revealed to Paul that man is a tri-part being – a spirit-being with a soul that lives in a body. The battle ground over right and wrong believing is in the soul – one's natural mind, will and emotions – rather than in a believers' spirit-self. Why? Because one's *spirit* is either **in Adam** - and, therefore, dead to God - or is **in Christ** and, therefore, is alive to God through rebirth and is *not* subject to evil influence. Why? Because the new, inner man is seated **in Christ** in the heavenlies. There are no devils in heaven to bother you. The mental battleground is the believing, thinking, feeling and choosing powers of a believer's unsanctified soul and the appetites of his body that the devil tries to influence and manipulate in order to override the wisdom of your new spirit-self, now one with Christ Jesus. There may be a battle in your mind between the two, **unseen** spiritual kingdoms but you are now **in Christ**, and the devil's devices are no match for the Holy Spirit, living inside of each believer.

Why is one's soul the main battlefield with the devil? Because the soul is where thoughts are weighed, beliefs are formed and then choices are made to accept or reject God's life and His wonderful ways, day by day. Each person's temperament, nurturing, perceptions, environment and experiences, both good and bad, can influence his choices – but don't have to. Trusting in and yielding yourself to the Holy Spirit as your Teacher, Guide, Counselor, Guard, Sanctifier, Friend and Enabler the way Jesus did, will produce the same fruits of the abundant life which Jesus walked in and which He now offers to all who focus on Him. That is what it means to make Jesus <u>your point of reference</u> – also known as meditating on and *consciously* interacting with Him as your constant companion. Jesus sent the Holy Spirit into you so that you can enjoy Jesus as your King and coming Bridegroom.

The Lust Of The Sarx

The believer's new heart and spirit-self is in union with God and, therefore, he has the mind of Christ *available* to him to think God's thoughts about anything and everything like Jesus did. However, the mental remnants from the believer's former conditioning such as negative habits (which might even be physically grooved onto the brain's surface), mind-sets ("I'm a sinner saved by grace" or "rich people are evil"), and strongholds (erroneous beliefs about God) etc., are opposed to the life-giving wisdom and blessings of the Holy Spirit. Again, Jesus sent Him to progressively transform the outer man into conformity with the way Father-God sees, thinks and operates. Initially, a new believer might feel swamped with the old mental patterns and dictates of the self-centered flesh (the *sarx*, in Greek) and continue to depend on his natural sight or on the letter of the Law. But often there is a God-given hunger for the truth of God's word to provide wisdom and direction as the Holy Spirit leads. Maturity is a process of learning to walk in accordance with the Spirit that is united with the believer's spirit, and think God's thoughts of what is true and lovely and worthy of praise etc. rather than according to the cravings of the flesh. It is our choice whether or not to "let your hearts be troubled" by casting your cares on Jesus and setting your mind on the things above instead of rehearsing and magnifying negative circumstances. It is the way to walk in Jesus' peace and victory.

316

That is why Jesus revealed the necessity of renewing one's mind after rebirth to be increasingly conformed to the power of His ways of life in His love-based Kingdom Why? So that the soul will operate in submissive harmony with the believer's sinless spirit-self that is one with God Himself. The carnal mind can be increasingly transformed through the ongoing sanctification and cleansing by the Holy Spirit, using the living Word of truth, especially Christ Jesus' **whole gospel** given to Paul. Trusting faith arises when we focus on God's love for us, clearly demonstrated in Jesus' **divine exchange** which He provided for all who believe **in Him**. Meditating on His glorious work and its implications, through the Holy's Spirit's revelation-knowledge of Jesus' **whole gospel**, renews one's mind beyond the limitations of the five senses. Thinking God's thoughts generates a love for God, based on eternal truth rather than on one's conflicting thoughts and fluctuating emotions which produce bad choices (see Ephesians 3:16-19). Because Jesus knows first-hand how wonderful His **unseen Kingdom** really is, He exhorts us through Paul in Romans 12:2 to:

> No longer be squeezed into the mold of this (temporary, **seen**) world, but instead, be transformed by the renewal of your (natural) mind, so that you may discern and demonstrate all that is good, acceptable and perfect, according to God's wonderful will (His intention and inheritance) for you (according to the Holy Spirit's wisdom).

His word tells us that the three forces that want to squeeze your outer man into godless conformity are:

1) the world system based on circumstances and selfish interests (yours or other people's)

2) your independent-minded flesh *dwelling in you* (which is reinforced by the *leftover,* wrong assumptions, impulses, self-centered habits, misguided desires, selfish motives, appetites, mind-sets etc. of the old, **in Adam** self, now crucified, buried and gone) and other people's flesh, and

3) the devil who is out to steal, kill and destroy God's best plan and purpose for you through deception.

Of the three, the most insidious enemy against your new spirit-self is the flesh because it *dwells within* and is spring-loaded to focus on your soul's self-centered interests, passions and self-preservation. This fleshly mind-set of "looking out for # 1" as one's point of reference, competes with the believer's new heart and spirit-self which are united with **Christ** and which are spring-loaded towards God and in harmony with the Holy Spirit.

I Am Not The Enemy

In Romans 7:17 and 21, Paul says that the flesh, where "no good dwells," is *not* himself but it is "sin dwelling in me." He is careful to distinguish between his new spirit-being, soul and body (which are *not* sinful, per se) and the "flesh" that *dwells in him* and *is* "sin." The flesh is *not* the same as the old, **in Adam** self because the latter was crucified upon rebirth and is now gone. Paul also describes this as a war between the Mosaic Law, (given only to the Jews to whom Romans Chapter 7:1 is addressed) and a "law of sin being in my members" – the flesh – in verse 23. Some have described the flesh as a monster that "makes" us feel and do hideous things. Paul *sounded* helpless in this struggle between the demands of the Law (and his inability to keep them perfectly) and the flesh bent on trying to justify itself. The Law is not the monster but it exposes and arouses the monster *dwelling in us*. So what is the remedy? In Romans 8:1-2, Paul triumphantly declares that, despite our failures to "do good:"

> There is therefore now no condemnation for those who are **in Christ Jesus**. For the (higher) Law of the Spirit of life set me free from the (Mosaic) law of sin and death.

Jesus fulfilled and replaced the Law of the Jews (for Jewish believers) and gave both Jews and Gentiles (who entrust themselves to Him through rebirth) a **New Covenant** of total grace in which He supplies everything that is needed for life and godliness. By degrees, Paul learned to rest and be content in God's generous supply, despite what went on around him in the **seen realm**. That is also why Jesus sent the Sanctifier inside of me and you to *replace* wrong beliefs and *law-mindedness* and our former self's polluted ways. Why? Because they are incompatible with who I now am **in Christ**. My inner spirit self *is* now compatible with God's heavenly ways of dependent faith, agape love and liberty **in Christ Jesus**. They characterize the real me, in unity with the Holy Spirit.

But, like Paul, our mind must be willing to partner with and yield to the Holy Spirit to progressively overcome, by His power, the three enemies of our real self. The key to willingly trust and cooperate with the Holy Spirit is to come to deeply know and to personally embrace Abba-Father's unconditional love for *you*, demonstrated through what He did for you through Jesus' **divine exchange**. Then, you will be increasingly free *mentally* to let Him express His life through your yielded soul and body. That is the essence of Jesus' prayer through Paul in Ephesians 3:14-19 that He prayed for them and for us. <u>Our role is to keep our eyes of faith focused on Jesus and His **whole gospel of grace** that realigns our beliefs with the truth of how good Father-God really is and who we now are **in Christ Jesus.**</u>

> By reason of God's grace, I bend my knees to the Father of our Lord Jesus Christ, from whom every family in heaven and on earth takes its name. I ask Him to grant to you, in accord with the wealth of His glory and by His power, to become mighty through His Spirit in the *inner man* so that Christ may live in your hearts through faith, <u>having been rooted and grounded in (God's) love</u> (for you) so that you may be given strength to know and to embrace, with all the saints, what is the width and length and height and depth of <u>Christ's love for you</u>, that surpasses all knowledge, so that you may be filled with all the fullness of God.

Dead To Self, Alive To God

Before His own crucifixion, Jesus said to His disciples: 'If anyone desires to come after Me, let him utterly deny (disown, reject) himself and take up his cross, and follow Me" (Matthew 16:24). Now that you understand that:

1) every human being (except Jesus) starts off with a corrupted, **in Adam** nature, totally incompatible with heaven, and that

2) Jesus would later ascend into heaven and sit next to His perfectly holy Father, the necessary transaction He was pointing to becomes clear. By accepting Jesus' offer of salvation by faith **in Him**, our original nature **in Adam** dies through identification with Jesus' death. Then, we instantly receive a new, reborn nature, compatible with divinity by being made one with God **in Christ**. That is accomplished by agreeing to be reborn of God by faith in Jesus' **finished work.** It is never about what we "do" by our own initiative but about receiving what Jesus did 2000 years ago by His obedience of faith, as Paul states in Romans 1:5.

Again, this **unseen** transaction, revealed in the **whole gospel of grace** included:

1) our own crucifixion, death and burial of our old, **in Adam** self, with Christ and

2) the regeneration of our new, spirit-self in its place and

3) our ascension with Jesus into the heavenlies – all by identification with Jesus, by faith.

But God's regeneration of our spirit-self does not automatically defeat the flesh that dwells within us. Nor does it automatically transform our outer man – our soul and body side. So the Holy Spirit, dwelling in our inner, spirit-self, works to:

1) neutralize the impact of the negative impulses of the flesh as we learn to yield, instead, to His life through us and

2) to renew our soul with the revelation knowledge of our **divine exchange** with Jesus so that we can rightly believe, think and walk victoriously on earth, day to day, the way Jesus walked.

We have the same Holy Spirit in us that Jesus needed to respond to Father-God's voice out of love for Him while on earth. That is the **butterfly life** of faith, love and liberty **in Christ Jesus** that He died to provide to us, as God's own, beloved children.

Resisting The Adversary

However, there is spiritual opposition that would use the flesh and our unsanctified, soulish ways against us to undermine a victorious walk here on earth. Jesus revealed the source of this opposition to John in Revelation 12:10-11.

And I (the Apostle John) heard a great voice in heaven, saying: 'Now salvation and power and the Kingdom of our God and the authority of his Christ has come. For the accuser of our brothers (Satan) has been thrown down (from heaven to earth), he who accused them (the righteous saints) before our God day and night. And they (the saints) overcame him by the blood of the Lamb and by the word of their testimony and they loved not their own soul, even unto death.'

How did the saints defeat the Accuser? Satan is defeated by:

1) the blood of Jesus – which I take to mean walking by receptive faith in the benefits of His blood-bought **divine exchange** with me and, then, enforcing His victory through the Holy Spirit over the world system, my own flesh and the Kingdom of Darkness which is done by

2) declaring the word of my testimony – the truth of God's love and goodness towards me. He demonstrated His love when He made me one in spirit with Him, **in Christ Jesus**, through the resurrection power of God's own life in the person of the Holy Spirit and

3) being reborn of God gives me a new spiritual identity as His child and places me in His Kingdom of authority and power, with a new focus and purpose – God Himself – instead of being focused on justifying or preserving myself.

The result is a return to God's original intention for mankind: to know Him, love Him and abide with Him forever <u>as our primary reason for existing</u>. It is a return to depending on God as our true point of reference. Paul referred to this new reality as being "dead to self and alive to God" and "crucified to the world" because we are no longer of it, just in it, the same way Jesus was, **pre-cross.** That new mind-set is a huge difference from **seen-based** thinking because it emphasizes the reality of our new, **unseen unity** with the triune God, through Christ Jesus' **New Covenant,** which He ratified permanently for us in His own blood. <u>That is our new testimony</u>.

This change of perspective (repentance) is more than just some esoteric theory with me. Not long after being saved and baptized in the Holy Spirit, I was using a cheap, electric door plane at my home. Accidentally, my right index finger (which I use to play saxophone and guitar) slipped into the whirling blade. In a blink of an eye, I pulled it back to discover that my finger-print area was badly lacerated, even though my fingernail and bone were not affected. Upon seeing my blood squirting out, I could feel myself begin to faint, probably from shock. Just then, a thought, clear as if spoken, said: "That is not you." The revelation that my *life* was **not** ebbing away (because my mutilated body part was not the *real me*) brought me back to my senses. I then calmly put a <u>butterfly</u> bandage on it and it healed in a few days. The faint scar that remains there reminds me that my body is but a tent in which my soul and my true, perfect spirit-self reside - temporarily.

The New Sight Of Divine Faith

Jesus' **whole gospel** unveiled to Paul reveals that my new spirit-self, within my physical body, is a temple of God here on earth and that I am also **in Christ** in heavenly places. He lives in me and I am **in Him,** which means that my spirit-self is not confined to my physical body. Seeing yourself **in Christ** positionally in the heavenlies, by faith, enables you to learn to operate *from* Jesus' victorious position of authority and power to *enforce* His victory over the devil - rather than *trying to gain* victory over him by one's inferior, soulish strength. It is not by the puny might or power of the believer's unsanctified outer man that can successfully engage the two **unseen** Kingdoms. Instead, it is by the might and power of the Holy Spirit within - who is now in unity with every believer's spirit-self **in Christ**. Our position **in Christ** is obviously superior to the Kingdom of Darkness, which Jesus defeated at Calvary.

But we can only enforce that victory by operating in the power of the Holy Spirit by faith in Jesus' victory over Darkness and in His subsequent **divine exchange** with us. Knowing and believing in the truth of our righteous standing **in Christ** equips us to discern and confidently stand against the devil's wiles and snares through groundless accusation and lies. As always, keep your <u>focus</u> on Jesus and on the truth of His **whole gospel of grace** rather than on yourself or on others or on the Law or on the lies of the devil, who still tries to use the law to distract, condemn and defeat you. Remember: It is always about Jesus!

Standing Firm In Christ, My Armor

Jesus revealed to Paul that the reality of spiritual warfare is against Darkness, not with other humans, per se, according to Ephesians 6:12. But again, our proper role is in *enforcing* Jesus' victory over Darkness that He accomplished at Calvary, not trying to *cause* victory by our own, inferior strength. He emphasizes the importance of operating from our position of strength and victory **in Him** and describes His protection over us by appropriately using the analogy of battle gear in Ephesians 6:10-18.

> … be empowered in the Lord, by the might of His strength. Be clothed in the armor of God, so that you may be able to stand against the treachery of the devil. For we are not wrestling against flesh and blood, but against principalities and powers, against the rulers of this world of darkness, against the spirits of wickedness in high places. Because of this, take up the whole armor of God, so that you may be able to resist in the evil day, having worked out all things, to stand. Therefore, stand firm, having been girded about your waist with the <u>belt of truth</u>, and having been clothed with the <u>breastplate of righteousness</u>, and having <u>feet shod with the preparation of the Gospel of peace</u>. Above all things, take up the <u>shield of faith</u>, with which you will be able to extinguish all the fiery darts of the devil. And take up the <u>helmet of salvation</u> and the <u>sword of the Spirit</u> - which is the Word (voice) of God. Praying always with all prayer and supplication and perseverance in the Spirit for all the saints.

All this is another way of stating that victory over Darkness can only be ours by being clothed **with** and **in Christ Jesus Himself** as our armor, then exercising His authority over the enemy from our position of victory **in Him**. Remember, in God's **unseen Kingdom**, the Giver is the gift. He does not give us pieces of armor or other spiritual gifts apart from Himself – like the material gifts we give to others in the **seen realm.** No, Christ Jesus *is* my armor and no evil can pierce through Him to get to the real spirit-me because it would have to go through the now triumphant and exalted Christ Jesus first. Why? It is because of my new position as a reborn saint, **in Him**. Christ Jesus is now my eternal fortress, refuge and security. Like David, who met Goliath, yet focused on God, my confidence is in Jesus' victorious power, not in my doing.

Jesus Is My Belt Of Truth

However, my unsanctified soul and body are vulnerable to the devil's deception, tempting me to remain **seen**-focused, so I need to replace his lies and accusations with the revelation of Jesus' **divine exchange** with me. Understanding this transaction reveals the full extent of His salvation for my perfect spirit-self and His corresponding provision for my soul and body. This monumental revelation proves how wonderful and inclusive God's love for me really is, demonstrated by all that I now am and have **in Christ**. Like a belt holds my physical clothes in place, the <u>truth</u> of Jesus' **whole gospel of grace** sanctifies, integrates and unifies my soul with my inner man, now unified with Jesus, who *is* my belt of truth. That union is the central revelation of God's purpose for the various benefits of Jesus' salvation, righteousness and abundant life. Jesus is my *way* to Father-God, my *truth* that defeats the devil's lies and my *life* source - the very reason for my existence because He created me and holds all things, including me, together. When I died to my old, **in Adam** self, Jesus, the last Adam, became my new point of reference. I am now free to focus on Him, instead of being pre-occupied with me and my needs as the devil wants me to do. Believer, it really *is* all about Jesus!

Jesus is now my new reality, whether I am mentally conscious of Him that way or not at any given time. However, when I consciously choose to see Him as my way, my life and my truth belted around me, it encourages me to mentally focus on Him for everything else - as my source and provider, my all-in-all. This is the central meaning behind Jesus' direction through Paul to "bring into captivity every thought into the obedience of Christ," according to the original Greek text of 2 Corinthians 10:5b. In other words, we are to focus on Jesus' perfect performance, not our obedience to Him, which sometimes falters and fails.

What was the ultimate result of "the obedience of Christ" to His Father? It was the **finished work** of His **divine exchange** offered to mankind! It is faith in that revelation of His unselfish love in action which produces the freedom from all forms of bondage such as disease, mental strongholds, addictions, oppression, depression etc. that have plagued even believers for 2000 years. Yes, it was for freedom that Christ Jesus set all believers free – from His viewpoint – as new creation spirit-beings. This *legal* inheritance of the **unseen Kingdom**'s benefits becomes our *vital experience* in the **seen realm** through exercising a dependent, trusting faith in the whole Word of Christ, the **gospel of grace** and love, unveiled to us and through us by the Holy Spirit.

Jesus Is My Breastplate of Righteousness
Jesus is also my righteousness, the breastplate meant to protect my vulnerable soul from the arrows of Satan's accusation which cause needless stress, fear, shame and guilt which come from groundless condemnation against believers. The devil uses the **elephant of mixture** to confuse God's righteous saints **in Christ** about the basis of their righteousness. He wants you to put your eyes on yourself and measure your behavior against some standard to determine if God still loves you and/or is pleased with you. Then he will tell you that any wrong behavior makes you "unrighteous" so you must "repent" by confessing your sins to get God's forgiveness in order to restore your right-standing with God. This works-based process is no gospel at all but the heresy of Galatianism. Why? Because it is based on your doing, not on the gift of Jesus' **finished work** of total forgiveness of all mankind of all sin for all time. Jesus is my righteousness - right standing - with my Father-God, 24/7, regardless of what I do, because true Christianity is about depending on the gift of His **finished work** for me, not putting faith in my doing. See Chapters Thirteen and Fourteen if you need a refresher of this vital revelation. Through rebirth, by faith in Jesus' doing, I am now the righteousness of God **in Christ**. He has imparted His gift of righteousness to me as part of His **divine exchange**.

My Feet Are Shod With The Gospel Of Peace
How beautiful upon the mountains are the feet of the messenger and the preacher of peace! Announcing good news and preaching peace, they are saying to Zion, 'Your God reigns!'(Isaiah 52:7).

Imagine the jubilation when a runner come back to Jerusalem and announced to its fearful inhabitants that God had just enabled the shepherd boy named David to win a decisive victory over Goliath and his hoards. Yet, how much greater for *all* of mankind it is that King Jesus has forever won the colossal battle over Satan who held mankind captive since Adam? There is no more important victory in human history. But the news of God's forgiveness and reconciliation toward mankind has been greatly blunted and distorted by the **elephant of mixture** for some 2000 years. Consequently, believers sometimes try to *cause* victory against an **unseen** enemy by their well-intentioned but useless efforts. Instead, our call is to rest in Jesus' **finished work** of His **divine exchange,** which equips us saints to enforce His victory over Darkness at Calvary by declaring the **whole gospel of grace** from our secure position **in Christ** in the heavenlies.

Again, it is the difference between attacking an enemy's mountaintop stronghold, by starting from the valley floor as opposed to operating from a superior position in the heavenlies **in Christ** over an already defeated, groveling foe. We were no match for the devil in our former selves. But the good news is that we are no longer our former selves or still under the devil **in Adam**. We have been placed **in Christ** Jesus, our Victor. So, "... in all these things (attacks) we are more than conquers through Him (Jesus) who loves us" (Romans 8:37).

That revelation of the shoes of Jesus' **gospel of grace** and peace with God **in Christ**, assures me ultimate victory, no matter what happens to my body. Wow! As I learn to mentally abide in that good news of my eternal inheritance **in Christ Jesus**, I increasingly *experience* the **unseen reality** of peace *with* God which produces the fruit of the peace *of* God through me as His ambassador in day to day circumstances. It is the ultimate stress eliminator. Walking daily in the shoes of His Kingdom-based gospel of righteousness, peace and joy in the Holy Spirit, surpasses all natural understanding This experience cannot be duplicated by the world system which is circumstance-based. No, it is the work of the Holy Spirit, producing His fruit of peace, as I set my natural mind on the eternal, **unseen** realities above - which I am now a part of. That is how Jesus walked and brought the life and freedom of heaven to earth.

Letting the Holy Spirit live His life through the new me produces the fruit of His enduring peace. But those still **in Adam** are often tossed to and fro by the evils of confusion, disorder, disease etc. - caused or facilitated by this world's **unseen** rulers of Darkness. This also can be the *experience* of the "city dog believer," still mentally under law. "My people perish for lack of knowledge" is primarily referring to the ignorance of how the two **unseen** Kingdoms operate and about the spiritual war in progress all around us. Now that I am on God's side **in Christ Jesus**, I am, de facto, at war with Darkness. Jesus is my safety and security and He offers me His wisdom and confidence to *enforce* His victory over Darkness through the love and almighty power of the Holy Spirit living through the new spirit-me **in Christ Jesus.**

Quenching The Devil's Darts.

"Above all, take up the shield of faith, wherewith ye shall be able to quench all the fiery darts of the wicked one" (Ephesians 6:16). God's gift of faith enables the believer to focus on Jesus and to rely on His **finished work** and to comprehend His **divine exchange**. This focus acts like a mental shield against the *external* darts of negativity and accusations and condemnation, designed to cause doubt, fear, anxiety, worry, and stress which steal a believer's peace and joy and even physical health. What does God's *gift of faith* help me to see additionally? It enables me to see Him and my redeemed self and others as *He sees* – with the mind and vision of Christ Jesus. His sight protects me against the fiery darts of deception and accusation of the devil, which caused even sinless Adam to fall.

Jesus Is My Helmet of Salvation

While the shield of faith defends against external, negative influences, the helmet of salvation – the revelation of Jesus' **whole gospel of grace** - is given to redeem, renew, reorder and, thereby, progressively renew the saint's natural mind. Remember, the mind of man was programmed to be self-centered by the old, **in Adam** nature that was "dead to God" by being spiritually separated from Him. Rebirth regenerated the believer's spirit-self, now alive **in Christ,** but it did not automatically perfect the soul or body. Again, the new believer's mind is still corrupted from all the internal programming left over from being **in Adam** - the "old" you, now gone - which was legally under the dominion of the devil before rebirth. As a result, there is often an internal, soulish battle of conflicting thoughts, emotions and choices that is limited to functioning only in the **seen realm.**

Internal doubt, fear, worry condemnation, stress and unbelief are all caused by placing and magnifying anything above Jesus. It is "natural" for my **seen-based mind,** influenced by the flesh (sarx), to

1) focus on myself and the **seen realm** and

2) depend on myself or the world system or on others to meet my needs rather on the wisdom and supply of the Holy Spirit and/or

3) keep trying to win or maintain God's acceptance and approval by my efforts etc. rather than to learn to rely on Father's approval of Jesus *and* me *because I am one with Him.*

In other words, why waste time and effort trying to obtain by soul power what Jesus has already revealed and supplied by operating in "the mind of Christ" available to all believers? Whatever we truly need for life down here and godliness up there was purchased for all believers almost 2000 years ago and supplied through rebirth **in Christ Jesus**. That is why He told His disciples, **pre-cross,** to "Seek first the **(unseen)** Kingdom of God and His (gift of) righteousness and all else will be given unto you as well (Matthew 6:33)." That is how Jesus lived and He invites us to live His way, not Adam's. "Acknowledge Him in all your ways and He will direct your Pathways." That **pre-cross** proverb can now be updated to "Consciously communicate with Daddy-God and He will be your guide and supplier through the Holy Spirit living within." David was victorious in the **seen realm** when he depended on God. Now we have a far better covenant than all the others.

From God's perspective, all believers already have the fullness of God's gift of salvation for their whole being, even in this life. That is why He calls it a **finished work**, done in the **unseen realm**. The more you see this reality by faith and receive the extent of that free gift of God's supply that is yours **in Christ Jesus**, the more you will experience the protection of the helmet of salvation for your natural mind. God's blessing of His righteousness, peace, joy and rest - His abundant life in the Spirit in the **unseen realm** - are given to retrain your mind to think from

God's perspective so that sharing in His abundant life increasingly becomes your normal experience in the **seen realm**. In other words, you become mentally established in the revelation of God's view of you as righteous **in Christ**.

That is why Jesus exhorts us, through Paul, to "set your mind on things above, not on things of earth" because this world can't supply lasting peace and joy and rest. We are given the shield of faith to believe in Jesus' perfect life and performance that has won full salvation for us as part of God's family. Renew your mind with this new reality: "Jesus, You are my life and salvation, my glory and the lifter of my head, my righteousness and my reason for existing." The song poems in this book will help renew your mind to think God's thoughts about Him and about who you now are because of Him.

Jesus Is My Sword Of The Spirit Of God

Jesus, the living and active Word of God, is sharper than any two-edged sword, slicing to the division between the soul and the spirit, as between the joints and the marrow, and so it discerns the thoughts and intentions of the human heart (see Hebrews 4:12). This living sword is our offensive weapon that Jesus, operating as a man, used against the devil in the desert temptations and is also part of our equipment, **in Christ.** The Bible is the Word of God but not all of it is helpful to use in the **unseen** war. The devil uses the law to confuse and condemn unwary believers who do not know the harsh realities of focusing on the law, as described in Chapter Nine. Mentally mixing opposing covenants advances the devil's agenda against believers. The **elephant of mixture** is the devil's favorite pet.

We are now **New Covenant** believers (not Jews or Judaizers) equipped with the revelation of Jesus' **finished work** that was not known or available to **pre-cross** people. Our **divine exchange** with Jesus has put Satan under our feet so that we can now enforce Jesus' victory from our new position **in Christ.** Also, the higher Law of faith, love and liberty – Jesus' **whole gospel of grace** – has legally defeated the devil's agenda of fear and hate and bondage over every believer's mind. That new freedom becomes experiential as we focus on who we now are **in Christ** (rather than mentally fall from grace by going back under law-mindedness and the devil's condemnation.) We now have Jesus' authority and power, through the Holy Spirit, to *speak* the pure truth of Jesus' **whole gospel** to set free all captives who desire to be free from the lies of the enemy of their souls.

Additionally, believers are offered the power of praying in the Spirit – speaking God's inspired words of power and authority by using the wonderful gift of tongues. God supplies this new prayer language (which by-passes our natural, limited, unsanctified minds) to effectively declare His pure word of truth to accomplish His will in the **seen realm**. It is a fool-proof way for the Lord of the universe to deliver the word of His power to the earth through us, His ambassadors. This mighty weapon – that is another manifestation of the sword of the Spirit - also enforces Jesus' defeat over the devil's spiritual schemes and activity in the **unseen realm.** God gave this power gift to His body at Pentecost but it has been mostly ignored or forgotten (and even denounced by some) for 2000 years. It is a very important benefit of the "all things new" **gospel of grace**, meant for all believers, according to 1 Corinthians 14. But here, again, God's own people have often needlessly suffered defeat for lack of knowledge of what armor gifts God has made available to us, His ambassadors.

Ground Zero Spiritual Warfare

It is for freedom that Jesus did what He did to free all **in Adam** humans from Satan's captivity through rebirth. The revelation packed in this chapter is more than just academic theory to me. In the early 1970's, while many were experimenting with drugs etc, my wife and I were seeking for more than the deadness of religious law and tradition. We were naive about the reality of spiritual warfare and we were intrigued with "spiritual experiences." So we began to blindly dabble in Satan's sandbox – the occult. We were mercifully delivered only by the love and grace of God after two troubled years. But that experience prepared us for other spiritual battles soon to follow, one of which involved my oldest daughter when she was only three years old.

A doctor determined that she should have her adenoids removed because of repeated ear and throat infections. During her hospital stay, she was traumatized by an intern who, unknown to us at the time, took a blood sample while we were briefly out of her room. Soon after, we noticed how our very friendly and outgoing little girl was growing increasingly shy and even fearful. We thought all would be well when she healed and returned to pre-school which she loved attending. She healed quickly but even after a month, she remained fearful and she even resisted going to school. It was then that I discerned in prayer, through the Holy Spirit, that a demon of fear was oppressing her. So rather than alarm her even more, we waited until she was soundly asleep and then, by faith in Jesus' power and authority over all Darkness, we rebuked that spirit in Jesus' mighty name.

When she awoke the next morning, it was like a switch had been turned back on. She was back to being her happy self, eager to go to school. Other similar experiences over the years have verified that Satan is waging a war to keep his hold on those ignorant of his schemes *and* he uses lies about God and accusations through the law to try to keep even believers in bondage if possible. Only by knowing the truth of Jesus' **finished work** and accepting Him and all that He freely offers, can **in Adam** sinners become regenerated into saints, positioned and victorious over all principalities and powers **in and through Christ Jesus,** our Deliverer.

As your mind is renewed by God's view of His salvation for your whole being, you will be equipped and motivated to speak His truth with conviction, using the mighty sword of Jesus' **whole gospel of grace** that has been so compromised by the **elephant of mixture** for 2000 years. Christ Jesus, the Living Word of God, *is* the Sword of the Spirit, the good news, who came to defeat the lies and tactics of the enemy, just as He used the truth against Satan in the desert.

Jesus Is My Armor

Unlike earthly armor that is worn only for periods of combat, we believers are *always* **in Christ Jesus** so we are never without His armor. That is crucial to know because the war in the **unseen realm** won't end until Jesus returns. The notion that we have to put on this armor daily implies that it must be "falling off" at some point – maybe while sleeping? But that notion is a deception. Jesus has permanently included and sealed every believer (as a new spirit-being) **in Himself** and He *is* the invincible, spiritual protection described in the passage above – because of who He *is* for every believer. It only *seems* to "fall off" when we mentally turn our attention from Him to concentrate on some task or to solve some problem etc. and forget to ask for His wisdom. But just because a believer chooses to shift his mind to some other focus temporarily –

or even sins - does not mean he "falls out" of Jesus, his holy armor. He is still spiritually united to God **through Christ Jesus**.

The supposed loss of God's fellowship or friendship or communion or acceptance or approval, (or as some teach, even the salvation of God) because of *wrong behavior,* is one of the most common lies in the devil's arsenal that comes from the performance-based mixture of law with grace – the **elephant of Galatianism**. However, giving in to sinning does have negative consequences in the **seen realm** that can be very costly. <u>Sinning can take you further in the **seen realm** than you want to go and cost more than you want to pay.</u> God wants us to reign victoriously by right believing that produces the Holy Spirit's fruit of right living. Therefore, resist Satan's temptations and lies by progressively renewing your mind with the higher law of the Spirit of life that Jesus gave us to keep all believers progressively free from the law of sin and death, as Jesus declares over us in Romans 8:2. <u>Focus on Jesus, not on the Liar or on the Law.</u> The following song poem keeps me mindful of the unseen spiritual war still being waged by our defeated foe and, more importantly, reminds me that there is no defeat for those **in Christ Jesus.**

THERE IS A WAR being waged for you're soul
Yes, Satan would sift you like wheat.
But be at peace for I am God,
In Me there is no defeat.

Equipped with My armor and shield
And strengthened by the joy of a thankful heart,
Attack with My sword that will set you free
For no weapon formed against you can prevail.
© Copyright 1988 by Leonard J. Ransil

Much more can be shared regarding this part of the believer's legal right and inheritance because of his spirit-oneness with God. (Appendix 5 has a list of recommended books by fellow saints who have helped me renew my mind and experience increasing freedom **in Christ Jesus.**) Thankfully, more and more saints are now discovering who they are as tri-part beings and just how wonderful and powerful and freeing is Jesus' **whole gospel of grace**. This revolutionary revelation that Paul walked in, slays the **elephant of mixture** in our thinking, freeing us to consistently walk according to the Spirit in the **seen realm** rather than according to the flesh.

Saints around the world are now renewing their mind with the mind of Christ to think God's thoughts and are speaking and sharing and praying and ministering and worshipping God according to the leading and empowering of the precious Holy Spirit. Relationship with the true God is replacing religion; transformation is replacing mere information; the fruit of the Spirit is replacing dead works; genuine worship is replacing mere singing; thankfulness is replacing complaining. God's life is overcoming death in all its forms thanks to the light of truth and freedom of Jesus' **whole grace gospel**. The rising tide of His grace and truth is triumphantly overcoming the counterfeits of Darkness – inside and outside of the Body of Christ. It's about time, don't you think?

Replace the Elephant With The Butterfly Life In Christ

My hope and prayer for you, my friend, is that you use the Law only for God's intended purpose (to bring people to Christ, as the Holy Spirit leads) and increasingly operate in the law of the Spirit of life, enabled by the power and authority of the Holy Spirit living within you and in every believer. God has made "all things new" through Jesus' **divine exchange** which is available to any and all who call on the name of Jesus to be saved and freed. Why go back under the shadow and curse of an obsolete Law system when you can walk in the light of God's full protection and blessing – Jesus' abundant life of grace and favor? This treasure is freely offered to all who choose to depend on what Father-God has already done for His children through our Elder Brother, Jesus the Christ. Choose His life on every level of your being – spirit, soul and body – by *consciously* abiding **in Christ Jesus** and His **finished work.**

The final chapter explores the age-old question "Who is God," according to what He says and reveals about Himself in the Bible. Now we know that the tragic events during the Mosaic Law period did not occur to reveal God's nature. Rather, they actually revealed man's fallen nature **in Adam.** Therefore, we can look through the kaleidoscope of the unconditional, unilateral and everlasting **New Covenant** of grace, which Father-God made with Jesus for our sake, to see the dazzling glory of Father-God's nature and ultimate intention. He triumphed over the devil's sinister plan to enslave mankind forever. And He triumphed over mankind's folly of cooperating with the devil's plans against Him. His heroic intervention through Jesus proved that God's foolishness is wiser than man's so-called wisdom. I am so grateful that God did not give up on us foolish rebels. He mercifully provided a way for us to come back to Him when there was seemingly no possible way. That underserved grace reveals who the God of the Bible *really* is and we will know Him best by experiencing what He has done for us through the **finished work** of Christ Jesus - His **divine exchange.**

Ultimately, it is the devil who steals, kills and destroys, never God. It was Adam who opened the flood gates of everything bad after God had supplied him and Eve with everything good. The following song-poem will help you put the blame for all that is wrong on the true source - and help you wholeheartedly side with our victorious Father-God Who wants you well in every way, spirit, soul and body. Shalom!

POVERTY AND SICKNESS DO NOT PLEASE YOUR HEART, O LORD.
They are part of Satan's plan to steal and kill.
Through his lies and trickery, he got Adam to rebel
Causing mankind to be poor and ill.

Yet many still believe that You send sickness and disease
And they think You want to keep them poor.
But, they turn around and pray to You for healing or a job
Not thinking what they're asking for.

They sadly cry to You, who they blame for all their pain,
To fix the very thing that they blame You for.
They're confused by Satan's lies, so have double-minded thoughts -
Ignorance and doubt have closed the door!

They trust in what tradition says instead on what You've done.
And they focus on the circumstance they see,
But healing comes from focusing on You and what You've done
For by Your stripes all healing is now free.

You only do good things and, with healing in Your wings,
Came to earth to set all captives free.
As a Man, You came with grace, to reveal our Father's face,
And to share Your Life abundantly.

So I thank You for Your mercy and Your sacrificial love
That destroyed the curse of poverty and shame,
And, by faith, receive Your **finished work** of resurrection life,
And authority and power in Your name.

Poverty and sickness do not please Your heart, O Lord.
They're from Satan who is here to steal and kill.
But You ransomed us from him and You paid for all our sin,
Through Your love, we're free to do Your will.
A Sermon Song © Copyright 2009 by Leonard J. Ransil

Dear friend, I pray that you may enjoy good health and that all things may go well with you, even as your soul prospers (see 3 John 1:2).

"Blessed be the God and Father of our Lord Jesus Christ who has blessed us with every spiritual blessing in the heavenly places **in Christ**" (Ephesians 1:3).

CHAPTER TWENTY ONE

WHO IS GOD, ACCORDING TO THE BIBLE?

Confused Concepts About God

Tragically today, believers and unbelievers alike have very distorted opinions about who the God of the Bible really is. The Bible itself seems to paint different pictures of God according to how He interacted with different people groups and individuals over the Bible's 6000 year record of events. Is He an indifferent Creator who fashioned the universe for something to do and is now working on another project elsewhere in the universe? Or is He a cold and cranky taskmaster who just likes to boss people around for the fun of it? Or is He a perfectionist who won't let anybody into His perfect space unless they somehow work to become as perfect as He is? Or is He someone who is warm and personal and welcoming toward everyone or to only a chosen few? Or is He a combination of all of these characteristics or someone else altogether? Whether or not you have ever consciously thought about who God <u>really</u> is, *you already have formed a set of assumptions about God which you routinely use to filter related ideas about Him.* In fact, just now, you used that mental filter to decide which of the above statements about God you think are true and which are not. But are you sure your filter is accurate? That question suggests four other crucial questions:

1) From what sources have you assembled your set of assumptions – your mental picture of God?

2) <u>How accurate are these assumptions that form your concept of God?</u>

3) Is knowing who God really is all that important?

4) Is it possible and desirable to have a personal, interactive relationship with Him?

When Did The Answers To These Questions Hit Home To Me?

You now know from my testimony in Chapter Three that I relied on many false assumptions about God over the first fifty years of my life. Only when I heard Dr. Robert Cornwall say in 1991 that *"Your relationship with God is only as good as your concept of God"* did I realize that my beliefs about God might not be very accurate. Furthermore, <u>Christianity is relational and based on faith, not on physical sight. Therefore, to the degree that my beliefs are off, so is my relationship with God, with myself and with others</u>. Why? Because only God has the right perspective about everything and everybody – including you and me. Wherever we think differently about something or someone than He does, we will relate to it "wrongly." Wrong believing among humans got started with Adam and Eve. A believer's rebirth **in Christ** does not automatically delete all wrong believing. That is why we need to have our minds bathed (renewed) in His truth in order to see everything the way He sees. There is no condemnation for "falling short" of totally right believing because Jesus paid the price for all of our sin. But we often still reap the consequences of our misguided thinking and actions which keep us from enjoying Father-God and His best blessings in the **seen realm**.

Morality Is Not The Main Goal Of Christianity

I soon realized in 1991 that living "morally right" is *not* the primary goal and the *basic* issue in Christianity, even though it is central to most religions, including Judaism. Bathing your mind in "morality" is not the same thing as renewing it with the truth because Jesus has <u>personally</u> become our way, our truth, and our life, now that we are alive **in Him**. He did not come to bring us the Law to focus on. The Jews already had that and it was not life-giving but actually a great burden, as Peter correctly stated in Acts 15:10, because they could not keep it perfectly. He, who *is* grace and truth, replaced the Law for the Jews with the **New Covenant** which is based entirely on grace, not on keeping any part of the Mosaic law.

The Jerusalem church missed that revelation and hung on to the Law as a way to be more holy and righteous. The focus on morality (instead of on Jesus) is a carryover from Adam's misguided choice to eat from the Tree of Law. It was reinforced by the Mosaic Law given to the Israelites. This focus is the smokescreen of law-based religion, the veil that blinded the law-based Pharisees and what I lived under for about fifty years. But Christianity is about having a personal relationship with our benevolent Father-God, now and forever. Thanks to Jesus, we can choose to receive or reject God's gift of righteousness which Jesus, the Tree of Life, made possible again to mankind at Calvary.

My religious training caused me to blend God's grace with my "right works" to hopefully earn heaven. But true Christianity is totally grace-based. This means that Jesus has already done *everything* required for **in Adam** sinners to become united with Father-God forever. Since He became the way back to God by what He did on Calvary, what is left to do? Simply believe and receive His offer of an everlasting relationship with God as now true for you. It is Father-God's free gift that you don't deserve and can't earn. His amazing generosity reveals <u>His true nature of unselfish love</u> that the heresy of Galatianism hides from us.

Theologians call the miracle of union with God through rebirth "being justified by faith." The basis of your acceptability to God is not your degree of moral "rightness" as religions teach. That false belief is the essence of self-righteousness. Oneness with God has *nothing* to do with your behavior and *everything* to do with your *belief* that Jesus is your righteousness because you are now united to Him who *is* the righteous Son of God. It is all based on God's lavish grace through faith, not on your meager efforts to be good - however you or your church or your culture define "good." The only way to manifest God's good fruit is to be grafted onto the right tree – the Tree of Life.

Learning to *believe and depend* on God's gift of right-standing through union with Jesus will produce the fruit of right-living, as God defines it. This fruit does not always agree with man's view of "right-living." The ultra-moral, self-righteous Pharisees had a negative view of the most righteous Man that ever walked on the planet. Obeying the Law did not change their basic, **in Adam** nature. Jesus produced the fruit of right living because He was in a dependent *union* with God as His Son. Reborn saints *legally* enjoy that same union with God as Jesus does through rebirth into a new nature. *However,* ignorance or wrong beliefs about who Father-God *really* is and what He *has done* for mankind through Jesus, can minimize (and even prevent) how much we *benefit* from His lavish goodness and victory here on earth, even as believers.

Our Relational Father

God revealed in the Bible that He exists as Three Persons in One God. God enjoys an eternal love-based relationship among these three Persons. He came to the Garden daily to relate to Adam. Even after he rebelled, God still discussed the situation with him because He is a compassionate, relational God who created us as social beings in His image originally. He sent Jesus as the last Adam to make it possible for us to be united with the Trinity in an eternally blissful relationship. What an amazing privilege! It begins when an **in Adam** person is reborn of God. So, it seems to me that relating to Him personally throughout each day (which some label as "prayer") is the most important thing we can do.

Who do you know that is more important than Father-God? Who has done more for you than He has? He caused your existence and sustains you. He has done everything that He can from His side to make relating with your outer man possible, by making you one with Him spiritually. Now your outer man is meant to benefit from this union by you choosing to focus on Him and ask for, receive and walk in the wisdom of the Holy Spirit. He then inclines you toward praise and thanksgiving for all God now *is* toward you and who you now are in Him. That is what Paul learned to do even in the most appalling **seen realm** <u>conditions</u> of prison and shipwreck etc. He magnified God - "made God bigger in his sight" - rather than complain about the conditions around him by worshipping and by praying in tongues. That didn't always change the immediate conditions but he *mentally* triumphed over them nonetheless, much to the devil's dismay. So did David when he told his soul (outer man) five times in Psalm 103 to "bless the Lord."

However, your *current* concept of God is the filter that you use to judge and decide whether or not what you just read in the above two paragraphs about relating to Father-God is true and, therefore, possible, safe and desirable. If you are still law-minded, then the idea of relating intimately with God probably sounds impossible or feels awkward or threatening - or at least not always pleasant and positive. Why? Because you still wrongly think God's acceptance and approval of *you* is based on your performance. The result is that your relationship with God seems to fluctuate like a yo-yo, even on your best days. That is why I have been emphasizing the importance of believing in Jesus' **finished work** because it is the over-riding reality that placed you, believer, in a permanently righteous relationship with God, <u>in spite of your day to day behavior and experiences</u>. Because you are **in Christ,** Father-God sees you and treats you like He does Jesus, not according to your behavior. Sinful behavior might ruin your relationship with other people but not with God, <u>from His perspective,</u> because our **New Covenant** is based on Jesus' doing, not on ours. That alone is what makes Christianity different from any other belief system.

As you become established in this grace-based revelation and willingly yield to the Holy Spirit's direction (instead of depending on law-based thinking for worldly or religious "wisdom" and direction), the behavior of your outer man will increasingly line up with God's ways as you let Him live His life through you, as you. I know it seems counter-intuitive. That is because law-based thinking is more focused on "justice" than on grace. But Jesus justly paid for all of your wrong doing, forever, and now God looks favorably on you and every believer through His eyes of underserved favor – abundant grace. It is when we look to the law that we fall *mentally* out of grace because we are depending on ourselves and our imperfect efforts to "stay-right" with God. That is the heresy common to world religions but that is *not* Christianity.

As a believer, your behavior only affects your external circumstances and relationships, *not* your intimate oneness with Father-God because the real spirit-you is *permanently* **in Christ Jesus** through the **divine exchange** with Him. Does improvement need to happen in the outer man so that things go better for you in the **seen realm**? Most likely. But that is the beauty of how God has arranged things. He sent the Holy Spirit inside of you to bring about the renewal of your mind through His doing. "… it is God who works in you (as a believer), both to choose and to work in accord with His delight," according to Jesus' word through Paul in Philippians 2:13. Again, it is about the "sanctification" of your outer self by yielding to the Holy Spirit's promptings to increasingly conform it to your new, perfect, spirit-self, already seated in the heavenlies **in Christ Jesus**. Letting the Holy Spirit have His way in and through you yields the fruit of victory in the **seen realm**.

Do you see how loving Father-God really is? He thinks of everything for us, His holy children. The more you receive from the Holy Spirit the reality of all that Father-God did through Jesus, the better They like it. That is who They are. They want you to be totally free to enjoy relating to Them – abiding consciously in Them – 24/7. They are the *only reliable source* of true love and acceptance and approval and *real life* - which we all need and crave - in the whole universe. Only wrong believing stands in the way of living by biblical faith in God's overwhelming love for you that produces liberty. God's view of you is the only one that really matters. Invite the Holy Spirit to show you what His view of you is by bathing your mind in the results of Jesus' **finished work** of His **divine exchange** *with you*, presented in Chapters One and Two. It is written to *you* about *you*, dear believer and so why not start agreeing with God's view of you.

Renewing Your Mind

I can clearly see now, in hindsight, just how right Dr. Cornwall was in emphasizing the importance of relating to God according to who He says He really is, *especially as revealed through Jesus' earthly life and in Jesus' gospel given to Paul.* Jesus graphically demonstrated Father-God's compassionate nature through His earthly life. So don't rely on the hear-say of other people's impressions and misgivings about God. They often come from the "traditions of men" who do not properly interpret the Bible (divide the Word rightly) according to the varied terms of the five main covenants. Consequently, people's opinions about Father-God and Jesus vary over a wide spectrum, both positive and negative, just as even occurs within the Bible itself. For example, Peter had the revelation from God (from above Line A, as pictured in Chapter Sixteen) that Jesus was God's son, as stated in Matthew 16:16. However, some Pharisees believed that Jesus was a liar and had a demon. Where do you think they got that blasphemous opinion?

As always, those who risked walking by biblical faith received the truth of who Jesus is and experienced the **unseen** benefits that Jesus came to offer. Those who walked by sight only saw and experienced the limits and distortions of what the **seen realm** of this world and the flesh and the devil could offer. The same is still true today. The sure way to see and appreciate and benefit from what God offers **in Christ Jesus** is to meditate on the profound revelation of the following *pivotal* scripture from 2 Corinthians 5:16-21, which explains Jesus' **divine exchange** that made our entrance into the **unseen realm** possible. I am presenting it yet again because it also shows to what outrageous lengths Father-God was willing to go to in order to include all who freely choose, by faith, to be received into His everlasting family.

> And so, from now on we know no one according to the flesh. And though we have known Christ according to the flesh, yet now we know Him in this way no longer. So if anyone is **in Christ** (by rebirth), he is a **new creature**; the old things passed away (the old Adam nature is gone). Behold, all things have become new. Now all this is from God, having reconciled us to Himself through Christ, and who has given us the ministry of reconciliation. For God was **in Christ**, reconciling the world to Himself, not reckoning their sins against them. And He has placed in us the word of reconciliation. Therefore, we are ambassadors for Christ, so that God is beseeching you through us. We beg you (those yet not reborn of God) on Christ's behalf: be reconciled to God. For God made Him (Jesus) who did not know sin to become sin on our behalf so that we might become the righteousness of God in Him.

Can you sense the passion in Father-God's heart to welcome and include every man, woman, and child into His arms, now that Jesus' sacrifice has removed all barriers to relationship with Him – from His all-knowing viewpoint? All He is waiting for is each person's acceptance of His invitation and blessings. The next scripture from Romans 5:9-11 mirrors that same stupendous revelation that has been mostly eclipsed by the **elephant of mixture** for 2000 years:

> Therefore, having been justified now by His (Jesus') blood, all the more so shall we be saved from (God's just) wrath through Him (Jesus). For, when we were still enemies, we were reconciled to God through the death of His Son. All the more so, having been reconciled, shall we be saved by His life. And not only that, but we also glory in God, through our Lord Jesus Christ, through whom we have now received reconciliation.

Father-God's love for mankind is so magnanimous that He sent Jesus to become like us in all things except sin. Then Jesus *became* sin in order to *crucify the Adamic nature* and, thereby, eliminate the three things that prevented relationship with Him:

1) our fallen nature **in Adam**

2) all the sins of all mankind for all time and

3) all the curses caused by Adam's fall.

None of those evils were God's fault but He justly and totally paid our debt through Jesus. Why? In order to restore the *option* to us to *choose* to believe and receive eternal oneness with Him and His family. Jesus exchanged all the privileges and blessings that He, as God's beloved Son, deserved with all the bad that we, as God-hating rebels, deserved. Consequently, all reborn saints are **new creations,** made righteous and totally accepted and approved by Abba-Father forever. What does this accomplishment of God's extravagant love through Jesus demonstrate about His nature?

> So why did Christ, at the proper time, while we were helpless sinners, suffer death for the ungodly? … Because God <u>demonstrated His love for us</u> in that, while we were yet sinners **(in Adam)**, Christ died for us (Romans 5:6 and 8).

Mercy, Not Justice

So rather than justifiably exacting judgment and destruction on mankind for executing His Son, God actually sent Jesus to purposely go through all the horrors of Calvary - and even be forsaken by God, His own Father, when He became our sin. Why? To demonstrate His love and commitment to Their divine plan to include into His eternal family whosoever is willing. Even before Calvary, Jesus demonstrated His Father's gracious love for all those He encountered while on earth in countless ways. We know that because Jesus said that He only did what His Father told Him to do. So by following Father-God's instructions, Jesus forgave some people's sins even before they asked. He healed their bodies, raised dead people to life, supplied wine to keep a wedding celebration going, fed thousands of hungry listeners, saved an adulterous woman from a Law-required stoning and did *not* condemn her, touched and healed lepers, healed blind and deaf and crippled people, went out of His way to impart a word of life and hope to a licentious Samaritan woman, freed a man of 2000 demons, delegated authority to His **in Adam** disciples to go out and do some of these same things **(pre-cross)**, calmed a raging storm, enabled Peter to walk on water, loved His disciples enough to put up with their ignorance and antics and unbelief for three years, and far more. In fact, John comments in John 21:25 that:

> Now there are also many other things that Jesus did, which, if each of these were written down, the world itself, I suppose, would not be able to contain the books that would be written.

At first glance, the focus of the four gospels seems to be on what <u>Jesus</u> said and did. <u>But actually He was acting as an ambassador of His wonderful Father</u>, demonstrating how loving, merciful, powerful, forgiving, gracious, committed, faithful, friendly, empathetic etc. Father-God has always been because He *is* love by nature. Jesus' life here is a peek into the **unseen** quality of the family life that the Trinity has always enjoyed and what all who have been reborn of God have inherited as the DNA of Jesus' **divine exchange** with us. Do we have to wait to physically die before we can experience this **unseen reality** in Christ? Well Jesus reveals to Paul some of what is possible to us even now in 2 Corinthians 3:17-18 and in 4:6-7:

> Now the Spirit is the Lord. And wherever the Spirit of the Lord is (inside each believer's spirit-self), there is liberty. Yet truly, all of us, <u>as we gaze upon the unveiled glory of the face of the Lord,</u> (the unseen, exalted Christ Jesus), are transfigured into the same image, from one glory to another. And this is done by the Spirit of the Lord (not by our doing).

> … For God, who told the light to shine out of darkness, <u>has shined a light into our (new) hearts to illuminate the knowledge of the splendor of God, in the person of Christ Jesus.</u> But we hold this treasure in earthen vessels (our **seen**, outer tent), so that what is sublime may be by the <u>power of God,</u> not by us.

Now, just in case you missed it, I will repeat Jesus' *secret* to knowing God and experiencing the life and liberty that He walked in:

> ...as we gaze upon the unveiled glory of the face of the Lord, (the unseen, exalted Christ Jesus), we are transfigured into the same image, from one glory to another. And this is done by the Spirit of the Lord (not by our struggling efforts).

One Thing Is Needful

It boils down to one thing that is "needful": focusing on the love and goodness of Father-God, revealed through Jesus' earthly life and the **finished work** of His **divine exchange** on Calvary that has made *all things new* for those **in Christ**. That was the essence of Jesus' loving rebuke to Martha when she complained to Jesus that her sister Mary was absorbed with listening to Jesus instead of helping to serve Him a meal (Luke 10:38-41). And it was Mary who was with Jesus when it mattered to Him the most – at Calvary. What better things or events or persons are there for you to focus on than on Father-God and Jesus and on His **whole grace gospel**, which enables us to partake of His own divine nature as part of His family?

So why don't we see more of this heavenly life manifest down here? It's certainly not because God is holding anything back. He gave His best gift – Jesus – to us 2000 years ago. Rather, it is most often because we are relying on our religious efforts to accomplish what Jesus has already done for us in His **finished work**. A major premise of this book is that, by and large, the church has been tricked into looking at everything else *but* at Father-God and Jesus and what He *has done* on our behalf. And the biggest culprit is the devil who uses the law as a veil over our eyes and as a club to fool unwary believers like he did in the Jerusalem church.

The futile and failed tradition of trying to fix our earthen vessel - our outer man - through religious law-keeping and self-help books, has kept us focused on the **elephant of mixture**. Ironically, that focus distorts our concept of Father-God, Himself, so that He *seems* to be a distant, angry, hard, demanding, perfectionistic Judge. These are behavioral traits that we sometimes see in ourselves, our parents and other authority figures all around us. So, we tend to project them on to God, causing confusion and frustration. But that is all a distraction by the **seen** world, our flesh and the devil, using law and condemnation to distort the truth and causes us to forget how good, loving and faithful Father-God really is.

Our Prodigal (Extravagant) Father-God

Did the Holy Spirit inspire any word pictures in the Bible to help us understand and relate to Father-God? Yes, there are many such stories and parables in the Bible that give us glimpses of His true nature, when viewed through the glasses of grace instead of law. A classic favorite is what is often referred to as the parable of the "Prodigal Son." The title itself betrays the fact that we humans are self-occupied rather than focused on God. Jesus presented this parable to a bunch of self-righteous, fault-finding law-keepers to show just how extravagant is Father-God's love, mercy and grace. Therefore, a better title would be "The Prodigal Father." Predictably the Pharisees were scandalized more by the father's actions in the story than by what the two sons did. Why? Because the father seemingly let the situation get out of hand by being supposedly too lenient, rather than being a "responsible" father who strictly enforced the Mosaic Law. (Jesus faced this same challenge, in principle, when these law-types threw the woman they had caught in the act of adultery down in front of Him in public.)

How would a good Pharisee have told the story – according to what the Law demanded? Well, when the youngest son asked his father for his own share of his dad's estate, the father should have (at the very least) refused because it was an insult for a Jewish son to even *think* of getting any of his father's estate before his father's death. It is like blatantly saying "Your stuff is more important to me than you are." (In spiritual terms, it is idolatry – putting created things above the Creator.) And if the son stubbornly refused to take "no" for an answer, right then and there, the "correct" thing for the father to do, according to the Law, was to have his disrespectful son stoned to death as an example to other sons in town not to be presumptuous, greedy and rebellious.

Their thinking was "If you don't control the people with the law, they will become lawless." However, God gave them the Law to prove that kind of thinking is a lie. Law actually arouses more sin and causes death to **in Adam** sinners, as we saw in Chapter Nine. Jesus operated from the higher law of faith in His Father's love for Him, which engendered love for God and liberty from the world system and the devil's devices. The parable was a way to show what happens to sons who are self-focused rather than living consciously in a love-based relationship with their father. Two opposite extremes are presented through the behavior of the two sons: license and legalism, already discussed in Chapter Nineteen.

Both sons were in bondage to "self" but neither knew it nor cared. While the sons focused on their self-centered goals, the father focused on *their* welfare out of His unselfish love for them. Yes, they were *legally* related to their father. But their self-focus prevented the sons from seeing their true needs. Just owning his "stuff" in the **seen realm** could not provide lasting fulfillment or satisfaction because "stuff" is temporary. But they could not grasp that reality unless and until they would come to the end of their stubborn self-centeredness and the self-sufficiency of their flesh. They were their own point of reference, not their father.

God's Way Of Sacrificial Love
But rather than follow the Mosaic Law, he spared his youngest son's life and gave in to his demands, which probably caused the father great embarrassment and ridicule locally and shocked the older, law-abiding brother. The younger son's downfall forced him to eat food meant for pigs. In desperation, he "came to his senses" and decided to return home, beg for forgiveness, and ask to be treated as a hired servant. Now, here is where the Pharisees were shocked beyond belief. They expected that the father would stone him or certainly disown him or at least refuse to let his son return home. But no, he did none of that. He didn't even require him to confess all his sins and promise to "mend his ways."

Instead, this loving father left his dignity behind when he pulled up his robe and then ran to his son while still far-off, kissed him, and restored the *privileges* of son-ship that he had legally forfeited. The joyful, grace-based father even threw a party for him which brought to light the older son's pride in his dutiful law-keeping and hidden resentment for his brother. His relational father was now grieved that his oldest son's objections proved that he was also self-centered. He neither loved his dad nor his brother. His anger revealed that he, too, was focused on himself and what was in it for him - his dad's stuff - that was now supposed to be all his. He had worked for his father out of duty, not thankful devotion and love.

Jesus did not tell us what the oldest son decided to do – continue to pridefully create division and discord or change his mind (repent) and be grateful to his loving dad and join the party. But one thing was made clear. Legalism and license are both symptoms of dysfunctional, loveless mind-sets. In contrast, heaven operates on faith, love and liberty which is how God operates and how He graces us to operate, too, as His children. If Father-God or our elder brother, Jesus, were legalists, Jesus would not have come down to rescue us so that we could join their party in heaven. Everything they did and do for us is always motivated by God's extravagant love, just like the parable demonstrated. Jesus correctly portrayed His Father as a loving, faithful and longsuffering giver, not as an exacting, selfish judge like the Pharisees believed Him to be.

Jesus indirectly addressed this common negative misconception about His Father in the following parable about prayer from Luke 18:1-8:

> How he (Jesus) also told them a parable that we should continually pray and not cease, saying: 'There was a certain judge in a certain city, who did not fear God and did not respect man. But there was a widow in that city who went to him, saying, 'Vindicate me from my adversary.' And he refused to do so for a long time. But afterwards, he said to himself: 'Even though I do not fear God, nor respect man, yet because this widow is pestering me, I will vindicate her, lest by returning, she may, in the end, wear me out.' Then the Lord said: 'Listen to what the unjust judge said. So then, will not God grant the vindication of his elect, who cry out to him day and night? Or will he continue to endure them? I tell you that he will quickly bring vindication to them. Yet truly, when the Son of man returns, do you think that he will find faith on earth?'

If you string all the negatives about this judge together you get a very bleak picture. He was unjust, he did not respect people, he refused to do his job for this needy widow and, finally, he reluctantly did what he should have done to begin with only because he feared she would wear him out. Does this sound like a fair description of God to you? Well, I hope not - but it *is* for many believers who are confused by the **elephant of mixture**. Why? Because they are trying to obtain from God what He has <u>already provided through Jesus</u>. Ignorance, doubt and unbelief about who He <u>really</u> is, traps them into relating to God as a fickle judge who gives blessings and healing and miracles arbitrarily to some - but not to them.

Eventually, they conclude that "He does not really love me" or "I am not worthy" or "God stopped doing all that when the last Apostle died, centuries ago." We tend to form our concept of God according to human experience in the **seen realm** instead of on the **whole gospel of grace** from Jesus. It seems easier to focus on the world around me rather than discover and operate from the "word of Christ" that reveals God's **New Covenant realities in Christ**, apprehended by faith. It *seems* easier - until we get desperate when the answers from the **seen realm** "don't work."

This parable has some parallels to the Israelite's plight in Egypt, discussed in Chapter Sixteen. When things got really tough, they "cried out to God" who apparently did not come running immediately. They persisted and He eventually raised up Moses. But, at first, Moses tried to save them *his* way. This cost them 40 years while Moses got his head straight shepherding sheep. (This is about faith in God's strength, not ours.) Then, those who trusted in God's direction about putting a lamb's blood on the door post were spared the death of their firstborn son. Those who followed Moses out of Egypt left healthy, rich and free, all by faith. But later, they failed many faith tests by focusing on the **seen** circumstances, not on God. It cost the first generation the blessings of the Promised Land. It was theirs by grace through faith but unbelief, not God, kept them out. So it is no coincidence that Jesus ended the parable above by saying:

Yet truly, when the Son of man returns, do you think that he will find faith on earth?

Most believers think that this refers to Jesus' second coming and it probably does. But even when Jesus walked on earth, He experienced more unbelief than belief, even among His own disciples. This is even after they witnessed many miracles in the **seen realm**. Then, even though He told them of His coming death, they did not believe Him. They clung to their hope that He would conquer the Romans, not to His word to them. Consequently, when He died, they were fearful and demoralized and so, before He arose, there was no expectant faith. Their wrong beliefs were always founded on what they saw, not on what He said. No wonder they often missed it and why we can miss Father-God's best sometimes too.

Vindicated By Our Just Judge And Father

Believer, as you increasingly embrace Jesus' **whole gospel of grace**, you will understand that you already have been "vindicated" by Jesus. God judged and defeated the devil through Jesus, removed your sin nature and gave you a new one now compatible with Him, positioned you in heaven **in Him** and He has provided everything you need for life and godliness – just by believing His revelation to Paul. You reside in the **unseen** Promised Land of heaven now and the **unseen** King of all Kings resides in you. What more do you need? Persistently asking for what you already have or trying to get it through your efforts, produces needless frustration and anger, depression and even despair. It comes from being tromped on by the **elephant of mixture** instead of from living the **butterfly life** of dependent faith in God's love for you that leads to experiencing the liberty of resting **in Him.** That is God's will for everyone because He is not partial to a chosen few. It is God's enemy who steals the word of Jesus' **whole gospel of lavish grace and truth** from us and plants weeds of deception and lies about Father-God's true nature.

Misconceptions From Translations

Another source of potential misconceptions about Father-God's nature and about our new nature (as well as other key concepts) can come from translations of the Bible that ignore the culture and context of the passage. (I elaborate on this and other causes in Appendix # 12.) One of my own misconceptions about Father-God came from a common translation of John 15:1-3:

I (Jesus) am the true vine, and my Father is the vinedresser. Every branch in Me that does not bear fruit, He removes. And each one that does bear fruit, He will prune, so that it may bring forth more fruit.

340

Taken at face value, this <u>translation</u> says, in effect, that all believers (branches) are under pressure to "bear fruit" or God "removes" or "cuts us off" from Jesus. Of course, that can only mean one thing - being hell-bent since there are only two kingdoms in the **big picture**. That frightening thought undermines any sense of relational security with Father-God. Of course, it is consistent with the **pre-cross** time period under the Mosaic Law that Jesus came to fulfill and replace. Simply put, this *translation* uses words that describe God's conditional acceptance of the Jews (not me), based on their performance - Galatianism - *not* on grace. If that was still true under the **New Covenant**, it would deny Jesus' **finished work** and nullify His **divine exchange** with us. And that is probably what a lot of law-minded believers still think this passage is meant to convey. The **elephant of mixture** is the wrong belief that is mentally condemning its victims.

How relieved I was to discover that the exact opposite is true - according to the grape-growing practices of the day and the *primary* meaning of the Greek verb "airo," which is "to lift," *not* "to remove." It turns out that both definitions (lift and remove) are possible but vinedressers typically do not cut off and remove grape branches during growing season. Why? Because they won't be able to reap any fruit - which is the whole reason for having a vineyard. Instead, the vinedresser <u>lifts up</u> the sagging branches, possibly dust or mud-covered etc., and ties each one carefully to the sturdy trellis. This is regarded as "training" the branch, giving it the support it needs to be cleansed by the rain and to yield fruit.

The vinedresser may also prune off unneeded *shoots* on the branch that waste the energy of the sap in order to encourage *more* fruit-bearing. That is a description much more in keeping with the merciful, magnanimous heart of our Father-God who sent us the Holy Spirit to sanctify our outer man. Unfortunately, a translator's ignorance of vine dressing (or his bias about who God really is etc.) can influence the choice of alternative English words for a particular Greek word and, thereby, distort the true meaning of Bible passages. The **New Covenant** is *unconditional* and *unilateral* and *eternal*. Salvation and all of God's other blessings are based on our faith in the fruit of Jesus life, not on what we "produce," otherwise our salvation would be based on the "works of the law" – Judaism.

Another major misconception about Father-God's nature of love and mercy comes from an unfortunate carryover from the Mosaic Law which sets the tone in Hebrews 12:5-11:

And ye have forgotten the exhortation which speaketh unto you as unto children, My child, despise not thou the chastening of the Lord, nor faint when thou art rebuked of him. For whom the Lord loveth he chasteneth, and ***<u>scourgeth</u>*** every child whom he receiveth. If ye endure chastening, God dealeth with you as with sons; for what son is he whom the father chasteneth not? But if ye be without chastisement, whereof all are partakers, then are ye bastards, and not sons. Furthermore we have had fathers of our flesh which corrected us, and we gave them reverence: shall we not much rather be in subjection unto the Father of spirits, and live? For they verily for a few days chastened us <u>after their own pleasure</u>; but he for our profit, that we might be partakers of his holiness. Now no chastening for the present seemeth to be joyous, but grievous: nevertheless afterward it yieldeth the peaceable fruit of righteousness unto them which are exercised thereby. (KJV Public Domain)

This passage is often used by law-minded pastors and teachers to say or imply: "No pain from God, then no gain from God." Where does this notion of punishment and pain come from? It is found in verse six, which is a quote from the **pre-cross** book of Proverbs 3:11-12. Hopefully that realization should trigger a red flag and raise this question for a **New Covenant** grace-based believer: "Does that Old Testament verse apply to me as a totally forgiven, righteous saint **in Christ** or not?" If God now punishes believers by scourgings and whippings, **post-cross**, then Jesus' died in vain because that would mean that His substitutionary suffering and death changed nothing. But the glorious truth of the **whole gospel** is that Jesus' cross changed everything for believers. Consequently, passages from the whole Old Testament, and especially from the Mosaic Covenant, must be discerned properly in light of Jesus' **finished work** of His **divine exchange** with all believers in order to avoid being mentally stomped on by the **elephant** of Galatianism.

The author of Hebrews quoted the above passage from Proverbs accurately. But by introducing it, he brought the negative concept of "punishment" into the **post-cross** era, even though God's entire wrath was exhausted on the body of Jesus when He became mankind's sin. That is why God had to forsake Jesus just before His death. But now, the good news for us is that Father-God views and deals with us believers as He sees and relates to the exalted Christ Jesus because we are united with Christ in God. So, the unfortunate inclusion of this passage potentially casts a negative bias in a translator's choice of which word he picks among the various possibilities for the general notion of "correction" found in a Greek concordance. In this case, all the Greek words related to "correction" in this passage (that do not come from Proverbs 3:11-12) come from the same Greek root word and they all carry the *primary* meaning of "training, teaching, educating, nurturing and disciplining." However, the Old Testament form of correction was apparently punishment by whipping and or scourging, so a *secondary* "implied" meaning is "punishment." That is a big difference in tone and practice from the process of teaching and training to help change wrong assumptions and beliefs that lead to unprofitable behavior. The goodness of God leads to repentance, says Romans 2:4b, while punishment causes fear, alienation and distance. It is not uncommon for people to come to hate what they are afraid of.

Training up a child by beating him is obviously not the same form of "correction" as training him through teaching and discipling the way Jesus did with His disciples. Did He beat or punish any of them? Of course not. When He did speak pointedly to Peter or to the Pharisees, for example, it was to get them to change their mind (repent) to agree with God. He was motivated by love, not hate. Jesus even restored the ear (that Peter had impulsively cut of) of the man who came to help arrest Him in the garden. It was another grace-based demonstration of Father-God's mercy. In fact, Jesus was in the process of going to Calvary to absorb the punishment we all deserved, *not to dish-out even more*! Similarly, Paul mirrors the tone of the **New Covenant** by reminding them, in 1 Thessalonians 2:11-12, what kingdom they are a part of now as God's children:

> For you know that we treated you as a father treats his own children, encouraging, comforting and urging you to live lives worthy of God who calls you into His Kingdom and glory.

Now can you see how the above translation of this passage could imprint or reinforce a very grim mental picture of God's nature in your mind – especially if your natural father used hurtful punishment rather than godly discipline to correct you? This is another area where believers often need the renewing of their mind by the Holy Spirit to properly process negative past experiences so that they can then train up children God's way, which leads to life, not death – physically, mentally, emotionally and spiritually. It starts with coming to know who your loving Father-God really is, despite whatever lies and hurtful experiences the world system, other people, your flesh or the devil have planted in your mind. Coming to know and believe the truth will progressively set your mind free to see and think the way Father-God does, according to 2 Corinthians 5:16.

Setting The Record Straight

In short, God is not a withholder or an ogre or a hateful judge or a mean punisher at His core. And He sends no one to hell. Adam's rebellion back in the Garden put mankind on a train bound for hell. God is legally able to offer mankind a new train – *the Romans 10:9-13 Express to heaven* - because Jesus willingly absorbed all just punishment for all sin, forgave all of mankind, and paid for everyone's ticket to heaven with His own life. Now it is up to each person to freely choose to repent – to "change trains" - by accepting and redeeming God's free ticket of salvation, bought for you by Jesus' own blood. This qualifies anyone who receives Jesus' free gift to be part of God's family forever – and to be Jesus' Bride to boot. This is what it means to be fully "reconciled to God."

God's view of Jesus' **new creation** Bride is as a righteous, blameless, glorious, beautiful, regenerated creation and all believers, collectively, are **in Christ Jesus** already – spiritually speaking. That is God's perspective of Jesus' accomplishment. Again, what "works" do we have to **do** to be Jesus' spotless Bride? None! It was all done 2000 years ago for all who would believe and receive Him down through the corridors of time. Now finally, that **unseen reality** is increasingly being manifested on earth like God wants it to be and the **elephant of mixture** is being overcome. How? By God's saints discovering, living in and enjoying the **butterfly life** of Jesus' radical **grace gospel** and spreading the truth about Jesus' **finished work** to all mankind, according to the will and plan of our gracious Father-God.

Our Message As God's Ambassadors: Love Has Made A Way Across The Chasm

Therefore, as Father-God's ambassadors, we are commissioned to *lovingly announce* to unbelievers God's exceptionally good news to them from 2 Corinthians 5:19. And what is that again? Jesus' **finished work,** done on behalf of fallen mankind, accomplished:

1) the total forgiveness of all of mankind's past, present and future sins and consequently

2) all of mankind is now reconciled to God - from God's viewpoint. (Please don't forget that important qualifier).

It's *almost* as if the spiritual separation between God and Adam never happened. Metaphorically, Jesus' cross was the missing plank that bridged the yawning chasm. What remains for unbelievers to "do?" Be reconciled to God by grace through faith in what Jesus has already done. How? Just walk across the "plank" of Romans 10:9-13, into our loving God's waiting arms. Isn't this the sense of what the angels prophesied at Jesus' birth when they announced new hope to a fallen mankind: "… (God's) peace on earth, (His) good will toward mankind" (Luke 2:14b). That is why the Savior's coming was such *good* news that replaced all the bad news from Adam to Calvary. He brought the grace and truth of His supply instead of the demands of more Law. He made *all things new* for you to receive, believer!

I hope you have enjoyed this exploration of God's offer of the **butterfly life** and have been invigorated by inhaling the freeing atmosphere of Jesus' **whole gospel of His grace.** This final chapter repeated some of the key truths that prove and highlight just how wonderfully good Father-God really is now, *and has always been*, despite the devil's lies and the misgivings and chaos caused by Adam's Fall. Appendix # 9 presents a summary of 45 key biblical truths, offered as a review and resource to equip the saints to help combat the lies so common in circles where the **elephant of mixture** reigns - even in churches. Equip yourself with **big picture** thinking – the way God sees - to enable you to resist the lies of the devil who is bent on stealing the truth of your true identity and the other blessings and benefits of Jesus' **divine exchange.** Jesus reversed what Adam did to the human race so that, never again, must the world system, the flesh or the devil reign over those **in Christ**. We have Father-God's promise, actualized **in Christ Jesus** through His **finished work.** Again, He declares it like this in Romans 5:17:

> For though, by the one offense, death reigned through Adam, yet so much more shall those who receive both an abundance of grace and (God's) gift of righteousness, <u>reign in life through Jesus Christ</u>.

When Jesus declared "It is finished," He meant it! His grace-based gospel is "Jesus + nothing else!" Accept and rest in all He has done for you so that you can enjoy the **butterfly life in Him** and pollinate others with Jesus' **whole gospel of grace.** It is the revelation of Father-God's true nature and His ultimate intention to include every willing human in His family forever.

> The thief (the devil) comes only to steal and slaughter and destroy. But I (Jesus) came so that they might have life and have it more abundantly (John 10:10).

Thank you, Father, Son and Holy Spirit for ALL You have done. Help me to bathe my mind in your true truth, now and forever. Amen

These last three song-poems offer a simple but profound overview of what Jesus has provided for us for which we give Father-God, Christ Jesus and the Holy Spirit thankful worship eternally.

MORE THAN FORGIVENESS of all my sins, amazing as that is.
More than deliverance from death and hell, fantastic as that is.

For all of the prophets of long ago tried to look but could not see
That You, the Messiah, would share true Life by dying on a tree.

What could be wiser than freeing me from sin and slavery
By nailing me to the cross with You to put an end to me,

Then raising me from the grave with You, brand new, completely free
And able to know and worship You, my Lord, my victory!

What could be greater than lifting me by resurrection life
To heavenly places to reign with You above all fear and strife?

It's making me one with You, my Life, my hope, my everything,
Secure in Your love, forevermore, my joy and covering.

Then, helping me share Your love and Word with those who doubt You care,
Inviting them into life in You, in answer to Your prayer. (John 17:21)
© Copyright 2003 by Leonard J Ransil

LAUNCHING OUT IN FAITH,
Trusting in Your lavish grace
Overflowing joy,
Focused on Your glorious face
Captured by Your love,
Melting in Your warm embrace.
As I worship You, Jesus (2x)

Righteous through Your cross,
Privileged to abide in You.
Sharing heart to heart,
Living to commune with You.
Following Your will,
All my needs are met in You.
As I worship You, Jesus (2x)

Held secure in You,
Reigning in the heavenlies.
Loving not my life,
You've become my destiny.
Tested by the storm,
Drawing on Your victory,
As I worship You, Jesus (2x)
© Copyright 1999 by Leonard J. Ransil

You're the **LORD OF MY HEART**,
You're the Savior of my soul
Sweet Messiah, Son of God.
You're the One who made me whole
King of kings, Lord of lords,
You're the bright and Morning Star.
I just can't express how wonderful You are.

Your name is Jesus, Jesus,
The Word made flesh. King of glory,
Emmanuel, You are the Way,
You are the Truth, You are the Life.

You're the Light of the world,
 Friend of sinners, Mighty King.
You're the God of all the earth,
You created everything.
Man of sorrows, Prince of peace,
You're the chosen one of God,
And His covenant you sealed with Your blood.

I give You glory, Jesus, the Lamb of God.
Lord most holy, You have delivered me from death.
You are the Vine that gives me life.

You are faithful and true,
You're my Healer and my Rock.
You're the precious Gift of God,
The great Shepherd of the flock.
My Foundation, Bread of life,
You're my Master and the Door.
And I long to live with You forevermore.

So I surrender, Jesus, I belong to You.
You're the sacrifice that ransomed me
You paid the price,
You set me free, now I am Yours.
© 1980 John J. Heintzel
Permission is granted to Leonard Ransil for use in this book.

POSTSCRIPT

Dear Saint in Christ,

Thank you for joining me on this rather lengthy journey of an overview of Father-God's grace and truth. I hope it has been an enlightening, refreshing and enjoyable one for you. I purposely repeated many key points (and scriptures) expressed in different and expanded ways because many of these insights are so new to most believers today. Brain research indicates that spaced repetition is needed to help people replace wrong concepts with true ones. Also, I took extra care to provide and repeat many in depth proof texts and sources to back up my content. All that added another 100+ pages to this study book.

Please be sure to check out the Appendices and Endnotes which greatly elaborate on some of the more "controversial" topics of this book. The song-poems, included in many of the chapters, focus on Jesus' **whole gospel of radical grace**. They are offered to help you further renew your mind with the truths about Jesus' **finished work** described in this book. They and many other of my scripture-based songs are a staple at my own men's weekly Bible class and at my pastor's Bible study night at church. I plan to offer a CD recording of the 33 songs in this book on Amazon entitled *Songs of Grace and Truth*, as well as publish at least four other books on Amazon. I also hope to have an interactive blog at www.**totaltruth.org** - as time permits.

I am available to give seminars and retreats on this book's content. <u>Have guitar, will travel!</u> I welcome any requests, questions, constructive comments, suggestions - pro or con - regarding the content of this study book by using my e-mail address   ljrmsn562@msn.com

God's grace and peace to you and yours in abundance, now and forever! Amen

Leonard John Ransil

APPENDICES CONTENTS

APPENDIX # 1

DATES OF THE NEW TESTAMENT BOOKS

The following chronological order of the New Testament books is based on the opinions of several hundred conservative and liberal scholars. The listing of individual scholars and their dates for each book of the New Testament is provided in the links at:

http://www.evidenceforjesuschrist.org/Pages/bible/dating-nt-chronological_order.htm

The data for this list will always be a work in progress and is constantly changing as it is being updated. I do grant permission for a link to this page if proper credit is given. Permission to copy this data for written publications or classes can be obtained by writing Gary Butner at DrGary777@aol.com. Copyright 2014, EvidenceforJesusChrist.org.Data content collected and input by Gary Butner, Th.D. Original spreadsheet designed by R.A.Sickler, Ph.D.
(1) John Mark - John was his Hebrew name and Mark his Latin name.
(2) Author unknown. Opinions include Luke, Paul, Barnabas, Apollos, Priscilla and Aquila.
(3) John the Apostle or John the Elder. The evidence is strongest for the apostle.
(4) There is a pronounced difference between scholars for the book of James, and so we have excluded the scholars with higher dates from Modified James.
Protected by Copyscape - Electronic Copies Are Not Allowed. Permission is granted for up to 100 copies on printed paper for classroom use.

Updated 1/1/2014. Copyright Errant Skeptics Research Institute. Copyscape Protected. Do not copy without written permission. Permission is granted for up to 100 paper copies for Sunday School classes. Electronic copies are not allowed.

Permission to use the above chart was received from author confirmed by these e-mails: on December 3, 2014, Leonard Ransil wrote:

Dear Dr. Butner,
I am writing a book on the early church and find your "range" approach to bible book dates novel and very sensible. I would like to include it (or the data only on Paul's books and James' book) in an appendix in my book with due credit to you, of course. I am referring to the site:
Sincerely,
Leonard Ransil

Dear Mr. Ransil
You have my permission to put my chart or a link in your book. The site's name has been changed to EvidenceForJesusChrist.org. The information is in Excel format. Proper credit is required.
Grace and peace,
Gary Butner, Th.D.

N.T. ORDER	CHRONO-LOGICAL ORDER	DOCUMENT	NUMBER SCHOLARS	RANGE OF DATES EARLY	LATE		YEAR AD 33	AUTHOR
		Jesus Christ's Death and Resurrection						
13	1	1 Thessalonians	41	50.8	51.4	A.D.	51.1	Paul
14	3	2 Thessalonians	33	51.2	51.9	A.D.	51.5	Paul
9	2	Galatians	40	50.8	52.4	A.D.	51.4	Paul
7	4	1 Corinthians	43	55.0	55.5	A.D.	55.2	Paul
8	5	2 Corinthians	39	55.7	56.2	A.D.	56.0	Paul
6	6	Romans	43	56.7	57.2	A.D.	56.9	Paul
11	8	Philippians	41	60.1	61.0	A.D.	60.6	Paul
18	7	Philemon	37	59.9	61.1	A.D.	60.5	Paul
12	10	Colossians	39	60.2	61.3	A.D.	60.7	Paul
10	11	Ephesians	38	60.8	62.2	A.D.	61.5	Paul
2	12	**Date for the Gospel of Mark**	72	58.9	64.3	A.D.	61.8	John Mark (1)
20	9	James	70	51.9	69.0	A.D.	60.4	James
	N/A	James (Modified)	51	47.0	54.6	A.D.	50.8	James (4)
15	13	1 Timothy	36	62.9	64.6	A.D.	63.8	Paul
17	14	Titus	32	63.2	65.0	A.D.	64.1	Paul
16	17	2 Timothy	35	65.2	66.4	A.D.	65.8	Paul
1	16	**Date for the Gospel of Matthew**	71	62.1	69.0	A.D.	65.5	Matthew
21	15	1 Peter	32	63.1	65.9	A.D.	64.5	Peter
3	18	**Date for the Gospel of Luke**	70	64.1	68.4	A.D.	66.3	Luke
19	20	Hebrews	39	64.6	70.3	A.D.	67.4	Unknown(2)
5	19	Acts	62	66.6	68.1	A.D.	67.4	Luke
22	21	2 Peter	33	67.1	69.5	A.D.	68.3	Peter
23	22	Jude	30	68.0	75.4	A.D.	71.7	Jude
4	23	**Date for the Gospel of John**	60	83.5	89.4	A.D.	86.5	John the Apostle
24	24	1 John	33	85.8	93.3	A.D.	89.5	John (3)
25	26	2 John	33	86.8	93.8	A.D.	90.3	John the Apostle
26	25	3 John	33	86.3	92.8	A.D.	89.6	John the Apostle
27	27	Revelation	39	90.1	94.4	A.D.	92.2	John the Apostle

APPENDIX # 2

THE "OUR FATHER," FULFILLED IN JESUS' FINISHED WORK

As we saw in Chapter Twelve, there are many scripture passages that are still unwittingly used today to promote and reinforce the **elephant of mixture**. This is because Jesus' **gospel of grace**, revealed to Paul in about 42 AD, is not used as the plumb line to divide the word rightly by understanding the purpose and terms of the various covenants in the Bible. What were mere types and shadows from Genesis to Calvary are now a reality for believers who are **in Christ Jesus.**

Matthew 6:9–13 is often referred to as the "Our Father" prayer and is quoted in the chart below. I am using it here as an *example* of how to discern, by the Holy Spirit, the difference between what Jesus taught the disciples under the Law covenant, **pre-cross,** in contrast to the realities of the **New Covenant's** pure, unfettered grace, **post-cross.** This differentiation is based on Jesus' **divine exchange** revealed directly to Paul.

If we keep asking for what we already have, we are *not* understanding and enjoying what His **finished work** has already provided for us. For example, this **pre-cross** prayer asks for "His Kingdom to come on earth" even though He has already sent His Kingdom (righteousness, peace and joy) into every believer in the Person of the Holy Spirit, according to 1 Corinthians 6:19. Wherever the King lives is where His Kingdom is. "The Kingdom of God is within" means what it says, according to Luke 17:21. Asking for what has already happened within us, means we either are in ignorance, denial, doubt or unbelief that we are now temples of God Himself. What could be more important than the miracle of God living inside of you and you living **in Christ Jesus**? Walking in this **unseen reality** by faith will produce the fruit and freedom of love that is found only **in Christ.**

God is not a distant, unapproachable Being, far beyond the reach of human experience, as many people, who call themselves Christians, believe and confess. I know Him as my personal Baptizer, Counselor, Guide, Teacher, Comforter and Friend etc. He does *not* convict me of my sin, which has been fully forgiven and not joined to me (not "re-membered" by God), according to the terms of the New Covenant, found in Hebrews 8:12 and 10:17. But He was sent by Jesus to *convince* me of my right-standing with God even when I do sin. That was not true for the heroes in the Old Testament who longed for such a covenant that we believers now have. The present-day believers, who are experiencing this Kingdom relationship, are thanking God for His gifts and blessings and equipping others for the work of the ministry, rather than passively praying for His Kingdom to come. They agree with God that "Where the King resides, there is the Kingdom" and delight to worship Him and fellowship with Him day in and day out. If we limit our thinking to just longing for the Kingdom's full manifestation in the end times, we risk missing the benefits of reigning here on earth now, as Romans 5:17 says is possible to those **in Christ Jesus.**

The phrase "…forgive us our sins as we forgive those who sin against us …" is another **pre-cross** statement that confuses believers today. Since Jesus said it, it must be true. Well, yes, it *was* true at the time He said it. But He said it to His disciples, <u>not to us believers today</u>. Why? Because things changed drastically for the better at Calvary when He became our sin and forgave the sins of the whole world, according to 2 Corinthians 5:19 and 1 John 2:2. Again, He made "all things new" spiritually. Consequently, the forgiveness of sins is not contingent on how well I forgive other people's sins. Such a requirement would put me back under the "works of the law" and under a curse. His forgiveness of all my sins, past, present and future, and His **divine exchange** with me, is a gift based on faith alone, not contingent on my efforts to get forgiven by God. That is good news. Chapter Fourteen and Appendix # 4 discuss all this at length.

Another phrase that needs rethinking is "and lead us not into temptation." Since God hates sin because of what it does to us, why would He tempt us to sin? Just because the Spirit led Jesus into the desert, that does not mean that He also led Him into temptation, per se. It was the devil who chose to tempt Jesus there. Another legitimate translation of the Greek word is "**adversity.**" God led Jesus into the adversity of the desert but God did not make the devil tempt Him. Nor does He lead us, His precious children, into temptation to sin. Rather, He provides a way of escape when it comes. James 1:13-14 and 1 Corinthians 10:13 tell us that temptation is often triggered by our own misguided craving and curiosity. Temptation appeals to our own carnal/soulish/fleshy desires. The prayer would be better <u>translated</u> "and lead us not into adversity but deliver us from that evil." Jesus bore all the adversity of Satan's hate and fury and God's wrath when He became sin who knew no sin on Calvary so that we would not have to suffer from those sources. The world and the flesh are adversarial enough. Jesus conquered Satan so that we can enforce His victory over our Adversary, the devil.

A man who hates broccoli will not be tempted to covet or steal another man's broccoli. The answer is not to focus on the law which only arouses carnal desires and brings condemnation and death (see 2 Corinthians 3:6-9). Rather, prevention is far better than a cure. Therefore, the more we focus on Jesus and His **finished work** the more we will walk according to a Holy Spirit-led life as He guides us from within, instead of walking according to the natural mind focused on the law and the flesh. His fruit such as love, joy, peace, patience and self-control is the power needed to resist temptation from the world system, the flesh and the devil. Resistance to these influences is not by one's might or soulish will power, but by resting and depending on the power of the Holy Spirit. Right believing about *who* you belong to (Jesus who bought you) and, therefore, *who* you are now **in Christ Jesus,** produces His fruit of right living.

In contrast to the *Our Father* prayer, the coming of God's New Order of radical grace was announced when Jesus prayed the true "Lord's Prayer" in John 17:21 which was then manifested at Pentecost. Among other wonderful things, Jesus asked Father-God to make believers *one* with Jesus Himself, just as He is *one* with Father-God. This momentous miracle happens whenever an **in Adam** sinner is reborn of God, making him or her a righteous saint **in Christ Jesus** - regardless of his or her behavior. Oneness with God happens by a divine exchange of natures with Jesus. In order to transform sinners into holy saints through rebirth, Jesus first had to make the answer to His prayer possible by dealing with the "nature issue" and then the "sin issue" (which is really a "law issue") by becoming sin and then paying mankind's sin-debt in full and nailing the Law to the cross. As we have quoted repeatedly with joy, sin is not imputed where there is no performance-based law, as Jesus declares through Paul in Romans 4:15. Do you see how wonderful and radically different Jesus' **grace gospel** really is?

The chart below compares and contrasts the **pre-cross** prayer Jesus gave to His disciples while they were all still under the Law, with a list of **New Covenant** realities for believers, based on Jesus' **divine exchange** with us. The most important two-fold provision, which made possible all the other blessings of this **New Covenant,** was 1) Jesus' blood sacrifice for all sins of all mankind for all time by 2) becoming sin – taking on the Adamic nature which was crucified at Calvary. How else could mankind be reconciled to God unless all that Adam *was and did – a traitorous rebel* who caused mankind's spiritual "alienation" from God – was crucified and eliminated in the body of Christ Jesus on Calvary for all those **in Christ**?

This **post-cross** update of the *Our Father*, based on a believer's **New Covenant** which God made with Jesus on our behalf, is *not* intended to be an official replacement for the *Our Father*, per se. That prayer was appropriate for the **pre-cross** time period. Rather, it is cited as yet another example of the **elephant of mixture** that is confusing many saints today because they fail to fully understand the radically different grace-based *terms* of our **post-cross New Covenant,** all because of Christ Jesus' **finished work** nearly 2000 years ago.

Matthew 6:9–13 Pre-Cross	The Post-Cross Gospel Of Jesus' Finished Work
Our Father in heaven, hallowed be your name.	My Abba-Father in heaven, holy is Your name. Romans 8:15-16 and Galatians 4:6
Your kingdom come	Thank you Father that Your Kingdom of righteousness, peace and joy in the person of the Holy Spirit, dwells in my new heart so that I can reign on earth by grace through Your gift of faith. Romans 14:17, Luke 17:21, Romans 5:17 and Ephesians 2:8-9
Your will be done, on earth, as it is in heaven.	Thank you Holy Spirit for living Your life through me as You lived through Jesus so that You can lead and guide me in Father's will and purpose for me here on earth. Romans 5:13, Galatians 5:18 and 25, Ephesians 2:10
Give us this day our daily bread	Thank you for providing everything I need for life and godliness by placing me **in Christ Jesus and being my supplier.** 2 Peter 1:3
and forgive us our (sin) debt , as we also forgive our debtors	Thank you Father for Jesus' full payment and forgiveness of all my past, present and future sins and removing all curses over me on Calvary. 2 Corinthians 5:19, 1 John 2:2 and Colossians 2:13
And lead us not into temptation, but deliver us from evil	Thank you Father for rescuing me from Darkness and for placing me **in Christ Jesus** who defeated Satan and now reigns over all Principalities and Powers on earth through us. I now enjoy and enforce Jesus' glorious victory by providing me with a way of escape for every temptation. Colossians 2:13-15, 1 Corinthians 10:13, Colossians 1:13.
For Yours is the kingdom, and the power, and the glory, forever and ever. Amen	Thank you, Father-God, for including me in your everlasting Kingdom to love and to worship you in spirit and in truth with all the other saints as we share in Your glory forever. Amen John 4:23, Romans 8:17

The following prayer includes the central purpose of Jesus' salvation offered to mankind: to transform **in Adam** sinners into **in Christ** saints so that they can be **one** with the Trinity forever, fulfilling what Jesus prayed for His disciples and us, according to John 17:21.

Dear Abba-Father,

*Thank You for placing me next to You **in Christ Jesus** in heavenly places by faith so that I can be one spirit with You and glorify Your holy name forever. You sent Your Kingdom within my new spirit-self in the Person of the Holy Spirit so that I can do Your will consistently on earth, even as it is lived here in heaven. Thank You for totally forgiving and forgetting all of my past, present and future sins at Calvary and making me a partaker of Your divine nature as Your favored child so that I am now free to live according to Your plan and purpose for my life - to know, love, and glorify You, now and forever. Thank you for making me an overcomer over all temptations and lies of the world, the flesh and the devil by letting You, the Spirit of truth and love, live and reign in and through the new me as my Sanctifier. Thank you for supplying everything I need for life and godliness and equipping and positioning me to be a blessing to others as Your Ambassador on earth. Thank You for including me in Your everlasting Kingdom to enjoy and worship You forever, in spirit and in truth, with all the other new creation saints, reborn **in Christ Jesus.** Amen !*

APPENDIX # 3

MIXTURE IN JOHN CALVIN'S
INSTITUTES OF THE CHRISTIAN RELIGION

A careful reading of Book Two, Chapter Seven, sections 11-15 of Calvin's famed *Institutes of the Christian Religion*, reveals an alarming degree of Galatianism – the mixture of opposing covenants. Calvin quotes many of Jesus' revelations to Paul but then charges through these "stop signs" as though the **finished work** of Christ Jesus makes no real difference in the believer's very nature. For example, in section #10 he quotes Timothy 1:9 (which coupled with verse 8) states that:

> But we know that the Law is good, if one makes use of it properly. Knowing this, that the law was not set in place for the righteous (those **in Christ**), but for the unrighteous (those in Adam) – rebels, ungodly, sinners....

Can this be said any more clearly? The Law was not made for righteous saints who are, by definition, **in Christ**. Certainly, the law is good in and of itself. (And so was the Tree of the Knowledge of Good and Evil – but it was not good for man.) But it has a proper use and was given only to the Israelites for a specific purpose. This purpose was to reveal mankind's real problem, the corrupted seed of the **in Adam** nature, caused by eating the Law Tree, as we proved in Chapter Eight. Adam's nature was corrupted precisely because he ate of the Law Tree instead of the Life Tree – Jesus. The Mosaic Law as not given to save the Jews spiritually but to reveal how condemned they already were by being **in Adam**. Why? So that when their only hope for being rescued and transformed came to earth – the Man Jesus – they would quit relying on their own law-keeping (morality) and accept and depend on Jesus' **finished work** of the cross for His gift of justification. Nonetheless, Calvin is unwittingly telling believers to still focus on law-keeping as a "duty" and a help to believers. This is the very temptation from the Judaizers that bewitched the foolish Galatians (see Galatians 3:1).

Unfortunately, Calvin is promoting the same heresy – **the elephant of mixture** - that the Jerusalem church retained and defended. This was even after God revealed His perspective on Law-mindedness to Peter at Cornelius's house and Paul's testimony at the first Council in Jerusalem. Like the Catholic church before him, Calvin fails to help the believer to discern the monumental differences between the Mosaic Covenant and Jesus' blood Covenant which all believers are included into, by faith alone. The former covenant is based on man's efforts to achieve or maintain justification – an impossibility. The latter covenant is based on Jesus' **divine exchange** that totally justifies a rebel by being reborn of God – by grace through faith alone.

The Law's function was to arouse sin, cause death and bring the **in Adam** Jew to the end of himself so that he would become desperate to receive Jesus. And since the law was never given to the Gentiles, Paul did not teach on obedience to the law or even obedience *to* Christ, per se, but said "bring into captivity every thought to the obedience *of* Christ" (2 Corinthians 10:5). That way, dependence on Jesus and on His **divine exchange** is one's constant focus, not on self. The law always demands perfect obedience to achieve or maintain righteousness – an impossibility for us. Jesus' gift of grace supplies His gift of righteousness by faith in what He did for mankind nearly 2000 years ago. The law is a collection of relatively weak and inadequate principles. They are unable to make **in Adam** sinners righteous. So the law was made obsolete and nailed to the cross for all believers. That is good news. But Calvin insists that believers can profit from obedience to the Mosaic Law – which he wrongly asserts is written on the believer's heart. (Why would God write an obsolete law which ministers death and condemnation on our new heart?) According to section 12 in Book 2, Chapter 7 of Calvin's Institutes:

> The third use of the Law (being also the principal use, and more closely connected with its proper end) has respect to believers in whose hearts the Spirit of God already flourishes and reigns. For although the Law is written and engraven on their hearts by the finger of God, that is, although they are so influenced and actuated by the Spirit, that they desire to obey God, there are two ways in which they still profit in the Law. (1) For it is the best instrument for enabling them daily to learn with greater truth and certainty what that will of the Lord is which they aspire to follow, and (2) to confirm them in this knowledge; just as a servant who desires with all his soul to approve himself to his master, must still observe, and be careful to ascertain his master's dispositions, that he may comport himself in accommodation to them. Let none of us deem ourselves exempt from this necessity, for none have as yet attained to such a degree of wisdom, as that they may not, by the daily instruction of the Law, advance to a purer knowledge of the Divine will.

If the law was not made for the righteous (see 1 Timothy 1:9) and is now obsolete (see Hebrews 8:13), how can it embody the will of the Lord for those **in Christ**? Some teach that Jesus sent the Holy Spirit to help believers keep the law. But Jesus revealed to Paul that the law is not of faith and whatever is not of faith is sin. When you focus on the law, you are walking by natural sight; when you walk according to the Spirit, you focus on Jesus by faith. It was the Pharisees' pre-occupation with the law that blinded them to their true salvation standing right in front of them - Jesus. How can obedience to the law that is impossible for us to keep perfectly, possibly gain the Master's approval? That is works-based thinking – Galatianism. Believers are already accepted and approved by God just by being **in Christ**. A daily focus on the law will arouse sin, bring death and cause the *feeling* of condemnation to any saint who takes Calvin's advice. He or she is in danger of **falling from grace** by going back under obedience to the law to achieve or maintain God's acceptance or approval.

But Calvin insists that obedience to the law is a remedy for sin. The Judaizers believed this too and constantly harassed Paul about it. Calvin continues:

> Then, because we need not doctrine merely, but exhortation also, the servant of God will derive this further advantage from the Law: by frequently meditating upon it, he will be excited to obedience, and confirmed in it, and so drawn away from the slippery paths of sin. In this way must the saints press onward, since, however great the alacrity with which, under the Spirit, they hasten toward righteousness, they are retarded by the sluggishness of the flesh, and make less progress than they ought. The Law acts like a whip to the flesh, urging it on as men do a lazy sluggish ass. Even in the case of a

spiritual man, inasmuch as he is still burdened with the weight of the flesh, the Law is a constant stimulus, pricking him forward when he would indulge in sloth.

David had this use in view when he pronounced this high eulogium on the Law, "The law of the Lord is perfect, converting the soul: the testimony of the Lord is sure, making wise the simple. The statutes of the Lord are right, rejoicing the heart: the commandment of the Lord is pure, enlightening the eyes," (Ps. 19:7, 8). Again, "Thy word is a lamp unto my feet, and a light unto my path," (Ps. 119:105). The whole psalm abounds in passages to the same effect. <u>Such passages are not inconsistent with those of Paul</u>, which show not the utility of the law to the regenerate, but what it is able of itself to bestow. The object of the Psalmist is to celebrate the advantages which the Lord, by means of his law, bestows on those whom he inwardly inspires with a love of obedience. And he adverts not to the mere precepts, but also to the promise annexed to them, which alone makes that sweet <u>which in itself is bitter</u>. For what is less attractive than <u>the law, when, by its demands and threatening, it overawes the soul, and fills it with terror</u>? David specially shows that in the law he saw the Mediator, without whom it gives no pleasure or delight.

Calvin says confidently that by frequently <u>meditating upon the Law</u> the believer will be drawn away from the slippery paths of sin. But Jesus told Paul that "The strength of sin is the Law "(1 Corinthians 15:56) and "… sin, seizing the opportunity <u>afforded by the commandment</u>, deceived me, and, <u>through the commandment, put me to death</u>" (Romans 7:8-11). It is the Law that arouses sin and brings death to those who focus on it instead of on Jesus. We covered all this in Chapter Nine. Somehow, Calvin missed the implications of the hazards of the Law for believers that Paul clearly explained. Consequently, his teaching has helped keep the **elephant of mixture** alive for centuries.

In all due respect, this is a grim picture of Christianity as defined by Calvin. No wonder so many unbelievers are turned off by people who believe this sordid view of God and His kingdom ways. No wonder Calvinists often seem so joyless in their daily lives if they use the law to whip their flesh (and probably other people's too). Do they really think that being under the law is somehow supposed to be a blessing. No wonder so many Christians are depressed and defeated and reject what they have been wrongly taught is the gospel - but is actually "no gospel at all." On the contrary, the true gospel is the experience of God's perfect love and grace that <u>casts out all fear and terror of Him</u> and of everything else. And it is the goodness of God that brings us to repentance, according to Romans 2:4. If the law had the power to help David "hasten toward righteousness" – defined as "right behavior" *only* under the Mosaic Law Covenant – why did he fall so badly?

But the most alarming thing about this section is that Calvin accuses Paul of promoting the very thing Paul railed against after he personally experienced the grace-based love of Father-God through Jesus. Calvin is reinforcing the lie that Mosaic Law righteousness (which is based on man's perfect performance) is the same as **New Covenant** righteousness that is based on Jesus' performance and given as a free, underserved gift, received by faith alone.

But Calvin doesn't stop there. In section 13, he rails against those who would dare teach the truth of Jesus' **radical grace-based gospel**, as follows:

Some unskilful (sic) persons, from not attending to this (Calvin's perspective), boldly discard the whole law of Moses, and do away with both its Tables, imagining it unchristian to adhere to a doctrine <u>which contains the ministration of death</u>. <u>Far from our thoughts be this profane notion</u>. Moses has admirably shown that the Law, which can produce nothing but death in sinners, <u>ought to have a better and more excellent effect upon the righteous.</u> When about to die, he thus addressed the people, "Set your hearts unto all the words which I testify among you this day, which ye shall command your children to observe to do, all the words of this law. For it is not a vain thing for you; <u>because it is your life</u> (Deut. 32:46, 47).

Again, for the Israelites living under the Mosaic Law, that was the only "light" that they had. So all they could do was to "try your best to obey the Law." But we know now that if they broke any part of it, they broke the whole Law. And no one but Jesus could keep it. That is why Jesus' fulfilled it, replaced it and gave us the higher law of the Spirit of life of the **New Covenant,** based on Jesus' performance, not on ours. It is a grace-based covenant, totally of faith in what Jesus has DONE, received as a totally free gift. Telling believers to combine the two opposing covenants nullifies both. Galatianism is a heresy and Calvin should have known better by properly dividing the word rightly, according to the terms of the various covenants. Instead, he put an obsolete covenant on par with the **New Covenant** that replaced it. In doing so, he unwittingly put Moses and Jesus as equals.

Why would God tell a reborn Christian to focus on anything that "arouses sin and administers death?" Jesus, through Paul, also said in the same passage that the law brought condemnation to the Jews but the **New Covenant** brings righteousness – justification by faith to believers. Inexplicably, <u>Calvin ends up reversing the intent of this very passage to insist that the Law, not the Holy Spirit, should be the focus and guide for the believer **in Christ**</u>. No wonder the **elephant of mixture** has had such a field day in many Protestant circles just like he did in the Jerusalem church and does in the Catholic church. Only Jesus is our way, our truth and our life – not the obsolete Mosaic Law. It is a mere shadow of the true source of grace and peace – Jesus Christ, who came to make all things new **in Him.** By living according to the Holy Spirit by the higher law of faith, love and liberty, believers will live the way Jesus lived on earth. He focused on His Father in the power of the Holy Spirit, not on "doing the works of the Law," per se. Otherwise, He would not have touched the leper or forgiven the woman caught in adultery. He focused on hearing His Father and now we can too.

More could be said about this section and the next two sections of *The Institutes* but, frankly, it is a depressing study. It so reminds me of the mind-set I learned and practiced diligently for much of my life. I am so grateful to have escaped into the arms of my loving Father-God, thanks to a revelation of Jesus' **divine exchange**. Unfortunately, Calvin just mimicked the diatribe that was begun by the Judaizers in Paul's day, echoed by the mainstream church through the centuries and is now being trumpeted like a herd of elephants today against the teachers of Jesus' **grace-based gospel**. I am glad to count myself among those walking increasingly in grace-based faith, love and liberty – the higher law. Apparently, John Calvin had no deep, personal revelation about the core of Jesus' **whole gospel** revealed to Paul in 42 AD and wonderfully unveiled in his writings. May we all embrace Jesus' **grace-based gospel** to Paul as God's plumb line, revealed to properly discern and interpret all the other books in the Bible.

APPENDIX # 4

AN EXPLANATION OF 1 JOHN 1:9 -
A FOLLOW UP OF CHAPTER FOURTEEN

Many, if not most, preachers and teachers in most Christian denominations today teach that 1 John 1:9 is written by John to born-again believers as a necessary condition for staying in right relationship and/or in fellowship with God. I already gave six reasons in Chapter Fourteen why 1 John 1:9, which "requires a confession of one's sins to God before He grants forgiveness," could not have been written to reborn believers. Why? Because we now know from Jesus' revelation to Paul that all of mankind's sins were forgiven at Calvary, according to 2 Corinthians 5:18-19 and John 2:2. So, the only thing that makes historical sense is that John wrote the first chapter of First John primarily to Jewish Gnostics in the Diaspora.

Why Was John Writing To Gnostics?

To understand why, it is necessary to understand the time and context in which the letter was written and to whom it was written. **First,** unlike most of all the other letters contained in the New Testament, John did not address this letter to a specific group in the beginning of the first chapter. However, he did address what we now call "Chapter 2" to "my dear children," a term of endearment in the actual Greek. The assumption is that he was addressing Chapter 1 to them as well. That is a false assumption. Let's see why.

First, one of the tip-offs to who he was addressing in Chapter One is verse eight: "If we say that we have no sin, ...". No orthodox Jew or true Christian would deny they have "sin." The essence of Judaism is knowing and obeying the Mosaic Law and having a sin-removing system of sacrifices to cover disobedience to avoid God's punishment, according to the terms of that particular covenant. Likewise, most Jewish Christians would understand, hopefully, that Jesus was the Lamb of God, the One, perfect sacrifice who took away all the sin of the world. In both cases, the reality of sin would be understood and God's provision for dealing with the sin problem would be welcomed, not denied. So, when and to whom was John addressing the first chapter of this letter?

Second, it is important to understand the ideas of that period that challenged Christian beliefs. The general consensus is that John wrote this book about 90 AD, which was about 60 years after Pentecost (see Appendix # 1). During that time, the heresy of Gnosticism was gaining a following among some Hellenistic Jews. John either knew about or anticipated that some of the Hellenistic Jews, who would read this letter, believed parts of this heresy or were tempted to accept this as a new fad that appealed to the Greek intellectuals of the day.

Therefore, being a good apologist, he used eye-witness testimony to dispel these lies. First, he assured his readers that he personally saw and experienced God come-in-the-flesh, in the Man, Jesus Christ, the long awaited Jewish Messiah. Secondly, in verse 10, he refuted the lie that mankind is sinless, a crucial point because being "sinless" implies that mankind is already perfect and, therefore, does not need a savior. Denying the need for salvation, given as a free gift

359

by Jesus Christ, is one of Satan's main tricks to mentally hamstring people from being reborn of God. (The modern counterpart is the heresy of Humanism which insists that man is basically good and, by implication, does not need a savior to give one a new nature.) This gift of rebirth, which is received by faith, is required in order to become compatible with God and live with Him eternally, rather than exist forever in the kingdom of Darkness under Satan. Rebirth is also necessary to have true fellowship with other believers, as John indicates.

The following two quotes further explain the seriousness of the heresy that John was writing against. They are penned by noted Bible commentator, William Barclay in Chapter Eight of his book *Many Witnesses, One Lord.* (see: http://www.religion-oline.org/showbook.asp?title=1112)

> The heretics denied the fulness (sic) of the incarnation; they refused to believe that Jesus came in the flesh (4:2, 3). It was the incarnation that any Gnostic was bound to deny. They could not believe that God could take manhood upon him, and so they presented men with a Jesus who was no more than a phantom in human shape. They thereby destroyed the work of Christ for, as Irenaeus said, "He became what we are to make us what he is." Docetism in a kind of mistaken reverence took the meaning out of the life of Jesus Christ."

Of course, the obvious problem with this lie is that, if Jesus was not fully man as well as fully God, He could not legally represent mankind before God as the last Adam and become our perfect Substitute to undergo all God's just wrath and punishment for all of mankind's sin. But the next paragraph by William Barclay explains why that was not a problem for the Gnostics because they did not believe they had a "sin problem" that needed a Savior.

> Their ethical teaching was wrong and dangerous. They claimed to have fellowship with God and yet they walked in darkness (1:5). That is to say, they claimed to be walking with God and yet went on sinning. They in fact denied that they sinned at all (1:8-10). They would have said that a truly spiritual man may allow his body to do as it likes, for his body thereby simply fulfils its nature, and that cannot be called sin. John insists that no one who abides in God sins, that the righteous man is he who does righteousness. No one born of God commits sin, for sin is of the Devil (3:6-10). To love God is to keep God's commandments (5:3). He who is born of God does not sin (5:18). This is directed against the Gnostics who claimed that they were in the most intimate possible fellowship with God, fellowship not even possible for the ordinary man, and who yet wallowed in sin, either on the principle that the body is evil and therefore it does not matter what is done with it or in it, or on the principle that in sin the body does no more than fulfil (sic) its own nature, and that in either case the spirit is left quite untouched. To the Gnostics an unethical religion was perfectly natural; to John it was a blasphemous contradiction in terms.

Third, as stated above, the general consensus is that John wrote this letter in about 90 AD, which was about sixty years after Pentecost. This time gap is very significant because if 1 John 1:9 was meant to be a central doctrine of Christianity (as many teach), then how could the early church have flourished for its first sixty years with so much unconfessed sin? That gap, in itself, should settle the "confession" issue. (The Roman Catholic denomination, in particular, has made it a central requirement by enthroning it into its sacramental system.)

But how can we be sure that it is not a core doctrine? Because Jesus' direct revelation to Paul about the **New Covenant** and His **finished work** includes no requirement of confessing one's sins to God before He grants forgiveness. In fact, the most Biblical so-called "sinners prayer" is in Romans 10:9-10 which does not even mention, let alone require, the need to confess one's sins but, rather, the need to "confess with one's mouth that 'Jesus is Lord'" (see more below.) But most every evangelist today feels compelled to make "confessing sins" a requirement for salvation. This is a carry-over from the **pre-cross** practices of John the Baptist and even Jesus' disciples. But if God did not require it for Cornelius and for his whole household to be saved, why are we including it in the mix? The **elephant of mixture** is at it again. Tradition masks the truth.

The Fallacious Mixture Of Two Covenants

So what is the unadulterated truth - which I already focused on in the book? Jesus revealed to Paul in approximately 42 AD that His sacrifice already paid the total sin debt for all mankind for all time. Therefore, God no longer remembers (chooses to be mindful of) that debt (see Hebrews 8:12 and 10:17). All sin was transferred to Jesus who "became sin" so that we believers could now focus on Him and His **finished work** on our behalf, rather than on the Law and our imperfection compared to it. <u>Father-God now regards each true believer as He does Jesus because we are **in Him**.</u> That is the gospel of lavish grace that has been buried under the preoccupation with law and confession of sins for two millennia – starting from day one in the Jerusalem church by mixing the two covenants, now called Galatianism.

Paul made this error crystal clear when he said:

> … yet knowing that a man is not justified by the works of the law but through faith in Jesus Christ, even we believed on Christ Jesus, that we might be justified by faith in Christ, and not by the works of the law: because by the works of the law shall no flesh be justified (Galatians 2:16).

Then he followed it up with these clinchers:

> I do not make void the grace of God: for if righteousness is through the law, then Christ died for nothing (Galatians 2:21).

> So the law is become our tutor to bring us unto Christ, that we might be justified by faith. But now that faith has come, we (the Jews) are no longer under a tutor (the Law – speaking only to the Jews) (Galatians 3:24-25).

Luther then used Jesus' gospel to Paul to make it clear that one's justification / righteousness was a gift from God received by "faith alone." So, this gift of "right standing with God" can't be maintained by a believer's effort of constant confession of sins - already forgiven and forgotten – or it would no longer be by the gift of grace.

> For if they (Jews) that are of the law are heirs, faith is made void, and the promise is made of none effect because the law brings wrath. But where there is no law, there is no transgression (Romans 4:14-1).

Again, if any more proof is needed, the terms of our New Covenant, which are spelled out in Hebrews 8:10-13 and 10:16-18 and kept for us by Christ Jesus, assures that God forgave all our sins and no longer remembers them. This is all because of the **finished work** of Jesus 2000 years ago. We need not confess what has already been paid for and forgotten. What we should confess is the reality of this glorious **divine exchange** that causes our Father-God to view us, His beloved children, the same way He views the glorified Man, Jesus, our eternal High Priest. What is true for Him is now true for us who are **in Christ**. "As He is so are we in this world" (1 John 4:17b).

Jesus Warning, Through Paul, To Teachers Who Teach 1 John 1:9 to Believers

Jesus revealed the whole New Covenant grace-based gospel exclusively to Paul in 42 AD. Knowing this, Paul wrote the following warning to the Galatians not to listen to any gospel from any other source if it differs from what Jesus revealed to him.

> I wonder that you have been so quickly transferred, from him (Paul) who called you into the grace of Christ, over to another gospel. For there is no other (gospel), except that there are some persons who disturb you and who want to overturn the Gospel of Christ. But if anyone, even we ourselves or an Angel from Heaven, were to preach to you a gospel other than the one that we have preached to you, let him be excommunicated. Just as we have said before, so now I say again: If anyone has preached a gospel to you, other than that which you have received (from me), let him be excommunicated. For am I now persuading men, or God? Or, am I seeking to please men? If I still were pleasing men, then I would not be a servant of Christ

These strong words apply to any other perceived "pillars" of the church, then or now. Why is that warning so strong? Because *anyone* who dilutes the glorious message of Jesus' **whole, grace-based gospel** misrepresents what Jesus accomplished on Calvary which is beyond unaided human understanding. Adding

1) any part of the Mosaic Covenant that is based on human works and

2) was abolished for the Jews at Calvary or

3) minimizing the immensity of Jesus' **finished work** by

4) filtering it through the limitations of human reasoning, robs God of His rightful glory and robs mankind of the revelation of the fullness of His intended purpose and benefits for mankind.

Kingdom living and reigning on earth as God intends for His saints, according to Romans 5:17, is hampered if not prevented when believers are not taught to believe in Jesus' **whole, grace-based gospel**.

Paul used the phrase "the gospel of Christ" eleven times in his writings to distinguish Jesus' revelation to him from any other message from any other source – including from the Jerusalem church under James. It is this pure "gospel of Christ" that Paul celebrates in Romans 1:16-17:

For I am not ashamed of the gospel of Christ because it is the (miraculous) power (ability) of God into salvation to everyone believing – to the Jew first, and to the Greek. For within it (the gospel of Christ), the righteousness of God is revealed, from faith to faith, just as it was written: 'For the just one shall live by faith.'

The gospel is Jesus plus nothing else. This was a totally new revelation, completely distinct from the religion of Law-based Judaism. It unveiled the intricate mysteries of how God fulfilled His promise of salvation through a crucified Savior for every believing Jew and Gentile. Since the law is not of faith, Jesus' whole gospel had nothing to do with a belief system based on the Tree of Law - people keeping or not keeping laws to qualify themselves for eternal salvation. Why? Because law-keeping cannot make men perfect since it is based on man's imperfect performance to achieve perfection. Only God's "doing" is perfect. Only faith in what He has already *done,* through trusting in Jesus' **finished work**, can justify (make righteous and perfect spiritually) an **in Adam** sinner. If a believer adds a requirement such as "confessing his sins" to get or remain justified, he is adding to Jesus' perfect **finished work**. That is why understanding that "the gospel of Christ" is the only true gospel is so essential to victorious living **in Him**.

Again, Jesus revelation to Paul is the only "gospel" personally endorsed by Jesus and, therefore, should be the *plumb line* that is used to discern the "four gospels" and all other **post-cross** writings. This is especially necessary because we now know that the other writers were influenced in varying degrees by **the elephant of mixture** practiced in the Jerusalem church under James' leadership - as already documented in this book.

While all scripture is inspired by God – including the 82% that presents the Mosaic Law and the life of Jesus up to the cross – it is not identical to "the gospel of Christ" revealed to Paul in 42 AD. Act One and Act Two are very important to better understand and enjoy Act Three of the Bible – "the gospel of Christ - but they are mere shadows of the "substance" – the now exalted Christ Jesus Himself and the new **unseen** reality, now opened to those who believe and receive from Him. Any other gospel is no gospel at all and is not true Christ-ianity. That is why Paul urged the Corinthians to "… no longer regard anyone from worldly point of view. Though we once regarded Christ in this way, we do so no longer." Why? Because all things are *new* from God's point of view! Any mixture of opposing covenants is religiosity that nullifies both. It is teaching the Bible as a book of requirements needed to earn or maintain salvation rather than focusing on Jesus' **grace-based "gospel of Christ."** He is the only Tree of life and salvation.

Comparing and Contrasting Two Salvation Scriptures

Because Jesus' **whole gospel of radical grace** was given expressly to Paul, it follows that Romans 10:9-13 would be the definitive statement on what is necessary for an **in Adam** sinner to be saved by rebirth. It reads:

… if you confess with your mouth the Lord Jesus, and if you believe in your heart that God has raised him up from the dead, you shall be saved. For with the heart, we believe unto righteousness and with the mouth, confession is unto salvation. For Scripture says: 'All those who believe in him shall not be disgraced.' For there is no distinction between Jew and Greek. For the same Lord is over all, richly in all who call upon him. For all those who have called upon the name of the Lord shall be saved.

Paul characteristically focuses the unbeliever on the person of Christ Jesus, not on himself or on his sins. This is because God is focused on the Lamb of God like the priest was focused on the perfection of the lamb, not on the sin or on the sinner, under the Mosaic Law. If the lamb was perfect, the **exchange** of his perfection (righteousness) in the eyes of God could be transferred to the sinner. When the lamb was sacrificed, the exchange of the lamb's perfection for the sinner's unrighteousness was accomplished. The sinner went home acquitted of the sin debt because our righteous Lamb paid it with His own precious blood.

The transaction was made possible because God ordained this process to satisfy His justice at that time - in anticipation of what Jesus' cross would later accomplish for mankind. The sinner demonstrated his faith in God's promise of forgiveness by complying with the process. The priest carried out the required process and the sinner got the benefit. All he had to do was supply the perfect lamb and believe it was sufficient. No "confession of sins" was required although one would assume that bringing a lamb to the priest was an admission of a sin problem. That whole process was part of the covenant that the Israelites made with God (bilateral), for a specific time period (temporary) which required certain conditions be met before the blessing was given (conditional). In this case, the lamb had to be supplied.

However, at Calvary, a totally **New Covenant** has been inaugurated by mankind's new representative Jesus Christ, the Lamb supplied by God. The terms are drastically different because of who Jesus is and what He did for mankind. So now, all reborn believers benefit from a covenant that He provided for everyone **in Christ** (unilateral), that is not temporary but permanent (eternal) and one in which He fulfilled all the conditions (unconditional). So, in accordance with to Romans 10:9-13, there is nothing left for any unbeliever to "do" to be reborn into God's Kingdom except:

1) speak in agreement with God that Jesus is Lord of the universe because He proved it by His resurrection, orchestrated by God, His Father and

2) believe for and receive His gift of rebirth into righteousness and speak in agreement that you are now saved through rebirth and set free from your old **in Adam** nature.

Now ask the Holy Spirit, who now lives in you, to teach you and lead you into all truth which will progressively renew your mind to think and see the way God does, now that you are His child, so that you can begin to enjoy Jesus' abundant life. (This last section is a review of a section in Chapter Eighteen.)

APPENDIX # 5

RECOMMENDED READING

Destined to Reign Devotional: Daily Reflections for Effortless Success, Wholeness and Victorious Living by Joseph Prince. This is a treasure house that I have used daily since 2008 and regularly teach from in my Bible classes and at prayer meetings. It was this book the Lord used to inspire a particularly rich, spiritual download of 13 "sermon songs" in the fall of 2009 and others since then. I'm not sure if Pastor Prince realizes just how profound this really book is. The key topics he picked that are listed in the back of his book and the depth of progressive revelation through the year, is like a corkscrew of truth opening up the wells of salvation – Jesus' **finished work** of His **divine exchange**.

Unmerited Favor by Joseph Prince

The Power of Right Believing: 7 Keys to Freedom from Fear, Guilt, and Addictions by Joseph Prince (and all his other books).

New Creation Realities by E. W. Kenyon (and all his many other books are a treasure of revelation knowledge.)

Grace Walk by Steve McVey (a classic book)

52 Lies Heard In Church Every Sunday (And Why The Truth Is So Much Better) by Steve McVey

The Rest Of The Gospel: When the Partial Gospel Has You Worn Out by Dan Stone and David Gregory

The Gospel [un]Cut: Learning to Rest in the Grace of God by Jeremy White

Pure Grace by Clark Whitten

You've Already Got It! (So Quit Trying To Get It) by Andrew Wommack

Effortless Change by Andrew Wommack

War is Over: God is Not Mad, So Stop Struggling with Sin and Judgment by Andrew Wommack

Living in the Balance of Grace and Faith by Andrew Wommack

The True Nature of God by Andrew Wommack

Spirit, Soul and Body by Andrew Wommack (Also see his web site: awmi.net for a wonderful wealth of free teaching.)

Classic Christianity by Bob George

Jesus Changes Everything by Bob George, and excellent follow-up to avoid Galatianism

Sit, Walk, Stand by Watchman Nee

The Normal Christian Life by Watchman Nee

The Gospel in Ten Words by Paul Ellis

The Hyper-Grace Gospel: A Response to Michael Brown and Those Opposed to the Modern Grace Message by Paul Ellis

The Naked Gospel by Andrew Farley

Relaxing With God by Andrew Farley

2000 Years of Charismatic Christianity by Dr. Eddie Hyatt (chronicles the doctrinal struggle between Law and the whole gospel of grace that Jesus revealed to Paul).

Are We Preaching Another Gospel by C. D. Hildebrand

More recommendations by Paul Ellis's:
http://escapetoreality.org/resources/book-reviews/

You will also find more recommendations - as I discover them - on my web site:
www.totaltruth.org

APPENDIX # 6

THE THREE NEW TESTAMENT SCRIPTURES THAT TIED ME UP IN KNOTS

Examples of Mixture In The New Testament

Most of what I am sharing in this book was not at all clear to me in my early years as a reborn Christian because of wrong believing. Even though it was true that all things are new in the **unseen realm** for every reborn saint **in Christ**, my dependency on law-based living blinded me from seeing and walking in the Spirit. Here, again, are three New Testament scripture passages that tied me up in mental knots, and kept me living the sub-standard life of the city dog under mixture until the **whole gospel** of Jesus and His **divine exchange** began to replace my wrong believing. This is a reiteration from previously covered content but since these verses are still very often used to stomp on the revelation of the **total grace gospel**, they deserve emphasis because they can be used as lightening rods for mixture when not rightly divided by Jesus' revelation to Paul.

The first (in no particular order) is from John14:21 "He who has my commandments and keeps them, he it is who loves me. And he who loves me will be loved by my Father and I will love him and show myself to him." Taken literally, without looking through the lens of the **whole grace gospel**, my unrenewed mind, steeped in law-based thinking, concluded that:

1) God demands that I love Him first, which is

2) proven by keeping all the commandments in the Bible, before

3) I have any hope of Him loving me or before

4) Jesus reveals Himself to me.

In short, the success of my whole Christian life depended on my ability to love God perfectly, proved by keeping His commandments. That is the choke-hold that Satan had on me and has on many Christians today, due the **elephant** stomping around in their head. But for a believer who has been crippled by a church culture of law-based wrong believing - which is no Christianity at all - it seems normal.

It is akin to third generation slaves living on a Southern plantation in 1850 who have no concept of personal freedom or individual identity and purpose apart from their master's. God's-kind-of-love cannot be demanded, coerced or produced by a bankrupt human race that is under the slavery of Darkness. Other-centered, agape love must first be supplied by God through the Holy Spirit who *is* love, which then enables us to respond to God with His unselfish love. It is similar to a youngster giving a birthday gift to his dad that the child bought with some of the money that his dad had given to him for Christmas weeks earlier. Instead of spending all of it on himself, he shows his love and appreciation for his dad with a gift made possible by his dad.

Remember: the grace of true love and generosity originated from God, not Satan who is only out to steal, kill and destroy. But God loves you as much as He loves Jesus – who He sent to buy you back from Satan. He has already fully forgiven you and has supplied you with His gifts of faith, love and liberty through Jesus' resurrection victory. The more that you focus on Jesus and on what you already have **in Him**, faith and joy and love for God will arise from your new spirit and progressively heal and renew your mind and body.

But for all this to be possible to **in Adam** sinners, it was first necessary that God, who loved the whole world before we could love Him, sent Jesus to be our mediator and payment for all our rebellion and disobedience. But that was not enough. Each person must believe God's offer of rebirth by faith in order to be regenerated as holy and perfect new wineskins **in Christ Jesus**. Only then, can Jesus send the Spirit of God's love, the Holy Spirit, into you as a **new creation** spirit being, equipped with a new heart that is in union with Him and now able to respond to Him in loving adoration and gratitude that He so richly deserves. His radical grace gospel is not about me and my doing; it is all about Him and receiving *His* doing. But my "yes and amen" are needed because He does not force compliance on anyone but graciously waits for our agreement - as a loving suitor would do for the girl of his dreams. It is the Holy Sprit's job description to facilitate our compatibility with God in our outer man. Of course, this transformation has already been accomplished in our new, inner man by receiving His lavish grace of rebirth through faith.

Being a **New Covenant** son of Abba-Father is founded on a mutual, love-based freedom of continuous, intimate, spontaneous relationship in the **unseen realm** between our spirit and the Holy Spirit, who was sent to progressively produce the likeness of Jesus in our outer man - without the drudgery of "duty." It is the outworking of Jesus' prayer: "Father, make them one in Me as I am one in You." How "one" is "one?" It is as close as Spirit to spirit can be, **in Christ**, in God. It is as close as the three divine Persons of the Trinity are to each other. And that is the new starting point of our spirit-self that our outer man can now submit to – all part of Christ Jesus' abundant life of a dependent relationship with our Bridegroom. It is a life lived **in Him** and **through Him,** as me, His precious **butterfly**. His life through us overflows as worship to our Abba-Father through the Holy Spirit's enablement in all that we believe, think, say and do – for His glory and our good as His precious children, permanently united to God through His beloved Son. Walking in the revelation of Jesus' **whole grace gospel** will produce the fruit of right living, the fruit of the Holy Spirit reigning in and through you. Let Him always have His way! And when you don't, know that His forgiveness has already been given 2000 years ago. "There is therefore <u>now</u> no condemnation for those who are **in Christ Jesus**" (Romans 8:1)

Confusion Over Confession

The second and third scriptures that have caused great confusion to reborn saints are 1 John 1:9 and John 16:8-11 that deal with the topic of "righteousness." I will not repeat the detailed explanations given in Chapter Fourteen and Appendix 4 of how and why these two scriptures have been misunderstood and misapplied. But the fact is these misinterpretations are the result of a law-based bias that has served the devil's purpose to undermine two key revelations of the New Covenant. The first truth is that Jesus' perfect blood sacrifice has totally paid for, forgiven and removed before Father's eyes all of the sin of the whole world for all time, *and, therefore, for you because Jesus paid for <u>all</u> sin.* His unilateral action does not require a saint's on-going "confession of sins" to remove supposed continuous "unrighteousness."

Doubting Jesus' **finished work** is big time **elephant** thinking, which has been a source of condemnation for 2000 years for most believers. The "dead work" of confessing one's sins to God is based on the lie that it is one's "doing" (confession) that regains God's gift of righteousness and/or fellowship – rather than righteousness being a permanent gift, won for the saved believer by faith in Jesus' blood alone. It unwittingly promotes law-consciousness which, then, arouses sin and prevents Jesus-consciousness (which is what actually conquers sin.) The revelation of God's *total forgiveness of all sin* is the bedrock upon which the gift of justification/righteousness and God's acceptance and approval of every believer rests. It is a lie from the devil that the Holy Spirit is on a constant, fault-finding hunt for a believer's every sin. On the contrary, He was sent to reveal, seal and enforce the victory of Jesus' **divine exchange** in every believer by *convincing* him that he is the righteousness of God **in Christ Jesus**. Only by reckoning that to be true can a believer learn to freely walk in the Spirit's power, love and a sound mind, instead of under the evil of fear and insecurity (see 2 Timothy 1:7).

The confusion over the third scripture - John 16:8 11 - compounds the problem because the misinterpretation insists that the Holy Spirit acts like God's policeman over every believer, pointing out every sin he commits. This is actually accusing the Holy Spirit of doing exactly what Satan does as the "accuser of the brethren." No wonder so many saints are depressed and even "quit" this brand of Christianity – which is not Christianity at all. It is insanity orchestrated by he who is out to "steal, kill and destroy" the saints by the mayhem of mixture, the misrepresentation of the purity of Jesus' **grace-based gospel**.

While the Holy Spirit does mercifully convict the world's sinners who are still **in Adam** of their sin of unbelief in Jesus (so that they come to Him), He was sent by Jesus into believer's spirits to convince them of their *"all things new, permanent right-standing"* with Father-God, thanks to what Jesus did 2000 years ago. It is that central truth of the **New Covenant** that the devil fears the most because our new standing has provided us with all God's power and authority over him and his minions – as well as provided all the other benefits of Jesus' eternal inheritance freely given to us. Hallelujah

APPENDIX # 7

JESUS IN EVERY BOOK OF THE BIBLE

"Jesus in every book of the Bible" is on many web sites in many forms. Here is just one good example. Enjoy!

http://www.jesusplusnothing.com/jesus66books.htm

APPENDIX #8

AN ALPHABET OF SOME CHRISTIAN BASIC TRUTHS

Below explores Who God *really* is by describing what He has done, reflected by whom and where I am *now*, **in Christ Jesus**, because of what He *has done* for me:

A

God's _ABUNDANT LIFE_ is now mine **in Christ Jesus** because His blood totally paid my sin debt – past, present and future – so I am totally forgiven (Galatians 1:3-5, Hebrews 9:28 and 10:2, 10). Therefore, God is no longer mindful of my sins - as prophesied in Jeremiah 31:34 and which became true under the New Covenant (Hebrews 8:12 and 10:17), thanks to Christ Jesus' **finished work** (His righteous behavior and His perfect sacrifice on Calvary).

Consequently, I am the _APPLE_ of Abba-Father's eye and _ASCENDED_ **in Christ Jesus**. Now, I am freed to be God-conscious rather than Law, sin, guilt, shame and, therefore, self-conscious (see Hebrews 10:22). I *am* the righteousness of God **in Christ** who *is* my righteousness – thanks to His gift to me, not by my own doing (see 2 Corinthians 5:21 and Romans 4:24-25).

B

Because I am _BORN AGAIN_ by the _BLOOD_ of Jesus, all of Father-God's _BLESSINGS_ are now mine **in Christ Jesus** because He died on a wooden cross (not by stoning) to bear every curse against me. "Cursed is every man who hangs on a tree." Now, all the _BLESSINGS_ (and none of the curses) of Deuteronomy 28 are mine in Christ Jesus, my Savior and elder Brother. This is just part of the _BIG PICTURE_ of the **whole gospel of grace**

C

Thanks to _CHRIST JESUS_ and His **finished work** on the _CROSS,_ He is now my everything, my all in all, in Father-God.

D

Because I _DIED_ with Christ Jesus by faith, I am _DESTINED_ to reign in life (Romans 5:17) (not over people) because Christ Jesus defeated the devil and his hosts who had stolen Adam's authority over earth through deception. Jesus took back the keys of authority and power from Satan after He died and arose triumphant. He has given them to those who believe and receive them as part of His _DIVINE EXCHANGE_ so that believers can and operate in this aspect of redemption by enforcing His victory over all Darkness, in the name of Jesus, the ascended, victorious Christ.

E

ETERNAL, God-kind-of-Life (zoe) began in me when I was born again, this time of God, not of natural parents. His resurrection life lives and operates within me in the person of the Holy Spirit as the sanctifier of my outer man, producing the fruits of the Holy Spirit by His life through me as I rest in Jesus' **finished work**. The *ELEPHANT* of mixture prevents believers from experiencing God's best for them on earth.

F

I am walking in Jesus by *FAITH* in the unseen realm, not by natural sight, trusting and resting in Jesus and His ***FINISHED WORK*** as my source and stability.

G

I am a constant receiver of the *GOSPEL* of *GOD'S* lavish *GRACE* – God's Righteousness At Christ's Expense - through faith **in Christ** (Ephesians 2:8-9) - receiving all of God's blessings that I don't deserve but, by being one with Christ Jesus, I have been made worthy to receive His inheritance.

H

I am *HOLY* (set apart) through rebirth **into Christ Jesus**, who is my holiness, my wisdom, my redemption and my righteousness (see 1 Corinthians 1:30).

I

I was born ***IN ADAM*** through my natural birth. Now I am ***IN CHRIST*** through rebirth by being *IDENTIFIED* with Christ Jesus at Calvary by faith. So I am one with Him in God (see John 17:21, and 1 Corinthians 6:17, 19-20).

J

I am now *JUSTIFIED* – made righteous – in "right standing" eternally with God, my Father, by the perfect blood sacrifice of *JESUS CHRIST*, my Savior and Lord (see Hebrews 10:13-14).

K

I am in God's *KINGDOM* operating as a prophet, priest and *KING* **in Christ**, to speak His living truth in love as His ambassador.

L

I am a *LIVING SACRIFICE* of praise and thanksgiving, made holy and acceptable to God by Jesus, which is my service to Him.

M

I am a constant receiver of God's *MAGNANIMOUS* MERCY because Jesus fully paid for all of my past, present and future sin and absorbed all Father-God's just wrath and punishment that I deserve for my sin. What is true for Jesus is now true for me **in Him.**

N

Through rebirth, I have a *NEW NATURE* so am a *NEW CREATION* **in Christ**, included in God's *NEW COVENANT,* made between God and Jesus for me, through which all spiritual things have been made *NEW*. Consequently, I am greatly blessed, highly favored and deeply loved by Father-God, Jesus and the Holy Spirit who lives within me. (see 1 Corinthians 6:19)

O

There is only *ONE* true God, the Triune God, creator of the universe, almighty, omniscient and all loving.

P

I am *PERFECT*, complete in Christ in my new creation spirit being – in my inner man (see Colossians 2:10 & Hebrews 10:14).

Q

I am now legally *QUALIFIED* for all the **New Covenant** promises and blessings by rebirth **in Christ Jesus.**

R

By God's lavish grace through faith in Jesus' **finished work**, I am:
RECONCILED to God,

RESCUED from the dominion of Darkness,

RESURRECTED in Christ,

REGENERATED – *REBORN* of God my new Father,

REDEEMED from the curse of sin and death

I enjoy the *REMISSION* of all my past, present and future sins – totally forgiven,

I enjoy ongoing *REPENTANCE* = *RENEWAL* of my natural mind (change of thinking) by the washing of the whole gospel of Christ, God's revelation of His New Covenant Realities,

RANSOMED from slavery,

I am now the *RIGHTEOUSNESS* of God in Christ,

I enjoy *REVELATION* of God's word,

RESTING in Christ who is my *REWARD,*

I enjoy His *RICHES,*

REIGNING in life through Christ Jesus because I receive God's abundant provision of grace and His gift of *RIGHTEOUSNESS* to me (see Romans 5:17)

RULING over powers and principalities and

RECEIVING Jesus' inheritance – thanks to being one in Him forever.

S

I am a *SAINT* who sometimes still sins in my outer man yet fully *SANCTIFIED* in my inner man *SECURE* **in Christ,** now and *SEATED* with Him in heavenly places.

T

The Spirit of *TRUTH* uses my *TONGUE* as the Sword of the Spirit to speak His Word of life and *TRUTH* in Love.

U

I am enjoying the *UNITY* of the Holy Spirit in the bond of peace, thanks to His *UNMERITED* favor and blessings and protection. The *UNSEEN REALM* is much more real than what we see down here (see 2 Corinthians 4:18.
.

V

The *VEIL* of law between me and God has been removed and I am saved and *VICTORIOUS* **in Him,** seated with Him in heavenly places.

W

I am enjoying the privilege of *WORSHIPPING* my heavenly Father-God and Christ Jesus in Spirit and in truth as revealed in Jesus *WHOLE GOSPEL.*

X

The *CROSS* of Jesus "X'd out" the "old me" and I am now a new creation spirit being. The old spirit me in Adam was crucified, died and was buried and so is now gone. Praise the Lord.

Y

If YOU are not yet born again, YOU can be just by agreeing with what Paul said in Romans 10:9-10 – by believing and receiving Jesus as your Savior and Lord.

Z

My *ZEAL* for Father-God, Christ Jesus and the Holy Spirit comes from a deep and abiding personal relationship with them, the only true God. He alone is the *ZENITH*, the highest of the highest, beyond all other belief systems and natural human experience.

APPENDIX # 9

45 WRONG BELIEFS, BASED ON COMMON LIES

Right Believing Leads to Active Receiving Which Produces the Fruit of Right Living

"The righteous one lives by faith" (Hebrews 10:38). "Without faith (in God) it is impossible to please Him because whoever worships God must (obviously) believe that He exists and that He rewards those who worship Him," according to how the Greek text in Hebrews 11:6 can be translated. But what is faith? Biblical faith is the gift of certainty and confident expectation that whatever God reveals about the **unseen realm** is true and reliable, according to how the Greek text in Hebrews 11:1 can be translated. In summary, God's righteous ones live by a confident expectation of good from God who is **unseen** yet rewards those who seek and worship Him. Why? Because of who He is as demonstrated by the **finished work** of Jesus. This is the nuts and bolts of "walking by faith," biblically speaking.

Now, every functioning human being walks by faith in something or someone even if they do not realize it. Even the most hardened atheist lives day to day believing with certainty that there is no **unseen realm**. He has convinced himself that only the physical realm exists. But he can't prove a negative theory. His belief does not necessarily make true what he can only perceive with his five senses to be all that exists. The only Being that knows about everything with certainty is the One who created and sustains everything. The incarnation of this Being's Son and the testimony of His sinless life and sacrificial gift of Himself, demonstrated that there is an **unseen realm** that we can be certain of – based on Jesus' life of faith in His unseen Father. The validity of true Christianity rests on faith in the testimony of those who witnessed Jesus' resurrection and experienced the transforming power of God living in them. They personally discovered how good and faithful God is even though they were not. They discovered the God of love who loved them. They walked in biblical faith with this living, loving God who they grew to personally know, love, worship and gladly serve and die for. He became their point of reference forever!

But not everyone walks by this kind of faith, largely because of the **elephant of mixture**.

Here are some examples of wrong believing which leads to wrong living, many of which are discussed in this book:

Lie # 1 "The Mosaic Law reveals God's true character."

No, the Mosaic Law was given to reveal *man's evil nature* **in Adam** and, therefore, man's desperate need of a new nature made possible by believing and receiving Jesus' **divine exchange**. Jesus revealed God's true nature of love and mercy, for He was the exact representation of our Father-God. If the Mosaic Law reveals God's true character, 1) why did Jesus fulfill it and replace it (for believers) with the higher law of faith, love and liberty of the **New Covenant** 2) why did Jews have to die to it to be married to Jesus, and 3) why were the Gentiles never given the Law if it was as good for us as He is? It was the Law Tree that got us into trouble through Adam. For more on this topic, see Hebrews 1:3 and Chapter Eight of this book.

Lie # 2 "Man's nature consists of only a body and a soul."

No, Jesus revealed to Paul that man is a spirit being (like God) who has a soul that lives in a physical body until death. See chapters Sixteen and Seventeen for documentation on this vital issue. Until you agree with God about His revelation, you won't be able to fathom Jesus' **whole gospel** revealed to Paul.

Lie # 3 "Christians must keep the Ten Commandments to reach heaven."

No, the "good thief" was a lawbreaker and is in heaven today. Only perfect people qualify for heaven and only being reborn of God qualifies an **in Adam** sinner for heaven through rebirth by faith alone, not by obedience to any standard of behavior. The Law is not of faith. Anything not of faith is sin, says Paul. See Lie # 19 and Chapters Eight and Nine for more details.

Lie # 4 "The four gospels are the same as the gospel that Jesus revealed to Paul."

No, the four gospels focused mainly on Jesus' earthly life before Calvary which He lived under the Law. Jesus' **whole gospel of grace,** revealed exclusively to Paul in about 42 AD, is about what Jesus accomplished for us at Calvary, and beyond, when He replaced the Law covenant with the **New Covenant** of grace, opening heaven to reborn believers. See Chapters One and Twelve for more explanation.

Lie # 5 "The four gospels are the only true gospel of Jesus Christ."

Not so. While they reveal God's true nature through the life of Jesus, who focused on His Father rather than on the Law of Moses (which became obsolete and was replaced for Jewish believers), they mainly describe His earthly life. They only briefly touch on the most important event in history – His death and resurrection that opened heaven to everyone who believes and receives His **divine exchange.** But the **whole gospel** that describes how that happened and what it means for mankind was revealed in its fullness to Paul by Christ Jesus Himself. In Paul's gospel, Jesus explains how to see and enter into the Kingdom life of victory in the **unseen realm,** in and through accepting Christ's **finished** work by the enablement of the Holy Spirit living inside each reborn believer. See Chapter One and Eighteen through Twenty.

Lie # 6 "The Word of God is the same as 'the gospel of Christ.'"

No, not technically. The whole Bible is the word of God but Paul referred to Jesus' revelation to him specifically as the gospel of Christ (the **whole gospel of lavish grace**) as he called it in Philippians 1:27. Chapters Six, Seven and Twelve offer more distinctions.

Lie # 7 "All the Apostles shared the same revelation knowledge of the whole gospel."

No, not according to Paul. He called what he preached "my gospel" in Romans 2:16 that he received, in its totality, directly from Christ Jesus in about 42 AD. This revelation was decidedly different from the four gospels (see Chapters Six and Twelve).

Lie # 8 "God is angry at you when you sin."

No, Jesus received all of God's just wrath against all sins on Himself, and His perfect sacrifice <u>for all sin for all mankind for all time</u> caused mankind to be reconciled to God <u>from His viewpoint</u>. God's wrath will come on those at the final judgment who chose not to *believe* and receive God's offer of salvation and refused to be <u>reconciled to God</u> through rebirth– even after God reconciled the whole world to Himself through Jesus (see 2 Corinthians 5:18-21, John 3:16-18, Romans 5:9-11, 1 John 2:2). As in any marriage based on love and respect, both parties must agree to the **New Covenant.**

Lie # 9 "Repentance in both the Old and the New Covenant means the same thing – be sorry for and confess your sins to God."

No, because the terms of the **New Covenant** radically changed mankind's relationship to God. Repentance under the Mosaic Law focused on *turning from sins* and back to God. But Jesus' **finished work** won forgiveness of the sins of the whole world and reconciled mankind to God – <u>from His viewpoint</u>. Now, what is required is a *change of mind towards God* (**New Covenant** repentance) by each individual to be humble enough to believe and receive what Jesus has done in order to be reborn of God. No Israelite was reborn of God before Calvary so God gave the sacrificial system for forgiveness of sins under the Mosaic Covenant. No sins were imputed before the Law was given. 1 John 1:9 is not addressed to believers. See Chapter Fourteen and Appendix # 4 and Lie # 18 for a thorough discussion of this vital topic.

Lie # 10 "Jesus sent the Holy Spirit to convict every believer of every sin so that they repent by confessing their sins in order to stay in fellowship with God."

No, but the Holy Spirit does still convict **in Adam** sinners of their sin to bring them to Christ for salvation. But Jesus sent Him into believers to convince them of their righteousness **in Christ** so that they live consistently out of the new creation being that they now *are,* **in Christ**. Believers are spiritually united with God and sinning does not break fellowship <u>from God's point of view</u> because He forgave and forgot the sins of the whole world through Jesus some 2000 years ago. It is wrong believing that makes the believer *think* he loses fellowship with God. It is precisely when a believer sins that he needs God's help the most – not His rejection. God forsook Jesus at Calvary so that He would never leave or forsake any believer or refuse fellowship with His children. See a detailed exegesis of this very important issue in Chapter Fourteen.

Lie # 11 "The Holy Spirit uses every believer's conscience to convict him of his sins."

No, the Holy Spirit was sent by Jesus to believers to convince them of their righteous position and condition **in Christ.** Because a believer is not under law, he need not be sin-conscious but can now be Jesus conscious. This provides a clear conscience (see Hebrews 9:9-10). It is one of the many benefits of *being in the* **New Covenant** that the Law covenant could not provide. See Lie # 10 and Chapter Fourteen for more explanation.

Lie # 12 "God only forgives your sins to the same degree that you forgive the sins of others."

No, that fortunately is not true now for New Covenant believers. Jesus gave that direction to His disciples, **pre-cross,** in what is now called the *"Our Father."* This was a seeming improvement over animal sacrifices for sins. But one's forgiveness was conditional on how well he "performed" by forgiving others. This is still based on the "works of the Law" rather than on grace. But that all changed with the **divine exchange** when Jesus paid for the sins of the whole world and then gave believers the terms of a **New Covenant** that made all things new. See Appendix #2 for a fuller explanation.

Lie # 13 "God is personally offended by all sin and must be appeased by confessing sin."

No, 2 Corinthians 5:18-21 and 1 John 2:2 state that God forgave the sins of the whole world and Hebrews 8:12 states that God remembers our sins no more. See Chapter Fourteen for more insight.

Lie # 14 "You must regularly confess your sins to God to remain in fellowship with Him." See answer under Lie # 10.

Lie # 15 "Sinning causes a Christian to fall from grace."

That is not what Jesus revealed to Paul, according to Galatians 5:4: "You who are (attempting to be) justified by (keeping) the law have done away with Christ. You fell from grace." Sinning does not cut a believer off from Christ Jesus and His abundant grace whose perfect sacrifice won forgiveness for the whole human race, according to 1 John 2:2. Where sin abounds grace abounds much more, says Romans 5:21b. But depending on obedience to the law to stay right with God means adding one's works to the **grace gospel** which results in having no gospel at all. Falling from grace comes from living according to the **elephant of mixture** instead of under Jesus' **gospel of lavish grace.**

Lie # 16 "It is God's will that you suffer for Him to gain heaven rather than prosper in this world."

No, it was not God's perfect plan for Adam to ever suffer in the perfect Garden of Eden that He created for him. All of mankind's suffering, sickness, pain, lack, torment and all other forms of death resulted from Adam's rebellion against God's will for Adam. Jesus entered into the suffering of our human condition **in Adam** to offer an alternative to Adam's fall – salvation on every level. Suffering still comes from poor choices made by us or others – including persecution for the gospel of Christ like Paul suffered from even members of the Jerusalem church. But the true heart of God is not to steal, kill and destroy like His enemy does but to heal and set captives free. Also, no one can "gain" heaven by suffering because it is given as a free gift through rebirth. He sent Jesus to accomplish this for all who trust and rely on His **divine exchange**. Your concept of God greatly effects how much you personally experience His tangible love and blessing in the **seen realm**. See Chapter Twenty-One and Appendix #2 for more revelation.

Lie # 17 "A sinner is anyone who sins."

No, not according to Jesus' biblical definition given in Romans 5:19 that states, "By the disobedience of one man (Adam) the many were made sinners." Therefore, because everyone is born **in Adam**, everyone is a sinner by nature even before he/she does any sinning. You can only change your nature and destiny by being reborn of God (see John 3:3-7). A believer is a saint who sometimes sins. Believer, agree with God about your new identity **in Christ Jesus** that gives proper credit to Father-God's love for you, proven by Jesus' **divine exchange** with you.

Lie # 18 "To be saved, a sinner must confess his sins, believe in Jesus and do good deeds."

No, salvation is a free gift paid for by Jesus. According to what Jesus told Paul, recorded in Romans 10:9-13, **in Adam** sinners, who are automatically in Darkness and bound for hell, do *not* have to "confess their sins" to be saved, even though the **elephant of mixture** says you must. Salvation is about believing, receiving and professing Jesus' and His **divine exchange** by faith alone. Jesus has already done for us all the "good deeds" needed with His life and His sacrificial death on Calvary to accomplish your rebirth. John 6:40 states: "It is my Father's will that everyone who looks to the Son (Jesus) and believes **in Him** shall have eternal life." Jesus plays no favorites! See and believe Romans 10:9-13.

Lie # 19 "God gave the Mosaic Law to mankind so that all who obey it can go to heaven."

Not true. The Mosaic Law was given only to the Jews. It was meant to show God's wisdom to improve the health and social order in the seen realm (see Deuteronomy 4:5-6) so it is a great code of civil law for nations. But it never offered eternal life to mankind because it only addressed outward behaviors which cannot change one's nature **in Adam.** Hebrews 7:8-9 describes the Mosaic Law as *weak and unprofitable* for achieving salvation because it only shows where you are wrong (always falling short of perfection) but gives no power to keep it. Read about the purpose and proper use of the Law, according to Jesus' gospel to Paul in Chapter Eight and the law's harsh realities presented in Chapter Nine.

Lie # 20 "Anyone teaching the gospel of radical grace is lawless or "antinomian" and, therefore, a heretic."

No, that trick of the devil is spoken by well-meaning but deceived pastors, just like the Judaizers spoke it about Paul. Jesus' **grace gospel** is based on a higher law – faith, love and liberty - found in Galatians 5:1-6 (and elsewhere in separate verses) that reveals how God's Kingdom works. This is what Jesus lived by rather than being limited by the minimums of the Mosaic Law – now made obsolete for Jews at Calvary and replaced by the **New Covenant** with

God's higher law of the Spirit of life. The law principle still operates to bring in Adam sinners to Christ. But it is not for believers. Unfortunately, most early Jewish believers held on to and mixed their roots in the Law with grace and spawned the **elephant of mixture** that still mentally confuses, condemns and confounds believers today (see Chapter Three and Appendices # 3 and # 11 for examples). One of the main reasons for this book is to expose that 2000 year old lie.

Lie # 21 "All true miracles ended when the last apostle died."

No, the Doctrine of Cessation was instituted to cover up the deadness in institutional, law-based churches. When Jesus' **grace gospel** is ignored, the vibrant life of the Holy Spirit in believers is stifled to prevent possible "disorder" in the church. Law-minded people are often about the control of other people and "the flesh" rather than depending on the fruit of self-control through the Holy Spirit. People can abuse the power of guns or automobiles, but banning them by external law will only arouse more rebellion and abuse. America's ill-advised Prohibition Laws bore that out. Infinitely better is the law of the Spirit of Life that sets believers free of the constraints of the law of sin and death that causes condemnation (see Romans 8:1-2). He gives His beloved children the power and grace to live the higher law of faith in Him and His direction, out of love for God (not slavish fear) and for others, in His liberty. See Chapter Nineteen to discover more about God's alternative to living under the curse of the law.

Lie # 22 "Jesus came to earth and lived as both fully God and fully man."

No, otherwise John 5:30 makes no sense: "By myself I can do nothing." Though He was fully God and fully man, He laid aside His deity (He "emptied Himself" - see Philippians 2:5-9) and operated as the Son of Man in order to identify with us in all things except with our **in Adam** fallen state of being - until at Calvary. There He became sin by taking on the Adamic nature of mankind, thereby crucifying it so that all those who believe **in Him** could be raised as **new creations**, having died to the former **in Adam** old man with Christ. If Jesus operated on earth as our perfect holy God, he could not have died let alone "become sin." He **exchanged** all His "good" – from living a perfect life, for all our "bad" – the very evil, depraved nature of Adam - so that all believers are now the righteousness of God **in Christ Jesus,** according to 2 Corinthians 5:21. What is true for Christ Jesus is now true spiritually for those in Him – from God's viewpoint.

Lie # 23 "Every Christian must put on the armor of God every day to stay protected from the devil's attacks."

No, because all those **in Christ**, who *is* our armor, are clothed in Him 24/7. See Chapter Twenty for full details of how you are equipped for battle. But it is good to be continually *mindful* of being **in Christ** and renew your mind on what Jesus whole gospel offers.

Lie # 24 "There are many ways to God besides Jesus."

No, not according to Jesus who said "No one can come to the Father unless by me" (John 14:6). Only Jesus, as fully God and operating on earth as fully Man, could do for us what was necessary for our redemption and salvation – the **finished work** of His **divine exchange**. He made a way back to God when there was no other way.

Lie # 25 "Because God is so loving and merciful, eventually all mankind will inhabit heaven."

No, this doctrine of Universalism is not conclusively substantiated in the bible. This is the extreme opposite of Calvin's doctrine of predestination which states that only certain, pre-selected humans are going to be in heaven. Both doctrinal extremes negate the gift of free choice that Jesus restored to mankind at Calvary - regarding salvation. The requirement of being "reborn of God by faith," in order to be compatible with a perfect heaven, is a choice offered by grace through faith, not accomplished by God's sovereign, unilateral dictate. The Bride's marriage to the Lamb is not a shotgun wedding (see Chapter Thirteen).

Lie # 26 "According to God, every Christian is a sinner saved by grace."

No, not according to Romans 5:19. "For, just as through the disobedience of one man (Adam), many were established as sinners, so also through the obedience of one man (Jesus), many shall be established as righteous." So, every Christian reborn of God and, therefore, is a righteous saint who sometimes sins, now that he is no longer **in Adam** but **in Christ**. One's nature i. (who one actually *is)* is determined by birth not by behavior. See Lie # 17 for more.

Lie # 27 "Currently, there are three spiritual kingdoms: heaven, hell and the one you are in now until you decide which one of the other two you will permanently join."

No, this common, sometimes unconscious, belief hides the desperate condition of mankind's existence because of Adam's fall. All created human beings descend from Adam and, therefore, inherit his fallen nature which is disconnected from God spiritually. Every human is under the power of Darkness until and unless he/she chooses to be reborn of God and, thereby, be delivered from that power by being translated into the Kingdom of God's beloved Son, Christ Jesus, according to Jesus' revelation to Paul in Colossians 1:13.

Lie # 28 "Everyone on earth is God's child automatically."

No, even Adam was not a child of God because God had not yet made rebirth possible through Jesus. John 1:12 clearly states that only those who receive and believe in Jesus can become children of God. Possibly, Adam might have become born of God by eating of the Tree of Life, but that is speculation. However he was just a creation from the earth who rejected the Tree of Life offered to him in the garden. See Chapter Thirteen for more explanation.

Lie # 29 "God gives sickness to teach believers a lesson and test their trust in Him."

Fortunately for us, Father-God is not like that. He sent Jesus to offer freedom to the human race from all that came down through Adam's Fall, which included being dead to God spiritually and the many symptoms of that death such as sickness and lack naturally flow from that fallen condition. Salvation from Jesus is offered for every level of the believer's being, starting with his spirit-self **in Christ.**

Jesus never taught such a lie or made people sick. Rather, he set people free of all manner of oppression and bondage because He came to set captives free from the effects of Darkness. He came to give abundant life, not disease and death. If God gives sickness, **post-cross**, then praying to be healed or going to a doctor to get well would be defying Him. How many parents do you know want their children to get sick? How can you trust someone who is out to make you sick? It is the devil who is out to steal, kill and destroy your health and Adam's rebellion opened the door to the devil's devices, not God. Let the Holy Spirit renew you mind about who Father-God really is. One main purpose of this book is to confront and dispel many common lies about Father-God's nature that the **elephant of mixture** implies or suggests. Chapter Twenty One is specifically dedicated to help you discover His true nature.

Lie # 30 "God gave the Law to Moses to fix our sinfulness."

No because the law arouses sin rather than fixes it. The purpose of the Law was to reveal mankind's sin nature from Adam. External rules or guilt or condemnation only show the deeper problem but can't fix it. Only being reborn of God by the Holy Spirit provides a new *nature* **in Christ** that makes right believing and living possible (see John 3:3). See Chapter Eight for a full explanation of God's purpose for the Mosaic Law.

Lie # 31 "Believers must balance grace with the Mosaic law."

The Mosaic Law was given only to the Jews and is now *obsolete* for them as the means or measure of righteousness since the Temple was destroyed. It was never given to the Gentiles by God. Mixing or "balancing" the two opposing covenants of Law and grace is the heresy of Galatianism that became entrenched in the early Jerusalem church. But in the **New Covenant** there is now "the law of the Spirit of life" – the higher law of faith, love and liberty - which is the means of radical grace-based living for everyone. You can find much more about that on page 54, in Chapter Four and Chapter Nineteen in Part Three of this book and in Endnote # 13.

Lie # 32 "A Christian's degree of holiness is based on how well he obeys God."

No, our holiness is not based on our performance like religions teach but only on our *position* of being set apart **into Christ Jesus** who is now our holiness, wisdom, redemption and righteousness by identification with Jesus by faith, according to 1 Corinthians 1:30. But our new position **in Christ** is meant to have a positive impact on our outward behavior as new creations as we allow and depend on the Holy Spirit to sanctify and live through our unsanctified outer man.

Lie # 33 "Holiness is another name for right living. The more that you do right the holier you are."

No, the Bible defines holiness as being "set apart," consecrated for God's service. Every believer was set apart spiritually at rebirth and is therefore holy by being **in Christ Jesus.** Again,

Jesus is now the believer's "holiness" according to 1 Corinthians 1:30. This has nothing to do with what you do, per se, but with *whose* you are, who you are and *where* you are now, spiritually speaking. It describes your position, not your behavior. However, there is a link. The more you believe the truth of who you are **in Christ**, the more consistently you will let His Spirit live through you, producing the fruit of holiness – right living.

Lie # 34 "The New Covenant begins at Matthew 1:1."

No, what we call the New Testament begins there but God made the **New Covenant** with Jesus at Calvary, not when Jesus was born. This a *very* important distinction because Jesus was born under the Law, fulfilled the Law and then replaced it with the **New Covenant** as a means of right-standing with God. The **New Covenant** began with Jesus' death, not with His birth.

Lie # 35 "Every Christian has two natures until he dies."

While this is a common misconception in the church today, we can only have one nature or "essence" at a time. Jesus revealed to Paul that at rebirth, the old, **in Adam** nature is spiritually circumcised away, replaced by a regenerated, new creation being that is part of a new race and a partaker of divine nature because of now being **in Christ Jesus** (see 2 Corinthians 5:17). This revelation can only be reckoned by faith, not by observing one's unsanctified soul life. Yes, there is a battle in the mind of every believer because the soul and body was running things before the saint's spirit-being was regenerated and plugged into God. The mind does not automatically start thinking like God immediately upon rebirth, (after being spiritually under Satan's power and at enmity with God before rebirth.) That is why mind renewal is so very necessary to live victoriously on earth. But the reality of having an *unsanctified outer man* should not be mistaken for still being **in Adam** and being **in Christ** at the same time. Light does not mix with Darkness. "We were Darkness but now we are light in the Lord so walk as children of the light" (Ephesians 5:8 and 2 Corinthians 6:14).

Lie # 36 "I must love God and keep His commandments so that He will love me and reveal Himself to me."

No, this is like putting the cart in front of the horse. This is what John 14:21 *seems* to say but *that* interpretation does not square with 1 John 4:19: "We love because He first loved us" and John 3:16, of course. All mankind starts off **in Adam**, at enmity with God, incapable of loving God without Him first supplying His gift of love, in the Person of the Holy Spirit, into our new spirit-self. John 14:21 seems to mirror the impossible situation the Israelites put themselves in by rejecting the grace-based covenant under Abraham and embracing the Law Covenant at Sinai (see the end of Chapter Nineteen). A later verse can be rendered: "If anyone loves me he will keep his eye upon my word and my Father will love him and we will make our abode with him" (John 14:23). That corresponds with "looking to" (keeping your eyes on) Jesus, the Author and Finisher of your faith (see Hebrews 12:2). God loved us while we were *yet* sinners.

Lie # 37 "The whole Bible applies directly and equally to me so I must study it to receive God's approval and reach heaven"

No, not every promise or command was given directly to you nor was the Law Covenant given to non-Jews. God did not make you the "father of many nations" because that promise was only given to Abraham. God loves everyone. He approves of and accepts into heaven all who are reborn **in Christ,** even if they never read the Bible.

Lie # 38 "Because God is absolutely sovereign over everything, He determines every detail of everyone's life." So, before time began, God sovereignly decided unilaterally who He would save and everyone else would be condemned to hell."

Not so. God does not send anyone to hell. It was Adam's choice as mankind's Federal Head that put humanity on the road to hell and Jesus came to reverse that calamity by restoring choice to mankind as the last Adam (John 3:16-18). Space is too limited here to fully expose this lie so please see Endnotes # 8 and #22 for my answer to those who teach the twin doctrines of "God's absolute sovereignty" and "Predestination," according the doctrine of hyper-Calvinism.

Lie # 39 "The "Baptism in the Holy Spirit" that the Book of Acts presents is not needed or even desirable today.

True – if you mean not needed for salvation. Not true if you mean a believer does not need the immersion into the life of the Holy Spirit for victory on earth. If the perfect Man Jesus needed to be baptized in the Holy Spirit to be empowered to fulfill God's ministry through Him, can you afford to do without His empowerment and personal hot line to heaven – tongues? Desire the gifts of the Spirit, says Jesus through Paul in 1 Corinthians 14:1 and following. They are an integral part of the **grace-based gospel.** Being reborn is like having a drink at the well of the Holy Spirit; being baptized into Him is like diving into the river of life Himself so that He can support and carry you along. Ask the Spirit of Life to set you free from the constricting **elephant of mixture**, the law of sin and death, so that you can experience His abundant river of life flowing through you to others. We are but a branch, one with the Vine. He is the sap which produces His fruit through us when yielded to Him.

Lie # 40 "No one can be sure they are saved until they die."

The apostle John offers believers (all those who have been reborn of God according to what Paul wrote in Romans 10:9-13) the assurance that they have God's own eternal life within them. "I am writing this to you, who believe in the name of the Son of God so that you may *know* that you have eternal life" (1 John 5:13). Having eternal life *is* salvation because "having eternal life" is having Jesus by being *one* with Him. Again, all those **in Christ** are already seated in heavenly places where He sits, according to Ephesians 2:6. See Chapters Eighteen and Nineteen for more specifics.

Lie #41 "I get closer to God by doing good things instead of bad things."

This might seem true mentally but it is not true spiritually for a reborn saint. You are either **in Adam** and therefore, dead to God **spiritually**, or **in Christ** and, therefore, one spirit with the Lord according to 1 Corinthians 6:17. Union with Christ Jesus is not based on your behavior but based on believing and accepting the gift of His **divine exchange**. It is impossible to earn or maintain the gift of salvation and fellowship by your works. How can you get "closer" than "*oneness*?" Being **in Christ** means that you are *one* with Him, spirit to spirit not "drawing closer" until you die physically.

If you are inside your car, how can you "get closer" to it. That notion comes from works-based, religious thinking. Your <u>outer man</u> may be "far away from God" in thought and/or behavior, but the real you, believer, your **new creation** self, is never apart from Father-God because you are **in Christ**, by definition, and one with the Father in spirit (1 Corinthians 6:17). The more that you grasp this revelation, the more you will reflect that unity in your behavior out of love (not duty) for your loving heavenly Father. Don't let your natural mind or emotions trick you into thinking or feeling that you live a yo-yo life with Christ Jesus.

Lie # 42 "God helps those who help themselves."

Contrary to common beliefs, this statement is not a Bible verse. It was coined by Ben Franklin and reveals his humanistic thinking. There are some things that only God can do for you such as qualify you for heaven. Since you did not create yourself, you cannot sustain yourself. Therefore, in a fundamental sense, you can do nothing without God's help. Until you see yourself as helpless without Him, you won't be fully dependent on Him and so can't benefit from all He has done for you in the **divine exchange**. <u>When you work in your own strength, God rests; when you rest in Him, He is free to work on your behalf - in you and through you.</u> Big difference. Christian life is one of trust in His ability, not in yours or in things or in other people. Only God is a reliable point of reference. He really *is* our all in all and our "everything." In contrast, everything the **seen realm** is temporary and will eventually pass away, according to 2 Corinthians 4:18.

Lie # 43 Even though Jesus is merciful, God is wrathful and judgmental.

See Chapter 21 for a full debunking of this pernicious and pervasive lie.

Lie # 44 "A Christian must bring every thought captive to obey Christ."

The law's function was to arouse sin, cause death and bring the **in Adam** sinner to the end of himself so that he would see his desperate need to receive Jesus. And since the law was never given to the Gentiles, Paul did not teach on obedience to the law or even *to* Christ, per se, but on "bring into captivity every thought to the <u>obedience *of* Christ</u>" (2 Corinthians 10:5b). The law always demands perfect obedience to achieve or maintain righteousness – an impossibility for us. However, Jesus' gift of grace supplies His gift of righteousness by faith in what He did for mankind some 2000 years ago. Since the law is weak and incapable of making **in Adam** sinners perfect, it was made obsolete for Jews and nailed to the cross.

Lie # 45 "Every statement in the bible is absolutely true."

No, or that would mean that all the terrible statements that the Pharisees and others made about Jesus, for example, are true. "Many of them said 'He is possessed by a demon and is raving mad'" John 10:20. It is a true account of what people said but it is not a true statement.

This is why we need the Holy Spirit, who inspired people to write down what we call the Bible, to lead and guide us into all truth by rightly dividing the word of truth. See Chapter Twelve for more on how to properly interpret the Bible as we have it today.

The book *52 Lies Heard In Church Every Sunday: And Why The Truth Is So Much Better* by Steve McVey is another good resource for renewing your mind with Jesus' **whole gospel of grace.**

Appendix # 5 recommends other grace-based books too.

APPENDIX # 10

James' Beliefs,
Which Dictated His Leadership Decisions ...
A Follow-up of Chapters Seven and Thirteen

It is an historical fact that the Gentiles in Jerusalem were required by James to first be circumcised before they could become saved Christians. **#45** This requirement was enforced by all Hebrew bishops in Jerusalem until circumcision was officially banned by the Romans in 132 AD. So why would James continue to officially insist on circumcision for Gentiles in Jerusalem when he agreed at the first council in 50 AD that it was unnecessary for Gentiles elsewhere? And worse yet, why would he endorse and practice the now obsolete Mosaic Law system that no one could keep and which arouses sin, brings condemnation and causes death, according to Jesus' revelation to Paul (see Chapters Eight and Nine)?

A Jewish View Of The Law's Purpose

This mysterious picture becomes clear when we connect the dots from William Barclay's explanation of 1) the way the Jews viewed the purpose of the Law in Paul's day (a view that Paul rejected after Jesus' revelation in 42 AD) and 2) James' personal lifestyle and continued commitment to Moses' teaching that influenced his policy-making as the leader of the Jerusalem church. The following quote comes from page 156 of Barclay's book, *The Mind of Paul* which, he says, describes the Jewish view in 50 AD of why God gave them the Law, according to the Mishnah, (which is both a collection of laws to be followed by the Jewish people and a study book for deriving more laws):

> In the Mishnah there is the sentence: 'It was because the Holy One (God) wished to give Israel an opportunity to acquire merit that He gave them so much Torah (Law) and so many commandments.' The Law was designed to enable a man to amass and to acquire credit in the sight of God. Everything depends on the assumption that, 'Man has got the ability to acquire merits before the heavenly Father.' However weak and frail man may be, physically and morally, he is in a position to gather merits in the eyes of God.

And what does Barclay say was Paul's enlightened view of the Law?

> Nothing could be more diametrically opposed to the conception of Paul. Grace means that no man can ever acquire anything in the sight of God; all that man can do is wonderingly to accept that which God freely and generously gives.

He then cites 20 of Paul's scriptures that document Jesus' **grace-based gospel** of God's unmerited favor, given as a totally free gift with no strings attached. But of course, we know in retrospect that Paul did not start out at his conversion with this revelation of Jesus' **whole gospel of grace**. And neither did the disciples - who walked and lived with Jesus for three years, **pre-cross** - comprehend how radical Jesus' **whole gospel of grace** would be, even after what they experienced at Pentecost. They just assumed that they were to live under the Law of Moses as they had done with Jesus, **pre-cross**.

Once Jesus revealed the truth to Paul years later, in 42 AD, he realized that the law is the polar opposite of grace. That is why Paul was so adamantly against the **elephant of Galatianism,** as is evident in Galatians. He saw that the Mishnah's teaching that man can earn merits that somehow obligate God to reward him, is an insult to the loving and gracious nature of Father-God. But that was not clear to anyone before 42 AD. (However, it had been true for Abraham who walked with God by faith and was declared righteous, not by his works.)

It is easy to understand why they would all arrive at the wrong assumption initially. Why? Because the blessings and curses tied to the Mosaic Law Covenant are based on the Israelite's performance, not on God's free grace. So their assumption presupposes that right behavior is all that is required to be compatible with heaven. As we know now from Jesus' revelation through Paul, Adam's fall gave every human, thereafter (except Jesus), a fallen, **in Adam** nature, from which springs wrong behavior. The Law was given to reveal this fact to prepare mankind to see their desperate condition spiritually and accept Jesus as Savior. He is the only One qualified to make it possible for humans to receive a new nature through being reborn of God Himself. But to trust in and therefore benefit from this totally grace-based offer, one *must* reject the lie that says that Jesus' efforts were not enough and, therefore, each person must continue to work to add to Jesus' **finished work** on Calvary to help earn (or to at least maintain) one's salvation.

The corollary to the lie of works-based salvation is that each person can take some credit for getting himself (and even others) to heaven by his praying and fasting and obeying the Big Ten etc. This deception is so ingrained today that many fear if they don't follow the Law and do all the above, they won't make it to heaven. That poisonous mixture of two opposing covenants – law vs. grace – is the norm today among many who call themselves Christian. In fact, it might very well be the norm taught in the church that you currently pastor or attend. It certainly was the case for me for most of my life and is a main reason for this book that <u>seeks to get to the root cause of this heresy and how and why it is still so entrenched in the Body of Christ today</u>.

So, on to the second point: what was James' core belief system and the role that he played in furthering (rather than helping to stop) this mixture of opposing covenants, practiced under his leadership? Barclay collected many more important dots about James' life and thoughts in *The Letters of James and Peter* which is a book from his popular Bible commentary collection called *The Daily Bible Series*.

The first quote, found on pages 12-14, is a lengthy and highly relevant account of the life and death of James as first recorded by Hegesippus (c. 110 - c. April 7, 180 AD) who was the first Christian chronicler of the early Church. He was most likely a Jewish convert to Christianity and therefore quite conversant with Jewish ways of thought and action. This detailed account was preserved by Christian historian Eusebius who lived from c. 260/265 – 339/340 AD. **#46**

> James, the Lord's brother, succeeds to the government of the Church, in conjunction with the apostles. He has been universally called the Just, from the days of the Lord down to the present time. For many bore the name of James; but this one was holy from his

mother's womb. He drank no wine or other intoxicating liquor, nor did he eat flesh; no razor came upon his head; he did not anoint himself with oil, nor make use of the bath. He alone was permitted to enter the holy place: for he did not wear any woolen garment, but fine linen only. He alone, I say, was wont to go into the temple: and he used to be found kneeling on his knees, begging forgiveness for the people - so that the skin of his knees became horny like that of a camel's, by reason of his constantly bending the knee in adoration to God, and begging forgiveness for the people. Therefore, in consequence of his pre-eminent justice, he was called the Just, and Oblias, which signifies in Greek Defence (sic) of the People, and Justice (righteous before God), in accordance with what the prophets declare concerning him. (The question is: were these "declarations" about John the Baptist, James or Jesus. They could have been misapplied.)

Now some persons belonging to the seven sects existing among the people, which have been before described by me in the Notes, asked him: "What is the door of Jesus?" And he replied that He was the Saviour. In consequence of this answer, some believed that Jesus is the Christ. But the sects before mentioned did not believe, either in a resurrection or in the coming of One to requite every man according to his works; but those who did believe, believed because of James. So, when many even of the ruling class believed, there was a commotion among the Jews, and scribes, and Pharisees, who said: 'A little more, and we shall have all the people looking for Jesus as the Christ.

They came, therefore, in a body to James, and said: "We entreat thee, restrain the people: for they are gone astray in their opinions about Jesus, as if he were the Christ. We entreat thee to persuade all who have come hither for the day of the Passover, concerning Jesus. For we all listen to thy persuasion; since we, as well as all the people, bear thee testimony that thou art just, and showest partiality to none. Do thou, therefore, persuade the people not to entertain erroneous opinions concerning Jesus: for all the people, and we also, listen to thy persuasion. Take thy stand, then, upon the summit of the temple, that from that elevated spot thou mayest be clearly seen, and thy words may be plainly audible to all the people. For, in order to attend the Passover (sic), all the tribes have congregated hither, and some of the Gentiles also.

The aforesaid scribes and Pharisees accordingly set James on the summit of the temple, and cried aloud to him, and said: "O just one, whom we are all bound to obey, forasmuch as the people is in error, and follows Jesus the crucified, do thou tell us what is the door of Jesus, the crucified." And he answered with a loud voice: "Why ask ye me concerning Jesus the Son of man? He Himself sitteth in heaven, at the right hand of the Great Power, and shall come on the clouds of heaven."

And, when many were fully convinced by these words, and offered praise for the testimony of James, and said, "Hosanna to the son of David," then again the said Pharisees and scribes said to one another, "We have not done well in procuring this testimony to Jesus. But let us go up and throw him down, that they may be afraid, and not believe him." And they cried aloud, and said: "Oh! oh! the just man himself is in error." Thus they fulfilled the Scripture written in Isaiah: "Let us away with the just man, because he is troublesome to us: therefore shall they eat the fruit of their doings." So they went up and threw down the just man, and said to one another: "Let us stone James the Just." And they began to stone him: for he was not killed by the fall; but he turned, and kneeled down, and said: "I beseech Thee, Lord God our Father, forgive them; for they know not what they do.

And, while they were thus stoning him to death, one of the priests, the sons of Rechab, the son of Rechabim, to whom testimony is borne by Jeremiah the prophet, began to cry aloud, saying: "Cease, what do ye? The just man is praying for us." But one among them, one of the fullers, took the staff with which he was accustomed to wring out the garments he dyed, and hurled it at the head of the just man.

And so he suffered martyrdom; and they buried him on the spot, and the pillar erected to his memory still remains, close by the temple. This man was a true witness to both Jews and Greeks that Jesus is the Christ.

The fact that he was known for "begging forgiveness for the people" would, in itself, indicate that he did not yet understand the full efficacy of Jesus' **finished work** for believers and unbelievers. 2 Corinthians 5:18-19 declares that God, in effect, no longer counts men's sins against them. Begging God for something He has already supplied proves that James was still focused on the requirements of the Law rather than on Jesus and His **whole grace gospel**.

The account states that "He has been universally called *the Just* (righteous), from the days of the Lord down to the present time." This indicates that even the non-Christian Jews greatly respected him for his *holy lifestyle* and regarded him as "righteous" or he would not have had access into the Holy of Holies or regarded as a man "whom we are all bound to obey." Apparently, he was born and lived as a Nazarite until his martyrdom, generally thought to be in 62 AD. This would explain why he did not challenge the Jewish establishment like Jesus, Stephen and Paul routinely did regarding its focus on the Law for righteousness. But Jesus made it clear to Paul that before Jesus' perfect sacrifice on Calvary "There is no one righteous, not even one" (see Romans 3:9-10). James and the Pharisees were judging people based on outer appearances, not on their **in Adam** condition, **pre-cross**.

Apparently James believed that his law-based thinking and lifestyle was an inherent part of being a Christian or he would have rejected it as unnecessary as Paul did after 42 AD. His revered lifestyle prevented any kind of conflict with the Jewish establishment that would risk another persecution like had happened after Stephen's death. So he was able to hold to his very strict, Law-centered, Nazarite beliefs yet quietly convince some Jews that Jesus was the Savior. Unwittingly, James boasted that the mixture of law with grace was practiced by thousands of Jewish Christians. Acts 21:20 states that James said the following to convince Paul to try to keep the peace by paying for and undergoing a Jewish rite.

You understand, brother, how many thousands there are among the Jews who have believed, and they are all zealous for the law.

Talk about being pressured by a pastor to squeeze you into a mold of law! Paul could have replied that "being zealous for the law keeps you from being zealous for Jesus" like he was. By then, he knew from Jesus about the evil results of mixture which he had detailed in Galatians. Yet, here is the half-brother of Jesus, who is regarded as "the holiest man in Jerusalem," insisting that Paul endorse the mixture of two opposing covenants because, in effect, "I am in charge here and you are on my turf where there are many thousands of Jews who have believed (presumably in Jesus) and they are all zealous for the law."

But why are they still zealous for Moses and the law instead of for Jesus? Because the Jerusalem church was unknowingly mixing law with grace, starting at Pentecost, and then rejected at least two opportunities to "repent" about that heresy and become Jesus-centered. And now James was endorsing and even boasting about the mixture and pressuring Paul to do the same. If James was living in the purity of the **whole gospel of grace** from Jesus, he would have been preaching against their misplaced zeal for the law and urging Paul to preach the truth about Jesus' **finished work** in power, as he had done in many other cities. But the Pharisees would not be happy.

No Compromise

Paul taught that righteousness was a gift from God, apart from works of the law. James was living a lifestyle that said works were necessary for righteousness and proud of the fact that thousands of Jews agreed with him. There is no reason to be zealous for a law system that arouses sin and causes death unless you think it is necessary to follow, due to ignorance or unbelief. After the council, James could not claim "ignorance" and so, apparently, he was operating in unbelief of the **grace gospel** that Jesus revealed to Paul. According to Galatians 5:4, that is a recipe for falling from grace and being under the curse of the Law. Ouch

On top of that churning tornado, is the added fact that Paul's reputation for exalting Jesus instead of Moses had preceded him, as related in Acts 21:21. James continues:

> Now they have heard about you, that you are teaching those Jews who are among the Gentiles to withdraw from Moses, (which Paul was actually teaching because the law had been nailed to the cross) telling them that they should not circumcise their sons, nor act according to tradition (adhere to the requirements of the Law and observe feast days etc. to be righteous).

Yes, of course, Paul taught that the **New Covenant** replaced the Mosaic Law Covenant for Jewish believers. Therefore, the only circumcision that counts for anything spiritually is the circumcision of the heart by being reborn of God who gives a new heart and a new spirit. In fact, Paul told the Galatians even more pointedly in 5:1-3:

> Stand firm, and do not be willing to be held by the yoke of servitude (the Law). Behold, I, Paul, say to you, that if you have been circumcised, Christ will be of no benefit to you. For I again testify, about every man circumcising himself, that he is obligated to obey the entire law.

This was the eye of the doctrinal storm, and James was giving Paul a chance to recant the "rumored" position that he was teaching Jews to disregard the Law of Moses, shown by discarding physical circumcision and many other Jewish customs and traditions. We know that

Paul was guilty as charged because he challenged that very requirement at the Jerusalem Council in 50 AD and <u>won that concession from James himself at that point</u>. (see Chapter Seven for the details). Paul was also quoted by Luke in Acts 13:38-39 as saying:

> Therefore, let it be known to you, noble brothers, that through Him (Jesus) is announced to you remission from sins and from everything by which you were not able to be justified in the law of Moses. All who believe **in Him** are justified.

That meant that circumcision and the whole sacrificial system was not necessary because Jesus accomplished justification for everyone who believes **in Him** – period. Was Paul guilty of teaching this and more? Absolutely! That is what Paul meant by "counting all else rubbish for the sake of knowing Christ." James' practices would be especially "rubbish" if James kept the Law and followed Moses because he still thought they would enable him and the Jerusalem church to merit salvation – as the Mishnah taught. In principle, this is the same test Luther faced before the established church of his day. Was James' obedience to the Law still needed to be "just" (righteous before God) or was Jesus' revelation to Paul the truth, succinctly expressed in Romans 3:20-22:

> Therefore, <u>no one</u> will be declared righteous (just) in God's sight by observing the Law. Rather it is through the Law that we become conscious of (our) sin (nature.) But now, a <u>righteousness apart from the Law</u> has been made known, to which the Law and the prophets testify. This righteousness from God comes through faith in Jesus Christ to all who believe. ...

Paul knew by revelation that being a Nazarite gets you no more points from God than being a tent maker or a fisherman because righteousness is a <u>gift of God's grace through faith alone</u>, not by "holy behavior" measured by obeying the law code of the day. Being zealous for the Law (like the Pharisees, James and his congregation were) will keep your eyes on yourself rather than on Christ Jesus. Mixture is deadly, no matter who is promoting it:

> But even if we or an angel from heaven (or a "just" man in Jerusalem) should preach a gospel other than the one we preached to you (that came directly from Jesus), let him be eternally condemned (Galatians1:9).

But James was apparently determined to prove publically that Paul agreed with him and that believers should be following the law, as recorded in Acts 21:22-25. So he misused the authority of his office as the head leader in the "first Christian church" by declaring:

> So, what should we do next? The multitude must be convened because they will hear that you have arrived. Therefore, do what we say to you: We have four men who are under a vow. Take these and <u>sanctify yourself</u> with them, and <u>require</u> them to shave their heads. Then everyone will know that the things that they have heard about you are false, <u>but that you yourself walk orderly, keeping (obeying) the law.</u> And as for those Gentiles believers, we have written a judgment that they should keep themselves from what has been immolated to idols, and from blood, and from what has been suffocated, and from fornication.

There he goes again. James is so focused on keeping the law and remaining "just" in the eyes of the other Judaizers and the Jewish leaders that he wants Paul to demonstrate his commitment to the law by submitting to a "purification" rite and making an offering. To add insult to injury, James also saves face with the Jews regarding the Gentile believers by reaffirming the four rules he persuaded the Council in 50 AD to impose on them. Yet we now know from Paul's writings that he knew that "sanctification" was the work of the Holy Spirit, not achieved by keeping external rituals, and that he did not preach James' edict to the Gentiles after the council. So, the big question is: "Why did Paul choose to cooperate with James' plan rather than confront James with the truth in love?"

One plausible answer is that Paul was listening to the Holy Spirit and this was not the time or place to risk an openly public schism. It was bad enough that James had caused a subtle but significant "split" by dividing the Body of Christ into two groups with two different sets of doctrines regarding the Gentiles back at the council. Yet, embarrassing James publically would cause James irreparable insult and harm and maybe even cause a riot. Also, James was the acting leader of that local flock and Paul wisely continued to <u>honor the office</u> of God-given authority, as he had in the past and taught in Romans 13:1. Additionally, Paul knew from personal experience that it took the grace and miraculous power of the Holy Spirit to replace his own previous law-entrenched paradigm with a totally new one and that mental repentance did not happen overnight. So probably, the best answer to that intriguing question is given by Paul himself in 1 Corinthians 9:19-23:

> Though I am free of all (obligations to) men, I made myself the servant of all, <u>so that I might gain all the more (converts to Christ)</u>. And so, <u>to the Jews, I became like a Jew</u>, so that I might gain the Jews. To those who are under the law, I became <u>as if I were under the law</u>, (though I was not under the law) so that I might gain those who were under the law. To those who were without the law, I became as if I were without the law, (though I was not without the (Mosaic) law of God, being in the <u>law of Christ</u>) so that I might gain those who were without the law (Gentiles). <u>To the weak, I became weak, so that I might gain the weak.</u> To all, I became all, so that I might save all. And I do everything for the sake of the Gospel, so that I may become a fellow-partaker.

Possibly, too, by obeying James who was "weak" in believing the **whole grace gospel**, God could present a teachable moment to James when his law-centered plans went south – as they soon did. So Paul followed suit as recorded in Acts 21:26-28 as follows:

> Then Paul, took the men the next day and was purified with them and he entered the temple, announcing the process of the days of purification, until a sacrifice would be offered on behalf of each one of them. But when the seven days were reaching completion, some Jews who were from Asia, saw him in the temple and <u>incited all the people</u>. And they laid hands on him, crying out: 'Men of Israel, help! This is the man who is teaching, everyone, everywhere, against the people and the law and this place. Furthermore, he has even brought Gentiles into the temple, and he has violated this holy place.'

As usually happens, man's plans backfired with unintended consequences that we are still paying for after some 2000 years. Challenging Paul to deny what Jesus had revealed to him and pressuring Paul to endorse the Law again, did not bode well for James. This is especially true, given the effect his blatant mixture of two opposing covenants has had on believers, consciously and unconsciously, for these 2000 years.

God gave the Law to reveal mankind's **in Adam** nature, not to merit heaven. Perverting the purpose of the Law into a merit system to gain or maintain God's acceptance and approval is to devalue the perfect, substitutionary, blood sacrifice of God's own Lamb. Putting Moses on the same plain as the risen Christ is blasphemy, no matter who does it. Only God knows for sure if James or any other Jew of the day was condemning themselves by the sin of unbelief towards Christ Jesus and His **divine exchange**. We do know that Jesus' words to Paul regarding mixture are very strong. Unfortunately, Paul's decision to submit to James is used today to "prove" that Paul also focused on and adhered to the Law for righteousness, despite all his rhetoric to the contrary in his writings.

So what was the result of all of James' maneuvering to keep the peace by getting Paul to "uphold the law?" Acts 21:29-36 describes the ensuing chaos:

> For they had seen Trophimus, an Ephesian, in the city with him, and they supposed that Paul had brought him into the temple.) And the entire city was stirred up. And it happened that the people ran together. And apprehending Paul, they dragged him outside of the temple. And immediately the doors were closed. Then, as they were seeking to kill him, it was reported to the tribune of the cohort: "All Jerusalem is in confusion." And so, immediately taking soldiers and centurions, he rushed down to them. And when they had seen the tribune and the soldiers, they ceased striking Paul. Then the tribune, drawing near, apprehended him and ordered that he be bound with two chains. And he was asking who he was and what he had done. Then they were crying out various things within the crowd. And since he could not understand anything clearly because of the noise, he ordered him to be brought into the fortress. And when he had arrived at the stairs, it happened that he was carried up by the soldiers, because of the threat of violence from the people. For the multitude of the people were following and crying out, "Take him away!"

Regardless of why Paul succumbed to James' pressure, the end result of James' strategy to placate the Law-minded Jews failed miserably. Why? Because law-based people are going on their own "knowledge of right and wrong" rather on the Lord's Spirit-led direction the way Jesus lived. But perhaps this episode and Paul's humility to submit to James' misguided leadership (in order to "win some to Christ") caused James eventually to repent of his dependency on the Law for righteousness at some point, in favor of living and dying only for Jesus.

Whether James eventually rejected mixture before he died or not can't be known definitively because it is ultimately a heart matter. But we do know from Hegesippus' account that when the Pharisees forced James to deny Jesus in about 62 AD, he publically declared that Jesus is the Savior of the world to a huge number of Jews and was thrown from the temple heights and clubbed to death for declaring the truth. Tragically, history confirms that the legacy of circumcising Gentiles as a requirement for salvation continued in Jerusalem until 135 AD. Obviously, James stuck to his life-long convictions or he would have changed the policy before he died. He kept the peace in Jerusalem by feeding the **elephant of mixture.** But, ironically, his death apparently also triggered a riot. #47

Is There Mixture In The Book Of James?

The Book of James was addressed specifically to the "twelve (Jewish) tribes scattered abroad." This group would have included both Christian and non-Christian Jews but, obviously, not Gentiles. Now, you know that only Paul was given the **whole gospel of grace** by Jesus who revealed that the Law was not given to Gentiles or to believers. Therefore:

1) Is there any significant revelation in James' book to benefit Gentile believers that is not found in Paul's gospel from Jesus? If so, it would mean that Jesus revealed essentials to James that He forgot to tell Paul. That would mean that there is more to Jesus' **grace gospel** than Paul knew about and therefore, more to Jesus' **finished work**.

2) Is there anything in James' book that Jesus "updated" or redefined or balanced in His gospel revealed to Paul? No, because James' content was not even as full of revelation as the "bare bones gospel" found in the book of Acts. In fact, Luther dubbed is as "the book of straw" because it had no "Christology" in it.

3) Is there anything in James' book that could be easily interpreted to feed the **elephant of mixture** in churches today? That is likely because it is written from a Jewish mindset, modeled on what all good Jews should *do* rather than on who reborn Jewish believers *are* - **new creations in Christ Jesus.** To emphasize the former before (or instead of) the latter reality is to risk reinforcing the works of the Law instead of the **finished work** of Christ Jesus' **divine exchange** on Calvary. Any hint that it is possible to "do good" in God's eyes while still **in Adam** is not the gospel of Jesus. It would imply that there is a source of "good" apart from God. A polluted stream cannot provide pure water. Giving good advice to change the behavior of spiritually dead people is behavior modification, not the **whole grace gospel** of Jesus. In short, there is no presentation of Jesus' **whole grace gospel** in the book of James to learn from and feed on. Furthermore, it makes no distinction between the proper use of the Law (to bring sinners to the end of themselves) from the improper use of the Law (to insist that believers have to follow it to be saved or to remain righteous).

Does this possibility imply that James' book is not inspired or canonical? Not if one understands the dynamic of progressive revelation? Why? God unveiled more and more of His ultimate purpose and the process of salvation over the 6000 year history recorded in the Bible. Even as Jesus revealed many new things about the Kingdom to his followers, **pre-cross,** He also stated that much more would be revealed to them **post-cross** through the Holy Spirit. That is an historical example of progressive revelation. However, James did not travel with Jesus and, in all likelihood, was embarrassed by Jesus' run-ins with James' friends, the Pharisees, who thought so highly of James and called him "James the Just."

Unfortunately, by the conventional placement in the Bible of the book of James *after* Paul's writings, a reader might unwittingly be led to think that the book's content is on a par with or "better" (progressively speaking) than is Jesus' **whole gospel of grace**, revealed directly to Paul in 42 AD. However, in the light of the overall progression of revelation in the Bible, James' book would fit more logically *after* the four gospels but *before* the book of Acts. Why? Because the content reflects the entrenched Jewish thought and practice in the Jerusalem church – mixture – and, therefore, is decidedly different than the bare bones gospel and miracles written about in Acts and in the **whole grace gospel** later revealed to Paul. James' lifestyle as a Nazarite kept him focused on the requirements and practice of the Law. Again, the historical proof of this fact is that he insisted that Gentles be circumcised, and do as he did, to secure salvation, as presented above. (Actually, James' book is in the style of some Old Testament books and, lacking in Christology, could logically fit before the Gospel of Matthew, though that placement might detract from the centrality of Jesus life in the four gospels.)

The Book of James, like all the other books in the Bible, should be viewed through the lens of Jesus' **whole grace gospel** to Paul, much like the Final Act of a good play supplies the meaning and ultimate context and the best interpretation of the two (or more) previous Acts. Jesus' own explanation of the **finished work** of His **divine exchange** is the most complete and reliable commentary to properly interpret all the other books of the Bible. Any other book that combines law with grace to be saved is not the gospel that Jesus revealed to Paul, no matter who penned it. The Book of Psalms, for instance, are the inspired word of God but are *not* the pure **grace gospel** because it focuses on keeping the Law – consistent with the covenant it was written under. Care should be taken to see it through **New Covenant** eyes because you and I live under that decidedly different grace-based Covenant. No need to ask God "to create in me a clean heart" (see Psalm 51) if you are reborn of God. You already have a new heart, thanks to Jesus **divine exchange**. It is not clear from James' book that he really had that revelation about himself or any other believers. Again, that is why Luther called it a "book of straw." Not much meat. A much more thorough treatment that closely compares Jesus' revelation to Paul with the Book of James will be one of my future publications on Amazon.

APPENDIX #11

A REPLY TO JOHN F. MACARTHUR

Law-focused teachers often accuse grace-based teachers of antinomianism – defined as rejecting the law. They insist that if you don't tell a believer to live according to the Ten Commandments then you are, by default, giving that believer a license to sin. In their mind, there are only those two options. But as noted many times in this book, the law was not given to Gentiles and it is not made for the righteous, according to 1 Timothy 1:9. The "righteous" are all those reborn saints who are **in Christ**. So was Paul an antinomian? No, and neither are the authors whose books are recommended in Appendix #5. In fact, these **grace gospel** teachers have a higher view of the law than those who feed on and teach the **elephant of mixture** like the Jerusalem church did. What is the difference?

Grace-based teachers use the law the way Jesus did in the four gospels - as needed - to bring unbelievers to realize that their efforts at law-focused living are as filthy rags. Earning heaven through law-keeping is not an option. Only faith in Jesus and in His **finished work** provides God's gift of righteousness through rebirth. From then on, the Holy Spirit, not the law, is to be their Friend, Guide, Teacher, Enabler, Sanctifier, Comforter, Empowerer, etc. Learning to hear and depend on Him like Jesus did enables every saint who seeks Him to live the higher law of faith, love and liberty **in Christ**. This is the third option that Jesus revealed to Paul as part of His **grace-based gospel**. It is the third alternative - the **butterfly life** - that the **elephant of mixture** has stomped on for 2000 years.

The demands of law cannot be kept perfectly and so they cause fear of failure that brings torment and condemnation to those trying to *earnestly* live under the law. It is all part of the harsh realities of the law discussed in Chapter Nine. Law-consciousness causes sin-consciousness that prevents Jesus-consciousness. This performance-based mind-set breeds many misconceptions about God's true nature and is commonly taught by popular preachers and authors today.

Rather than just talk in generalities, I want to give examples of how this 2000 year old doctrinal war between law vs grace is being fought today. One of many examples is the popular author, teacher and pastor, John MacArthur, chosen because he called out Bob George (one of my favorite **grace-based gospel** teachers) by name in his book, *The Freedom and Power of Forgiveness,* published in 1998. He did this because Bob believes that 1 John 1:9 was *not* written to believers but to Gnostic Jews.

As previously noted in Chapter Fourteen of my book, this verse is a lightning rod that is used by law-based teachers to insist that believers must confess their sins to stay right with God. I gave six reasons why this assertion *cannot* be true.

Now, to his credit, Mr. MacArthur *correctly* states on page eight of his book that:

What we believe determines how we think, how we behave, and how we respond to life's trials. … A right belief system therefore lies at the foundation of all truly righteous conduct.

This is another way of stating that right believing yields the fruit of the Spirit of right living. While all this is certainly true, it is also true that our beliefs determine how we respond to God, as emphasized in this book. On page 28, Mr. MacArthur beautifully summarizes many essential truths of Jesus' **divine exchange**, including the revelation that there is no condemnation for those **in Christ** and, therefore, all their sins are totally and eternally forgiven by just believing it is true, in agreement with Romans 8:1.

Unfortunately, Mr. MacArthur does an-about-face and devotes all of Chapter Three to insisting that 1 John 1:9 is written to every believer. He seems to have forgotten that 1 John 2:2 agrees with Jesus' revelation to Paul that Jesus' perfect sacrifice paid (past tense) for the sins and punishment of the *whole world* – before anyone confessed any sins, **post cross**. It was one of the terms of the *unilateral* covenant Jesus made with Father-God on Calvary as mankind's new representative. Since "Jesus was the atoning sacrifice for the sins of the whole world," both an unbeliever's and a believer's sins are eternally forgiven (and forgotten) by God. *That alone* is why there is no condemnation for those **in Christ** – not because the saints are confessing their sins. In fact, Jesus' teaching through Paul never told believers to confess their sins be reborn or to *stay* righteous or restore fellowship with God.

Nor does Jesus require unbelievers to confess their sins *to be saved,* according to Romans 10:9-13. God's **post-cross** "issue" with unbelievers is their *unbelief* that Jesus is who He says He is and will do for them what He came to do – save them from hell by grace through *belief* in Him. The Holy Spirit convicts unbelievers of the specific sin of unbelief (even though that sin is already forgiven) because of their mistrusting disbelief which prevents them from accepting salvation. Even though God is now reconciled to unbelievers (thanks to Jesus' sacrifice for mankind - 2 Corinthians 5:18-19), the unbeliever must choose to receive God's offer of that gift to be reconciled to God, as verse 20 states. Influenced by the **elephant of mixture**, law-minded teachers still focus on people's law-breaking behavior rather than on what Jesus did about mankind's sinning some 2000 years ago. They just can't fathom that God could be that merciful and good to mankind through Jesus' **finished work** as mankind's last Adam and through His **divine exchange** with believers that made all spiritual things new from God's point of view.

So why is Mr. MacArthur insisting that all believers must regularly confess their sins to God for the rest of their lives to receive God's on-going forgiveness? Because he mistakenly mixes the terms of two opposing covenants. This is a blatant example of inviting the **elephant of mixture** to stomp on the minds of the saints reading his book.

But, not content to just air his law-minded beliefs, he ironically does the same thing that John Calvin did, as documented in Appendix # 3. He accuses grace-based teachers of serious error if "They insist that 1 John 1:9 has nothing to do with Christians." Directing his attack on Pastor Bob George, Mr. MacArthur states:

A handful of popular teachers are claiming that since Christians are *already* forgiven, they should never ask God for forgiveness, and to do so is an expression of unbelief. They insist that 1 John 1:9 has nothing to do with Christians.

One of the best known proponents of this view is Bob George, popular author and radio speaker. George characterizes Christians who pray for forgiveness as people 'who live in daily insecurity ... Christians who doubt whether all their sins are forgiven' (page 53).

We already extensively discussed 1 John 1:7-9 in context in both Chapter Fourteen and in greater depth in Appendix #4 because this is such a pivotal point for believers today if they are to walk in faith, love and freedom rather than in bondage to the law. But let's look closely at this single verse to see if it could cause doubt and insecurity in a believer's mind as Bob George stated.

(Note: I am doing this analysis again for a very personal reason. In 1980, I put 1 John 1:9 to music, along with many other single verses, from a well-known memory system and this is what played over and over in my mind for decades and *reinforced* a works-based mind-set that caused unconscious doubt and insecurity in me. Many students and adults I have taught in earlier years have this same catchy tune still rolling around in their heads, probably still thinking it applies to them. I regret that and trust God to intervene in their lives with His truth.)

> If we confess our sins, then he is faithful and just (holy, righteous) to forgive us our sins and to cleanse us from all iniquity (unrighteousness) (1 John 1:9).

Proper exegesis of this particular verse is so important because it is a key verse that the world-wide Catholic church uses to justify the necessity for the sacrament of Penance (confession of sins). They claim that this sacrament is "instituted by Christ to give grace." How could that be true when Jesus revealed to Paul that being law/sin-conscious causes believers to "fall from grace," according to Galatians 5:4. So let's unpack this verse carefully – again.

The very first word "if" is a conditional participle which means that you can't get the benefit unless you meet the condition. Does that sound familiar? Yes, it is the bottom line of the Mosaic Law. "If you obey the Law (perfectly), I will bless you; if not, you will be subject to the list of curses." In 1 John 1:9, forgiveness is not a gift of grace accomplished at Calvary for mankind <u>but presented as a result of one's obedience to a requirement which depends on my continuous performance</u>. If it is true for me, it obligates me to:

1) confess <u>all</u> of my sins to God until I die,

2) be sure to get God's forgiveness in order to regain right-standing with Him and,

3) do all this so that I can "go to heaven."

To accomplish this (impossible) task, I will have to continuously monitor all of my thoughts and words and deeds, measuring them against some standard of right and wrong – some law code.

Those who are law-minded would ask "So what's wrong with that? That's how to be a good person so that you can go to heaven. God gives you His grace so that you can faithfully keep the law." But what if I forget to confess even one sin? Since under the law, ignorance is no excuse, what if I sinned without knowing it? Do I have to be fully up on *all* the law's 613 requirements, like the Pharisees tried to be, and to be sure I confess every one? Well the dirty little answer to these three questions is "Yes." Living by the law to stay in right standing with God requires perfect obedience to all the demands of the Law. And that includes all of the Mosaic Law, not just the Big Ten. As Paul stated in Galatians 5:3: "Again, I declare to everyone who lets himself be circumcised, he must obey the whole Law." Choosing some parts and not other parts is not an option if law-keeping is your focus, according to James 2:10. So, if you break just one part of the Law, you break the *whole* Law.

So if that is what you believe Christianity is, how is this working for you? It didn't work for Paul or for Martin Luther. It is the same yo-yo life the Israelites lived under and Jesus saved us from. And even if somehow you are able to keep 90% of the law, you will fall from God's grace by being under the curse of the law and you will actually be arousing sin to boot. Then you will have more sins to confess. This describes the wretched predicament that Paul described at the end of Chapter Seven in Romans. He was addressing the law-minded Jews "who knew the Law," backwards and forwards, just like he did as a Pharisee.

The only way a believer would be aware that he is sinning is by some memory or reminder or outright focus on the "requirements and demands of the Law," the one nailed to the cross and that is now obsolete for Jews (and never given to Gentiles). Such awareness necessarily indicates that he has his mind *focused on the Tree of Law rather than on Jesus,* the Tree of Life - *not* on "the things above but on the things of earth." That is the opposite of what Jesus told us to do in Colossians 3:1-3. When a believer wrongly thinks that this verse is addressed to him, he will, at that point, put himself under the law and fall from grace. He will experience the insecurity that performance-based acceptance and approval brings and open himself up to condemning thoughts from the devil, a corrupted conscience and the mixed message of law-minded pastors and teachers and denominations. This is the bondage of the law that Jesus warned Paul about - and which got him so angry with the Judaizers in Jerusalem.

Must You Confess Your Sins?
Believer, you can confess your sins to God if you want. But it won't be because the Holy Spirit is "convicting you of sin." It is His job to convince you of your righteous oneness with Jesus and encourage you to listen to His voice instead of the obsolete law causing sin-consciousness. Be aware that confessing sins pre-supposes and requires a degree of *self-focus* and introspection on your part, an awareness of the law that could also include a false sense of guilt, shame and condemnation. The devil facilitates this process by "accusing the brethren." All of this can contribute to a *feeling* of distance from Abba-Father, something that law-minded believers apparently assume is the norm. They believe God is always looking at their sin instead of seeing them as righteous and holy saints **in Christ**, regardless of their behavior. Because they are law-minded, they think and teach that Father-God is law-minded instead of love-natured.

Mr. MacArthur reaches this wrong conclusion because he also refuses to accept the very important distinction Bob George makes between punishment and discipline (found in the same

401

chapter) as they apply to a believer. Instead, he <u>fabricates a supposed distinction</u> between God's unconditional forgiveness as a <u>Judge</u> and His *conditional* forgiveness as a <u>parental Father.</u> He correctly insists that God's "judicial forgiveness" was purchased by Jesus' atonement and never needs sought again. It "frees us from any kind of eternal condemnation. It is the forgiveness of justification." **However,** he insists <u>that God's "parental forgiveness" is different because it is given only when a believer confesses his sins to God,</u> the Parent. Here are some of his quotes:

> Sin needs to be confessed and forsaken regularly, and the pardon of a loving but <u>displeased Father must</u> be sought (page 57).

> Parental forgiveness sets things right with a grieving and displeased but loving Father (Page 58).

> So the notion that God is always benign, never displeased with His children, is quite foreign to Scripture (page 64).

> Christians never need to fear facing God's wrath as their Judge, but they will definitely face His fatherly disapproval and correction when they sin (page 64).

> Again, 1 John 1:9 is simply speaking about an attitude that is characteristic of <u>all true Christians: they are the ones who as a pattern are saying the same thing as God about their sin</u> (page 74).

Repent – Agree With God's Miraculous Salvation

Ironically, Mr. MacArthur "supports" his position by quoting from the same book where God *twice* declares: "<u>I will forgive their wickedness and I will remember their sins no more</u>" – Hebrews 8:12. Why? <u>Because God has already forgiven and reconciled the whole world to Himself – from His viewpoint.</u> *That,* believer, is what God says about *every* believer's sin in His New Covenant. And I agree with it and that is why I wrote this book! Apparently, Mr. MacArthur thinks that God switches hats and now "remembers your sin no more" <u>only *after* you remember and confess each one.</u> Again, Mr. MacArthur obviously rejects Jesus' **whole grace gospel's** blanket coverage of His forgiveness of the sins of the whole world that both 2 Corinthians 5:19 and 1 John 2:2 declares. If you believe Mr. MacArthur's perspective of God, how could you *not* "live in daily insecurity" as Bob George correctly states in the above quote? I guess he thinks that God just can't possibly be *that* good – at least as a parent.

Am I making light of the seriousness of sinning? Absolutely not! I know it can have devastating consequences in the **seen realm** and can open up a door for the devil to spoil one's victory in this realm. So, no, I am not making light of sinning. <u>But I am making much of Jesus blood sacrifice for all sinning</u> from God's viewpoint. "For where sin abounds, grace superabounds!" Therefore, I also now know I am no longer "under sin" because Jesus actually "became sin." Consequently, the **in Adam** sin nature of mankind was crucified on Calvary. He did that so that I could now be the righteousness of God **in Christ Jesus** by faith in His accomplishment. Adam's sin nature was imparted to Him and I was crucified with Him so that the new righteous nature He arose with was also <u>imparted</u> to me by virtue of being **in Him,** by faith alone. "[God] made Him who knew no sin *to be sin* on our behalf." This revelation from Jesus to Paul so confounds Mr. MacArthur's natural mind that he insists that:

> It cannot mean that Christ *became* a sinner. It cannot mean that He committed any sin, that His character was defiled, or that He bore our sin in any sense other than by legal imputation (page 25).

Why not? Who are we to reject what God said He did and how He did it? What more permanent way to legally end the devil's dominion - which Adam's rebellion relinquished to the devil and which made him the "god of this world" - than putting an end to the "Adamic nature" itself. By operating as fully man, Jesus was the last Adam sent here by God. He identified Himself with our **in Adam** nature "by *becoming* it" so that it could be destroyed. It is the same way humans became **in Adam** sinners without first sinning - by "impartation." A sin nature is not just imputed to each human being but *imparted* to each one "born of woman."

Likewise, when reborn of God, a new, righteous nature is not just imputed but *imparted* to every believer. (Romans 5:15-21, and especially verse 19, explains this grace-based reality in detail.) Otherwise, he or she could not be **in Christ** without "polluting Him." It is a transaction on the level of one's very *nature* or essence, more than just about one's behavior. When a believer gets a revelation of just how deep a transformation has *already* happened to his core self, his spirit man, through rebirth, <u>he is then freed to learn to live out of that new identity **in Christ Jesus**</u>. Spiritually, he is now of royal DNA, no longer a rotten sinner **in Adam**. "The old has passed away; behold, the new has come." That is God's perspective of His handiwork, accomplished by Jesus' **finished work** of His **divine exchange** which we can only "behold" by faith, not sight. It is always best to agree with God!

So now those who believe are *identified* with the <u>last Adam</u>, who God raised from the dead as the first of many brothers of a <u>new, holy nation</u> - no longer of the **in Adam** nation but of the royal priesthood of Christ Jesus (see 1 Peter 2:9-10). He becomes a child of God, a partaker of His divine nature, because of Jesus' **divine exchange.** This is the fulfillment of the "all things new" reality **in Christ**. I now know much more clearly what my sin cost Jesus (to be forsaken by Father-God) and how much I have been forgiven and it is that revelation of God's astounding goodness and love that keeps me in ever-deepening repentance (mind renewal) of how much Abba-Father loves me. His perfect love <u>casts out all fear</u> of His <u>alleged</u> "disapproval or punishment." All sin has been forgiven and forgotten because of Jesus **divine exchange** of natures and I am now "one spirit with my Father" (1 Corinthians 6:17). He who he is forgiven much, loves much! Amen.

So to summarize, there are many good reasons why the first chapter of 1 John does not apply to believers. The assumption that it does, forces a focus back on the **seen realm** of law and sin and self, rather than on the freedom of setting one's mind on the **unseen** things above, on Jesus, the Author and Finisher of our faith **in Him.**

Trashing God's Goodness
But even more importantly, the law/sin focus impacts a believer's concept of God and therefore his response to God. Since His infallible Word states that God truly forgave and no

longer remembers my sin, why would He be displeased with me and "chastise" me for what Jesus was already chastised for? (See 2 Corinthians 5:18-19, 1 John 2:2, Hebrews 8:12 and 10:17).

What does Mr. MacArthur think every believer must do to get this forgiveness? He must regularly apply 1 John 1:9 to keep short accounts with God in His role as our parent Father. This puts the believer back under a sin-centered focus on law. The believer must continually work his way back into fellowship with a (supposed) consistently *displeased* Father by regular confession of his sins. "So the notion that God is always benign, never displeased with His children, is quite foreign to scripture." (page 64). This statement is, itself, a display of the **elephant of mixture**. Let's take it apart. Is God always benign? No. For example, there are many **pre-cross** instances with the Israelites where He showed His displeasure by punishing their idolatry. They were "His people" *but* they were not "His children" in the **New Covenant** sense.

All of them were still **in Adam**, not reborn saints **in Christ**, because they lived before Jesus' **divine exchange**. To equate their position of servitude **in Adam** with a believer's position of son-ship **in Christ** is to devalue the cross and the blood of Jesus. For those who are **in Christ**, the question is now "Is God ever displeased with Jesus and therefore all the saints that are **in Him?**" The answer to that question is unequivocally and absolutely "No!" Why? Because Father-God is totally satisfied with what Jesus accomplished for mankind on Calvary. Consequently, God forgave all the sins of the whole world and, more radically, eradicated every *believer's* sin nature **in Adam**. The axe had be laid to the root of the tree so that we could be compatible with God by being **in Christ**. Could Jesus' parable of the prodigal son be a foretaste of His grace-based gospel – knowing what He would do for mankind on Calvary? I see no hint of displeasure or a requirement of a sin-confession in the father's reaction to the sins of either son. If he was disappointed, it would have been with the legalism of the elder brother, who resented his father's mercy and grace toward his younger sibling. Hmmm.

Slay The Elephant Still In Your Mind With Jesus' Finished Work

Question: Since 1) an **in Adam** sinner, who is at enmity with God, does not have to "confess his sins" to be born again, according to Jesus' revelation to Paul in Romans 10:9-13, and since 2) God forgave all mankind's sin and reconciled the whole world to Himself through Jesus, according to 2 Corinthians 5:19, why would a blood washed, **new creation** saint **in Christ** have to keep track of a law system that is now "obsolete" for believers (1 Timothy 1:9) so that he knows when he sins and then remember to confess *every one* of them to remove God's supposed displeasure with him – until he sins again?

That is the very treadmill of law-based bondage that Jesus died to free the Jews from forever when the law was nailed to the cross (Colossians 2:14). It produces a never-ending cycle of mental bondage to guilt, shame and condemnation. It prevents fellowship and intimacy with Abba-Father. It helps Satan in his goal to accuse and discourage the saints so that they give up and despair. It is the very way I tended to treat my children because I was brainwashed by law-based teaching that said God treated me that way. But the good news in Romans 4:15b is that "Where there is no law, there is no transgression." It is not the Mosaic Law that is written on every believer's heart because God never gave it to Gentiles and He declared to be "obsolete" in the same passage describing the terms of the **New Covenant** that Jesus made with Father-God (see Hebrews 8:12-13).

This erroneous <u>doctrine of demons</u> is the **elephant of mixture,** tragically being paraded around and endorsed by many respected and very high profile pastors and teachers. Like John Calvin, Mr. MacArthur is inexplicably mixing the requirements of the Mosaic Covenant with the **New Covenant** and sowing insecurity into many believers' minds who accept his brand of Galatianism. Hopefully he has repented (changed his mind to the grace-based thinking of Jesus' gospel revealed to Paul) since he wrote this book in 1998. That happens to be the very year that God told Joseph Prince that he, himself, was not teaching the gospel of radical grace. Fortunately for the Body of Christ, Joseph Prince did repent of mixture. Subsequently, I have personally benefitted enormously from Joseph's teaching and from other grace-based teachers, as have millions of other saints, world-wide. See Appendix 5 (the biblical number for "grace") for a list of recommended books that effectively declare Jesus' **whole grace-based gospel** of His **divine exchange.**

APPENDIX # 12

CREDITING SCRIPTURE QUOTATIONS USED IN THIS BOOK

Normally it is expected in a book of this scope that quotes so many scriptures, that the author give credit to every translation used. My own training and certification and experience as a former high school A. P. English teacher would also dictate that protocol. My third book, *God's Solution For A Fractured America*, published on Kindle, made a point to meticulously credit sources.

However, my four-year-long research for this book took me on a trail that led to places I did not anticipate as I sought to answer the question "Why, after 2000 years, is the Christian church, in general, still so mired in the pit of legalism?" During the search for the answer, I realized that in some cases, well-regarded translations were not always faithful to the original Hebrew or Greek text and disagreed among themselves on key concepts that I was investigating.

As an example, the word Elohim in Hebrew refers to God as the Creator and Judge of the universe according to the traditional Jewish view. However, in most translations of Psalm 8, it says that "man is little lower than the angels" or "beings," not a little lower than Elohim (God) as the Hebrew text says. In other words, the idea that every word of every translation of the Bible is inerrant is *not* necessarily true. Of course, all of the original texts (and perfectly accurate copies) of the original Hebrew and Greek texts were the inerrant Word of God. Unfortunately, that claim cannot be made about *any* translation of the complete Bible. Why? Because translators are fallible. Words in the original text (none of which we have) or accurate copies often have many meanings. Context gives clues but there is often no one-to-one correlation of words from one language to another. Also, a translator's theological bias can dictate his word choices. The translation of "Elohim" in Psalm 8:5 is a case in point. Look at the differences in the following translations, noted in the article *Why Angels Are Called "gods" In The 8th Psalm*? taken from: https://answers.yahoo.com/question/index?qid=20100122035722AAifbHT as follows:

> **Hebrew:**
> מֵאֱלֹהִים מְעַט וַתְּחַסְּרֵהוּ
> Interlinear:
> And you-made-lower him little than gods

> **Septuagint**:
> ἠλάττωσας αὐτὸν βραχύ τι παρ' ἀγγέλους

> **Greek Interlinear:**
> You-made-less him little some than angels

Various Translations:

> You made him a little lower than the angels

KJV: For thou hast made him a little lower than the angels

NIV: You made him a little lower than the heavenly beings

ESV: Yet you have made him a little lower than the heavenly beings* (footnote: Or, than God; Septuagint, than the angels)

AB: Yet You have made him but a little lower than God [or heavenly beings]

CEV: You made us a little lower than you yourself* (footnote: you yourself: Or " the angels" or " the beings in heaven.")

NLT: Yet you made them only a little lower than God* (footnote: Or, Yet you made them only a little lower than the angels; Hebrew reads Yet you made him [i.e., man] a little lower than Elohim)

Tanakh, The Holy Scriptures: You have made him little less than divine* (footnote: Or, "the angels")

JB: Yet you have made him little less than a god

NAB: You made him for a little while lower than the angels* (footnote: Little less than a god: Hebrew 'elohim, the ordinary word for "God" or "the gods" or members of the heavenly court. The Greek version translated 'elohim by "angel, messenger"; several ancient and modern versions so translate. The meaning seems to be Hebrews 2:9 finds the eminent fulfillment of this verse in Jesus Christ, who was humbled before being glorified. Cf also 1 Cor 15:27 where St. Paul applies to Christ the closing words of Psalm 8:7.)

The NAB footnote concludes that "the meaning seems to be that God created human beings almost at the level of the beings in the heavenly world" rather than "it means God." Is it possible that man is higher than angels in God's big picture view? Hebrews 1:4 provides the true perspective when it says "Are they (angels) not all spirits of ministration, sent to minister for the sake of those who shall receive the inheritance of salvation (reborn saints)?" The role of angels will forever be as servants. Reborn human beings have the privilege of being God's own children, a part of His forever family. Therefore, who is superior to whom? The word the translator chooses to use in all likelihood indicates whether he has a "low view" of man or a "high view" of man. These two different views are, in fact, part of an ongoing theological debate in some circles.

In another example, older versions (1984) of the NIV Bible translate the Greek word "sarx" as "sinful nature" instead of "flesh" or "earthly mind" as others do for Romans 8:8. By using "sinful nature," it implies that reborn saints now have two natures, which is another hotly debated topic and calls into question if "all things are new." (Fortunately, NIV corrected the error in additions printed some twenty years later.)

The revelation of Jesus' **divine exchange** makes clear what happens at rebirth. I had the nature of an **in Adam** sinner and, therefore, was condemned to hell. When reborn by faith in Jesus, I died to the old Adamic nature when Christ did (when He "became sin") and I arose with Him as a **new creation** and partaker of His divine nature by being placed **into Christ**. My original nature **in Adam** is now gone – crucified and buried – and I am a regenerated, perfect spirit-being (or I could not be compatible with the perfect Christ Jesus who I am now *one* with). But I still *have* an unsanctified soul and body. They are not my core self but my "outer man" as Paul says. If not submitted to my spirit-self, they can produce the "works" of the "false self," the flesh, which is at enmity with my spirit (as opposed to the fruit of the Holy Spirit who is alive in me and living through me). Experientially, it seems like I have two opposing natures but that conclusion is based on "appearances" in the **seen realm**, not on Jesus' **whole grace gospel** that reveals the truth of my completely new identity **in Christ**, in God.

Related to this important revelation is another passage that is not well translated from the Greek by the NIV where, in 2 Corinthians 3:18, it says:

> And we, who with unveiled faces all **reflect** the Lord's glory are being transformed into His likeness ..." (with a footnote "contemplate").

.

But the Greek unequivocally states, as does the KJV:

> But we all, with face having been unveiled (the veil of law-mindedness having been removed), **beholding** in a mirror the glory of the Lord, are being changed into the same image from glory to glory as from the Lord Spirit.

Effortless change

Why is this distinction important? Because Paul is sharing about how the process of a gradual sanctification of the outer man can happen - by cooperating with the Holy Spirit. First, the believer must stop focusing on keeping standards (law) as a means of righteousness because law acts like a veil over the mind that blocks the revelation of the reborn saint's state of righteousness (just by him being **in Christ)**. Rebirth automatically qualifies him for the gift of righteousness by faith, never ever by his human efforts. Trying to become in the inner man what he already is **in Christ**, actually frustrates the sanctification of the outer man. So what should the believer focus on if not on keeping standards? He should view himself as God now does, *one* with the glory and perfection of Jesus as a partaker of God's **divine nature**. How? By looking intently in the mirror of the **whole grace gospel** that reveals his new self. Focusing his mind on Jesus and the **finished work** of His **divine exchange**, will renew – reprogram, sanctify - his mind to the **unseen reality** of his true, new identity so that his outer man will be progressively conformed to this revelation. By knowing this truth, he will be increasingly free to live consistently with who he now *is* **in Christ**, by the ability of the Holy Spirit.

This is just one example of thinking according to the mind of Christ. What we truly believe about ourselves causes how we think and act. Sanctifying one's mind with the truth of Jesus' **whole grace gospel** increasingly causes right believing which, in turn, manifests the Holy Spirit's fruit of right living through reborn saints. The NIV translation does not suggest this *process* of what to focus on – Jesus and the handiwork of God that we now *are*, due to being reborn **in Christ**. We can only manifest the Lord's glory by beholding Him, not the law. In fact, the definition for the Greek word translated "glory" is "nature."As we behold His nature, revealed in His glorious work through Christ Jesus, our minds will be renewed with the eternal, **unseen realities** found **in Christ**. We will "see" who we actually are as a result of Jesus' **divine exchange** with each of us.

To, repeat, a Hebrew or Greek word can have a wide range of meanings and which word is selected (or rejected) can be because of the theological bias of the translator. If he has a law-based mind set, he might use the word "dogs" in the gospel passage referring to a certain Gentile woman where the softer meaning of "puppies" is more accurate, indicating Jesus' more gracious perspective towards her. <u>All this is to say that translations are somewhat subjective and words often carry connotations that flavor it according to the bias of the translator.</u>

Therefore, given the above dynamics, my general approach in this book was to consult such research tools as a Greek interlinear text, two different exhaustive concordances, the *26 Translations of the Holy Bible* and on-line Bible translations, including an older public domain version which I often used as a base text and tweaked for accuracy when necessary for the longer scriptures. The bottom line is that if there are any scriptures that are identical to any copyrighted translation, it is coincidental rather than intended, except where so noted.

Also, to accentuate longer quotations, I indented them. Then I used parenthesis to clearly indicate my own comments, added to help the flow or understanding of the text.

Also, in the book as a whole, I often <u>underlined a particular text,</u> made it **bold** or used *italics* to highlight its importance. I did this in the case of key words that introduced ideas that are new to many people such as **finished work** or **in Adam.** Hopefully, all these mechanisms work together to help you, the reader, to understand and benefit from the rather complex but very important distinctions between a religion-based focus on law versus enjoying a vital relationship with Father-God, made possible by Jesus' **finished work** – the wondrous revelation of His **divine exchange.**

APPENDIX # 13

EXPLORING THE "WRATH OF GOD" IN THE NEW TESTAMENT

It is no secret that the Israelites suffered under the wrath of God for their wicked ways during the Mosaic Covenant period according to the performance-based terms of that covenant. The Law was given to reveal mankind's fallen nature **in Adam** - not God's loving, other-centered nature. God sent Jesus as man's second representative to <u>reverse</u> the incomparable damage Adam's fall caused to mankind. How? By becoming the very nature of Adamic sin and receiving all of God's just wrath and punishment justly due to mankind. Why? So that every hindrance to sinners becoming united to God spiritually could eliminated. That expiation (total removal) of sin, guilt, shame and condemnation is just one part of the **divine exchange** of Jesus' **finished work.** This made God's reconciliation toward man (propitiation) possible by Jesus' unilateral performance, not by man's own effort or confession of sins.

So now that God's wrath for all sin has been exhausted on Jesus at Calvary, why does the New Testament still have scriptures about God's wrath? Like always, each scripture's context and also when, where, why how and to whom it was given matters greatly if one is to interpret scripture rightly. The following collection of New Testament scriptures regarding God's wrath are grouped according to how they fit these criterion and, therefore, share a common explanation. First, the good news for believers.

Reborn Saints In Christ Are Forever Spared God's Wrath
We have been justified freely by His grace through the redemption that is in Christ Jesus, whom God has offered as a propitiation, through faith in His blood, to reveal His justice for the remission of the former offenses, and by the forbearance of God, to reveal His justice in this time, so that He Himself might be both the Just One and the Justifier of anyone who is of the faith of Jesus Christ (Romans 3:24-26).

Therefore, <u>God has not given wrath to us (believers)</u>, but the possession of salvation by our Lord Jesus Christ. He died for us, that, whether we are awake or asleep (physically dead), we should live together with Him (1 Thessalonians 5:9-10).

Christ died for us. Therefore, having been justified now by His blood, all the more so shall we be <u>saved from wrath</u> through Him (Romans 5:9).

And to the expectation of his Son from heaven (whom He [God] raised up from the dead), Jesus, who has <u>rescued us</u> from the approaching wrath (1 Thessalonians 1:10).

The Coming Wrath For Unbelievers Who Reject God's Only Solution
As has been stressed all along, Christianity is not a religion but a relationship-based belief system where God's gift of free will to man is honored. Jesus freely chose to do everything necessary for human beings to become part of God's family forever through rebirth by faith alone. But just because it is God's will that all be saved by each one accepting His offer of

marriage to His Son, scripture says that not everyone will *believe* that generous offer and accept the hand of the Bridegroom. The reasons for such unbelief are many and varied but the *key,* given throughout the Bible to be in harmony with God, is to *believe* and *receive* His offers and promises addressed to *you.*

> But without faith, it is impossible to please God. For whoever approaches God must believe that He exists, and that He rewards those who seek Him (Hebrews 11:6).

In our traditional American culture, courtship sometimes leads to an engagement when the guy proposes marriage to the girl of his dreams. If she agrees to an engagement, there is time to explore and confirm if there is a mutual desire to freely agree to a life–long covenant relationship that we call "marriage." But, of course, not all engagements end with marriage because one or both parties may decide not to become united together as "one flesh." Even if one party is totally committed to marrying the other, both have to freely agree to have a valid union in America.

And so it is with God's desire that all people be saved and come to the knowledge of the truth by rebirth into an everlasting union with Christ in God. By Jesus' perfect propitiation and by becoming mankind's new representative, God is now reconciled to the world from His viewpoint. Now, the Holy Spirit is about wooing willing people to union with Jesus. However, after all of God's love-motivated, sacrificial efforts are spurned by an unbelieving sinner, there can be no marriage with Jesus, the Lamb of God. This is so even though the sin of unbelief itself has been paid for at Calvary. Why? <u>Because God honors the unbeliever's rejection of God's offer through Jesus and there is only one alternative to heaven</u> – hell. It is not God who sends people to hell. Rather, people who are still spiritually dead **in Adam** and, thereby sentenced to hell, reject God's magnanimous offer of life. And the consequence for rejecting Jesus (and the **divine exchange** of His new nature for the unbeliever's **in Adam** nature) is to receive the just debt due to the unbeliever's Adamic nature – permanent separation from God in the place originally established for the devil. The following scriptures reflect that common theme of what happens to people who reject God's grace by unbelief and so are eternally confined to hell.

> And we too were all involved in these things (sins), in times past (before conversion), by the desires of our flesh, acting according to the will of the flesh and according to our own thoughts. And so we were, by (our Adamic) nature, sons of wrath, even like the others (unbelievers) (Ephesians 2:3).

> For the wrath of God is revealed from heaven over every impiety and unrighteousness among those men who fend off the truth of God with unrighteousness (Romans 1:18).

> They (certain men) prohibit us to speak to the Gentiles, so that they may be saved, and thus do they continually add to their own sins. But the wrath of God will overtake them in the very end (1 Thessalonians 2:16).

> But in accord with your hard and impenitent heart, you store up wrath for yourself (by rejecting Jesus) unto the day of wrath and of revelation by the just judgment of God (Romans 2:5).

What if God, wanting to reveal His wrath and to make His power known, endured, with much patience people (unbelievers) deserving wrath and fit to be destroyed (Romans 9:22).

Let no one seduce you with empty words. For because of these things, the wrath of God was sent upon the sons of **unbelief** (Ephesians 5:6).

Deaden (subdue, control), therefore, the members of your body which are upon the earth (which might tempt you to) fornication, uncleanness, inordinate affection, evil lust, and covetousness, which is idolatry by which things the wrath of God comes on the children of disbelief (all still in Adam) in whom which you also walked at one time, when you lived among them (Colossians 3:5-7).

And the third Angel followed them, saying with a great voice: "If anyone has worshiped the beast, or his image, or has received his character on his forehead or on his hand, he shall drink also from the wine of the wrath of God, which has been mixed with strong wine in the cup of his wrath, and he shall be tortured with fire and sulphur in the sight of the holy Angels and before the sight of the Lamb (Revelations 14:9-10).

And I heard a great voice from the temple, saying to the seven Angels: "Go forth and pour out the seven bowls of the wrath of God upon the earth." And the first Angel went forth and poured out his bowl upon the earth. And a severe and most grievous wound occurred upon the men who had the character of the beast (**in Adam** unbelievers), and upon those who adored the beast or its image (Revelations 16:1-2).

And from His mouth proceeded a sharp two-edged sword, so that with it He may strike the nations (of unbelievers). And He shall rule them with an iron rod. And He treads the winepress of the fury of the wrath of God Almighty and He has on his garment and on His thigh written: KING OF KINGS AND LORD OF LORDS (Revelations 19:15-16)

New Testament Scriptures Regarding Old Testament Israelites
For this reason, I was enraged against this generation (the **in Adam** generation under Moses), and I said: 'They always wander astray in heart. For they have not known My ways.' So it is as I swore in My wrath: 'They shall not enter into My rest' (Hebrews 3:10-11).

For the law works unto wrath. And where there is no law, there is no law-breaking (sin) (Romans 4:15). (Remember: a Jewish Christian is dead to the Law and it was never given to Gentiles.)

Respond To Others In Love, Not In Wrath
Do not avenge yourself, dearest ones. Instead, allow room for (God's) wrath. For it is written: 'Vengeance is Mine. I shall give retribution, says the Lord' (Romans 12:19).

Civil Government Official's Wrath Against Lawbreakers In The Seen Realm

For he (a government official in legitimate authority) is a minister of God for you unto good. But if you do what is evil, be afraid. For it is not without reason that he carries a sword. For he is a minister of God; an avenger to <u>execute wrath</u> upon whomever does evil (in the **seen realm**) For this reason, it is necessary to be subject to (the authority), not solely because of wrath, but also because of conscience (Romans 13:4-5).

In Summary, Jesus' **finished work** changes everything for mankind by making it possible for sinners to choose to be reconciled to God (2 Corinthians 5:19). God will never be angry with anyone who becomes united with Jesus through rebirth by faith. God regards all those **in Christ** Jesus as He regards Jesus. Why would anyone not choose to receive - by faith in Jesus' **finished work** – His abundant blessings and favor while still on earth and have his spiritual residence in to heaven? Doubt and unbelief about God's grace-based offer are killers. Make Romans 10:9-13 your own heartfelt statement of belief to God and, thereby, personally receive all that God has done for you through Jesus.

APPENDIX # 14

BEWARE OF PITFALLS IN MANY POPULAR BOOKS

Promise Books

There are many popular devotionals and "promise books" that are potential pitfalls for mixture because they are usually topical and, therefore, quote scriptures on the same topic without regarding 1) the context in which each one was written 2) to whom each one was written to and why and 3) under what covenant terms was each written. If you look up the section on "obedience," for example, you will probably find a long list of scriptures from both the Old and New Testaments lumped together. This implies to the undiscerning reader that Jesus' **grace-based gospel** really is no different than the Mosaic Covenant. So the believer might mistakenly think: "It is all the 'Word of God' for me to learn and to obey." However, they are not automatically all a part of the "gospel of Christ" as revealed to Paul by Jesus in 42 AD that *changed everything for believers.* The Law was never given to Gentiles *and* it was made obsolete for Jewish believers at Calvary, according to Hebrews 8:13.

So it is not my obedience to an obsolete Law that earns blessings from God, as was true under the harsh terms of the Mosaic Law for the Jews. No, under the **New Covenant**, it is believing in Jesus' obedience to God and Jesus' **finished work** on my behalf which provides the revelation and experience that only good things come from God – including total forgiveness of all sins for all time. They are His generous gifts that are based on receiving what Jesus did 2000 years ago. So, to avoid having the **elephant of mixture** tramp around in your mind, focus on the scriptures that exalt the **finished work** of Jesus *until* you can learn to see for yourself what Appendix # 7 helps you to do – see Jesus in every book of the Bible. If what you are reading puts the demands of the Law upon you, then move on to something else that reveals Jesus' **divine exchange** that shows you what He already has supplied to you **in Himself.**

My Utmost For His Highest

Speaking of books that heap demands on you, it doesn't get much more demanding than this title: *My Utmost For His Highest.* It mirrors the demands of the First Commandment, described by Jesus in Matthew 22:37-38:

> Jesus said to him: 'You shall love the Lord your God from all your heart, and with all your soul and with all your mind.' This is the greatest and first commandment.'

If you still believe that is what you have to do to reach heaven - like the rich young ruler apparently concluded - you are being stomped on by the **elephant of mixture.** Jesus knew that no **pre-cross, in Adam** human being could measure up to that impossible standard by himself. So Jesus used the law to hopefully bring this man to the end of depending on himself to *do his utmost* for God - self-righteousness. (Jesus' encounter with the rich young ruler is discussed in detail in Chapter Twelve.) My utmost is never good enough to reach perfection. If you are still trying, how is it working for you? God wants *you,* not what you can do for Him. When you are busy working for God, He rests. When you come to the end of your meager resources, you are then a position to begin depending on God for His supply - like Jesus did all of His life on earth.

414

It is not about *your* doing but about enjoying *His* **finished work**. Walking in the Spirit like Jesus did produces the fruit of faith, love and liberty, **in Christ Jesus.**

Even under the New Covenant, as a **new creation** saint, it is impossible for your unsanctified outer man to love God perfectly, 24/7/365. Even on your best day, your outer man falls short. That is why the law was nailed to the cross for Jewish believers and Jesus sends the Holy Spirit into each one of us believers so that He can love God perfectly through us, as us, – Spirit to spirit. In short, <u>God has already supplied to us what He could rightly demand from us because we can't possibly produce it by ourselves.</u> So again, the good news of the **whole grace-gospel** is that He *has supplied* His love to us in the Person of the Holy Spirit. In turn, He lives through us, as us **in Christ**, to manifest His good fruit, including love for God and others <u>as He loves us</u>. Thus, we can love God back as He deserves in a mutual, intimate relationship as our Daddy-God. (The alternative is to walk according to one's flesh and reap the negative consequences in the **seen realm**, as described in Romans, Chapter Eight and presented in Chapter Nineteen of this study book.)

If you want to read a really <u>great</u> devotional that won't tie you up in mental and theological knots, refresh your soul daily by renewing your mind with Joseph Prince's *Destined To Reign Devotional*. God's revelational wisdom packed in this book will feed your faith and inspire love for Jesus and for Father-God <u>year after year</u> by revealing the vast implications of His **finished work – the divine exchange** – in practical terms. Joseph Prince effectively communicates the truths and benefits of the **unseen** Kingdom of Jesus' **grace gospel** to enable the reader to enjoy them in the **seen realm.** It is the unveiling of Jesus' abundant life that He came to supply by giving His Utmost for our sake. It is not about what you can try to do for Jesus. Your "utmost" isn't good enough. It is about learning to live in what Jesus has already *done* for you, dear saint, then responding to Him by the enabling Power of the Holy Spirit. That is the good news!

As you renew your mind with Jesus' **whole gospel of grace**, you will be able to spot the thread of law-based sermons or writing that places demands, "challenges" and burdens on believers or focuses on sin management through self-help and guilt. Simply chew the meat and spit out the bones. Or, better yet, feed on pure grace-based book like the ones listed in Appendix # 5.

APPENDIX # 15

MORE ABOUT THE "SARX"

Throughout the book, I have used the word "fleshy" to describe the self-centered, natural, carnal mind-sets, habit patterns, attitudes, passions, addictions and appetites of our unsanctified outer-man that can dominate our behavior - as always happened while still **in Adam**. It is living like a "city dog." In Romans, Chapter Eight, Paul contrasts this as yet unsanctified, soulish-side of believers with the new creation spirit-self, recreated in Christ Jesus through rebirth. This extremely important distinction between the outer-man vs. our inner-man is based on the revelation of our tri-part nature - body, soul and spirit - as presented and defended in Chapters Sixteen and Seventeen. Because of rebirth, believers are no longer a slave to the old **in Adam** nature, now crucified with Christ on Calvary and gone. However, we still have the continuous choice to walk according to the "*remnants*" of our former self (which Paul now calls "the flesh") or according to the direction and power of the Holy Spirit living through us, as us, as presented in Chapter Nineteen.

Unfortunately, the Greek word "sarx" that is translated as "flesh" has various meanings that can cause confusion while reading the **New Covenant** writings of Paul. The word "sarx" can mean the meaty substance below the skin of an animal or person, such as "the circumcision of one's flesh." By extension, it can mean one's physical body, which is not evil, per se. However, the body can be used by the "flesh" to do evil things. It is this last sense, described above as the unsanctified soul – our mind, emotions and will - that Paul contrasts with walking according to the Spirit. That is why he exhorts believers "Do not be conformed to this age but be transformed (in the outer man) by the renewing of your mind (to think as God thinks) to show forth what is the good, well-pleasing and perfect will of God" Romans 12:2). That happens over time as we let the Holy Spirit have His way in our whole being as He leads, teaches, guides, guards, sanctifies and comforts us, manifesting the fruit of a Spirit-led life in Christ Jesus. Against such there is no law needed or desired - except the higher law of faith, love and liberty that Jesus walked in and that operates in Heaven.

ENDNOTES

Foreward
1. Many terms that are essential to understanding Jesus' **grace-based gospel** are in **bold** print throughout this book to emphasize their enormous importance. In John 17:4, Jesus stated that "I have glorified You (God) on earth. *I have completed the work that You gave me to accomplish.*" Of course, He was referring to all that He was about to undergo from the garden to finally being seated next to God in heaven. Being seated there indicates that He is now totally done with the **finished work** of offering salvation to the world, which Father-God sent Him here to make possible. This book will unpack what all that means, which includes the **divine exchange** between Him and all who are reborn of God by faith in Jesus and His **finished work**. The more we understand what He has already done for us some 2000 years ago, the more we will fathom His love for us which progressively frees us to fully trust and rest in His **finished work** rather than in our feeble efforts to earn or maintain His free, grace-based gifts and blessings of salvation.

Chapter One
2. New Testament scholar, F. F. Bruce, verifies this date for Paul's astounding experience of "seeing" the reality of Jesus' **divine exchange** in the heavenlies on page 134 of his detailed account of Saint Paul's life entitled *Paul: Apostle Of The Heart Set Free.*

Also, noted author John Pollock, a biographer of Billy Graham, calculated a date of "A.D. 41 or 42 A.D." as the time of Paul's "vision and revelation of the Lord" and described on page 38 of his book *The Apostle, A Life Of Paul* published by Doubleday and Company, copyrighted in 1969.

Charles Swindoll also makes mention of "the divine revelations he (Paul) received from the Lord Jesus," while waiting in Tarsus, as happening fourteen years from the time Paul wrote Second Corinthians. This reference is on page 86 of his book Paul, *A Man Of Grace And Grit.*

3. The Second Jewish Revolt

The Second Jewish Revolt (AD 132–135), a Jewish rebellion against Roman rule in **Judaea**. The revolt was preceded by years of clashes between Jews and Romans in the area. Finally, in AD 132, the misrule of Tinnius Rufus, the Roman governor of Judaea, combined with the emperor **Hadrian**'s intention to found a Roman colony on the site of **Jerusalem** and his restrictions on Jewish religious freedom and observances (which included a ban on the practice of male circumcision), roused the last remnants of Palestinian Jewry to revolt. A bitter struggle ensued. **Bar Kokhba** became the leader of this Second Jewish Revolt; although at first successful, his forces proved no match against the methodical and ruthless tactics of the Roman general Julius Severus. With the fall of Jerusalem and then Bethar, a fortress on the seacoast south of Caesarea where **Bar Kokhba** was slain, the rebellion was crushed in 135. According to Christian sources, Jews were thenceforth forbidden to enter Jerusalem.
See http://www.britannica.com/EBchecked/topic/303635/Second-Jewish-Revolt

In the years following the revolt, Hadrian discriminated against all Judeo-Christian sects, but the worst persecution was directed against religious Jews. He made anti-religious decrees forbidding **Torah** study, **Sabbath** observance, **circumcision**, Jewish courts, meeting in **synagogues** and other ritual practices. Many Jews assimilated and many sages and prominent men were martyred including **Rabbi Akiva** and the rest of the Asara Harugei Malchut (ten martyrs). This age of persecution lasted throughout the remainder of Hadrian's reign, until 138 C.E.
See http://www.jewishvirtuallibrary.org/jsource/Judaism/revolt1.html

4. "Paul did not invent Christianity or pervert it: he rescued it from "extinction."Paul was the first pure Christian: the first fully to comprehend Jesus' system of theology, to grasp the magnitude of the changes it embodied, and the completeness of the break with Judaic law." This quote is by noted historian, Paul Johnson, from his *A History of Christianity*, published in 1976 by Simon and Schuster, page 35

5. "The early believers maintained a close tie with Judaism, and to most observers Christianity would have appeared to be just one more sect within Judaism." "The connection with Christianity with Judaism was also made more apparent by the presence of converted priests and Pharisees in the Christian brotherhood." These two quotes are from New Testament History by Richard L. Niswonger, published by Zondervan, first cover addition in 1992, page 190. Also see Endnote # 15.

6. From God's standpoint, there are ultimately only two kinds of people. Everyone born of natural parents are automatically **in Adam**. All those who become reborn of God by faith in Jesus' as Savior are, thereby, **in Christ**. Adam was the first parent of the human race and, because of Adam's choice to fall into rebellion, the whole race is in Darkness and condemned to hell, according to John 3:17. It is not God's fault that this happened and He sent Jesus to become mankind's second representative to reverse all that Adam's fall caused and to offer the free gift of God's eternal life in heaven. This is foundational biblical theology that even many Christians do not know, let alone unbelievers.

7. From God's standpoint, there are ultimately only two kinds of people. Everyone born of natural parents are automatically **in Adam**. All those who become reborn of God by faith in Jesus' as Savior are, thereby, **in Christ**. Adam was the first parent of the human race and, because of Adam's choice to fall into rebellion, the whole race is in Darkness and condemned to hell, according to John 3:17. It is not God's fault that this happened and He sent Jesus to become mankind's second representative to reverse all that Adam's fall caused and to offer the free gift of God's eternal life in heaven. This is foundational biblical theology that even many Christians do not know, let alone unbelievers.

8. This is a greatly condensed version of a seven frame chart I gleaned from Jesus' revelation to Paul of His grace-based gospel that focuses on the **unseen realm** that we are now a part of. I taught the larger version to students at Word of God Academy with great effect and I use it today in Bible studies. It gives a **Big Picture** view of the scope of the Bible and our position as believers **in Christ** that is a *now* reality.

9. There are no Robots in Heaven. To all my brethren **in Christ** that are convinced of the "doctrine of election" by qualifying "the whole world" to mean only those who God chose to specifically predestine to save – and to hell with the rest – I beg to differ. I am aware that Calvin just expanded St. Augustine's interpretation of Paul's use of the word "predestination." But I am also aware of how they both assumed that the Mosaic Law had relevance for believers even though it was never given to the Gentiles – which I will discuss and prove in later chapters.

So, I believe that the **divine blood** of the Savior of the world was so powerful that His perfect sacrifice paid for all sins for all time for all people and effected the reconciliation of the whole world to God – *from God's viewpoint* - just as 2 Corinthians 5:17-21 and 1 John 2:2 clearly state.

In other words, Jesus, the **last Adam,** restored to mankind what was lost to mankind by the **first Adam** when Adam ate of the wrong Tree. And what was lost? The personal choice to eat of the Tree of Life, Jesus. But thankfully, His perfect sacrifice restored the gift of free choice to mankind, by grace through faith, rather than each person's fate decided "arbitrarily" by God, as predestination asserts. Otherwise, God would be violating His own principle, given through Paul and James, where He exhorts believers not to play favorites. Yes, God chose all He foreknew (and He knew everyone) to be predestined to be conformed to the likeness of His Son etc. (see Romans 8:29-30). But doing this *unilaterally*, without the consent of those He picked and those He supposedly rejected, negates the most sacred part of every human being made in His image – free will. Do you honestly think that 1 Corinthians Chapter 13 describes a god who "intends everyone to go to hell unless he intends you to go to heaven?" Satan wants you to think so.

The election doctrine reduces everyone to the status of mindless robots, based on the biased "doctrine" that God is absolutely sovereign and, therefore, is in absolute control of every detail of everything all the time – a perfectionistic micro-manager. That then, implies that He is responsible for Satan's fall and Adam's fall because they had no choice in the matter. That lie, my friend, makes Him effectively responsible for *all* the evil in the world – exactly what the devil wants you to think and, thereby, be mentally alienated from a "ruthless" God . This is the doctrine of demons that shifts all blame from Satan and Adam and us on to God. That is what the Gnostics also thought. The Accuser of the brethren delights in all who propagate his dirty work against Father-God. (They miss the fact that God, in His "absolute sovereignty," freely chose [and I believe did choose, according to what is stated in many scriptures like John 3:16-17] to honor His gift of free will and arrange, in His infinite wisdom, to provide that choice, somehow, some way to each human being.)

Well, as for me, I am standing up as His precious son and declaring that my Daddy is *not* an evil, ruthless dictator. On the contrary, it is His will that all mankind be saved and come to the knowledge of the truth – Christ Jesus. And He did everything possible on His side, through Jesus, to make salvation available again (but not guaranteed), by forgiving all sin and now leaving it up to every human to personally choose or reject Him. The first Adam took away our choice – the last Adam restored it. I believe that Jesus' parable of the wedding feast was a type of this very offer. The king invited "his chosen people" and they chose against him. Notice that he did not exercise his military might and drag them all into the wedding feast anyhow – and leave all others in the cold. Instead, he welcomed the others into the hall who chose to come but then rejected one individual who *chose* to refuse a free wedding garment *supplied* in the vestibule of the palace – according to the custom of the day. (That garment is a "type" of His free, undeserved gift of the robe of righteousness, given to every reborn believer.)

Yes, the king has a right to make requirements of who he accepts but our King "graciously" supplies anyone who asks for, believes and receives whatever is needed to qualify them to enjoy Him – and His feast. *Your concept of God will determine how open you are to Him and, therefore, what you will receive from our generous Father-God.* John 7:17 implies that you have to *choose* to know God's will, which is a gift of His grace, before you know something is God's will for you. His will is to have you (and the whole world) with Him in heaven. But you must want union with Him too.

I believe our wonderful Father is not about exclusion but inclusion and provides whatever is needed to anyone who wants to be included. But one must be humble enough to recognize his need and receive, looking only to God, not to himself. That is a choice all are capable of making – and I believe Jesus restored the choice to say "yes" or "no" to His merciful invitation. This is my bias because it is the only possible way for anyone to have a *mutual*, love-based relationship with Jesus and Daddy-God. There are no pre-programmed robots in heaven. It was for freedom that Jesus came to offer freedom to all captives – right? And the basis of all true freedom is the freedom to choose.

Yes, we can make pro and con lists from the Bible to support and debate either position till we die and see the truth first hand. But I believe Jesus revealed the true heart of our loving Father in His compassionate dealings with those who realized and admitted their deep need. The terms of the Law covenant, based on man's doing, required justice. The **New Covenant**, based on Jesus' doing (which fulfilled the demands of justice), supplies His mercy and grace when He says, through Paul, that "*Everyone* who calls upon the name of the Lord will be saved," according to Romans 10:13. That verse, which is repeated in other places in the Bible, has no meaning if everyone was a pre-selected and pre-programmed robot. In John 5:24, Jesus said: "Truly, truly I say to you: He who hears My word and believes Him who sent Me has eternal life, and does not come into judgment but has passed from death to life." Do you honestly think, Mr. Predestinationist, that God <u>made</u> Adam eat the tree of Law so that he would die so that Jesus could make such an offer to people but which they could not choose to accept? This is utter nonsense to anyone who knows just how good God really is. Endnote #22 adds more insight into this topic.

Chapter Three

10. After Jesus had radically changed Paul's mind in 42 AD, he gave Jesus' view of this matter by writing: "I know, and am persuaded by the Lord Jesus, that there is nothing unclean of itself: but to him that esteems anything to be unclean, to him it is unclean" (Romans 14:14). This is an example of the "new law of faith" in Christ's **finished work,** trumping the specifics of the Mosaic Law. The degree to which one relies on "the law principle" for direction, "using natural sight" instead of "the sight of faith from first to last," he will, by definition, be focusing on that rather than on Jesus. Thus, he will be putting some behavior-based law above the higher law of faith, love and liberty. This nullifies both opposing covenants in his mind and he falls from grace. He risks not being able to clearly hear the Holy Spirit's direction the way Jesus did.

Unfortunately, for 2000 years, the church has typically taught that it is the Holy Spirit's job to "convict you of sin" – law breaking – when, in fact, the Law (which was only given to the Jews and that "arouses sin and causes death") has been replaced with the "law of the Spirit of life." I will more fully explain this difference between religion and grace in the next chapter.

11. That intense, daily bible study amassed 600 + scriptures that eventually morphed into a self-published devotional handbook titled *Every Christian's Testimony: Discovering the New And True You In Christ*. The text of each chapter consists of only personalized scriptures of the truths of our New Covenant realities woven together into a flowing stream. I intend to update and publish it on Amazon in 2016.

12. Quoted from *Jesus Changes Everything* by Bob George, published by Harvest House Publishers, Published in 2013, p 45.

13. 1) The *law of faith* is found in Romans 3:27, which Paul contrasts with the law of works.

2) The *law of love* for God and neighbor is found in Matthew 22:37-40. Jesus made it possible in the New Covenant for reborn believers to love God and others with God's agape (unselfish) love by sending the Holy Spirit into every believer.

3) The *law of liberty* is cited in James 1:25. While James may have mistakenly thought that attempting to keep the Mosaic Law brings freedom, we know now that it actually arouses sin and causes death – as explained in Chapter Nine. However, the interconnectedness of all three laws is summarized in Galatians 5:1 and 6 as follows:

> Stand firm in the liberty in which Christ has made us free and do not be willing to be bound again by the yoke of slavery (to the Mosaic Law of works). ...For **in Christ Jesus**, neither circumcision nor uncircumcision has any strength, but (only) faith working through love.

It is the law of the Spirit of Life – the Holy Spirit living through the believer, as the believer – that produces the fruit of the Holy Spirit "against which there is no law." In other words, living by the Spirit of love, by faith in Father-God like Jesus did, actually results in not only "filling full" the "demands" of the Mosaic Law but goes far beyond the law's limited scope. Not only did Jesus *not* keep the letter of the Mosaic Law when He did not stone the adulterous woman; He kept the higher law of love by forgiving and freeing her - just as His Father instructed Him to do. Jesus' obedience of faith in His Father's word was the freedom to operate according to Father-God's love in the Spirit. That produced freedom from bondage for whoever chose to receive what he offered. Much more about this **butterfly life** is explained in Chapter Nineteen.

14. A quote from *Complete in Christ* by Bob George, published by Harvest House Publishers, Published in 1994, p 36-37:

> The moment you put your faith in Christ Jesus, you step out of Adam into Christ, and Christ steps out of heaven and into you, and He makes you into a new creation: "Therefore, if anyone is in Christ, he is a new creature; the original (one) perished. Behold, everything has become new!" (2 Corinthians 5:17). Paul summed up his ministry as the proclamation of "the mystery that has been kept hidden for ages and generations, but was now revealed to His saints ... which is Christ in us, our hope (confident expectation) of glory" (Colossians 1:26-27).
>
> Being made into a "new creation" is somewhat like the caterpillar that has emerged from its cocoon as a new creature – a butterfly. As a caterpillar, it viewed life from the ground up. As a butterfly, it views life from the sky downward. In the same way, as a new creature in Christ, you are invited to begin to see yourself *as God sees you*.
> Look at a butterfly we don't say, "There's a converted caterpillar!" Although it was originally a caterpillar, and it was "converted," all we now see is the beauty and grace of this new creature. The same is true of God. He only sees you as a butterfly now, His **new creation in Christ.**

Chapter Four
15. Besides endnotes found at # 5 and # 18, the following quote gives a bigger overview of how the early Jewish Christians intertwined the two opposing covenant in their minds.

"The Christian faith, so deeply rooted in Judaism, began to increasingly assert its independence and distinctiveness by AD. 100. Paul's battle against legalism, the development of large Gentile churches as at Rome, the destruction of the temple in 70 with consequent weakening of the Jewish Christian movement centered in Jerusalem, all contributed to the separation of the two faiths. Hostilities between Christians and Jews increased as the church entered the second century" New Testament History by Richard L. Niswonger, published by Zondervan, first cover addition in 1992, page 282.

16. *The Gospel [un]Cut: Learning to Rest in the Grace of God* by Jeremy White

17. A reference to James the Just as a Nazarite and a definition of the term comes from a web site **at:** http://www.jewishencyclopedia.com/articles/11395-nazarite:

> The description of James the Just which Eusebius ("Hist. Eccl." ii. 23) quotes from Hegesippus indicates that James may have been a Nazarite for life, though the name is not applied to him.

> One who lives apart; one who has made a vow of abstinence; in the former sense used as early as Sifra, Emor, iv. 3; Sifre, Num. 23.

Nazarite Laws:
> Three restrictions are imposed upon the Nazarite, according to Num. vi.: he may not take wine, or anything made from grapes; he may not cut the hair of his head; he may not touch the dead, not even the body of his father or mother. If a Nazarite has become unclean by accident, he must offer a sacrifice and begin the period of his vow anew. He is "holy unto the Lord" (Num. vi. 8), and the regulations which apply to him actually agree with those for the high priest and for the priests during worship (Lev. x. 8 *et seq.*, xxi.; Ezek. xliv. 21). In ancient times the priests were persons dedicated to God (Ezek. xliv. 20; I Sam. i. 11), and it follows from the juxtaposition of prophets and Nazarites (Amos ii. 11-12) that the latter must have been regarded as in a sense priests. Young men especially, who found it difficult to abstain from wine on account of youthful desire for pleasure, took the vow. ... (Num.*l.c.*; Jer. vii. 29).

Chapter Six

18. "Palestine Judaism was not a unitary religion but a collection of sects. It is possible, even from the fragmentary sources, to enumerate as many as twenty-four." *A History Of Christianity* by noted historian Paul Johnson page 14-15. Also see Endnote # 15.

19. For believers to reign in life through Jesus while still on earth (see Romans 5:17), it is essential to understand that Jesus laid aside His deity and lived as a pre-Fall, sinless man while on earth. He operated as an extension and Ambassador of His Father's will and power through the Holy Spirit living within Him. He did the works of His Father, *not His own works*. He was totally dependent on His Father's provision and direction, acknowledging Him in all His ways so Father could direct His paths. It is obvious Jesus operated as a man because it is not possible to tempt God to sin and certainly not possible to crucify God. When God raised Jesus from the dead "God <u>made</u> Jesus (the Man) both Christ and Lord" (see Acts 2:36). How did they arrange all that? You will have to ask them when you get the opportunity.

So, the way Jesus walked on earth - focused on His Father and on living according to the Spirit within Him- is the pattern and process available to any reborn saint who is also baptized in the Holy Spirit like Jesus was. Why did Paul promote an <u>immersion (baptism) in the Holy Spirit</u> rather than just water baptism? In order to do greater works than Jesus did, manifesting our Father's loving heart and power to give dead people life – in all its forms. We are to be His Ambassadors just like He was our Father's Ambassador, living according to the Spirit of life, not under the **elephant of mixture** that has prevented the church from living fully **in Him** for 2000 years (except for occasional outbreaks of the manifested life of the Holy Spirit as recorded in Acts). But, over time, the law-minded believers squelched the life in the Spirit. Consequently, the *lack* of His manifested life through believers became the accepted norm for 2000 years. Cessationists foolishly promote the lie that miracles and other manifestations of the Holy Spirit ended with the death of the apostles. I've been on both sides of that ongoing battle over the reality of "the baptism of the Holy Spirit" so I write this from first-hand experience, not theory. It would take another book to describe and explain the unique experiences of the Spirit's many gifts my wife and I have had on our journey **in Christ** over the years since being reborn. A good overview of this vital role the life and gifts of the Holy Spirit can be found *in* ***2000 Years of Charismatic Christianity*** by Dr. Eddie Hyatt.

Chapter Seven

20. But then again, James said in the letter sent to the Antioch church, after the council, that he did not specifically <u>authorize</u> the Judaizers to "trouble your minds by what they said," according to Acts 15:24. That statement would seem to suggest that the confrontation with Peter in Antioch is what precipitated the need for a council to settle the matter. That is why there is an unresolved debate among scholars about the sequence of these events still today. But note, also, that James did not deny Paul's assertion that James had sent these Judaizers to Antioch. The real question is … why?. It would make sense only if he was acting as a policeman, suspicious of what Paul was saying and doing. Was James acting on his own orders or on God's direction? If his motive was to defend and foster Judaism, you can guess the answer to this crucial question.

Chapter Eight

21. The noun "adam" is also the masculine form of the word "adamah" which means "ground" or "earth." Adam was "of the earth."

22. A true, agape (God-kind-of-Love) relationship of total self-giving – as opposed to a robotic or slave relationship – can only exist when both parties are mutually free to choose to share it. In effect, Jesus has restored the option of freedom to the human race that Adam first enjoyed by reversing what Adam's rebellion accomplished. Denominations that deny the **New Covenant** dynamic of freedom **in Christ** by insisting on an extreme version of God's "absolute sovereignty," wrongly portray our loving Father-God as an iron-fisted taskmaster over the human race that has whimsically pre-selected who He will allow into heaven – with no agreement on our part. To be sure, there are scriptures that can be used to support both positions on man's free choice, a debate that has gone on for millennia. See Endnote # 9 for more in this topic.

But, your concept of God, which determines how you relate to and receive from God, is generally determined by your personal history and on which part of the Bible you focus: 1) on the Mosaic Covenant that covers 82% of the Protestant Bible and which focuses on the Law or 2) on the **New Covenant** of pure grace that focuses on who Jesus is and what Father-God sent Him to do for you. To repeat a crucial fact: the Mosaic Covenant was given to reveal man's fallen nature – not God's nature. Look to Jesus to see Father's true, sacrificial, long-suffering, loving nature. He is not the hostile, revengeful task-master that the devil wants you to think He is. On the contrary, that is an accurate description of the devil himself – the father of lies and lord of the flies.

Chapter Nine

23. James' continued association with (or maybe even dependence on) the Law as a committed Nazarite, probably influenced him to blur the Bible's continuous emphasis that <u>only by faith in God's performance, *not* in one's own efforts, is a person reckoned righteous in God's sight</u>. James introduced the potential confusion by stating that "faith without works/action is dead" (see James 2:17) Implied in his statement is "good" (not evil) action, of course – which puts the focus back on the Law Tree and self. His attempt to evaluate a person's faith by the person's outward behavior is, admittedly, the only way <u>fallible humans</u> can *try* to determine whether that person is saved and trustworthy. But fortunately, God sees everyone's heart and motives and knows who are is His own children - by rebirth through faith alone - from His infallible perspective. James' emphasis on a person's lifestyle is a *carryover* from how people were judged under the Mosaic Law – by external words and actions.

If we take James at his word and go down the dangerous road to evaluate the condition of his faith and salvation based on his actions, he might come up short. Why? Because he insisted on ignoring God's revelation to Peter and Paul about Gentiles because he required them to be circumcised before they could be saved. That is front-loading the Gospel – which is no gospel at all. (See Endnote # 37.) So this fact calls into question just what gospel was he actually depending on – one based on his works or on God's grace, on Moses or on Jesus.

James himself was called "James the Just" in Jerusalem apparently because of his life-long, strict, law-based, Nazarite lifestyle – considered to be the "holiest" way to live in the Jewish system. But Jesus said that the greatest of all men born of woman was John the Baptist (not James) and that the least in God's kingdom (those reborn **post-cross**) are greater than John the Baptist was, at that **pre-cross** point in time. What does that tell you? Well, Jesus endorsed John the Baptist who focused on Jesus, not on the Law, and revealed that even the "best" of the law-keeping Jews could not compare with becoming a righteous child of God through rebirth. In other words, one's life-style alone is no sure indicator of **New Covenant** righteousness. Justification is a gift received only by faith alone. But right believing, apart from the knowledge of the law, will produce the fruit of right living through a Holy Spirit-led life, not through depending on a law-led life.

When Jesus inaugurated His totally **New Covenant** of grace with Father-God for us, He took full responsibility for all of mankind's sin-debt, thus reconciling mankind to God – from God's viewpoint. So, true righteousness is His gift to **in Adam** sinners who receive it and continue in it by faith – apart from *any* works of the Law. (Otherwise, it would no longer be a free gift.) James' emphasis on judging another's faith according to his actions quickly bleeds over in most people's minds into actions becoming the requirement for salvation. Their equation easily becomes: "No good works = no good faith, therefore, not saved." Soon, a list of necessary "works" - moral standards or dress codes or types of music etc. - of what "good Christians" say and do (or avoid doing) becomes the external "law" that people *must* follow to be acceptable to the current law-givers.

In the Jerusalem church, the Gentiles were required to first be circumcised into Judaism and then expected to obey the Mosaic Law and only then be reborn of God through faith in Jesus. That was the only way to stay in good standing with that local "Christian" church. Fraternizing with "unclean Gentiles" was a no-no, even though God had already forgiven and reconciled them to Himself, according to Jesus' revelation to Paul in 2 Corinthians 5:17-19 and 1 John 2:2. Obviously, requiring circumcision and those other "good works" were *not* considered good in God's eyes, proved by the miracle of salvation freely given to Cornelius and his household. Galatianism in any form is heresy.

The Law-minded, seen-focused James, blurred this important distinction between faith that focuses on the **unseen realm** and actions that are done in the **seen realm.** He tried to prove his belief by stating, in effect, that Abraham's right standing before God was because of the combination of his faith and works when he (nearly) sacrificed his son Isaac. Fortunately for us, Paul corrected James' erroneous "mixture" by pointing out that Abraham was declared righteous by God about 20 years before God called him to be willing to do that sacrifice. The righteousness that James was focused on was works-righteousness before man – actions done in the **seen realm** – rather than God's gift of faith-based righteousness received from God in the **unseen realm.** They are not identical any more than angels and apples are identical.

The Pharisees followed the law more strictly than Jesus did but that did not make them more holy or righteous in God's eyes. On the contrary, the Law was a veil over their eyes that kept them from seeing Jesus, the embodiment of grace and truth and righteousness. Their law-mindedness kept them from seeing that Jesus and His Father were "one." Apparently, James was more in agreement with the Pharisees than with Jesus – until Jesus appeared to James on resurrection day. But even then, Jesus gave Paul, not James, the revelation of the **whole gospel of grace.** The veil of the Law can also keep believers today from seeing that they are righteous *only* because they are "one with God **in Christ.**"

Only God knows for sure who has received His gift of righteousness - by faith alone before Him. He gives assurance to the believer by the revelation and witness that He is now his or her Abba-Father through the Holy Spirit. External human actions, judged by fallible humans, are not an infallible indication of one's right-standing before God, who infallibly sees everyone's state of being - **in Adam** or **in Christ.** The **elephant of Galatianism** has thrived because this key distinction between these two perspectives has been ignored through the ignorance of Jesus' **whole gospel** – or, possibly, intentionally covered over to accommodate or even justify law-minded thinking within various denominations. This was the essence of the "faith alone" battle between Luther and the Roman Catholic Church that was (mostly) resolved by theologians of the two sides which was announced in 1999 and then reaffirmed in 2015.

Jesus never referred to anyone's faith as "dead" or "incomplete" like James does in his book. Jesus pointed out those with little or with great faith. Predictably, the ones He praised for their "great faith" were non-Jews, presumably because they were not depending on the Law for righteousness with God. They looked to Jesus directly for help (not to their "good behavior") and got it. But even the Jewish disciples who walked with Jesus were not commended for great faith by Jesus. They trusted in their identification with Moses – even in varying degrees after Pentecost. Only Paul got the **whole gospel of lavish grace** from Jesus in 42 AD.

Conclusion: Luther's "faith alone" revelation from Romans is true. Salvation by faith plus works is heresy. Only accepting the **total truth** of Jesus' **whole gospel of grace** will overcome such law-based error. Depending on works to ascertain one's spiritual state is not an infallible guide. <u>True biblical righteousness is a gift received from God, not a moral lifestyle achieved by man</u>. The former is a matter of one's *being*; the latter of one's *doing*. Believing Jesus' **grace-based gospel** revealed to Paul, will produce the Holy Spirit's fruit of right living. See Appendix # 10 for more on James and Chapter Eighteen for more details on every believer's righteous position **in Christ**.

Chapter Ten

24 This Endnote is repeated from Chapter Six because of its importance. "Verse 14a has asserted that this bond or indictment has been 'canceled out'; v.14b now adds that God (or Christ) 'took it away, nailing it to the cross.' In other words, the bond (the Mosaic law) has been removed permanently, so that its claims against us can never again alienate us from God. … To sum up, the great principle asserted in v.14 is the destruction of the law in and by the cross of Christ." Quoted from NIV *Bible Commentary, Volume 2 New Testament*, Copyright 1994, published by Zondervan Publishing House, page 829-830.

25. The two covenants are diametrically opposed because of their opposing terms. Mosaic Law is based on man's imperfect performance and the **New Covenant** is based on Jesus' perfect performance. Additionally, the Ten Commandments state many requirements negatively such as "Do not steal." It tells you what not to do but gives no power to obey it and, in fact, arouses sin. However the <u>higher law</u> of faith, love and liberty **in Christ** is lived through us by the Holy Spirit. He is the love of God shed abroad in our new heart, sent to enable all believers to progressively think like God thinks and act accordingly. This is far beyond just refraining from stealing. It mirrors the nature of God as the giving lover and supplier that He is. This revelation is befitting of us, His children, and it more than fulfills the demands of the Ten Commandments that are impossible for **in Adam** sinners to keep perfectly, and was never given to Gentiles anyhow. It is this new, <u>higher law</u> of the Spirit of life that God writes on our new hearts, according to Hebrews 8:10 and 10:16. Depending of God's supply is far more profitable (as Paul would say) than stealing what others have.

Note: The following command in Deuteronomy 10:12 seemed to be positive:

> And now, Israel, what does the Lord, thy God, require of you but to fear the Lord thy God and to walk in all His ways and to love him and to serve Him with all thy heart and with all thy soul.

But that was impossible for the Israelites to do because they were still **in Adam**. It is now part of the **divine exchange** where God has made that a reality, now that we believers are one spirit with the Father and have the love of God shed into our hearts in the person of the Holy Spirit so that we can now love God in return. It is all about Him and the **finished work** of His **divine exchange** with all believers!

26. Bishops of the Circumcision:
The following article comes from *The Hebrew Catholic* #82, Fall 2005 - Winter 2006. On the web at:
http://hebrewcatholic.org/HCLives/Sholl-Andrew/hebrewcatholicbi.html

Hebrew Catholic Bishops of Jerusalem by Andrew Sholl:

According to the early Church historian, Eusebius, himself a Gentile Bishop of Caesarea Maritima in the Holy Land, from 314 to c..338, he provides a surprisingly long list of 13 successive Bishops of Jerusalem between the death of St. Simeon in 107 A.D. and the second Roman destruction of the Holy City at the end of the Bar Kokhba revolt in 135 A.D. and, interestingly, remarks that "they were all Judaeo-Christians. But from Mark of Caesarea (135-136) on, all the Bishops of the rebuilt city (Aelia Capitolina) were of non-Jewish origin." [1]

Why did the Hebrew Catholic line of bishops come to an abrupt end? When the Roman Emperor Hadrian put down the Jewish rebellion, leveled the City of Jerusalem, and then bebuilt (sic) it according to his own plan, while ('modestly') renaming it in his own family name of Aelius, without, of course, forgetting the chief of the Roman gods, Jupiter Capitolinus (hence, Aelia Capitolina), he forbad any Jew to enter the city, or reside there, on pain of death: hence, no more Jewish or Hebrew Catholic bishops! …

Jerusalem Bishops of Hebrew Origin

Eusebius goes on to tell us in his History of the Church from Christ to Constantine that when "Symeon had found fulfillment in the manner described, his successor on the throne of the Jerusalem bishopric was a Jew named Justus, one of the vast number of the Circumcision who by then believed in Christ." (p.145)

On page 156 he continues:

Of the dates of the bishops of Jerusalem I have failed to find any written evidence – it is known that they were very short-lived – but I have received documentary proof of this, that up to Hadrian's siege of the Jews, there had been a series of fifteen bishops there. All are said to have been Hebrews in origin, who had received the knowledge of Christ with all sincerity, with the result that those in a position to decide such matters, judged them worthy of the episcopal office. For at that time their whole Church consisted of Hebrew believers who had continued from Apostolic times down to the later siege (i.e., A.D. 135) in which the Jews after revolting a second time against the Romans, were overwhelmed in a full-scale war. As that meant the end of the bishops of the Circumcision, this is the right moment to list their names from the first."

He then lists the 15 bishops as follows:

• James, 'the Lord's brother,' First Bishop of Jerusalem
• Symeon, Second Bishop of Jerusalem
• Justus, Third Bishop of Jerusalem
• Zacchaeus, Fourth Bishop of Jerusalem
• Tobias, Fifth Bishop of Jerusalem
• Benjamin, Sixth Bishop of Jerusalem
• John, Seventh Bishop of Jerusalem
• Matthias, Eighth Bishop of Jerusalem
• Philip, Ninth Bishop of Jerusalem
• Seneca, Tenth Bishop of Jerusalem
• Justus II, Eleventh Bishop of Jerusalem
• Levi, Twelfth Bishop of Jerusalem
• Ephres, Thirteenth Bishop of Jerusalem
• Joseph, Fourteenth Bishop of Jerusalem
• and Judas, Fifteenth Bishop of Jerusalem, and the last Jew to hold that office till modern times. Eusebius then finishes by saying that "that was the number of bishops in the city of Jerusalem from Apostolic times to the date mentioned (i.e., A.D. 135), **all of them of the Circumcision.**

Jerusalem Bishops of Gentile Origin

We know that in A.D.135, the Emperor Hadrian banished all Jews from Jerusalem, and its surrounding area, and for the very first time put an end to the Jewish name of the country/province of Judaea, by renaming it Syria Palaestina, making it the first record ever that the name Palestine was used by anyone.

It is interesting for us Hebrew Catholics to note how different the name of the next fifteen bishops of Jerusalem are, since A.D. 135, all of whom, of course, are Gentiles. Eusebius lists them as follows:

• Marcus, Sixteenth Bishop of Jerusalem
• Cassian, Seventeenth Bishop of Jerusalem
• Publius, Eighteenth Bishop of Jerusalem
• Maximus, Nineteenth Bishop of Jerusalem
• Julian, Twentieth Bishop of Jerusalem
• Gaius, Twenty-first Bishop of Jerusalem
• Symmachus, Twenty-second Bishop of Jerusalem
• Gaius II, Twenty-third Bishop of Jerusalem
• Julian II, Twenty-fourth Bishop of Jerusalem
• Capito, Twenty-fifth Bishop of Jerusalem

• Maximus II, Twenty-sixth Bishop of Jerusalem
• Antoninus, Twenty-seventh Bishop of Jerusalem
• Valens, Twenty-eighth Bishop of Jerusalem
• Dolichianus, Twenty-ninth Bishop of Jerusalem
• Narcissus, Thirtieth Bishop of Jerusalem
Found at: http://www.keithhunt.com/Sunday2.html

> *.. The more probable explanation, as we shall see shortly, is that after the disappearance of the Bishops of the circumcision (ca. A.D.135), a group of into the majority, adopted the observance of Sunday in addition to the Sabbath.*

> *(3) The Bishops who administered the Church of Jerusalem after the year 70, continued to be of the circumcision. Eusebius, after having listed their names until the time of the seige of Hadrian, adds: "Such were the bishops in the city of Jerusalem, from the Apostles down to the time mentioned and they were all Jews. 39*
> *Not only the Bishops were from the circumcision, but, according to the same historian, "the whole church at that time consisted of Hebrews who had continued Christians from the Apostles down to the time when the Jews again rebelled from the Romans and were beaten in a great war." 40*

> *The fact that the Jerusalem Church up to 135 AD was administered by and composed of Judeo-Christians who as Eusebius writes "were zealous to insist on the literal observance of the Law" 41 would make it unreasonable to suppose that they would have taken the initiative to abandon Sabbath keeping and introduce Sunday observance.*

Further corroboration:
http://www.studylight.org/desk/interlinear.cgi?search_form_type=interlinear&q1=Genesis+26%3A5&ot=bhs&nt=wh&s=0&t3=str_nas&ns=0

The Seven Noahide Laws actually encompass numerous details and applications within hundreds of laws, each with specific applications. One should also keep in mind that these laws are only the minimal basis for a Hasidic gentile's service to G-d, since there are many Jewish mitzvos that non-Jews are encouraged to adopt to accomplish more. Through these laws a gentile refines himself and the Creation as a whole, fulfilling his purpose for existence.

For a detailed listing of the Noahide Laws, visit our sister site - Hasidic University
http://www.noahide.com/7laws.htm

Chapter Eleven

27. The following verses from Genesis 15:5-7 seem to contradict what God told Isaac in Genesis 26:3-5 quoted further below.

> And He (God) brought him (Abraham) outside, and He said to him, "Look at the heavens and number the stars, if you can." And then He said to him, "So also will your offspring be." <u>Abram believed God, and it was imputed to him as righteousness.</u> And He (God) said to him, "I am the Lord who led you away from Ur of the Chaldeans, so as to give you this land, and so that you would possess it."

> For to you (Isaac) and to your offspring I will give all these regions, completing the oath that I promised to Abraham your father. And I will multiply your offspring like the stars of heaven. And I will give to your posterity all these regions. And in your offspring all the nations of the earth will be blessed, <u>because Abraham obeyed my voice, and kept my precepts and commandments, and observed the ceremonies and the laws.</u>

The first passage clearly indicates that God blessed Abraham with the gift of right standing with Him because he believed what God promised – even though he did not yet tangibly see what was promised (multitudinous offspring.) But the second passage states that God will bless Abraham's son Isaac because Abraham obeyed God's commands and laws. This is puzzling since all this happened long before God gave the Law covenant to Moses.

Fortunately, the matter is clarified by Jesus' revelation to Paul that confirmed that Abraham's righteousness was a gift of undeserved grace by faith in what God promised to him as explained in Romans 4:1-5.Good works cannot achieve righteousness but are the *fruit* of right believing and depending on Jesus and His divine exchange.

> So then, what shall we say that Abraham, our forefather had discovered (about faith in God)? For if Abraham was justified by works (not by faith alone), he could have boasted, but not before God. For what does Scripture say? "Abram believed God, and it was reputed to him as righteousness." When someone works, his wages are not counted as a gift but as something he earned by his work. However, for he who does not work, but who believes in him (God) who justifies the wicked, his faith is counted to him as righteousness (Romans 4:2-5)

And so it is with the new, grace-based covenant that Jesus made for us with God. Viewing the Bible through the lens of Jesus' **whole gospel of grace** will straighten out twisted beliefs.

28. John 1:29 states that Jesus "takes away the sin of the world." This is a correct statement for the **pre-cross** period that John was writing about. However, on Calvary, Jesus TOOK away all the sins of the whole world, for all time, for all people, as 2 Corinthians 5:18-19 and 1 John 2:2 clearly state. Now it remains for each person to choose to be personally reconciled to God by agreeing with Romans 10:9-13.

29. *Could it be that those who make the Law their standard of the truth, are, thereby, not actually glorifying Jesus who is the Truth?* Yes, because Jesus is to be our focus, not a law or a standard that falls short of His fullness. The Ten Commandments were placed in the Ark in heaven under the mercy seat and under Jesus' blood, never to be looked on again. Morality is generally understood to be a given set of standards that dictate what is considered to be right behavior and wrong behavior, personally or culturally. And now you know which tree in the Garden gave us the principle of Law.

If the Ten Commandments are a part of the Universal Moral Law that people must obey perfectly to become or stay righteous, why did God call these same Commandments, which can only condemn mankind, the "ministry of death" and nail them to the cross? It is because moral laws, by definition, have to do with the notion of right and wrong behavior which is <u>not</u> the same as God's <u>gift of righteousness</u> in the **New Covenant**. Law minded people are focused on morality – right and wrong behavior - like the Israelites were under Moses. That was the basis of the terms of their covenant with God. Thankfully, the terms of the **New Covenant** are not based on a person's moral behavior but his <u>belief and acceptance</u> of Jesus' perfect behavior from His cradle to His grave and what He accomplished for us in that **finished work**. God gave us a better covenant than the Israelites had which He keeps for us. All this is a gift of His **finished work** that can't be added to or improved. This is why being "moral" is not the same as being in right-standing with God. The two are not incompatible, of course, just not synonymous.

Can you be righteous without focusing on the Law? Yes. Abraham was in right-standing with God and a friend of God before the Law was ever given. Abraham's behavior was not always "moral" (according to the Mosaic Law that came about 430 later) but he remained in right-standing with God because of the covenant of grace which he accepted on the basis of faith, not on the basis of his behavior. And despite what James 2:17 says, Abraham's faith was not regarded by God as "dead" or "incomplete" by not behaving perfectly.

Why did God tell Adam not to eat of the Tree of the Knowledge of Good and Evil? To keep him from contaminating himself and dying spiritually by **knowing** – being <u>one</u> with - evil thus separating himself from Him who is all holy and perfect and is the only source of eternal Life.

Chapter Twelve

30. Of course, historically, some Gentiles asked to be circumcised into the Jewish faith, **pre-cross**, and therefore came under the law by choice. Also, James erroneously thought that practice must continue **post-cross** – at least for Gentiles in Jerusalem. Had he totally agreed with Paul and Peter at the first Jerusalem Council, the **elephant of mixture** would have not gained such a strong foothold in the church. The **butterfly life** of the higher Law of faith, love and liberty might have been <u>mainstream Christianity</u>! But there is now a world-wide awakening to Jesus' **whole gospel** in progress. See Appendix # 5 for recommended reading materials.

31. Myles Coverdale (c. 1488 – 20 January 1569) was a 16th-century Bible translator who produced the first complete printed translation of the Bible into English and served as Bishop of Exeter from 1551 to 1553. https://www.goodreads.com/quotes/115190-it-shall-greatly-help-ye-to-understand-the-scriptures-if

32. However, in Abraham's case, God's gift of righteousness was *credited* to him by a <u>grace-based covenant</u> through God's gift of faith to believe that God's **unseen** promise was true. It anticipated what Jesus' blood would do for all believers. But Abraham was not yet reborn and **in Christ** or a partaker of divine nature and seated in heavenly realms like all **post-cross** saints are. Even the least in God's Kingdom is greater than he was, according to Jesus (see Luke 7:28).

Chapter Thirteen

33. There are some New Testament scriptures that seem to imply that one has to wait to eventually receive eternal life at physical death, such as Jude 21. But, again, Jude apparently did not know about the fullness of the **whole gospel** of the **finished work** of Christ Jesus. Rather than starting with the revelation that 1) a believer is One with Christ who *is* our eternal life, and that 2) we are seated with Him in Heavenly places and also that 3) we are one spirit with Father-God, law-based thinking leads one to rely on the works of the law (being moral/holy) to ensure one's salvation – finally decided at death. But karma is no gospel at all.

34. Yet, even then, God made a provision of grace in this covenant by establishing six cities of "refuge" to help insure justice but balanced with a degree of grace and mercy. There are many web sites that explain the purpose and meanings behind the names of these cities that testify to God's lavish grace and mercy, fully realized in our **New Covenant**.

Chapter Fourteen

35. *Paul and Jesus* by James D. Tabor, published by Simon & Schuster, copyright 2012. Also see endnote # 5 above.

Chapter Sixteen

36. Again, this chart is a small part of my Big Picture overview chart of the whole Bible, presented in seven frames. It is not the same as charts on dispensations etc. One frame is a graphic of our position in the heavenlies in Christ. I will include it in a future book.

37. Jeremy White describes many other tip-offs under the creative headings of "front-loading " and "back-loading" the gospel in his excellent book *The Gospel [un]Cut: Learning to Rest in the Grace of God.* Appendix # 5 lists this and other helpful books to help you separate the wheat of the **whole gospel** from the tares of the law-mindedness so that you can rest peacefully in Jesus' **finished work** .

38. http://www.pickle-publishing.com/papers/soul-and-spirit.htm WORD STUDY Greek Hebrewhttp://www.jba.gr/Articles/nkjv_jbamay96.htm more on topic (blog

39. Since God's gift of tongues originates from a believer's spirit, not from his mind, he does not mentally comprehend what he is praying privately or saying publically. This difference is self-evident to anyone who speaks in tongues. And this wonderful gift from God, in turn, confirms to the believer that he is a spirit-being with a soul. It is a similar dynamic with the gift of prophecy which comes from God through the believer's spirit then is "filtered" through his mind. In other words, true prophecy is an expression from the mind of Christ, who is one with the believer's spirit-self, not originated from the believer's own, natural mind. That is why it is an inspired gift from God! Like any power or gift in the natural realm, God's gifts, including grace, can be abused or misused but that does not negate their reality or worth to yielded believers. They are given by the Holy Spirit to build up and encourage the Body of Christ. Tongues are given to edify both the Body publically and the individual privately. We need all the help we can receive in the spiritual war zone called planet earth.

Believers who have fallen for the lie that "tongues is of the devil" or other similar deceptions about the gifts of the Spirit that Jesus died to provide, are victims of the devil's propaganda campaign whose aim is to steal the benefits of the **unseen realm** that are powerful weapons against his devices. Paul stated that he prayed in tongues more than anyone else.

Now I *want you all to speak in tongues*, but more so to prophesy. For he who prophesies (helps) more than he who speaks in tongues, unless perhaps he interprets, so that the Church may receive edification (1 Corinthians 14:5).

I thank my God that I speak in tongues more than all of you (1 Corinthians 14:18).

Could that be why God was able to reveal so much to Paul? It is a great way to pray perfectly and to declare God's perfect will to happen on earth, since He inspires what is spoken, not the fallible mind of man. Many people have testified that they were saved when they heard a believer speak in a tongue that was foreign to the speaker but known to the hearer. Faith comes by hearing and hearing by the word of God – including tongues. Ask the Holy Spirit, the Giver of good gifts, which particular ones He has for you as His ambassador of reconciliation to this fallen world. But also know that the Holy Spirit's gift of tongues is offered to all believers – including you.

Chapter Seventeen

40. Regarding Saint Thomas:

St. Pius V proclaimed St. Thomas a Doctor of the Universal Church in the year 1567. In the Encyclical "Aeterni Patris", of 4 August, 1879, on the restoration of Christian philosophy, Leo XIII declared him "the prince and master of all Scholastic doctors". …

On 6 December, 1273, he laid aside his pen and would write no more. That day he experienced an unusually long ecstasy during Mass; what was revealed to him we can only surmise from his reply to Father Reginald, who urged him to continue his writings: "I can do no more. Such secrets have been revealed to me that all I have written now appears to be of little value" (modica, Prümmer, op. cit., p. 43). The "Summa theologica" (regarded as his best work) had been completed only as far as the ninetieth question of the third part (De partibus poenitentiae).

Quoted from the Catholic Encylopedia: The Life Of Saint Thomas
http://www.newadvent.org/cathen/14663b.htm

41. CHRISTIAN ARISTOTELIANISM/ THOMISM

"He (Thomas Aquinas) was highly regarded by several popes, who sought his advice, but he refused the offer of the Archbishopric of Naples in favour of the religious life. He spent ten years from 1259 preparing commentaries on Aristotle's works, teaching again at Paris and becoming embroiled in several academic and administrative controversies. He lectured at Naples in 1272 and became a member of the papal court. He died while on the way to attend the Council of Lyons where he would have defended the use of Aristotle in theology.

http://www.philosophos.com/philosophical_connections/profile_047.html

42. The WORKS OF MARTIN LUTHER - THE MAGNIFICAT - TRANSLATED AND EXPLAINED 1520-1
http://www.godrules.net/library/luther/NEW1luther_c5.htm WEB
Found on the Web: Two other descriptions of the Tri-part Doctrine:
http://www.antipasministries.com/newantipaspapers/chapter1.htm
http://www.contendingforthefaith.org/res....pirit-same.htm

Chapter Eighteen

43. Why Call It "Radical Grace?" -- A Summary

By now it should be abundantly clear to you that, while the other apostles spread variations of the **bare bones gospel**, only Paul was specifically anointed and appointed to preach Jesus' **whole gospel** of radical grace. It was a radically new revelation for the Law-minded Jews as well as for anyone today still depending on his own behavior (law-keeping), instead of totally on Jesus' **finished work**, in order to be declared "right," accepted and approved by God and to be able to operate by faith alone in Him. The word "radical" in English comes from the Latin word "radis" which means "root". Jesus' **whole gospel** is "radical", first of all, in the sense that rebirth **into Christ** replaces the "root" of evil (one's sin nature **in Adam**), in contrast to the futility of changing one's outward behavior. Behavior modification does not affect one's rotten core self **in Adam**. Only by dying to the **in Adam** self, through identification with Jesus by faith, can my old self be spiritually circumcised away, forever removing my bad core. But that is only a small part of the radical gospel.

Secondly, Jesus reconciled the whole world to God from God's viewpoint and completely paid for everyone's sin debt - including future sinful thoughts and actions - with His blood. This is certainly a radical reversal of the **pre-cross** mode where the wages of my sin would spell my death. This holy transaction must be believed and received personally through being reborn from above, by grace through faith.

Thirdly, all believers "died to the (Mosaic) Law" by identification with Jesus' death (Romans 7:4-6). The Law was nailed to the cross - including the Ten Commandments - to remove the instrument the devil uses to "arouse sin" and bring guilt, shame and condemnation, and cause death. (See Chapter Nine.)

> And when you were dead in your sins and in the uncircumcision of your flesh, He (God) enlivened you, together with Him (Jesus), forgiving you of all sins, and wiping away the handwriting of the decree (the Ten Commandments) which was against us, which was contrary to us. And He has taken this away from your midst, affixing it to the Cross and thereby, despoiling principalities and powers, He has led them away confidently and openly, triumphing over them in Himself (Colossians 2:13-15).

Jesus nailed the Law to the cross - including the Ten Commandments. That is a radical alternative to Judaism and every other religion that requires obedience to a moral code for acceptance into heaven.

Fourthly, it was not enough for God to remove all the bad and quit. He must supply His good to us or we miss heaven anyway because we can't reach there by trying. So Jesus supplied all His good to us through His **divine exchange** when we rose and ascended to heaven with Him. As Titus 3:5 clearly states:

> And he (Jesus) saved us, not by works of justice that we have done but according to His mercy by the washing of regeneration and by the renovation of the Holy Spirit".

Jesus + nothing = the radical gospel of Christ Jesus. All those reborn **in Him** automatically receive His new life in the Spirit of God who then provides the gifts of faith, love and liberty to live life in the **seen realm** victoriously. Taken together, can you think of anything more radical than Jesus' **whole gospel of grace**? Unfortunately, all this comes as a radical surprise to most Christians because the **elephant of mixture** stomps on the **butterfly life** of radical grace in many churches and believer's minds today. Chapter Nineteen endeavors to put some feet to Jesus' gospel, the invitation to learn to walk according to God's higher law of faith, love and liberty in the Holy Spirit.

Chapter Nineteen

44. Know and reckon as true that your **in Adam** nature is totally dead and gone. You have been reborn, alive in Christ Jesus and dead to the sin nature that was crucified and buried with Jesus. However, you are not necessarily yet dead to "sinning." Why? Because you can still choose to follow the dictates of your body and your unsanctified soul. Even though you no longer are bound to Adam's sin nature, sinning is still a possibility until you die physically. But the good news is: God has already forgiven all your past, present and future sins. "There is, therefore, now no condemnation for those who are **in Christ Jesus**" (Romans 8:1). Halleluiah!

Appendix # 10

45. McGrath, Alister E., *Christianity: An Introduction*, Blackwell Publishing,(2006), ISBN 1-4051-0899-1, Page 174:

> In effect, they [Jewish Christians] seemed to regard Christianity as an affirmation of every aspect of contemporary Judaism, with the addition of one extra belief — that Jesus was the Messiah. Unless males were circumcised, they could not be saved (Acts 15:1).

Again, there are many early and contemporary books on very early church history that document the split that occurred at the first Jerusalem Council in 50 AD, that is, unfortunately, ignored or covered over by most theologians who apparently accept Luke's version of the council rather than Paul's. All objective evidence points to the fact that James was well respected for his ascetic, if not Nazarite, lifestyle that was based on practicing the Law of Moses personally and enforcing it corporately as the main and most respected leader in the Jerusalem church until he was martyred in about 62 AD. It is obvious that he mistakenly thought that Jesus came to *reform* Judaism rather than <u>to replace it altogether.</u> The passages of early church history cited above indicate that James was, in fact, a Nazarite and I find no reason to dismiss their claims. Therefore, I chose to include that as a "fact" in this book since it would explain many aspects of his reputation and leadership decisions that conflicted with Paul's vision and teaching. I will leave it to you, the reader, to make your own conclusions regarding this fascinating, though quite controversial, topic.

http://www.biblesearchers.com/hebrewchurch/primitive/primitive11.shtml re: James the Just–role of the high priest and leader of Nazarene church http://www.earlychristianwritings.com/text/hegesippus.html

See http://www.newadvent.org/fathers/250102.htm, the actual book of Eusebius re James and the early church Volume 3 chap 18 (number 23)

> And immediately Vespasian besieged them." James was so admirable a man and so celebrated among all for his justice (righteousness), that the more sensible even of the Jews were of the opinion that this was the cause of the siege of Jerusalem, which happened to them immediately after his martyrdom for no other reason than their daring act against him.
>
> 20. Josephus, at least, has not hesitated to testify this in his writings, where he says, "These things happened to the Jews to avenge James the Just, who was a brother of Jesus, that is called the Christ. For the Jews slew him, although he was a most just man."
>
> http://www.ccel.org/print/schaff/npnf201/iii.vii.xxiv

NOTE: It became clear to me as I researched the life of James and the split in the church in 50 AD that, in general, most theologians tend to ignore or downplay the facts of the doctrinal war between James and Paul like Luke also did. However, historians are more objective and cite many early historical sources that verify the differences between the two men and their beliefs and the fallout from that. By now, it should be apparent to you that the cover-up was not helpful in the long run. In fact, the "inconvenient" facts that the Bible contains serve to validate its authenticity. Being less than accurate helps no one. I have done my level best to be as accurate as possible and let the chips fall will they will.

46. Ibid

47. Ibid

A Brief Bio

My wife Elaine and I live in Erie, Pennsylvania. We have four wonderful grown children and ten terrific grandchildren. I graduated from a Catholic prep high school in my hometown of Pittsburgh, Pennsylvania and then attended a Catholic seminary for three years. By working my way through college as a carpenter and musician, I earned a B.S. in Secondary Ed. English at Duquesne University. After getting married, I taught English for a year at my old high school.

Then Elaine and I moved to Alexandria, Virginia to follow my dream to earn a Montessori Elementary Diploma from WMI in Washington D.C. After teaching in Fairfax, VA, I became the principal and teacher at Richmond Montessori School in Virginia.

Previously, at Duquesne University, classes such as Existential Phenomonology and Eastern Religion had lured me into New Age thought and practice and later into Humanism. But in 1972, I was captivated by a revelation of the sacrificial love of Jesus Christ for me and was saved at the age of 28. A year later, I was called to serve the Lord at Word of God Academy in Erie PA. I earned a M. Ed. at Gannon University in 1980 and I retired from WGA as principal in 2006

Father-God now uses my earlier "detours" to not only galvanize my trust and dependence on Him but also to understand and explain false belief systems as a former "insider." Additionally, I can now testify to the truth and present day reality of God's New Covenant promises in Christ that are offered to every believer. My second book, *Every Christian's Testimony*, integrates and personalizes over 600 scriptures that focus on this theme.

Proverbs 3:5-6 and Philippians 4:6-7 are my life verses. Using guitar and saxophone, I have served as worship leader for over forty years in various church and small group settings including Light of the World Community, Grace Fellowship Church International and Trinity United Methodist. I present seminars on comparative Worldviews and retreats on Jesus' **whole gospel of grace,** as presented in the songs in this book.

My Montessori training introduced me to the invaluable skill of Big Picture thinking, which I explained in my first book, *Pathways*. I wrote it in 1992 at the request of homeschool parents who wanted to teach their children to learn to think this way. I greatly enjoy passing on this approach to others, especially regarding our new identity in Christ, through workshops, books, songs and web articles. Elaine and I also enjoy visiting our kids and grandchildren who are scattered from Maryland to Illinois; remodeling; reading; composing and recording worship songs; writing; sports, gardening and traveling to tour museums and historical sites.

Through my website at totaltruth.org, I offer to the interested reader some of the insights I have gained through my varied experience over 50+ years of learning and teaching, including a free book on comparative Worldviews and American history. I welcome constructive comments and input - especially from those who disagree with my Christian Worldview.

NOTES